The Long Life and
Swift Death of Jewish Rechitsa

The Long Life and
Swift Death of Jewish Rechitsa

A Community in Belarus, 1625–2000

ALBERT KAGANOVITCH

THE UNIVERSITY OF WISCONSIN PRESS

The University of Wisconsin Press
1930 Monroe Street, 3rd Floor
Madison, Wisconsin 53711-2059
uwpress.wisc.edu

3 Henrietta Street
London WC2E 8LU, England
eurospanbookstore.com

Printed in the United States of America

Library of Congress Cataloging-in-Publication Data
Kaganovitch, Albert.
[Rechitsa. English]
The long life and swift death of Jewish Rechitsa : a community in
Belarus, 1625–2000 / Albert Kaganovitch.
p. cm.
Includes bibliographical references and index.
ISBN 978-0-299-28984-3 (pbk. : alk. paper) —
ISBN 978-0-299-28983-6 (ebook)
1. Jews—Belarus—Rechytsa—History. 2. Rechytsa (Belarus)—History.
I. Title.
DS135.B382R4313 2013
947.8´1—dc23
2012013015

To
TAMARA *and* BORIS KAGANOVITCH

Contents

Illustrations

Acknowledgments

This study is dedicated to Rechitsa, a town that evokes my fondest memories of childhood. Almost fifteen years ago, after I had begun writing my dissertation about Bukharan Jews' history in the Departments of Jewish Studies and Oriental Studies of Jerusalem University, I got the idea of researching the history of the Jews in Rechitsa as well. I began collecting relevant materials, but as it turned out, only in 2003 was I able to begin the actual writing of this study. I am deeply grateful to Shaul Stampfer, Michael Zand, and Mordechai Altshuler, whose scholarly advice, criticism, and intellectual guidance have been a tremendous help and from whom I have learned much during my studies.

I wish to thank my fellow townsman Leonid Smilovitsky, who not only kindly allowed me to copy some two dozen replies from letters to Rechitsa residents, but who also inspired me over many years to undertake this study and also allowed me to use his personal archive and library containing interesting documentary materials, books, and photographs. Among other colleagues and friends to whom I extend my heartfelt appreciation for their comments and assistance are Arkadii Zeltser, Vladimir Levin, Anthony Polonsky, Benjamin Baader, David M. Fox, Michael Gelb, Steven Feldman, and Benton Arnovitz. My special gratitude goes to Mark Tolts, whose meeting with me helped me find my way through several demographic issues in this study. The statements made and views expressed, however, are solely my responsibility. This book was made possible in part by funds granted to the author through a Matthew Family Fellowship at the Center for Advanced Holocaust Studies, United States Holocaust Memorial Museum. I am also grateful to the Emerging Scholars Publication Program at the Center for Advanced Holocaust Studies for its support in the preparation of the manuscript and of the book proposal.

I would also like to thank the staff of the Central Archive of the History of the Jewish People and all other staff members in archives and libraries who helped me find materials. Their attitude was uniformly helpful. For translations from Yiddish I am grateful to Aviv Shashar, my former colleague on the Appeal Authority of the Conference on Jewish Material Claims against Germany. I am also grateful to Ilana Guri, another former colleague, now with the Department of Encyclopedia of the Jewish Communities (Pinkas Ha-Kehillot) at the Yad Vashem Holocaust Museum. I cannot overstate the help provided by Dmitry Tolochko, who found many interesting documents for me in the Gomel archives.

My thanks go to all the Rechitsa natives who shared their recollections and photographs with me. Of particular help were Maria Rubinchik, Avraam Dovzhik, and Fridrikh Valler, who kindly and patiently answered my many questions. I wish to express my gratitude to the former head of the Rechitsa Jewish community, Alla Shkop, who provided me with a list of individuals buried in the Rechitsa Jewish cemetery, along with materials on Jews who were saved during the war and the people who saved them.

I am endlessly grateful to my wife, Svetlana, for her patience with this study, done "outside working hours," and for the several times she kindly read the whole manuscript and made detailed comments that were extremely valuable. I am indebted to her and to our children, Ayala and Benjamin, for the many evenings I spent away from them working alone at my desk.

The monograph presented here for the reader's critique is a variant, with significant changes and much fresh thinking, of the version already published in Russian. A substantial portion of these changes came in response to two editorial reviewers whose recommendations I found to be both fitting and very useful. It is a particular pleasure to acknowledge my debt to Jack Piotrow, my translator from Russian, whose knowledge of Russian history was most helpful. My special thanks go to Penny Rubinoff, who funded the translation in honor of her father, David Rubinoff, who lived in Rechitsa until his emigration to Canada in 1923. I am very appreciative of the editorial staff at the University of Wisconsin Press and particularly Barbara Wojhoski for her highly professional copyediting.

Transliteration Notes and Territorial Definitions

To make it easier for the reader, I have used familiar Anglicizations of the names of well-known figures like Khmelnitsky, Nicholas II, Trotsky, and Gorky. Given names like Maria and Iulia are rendered without the extra "i" that a strict transliteration requires. Given names such as Alexander and Eugenie have been left in their familiar Anglicized forms. For other proper names, as well as for place names, with the exception of those already in common use in the West, I have followed the standard transliteration model set by the Library of Congress, except that in the text I have not used diacritical marks.

In my text, for the biggest territorial units, *województwo*, in the Polish-Lithuanian period, and *guberniia*, in the Russian period, I use "voivodship" and "province," respectively. For medium-sized territorial units I use their original names—Polish-Lithuanian *powiat*, Russian *uezd*, Soviet *okrug* until 1926, and then *raion*. For the smallest territorial units I use the Polish-Lithuanian *starostwo* and the Russian *volost'*. The Soviet names "oblast" and "krai," on the other hand, are retained unchanged in the text. Together they designate some of the principal territorial administrative units in the Soviet system and survive at least in name in the post-Soviet Russian Federation. Oblasts, for instance, are in many cases the administrative replacements of former *guberniias* and outwardly resemble US states or German *Länder*. A "krai" is one of six thinly populated territorial-administrative-political subdivisions of Russia, often a border region such as the Maritime Krai in the Far East.

The Long Life and
Swift Death of Jewish Rechitsa

Introduction

In August 1898 a famous scholar of the history of the Jewish people, the social activist and journalist Semën (Shimon) Dubnov (1860–1941), recorded the deep impressions made on him by his visit to the Rechitsa synagogue accompanied by his friend Markus Kagan (Mordechai Ben Hillel ha-Koen, 1856–1936) on the ninth day of the month of Av (the Jewish Day of Mourning for the destruction of the First and Second Temples):

> I sat on the floor of the synagogue, on the same level as everyone else, read the "Eicha" and my beloved elegy "Belel ze ivkaiun" ("On this night my children weep and sob." S.D.). . . . Then, late in the evening of the same day, I sat on a bench I had built in a garden on the high bank of the Dnieper, looked at the enigmatic face of the moon floating above the river, and something new rose up in my soul, something distant from the impressions of this Day of Mourning. I felt that the message of nature was taking its place next to the message of history. . . . What had happened to me on this enchanting night on the Dnieper?[1]

He went on to describe the turning point in his life that took place on this night. He found here a cult of nature, expressed in lyric poetry, which led the historian's soul to harmony between two opposing principles: ardent historicism and cold cosmism. "From that time onward, the complex of Nature and History, pantheism and historicism, grew stronger within me and gave me spiritual support for my further life's journey amid the gathering social storms," wrote Dubnov.[2]

Semën Dubnov spent at that time two months in Rechitsa, residing a few kilometers from the town—on the dacha of Markus Kagan. He would take a daily walk through the pine forest and work in the carpenter's shop at the sawmill, taking pride in his callused hands. In the evenings all the residents on the dacha would gather on the large veranda. They would sing songs, recite poems, and read books aloud. Vera Gurovich, the private tutor of the Kagan children, was often present at these evenings, and the memories of her, along with nostalgia for the scenery of Rechitsa, later inspired Dubnov.[3]

Kagan himself would spend the summers there and return to his home in Gomel for the winter. He combined his business activities with social activism in the Zionist movement. His journalistic writings appeared in many Jewish publications. At the first Zionist congress in 1897, he was the only delegate who gave a speech in Hebrew. Like the majority of the Russian representatives, he expressed his support for the ideas of Theodor Herzl. Markus Kagan also took part in the second All-Russian Zionist Conference in Minsk in 1902. He was chairman of the Merchants' Society and participated in many Jewish and non-Jewish social organizations. The pogroms of 1905 led him to move to Palestine in 1907. After his repatriation, Kagan continued his work in journalism and in social organizations. He was one of the founders of Hebrew University in Jerusalem in 1918 and of the newspaper *Haaretz* in 1919.[4]

Leaving the Rechitsa dacha was difficult for Dubnov. When he returned to Odessa, he walked the streets like someone who had come from another world; he greeted his friends and acquaintances while bearing in his soul the ache of parting with the vision he had gained in the summer. To distract himself, Dubnov again immersed himself in the study of the history of Hasidism and wrote a long introduction to his future major work, *The Social and Spiritual Life of Jews in Poland in the 18th Century.*[5]

Over the next year the hospitable Markus Kagan built a wing in the courtyard of his dacha and in the summer of 1899 again invited Semën Dubnov and his whole family to use it. When the historian arrived, he immediately felt the influence of the Rechitsa countryside: "Exhausted by the heat of Odessa and still not fully recovered from a serious bout of the flu, I felt the 'curative powers of nature' the moment I arrived amid my native forests. What ardent prayers resounded in my soul amid the broad expanses of the fields, the colonnades of the forest temple, and on the high bank of the Dnieper! I observed the whole ritual of the cult of nature to which I had pledged my loyalty in the past summer in these same 'sacred environs.'"[6]

Dubnov and his family visited Kagan's dacha a third time in the summer of 1900—at the owner's invitation. The well-known writer-journalist, philosopher, and ideologist of spiritual Zionism, Asher-Hirsh Gintsberg (1856–1927)—better known as Ahad Ha'am—also came. He had just returned from a difficult trip around Erets-Israel and, along with his daughter, was happy to restore his health in the bosom of nature. News of the arrival of this important guest quickly spread throughout Rechitsa. Jewish cabdrivers at the station carefully looked over passers-by in hopes of seeing him.[7]

Ahad Ha'am, an admirer of urban life, did not share Dubnov's attachment to nature and teased him about his passion. Meanwhile, the great historian, inspired by nature, began writing his fundamental work—an eleven-volume world history of the Jewish people—at the Rechitsa dacha. "I worked zealously that summer," Dubnov recalled. "I would sit at a primitive desk in our hut and write until my mid-day stroll. . . . To the glorious melodies of the forest I would write of the era of the prophets and ancient culture. Then, in the late afternoon hours, all of us, along with an army of children, would walk through the fields and forest and fulfill all the commandments of our personal life. We would walk along the highway leading to Rechitsa."[8]

In the quiet of the Rechitsa landscape, Ahad Ha'am, exhausted by his travels and official meetings, could probably not tear himself away from social life as Dubnov could. Dozens of Ahad Ha'am's letters show that he spent the two and a half months in Rechitsa only physically, on the recommendation of his doctor,

Markus Kagan, Ahad Ha'am, and Semën Dubnov with their daughters in Rechitsa, 1900. From Ben Hillel Hakohen, 'Olami, vol. 3 (Jerusalem: Ha-poalim, 1927).

while his soul continued to live an intense life of editorial and social activity.[9] Recalling that time, Markus Kagan writes that Ahad Ha'am continually wrote letters, while Semën Dubnov would lock himself in his room from morning until two o'clock to write his book. After lunch, with about twelve people gathered at the table, the whole group would go for a walk in the forest, and there one of the girls would read aloud the stories of Chekhov, Andreev, or Gorky.[10]

On the evening of the ninth day of the month of Av they all went once more to the Rechitsa synagogue. Dubnov wrote: "Again, as two years ago, I sat on the floor of the synagogue next to Kagan, Ahad Ha'am and the children and repeated in chorus with the others the mournful verses of the 'Eicha.' News of this spread through the whole area and gave credence among the people to the old legend of my public repentance."[11] Unlike Dubnov, who in these moments felt a sense of unity with the people and their history, Ahad Ha'am was annoyed by the tears of mourning shed by Rechitsa Jews. What he saw in the synagogue reminded him of the Wailing Wall, which he had visited not long before in Jerusalem. Ahad Ha'am believed that a weeping people would be incapable of restoring itself. Kagan argued with him, maintaining the opposite view that the Jewish people had not forgotten their past greatness and so they were alive, as were their hopes for rebirth.[12] Kagan managed to combine relaxation and the pleasure of arguments with his friends with his business activities in Rechitsa and Gomel. That summer he also managed to write and edit several articles for Jewish magazines and anthologies.[13]

In the second half of August, Dubnov finished the first book of the first volume of his world history of the Jews, after which he decided to rest until September and devote more time to walks in the forest with his family. He wrote: "I had but one other true believer in my cult of nature, my fifteen-year-old daughter Sofia."[14]

Other places in Belorussia, including his native Mstislav Uezd, never evoked such love in Dubnov as did the environs of Rechitsa. In July 1901 he wrote from Propoisk (renamed Slavgorod in 1945) to Kagan: "I find that I can truly rest only in Rechitsa."[15]

In August 1901, Semën Dubnov came to Markus Kagan's dacha for the last time. There the historian again met Ahad Ha'am, his children, and other guests. As Dubnov recalled: "For me these were my farewell strolls through the places I loved. My fourth summer in Polesia turned out to be my last. We never gathered here again. At the end of August I bade farewell to the forest of Rechitsa and the banks of the Dnieper and returned to Odessa with Ahad Ha'am."[16]

I have dwelled in special detail on the impact that Rechitsa made on Dubnov because the beauty of its natural environment may have been an idiosyncratic feature of Rechitsa, distinguishing it from many other outlying towns of Belorussia. Despite its favorable location on the bank of the Dnieper, due to historical circumstances Rechitsa did not develop into a major city, for many Belorussian towns and shtetls were situated on rivers. From the perspective of Jewish history, Rechitsa is distinguished in that in 1941 it was almost the last place in Belorussia to be occupied by the Germans, which thus allowed many Jewish residents to flee to the east. After the war they returned and managed to influence the preservation of the town's prewar Jewish landscape, especially in its old urban districts, despite the fact that the proportion of Jews in Rechitsa had decreased during the war from a quarter of the population to one fifth. The great majority of them had been living in Rechitsa before the war. Such a high Jewish proportion did not exist in any other town in Belorussia or the Baltic States in 1947, and in Ukraine there were very few such cases. And although a dozen years later the proportion of Jews in Belorussian Minsk, Gomel, and Bobruisk was greater than in Rechitsa, this higher number was less the result of natural growth than of the postwar migration there of Jews from other regions.

Rechitsa was considered a town even during the period of the independent Lithuanian Duchy, when it was a *powiat* center; then, in the period of the Polish-Lithuanian Commonwealth, an important feature was its status as a town governed by the Magdeburg Law; and later, within the Russian Empire and, finally, in the USSR, it remained a town or city (*gorod*) according to the accepted criteria of population size. On the other hand, Rechitsa can quite legitimately be called a shtetl after the 1830s and 1840s because of the changes in its way of life resulting from the growth of the Jewish population there in the first third of the nineteenth century. A shtetl in Jewish tradition, or *mestechko* in Russian (*miasteczko* in Polish), was generally regarded as something between a town and a village. The status of mestechko in the Russian period gave a settlement a number of privileges, the most important of which for the local economy was the holding of markets at least twice a month. Many privately owned settlements within the Russian Empire had retained their status as mestechkos from Polish–Lithuanian times. But some of them received this status later, mainly during the first quarter of the nineteenth century. Often the conditions for a village to receive the status of a mestechko were the presence of an Orthodox church, markets (held at least once a week), and, paradoxical as it may seem, the presence of a Jewish population. The decision to give villages the status of mestechkos in the Russian Empire was a prerogative of provincial administrations.[17] At the end of the nineteenth century the Senate revoked this, its decision based on the fact that proclaiming villages as mestechkos gave Jews the right to settle in them.[18] Catherine II carried

out a policy of enlarging the mestechkos, the result of which was the forced settlement of Jews from villages into towns and mestechkos, where they became a
significant part of the population. Rechitsa retained the characteristic traits of
a mestechko until the early 1960s; therefore in this study I call it a town when
referring to its administrative relationship to the *uezd* center (and from 1924
to the *okrug* center and from 1931 to the *raion* center), and a mestechko when
discussing its sociocultural aspects. I use this approach for other similar administrative units as well.

Rechitsa is situated within the boundaries of the geographical territory that
became known as White Russia (Belaia Rus') in the fifteenth century. Later, from
the seventeenth century onward, this whole territory was called Belarus. Its name
and territory often changed; therefore, for the sake of consistency and not in any
political sense, I use the name that used in Soviet times, Belorussia, with its
contemporary political boundaries. I use the phrases "Belorussian peasantry"
and "Belorussian Jewry" in this work only in a geographical sense. Only after
1917 and within the territory of Soviet Belorussia did the Belorussian peasantry
generally consider themselves Belorussians; this happened even later in the parts
of Belorussia that were ceded to Poland. Until that time, the Belorussians, particularly the peasants, called themselves "local people" and were regarded by
the Russian administration not as a separate ethnic group but as a part of the
"Russian population." Therefore, they received unconditional support from the
authorities when they were involved in conflicts with Jews or Catholics (and by
the end of the eighteenth century the entire former Orthodox aristocracy of
Belorussia was Catholic).

Until the annexation of Belorussia to the Russian Empire, its residents were
subjects of the Grand Duchy of Lithuania, an autonomous unit within the Polish-
Lithuanian Commonwealth. Subjects of the duchy where called Litvins. I used
this term frequently in this study when speaking of the population. I also use
official terms such as "Lithuanian Hetman" and "Lithuanian State" relating to the
Grand Duchy of Lithuania.

The Jewish community of Rechitsa was an integral part of Lithuanian-
Belorussian Jewry known as the Litvaks (Yiddish, Litvakes), a group that experienced a prolonged development from its formation as a separate Jewish subgroup
in the Middle Ages until its distinctive identity was essentially lost during the
years of Soviet rule. The study devotes special attention to a comparison of
the mentality and other specific traits of the Litvaks with those of Polish and
Ukrainian Jewry. It also offers a detailed examination of Hasidic religious life in

Rechitsa, which was a constituent part of the distinctive Litvak Hasidism that developed dynamically within Belorussia and Lithuania. One should keep in mind that in the prerevolutionary period the authorities in Rechitsa regarded only one Jewish religious gathering place as a synagogue; others were called houses of prayer. In fact, in tsarist Russia the notion of a house of prayer could include a synagogue, a *beis-midrash* (*beit-midrash* in Hebrew), a *shtibl*, or a *kloiz*. In postrevolutionary times, all Jewish institutions of prayer were generally called synagogues, even though they might in fact differ substantially from a traditional synagogue. In cases where the actual nature of one or another religious institution was unknown, I have used the terminology found in my source.

Today most historians undertake studies of intellectual, global, or cultural history. Earlier studies focused more directly on the interrelationships of Eastern European Jews with the legal structure and the surrounding population on a national scale. Studies that concentrated on the life of the "little Jew," the Jewish family, and the Jewish community, on the other hand, ignored the influence of time and the environment on the subjects of their research. As a result the reader often formed an inaccurate view of the situation as essentially static. Nonetheless, it would have been wrong to picture the Jewish local society as something wholly dynamic.

Until recently many researchers who created these or other models for Jewish society in Eastern Europe in the premodern and modern periods relied on sources dealing with Poland.[19] But the situation of Jews in the Grand Duchy of Lithuania and later in the Russian Empire had its own unique features with regard to everyday life; religious, educational, social, and legal issues; and interethnic contacts. For example, Bernard Dov Weinryb estimates that in the fourteenth and fifteenth centuries in the Polish-Lithuanian Commonwealth on the average two or three outbreaks of violence against Jews occurred in each generation.[20] The cases he enumerates primarily involve Kraków, Warsaw, and Poznań. And although some additional cases of violence elsewhere cannot be known to historians, such a conclusion must not be extended to the Grand Principality of Lithuania, where attitudes regarding Jews at this time were more tolerant.

The number of scholars writing regional or local, "peripheral" Jewish history in Belorussia has increased in recent years. David Fishman has described the important spiritual transformation and the currents emanating from it that occurred in the early decades of Russian governance in Shklov.[21] In 2008 Mordechai Nadav published a revised and translated version of his previous book on the Jews in Pinsk.[22] Unlike Rechitsa, which did not leave a strong mark in

Jewish history as a great center of Jewish learning and traditional life, Pinsk is portrayed as a quintessentially Jewish town. In contrast to Rechitsa, the Russian period in the history of Pinsk became on the whole a history of the decay of Jewish life resulting from the decline in economic opportunities. Leonid Smilovitsky has depicted the life of the Jews in a shtetl against the backdrop of a broad domestic landscape.[23] Arkadi Zeltser has examined the sociocultural transformation of Jewish life in a provincial town modeled on Vitebsk.[24] Belorussian history, as is the case with many other ethnic histories (Tatar or Bashkir, for example), was for many years regarded as an adjunct to official Russian history, both in tsarist and Soviet times. In this regard, many historical events were treated in the context of their contribution to the development of the Russian state. Only in recent times have several interestingly argued "independent" scholarly works appeared.[25] I have attempted to draw on those that are relevant to my study.

A unique feature of my research is that it considers a long segment of time. I examine how Jewish Rechitsa developed and prospered during centuries, but also how tensions between Jews and Christians spread across the town. By focusing on a continuing period of time, I can, on the one hand, view a comprehensive picture and reveal nuances, and, on the other hand, better retrace the dynamics of change in the community and understand it retrospectively. From its local perspective, this study of Jews in a typical town in the Polish-Lithuanian Commonwealth, the Russian Empire, and then the USSR seeks to contribute to wider debates on the nature of central power, local authorities, Jewish institutions, and family life. The history of Jewish Rechitsa is presented here in the context of the major events and processes taking place in these states. Thus the analysis of Jewish life in Rechitsa serves as a lens that brings a larger process in Jewish history into focus. My aim was to show, insofar as possible, the particular features and principles determining the existence of the Rechitsa community; to this end, I compare the situation of Jews in Rechitsa with that of Jews in other mestechkos and towns of Belorussia, those nearby in particular.

I have attempted to trace the history of the Jews against the background of more general historical processes and show that their history was closely intertwined with that of the other ethnic groups living in the same territory, thus revealing the complex processes of their interaction and mutual influence. In this way, as far as possible given my subject, I have sought to avoid an "ethnicized" study that concentrates on one ethnic group while ignoring the population surrounding it or presenting it as somehow monolithic.

As John Doyle Klier rightly observes in his classic work, the history of Jews in Russia was frequently presented by Jewish historians as an infinite sequence of confrontations with non-Jews.[26] Finding themselves trapped by such an approach, they could not take a critical look at certain controversial problems of Jewish history in Eastern Europe, and in particular they accepted as axiomatic the notion that the dominating role of Jews in the economy of the region and particularly in leaseholder-tenant relationships was the cause of the anti-Jewish pogroms in Ukraine in the mid-seventeenth century. This view, which is rooted in Ukrainian folklore of the eighteenth century, especially the second half of the century, and subsequently established itself in Russian historical scholarship, directly contradicts relevant Ukrainian sources of the mid-sixteenth through mid-seventeenth centuries. Although the situation was somewhat different in the Grand Duchy of Lithuania on the eve of these dramatic events, I devote considerable attention to it inasmuch as Rechitsa, located within three hundred kilometers of Kiev (at the midpoint along the land route from Kiev to Minsk), suffered severely from the Cossack uprising.

Negativity in research on Jewish history received a substantial boost from Russian administrators seeking to blame the Jews for the difficult economic circumstances of the peasants. The present study demonstrates that with the exception of a few aggravations, interethnic relations in Rechitsa were marked by tolerance. In several sectors, economic relations between Jews and urban and peasant non-Jews might even be called symbiotic, a notion that was especially reinforced two decades later after the abolition of serfdom.

Many Russian civil servants did not understand the particulars of relations between Christians and Jews; thus the preference of the peasants for commercial relations with the Jews and not with other middlemen never ceased to amaze them. Like other colonized ethnic groups, the Jews were subjected to the discourse of *sliianie* (merger). Its effects, however, were torpedoed by administrators who gave priority to the nationalistic Russian Orthodox discourse, which was concerned with preventing "the plague of Jewish influence" from infecting the Russian people. A reflection of this resistance was the very involved complex of laws concerning Jews, which in terms of volume occupied a prominent place in Russian legislation. The process of formulating these laws created a major bureaucratic problem for the state that could be solved only by numerous committees. As a rule the new laws adopted in the wake of lengthy research on the problem of Jews in Russia did not satisfy any of the warring camps, not to speak of the liberals, who demanded equal rights for Jews.

The ponderous and contradictory legislation on Jews contained a multitude of reservations as well as circular local statutes that were not adopted in the regular legislative order but which nevertheless were considered even more important. As a result, the offices of all administrative and regulatory units were flooded with cases involving the adjudication of Jewish issues. Because of the numerous reservations and amendments in the legislation, decisions took a long time to be enacted; both the bureaucrats themselves and to a greater extent the Jews suffered from this protracted process.[27] Between 1817 and 1917, not a year passed without an edict or statute that dealt with Jews being enacted.

In this connection a conversation between soldiers overheard by an officer in the Russian trenches during the First World War is noteworthy. Fantasizing about the punishment to be meted out to German emperor Wilhelm II for unleashing the war, one soldier said that he would simply kill him. A second man suggested flogging him with a whip before shooting him. A third wanted to burn him at the stake, whereas a fourth soldier, a Jew, said the best way to punish him was by issuing him a Jewish passport to live out his life in Russia.[28] Although this conversation may have the ring of an anecdote or a tragicomic story from the pen of Sholem Aleichem, it very precisely conveys the attitude of Jews to their situation.

Although Jews suffered from their legal standing, their economic condition on the whole improved during tsarist rule. Even when one factors in the pogroms that occurred in the Russian Empire, the personal security of Jews nonetheless improved remarkably in comparison to the period of the Polish-Lithuanian Commonwealth. Both the personal security and the economic position of the majority of Jews were in danger after the October Revolution of 1917. Nearly two decades passed before a measure of economic stabilization was achieved. By this time, Jews had already lost many attributes of their national-religious life, thanks to the efforts of those in power. After a short-lived upsurge immediately after the Second World War, their consciousness of themselves Jews gradually disappeared. By the 1970s very little of such consciousness remained.

One my goals in this project was to inform the general reader, using the example of Rechitsa, about the various problems involved in the study of the history of the Jews in the territory of contemporary Belorussia and, to some extent, in the broader geographical area of contemporary Russia and Ukraine. I took advantage of the opportunity to introduce information from primary sources that was previously unknown to historians and that concerned both the history of the Jews of Belorussia and of the Russian Empire as a whole. Therefore, I submit this book to the judgment not only of those who emigrated from Rechitsa but also to other readers who are interested both in Jewish history and in the general history of Eastern Europe.

I have used a broad range of published and unpublished sources that can be divided into four basic types:

- Jewish sources, including Jewish newspapers in Hebrew and in Russian published during the period covered in the study, along with memoirs, letters, and written and oral family histories of Rechitsa Jews.
- General printed sources, including articles and commentaries in Russian newspapers, travelers' accounts, memoirs, and statistical reports.
- Archive materials held in Belarus, Russia, and Israel containing mainly statistical information and administrative correspondence about Rechitsa and Rechitsa Jews.
- Interviews with emigrants from Rechitsa in Israel, the United States, Germany, and Canada (letters and audio recordings held in my personal archive).

The book consists of eight chapters, divided at times thematically but maintaining an overall chronological progression. Chapter 1 discusses the history of Jewish Rechitsa beginning in the late sixteenth century, when official tolerance in the Grand Duchy of Lithuania combined with economic opportunity to attract Jewish settlement. After Rechitsa fell victim to the Khmelnitsky campaigns and invasion by Muscovy, the community began a demographic revival in the last third of the seventeenth century, but its economy overcame the consequences of those events only much later. The steady decline of the Polish-Lithuanian Commonwealth translated into hard times for the Jewish community in the eighteenth century, including a process of relative de-urbanization. The differing treatment and experience of the Jews in the former Lithuanian lands and those of Poland led to the development of a strongly differentiated ethnic subgroup, the Litvaks, in the Lithuanian lands of Belorussia and the Baltic.

The second chapter examines the abrupt changes that occurred after the Russian Empire acquired the area. Although this acquisition entailed the demolition of the old economic structure, it was somewhat softened by the existing system of communal responsibility for interactions with the government, such as payment of taxes and provision of recruits, inherited by the new authorities; thus Jewish distinctiveness from the rest of the population was reaffirmed. The growth of Hasidism (a revivalist movement with a distinctive social profile that stressed a joyous religiosity) reinforced this effect. As late as the mid-nineteenth century, membership in one's immediate religious community was a more important marker of identity for most Jews than adherence to Hasidism or membership in any ethnic subgroup. Attachment to one's own rabbi, particularly among Hasidim, might encourage or discourage migration, depending on how far away the rabbi lived. The abolition of the *kahal* system of communal self-government in 1844 weakened the internal bonds of the Jewish community just as the modernization of Russian society began to augment economic migration; at the same time gradual emancipation was increasing the number of Jewish youths who aspired to a secular education in the Russian language. The assassination of the "reformer tsar" Alexander II in 1881 shifted the government to a reactionary course under Alexander III and to a large extent under Nicholas II that predominated until 1917. The government's growing commitment to "Russification" and the re-imposition of legal restrictions on Jews had the countereffect of stimulating the national self-consciousness of the empire's non-Russian peoples; in the case of the Jews, the last decades of the empire witnessed an increased desire for national reorganization and recognition, emigration to America, the birth of the Zionist movement, secularization, and the growing attraction the revolutionary movement for Jewish youth. The revolution of 1905 reflected in large part the failure of Nicholas II's government to adapt to modernization. Although the establishment of the state Duma, or parliament, promised liberalization, the revolution was followed by a wave of reactionary violence that included widespread pogroms, including one in Rechitsa. When the government abruptly changed the electoral laws in 1907, any hopes that the Jews would receive equal rights were dashed. The growth of the Jewish population in the Pale of Settlement translated into a desperation auguring ill for the future.

Rechitsa's economy in the nineteenth and early twentieth centuries is the focus of the third chapter. After the incorporation of Belorussia into the Russian Empire, the authorities required Jews residing in villages to register as residents of towns (a move originally conceived to encourage urban development, if later represented as a way to shield the peasants from Jewish "exploitation"). This resulted in a shift in the Jewish population toward the towns and shtetls. Rechitsa's favorable location between economic districts, on the Dnieper River and close to Ukraine made it attractive to new migrants. During the first six decades of the new century, the number of artisans in Rechitsa more than quadrupled, significantly more than in most places in Minsk Province. Jews constituted the overwhelming majority of artisans and merchants in Rechitsa. Though most Jews no longer lived in villages, they retained their role in trade between villages and towns. The local trade fairs now ceded their preeminence to markets in the mestechkos. A peculiarity of Belorussia was that there the peasants (and others) tended to prefer the Jews to gentiles as middlemen. Despite this, before the 1880s the poverty of the peasants prevented Jewish artisans and traders from improving their situation. During the last decades of the century, however, the economic growth unleashed by Alexander II's reforms brought about improvements in the lives of the peasantry as well as their Jewish neighbors. For example, in Rechitsa several factories were operating by the end of the century, almost all of them owned by Jews.

Chapter 4 examines the urbanization of the Jewish population of Belorussia and of Rechitsa in particular. I compare population trends among the Jews with those of the non-Jewish population. I also explore trends and variations in Jewish migration and emigration. Using the microcosm offered by Rechitsa, this chapter examines marriage rates, fertility, mortality, infant mortality, and other indices to compare the Jewish community of Rechitsa with the gentile population and with other Jewish populations. Among my more interesting findings is that, contrary to the stereotypical belief widely adopted until the end of the nineteenth century regarding "the great fertility of the Jews," in fact, the birthrate of Jews was lower than that of Christians, but it was offset by a lower rate of infant mortality. The season of birth was an important factor in the survival rate of infants for reasons I discuss in this chapter. Jews married in August, and firstborn children appeared most often in May and the summer months; among the Orthodox population, who tended to marry in January and February, firstborns came in October to December. The peasants, needing women's hands to help take in the harvest, planned subsequent births to occur in late autumn or in winter. Given the relatively cool summer and the cold winter that prevailed in Belorussia, infants evidently died more often from respiratory diseases than from increased chances of infection in summer. The fact that the summertime mortality of infants was significantly lower in the southern Russian provinces than in the northern ones indicates that an increased chance of infection in summer was not a defining factor in infant deaths in Russia generally.

Chapter 5 addresses prerevolutionary social life. The late nineteenth century witnessed an increase in Jewish charitable activity, personified in the career of the *tzadik* (rebbe) Sholom-Dov-Ber Shneerson. By that time Rechitsa had become one of the most important centers of Hasidism in the empire. More widespread education in Rechitsa also contributed to the growth of the new Jewish intelligentsia. Rechitsa's reformist Jewish elementary school, one of the empire's first, founded in 1901 by proponents of Zionism to replace the religiously oriented traditional *heder*, manifested the intersection of charitable, educational, religious, political, and other trends at the beginning of the twentieth century. This chapter surveys these and other examples of the spiritual, charitable, and community life of a representative but unique early twentieth-century East European Jewish mestechko.

The interwar period is discussed in chapter 6. The February Revolution of 1917, when the tsar abdicated and was replaced by the so-called Provisional Government, opened unprecedented possibilities for the Jews of the Russian Empire, most immediately seen in the entry of larger numbers of Jews into the political life of the country. After the subsequent Bolshevik Revolution, political activity remained possible only within the framework of institutions created, or at least approved, by the ruling party. Jewish youths who had not emigrated before the early 1920s tended to be swept up in the revolutionary spirit of the Communist Party and the Communist Youth League (Komsomol). Any who were not motivated by the romantic idea of rebuilding the world were stirred into action by the endless new career possibilities: many abandoned Rechitsa for the cities. Still, in many respects the mestechko retained its traditional way of life, although the new authorities waged a (largely successful) campaign to suppress Jewish religious life. On the other hand, the "Jewish sections" of local party units promoted Yiddish culture, including government services, education, theater, and other avenues of cultural expression. The end of the mixed-market New Economic Policy in 1928 and the adoption of Stalin's crash industrialization program undercut the livelihood of self-employed Jews, many of whom now were marked (along with their families) as "class aliens"; these Jews found themselves second-class citizens deprived of many of their rights to employment, education, civic participation, and social services. Such difficulties motivated further out-migration. The population of the mestechkos grew older on average, and in many cases mestechkos collapsed or lost their Jewish character. The proportion of Jews in Rechitsa had fallen from one-half to one-quarter by the eve of World War II. And yet other Jews adapted to life in Rechitsa through the officially encouraged *artels* (crafts co-ops) or by becoming white-collar workers, managers, and officials. Life remained hard, and many breadwinners had to buy and sell on the black market, grow vegetables on private plots, or even keep a cow or some poultry. In Rechitsa as elsewhere, members of all ethnic groups fell victim to the purges that peaked in 1937 and 1938, carrying away a majority of the Soviet elite along with any members of the old elites still remaining at liberty.

Chapter 7 concentrates on the German occupation. Because Rechitsa was not immediately occupied, about 82 percent of its Jewish residents managed to flee to the East or to join the Red Army. Local authorities helped in this evacuation and even sought (unlike in most other places) to warn the Jewish population to leave. Among the Jews who remained were many elderly people and mothers with small children, who were less able to flee. Upon the arrival of the Germans, these people were subjected to humiliation and violence. Beginning in the third week of November 1941, the Jews were concentrated in stages into a ghetto (elsewhere this concentration took place in one step). From the beginning groups were taken to be executed, and the ghetto was "liquidated" on December 20, by which time the only Jews in Rechitsa—no more than twenty—were living in hiding or passing as gentiles. Some were found and killed, some escaped to join the partisans, but only five remained in Rechitsa to greet the Red Army on its return in November 1943.

Chapter 8 discusses the postwar period from 1945 until the collapse of the USSR. The German mass murders in 1941 and 1942 dealt an enormous blow to the mestechkos of the former Pale of Settlement. Most Belorussian, Ukrainian, and Baltic Jewish communities were destroyed. Jewish life could be restored after the return of the Red Army only in some communities, including Rechitsa, but none could be called mestechkos any longer, as all had permanently lost their Jewish character. Between 10 and 20 percent of those Jews who managed to evacuate Rechitsa died from illnesses and hunger on the way to or in the places to which they had fled. A certain number established themselves in their new locales; in any case most of their homes had been destroyed, taken over by their gentile neighbors, or demolished by the latter after the war for building materials. Still, most evacuees preferred to return. Some had to go through the courts to win their homes back, while new housing did not become available for some time. The issue of the return of Jewish property exacerbated anti-Semitism in Rechitsa, although the situation was not as bad as in neighboring Ukraine. The influence of German anti-Semitic propaganda may have played a role in this, but although the Soviet government suppressed openly violent expressions of anti-Semitism (and other ethnic conflicts), it did nothing to combat anti-Semitic attitudes. Indeed, Stalin's last years saw a new program of Russian chauvinism that translated into official and unofficial hostility toward Jews. Demobilized Jewish soldiers and returning evacuees found it difficult to reclaim their old jobs. Still, the shortage of qualified personnel permitted some Jews to find skilled or managerial work in Rechitsa, especially after the death of Stalin in 1953. For others the artels provided the way out of economic distress, although in the 1960s they were gradually merged into state enterprises.

On the other hand, and against the background of the arrival in Rechitsa in the first one and a half decades of the postwar era of a large number of non-Jewish migrants, which increased the size of the population almost 30 percent, Jews were broadly represented among the intelligentsia and administrators and were looked upon simply as established old residents who were also economically the most active part of the population, constituting an important part of the urban elite in the 1950s and 1960s. During the more stable Khrushchev and Brezhnev years, many of Rechitsa's remaining Jews sought to blend into the surrounding "Soviet" population. Others sustained an underground religious and Jewish cultural life. But out-migration to other parts of the Soviet Union, assimilation, and, later, emigration out of the USSR combined to erode the Jewish community of Rechitsa to under two thousand when the Soviet Union was abolished, a trend that only accelerated afterward.

1

Rechitsa and the Jews under the Polish-Lithuanian Commonwealth in the Seventeenth and Eighteenth Centuries

Rechitsa extends along the right bank of the Dnieper River in Eastern Polesia. The town's picturesque setting left its impression on travelers who came there. The writer and ethnographer Pavel Shpilevskii (1821–1861), who traveled in this area, wrote: "Rechitsa Uezd is particularly famed for its majestic oak groves along the banks of the Dnieper, places where, perhaps, the ancient Krivichi had their magical places, their sacred hills and places of worship. . . . In short, the forests in the Minsk area are marvelous."[1] Semën Dubnov described his impressions of the area surrounding Rechitsa very graphically:

> Each day I would walk through the pine forest that towered like a high wall around the field of rye adjoining our yard. On the boundary of field and forest, where the bright path among the ears of rye ended, began a dark forest path whose entrance looked like the maw of an enormous green beast. I would enter the forest's mouth as one enters into the semidarkness of a sacred temple and walk among the colonnades of pines until the land dropped sharply to a meadow, beyond which the glassy surface of the river sparkled in the sun.[2]

In the ninth century the territory of Rechitsa was at the junction point of the settlements of several Slavic tribes—the Radimichi to the east, the Dregovichi to the west, the Krivichi to the north, and the Poliane to the south.[3] It is most likely that the Krivichi and the Dregovichi, who moved into the Dnieper basin from the west, assimilated the population of Balts who had lived there since ancient times. Rechitsa's name (literally, "small river," Slavic) probably came from the river of that name that flowed into the Dnieper there. Today the river has all but vanished. It is assumed that a settlement already existed in this place in the second half of the eleventh century, and that it became a part of the Duchy of Pinsk-Turov in the middle of the twelfth century. By the beginning of the thirteenth century, Rechitsa was part of the Duchy of Chernigov. It was sacked by the Novgorod prince Mstislav Mstislavovich the Bold (?–1228) and by the Novgorod governor Tverdislav. According to the Gustyn Chronicle, this sacking took place in 1213; the Patriarchal or Nikonian Chronicle dates it in 1214.[4] It is likely that the settlement had already become relatively large, since the chronicler thought it necessary to mention the event. Through the entire thirteenth century, the princes of Turov, Polotsk, Kiev, Chernigov, and Smolensk laid claims to Rechitsa because it was located at the point where all their borders touched. In December 1240, the Mongol-Tatar troops of Subedei (Sabutai) passed through southern Belorussia, and it is likely that they also pillaged Rechitsa. Several decades later, in 1259, the united forces of the East Slavic princes inflicted a defeat on the Mongol-Tatar Golden Horde not far from Rechitsa.

At that time, the trading quarter of the ancient town (today, the site of the park on the Dnieper) was defended on one side by the Dnieper River, while the remainder of the quarter was laid out in a semicircle behind a fortified rampart. The Rechitsa River, which flowed alongside the rampart, made the quarter even more impregnable. It was here, between the rampart and the river, that the town market was held in times of peace.[5]

Gediminas, the Grand Duke of Lithuania, Ruthenia, and Zemgale (r. 1316–1342), who made almost all the territory of contemporary Belorussia along with the Kievan lands subordinate to him, probably never managed to seize Rechitsa from the Prince of Chernigov. Vladimir Pashuto believes that the absence of Rechitsa from the list of towns turned over to the new Grand Duke of Lithuania, Olgerd (r. 1345–1377), suggests this was the case.[6] Most probably, Olgerd conquered Rechitsa in the early 1350s during his campaigns against Chernigov, which itself fell in 1356. Nevertheless, in the Muscovite State, which also laid claim to Kiev, the towns of eastern Belorussia—Rechitsa, Gomiy (Gomel), Rogachev, Mozyr, and Turov—formally continued to be regarded as Kievan even in the last decade of the fourteenth century.[7]

When the Grand Duchy of Lithuania expanded eastward and southward, the influence of Orthodox landowners within its nobility grew stronger. This new influence found expression in the spread of the East Slavic proto-Belorussian language among the old Baltic nobility and in their acculturation to a certain degree. One such expression was Olgerd's having his children baptized in the Orthodox rite. All the inhabitants of the grand duchy were called Litvins in neighboring countries, and in Poland they were sometimes even called Rusins. For a long time legal proceedings, like business operations generally, were carried out in the proto-Belorussian language within the grand duchy.

Olgerd's son and heir Jagailo (ca. 1350–1434) married the Polish queen Jadwiga in 1385, and once he had accepted the Catholic faith under the name Wladyslaw, he became king of Poland as well. The role of the Catholic clergy in Poland was enhanced during his reign. Under the influence of the clergy, several anti-Jewish pogroms were instigated, and clerics persuaded Jagailo to issue a series of decrees against the Jews. The Litvin magnates, the vast majority of whom were Orthodox, disapproved of the grand duke's conversion to Catholicism, particularly after his attempt to spread this faith throughout the grand duchy. The united Polish-Lithuanian state faced the threat of a schism. With the aim of avoiding this, Jagailo in 1387 ceded a number of towns in Central and Eastern Belorussia, including Rechitsa, to his brother, Švitrigaila (Skrigaile, ?–1452), who was known for being more tolerant.

At the end of the fourteenth century, the Litvin magnates undertook a stubborn campaign to ensure the broad autonomy of Lithuania by resisting in all possible ways any plans for it to be absorbed by Poland. This resistance was destined to become a permanent and defining factor in the relationship of the two states for three centuries. Vladimir Picheta believes that the Old Lithuanian aristocracy entered the union with Poland out of fear of absorption by the Orthodox aristocracy and that nearly all the subsequent rivalry in the Lithuanian duchy between the opponents and proponents of the union can be explained by this threat. In actuality, the agreement of the Old Lithuanian aristocracy to this union was dictated in large measure by external politics, something Picheta himself writes about.[8] Therefore, in accordance with the views of Timothy Snyder, it is much more accurate to speak of the symbiosis and mutual acculturation of the Old Lithuanian and Orthodox aristocracies within the Lithuanian duchy.[9] The policies of the Old Lithuanian magnates, the Radziwills, who were opposed to closer relations with Poland, serve as an example of this.

The Litvin aristocracy had no desire to recognize Švitrigaila as their ruler, regarding him as no different from his brother. They therefore supported their cousin Vitautas, who seized the throne of the grand duchy in Vilna in 1392 and ruled it until his death in 1430. The result of military campaigns and diplomatic contention by both sides was the Treaty of 1413 between Vitautas and Jagailo, which recognized the Lithuanian duke's broad autonomy of rule along with formal acknowledgment of his status as vassal of the Polish king. Wishing to centralize his state, Vitautas, in the same year of 1413, granted broad freedoms to the *szlachta* (the noble, landowning class in Poland, Lithuania, Belorussia, and Ukraine), giving them, in fact, rights equal to those of the great magnates.[10] During his reign, Vitautas added to Lithuania the lands between the Dniester and the Dnieper as far south as the Black Sea and seized Smolensk and Viaz'ma as well.

Vitautas differed from his formal suzerain in his tolerance toward Jews, and he granted the Jewish communities in Brest, Grodno, and Troki a wide range of privileges aimed at developing the backward economy of his duchy. To end the widespread violence that was often inflicted on Jews at the time, he issued a document that imposed the death penalty and confiscation of property as punishments for the killing of a Jew; for a beating or injury the grand duke collected a fine and awarded the same amount of compensation to the victim as would be given to a noble. Jews were given a guarantee of the inviolability of their property. Strict punishment was imposed for disrupting Jewish religious services and for vandalizing Jewish cemeteries. Vitautas in fact offered Jews the same rights as Christians in commerce and in making loans and allowed them to engage in trades and farming.[11] The privileges Vitautas granted became a constituent part of the statute of the Grand Duchy of Lithuania in 1588.[12] This unique collection of judicial norms was ahead of its time in its defense of the inviolability of all the inhabitants of the duchy, including Jews, as well as of their property.

The provision of such broad rights for Jews was unprecedented in medieval Europe. In taking advantage of these rights, the Jews played a valuable role in the development of the duchy's economy. The surviving medieval chronicles, the records of legal disputes, and the grand duke's charters and decrees contain a great deal of evidence about the economic activity of Jews in the grand duchy. Jews in fact functioned as bankers, changing money, issuing receipts, becoming agents, and extending loans; they themselves borrowed money from the szlachta and the church, thus helping the lender by paying high interest. One cannot but agree with the well-known Russian historian Matvei Liubavskii when he argues that the great competitive ability of the Jews came from their willingness to accept responsibility as partners, their spirit of enterprise, and their mobility (at a time when Christians were reluctant to leave their place of residence for the sake of undertaking a new venture).[13] Collective responsibility had taught the Jews the value of solidarity, which in the marketplace took the form of mutual assistance and joint investment of resources. The latter was essential for them to carry out the banking operations mentioned, considering that, unlike the aristocrats, there few individual Jews possessed large capital. In essence, the system they followed was the prototype of the joint stock company.

The grandson of Jagailo, Alexander I Jagiellon (born 1460 and grand duke to his death in 1506), who had been installed as grand duke by the Litvin magnates, became simultaneously the king of Poland in 1501. He had been educated in the Catholic judeophobic tradition. Guided not by political but by spiritual and religious feelings, he was disturbed to see the Jews in Lithuania growing economically stronger and supplanting the Christians in business and trade. In 1495 Alexander I Jagiellon expelled all the Jews from the duchy, depriving them of their property and the right to collect their debts. Eight years later, in 1503, because of economic decline, he was compelled to summon them back, return the property taken from them, and restore their former rights.

Aside from his state interests, Alexander I Jagiellon also had a personal interest in bringing the Jews back and restoring them to their former position in society: taxes from Jewish communities in the Lithuanian duchy, the same as in many other European Christian lands as well as in all Muslim countries, were a basic source of income for the personal treasury of the ruling monarch. Everywhere the presence of Jews became much more significant during times of military campaigns, since heavier taxes could be levied on them to cover the costs of the army. This happened in Lithuania, for example, in 1565, 1566, and 1568, during the war with Muscovy.[14]

During the reign of Vitautas, Rechitsa had come under the authority of the Kievan *namestnik* (governor). At that time, a wooden castle-fortress with five towers was erected here. It was located in the center of the town, on a high bank of the Dnieper, and was surrounded by a deep moat, across which a drawbridge led into the town. The market square was located in the center of the town and near it the houses of the wealthy residents. Two lines of wooden fortifications surrounded the center of the town, and the largest part of the town's blocks of houses lay between them. The whole of Rechitsa encompassed an area of seven hundred by four hundred meters along the river and did not continue any farther west than the present-day Sovietskaia Street.[15] The Rechitsa castle-fortress, along with wooden castles in Dubrovno, Orsha, Kopys', Starosel'e, Shklov, Mogilev, Bykhov, Rogachev, Streshin, and Gorval', made up the Dnieper defense line that protected the Lithuanian duchy from the east. From the south, along the Pripyat' River basin, it was protected by castles in Bragin, Mozyr, Lel'chitsi, Turov, David-Gorodok, Pinsk, and Kobrin; because of the expansion of the duchy at the end of the fourteenth century, this had now become a second line of defense.[16]

From the end of the fifteenth to the middle of the sixteenth century, these fortress towns of southwestern Belorussia suffered from raids by Crimean Tatars, who had previously laid waste to Ukraine. The attacks were encouraged by the

Grand Prince of Muscovy, Ivan III (1440–1505), because the Crimean Tatars were his allies in the struggle with Lithuania and its ally, the Golden Horde. The Muscovite state itself, with its policy of expansion by military conquest, was an even greater threat for Rechitsa at the beginning of the sixteenth century. A particularly large number of raids on Rechitsa took place during the Muscovite-Lithuanian War of 1500–1503. During that period, forces from Rechitsa undertook counterraids in the Chernigov area and very often besieged Starodub.[17] The war ended with a treaty, according to the terms of which nineteen captured towns were ceded to Moscow.[18]

But the peace was a precarious one, and raiding by both sides continued. The most devastating raid on Rechitsa occurred in 1505, when the Muscovites "waged war on it to its very root"; in other words, they burned it to the ground.[19] In turn a deputy of Rechitsa, Simeon Polozovich (who assumed the post no later than 1518) attacked the borders of the Gomel and Starodub Volosts. The king of Poland, who was at the same time the Lithuanian grand duke Sigismund I the Old (1467–1548), and the Grand Prince of Muscovy, Vasilii III Ivanovich (1479–1533), exchanged mutual recriminations about these attacks in 1525. Because real accommodation was not achieved, Polozovich was induced in 1529 to petition Sigismund I the Old to fortify Rechitsa (Rzeczyca in Polish spelling). In that year, the king granted all the tax monies from his Rechitsa possessions, excluding those on honey, mead, and beer, for the fortification and restoration of Rechitsa castle. After strengthening Rechitsa, Polozovich launched a raid against Gomel and its environs.[20]

From the beginning of the sixteenth century, then, Rechitsa grew in importance as a strongpoint of border defense. In 1535, during the so-called rule of seven boyars period, Sigismund I the Old, taking advantage of the internal strife within Muscovy, sent the Lithuanian hetman (military commander) Jerzy Radziwill (like the other Radziwills, he was an ardent opponent of union with Poland)[21] to reconquer the territories on the right bank of the Dnieper that Ivan III had seized earlier. Reinforcements of several thousand Poles joined the Lithuanian force in Rechitsa, and the united forces crossed the Dnieper and captured Gomel, at that time a small mestechko.[22]

At the beginning of the sixteenth century, taxes in the town were collected by deputies of the chief state treasurer (*wielki litewski podskarbi*), Jan Abraham Ezofowicz Rebrikovich (1450–1519), a Jew who had converted to Christianity. The residents of Rechitsa were displeased by the multitude of taxes and requisitions; therefore, in 1511, they obtained from Sigismund I the Old a limited form of the Magdeburg Law permitting them to pay a single tax deposited directly into the grand duke's treasury.[23] Major Belorussian towns like Polotsk and Minsk had received the Magdeburg Rights not long before (in 1498 and 1499, respectively); Novogrudok received them in 1511 as well, and Mogilev and Vitebsk even later than Rechitsa, in 1561 and 1597, respectively. Rechitsa's Magdeburg Rights were confirmed in 1561 by Sigismund II Augustus (1520–1572) and in 1596 by Sigismund III (1566–1632).

The Magdeburg Law gave the town self-government by an elected town council, the *rada*. The rada consisted of a group of councillors who chose from among them the burgomasters who presided there. The rada was headed by a *voit* (elder) appointed by the grand duke. The organs of the town's self-government had at their disposal the income from weigh scales in the market, the collection of beeswax, the community baths, the mills, and from the taverns leased from the grand duke. The freedoms and privileges of the Magdeburg Law were not extended to the Jewish communities of Lithuania, however. Moreover, granting the law to the Lithuanian towns, that is, to their Christian population, restricted the rights of local Jews even more. The only exception was the extension of these rights to the Jews of Troki in 1441.[24] A few centuries later, several other Jewish towns of the grand duchy were given these rights. We know, for example, that they were extended to the Jews in Keydany (now Kiedainiai, Lithuania).[25] But granting the Magdeburg Law to the Jews also resulted in some harmful consequences for them. In particular, the laws of the town, and not the laws of the king, were endowed with legal force. The Jews much preferred the laws of the Crown.[26]

At the midpoint of the seventeenth century, Rechitsa paid a large amount of taxes into the state treasury: 50 copas of Lithuanian groshen, approximately the same amount as the more prominent cities of Minsk and Vladimir-Volynsky, but more than Slutsk and Borisov.[27] This apportionment of taxes points to the growing economic importance of Rechitsa. Therefore, it is no wonder that because of the administrative reform of 1565–1566, Rechitsa became the center of the largest of the three counties of the Minsk Voivodship (province). The towns of Gomel, Khal'ch, Bobruisk, Rogachev, Gorval', Belitsa, Kholmech, and others were included in this powiat. Rechitsa was allotted two seats in the rada of the grand duchy.

Under Jagailo's successors, the Litvin magnates continued to resist the absorption of the grand duchy by Poland. From Casimir IV Jagiellon (Grand Duke of Lithuania from 1440 and king of Poland from 1445), they obtained in 1547 a decree stating that only Litvins, that is, subjects of the grand duchy, could hold positions in the state and the towns, and only they could possess or rent crown lands in Lithuania.[28] Although the rulers of the two states signed the Union of

Melnik in 1501, the Lithuanian nobility campaigned against it, since they wanted only a defense treaty with Poland or a confederation that would preserve the duchy's independence. Because the Polish side was not prepared to agree to this, the Lithuanian rada refused to confirm the union.

Under the threat of Muscovite expansion during the Livonian War (1558–1583), Lithuania was compelled in 1569 to sign the new Union of Lublin and become part of a united state, the Polish-Lithuanian Commonwealth. Although the Grand Duchy of Lithuania kept its autonomy and could count on the retention of its army, financial system with its own currency, and its legal system, it was compelled to agree to transfer its most fertile voivodships—Volynia, Bracław, Podole, and Kiev—to Poland. Aside from that, several members of the Lithuanian state rada were not given seats in the united Polish-Lithuanian parliament, the Sejm, which, by a majority vote, decided that its permanent meeting place would be Warsaw. On the threshold of unification and immediately afterward, many state institutions, administrative units, and the nomenclature within the grand duchy were unified according to the Polish model. For example, in 1566, a land court (*ziemski sąd*) was introduced and counties were combined into voivodships; in 1569, the volost' (*włość* in Polish spelling)—small rural area—was renamed *starostwo*. In 1588 the Lithuanian statute was revised. As Timothy Snyder maintains, the union of the Grand Duchy of Lithuania and the Polish kingdom was organic, gradual, and meticulously negotiated.[29]

The new and closer union of the Grand Duchy of Lithuania with Poland changed the internal politics of the duchy. Before the union, the Orthodox population, which had their personal freedom, comprised the majority there, and this was something the ducal power had to consider. Although Orthodox Christians remained a significant factor in the united state, they were now only a minority. The Polish nobility and the Catholic Church considered them disloyal, so after the signing of the Union of Lublin, missionaries exerted increased pressure on them and on the elite in particular. In response, a number of Orthodox magnates, mainly those from the eastern regions of the duchy, pledged their allegiance to the ruler of Muscovy and detached themselves from the Polish-Lithuanian Commonwealth along with their ancestral lands. Some of the Orthodox landowners had to flee to Muscovy. The majority, however, gradually accepted conversion to Catholicism. This happened because the rulers of Muscovy used various means to encroach gradually on the lands of the boyars, transforming themselves into the sole owners of all state lands, which they then granted to a new nobility class (*dvorianstvo*) for temporary use. In the Polish-Lithuanian Commonwealth, by contrast, the relationship between the king and the landowners was based on vassalage. Thus the dedication and loyalty of the Russian nobility in the early modern period was not to the state but to the ruler; this allegiance, in turn, strengthened the monarchy but did not encourage the aristocracy to think in terms of the state, as was the case in the Polish-Lithuanian Commonwealth as well as in western Europe. The landowners of Muscovy, who were not assured of being able to hold on to their estates, attempted to squeeze as much as they could from the land and the peasants attached to it. The Russian nobility treated service to the state in the same manner, attempting to derive as much personal gain from it as possible. Enormous abuses resulted from this practice.

The two states also differed in their goals of governance. In Muscovy, the monarchy inherited the idea of extreme despotism from the rulers of the Golden Horde and saw their primary task as the strengthening of absolutism. The Grand Duchy of Lithuania was a constitutional monarchy in which the monarch, elected by representatives of the szlachta, granted the nobility civil and political rights, including the right of immunity. Such a system left the monarch no opportunity to concentrate all the power in his own hands. This form of democracy had become one of the values of many Litvin Orthodox magnates, and in cherishing it they preferred to remain loyal to the state rather than to Orthodoxy. The Ostrogskis, a dynasty of Volynian magnates, provide one of the most characteristic examples of the forced move of the elite from Orthodoxy to Catholicism. Its most noted member was the governor of Kiev Voivodship Konstanty Wasyl Ostrogski (1527–1608), a fierce opponent of union with Poland and an Orthodox zealot. Lev Ogiński (1595–1657), the vice regent of Troki and representative of an even more aristocratic, princely clan, shared these traits. In the war with the Muscovite state, he demonstrated loyalty to the Polish-Lithuanian Commonwealth and distinguished himself as a military leader. His son Szymon Karal (1625–1694) had already converted first to the Uniate Church and then to Catholicism. This did not prevent him from using his own funds in 1690 to rebuild the Orthodox Saint Mark Monastery in Vitebsk, which had burned down and which his late father had patronized.[30] Other offspring of Lev also converted to Catholicism. Among them were several Lithuanian hetmans. The Ostrogskis, the Ogińskis, the Wiśniowieckis, and many other representatives of the Lithuanian nobility following the Jagiellonian dynasty early in the contemporary era formed a significant segment of the Polish elite.

Since Orthodox peasants and town dwellers in the territory of contemporary Belarus and Ukraine did not want to convert to Catholicism, an intermediate variant in the form of the Uniate Church was invented for them. However, in both these regions the people adopted it differently. In Belorussia the Uniate

Church was successful by virtue of the smoothness of the transition. By the second half of the eighteenth century, up to 80 percent of the rural population was Uniate. In Rechitsa Powiat the Uniate faith probably spread more vigorously. At that time 89 percent of all Christian churches were Uniate.[31] In Ukraine the Uniate Church was less well accepted by the peasants because its introduction coincided with the time when Ukraine was transferred from the Grand Duchy of Lithuania to Poland, which meant that many former customs were summarily abolished. Also, right after this territorial transition an intense imposition of serfdom on the peasantry began. Polish magnates thus received ownership rights to noncultivated land (primarily pastures), which previously had been in common use. Under these conditions the acceptance of the Uniate rite by the Ukrainian people would also have been an admission of humiliating spiritual subordination. Religious and socioeconomic opposition led to peasant and Cossack uprisings, the first major one in 1594–1596.

One of the leaders of the uprising that broke out in Ukraine, Severin Nalivaiko, spread the revolt into the southeastern part of Belorussia in the autumn of 1595. After bands of Cossacks and peasants had laid waste to Slutsk and Mogilev, they suffered a defeat at the hands of a volunteer force assembled by Litvin magnates and led by the hetman. As he withdrew his two-thousand-man force back to Ukraine in early 1596, Ataman Nalivaiko looted Rechitsa. In Ukraine that same year, he lost a battle against the Polish army, was taken prisoner, and later executed. Over the following years, however, Cossack forces from Ukraine again invaded Belorussia, raiding towns and mestechkos. According to the Annals of Barkulabov, they held Rechitsa briefly at least twice—in 1600, under Hetman Samuil Koshka, and in 1602, under Hetman Ivan Kosoi.[32]

After these events the town was fortified. In 1634, the *voivoda* of Minsk and former elder (*starosta*) of Rechitsa Alexander Sluszka (who ruled in Rechitsa from 1612 until 1618), established a Dominican monastery in the town; this became the Catholic center of southeastern Belorussia for the next two centuries. At the beginning of the seventeenth century, Rechitsa had some two thousand residents.[33]

As far back as 1589, the Rechitsa subprefecture (starostwo) was included as one of the "household" possessions, the income from which went to support the Grand Duke of Lithuania and his court. In the fifteenth and sixteenth centuries, the principal income of the Rechitsa governors came from the collection of wild honey, which is shown by the royal charter of 1500 on taxes in regions along the Dnieper, including Rechitsa Volost'.[34] The Annals of Barkulabov, which tell of the damage done to the honey-gathering trade by the storms that passed through eastern Polesia in June 1592, also confirm that this occupation was the most important in the region.[35] Historian Boris Zakhoder posits that honey gathering was a traditional Slavic occupation at that time.[36]

Economic life in Rechitsa, which had suffered during the rebellion, began to revive. Jews, whom the szlachta had begun to employ on their estates, contributed to this recovery. Ivan Pryzhov, a scholar who has written on the history of drinking establishments in Russia, states that in Retchisk (he probably means Rechitsa) in 1596, the Jew Lazar leased a drinking establishment from a Polish gentleman, a *pan*.[37] Because he does not provide any sources and because his work has a markedly anti-Jewish bias, his statement may not be correct. In any case, a Jewish quarter already existed in Rechitsa in the second quarter of the seventeenth century.[38] At the same time, Jewish quarters appeared in other Belorussian towns and mestechkos as well: Bykhov, Gomel, Mozyr, Chausy, and Shklov. Jews from the more populated western part of the duchy came to these places. Even earlier, in the second half of the sixteenth century, Christians had made the same migration to the vacant eastern lands, which had been ravaged by the raids of Tatars, Cossacks, and Muscovites.[39] Evidently, the moves by both Christians and Jews were stimulated by the economic reform of 1560, which had replaced taxes in kind with monetary taxes and thus had promoted the development of trading and monetary relations and, consequently, the increased ability of peasants and craftsmen to market their goods.[40]

Overall, Jews tended to settle in separate quarters because of their desire to stay together and to keep themselves apart from the rest of the population. Isolation allowed Jews to live by their own laws and to reduce or completely avoid incidents of forced conversion to Christianity. As far as the Christians were concerned, the self-isolation of Jews increased the suspicions of the Christian population toward them, on the one hand, and on the other hand, allowed them to overcome their fear of Jewish "otherness."

The Jews enjoyed the privileges that Grand Duke Vitautas, mentioned earlier, had extended throughout the Duchy of Lithuania at the beginning of the sixteenth century. Since the Jews were not involved in local self-government, they secured the right to resolve civil disputes with Christians under the authority of the grand duke, an authority that had earlier tried Jews only for criminal matters. In privately owned mestechkos, criminal courts had been the prerogative of the owner since 1539.

The Litvin elite, the major landowners, needed Jews as a valuable intermediary link in various credit and trade dealings, and in the first half of the sixteenth century they had often pleaded on their behalf before the Lithuanian grand duke.

The lesser Litvin landowners, however, had no objection to taking on trade and conducting tax farming on credit operations themselves and therefore saw the Jews as rivals. After the signing of the Union of Lublin, the previous rights of the Jews to tax farming and leasing remained in force in the autonomous grand duchy; at the same time, apparently, in Poland itself restrictions had already been imposed on Jews in these same areas of enterprise.[41]

Despite the broad range of privileges that distinguished the legal position of Jews in the grand duchy from that in many other European countries of the time, they did not lead to an appreciable amount of Jewish immigration there, and the number of Jews in Lithuania increased because of the natural growth of the population; over the course of sixty years, from 1568 to 1628, the population of Jews within the duchy doubled—from twenty to forty thousand.[42]

By the end of the 1620s, Jews made up only a small portion of the population of what is now Belorussia—1.5 percent of the total number of inhabitants. In towns, however—and centers with a population greater than 1,500 people were considered towns—the proportion of Jews was considerably higher. It varied from 2 to 10 percent of all inhabitants.[43] There were particularly high numbers of Jews in the large towns in western Belorussia—Brest, Grodno, and Pinsk. They were noted for their keen competition in "Jewish" trades. Most likely, this led the Jews in Belorussia, as in the whole of the grand duchy, to internal migration. On the one hand, Jews moved from large towns to smaller, privately owned centers; on the other hand, they also developed the eastern territories, moving from western to eastern Belorussia and establishing new communities there and enlarging the existing ones. The Jewish population increased in Rechitsa as well.

Magistrates defending the rights of Christians impeded Jews who wanted to practice trades. Thus in Rechitsa, as in many other places, Jews most commonly engaged in small-scale retailing, selling alcohol, and brokerage. There were scarcely any large entrepreneurs in southeastern Belorussia at the time who were engaged in wholesale trade and leasing. Possibly many more of them lived in neighboring Ukraine.[44] They were invited to lease land there not only by Catholic magnates, as is generally believed, but also by Orthodox magnates—and possibly even in greater numbers. For example, the aforementioned Ostrogskis, who built a large number of Orthodox churches and only rarely allowed the building of Catholic churches, employed four thousand Jews on their extensive holdings in Volynia and Kiev districts, selling the vodka, beer, and mead that they produced.[45]

The view is widespread among current historians that Jews in Ukraine played a prominent part in the administration of landed estates and trade in the first half of the seventeenth century. In fact, these circumstances more closely correspond to the situation at the end of the seventeenth through the beginning of the eighteenth century. This administrative and commercial role of Jews was broadly reflected in the Ukrainian folklore of the eighteenth century that glorified the struggle waged by Khmelnitski's Cossacks against Jewish exploiters. "The Eyewitness Chronicle," compiled early in the eighteenth century, should be listed here also. And although the narrative in this work begins in 1648, it focuses on events in Ukraine since the mid-1670s. The Jews in the story enrich themselves as leaseholders and innkeepers whose prices compelled the Cossacks themselves to produce mead, Ukrainian *horilka*, and wine.[46]

Later this view was publicized and extended in the works of Ukrainian historians in the second half of the nineteenth and the early twentieth century: Vladimir Antonovich, Pantelemon Kulish, and Nikolai Kostomarov. Devoting themselves exclusively to explaining the cause of Orthodox Ukrainians' manifested hatred of the Jews in 1648, they demonized the caricatures of seventeenth-century Jews and accused them without proof of leasing churches.[47] Documents supporting this charge were not found by commissions analyzing ancient documents of southwestern Russia (usable name in the Russian Empire for Ukrainian lands), which published approximately ten collections of documents in the second half of the nineteenth century. It is also worth noting way that neither did these collections contain documents certifying a significant role for Jews in buying and leasing out property in Ukraine.

The nineteenth-century Russian Jewish historians Mark Vishnitser and Semën Dubnov also helped disseminate the notion that Jews played an important role in the Ukrainian economy. They used the conclusions of prejudiced Ukrainian research instead of ascertaining the truth about the share of activity by Jews in leasing and buyouts.[48] Under the influence of these references, other later and no less important researchers of Jewish history went even further and arrived at unfounded presuppositions regarding the dominant role of Jews in such activities.[49]

Meanwhile, documents in a collection of articles concerning economic activity in Ukraine prior to the mid-seventeenth century provide evidence that Jews played only a secondary role in the leasing, buying, and usurious administration of rural land. The magnates and the petty nobility, Polish as well as local, were more heavily engaged in this themselves.[50] The well-known collections *Regesty i nadpisi* published by the Society for the Propagation of Enlightenment among the Jews in Russia, which contain documents about Jews from numerous sources from the mid-sixteenth to the mid-seventeenth century, likewise did not contain proof of the dominance of Jews in the buyouts and leasing of land in Ukraine.

The work has documents only about leaseholding by Jews of the mestechko Gorokhov and eleven villages as well as by one Jew from Zhitomir Starostwo who was collaborating on a fifty-fifty basis with a wellborn Ukrainian. In addition to this work are materials concerning the purchase of tax collections by Jews in Lutsk and the water tax in Kiev.[51]

Documents about the economic and legal treatment of peasants in the sixteenth through eighteenth centuries in the collection titled *Arkhiv Iugo-Zapadnoi Rossii* (Archive of Southwestern Russia), the goal of which, as is obvious in the preface written by the editor, Ivan Novitskii, was to show the reader how peasants in Ukraine were oppressed, give us a basis for concluding, on the one hand, that more than half of the landed estates were not rented out but were managed by the owners themselves, and, on the other hand, that Jewish leaseholders constituted no more than 10 percent of the total.

The events of 1631 in Lubny (Poltava region) are testimony to the absence of any widespread hatred of the Jews. A certain Ivan with a group of supporters had declared himself king and had begun to pillage the Jews there. He appealed to the Cossacks to continue staging pogroms throughout Lithuania. At that point the local Cossack colonel, Minets, executed the bandits.[52]

The leader of the largest Cossack uprising (1648–1654), Bogdan Khmelnitsky (Khmel', in Jewish and some East Slavic sources), also made fighting the Jews part of his program. At the start of the uprising, he needed to recruit manpower, and the chance to pillage the Polish nobility and the Jews was tailor-made to attract a segment of the Ukrainian people to the rebel army.[53] An invitation to share in the spoils lurked beneath his appeal to the Crimean Khan to attack the Poles and the Jews on both banks of the Dnieper River.[54]

Townspeople (*meshchane*) were the only stratum of the population that might harbor hostility toward the Jews because of their economic competition, whereas the peasants had little contact with Jews and the Cossacks had even less. And although the townspeople frequently encountered Jews in their capacity as tavern owners, Jews did not form a majority of tavern keepers there, and they had to be regarded as a link performing useful services whose prices for alcohol were necessarily lower than those of their Orthodox competitors.[55]

It is also worth noting that in that period of Ukrainian history, as in the Lithuanian duchy, Jews were not "terra incognita" for the local East Slavic residents inasmuch as many of them spoke fluently *po Russku*, as the proto–East Slav language was then called. This is confirmed by their petitions for the translation of legal documents and charters of privileges into that language. Their nicknames testify to the serious cultural impact of the East Slav language on the Jews.[56]

Evidently Khmelnitsky was playing more to the religious fanaticism of the Orthodox, which was then at fever pitch. At that time the Orthodox magnates in Ukraine already were being compelled to convert to Catholicism or to do so indirectly through temporary acceptance of the Uniate Church. For this reason the Cossacks emerged as the only defenders of the Orthodox faith. The growth in the number of Catholics and Jews in Ukraine created the sensation of a need for religious expansion on the part of Orthodox Christians.

The manifesto in which Khmelnitsky addressed the Orthodox population in May 1648 reflects these feelings. In it he enumerates in detail the grievances afflicting Orthodox Christians caused by Polish "predators," on one occasion referring to "the Jews who collect their rent for them."[57] In contrast to Ivan, Khmelnitsky called for struggle primarily against the Poles. Only a little more than a month later, he stated his claims to Władysław IV Vasa. Begging forgiveness for the uprising and vowing to expunge his guilt with faithful service, the Cossack hetman was only deceiving the king, Khmelnitsky complained about the administration and added that the cunning Jews wanted to gorge themselves on Ukrainian landed estates.[58] Therefore, it is impossible not to agree with Salo Baron's conclusion that the complaint is not a biting one but is marginal in nature.[59] These two documents are the only evidence that Khmelnitsky and the insurgents were displeased with the Jews.

Here the chronicle *Yeven metzulah* (published first in Venice in 1653) should be mentioned, because the author, Nathan Hanover, considers the purchase of taxes by Jews as the cause of the uprising.[60] Hanover, however, presents no proof, and he makes this claim to explain the numerous Jewish victims of the uprising. The most recent studies show that Hanover has highly inflated their numbers.[61] The validity of Hanover's description of the participation of two Jews, Jacob and Zechariah, both Sobelenki, in the town of Chigirin, in Khmelnitsky's personal conflict is also questionable. Zechariah allegedly slandered Bogdan, while Jacob, a friend of Khmelnitsky, supposedly helped him.[62] No other sources, including archival sources, confirm the existence of these two Jews and their involvement in Khmelnitsky's fate.

Aside from inciting the people to rebel, Khmelnitsky, in a play for support, portrayed himself to Tsar Aleksei Mikhailovich (1629–1676) as a defender of the Orthodox faith. A note from the Russian envoy to Khmelnitsky's scribe, Grigory Kunakov, in Moscow is the only document of the period that directly explains the Cossacks' anti-Jewish pogroms as a reaction to oppressive acts committed by the Jews.[63] At that time the anti-Jewish discourse of Moscow with respect to the Polish-Lithuanian Commonwealth was widely known. In January 1638, despite a special request from Władysław IV Vasa to Tsar Mikhail Fedorovich (1596—1645), the father of Aleksei, the tsar refused to allow the royal intermediary, Aaron Markovich, to enter Russia to engage in trade.[64] The accompanying explanation that there had never been any Jews in Russia and that Christians did not have any contact with them contained a hidden rebuke to Władysław. The clarification also points to the religious reasons for Muscovite hostility toward Jews. John D. Klier attributes the intellectual Judeophobia in Russia at that time to fear of the influence of Judaism on Russian Orthodoxy.[65]

One might justifiably think that Jews were hardly in a position to present any kind of threat to Orthodoxy—except that a phobia then as now is formulated by means of overstating the imminence of the threat. The Russian decree of January 29, 1649, which subjected Jews to capital punishment by burning at the stake for seducing Orthodox Christians to convert to their faith, is a case in point of overstating the danger; initially intended for application to Muslims.[66] Therefore, it seems the Orthodox rebels staged anti-Jewish pogroms for religious, rather than economic, reasons.

I have focused special detail on the attitude of Ukrainian Orthodox Christians toward the Jews because during the uprising, Rechitsa became the object of a fierce struggle between Khmelnitsky and the Polish-Lithuanian state. The struggle began in May 1648, when Khmelnitsky and the Tatars, according to the record of the scribe Kunakov, "conquered . . . cities . . . Rechitsa . . . and beat Poles and Jews without mercy."[67] At the beginning of the summer of that same year, the Polish-Lithuanian Commonwealth retook the town. At the beginning of July 1648, the Cossack Ataman Pëtr Golovatsky attempted to seize the town once more; however, the head of the garrison, Major General Grzegorz Mirsky, managed to lure the Cossacks into an ambush and totally defeated them. Golovatsky was captured and impaled. Nonetheless, after the arrival of fresh forces from Ukraine in the autumn of that year, the Cossacks managed to capture Rechitsa once more and to spread their uprising across the whole of Belorussia.[68] Insurgent forces captured Brest and Pinsk, the most important Jewish centers of the Lithuanian duchy at the time. However, the majority of the Jews from these towns and the other important Jewish town, Slutsk, managed to flee across the Vistula or to Samogitia (Żmudź in Polish and Žemaitėjė in Lithuanian) province in the north of Lithuania. According to the previously mentioned chronicle by Nathan Hanover, the townspeople of Slutsk set a trap for the Cossacks. After inviting them into the town with a promise to hand over the Jews (who by that time had already fled), the townspeople opened artillery fire as the Cossacks came near the city walls, and when "the bandits fled, then the townspeople pursued them and defeated them utterly."[69]

Late in the winter of 1649, the forces of the Lithuanian hetman Janusz Radziwill recaptured Rechitsa. Radziwill installed a garrison and a temporary headquarters in the town, from which he continued the battle with the remnants of the Cossacks who had invaded southeastern Belorussia.[70] In early spring, Bogdan Khmelnitsky sent a ten-thousand-man Cossack force under Ataman Il'ia Golota to aid them, along with the Tatar mercenaries he had in his service. After a number of Belorussian peasants joined them along their march, Golota's force grew in number to thirty thousand. They succeeded in defeating Radziwill, who then fell back to Rechitsa. Over the next several months, the Litvin szlachta in the town assembled a volunteer force. In June 1649 this force, combined with Radziwill's, defeated Golota's army in the area of Zagal'e (Rechitsa Powiat). Golota himself was killed in the battle.[71]

After Golota's defeat, Khmelnitsky, concerned about an attack from the Lithuanian duchy, quickly sent a new ten-thousand-man force of Cossacks, commanded by Ataman Stepan Podobailo, down the Dnieper. The Cossacks burned Loev and built a fortified camp at the point where the river Sozh joins the Dnieper. At the end of June 1649, Janusz Radziwill left a large garrison in Rechitsa and launched a campaign against the Cossacks with an eight-thousand-man army reinforced by detachments of German mercenaries, along with a detachment of Orthodox volunteers commanded by Astroshka Shanchenko. At the same time, a thirty-thousand-man army under Mikhail Krichevskii came from Ukraine to aid Stepan Podobailo. He planned to seize Rechitsa immediately, but seeing that the town was heavily fortified, he abandoned his plan and hurried after Radziwill. Krichevskii caught up with him at the ravaged town of Loev and attacked the Litvin hetman. In the battle that raged, however, Radziwill managed not only to resist the sudden attack but also to gain the advantage, which almost turned into a complete defeat of the Cossacks. They withdrew into the forest and thus managed to save themselves. Podobailo, meanwhile, learned of the battle that had begun and undertook crossing to the right bank of the Dnieper. Radziwill then sank several Cossack boats with artillery fire, and those Cossacks who did manage to land were easily dispersed by his infantry. The next day, when Krichevskii's Cossacks hiding in the forest learned that the hetman was preparing to attack them, they attempted to flee but were decisively defeated.[72]

After his victory, Radziwill withdrew his forces to Rechitsa, where he created a fortified camp, since at the very beginning of August 1649, a sixty-thousand-man

Cossack army had again invaded southern Belorussia after crossing the Prypiat' River. However, on August 8 of that year, a peace treaty between Khmelnitsky and the Polish-Lithuanian Commonwealth was signed in Zbrov; as a result, the Cossack army returned to Ukraine.[73]

The peace turned out to be fragile. In the summer of 1650, the Chernigov ataman, Martyn Nebaba, taking advantage of the lack of funds in the grand duchy's treasury for maintaining its mercenaries, invaded Rechitsa Powiat in the area of Loev. He easily took Rechitsa with his Cossack forces and the peasants who had joined them.[74] Nebaba withdrew after looting the town, since he lacked the resources to hold it for long. Janusz Radziwill's headquarters was in Bobruisk at the time, and from there he directed defensive actions and sent regular proclamations to the szlachta demanding aid in the form of soldiers and money. The Cossacks were also short of troops; therefore Khmelnitsky in late 1650 sent his son Timofei to southeastern Belorussia with reinforcements. All the active Cossack forces in that region—the regiments of Chernigov, Nezhin, and Kiev— were placed at his disposal. Janusz Radziwill, who had moved his headquarters to Rechitsa, was in fact outflanked by Cossack forces. However, his troops were much better disciplined, and his voivodas were more skilled generals. Therefore, in July 1651 Radziwill managed easily to defeat the Nezhin and Chernigov regiments not far from Loev. Nebaba, who was leading them, was killed in battle. Military operations then shifted to Ukraine, where the remnants of the Cossack forces had fled.[75]

Several years later, military conflicts between the two sides resumed in southwestern Belorussia. After being defeated in January 1654, Bogdan Khmelnitsky transferred the territory he controlled in Ukraine to the protection of the Muscovite tsar, Aleksei Mikhailovich; this became the pretext for the Muscovite-Polish War (1654–1667). Unlike the Polish-Lithuanian Commonwealth, the Muscovite state had prepared in advance for war, assembling an army unprecedented in size. Henadz' Sahanovich, the single-handed creator of the Belorussian interpretation of the history of the war, came to the same conclusion.[76] The contemporary Belorussian approach differs from the Russian discourse and the Ukrainian, which is similar to it, in that the latter approach presents the role of Russia and Cossack Ukraine as that of liberation in nature. These discourses, basically antiPolish in their orientation, arose while Russia was still an empire, and the official propaganda of the USSR adopted them. They continue to be current in presentday Russia and Ukraine.

In May 1654, at the very beginning of the Muscovy-Polish War, a twentythousand-man Cossack regiment led by Ivan Zolotarenko came to the aid of the

Muscovite army that had invaded southeastern Belorussia. The szlachta of Rechitsa Powiat, led by Bobrovnitsky and Prince Zhizhemsky, tried to withstand their attack, but the forces were too unevenly matched. The relatively large garrison in Gomel was the first to be crushed, followed by the one in Rechitsa, after which both towns were looted. In an attempt to save themselves from the Cossacks, several hundred Rechitsa Jews, along with a number of the szlachta, fled to Stary Bykhov (today, Bykhov), where they found a strong Polish-Lithuanian garrison. Over the course of two and a half months in the summer of 1654, Zolotarenko besieged Stary Bykhov to no avail. Some of the townspeople wanted to surrender, but the Catholics and the Jews opposed them since they knew the fate that awaited them. Eventually, the Cossacks had to abandon the siege and leave.[77] Then the tsar's army tried several times to take the town, but only in December 1659, after a siege of seven months, did it manage to do so. The defense of Stary Bykhov became an example of the fortitude of the Litvin populace. The tsarist forces that invaded the town dealt mercilessly with the inhabitants. According to the evidence of an eyewitness, Rabbi Yehuda-Leiba Pukhovitser, some three hundred Jews were massacred during this action.[78] Some of the Jews accepted conversion and thus saved their lives, as documented in a letter by Pan Wojsza, dated 1662, on the forced baptism of Jews in Bykhov.[79]

By the end of 1665, almost all the territory of Belorussia, including Rechitsa, had been seized by Muscovite and Cossack forces, which robbed and murdered Jews. The forces of Aleksei Trubetskoi, which seized Mstislav in 1654, carried out a carnage whose victims were "szlachta, townspeople, and Jews, as well as simple people."[80] In that same year, after he entered Smolensk, which had surrendered, Tsar Aleksei Mikhailovich demanded that the Jews who lived there adopt Orthodoxy. Those who refused were driven into wooden houses and burned alive. It is most likely that the same fate was met by the Jews of Dubrovno, who comprised no less than a third of its defenders—ten detachments out of twenty-seven—before it surrendered.[81]

When the forces of Janusz Radziwill drew near Mogilev in 1654, the Jews there, who had come under Muscovite rule, were sent outside the town, where they were later killed. Only a few of them managed to accept conversion and thus save themselves.[82] In general, the Muscovite government demanded the annihilation or conversion to Orthodoxy of people of other faiths in the lands they seized: "There are to be no Uniates. . . . There are to be no Jews in Belorussia, and they are not to be left alive."[83]

In Vitebsk in 1655, during a two-week siege of the town, the Jews with their weapons "not sparing their own safety, defended themselves and fought off attacks by the enemy" and then were taken captive.[84] They had more to endure. After the city fell, the Muscovite voivoda, Vasilii Sheremet'ev, robbed them of all they owned and then exiled them to Russia. They were held for several months in the Novgorod prison, where they were fed poorly and were forced to convert to Orthodoxy. Then they were sent to Kazan.[85] According to an entry in the Russian book of military orders for 1654/1655, 176 Jews (27 families) were sent there from Novgorod, 3 of whom were held for christening while another 3 died on the road in transit. The presence of servants on the list indicates how prosperous some of these families were. Many of them were given the surname Iudin, denoting their Jewish origin.[86] According to other entries, 108 families and 24 individuals were sent via Kaluga to Nizhnii Novgorod, and 92 prisoners from Briansk were Litvins or Jews.[87]

The Muscovite and Cossack troops treated the Litvin Christians only slightly better. Both Catholics and Orthodox were robbed, and thousands of them were transported to Ukraine and Muscovy to become serfs.[88] The status of serfs there differed little from that of slaves.[89] In 1665, Patriarch Nikon wrote of the intention of Tsar Aleksei Mikhailovich to settle his lands with three hundred thousand enserfed Litvins.[90] Many serfs from the Lithuanian duchy perished from starvation on their journey. Many Litvin women were raped by their "liberators." To save themselves from the occupying forces, many local people fled to the forests, where from time to time they would be captured. Even in the early years of the war, many Orthodox churches in Belorussia were burned down, along with synagogues and Catholic and Uniate churches.[91] Thus within Belorussia, where the state had once been relatively tolerant of various faiths, existing religions were suppressed to achieve the spiritual submission of the population to the Moscow patriarchate.

In the course of the war the Muscovites destroyed and ravaged several hundred towns and villages in Belorussia.[92] Their behavior gave rise to a protest from the "liberated" Orthodox Litvins that found expression in a broad partisan movement. The partisans, or *shishaks*, as they were called by the Muscovite voivodas, attacked the Muscovites, the Cossacks, and local nobility who had sworn allegiance to the Moscow tsar.[93] The proportion of collaborators among the szlachta, the majority of whom were Catholic, was greater than that among the Orthodox peasantry of Belorussia. Unlike the nobles, whose personal safety and property were assured in exchange for their treachery, the loyalty of the peasantry to the new regime guaranteed them nothing. Disillusioned with the Orthodox tsar, the Litvin peasants sometimes established their own control over entire counties. Often, the szlachta who were loyal to Lithuanian authority joined them. With the growth of peasant resistance and the strengthening of the forces of Pawel Sapieha, who became the Litvin hetman after the death of Janusz Radziwill in 1655, increasing numbers of the Belorussian-Lithuanian nobility again became opponents of the tsar. This was the first large-scale popular resistance within Belorussia.

In the first half of the 1660s, the Polish-Lithuanian Commonwealth, with incredible effort and at an enormous cost in human lives, managed to push the Cossacks and the Muscovites out of most Belorussian territory, including Rechitsa. In 1666, not long before the war ended, the Cossacks abandoned Rechitsa and its powiat, carrying away the goods they had plundered and driving many inhabitants to Ukraine.[94] The war came to a formal end in 1667 with the signing of the Truce of Andrusovo; Christians and Jews then began gradually to return to Rechitsa.

In accordance with one of the provisions of this treaty, tsarist authorities were required to release their prisoners, and they did so, at least with respect to most of the imprisoned Jews from Vitebsk mentioned above. However, the stipulation that only those Jews who converted to Orthodoxy and did not want to return to the Polish-Lithuanian Commonwealth were allowed to stay in Russia opened up broad possibilities for violation of this provision. Also, Jewish women who had married Orthodox subjects of the Moscow tsar could not return, even if they wanted to go back. The case of a Jewish woman who persuaded her Orthodox husband after the couple had lived together for ten years to move their whole family from Russia to her hometown of Slutsk, whereupon she ran away from him with their children and her sisters, acquired considerable publicity.[95] In the last quarter of the seventeenth century more than ten families of baptized Jews who had been taken prisoner in what is now the territory of eastern Belorussia were then located in Moscow. Documents confirm that Jews at this time who rejected baptism were exiled from Moscow to Siberia.[96] Apparently baptized Jews from the Lithuanian duchy remained in still other central Russian cities.

A spirit of enterprise, on the one hand, and literacy, on the other, allowed some of the detained Jewish captives to move up the social ladder and, with time, even acquire the noble status. Noble families such as the Iudins, the Iudashkins, the Zhadovskis, the Evreinovs, and the Levitskis can trace their origins to these captive Jews. Evidently, Sen'ka Zhidovin was one of those forcibly converted; in 1674 he was sent to Kabul as Muscovy's ambassador. There he shifted his allegiance to serve the Afghan ruler.[97] In much the same way, Ivan Zhidovin, in service to Ivan Ipat'iev and evidently a Jew who was forcibly converted to Orthodoxy, was sent in 1677 to Shemakha in present-day Azerbaijan together with some Astrakhan merchants.[98]

The Cossack uprising and the Muscovite invasion caused huge economic losses to Belorussia generally and to Rechitsa in particular. The castle-fortress was destroyed and never again rebuilt. Russian officials at the end of the nineteenth century wrote of it: "On the bank of the Dnieper stands a small, ancient fortification called the castle, of which nothing remains, apart from some ruins and a moat."[99] The same fate was shared by many other towns of the grand duchy.

As a result of the war, Rechitsa's significance as an economic center declined and its population was reduced. Whereas in Belorussia population losses in the course of the war amounted to 53 percent, in Rechitsa Powiat they were 61.2 percent.[100] It can be estimated that the population of the town of Rechitsa was reduced by two-thirds. Although Rechitsa continued to be the administrative center of a powiat in Minsk Voivodship, its economic center moved to Rogachev. The organs of self-government of the powiat—the law court and the *sejmik* (the assembly of szlachta)—also moved there.[101]

In the last third of the seventeenth century, the Polonization of the Lithuanian population intensified. This happened in part as the population's reaction to Muscovite aggression, and in part because many towns and estates in the Grand Duchy of Lithuania had been transferred to the Polish nobility after their previous owners had perished during the war. The war undermined the autonomous position of Lithuania within the Polish-Lithuanian Commonwealth. A number of its prerogatives were revoked in the last third of the seventeenth century. In particular, Lithuania lost the right to maintain judicial and administrative records in the Belorussian language.[102]

In the last third of the seventeenth century, Rechitsa became of one the eight main towns levying customs duties within the autonomous Grand Duchy of Lithuania. In practice, this meant that all merchants who transported goods from central and southern Russia began stopping in Rechitsa to have their goods evaluated and to pay the customs duties imposed. Providing accommodation for goods and for merchants who had to stay in Rechitsa helped stimulate the town's economic life. In accordance with the instruction of King Jan III Sobieski in July 1693, the Jews Itsko Stolowicki and Shmerel Szereszewski, as superintendents collecting the royal customs duties, were entrusted with the duty of overseeing the transfer, through a staff of officials, of the *myta* (customs duties) of these eight towns into the royal treasury.[103] By the middle of the eighteenth century, trade with Ukraine via the Dnieper had lost its former significance in the Lithuanian duchy, and Rechitsa ceased to enjoy the status of a main customs town. Its customs agency fell under the jurisdiction of another town of eastern Belorussia, Glusk. Unlike the other towns within the autonomous duchy, however, Rechitsa levied other supplementary taxes, on land along the river and on oarsmen.[104]

In the 1770s the Rechitsa subprefecture paid to the royal treasury a "quarter" (*kvarta*, money for maintaining the army) totaling 2,585 zlotys, and to the treasury of the voivodship the sum of 1,159 zlotys. The *kvarta* was distributed in the following way: part of the income of the subprefecture was set aside for its maintenance; the remaining income was divided into four parts, one of which was earmarked for the army; a portion of the remaining three quarters of the money collected went to the voivodas and to the royal treasuries, but essentially they were spent on supporting officials and on the needs of the town. In general, the distribution of funds within the powiat was the subject of a fierce struggle between the Sapieha magnates, on the one hand, and the Radziwills and the Czartoryskis, on the other. Influential landowning families in Rechitsa—the Choleckis, the Chliawinskis, the Judyckis, the Kelcewskis, the Pruszanowskis, and the Skoryns—shifted their support from one side to the other.

In those years, the Rechitsa subprefecture paid fewer taxes to the state treasury than did the subprefectures of Bobruisk, Gomel, Rogachev, Chechersk, and Propoisk, which had become a part of Rechitsa Powiat, a fact that reveals the economic decline in the powiat center. This situation continued until the beginnings of the 1790s. At that time, the Rechitsa subprefecture paid the total sum of 4,018 zlotys to the royal treasury, which was a good deal less than the taxes collected from the other subprefectures of Rechitsa Powiat.[105]

Meanwhile, by the first quarter of the eighteenth century, the Jewish community in Rechitsa had become somewhat stronger. Indirect information on this comes from general court decrees imposing on the Rechitsa community a portion of the debts of other Jewish communities in the Lithuanian Vaad, the organ of Jewish self-government.[106] An independent Lithuanian Vaad was created formally in 1623 as a result of the division of the Polish Vaad into four "lands." The higher authorities did not oppose the formation of an independent Lithuanian Vaad, since it existed as a special tax unit both within the Polish-Lithuanian Commonwealth and within the Lithuanian duchy itself.[107]

The schism between Lithuanian and Polish Jews began to take shape as early as the first half of the sixteenth century. It was induced by the efforts of the latter to curtail the economic activity of the former in Ukraine. A reflection of this struggle was the indictment of Lithuanian Jews, who primarily were residents of Volynia, for secretly circumcising Christian children, converting them to Judaism, and subsequently shipping them off to Turkey. The charge was brought by

Polish Jews in 1540. An accusation of this kind brought before the Polish authorities could not help but lead to intensified antagonism toward Lithuanian Jews on the part of Christians. Therefore, Lithuanian Jews obtained from Sigismund I the Old an investigation and the issuance of a writ of actual innocence finding them blameless.[108] It is possible that after this accusation Lithuanian Jews began to act in their dealings with the central administration even more in the capacity of an independent representative unit. Such transition is confirmed in a grievance to the king from Nakhim Pesakhovich in 1555, which he submitted "on behalf of all the Jews of the Grand Duchy of Lithuania."[109]

In 1576 as a result of a wave of blood slanders in the duchy, Lithuanian Jews independently acquired charters from King Stephen Báthory (1533–1586) that consigned to the king's own courts the exclusive prerogative of trying them for ritualistic offenses.[110] Zenon Guldon and Jacek Wijaczka enumerate eight blood slanders occurring within the borders of the duchy beginning in 1574 and ending in 1766.[111] Not one of them happened in the territory of contemporary Belorussia, which points to the greater degree of tolerance on the part of the local population. This is a subject to which I shall return in the future.

The Lithuanian Vaad, just like the Lithuanian duchy, resisted merging with the counterpart Polish structures since both were striving for the same end: to spend independently the taxes they had collected and to preserve the autonomy of their political structures. Apart from collecting taxes, the Lithuanian Vaad defended Jewish interests before the authorities, dealt with questions of education, regulated the internal operations of the kahals (the Jewish communities), resolved disputes among them, and also chose the members of the Supreme Rabbinical Court, whose decisions were binding on the rabbinical courts of the kahals. Rechitsa, like other towns and villages of southwestern Belorussia, evidently did not have its own rabbinical court; disputes among the Jews of the town were resolved in the first instance in Rakov, and beginning in the eighteenth century, in Smilovichi, which had then become the center of the Minsk kahal division, which included Rechitsa as well.[112] This type of Jewish autonomy was not unique to the Polish-Lithuanian Commonwealth. Jewish communities in Muslim countries of the time, particularly in the Ottoman Empire, Persia, and Bukhara, functioned with exactly the same set of rights. The autonomous models in these countries were drawn from dhimma (Arabic, protected people) laws.

Jewish communities in Rechitsa Powiat were at the same time a component of the tax unit of the lands of Raisen (Rus'), which also included the voivodships of Vitebsk and Mstislav. In 1720, the kahals of Raisen brought the largest tax monies into the Vaad, 9,000 zlotys. The low status of these kahals within the Lithuanian

Vaad, governed by the five principal and largest kahals of Vilna, Brest, Grodno, Minsk, and Pinsk led, over the course of the next forty years, to an even greater increase in their tax burden. In 1761, in accordance with the decision of the Lithuanian Vaad, the kahals of Raisen were expected to pay 16,500 zlotys.[113] The communities of Rechitsa and Mozyr had long been in the sphere of influence of the Brest community. However, by the eighteenth century they, like the other communities of southeastern Belorussia, had fallen into dependence on the Pinsk kahal, which had amassed huge debts, primarily to the Catholic Church and the szlachta.[114] The debts of the Pinsk kahal had resulted from the postwar decline of the economy and huge tax levies. The Pinsk kahal attempted to spread its debts among the independent communities but met with their stubborn resistance. The Pinsk kahal nonetheless managed to achieve its end in 1763, after the Lithuanian Hetman Mikhail Masalsky gave instructions to send soldiers into the Jewish communities of Rechitsa, Mozyr, and Novogrudok Counties to collect these debts.[115] In an analogous situation the Shklov kahal, supported by the owner of this privately held mestechko, was able to withstand the pressure exerted on it by the Lithuanian Vaad to pay taxes assessed on the total debt that it owed.[116]

Similar conflicts between the kahals and sub-kahals within the Polish-Lithuanian Commonwealth led to many complaints to local and central authorities. They became one of the reasons for the abolition in 1764 of the central and division kahal organizations (including the Lithuanian Vaad).[117] Thereafter, all the kahals within the Polish-Lithuanian Commonwealth themselves became independent tax units responsible for collecting for the treasury the prescribed taxes—by means of a poll tax—from each member of their community. By contrast, the earlier system came from the arbitrary decision of the kahal, based on the arrangements made with the Lithuanian Vaad. Those who gained from this decision were the "new" eastern Belorussian communities of the duchy, including the members of the Rechitsa kahal. At the same time, the introduction of the poll tax undermined overnight the structure of Jewish autonomy in the Grand Duchy of Lithuania and in Poland as well.

In 1765, for purposes of the poll tax, a census of Jewish taxpayers was carried out in the Polish-Lithuanian Commonwealth. This census registered 4,125 Jews in Rechitsa Powiat, including 133 Jews (3.2 percent of the Jewish population of the powiat) in the Rechitsa kahal itself. In two other mestechkos in Rechitsa Powiat—Kholmech and Zhlobin—the same census recorded a greater number of Jews than in Rechitsa, 149 and 268, respectively. The largest mestechko in Rechitsa Powiat—Gomel—had 658 Jews. Significantly fewer Jews lived in the neighboring counties than in Rechitsa Powiat: In Mozyr there were 2,206, and in

Mstislav, 2,615.[118] It must be kept in mind that the census did not include infants less than a year old, who were untaxed, and those serving in religious posts. Some Jews, attempting to avoid taxation, hid from the census takers. The Jewish history scholars Mordechai Nadav and Shaul Stampfer, with some reservations, follow Raphael Mahler's belief that in order to obtain a relatively accurate figure for the Jewish population, the census figures should be inflated by 6.35 percent, to include the infants, and by 20 percent, to include those who hid from the census takers.[119] Even with these adjustments, however, the number of Jews in Rechitsa totals only 167.

The small number of Jews in Rechitsa can be attributed to the town's status as property of the crown and the applicability of the Magdeburg Law within its boundaries, which led the town's self-government, wary of competition in commerce and trades, to hinder the resettlement of Jews from other places. The magistrates' assault on the rights of Jews in the duchy occasionally was carried to extremes at this time. For example, Jews in Vilna were forbidden to cause any harm or loss to Christian merchants and craftsmen, including offering their goods and products to a buyer before their Christian competitors did the same.[120] Of course, this rule could hardly be strictly enforced as long as Jews for all practical purposes lacked any possibility of pursuing their own professions. Its negative effect for them, however, was obvious.

Still another source of confrontation between urban Jews and Christians that until now historians have not investigated were accusations that Jews were careless in using fire, which led to fires breaking out in towns. These accusations may have had some basis in fact. The Jewish calendar cycle stipulated that candles be lit in the evening on Fridays, on the eve of the Day of Judgment, during Hanukkah, and on days set aside for the commemoration of the dead. The Russian student of local history General Mikhail Bez-Kornilovich considers these accidental blazes as the reason why no love was lost for Jews in Mogilev; as a result of such fires whole sections of this town of wooden structures were burned to the ground. In 1626 Christians wangled from Sigismund III an order to remove Jews to an area beyond the town ramparts, but the latter succeeded in bribing the town elite to cancel the eviction. The question emerged again in 1633, as a result of which the Jews, hitherto living dispersed throughout the town, were resettled on the street where their synagogue was located. The magistrate prohibited Christians, already under the threat of bearing full financial liability for losses from a potential fire, from renting houses to Jews in other areas of Mogilev.[121] The accusations that Jews were responsible for fires may also have inspired the creation of ghettos in other towns.

The situation was different in the large, private mestechkos of the powiat, including Rechitsa Powiat; in the second half of the eighteenth century the owners of these mestechkos attracted Jews in order to develop the local economy. Exactly the same situation resulted in Poland and other counties of Lithuania.[122] For that period of time Shklov, a privately owned town in eastern Belorussia, was the most vivid example of the flowering of Jewish activity in the fields of economics and spiritual life.[123] The influence of the owners of mestechkos on the life of Jewish communities at this time was unprecedented in its extent. As Gershon David Hundert has noted, a rabbi at this time paid not only the local kahal as previously but also the owner of the mestechko for his appointment to the rabbinical office.[124]

On the other hand, even the Jews themselves preferred to live in the villages and small mestechkos of Belorussia since their principal occupation at the time was distilling alcohol, selling vodka, and leasing various sectors of the estates of the nobility. The lightly populated and impoverished Belorussian towns of that time could not guarantee a living for Jews who wished to settle there.[125] It is also possible that even the Jews did not want to live in Rechitsa because the community was burdened with the above-mentioned debts of the Pinsk kahal to the treasury. The situation was similar in the main kahals of Vilna, Brest, Grodno, and Pinsk, whose entire yearly income in 1765 covered only 4.5 percent of the total amount of the liability.[126]

It is difficult to say whether the total tax obligations of Jews who lived in privately owned mestechkos differed from those paid by the Jews in towns belonging to the king. In the first place, Jews were obliged to bring gifts to the owner of the mestechko and his family, to the Catholic Church, and to important administrators. Owners of mestechko competed with one another in inventing new levies; one such, a tax on using a chimney pipe, was by no means the most peculiar. In the second place, Jews were obliged to buy their food and goods from the owner at prices he set arbitrarily. In the mestechkos belonging to the king there were many more officials to whom presents had to be given or taxes paid that were entirely legal, for example, for the household maintenance of the voivoda or subprefect, to buy meat for the officers' hunting dogs, or to pay for ink used by the clerks. And in both places the Jews paid, apart from their municipal or property taxes, a special tax for the support of the army. They also collected a good deal of money for the *shtadlans* (intermediaries in Jewish affairs), who, by making generous gifts to influential people, were sometimes able to have revoked one of the anti-Jewish initiatives that abounded in the impoverished Polish-Lithuanian Commonwealth in the eighteenth century.[127]

The *hazaka* (literally, a "holding," Hebrew) occupied an important place in the realm of the Jewish economy, in internal kahal politics, and in relations with the nobility at this time. Initially in the Polish-Lithuanian Commonwealth, it merely prohibited the "sequestration" of a rental agreement that another Jew had with the owner of any property or other real estate, but later this monopolistic right became an important object of trade and income for the kahals. Because of the efforts of a majority of the members of the Sejm, this custom was officially prohibited in the Polish-Lithuanian Commonwealth in 1781 if it discouraged competition among Jewish entrepreneurs and for this reason did not promote a decrease in the payment by members of the nobility for the rental services of Jews. By the same token, some Jews grumbled about the hazaka. It follows from this decision, which interfered with the functioning of internal Jewish autonomy, that there were very few non-Jewish entrepreneurs at this time, and they were in no position to offer a price for a lease lower than the price offered by Jewish entrepreneurs. This was the case despite the obligation of the latter to pay the compulsory communal tax in full. Despite the decision to put an end to it, the hazaka continued to be levied unofficially even in the Russian period, and I shall revisit the topic later.

The fiscal system that existed until 1764, under which the taxation unit was not the adult male, the family, or the household, but the community as a whole, had irreversible ethno-cultural consequences for the Jews of the Polish-Lithuanian Commonwealth. The existence of autonomous Vaads with collective tax responsibility and the closed nature of the kahals contributed in the sixteenth century to the beginnings of a distinct mentality, particularly among the Jews of the Lithuanian duchy, that grew stronger over time and began to distinguish them from Polish and Ukrainian Jewry.[128]

The so-called Litvaks—Lithuanian-Belorussian Jews—by the end of the eighteenth century were speaking their own dialect; they dressed and cut their hair differently. The mentality they developed, which set them apart from the Ukrainian and Polish Jews who had once been very similar to them, was characterized by rationalism in behavior, a thirst for learning, a businesslike approach to work, purposefulness, and restraint in expressing their feelings. These qualities manifested themselves in both their everyday and their spiritual lives. One branch of the Litvaks, headed by the Vilna Gaon Rabi Eliyahu ben Shlomo-Zalman, did not generally accept Hasidism and came to be called Misnagidim ("those who oppose" or "those who object," Hebrew), the name given to their opponents by the Hasidim. The other branch, headed by Rabbi Shneur-Zalman of Liady, combined Hasidism with rabbinical scholarship and rationalism, thus creating their own independent tendency in Hasidism, the Chabad.[129]

A definite antagonism existed between the Litvaks and the Polish-Ukrainian Jews. Shlyoma Zaltsman writes of the mutual antipathy between Polish Jews and Litvaks in Warsaw, about which many anecdotes circulated in the city.[130] And if the Misnagidim's attitude toward Polish or Ukrainian Hasidism was definitely negative, it was a good deal milder toward Litvin Hasidism since the psychology of its followers was closer to their own. Marriages between followers of both Litvak religious tendencies were not uncommon in Belorussia.[131] A native of Kamenets in Belorussia, Yehezkel Kotik, who visited Warsaw in the last third of the nineteenth century, stated that the local Jews and the Lithuanian-Belorussian Jews, who formed a rather large community there, preferred not to rub shoulders with one another. The same author said that the Litvaks were called swine because of their asceticism in food and their way of life. Also, because of their thirst for knowledge—which among some of the Litvaks also included the study of secular sciences and was considered apostasy—they were also called *tselem kop* (literally "crucifix heads," Yiddish). In turn, the Lithuanian-Belorussian Jews scorned the Polish Jews for their acculturation and ignorance.[132] According to another source, the Litvaks acquired the name *tselem kop* from Ukrainian Hasidim because of their emotional restraint, something that in the latter's eyes bordered on atheism.[133] Since Kotik does not mention that the Polish Hasidim disapproved only of the Misnagidim, one can conclude that they had the same attitude toward the Litvak Hasidim.

David Asaf, who translated from Yiddish to Hebrew and edited and published Kotik's memoirs, has stated that the Warsaw Jews did not trust their children to the Litvak *melameds* (teachers in a traditional Jewish scool—*cheder*, Hebrew). One of them, a native of Minsk who was unable to find work in Warsaw in 1865, believed that his Litvak dialect was entirely to blame.[134] In fact, the reason was much more substantial; it was the difference in mentalities. Thus even the general acknowledgment that the Litvak rabbis and melameds were the best experts in Jewish scholarship meant almost nothing. Theodore Weeks has argued that Poles reacted badly to Litvaks in Poland because they saw them as a Russifying element.[135] It is likely that they acquired this attitude from Polish Jews, and in reality deeper roots of mutual antipathy lay behind the accusations of Russification.

The mutual disregard was based on the differences of these two ethno-cultural groups, which can rightly be regarded as separate Jewish subethnic groups. Everything served to alienate one from the other: behavior and external appearance, language, culinary preferences, and most of all, temperament. According to Shlyoma Zaltsman, outsiders were not accepted as community rabbis within the territory of contemporary Belorussia and Lithuania.[136] They did not look kindly on the Litvaks who moved to Ukraine. The Jewish writer Mordechai Ben-Ammi (the pseudonym of Mark Rabinovich, 1854–1932) describes the attitude toward a Lithuanian-Belorussian Jew who came to the mestechko of Verkhovka (Vinnitsa Province) in the 1860s:

> "Have you heard the news!" they would say to one another. "Some Litvak has fallen upon us. And you would look at his *treyf tsire* ["look, nonkosher appearance," Yiddish]. He doesn't have a Jewish face at all. *Tselem kop*," it was said. I have to admit that no one among us had ever seen a Litvak before. . . . Everyone stared at him, looking him over with the greatest curiosity and with much distrust, by no means in a friendly way, even with hostility. Children ran after him, as they would run after a monkey or a Gypsy leading a bear. A few of them . . . shouted to him: "*Tselem kop*, where are your sidelocks? Look, the rats have chewed off his sidelocks." Everyone watched with the same intense curiosity and sharply expressed mistrust as he prayed: Was he praying with heartfelt feeling? Was he praying with zeal?[137]

Later, the writer recalls that the Litvak behaved very modestly for several days, but then he stunned everyone. In the course of a heated discussion on one of the difficult places in the commentary to the Talmud, he asked the rabbi to consult a book, stating that he had once studied in a heder; and then he modestly and quietly made the correct interpretation. Everyone was amazed: "How do you like that *Litvekel*? It turns out that he's a genuine *lamdan* [scholar]. . . . That Litvak brain of his has some things to say after all. Still, there's something not right here." Then the author writes that if the new arrival had worn his beautifully tailored suits and worn his hair "like a human being," in Verkhovka they might well have suspected that he was a righteous man in hiding, "but no one could admit such a sacrilegious idea" that the Litvak could be a righteous man. "Among us," Ben-Ammi concludes, "Litvaks were all held in very low regard."[138]

The most strained relations developed between Litvaks and Ukrainian and Polish Jews in the southern regions of Russia, where they encountered one another in the framework of the government program to assimilate this territory. In Taganrog in 1868, a Ukrainian Jew said, "If I had known that Litvak blood was flowing in one of my veins, I would have torn it out."[139] Jewish journalist Kh. Tsybukmakher, who in 1880 visited the Jewish agricultural colonies in Kherson Province, wrote of the friction between Ukrainian Jews and the Litvaks: "The dominant element of the population—immigrants from Lithuania—treat the immigrants from Ukrainian provinces disparagingly, as ignorant people."[140] The reasons for mutual hostility in Novorossiya were economic. According to Shimon Yehuda

Stanislavskii, in the 1880s Litvaks, who were accustomed to being content with little, reduced the cost of goods in the Ekaterinoslav Province and thus stirred up the hatred of the Ukrainian Jews.[141]

In 1913, R. Samoilov, writing in the Saint Petersburg Russian-language Jewish newspaper *Rassvet*, described the differences in the mentality of Russian and Polish Jewry. Then he focused on the "southern Jewry" of Novorossiya, whom he defined as a recently educated blend of "Poles" and "Litvaks." Singling out the prosperity of Jews who had resettled in one of the mining towns of Ekaterinoslav Province, Samoilov provides an interesting description of the relations among three subethnic groups:

> First, there is no complete merging of the various Jewish groups. Even now you can pick out the southerners, "Ukrainians of the Jewish persuasion," completely ignorant of Jewish culture and influenced most of all by everyday assimilation. The "Litvaks" live separately, and the early pioneers among them attempted to transfer all the precepts of Judaism into their new homeland: it was they who organized the synagogues and charitable societies—in short, all the things that make up the life of contemporary Jewish society. The "Poles" also live apart, with their Hasidism and demonstrative orthodoxy.[142]

Most probably, the differences in mentality stemmed basically from the influence of the environment in which these Jewish subethnic groups had to exist. Unlike the Polish and Ukrainian Jews, the vast majority of Litvaks had to accommodate themselves to the difficult economic conditions of Belorussia and Lithuania, where, in view of the poverty of the rural population (which I discuss later), they had to expend far more effort in order to settle finally for very little. Economic conditions promoted the growth among Litvaks not only of asceticism but even of stinginess; Shlyoma Zaltsman compares it to the stinginess commonly attributed to the Scots.[143] It is possible that the Litvaks acquired this trait from the local population, of which the well-known scholar of the region, a Rechitsa native, Mitrofan Dovnar-Zapolskii writes: "The Belorussian is distinguished by his thrift, his near miserliness, by the economical management of his household."[144] It is most likely that only two factors—the relative tolerance of the population (which will be discussed in chapter 3) and the lack of keen competition among the Jews due to their small numbers in the sixteenth to eighteenth centuries—kept the Litvaks from migrating to other areas.

The particular Lithuanian-Belorussian, or northeastern, dialect of Yiddish that developed among the Litvaks was distinct from the southeastern dialect of

Ukrainian Jews and the central dialect of Polish Jews. Apart from a significant difference in phonetics, it is distinguished by the absence of the neuter gender, by peculiarities in conjugation and declension, and to some extent by vocabulary as well. For instance, the Litvaks call a cupboard an *almer*, the Ukrainian Jews a *shafe*, and the Poles a *shrank*. While the two latter groups use the word *libn* to mean "to love," the Lithuanian-Belorussian Jews say *golt gobn*. To signify *beautiful* Polish Jews pronounce the word as *shayn* (rhymes with English "shine"), whereas Litvaks say *sheyn* (rhyming with "lane" or "train").[145]

Litvak men did not wear the awkward, long-skirted garment. This gave rise to unfavorable comments from Ukrainian and Polish Jews but was encouraged by the Russian administration, which in the nineteenth century was waging a campaign against Jewish dress.[146]

The Litvaks and the Ukrainian Jews celebrated rituals such as betrothals and weddings, and marked the Sabbath in different ways.[147] In Litvak families, the man would consult with his wife on important matters, particularly those relating to trade, whereas in Ukrainian Jewish families this was usually not done.[148] In general, the woman in a Litvak family quite often made independent decisions.[149]

Because the distinctive character of Jews in Russia gradually eroded, today, aside from language differences, the only remnant of their former identity is culinary preferences. For the most part this comes down to the method of preparing gefilte fish, stuffed fish. Curiously enough, this very graphically identifies the subethnic origin of individual Jewish families from Eastern Europe. A century earlier culinary preferences were so clearly apparent that they were even noted by the Russian ethnographer Pavel Chubinskii. Very early in the 1870s he wrote that Belorussian and Lithuanian Jews loved rye bread whereas Ukrainians preferred wheat bread. According to him the borscht made by the Litvaks was sourer, and they liked to use more seasoning than did Ukrainian Jews.[150]

Although Rechitsa is located quite close to Ukraine, all Litvak traditions were specific and set in stone for its Jewish residents. This situation came about because there was practically no migration to Rechitsa from the south, whereas with varying intensity Jews migrated from Belorussian mestechkos and towns throughout the entire time under consideration (discussed further in the demographic chapter). Therefore, the cultural-geographical frontier between the two subethnic communities passed through the northern areas of the Ukrainian provinces.

The new socioeconomic conditions in which the former Jews of the Polish-Lithuanian Commonwealth found themselves in the Russian Empire promoted the rapid convergence of all three subethnic groups.[151] Processes of migration, which were particularly intense in the second half of the nineteenth and the beginning of the twentieth centuries, did more than anything else to erode ethno-cultural differences, an issue I treat in greater detail in chapter 3. In this connection the emergence of the new concept of Russian Jewry, into which the Litvaks were absorbed, does not seem unexpected.[152] As Benjamin Nathans has explained, the concept of Russian Jewry began to be used by Jews in Russia for self-identification early in the 1860s.[153]

As a result of the first partition of the Polish-Lithuanian Commonwealth in 1772, a sizable portion of Rechitsa Powiat, along with the mestechkos of Gomel, Rogachev, Khal'ch, Chechersk, and Propoisk, was attached to Russia. Of the remaining towns and mestechkos in the powiat, Rechitsa, Bobruisk, Liubonichi, and Parichi belonged to the king; Loev, Kholmech, Gorval', Streshin, Kazimirov, Karpilovka, Pobolov, and Zhlobin were owned privately by serving szlachta and clergy.[154] In 1776, a resolution of the Polish Sejm, which noted that the majority of the population of the towns were "engaged unsystematically in agriculture and [did] not aspire to retailing, commerce, or trades," conferred limited versions of the Magdeburg Law on eight towns; Rechitsa was not one of them, however.[155]

In 1789 a new census of Jews was conducted. It showed that the Jewish population of the town had not increased over a quarter-century. In Rechitsa 1,010 inhabitants were recorded, of which 134 (13.3 percent) were Jews, 68 men and 66 women. Since the last census, taken in 1765, the number of mestechkos in Rechitsa Powiat having greater numbers of Jews than Rechitsa itself had increased. In Loev this number reached 288 (22.4 percent of all inhabitants of the mestechko); in Bobruisk, 281 (31.6 percent); in Zhlobin, 201 (64.2 percent); and in Streshin, Gorval', and Kholmech their numbers were not much smaller than in the center of the powiat—113 (16 percent), 104 (14.4 percent), and 100 (12.9 percent), respectively. Among the mestechkos listed above, only Loev had a greater overall population than Rechitsa. There were 2,465 Jews living within the powiat, comprising 4.6 percent of the total population.[156] The same census shows that more than a hundred Jews belonging to the Rechitsa community were living in nearby villages outside the limits of Rechitsa.[157]

It is likely that the Jewish population in Rechitsa did not increase because Jews were migrating from the town to privately owned villages, which offered greater possibilities for earning a living through trade and leasing land. On the other hand, or rather in addition to this factor, some of Rechitsa's Jews had crossed the Dnieper into Russian territory by the time of this census, as Jews in the neighboring Ukrainian counties of Zhitomir and Kiev had done.[158]

The Jewish community in Rechitsa germinated during the heyday of the economic and legal flourishing of Jews in the Lithuanian duchy of the first half of the seventeenth century. Few of its members survived, however, after Orthodox insurgents from Ukraine seized the town in 1648. Although eighteenth-century Ukrainian folklore speaks of a dominant influence exercised by the Jews, there is no documentary proof for this claim; therefore the many anti-Jewish pogroms, like the anti-Catholic pogroms, can be attributed to the religious fanaticism of the insurgents. Numerous forced conversions of Jews to Orthodoxy confirm this interpretation. In the last quarter of the seventeenth century, Jews began again to settle in Rechitsa. Nevertheless, the huge debts of the Pinsk kahal, which they were saddled with; the weakening of royal authority; and economic stagnation did not permit the Jewish community in Rechitsa to recover its former status.

In the last third of the eighteenth century, the Polish-Lithuanian Commonwealth suffered a serious economic decline, something that had significant implications for Jews as well. Itskhak Shiper, a historian of the Jews of the Polish-Lithuanian Commonwealth, cites a description from 1790 by a contemporary writer that reveals the impoverished state of the Polish Jews: "Destitute Jews, without property and without work, surrounded by their small children, wander about the country, subjects of no one, receiving food from the kahals and sub-kahals."[159] In such conditions, the competition of Jews with Christian towns-people and the small and large landowners intensified in many economic spheres. Unable to contend with the Jews by economic methods, their competitors showered the king, the city authorities, and the Sejm with complaints against them; the result was a series of resolutions limiting the rights of Jews. The Lithuanian duchy was no exception to this trend.[160] Therefore, Jews of the duchy had to seek new ways to earn a living and also to become extremely active in commerce, competing not only with Christians but also with one another. The English historian William Coxe, observing this situation on his journey from Poland to Russia, described it in 1785 as follows:

Passing through Lithuania, we were struck by the swarms of Jews, who were more numerous than in other parts of Poland. It seemed that they had established their center in this duchy. If you seek an interpreter, they will bring you a Jew; if you come to a coaching inn, the owner is a Jew; if you are in need of post horses, a Jew will provide them and a Jew will drive them; if you need to buy something, a Jew will become your agent. It is possible that this is the only country in Europe where Jews work the land, and we often observed them busy at sowing, harvesting, haulage and other agricultural tasks.[161]

Thus the golden age of Rechitsa during the period under examination occurred in the middle of the seventeenth century; it was followed by a period of political and social decline that lasted until the end of the eighteenth century. The economic and legal status of the Jews in Rechitsa deteriorated correspondingly, something that was characteristic of the autonomous Lithuanian duchy as a whole. The alteration of the political map of Eastern Europe at the end of the eighteenth century brought changes to all spheres of socioeconomic, cultural, and community life, and these changes, naturally, touched the Jews as well.

2

Under Russian Rule, 1793–1917

DAILY LIFE IN THE TOWN AND THE JEWS

After the second partition of the Polish-Lithuanian Commonwealth, Rechitsa Powiat, along with the whole of the Minsk Voivodship, came under Russian rule. Rechitsa Uezd—as the former powiat was called in the Russian administrative system—was reconstituted at the end of October 1796 with the addition of the northern part of the former Kiev Voivodship. At the end of August 1797, the uezd became part of Minsk Province; some additional territory that had belonged to Rechitsa Powiat until 1793 but had been attached to Mozyr Uezd for four years was restored to it.

Rechitsa Uezd, along with the mestechkos of Bragin, Vasilevichi, Gorval', Kalinkovichi, Komarin, Kruki, Loev, Narovlia, Iakimovskaia Sloboda, Khoiniki, Kholmech, Yurevichi, and Ianovka, became territorially the largest in Minsk Province. Rechitsa's favorable geographical position was valued during the War of 1812, when it became the temporary residence of the governor of Minsk. Russian forces were concentrated there, and it was the location of the main supply depot of the southern army.

In Rechitsa Uezd, as throughout the whole province, the Russian administration initially preserved almost unchanged the former system of justice and judicial institutions and the former powiat confederation and its entire staff. However, the Rechitsa Powiat land court was transferred to Bobruisk in 1793 where it could be protected by the Russian garrison stationed in the town. Catherine II (empress from 1762 to 1796) was uncompromising only in respect to the Polish Constitution of 1791, which was the specific cause of the second partition of the Polish-Lithuanian Commonwealth among the three neighboring empires. All the articles of the constitution were annulled, and those who had taken part in adopting it were disgraced.[1]

54

On the other hand, the empress, attempting to enlist the support of the Polish szlachta, preserved all their former rights and freedoms. The szlachta of Rechitsa, like those in neighboring counties, were even permitted to go to Warsaw to the Sejm until the third partition of the already territorially truncated Polish-Lithuanian Commonwealth. At the same time, the empress, an admirer of Voltaire and a follower of the idea of an enlightened monarchy, prohibited fighting among the szlachta in the newly-acquired territories; she also prohibited acts of violence and abolished the death penalty, ordering that gallows be torn down. In the spring of 1793, the governor's office in the newly annexed lands recommended that the szlachta elect deputies to express their gratitude to Catherine II for preserving their former rights. All the uezds, through their deputies, obediently did so, while the Rechitsa deputy, I. Vishchinsky, on instructions from his electors, "made so bold" as to describe the impoverished situation of Rechitsa Uezd and petitioned the empress to take the uezd under her trusteeship and revoke part of the tax assessments at least until 1795. It seems that the economic situation in Rechitsa Uezd had remained grave since the mid-eighteenth century. However it may be, the petition of the Rechitsa szlachta had an effect on Catherine II: she issued a special decree freeing not only Rechitsa Uezd but also all of Minsk Province from all taxes (apart from customs duties) until the year requested.[2]

As noted, in 1764 the kahal's levy of taxes was replaced by a poll tax within the Polish-Lithuanian Commonwealth. This measure significantly reduced the power of the kahals, since their functions became mainly social and religious. The Russian authorities, in need of a Jewish fiscal body, not only maintained the kahals' responsibility for imposing taxes but also directed the Jews to establish kahals in places where none had previously existed. Moreover, through the passport system the Russian authorities attached those Jews who had moved to other areas to "its own" kahals. A legalized kahal in Russia had, as previously, the prerogative of deciding religious and civil legal matters among Jews, but its powers did not extend to "matters of exchange."[3] From 1820 to 1830, Russian legislative authority consolidated the power of the kahals even more. With the introduction of compulsory military service for Jews in 1827, the kahals became responsible for supplying recruits, and the Statute of 1835 included a paragraph stating that every Jew, except for landowners, was obliged to register his place of residence with the local Jewish community. In towns the Jewish population would choose a kahal committee of three to five representatives headed by an elder for a term of three years; the local administration would then confirm these candidacies. Among the duties of members of the kahal was the compilation of "electoral lists"

of Jews. The unenviable role that the government assigned to the kahals, particularly in the provision of recruits—many of them underage children—made
the Jewish population even more dissatisfied with them. The host of complaints
against the kahals, coupled with the Russian government's wish to promote the
fusion of the Jewish and Christian populations, led the government to revoke the
kahal system in 1844 and transfer some of its functions to town councils.

In the 1830s the Jewish community in Rechitsa was headed by the kahal elder
Iudka Bezborodkin. In 1831, before the eighth census of the Jewish community
was conducted, Shlëma Pinskii, Berka Mogilevskii, and Israel Shkolnik were
chosen as his deputies to assist in compiling the lists. It is likely that they had
responsible posts within the Rechitsa kahal at the same time. Israel Koparovskii
held an important position in the community, and he and Berka Mogilevskii sent
an official memorandum on the Jews living within the town of Rechitsa to the
uezd rabbinical commission.[4]

Until the second partition of Poland, many of the Jews who lived in the small
villages and towns scattered across Belorussia had made their livings by leasing
estate land or working in other branches of agriculture and by the production and
sale of vodka. The authorities, however, decided to treat the Jews differently in
the newly formed Minsk Province. By order of the Russian government in 1795,
the administration had to try to resettle them in uezd townships. There they
were supposed to register as members of the merchant or townsman class. In this
way Catherine II was hoping to enlarge the urban areas.[5] Local authorities then
wanted to enact exactly the same measures in the Mogilev and Vitebsk Provinces,
but manifold complaints from Jews and the appointment of more tolerant administrators there resulted in the cancellation of the arrangements that already
had been made.[6] A doubling of tax assessments was imposed on all Jews. In 1808
yet another decree was published, this time requiring all Jews to resettle in towns
and mestechkos within three years. Because they found it impossible to make a
living in their new places of residence, this resettlement was ended in Belorussia,
though only in 1822.[7]

Many landowners maintained their holdings after annexation. They received
the right to hold posts in local administrative and judicial institutions. Despite
the efforts of the Russian administration to return the population to Orthodoxy, Catholicism, the Uniate Church, and Lithuanian-Polish culture had become
deeply rooted among the East Slavic population of the territory of today's Belorussia. Not only landowners but also the peasantry were strongly attached to
that culture until the end of the nineteenth century. Polish was perceived as
the language of the elite, while their own language was considered countrified,

and Russian was seen as foreign. It is not surprising, therefore, that peasants who had become wealthy tried to adopt Polish culture and sometimes converted to Catholicism.[8]

The tsarist administration—which usually considered Belorussians, Great Russians, and Little Russians (Ukrainians) as parts of the greater Russian nationality and not as separate ethnic groups—took a very dim view of this gravitation to Polish customs and culture. One Russian official complained in the mid-1860s: "Polish propaganda has left deep and long-lasting traces in Rechitsa's first judicial uezd. The peasants, imitating the Catholic landowners as one must suppose, even now have the habit of referring disparagingly to anything coming from this bank of the Dnieper as 'Russian.' Certain Polish customs and habits inherited from those same Catholic landowners and priests, as well as their manner of speaking Polish, have become a part of the way of life and everyday existence of the peasants and have placed a special stamp on them, one not characteristic of the Russian peasant."[9] One of the reasons for the attraction to Polish culture was the difficult economic situation in which the Belorussian peasants found themselves in Russia (more about this later). On the other hand, it was also because the Belorussian peasants had a very vague conception of their own ethnic identity. They called themselves "local people" (*tutoshnie*), and even during the Polish censuses in Western Belorussia in 1921 and 1931, they had difficulty answering the question of which language they spoke.[10]

The sympathies of the uezd peasantry toward Polish culture and its representatives, the Catholic aristocracy, manifested itself as early as during the Polish uprising of 1830–1831. In the summer of 1831, when Russian forces had almost crushed the heartland of the uprising in Western Belorussia and Lithuania, it unexpectedly spread to Rechitsa Uezd, something that was possible only with the support of a certain number of local Uniate peasants, since relatively few Catholics lived there.[11]

Immediately after the final suppression of the Polish uprising, the government began a more active campaign of Russification of the entire territory of Belorussia. As part of this campaign, the administration began opening Russian-language primary schools, and by the middle of the nineteenth century, the language in all primary schools had been changed from Polish to Russian.[12] In the 1830s, many Catholic monasteries were likewise closed. One of the first to be closed, in 1831, was the Dominican monastery in Rechitsa, mentioned earlier. It had about twenty monks at the time of its closure. In 1858–1859, the monastery building burned to the ground.[13] In 1839, Nicholas I prohibited the Uniate Church (which at the time had the largest number of followers in Minsk Province), and in 1840 he

introduced the term "Northwest Region" to replace the previously accepted
names of Belorussia or Lithuania. Although the name Belorussia came into use
again during the liberal reign of Alexander II (1855–1881), it was frequently used
only to describe Mogilev and Vitebsk Provinces.[14] The central administration
feared even the slightest sign of a Belorussian national revival there, regarding it
as an integral component of Polish separatism and not an independent movement of the local population.

As Theodore Weeks correctly notes, the authorities naively supposed that
the effect of Russian civilization on Belorussians and Ukrainians would lead to
their acknowledgment of its superiority to theirs and to their voluntary assimilation with the Great Russian ethnic community. To safeguard this discourse,
the authorities tried to neutralize the influence of Polish culture and Jewish economic power, both of which they regarded as pernicious.[15] The most outstanding
scholar of Belorussian history, ethnography, and folklore, Rechitsa native Mitrofan Dovnar-Zapol'skii (1867–1934), writes that Russian writers of the 1860s
depicted the Belorussians as the unluckiest people on earth by foolishly doing
their utmost to present them as victims of the domination of Poles and Jews
in that territory.[16] This expert comments further that the Russian government
had tightened the grip of serfdom on Belorussians and that the situation of Great
Russian peasants under Orthodox landlords was no better. In the same place
he records the superficial judgments of Belorussia by the Russian civil servants
stationed there, people he characterizes as careerists and Russifiers.[17]

The comment of another social anthropologist of the Belorussian people,
Nikolai Ianchuk, correlates with Dovnar-Zapol'skii's assessment:

> I had the occasion to meet people who on their appointment to service in Belo-
> russia went there from the outset to do no less than save the Belorussians from the
> Yids. . . . And to their utter astonishment they saw that the very peasant whom they
> greeted with the outstretched hand of help reacted with nothing short of suspicion
> and ran away from them and always preferred to turn for advice and help to the
> Jew he knew and was comfortable with. . . . One must confess that now as before
> the peasant has more trust in the *lapserdak* [Jewish traditional long-skirted black
> coat] than in the frock coat [Russian officials' uniform], in which he is much more
> inclined to suspect his secret foe.[18]

Meanwhile, most Russian civil servants and landlords in the region, who had
obtained their land for a song when it was condemned for its owners' complicity
in the uprising or from emigrating Catholic aristocrats, did not change their

stereotypical convictions when they collided with the tolerant attitude of the peasants toward the Jews (to which I shall return in the next chapter); rather, they explained them by citing Belorussian backwardness. The new landowners together with the remnants of the old landed elite also did not harbor kind feelings toward the Jews because they competed with them for the peasant trade, especially after the abolition of serfdom. This approach was embodied in the many anti-Jewish ordinances adopted by public and administrative organs.[19]

Along with closing Catholic monasteries, the authorities in the 1830s began allocating more funds to restore and build more Orthodox churches within Belorussia. In 1838, funds were allocated for building the Uspenskii Cathedral in Rechitsa, since the existing wooden church there had by that time become quite decrepit. The contract was won by the lowest bidders, Soloveichik from Vilna and Gurvich from Minsk. Soon, however, they apparently realized that the job was more than they could handle and officially transferred their rights to several people from Minsk, Aron and Zisel' Rapoport and Faivel Zeltsman. In 1842, a contract was signed with the new group stipulating that they were to complete construction within three years, by 1844. The short deadline and insufficient funds did not lead to high-quality workmanship. This factor, and even more, several miscalculations in the project by the engineer-architect, led to the collapse of the almost completed bell tower in 1843; the cathedral building still under construction was damaged at the same time.[20] Apparently, the local residents, some of whom were very sympathetic to Catholicism and who regretted the closure of the monastery, took the structure's collapse as a bad omen. The years of judicial investigation that followed revealed serious defects in the construction. It is not known who was found to be responsible and what penalty he suffered, but the contract was annulled.[21] Not until 1872 was a cathedral finally built, thanks in large part to the financial support of the governor of Minsk Province, Vladimir Tokarev.[22]

Few noblemen lived in Rechitsa at the beginning of the nineteenth century. Statistics show that in 1800 the nobility comprised 2 to 3 per cent of Rechitsa's population; by contrast, in the provincial capital of Minsk they made up 15 per cent.[23] After 1817 the position of *marszalek* of the Rechitsa confederation was replaced by the marshal of the Rechitsa Uezd nobility, and that post was held mainly by Catholics until the beginning of the twentieth century. As noted, Catholics comprised the great majority in the uezd nobility.[24] The marshal of the nobility was simultaneously the president of the uezd Congress of the Nobility and of the uezd zemstvo assembly. Most major landowners in Rechitsa Uezd preferred to live abroad, mainly in France. Midlevel landowners also frequently traveled abroad. This was particularly so in Rechitsa Uezd, where they were wealthier and owned greater numbers of serfs than did midlevel landowners in the other uezds of Minsk Province.[25] It was mainly the minor nobility who lived permanently in the uezd. Until the 1860s the great majority of the noble class in the uezd remained Catholics, as was the case generally in the northwestern region.[26] Official Russian measures against the local Catholic elite stemming from the new Polish rebellion had a certain impact on the economic situation of the Jews, which I discuss in the next chapter.

For many years the post of military director of Rechitsa Uezd was held jointly with that of Mozyr Uezd. Since Mozyr had been chosen as the site of the administrative offices for both uezds, most of the uezd's governmental institutions were located there and not in Rechitsa.[27] Only in the 1870s did a separate military director begin to serve in the town. His duties included the supervision of reserve forces, the military draft, weapons depots, and food reserves for the army. The uezd military director served as a commandant and was chairman or member of many town committees that dealt with questions concerning the proper functioning of the rear areas in the event of war. He worked, for example, on committees supervising fire services, transport, food supply, epidemics, and medical services.

The administrators who dealt with civil matters in Russian towns were town governors. Decisions on a great number of everyday problems involving townspeople depended on the arrangements they made. In 1862, with the abolition of this post, its responsibilities were transferred to the uezd police chief, whose duties had formerly been confined only to police supervision of his uezd. The police chief had formerly been elected by the Assembly of the Nobility from among its members, but after 1862 he was appointed by the governor. Among the government institutions in the town in the late 1880s were four police stations; a jail to hold four people, built in 1864; and a civil court.[28]

Judicial disputes among the townspeople were resolved by the town council. Apart from this basic function, town councils in Russia were also responsible for levying property taxes; supervising the military draft; enumerating townspeople and merchants; selecting and approving candidates to serve on the boards of guilds; and assigning trades to guilds. The town council consisted of two burgomasters, four councillors, two judges, and an elder. Only those who were at least twenty-five years old and who owned property within the town or had paid town commercial taxes for no less than two years were eligible for these offices; incumbents served for three years.[29] Here, as throughout the territory of Belorussia, all official records continued to be kept in Polish for some time after annexation.

Map of Pale of Settlement, 1855. From Gershon David Hundert, ed., *The YIVO Encyclopedia of Jews in Eastern Europe* (New Haven, Conn.: Yale University Press, 2008), 1312; also available online at www.yivoencyclopedia.org. Courtesy YIVO Institute for Jewish Research.

The elder of the Jewish kahal, chosen by his coreligionists, also had a seat on the council. As early as 1783, Catherine II had issued an ordinance giving Jews the right to vote for the remaining members of the council and to hold posts on it. This was a major step toward the provision of rights for Jews that were equal to those of Christians. Jews had never enjoyed such broad electoral rights in either Poland or the Lithuanian duchy. The Christians of the town, however, were un-accustomed to seeing Jews in the local government and greeted this decree with hostility. Because of their complaints, this edict was cancelled in 1802, after the death of Catherine II. An unpublished ordinance allowed Jews to hold no more than one-third of the seats on town councils. Elections were conducted based on religion: Jews elected only two councillors, Christians two councillors and two burgomasters. Such a system of disproportional representation fostered antago-nism between the communities. In 1835, Abram Ezerskii and Evsei Rabinovich were elected to the two seat allocated to Jews on the Rechitsa town council.[30]

But even this unequal quota of Jews allowed to become magistrates was a positive deviation from the judicial norms of the aforementioned Statute of the Grand Duchy of Lithuania of 1588, and it remained in force in the united prov-inces until 1840.[31] This, progressive for its time because it guaranteed Jews secu-rity for their lives and property, became discriminatory against Jews in the late modern period inasmuch as it did not provide for their legal equality. It did not allow them to participate in urban self-government or testify in trials involving Christians. This last restriction was removed in 1814.[32]

However, over time, according to John D. Klier and Andreas Kappeler, the Russia learned Polish sophisticated Judeophobia, perceived the Jews as exploit-ers and parasites.[33] This new approach has found particular expression in the Law of 1839. In accordance with the law, Jews in the so-called western provinces (i.e., the Pale of Settlement) were not allowed to make contact with town mayors, councillors of the town police, and judges. Jews did not even have the right to elect Christians to these posts.[34] Their educational level was not high. Many had only a parish school education.

This law provided Jews only a third of all seats in urban community insti-tutions (the town council, the town duma, its board and committees). Elections for these posts were organized by community, as previously. It is interesting to note that such a division never took root in areas where it was unfavorable to Christians. Thus, because the Christian community was assessed a tax fine for incorrect assessment of property by Christian assessors, the law prescribed the election of assessors jointly by Christians and Jews so that the latter would share the burden of these expenses.[35]

In accordance with this same law, in Rechitsa—where Jews made up almost half the population in the mid-nineteenth century—only two of the six council-lors of the board of the duma (its executive organ) were Jews, Nokhem Roginskii and Aron Kom. One other Jew, Kiva (the Yiddish form of the name Akiva) Kotliar, served in the local government. He was one of three members of the housing committee that looked after the assessment of property, the care of state and church buildings, housing arrangements for the military and the police, and care of the poor.[36] From 1856 to the end of the 1870s, Rabbi Nokhem Pinskii was an elected councillor on the town duma; after 1864, Khatskel Frenkel was another councillor. Iankel Velenskii succeeded him in 1873 and remained in the post until at least 1885.[37]

Although none of the councillors of the town duma and members of its vari-ous committees received any salary for carrying out their duties, their presence enabled the community to have some degree of influence on many decisions taken by the town's government. However, Jews in the Pale of Settlement, who already were paying more than half of the town's taxes and fees—consisting mainly of property taxes and dues for the right to engage in commerce and trades—were unable to use their representatives to prevent the levying of additional taxes on them. This practice opened the way for abuse of power by the Christian majority in the town's government. In 1856, an audit in Rechitsa uncovered such an inci-dent, one that was subsequently heard in court. The court spent about ten years considering the case of some officials in the Rechitsa town duma who had ille-gally collected and appropriated money from Jews.[38] The mores of the time, so vividly depicted by Nikolai Gogol in his play *The Inspector-General*, give grounds to suppose that the majority of such audits ended "amicably."

On the other hand, the election of responsible officials predominantly from the Christian community significantly narrowed the choice for the population of the Jewish Pale of Settlement, and this adversely influenced the administration of towns. An auditor who inspected Mogilev Province in the 1850s reported that in all but two towns, the mayors had been elected from among "townspeople-ploughmen who did not have the least idea of the responsibilities entrusted to them." In Bykhov, where Christians comprised but one-fifth of the population of the mestechko and the council was supposed to consist of one burgomaster and two town councillors, no appropriate candidates for any of the three posts could be found among the Christians. Therefore, the local administration petitioned the tsar for permission to elect Jews as councillors, as an exception to the law.[39]

The Regulation on Towns issued in 1870 offered the Jews the right to take part in the elections for mayor and Christian duma councillors, which gave them a chance to influence the outcome of the voting. At the same time, the regulation preserved most of the former restrictions. The aforementioned Law of 1839 denied Jews the right to sit on town councils and as representatives of a distinct community. They could, however, influence the town council indirectly. The Jews lost this possibility in 1866, when town councils were abolished and judicial matters were transferred to the jurisdiction of uezd courts, where access by Jews as representatives of their communities was also closed.[40]

The situation of Jews deteriorated even more after Alexander III (r. 1881–1894) initiated a number of counterreforms in the late 1880s. The passing of a new Regulation on Towns in 1892 continued the policy of exclusion of Jews from town institutions. This new regulation stated that Jews were not permitted to participate in town election meetings and meetings of homeowners. Outside the Pale of Settlement they were generally excluded from local self-government; inside the Pale they were allowed to occupy only one-tenth of all the town duma seats. But Jews were not allowed to elect their representatives even to these seats. Unlike Christians they were appointed by the governor, so in the eyes of the Jewish community they were no different from the usual town officials. Counter-reforms also took place in the area of zemstvo administrative organs. As early as 1864, Alexander II had instituted the Regulation on Zemstvo Institutions, in which there were no restrictions on Jews; quite often, therefore, they became zemstvo councillors and members of zemstvo boards.[41] But in 1890, under Alexander III, a new zemstvo regulation was instituted in which Jews were excluded from any participation in zemstvo electoral meetings and congresses.

The disenfranchisement of Jews and the additional restrictions on their participation in local self-government denied them the opportunity to influence town politics. This, in turn, lessened their authority in the eyes of Christians. In many towns in the uezd, and probably in Rechitsa as well, Jewish property was taxed even more heavily. Jewish interests were disregarded even more in other issues such as the development of regulations on holidays and bazaar days and cleaning the streets on which they lived. As a result, the tolerant relationship between Jews and Christians that had existed previously began to deteriorate; the culminating point of these worsening relations was the anti-Jewish pogrom of the early twentieth century, something I discuss in detail below.[42]

The Regulation on Towns barred not only Jews from taking part in elections; poor and midlevel Christian residents were also disenfranchised, and as a result the number of voters for the town dumas was reduced by a factor of six to eight. A total of 290 Christians in Rechitsa, whose property was valued at three hundred rubles or more, had voting rights. These Christians comprised 2.4 percent of Rechitsa's total population. Nonetheless, this figure was somewhat higher than that of the rest of the empire, where the Regulation on Towns of 1892 enfranchised only 0.5 to 2 percent of urban dwellers. Such a low percentage for the whole of Russia occurred because many towns in predominantly non-Russian border areas did not receive any right of self-government. For example, the only urban area with self-government in the whole of the Turkestan region was the provincial capital, Tashkent. In towns that did receive self-government, the Regulation on Towns of 1892 not only diminished the number of voters but also reduced (on average in Russia) the number of councillors in town dumas by a factor of two. In Rechitsa, as in many other uezd towns, the new regulation introduced a simplified form of town government that replaced town dumas and councils with assemblies of twelve to fifteen local delegates; the town mayor was replaced by an elder elected for a four-year term. In Rechitsa the number of town delegates was set at thirteen.[43]

In the first decades of the twentieth century, the town elders of Rechitsa and their aides were Christians, despite the steady increase in the numbers of Jews within the overall population of the town. At the same time, however, in many mestechkos in the uezd—Bragin, Kalinovichi, Loev, Khoiniki, Komarino, Gorval', and Kholmech—the elders of town councils were Jews because there were not enough Christians to fill the offices.[44] The situation was the same in neighboring Mozyr Uezd. Although in Mozyr itself the elder and his assistants were Christians, in the majority of the uezd's mestechkos the elders were Jews. In Rechitsa many Jews sat on the committee that dealt with the allocation of commercial taxes.[45]

The basic question that the town's government had to address was the disposition of the town budget. Drinking establishments provided the largest source of income for Rechitsa. Thus, the tavern and the twelve other drinking establishments that had existed in the town in the 1820s provided almost a half (45 percent) of the town's income at the time. Profits from town property then comprised 35 percent, while taxes on the residents provided 20 percent of all town income. The basic expenses (46 percent) of the town were payments for the repair, construction, lighting, and heating of public buildings and for salaries of town officials. The police budget took up 21 percent of the town's expenses; 18 percent went to schools. Since all town buildings were wooden, special attention was paid to the fire department. In 1828, 15 percent of the town budget went to its support. Of all the towns of Minsk Province in that year, only Pinsk devoted more of its budget to its fire department than Rechitsa did.[46]

The fire department in this almost entirely wooden town functioned very well, since there were no serious fires—one of the major disasters of that time—in

Rechitsa. In the 1880s there were twelve men in the Rechitsa fire department. Such a small department could not have coped with fires without the help of the town's very active volunteer fire brigade. Six of nine members of its board of directors were Jews.[47] In Rechitsa as well as in other cities in the Pale of Settlement, the volunteer fire brigade was one of the few public institutions that admitted Jews as members; thus the Jewish elites of the city willingly took part in it in order to elevate their social status in the eyes of the local authorities and the residents of the city at large. Aside from that, membership created the illusion in their own minds that they were participating in the self-government of the city.

The steamboats that began sailing along the Dnieper in the 1820s and 1830s became a rapid and convenient form of transportation for the residents of Rechitsa. The Rechitsa dock became more important. Postal and other conveyances traveling on the roads were watched over by sentries in black-and-white striped booths. These sentries were usually called *budochniki,* soldiers on duty. There were a few of them in Rechitsa itself, and they helped maintain order. Such sentries were abolished in the second half of the nineteenth century, and town policemen became responsible for maintaining order. Almost all the private houses in Rechitsa—441 in all—were single-story. Orchards were attached to 60 percent of the houses of the nobility and functionaries. The vast majority of houses in Rechitsa (90 percent) had vegetable patches or gardens that provided their owners with vegetables and potatoes. In general, the large number of gardens in Rechitsa set it apart from other Belorussian towns at the time.[48] This practice persisted in Rechitsa even after the 1860s, when the first stone buildings began appearing in the town. In the 1860s, the total area of town land was 5,300 hectares, a territory greater than all but three Belorussian cities—Bobruisk, Minsk, and Mogilev. To be fair, it must be noted that 28 percent of the town's territory was taken up by forests, but even discounting them, the remainder of Rechitsa's area exceeded that of cities like Grodno, Brest, Borisov, Gomel, and Pinsk.[49]

By 1854 there were nine government and eight public religious buildings (two Orthodox and two Catholic churches, a synagogue, and three Jewish houses of prayer) in Rechitsa. Only two private houses were built of stone; the remainder were wooden.[50] Over the next decade, the number of houses in the town grew to 590. On average, seven people lived in each house. Many houses and streets were in very poor condition. A Russian official who passed through in 1870 offered the following impression: "Rechitsa is one of the most wretched towns, not only in Minsk but in the provinces adjacent to it. The Jewish population, the filthy, crooked streets, the wooden, half-collapsed hovels, and everything else. . . . Only the Dnieper, with its dock, gives this town some color of life."[51] However, at the

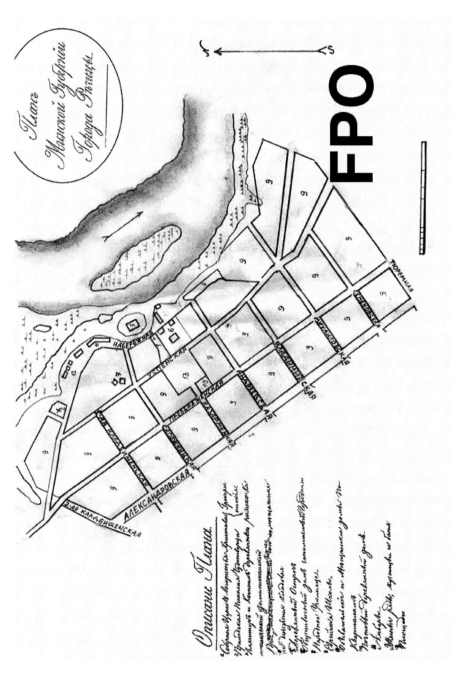

Restored segment of the plan of Rechitsa, from a mid-nineteenth-century original.

end of the nineteenth century, the ruins of the castle-fortress on the Dnieper, which had until then been used as a utility area, were cleared, and a park was laid out. This became one of the most picturesque spots in the town.[52]

By 1904 the number of residents in Rechitsa had grown to almost 11,000. They lived in 1,414 houses. Because construction lumber was cheap, the houses in Rechitsa were not as cramped as those in other towns of Minsk Province. On average, there were 7.7 residents in each house here, whereas in Minsk each house, on average, had twice as many occupants, 15.2 persons. Stone houses were expensive to build in Rechitsa; thus by 1904 there were only four such there. If we consider the overall number of houses in Rechitsa, the town lagged behind only Minsk, Pinsk, Bobruisk, and Borisov, but if we consider the number of stone houses, the town was almost in last place. The vast majority of roofs in the town had wooden shingles. Only 45 houses had tin roofs.[53] By 1917 there were about 10 stone buildings in Rechitsa. Jews lived in 6 of them: Beilia Shklovskaia, Freida Agranovich, the Sheindlin family (all on Kazarmennaia Street, now Koneva Street), Khaia Shklovskaia, and Leiba Livshits (both on Preobrazhenskaia Street, now Lenina Street). The Europa Hotel, the best in the town, was located in the building where its owner, Leiba Livshits, also lived. The stone, two-story house with a balcony that belonged to Irma Livshits was particularly lovely (this home later housed the city executive committee and later a savings bank).[54]

In 1910 the price of bread in Rechitsa was one of the highest in the province, while meat was cheap. The yearly rent for a small apartment (meaning three or four rooms, by the standard of the time) was 150–200 rubles; a midsized apartment (four to six rooms) cost 350–400 rubles; a large apartment (more than six rooms), 500–550 rubles. There were eight hotels and an inn to meet the needs of visitors to the town. All of them belonged to Jews and were situated in the area of today's square, between Preobrazhenskaia and Uspenskaia Streets. The others were on Aleksandrovskaia Street and Uspenskaia Street. There were a few restaurants and taverns where one could eat in Rechitsa, four cheap eating houses and a small cafeteria; drinks could be had in six wine shops and bars.[55]

The Jews of Rechitsa took part not only in the town's administrative bodies and community life but also in the sociopolitical movements of the country. The brothers Natan (b. 1847) and Leizer (b. 1857) Golubov studied at universities—one in Saint Petersburg, the other in Kiev—where in the 1870s they were drawn into the Narodnaia Volia (People's Freedom and Will) movement. In 1876 Natan's activities earned him a five-year exile to Arkhangelsk Province. He later settled in Warsaw. In 1884 he published a book in Saint Petersburg on asylum as an institution among the ancient Hebrews, Greeks, and Romans.[56] His brother

Leizer was arrested in 1875 and in 1877 was sentenced as part of the "Affair of the Fifty" to Arkhangelsk Province as well; he was marched there on foot and in handcuffs over the course of sixty-three days, from Veliky Ustiug to his place of exile in Shenkursk. He escaped from there to Paris in 1878, but returned to Russia a year later and was recaptured in Kiev and sentenced in 1880 as part of the "Affair of the Twenty-One." He was exiled to Irkutsk from 1883 to 1885, and after completing his sentence, he settled there.[57] Although the proportion of Jews within the Narodnik movement in Russia was no more than 5 percent, that is, a figure corresponding roughly to the proportion of Jews in the population as a whole, right-wing circles ranted about the significantly greater numbers of Jews in the revolutionary movement.[58]

In 1827, after the special tax for Jews had been replaced by active military service, the Jews of Rechitsa, along with other town residents, began to serve in the army. Unlike the Christians, however, Jewish children were taken away from their parents and placed in the army beginning at the age of eight; they then were sent to special military schools or "cantons" until they reached the age of eighteen. The young boys were forced to accept baptism by promises of privileges and psychological pressure. The twenty-five-year period of service began only at the age of maturity. Christian children were also sent to cantonist schools: for the most part, these were the illegitimate sons of soldiers' wives in military settlements, orphans, and the children of vagrants and participants in the Polish uprising of 1830–1831. In 1856, only a year after he assumed the throne, Alexander II ended military service for everyone below the age of fifteen, and in 1859 he signed a decree ending the institution of cantonists. However, the military authorities did not allow many Jewish children who had been called up for the army to return home until they had attained the age of majority. In 1867 retired Jewish soldiers who had served twenty-five years in the army were given the right to live anywhere in Russia.[59] Many Rechitsa residents who had been called up as cantonists took advantage of this right upon completion of their service and did not return to their native town.

Because of the administrative abuse of Jews in the army and the common anti-Semitism of their fellow soldiers, many Jews developed a strong antipathy toward military service and expressed it by trying to avoid the draft. This resistance increased in time of war, but the tightening of the mobilization policy toward Jews intensified it as well. A new statute on universal military service took effect in 1874. Although it reduced the term of service to six years, it also ended the draft exemption for sons of merchants.[60] Because many Jews suffered from poor nutrition and insufficient exposure to fresh air, they could not meet the existing medical standards for recruits. Therefore, these standards were set lower for Jews than for Christians. Nonetheless, many Jews did not meet even these lowered standards and so were exempted from service by the draft boards.[61] Other Jews were always taken to replace those who had avoided the draft or been exempted. Statistics show that the proportion of Jews in the army was even somewhat higher than their proportion in the overall population.[62]

In the battles for Plevna during the Russo-Turkish War (1877–1878), the Sixteenth and the Thirtieth Divisions particularly distinguished themselves. They had been formed in Mogilev and Minsk Provinces. A quarter of these divisions were Jews. One of the Russian generals described an instance of the bravery of a group of Jewish soldiers who broke through to a Turkish trench with cries of "Sh'ma Yisrael." Many Jewish soldiers perished in the battles for Bulgaria.[63] Among the participants of this war from Rechitsa, one of the best known was Berka Pasov.[64]

Despite their bravery in wars, the restrictions Jews faced in the army increased under Alexander III. Pëtr Vannovskii was responsible for this. Minister of war from 1881 to 1898, he was well known as the author of many pieces of anti-Jewish legislation.[65] In accordance with his directive of 1888, Jews and Karaites were not permitted to become officers or clerks in the military (an exception was made for doctors).[66]

The aggressive policies of Nicholas II toward China and Korea, along with the overestimation of Russia's military potential by the war minister, Aleksei Kuropatkin, led to the Russo-Japanese War of 1904–1905. Quite a number of Jews, including some from Rechitsa, served in that war.[67] Many Rechitsa Jews were mobilized for World War I. Rechitsa expatriate Shlëma Samsonov attained the highest rank possible for a Jew during this war, that of a noncommissioned officer. He was awarded four Saint George crosses.[68] Evidently, as had been the case earlier, the proportion of Jews called up for this war was greater than that of Christians. This inequity was one reason for the decline in the proportion of Jews in the population in Rechitsa (despite the arrival there of Jewish refugees expelled from the zone of the front line; see below) from 59.1 percent in 1914 to 52 percent in 1920.[69]

The Growth of Anti-Semitism and the Rise of Jewish Political Activism

Despite the service of Jews in the army, their participation in local government, and their significant role in the growth of the town's economy (which I examine in more detail in the next chapter), some Christians were prejudiced against them. Jews experienced the effects of this prejudice as early as 1881, when pogroms were took place in Ukraine and rumors were spreading about an imminent pogrom in Rechitsa as well. It cannot be ruled out that these rumors, which led to a curtailment of business in the town, had some real basis in fact. In any case, the local administration, in the persons of the police chief and the military director, let the townspeople know that they were prepared to take decisive measures to maintain order. Quite possibly, this firm policy avoided a pogrom in the town, and the population remained calm.[70] By contrast, the inaction of the local administrations during pogroms in other places encouraged the spread of rumors among the peasantry and the lower classes that the government had sanctioned the pogroms. An event that took place in the village of Novopavlovka in Ukraine in 1881 provides evidence for this. The peasants there had smashed up a Jewish tavern, but when a police officer arrived and told them that no ukase (decree) to rob Jews had been issued, the peasants at once repaired the damage and paid for the vodka they had spilled.[71]

Russian authorities considered pogroms to be not a singular manifestation of loyalty to the royal family but rather a genuine reaction to the alleged Jewish exploitation of the peasants, which, according to the decree issued by Tsar Alexander III on August 22, 1881, needed to be eradicated. Outraged by the decision that reverberated in the report on the session of the Minsk provincial committee on the Jewish question in December 1881, committee member Vladimir Rapoport, a first guild merchant, declared that manufacturers and merchants in civilized countries were considered a highly useful segment of society, not exploiters.[72] In May 1882 the government issued "Temporary Regulations," which prohibited Jews from settling in rural areas or owning and renting property there.

These regulations left the growing Jewish population without the means to support themselves and their families if they lived outside the mestechkos and towns. Although the "Temporary Regulations" prohibited Jews from "settling anew" in villages and towns, when the new measures were put into practice, Jews who had settled in villages and small towns even before the regulations were introduced were also expelled from these places. Prince Sergei Urusov, one of the few Russian administrators who showed tolerance toward Jews, observed: "Squeezing Jews out of rural areas and attempting to force them to 'stew in their own juice' was not limited to measures directed against new residents of rural areas. The government undertook, systematically and persistently, to drive those Jews whom the regulations have caught in villages into towns and mestechkos. With this intention, a number of shtetls have been redesignated as small towns, while an artificial constriction of territory has been imposed on the remaining towns and shtetls."[73]

By 1882, 573 Jewish families were living on peasant land—many more than in the other uezds of Minsk Province.[74] A certain number of Jewish families were also living on the property of landowners. Many of these Jewish families were forced to look for other places to live. With the passage of time, some of them, having found no steady source of income, returned to the villages until the next expulsion. Thus the end of the nineteenth and beginning of the twentieth century was a period marked by an endless struggle between the fiscal system and the Jews who were attempting to continue living in villages where they had a source of income. In this unequal struggle the Jews resorted to various tricks to somehow postpone their expulsion, since they were faced with cut-throat competition in the towns and mestechkos.

Typical of the trials faced by some Jews were those experienced by the Rechitsa townsman Berka Mnushkin, born in 1875 to a carpenter's family. The family had been living in a village in the uezd, but when the "Temporary Regulations" were issued, the authorities forced them to move to Rechitsa. After some time, Berka, who was now reaching maturity and could find no work there, moved to the estate of Balashovka in Rechitsa Uezd. In 1891 he was expelled back to Rechitsa again. Three years later, in 1894, Berka moved to the estate of Sviatoe and took up blacksmithing. Five years later, in 1902, the authorities again expelled him to Rechitsa. After a brief time the blacksmith returned to Sviatoe, but in 1913 the authorities again found him and expelled him once more. This time Berka Mnushkin settled not far from this estate, in the mestechko of Gorval'. Because of competition he was unable to make a living as a blacksmith here and so took up small trading. His business did not prosper. In 1914, in another of his appeals to the authorities, Berka wrote: "I am a man with a family and live in poverty. I earn my living only through my trade as a blacksmith, but since there are very many blacksmiths in Gorval', it is very difficult to survive and earn a mouthful of bread and some clothing. Since I have spent more than eighteen years in the village of Sviatoe, I wish to settle once more in some small village and work as a blacksmith."[75] At the same time, a large number of those expelled were forced to leave for good and go to large mestechkos like Rechitsa or to industrial cities, of which, by this time, Gomel was one.

Two decades after the restrictions of the early 1880s, the attitude toward Jews in Rechitsa took another turn for the worse: during the call-up for the Russo-Japanese War, there were demands for a pogrom.[76] Monarchists and "patriots" regarded Jewish involvement in the revolutionary movement as support for the

Japanese. The right-wing press very likely had spread this idea among the Christian population in Rechitsa at the very beginning of this unsuccessful military campaign. On March 4, 1905, Hillel Berlin, the owner of one of the pharmaceutical shops in the town, discovered a handwritten leaflet calling for Jews to be beaten up. It depicted a Jew holding a flag with the slogan *"Shlaboda"* (a distorted pronunciation of *"Svoboda"*—freedom). The text said that "mangy Yids" must not be spared but be beaten, expelled, and killed as betrayers of Christ. It ended with the words: "Yids out! Kill the democrats and sling mud at these Japanese trash!"[77]

The swell of political activity around the country in the summer of 1905 was felt in Rechitsa as well. The intelligentsia and young people held many democratic meetings. Thus, on the evening of June 9, about a hundred people gathered on Naberezhnaia Street for a rally. When it ended, the participants marched down Mikhailovskaia Street with shouts of "Down with autocracy!" and "Down with Nicholas II!" The next day, at about eleven o'clock in the evening, another group of about three hundred Jews and Christians marched down this same street carrying banners opposing the autocracy, the law courts, and the police.[78] Two weeks later, on June 23, socialists and democrats organized a rally next to the prison; about four hundred people attended. Then on June 28 and July 4 and 15, more demonstrations were organized in the town.[79] In August 1905, because of the growth of the revolutionary movement in Rechitsa and the uezd, a platoon of infantry from Gomel was stationed there.[80]

The general political strike across Russia in October that paralyzed the whole country and led to price increases and destabilization had a serious effect on the average citizen.[81] The strike led Nicholas II to issue the Manifesto of October 17, 1905, which offered several freedoms to the population, including the Jews. The tsar's concessions, which encouraged an even greater surge of democratic and socialist movements in the country, intensified the hatred of pro-monarchist circles for the Jews. On October 20 there were demonstrations and rallies of Zionist socialists, Bundists, and intelligentsia in Rechitsa. The large proportion of Jews among the participants particularly inflamed the local "patriots." The "patriots" in other areas as well regarded the many demonstrations and rallies in the same way. They held to the idea that the Jews had gained a victory over the tsar. Wishing to demonstrate their devotion to the monarchy and assuming that the bewildered administration wanted to punish Jews and liberals but were unable to do so because of the political situation, these "patriots" organized hundreds of pogroms across the country.

Nicholas II himself was personally impressed by the "patriot" response to the growth of the country's revolutionary movement that had compelled him to make concessions. But at the same time, as a political figure he could not but oppose the pogroms since they demonstrated the weakness of authority in Russia and its barbarity. The tsar was in a great dilemma, since he feared alienating the "patriots" as well. Indecisiveness in the battle against such disorders and the sympathies of the tsar for the Black Hundred movement influenced his ministers. Their inaction promoted the spreading waves of pogroms that washed over Russia. The confusion of the central authorities was transmitted to local administrations. They feared arousing the tsar's dissatisfaction, since they knew of his personal sympathies for the Black Hundred circles. In his memoirs, the director of a police department cites an instance of the tsar's direct incitement of the mayor of Rostov during an official visit of the latter: "You have an awful lot of Yids there in Rostov and in Nakhichevan!" And when the mayor tried to explain that many of them had perished when troops were putting down the revolutionary

Rechitsa clergy in 1914. Seated, from left to right: senior priest of the Uspenskii Cathedral, Archpriest Iosif Rybtsevich; senior priest of Saint Nicholas's Church, Nikolai Mozharovskii; inspector of church-parish schools, Ioann Kirkevich; priest of the Uspenskii Cathedral, Father Evstafii Lototskii. Standing: deacon of St. Nicholas's Church, Konstantin Brausevich. Courtesy of Rechitsa Regional Museum.

movement and during the pogrom, Nicholas II replied, "No! I had expected that many more of them would perish!"[82] The tsar's personal as well as official anti-Jewish stance, manifested in many restrictions on rights, revealed his attitude toward the Jewish question to the general population. As a result, many rank-and-file participants in the pogroms sincerely believed, just as they had almost a quarter-century earlier, that the tsar had given them permission to attack Jews for three days.

Despite the Christians' lack of antipathy toward the Jews in Rechitsa based on resentment of unspecified forms of economic competition, the wave of pogroms still rolled over the town.[83] Anti-Semitism in the town began to spread intensively after the pogroms in Kishinev and Gomel (both in 1903). The murder of a police inspector by revolutionaries in the neighboring uezd town of Mozyr doubtless fostered the growth of hostility toward Jews in Rechitsa.[84]

But more than any other manifestation of displeasure with the Jews, the blood slander that occurred there in 1904 did the most to promote it. Blood slanders were nothing new for the Belorussian provinces of Russia. In 1799 one occurred in Senno, in 1816 in Grodno, and in 1823 in Velizh. After a long interlude, the social-political contradictions of society led to the spread of a new wave of blood slanders in Russia: in Vilna in 1900 and in Dubossary in 1903. Inasmuch as the slander in Rechitsa and the subsequent trial are not even mentioned in studies of the period, I shall provide a brief description of them.

Karchev and Minevich, both Jews, were charged with enticing a thirteen-year old adolescent boy, Afanasii Gavnik, to their place, and after sharpening a knife in front of him that he could plainly see, they used it to draw blood from him. Although the preliminary investigation found the charge to be groundless, the minister of justice, Nikolai Murav'ëv, nevertheless decided to try it in a closed courtroom in Rechitsa. Ultimately the jurors, as occurred in the notorious case of Menachem Beilis, who was tried nine years later in nearby Kiev, acquitted the suspects in December 1904. As with the case in Kiev, most of the jurors at the Rechitsa trial were peasants.[85]

The central government's pressure on the judicial system, with the goal of eliciting proof of murder in Rechitsa, helps explain the staging of the subsequent Beilis trial. In connection with the Rechitsa court session, there was little basis to assign responsibility for initiating the Kiev trial to Minister of Justice Ivan Shcheglovitov (in office from 1906 to 1915). Rather, the idea of engineering such a high-profile case belonged to Nicholas II himself, and he followed its progress intently.[86] Uneasy about the involvement of Jews in the socialist movement, the highest echelons of central authority from the second half of 1880s obviously sought an expeditious means of isolating them from the non-Jewish sectors of the population. For example, one of the principal goals of the Numerus clausus (quotas) introduced in 1887 in institutions of higher and middle education was the isolation of pupils and students from Jews, which I shall discuss later. Another example of such measures was prohibited in 1893 to kheders' managers to teach Russian language and general subjects. These measures became the appreciable turn of authorities from the previous discourse of *sliianie* in Jewish politic. However, they realized that a merely restrictive measure would not achieve this goal and hence a more effective approach would be necessary.

The conditions under which the Rechitsa trial was conducted and the signatures of the defendants on a nondisclosure agreement ensured public ignorance of the scandal. The futile efforts of a journalist to inquire about these details indicates clearly that the censors suppressed publication of the entire story of the blood slander in Russian. The lack of public information about the trial combined with the rumors about it led to heightened antipathy toward the local Jewish population.

Archpriest Nikolai Mozharovskii, the senior priest in the oldest church in the town, Saint Nicholas's (founded in 1725), assumed the major role in spreading anti-Semitism there. He served at the same time as the head and teacher of religion in the two-year girls' school in Rechitsa and as the chairman of the uezd section of the diocesan academic council.

In his sermons, Mozharovskii declared that the Jews not only sympathized with the Japanese but also were working with them; that they hated the existing order and wanted to topple the government. From his pulpit he also gave the summons: "The Yids must be slaughtered down to the last one, for it is they who want to bring down the tsar." Indignant at this blatant anti-Semitic propaganda, the Christian intelligentsia stopped attending his church.[87]

In June 1905 tensions were mounting and rumors circulating in Rechitsa about preparations for a pogrom. Under these conditions conflicts between Jews and Christians erupted in the marketplace. One such clash ended in a fight that threatened to turn into a pogrom. To prepare for such an outcome, a self-defense force of seventy people, including about thirty Christian workers, was organized. But nothing came of this, possibly because of threats by some Jews to set the houses of the hooligans on fire.[88]

After the tsar's Manifesto of October 17 was issued, Mozharovskii summoned his congregants to struggle even more actively against the Jews. Police Inspector Fëdor Artemiev used the police hectograph to print many leaflets of at least four different types. These contained inflammatory slogans: "How long will we

tolerate Jewish dominance?" and "The time has come at last to settle scores with
these accursed enemies of Rus." One of the leaflets said that the State Duma,
which the revolutionaries were compelling the tsar to assemble, would be full
of Yids, Poles and Armenians. The constitution passed by such a Duma would
be directed against the old traditions, the Russian people, God, and religion.
Leaflets were handed out on the church porch. After a church service on October 21, a small band of hooligans, incited by Artemiev, attacked Jewish women
who were selling goods nearby, beat them, and took their goods. The situation
in the town became even more tense on the following day when, pressured by
Rechitsa's socialist parties, the shopkeepers went on strike. Artemiev, the police
inspector; Isidor Kovalchuk, the clerk at the military headquarters; and the sons
of Turënok, the leader of the local "patriots," began even more vigorously inciting
the Christian population to an anti-Jewish pogrom. As attested by Sara Rastrov-
skaia, Artemiev was handing out money to a band of ruffians on the evening of
that day. To respond to the threat of a pogrom, the Bundists and the Zionist-
socialists in the town formed a self-defense detachment. According to another
version, 70 people enlisted, including four Christians; yet another account states
110 people, including several dozen Russian workers.

The detachment was armed with twenty-five revolvers; they later managed
to acquire another fifteen. But few of the defense volunteers knew how to use
their weapons. When they learned that the defenders were armed, the "patriots"
tried to have the military director, Skvortsov, issue them rifles on the pretext that
they needed to defend themselves from armed Jews and democrats. Although the
uezd police officer Semën Zhitnikov did not approve of this request, Skvortsov
ordered his secretary, Kornilii Dmitriev, to issue a hundred rifles and cartridges
to the "patriots." While they were being handed out, a few Zionist-socialists
dressed like peasants tried to pass themselves off as Christians in order to get
some rifles as well, but they were recognized and beaten.[89] By that time, a wave of
pogroms had swept over the neighboring Ukrainian provinces. Anticipating the
worst, a number of Rechitsa Jews managed to flee in time to nearby villages.[90]

A deputation of Jews tried to complain to the police officer, Zhitnikov, but he,
accurately judging what was about to happen, had left town. Rechitsa Jews later
naively said that had Zhitnikov stayed in the town, he would never have allowed
the pogrom to happen.[91] Had the local administrators wished to do so, of course,
they could have dispersed the rioters with their force of twelve policemen, an
escort guard of fifteen soldiers, and a company of soldiers quartered in Rechitsa.[92]

Tension increased even more when a rumor circulated that Jews had killed
a sailor from a steamship that had arrived in Rechitsa from Kiev on Sunday,

October 23. In fact, some Jews in Loev, the steamer stop before Rechitsa, had beaten two hooligans who were traveling on this ship. That same day, an agitator from the Black Hundred arrived in Rechitsa from Novozybkov. In Saint Nicholas's Church he addressed the town's "patriots" and peasants who had arrived from nearby villages.

Then at two o'clock in the afternoon, at a signal of the bells of Saint Nicholas's Church rung by the verger, Raikevich, a large mob made up of peasants who had come to the bazaar, local criminals, and a few cabmen began smashing up Jewish stores and shops, stealing and destroying their contents. Yehuda Kom, a child at the time, was shaken by what he witnessed at the bazaar, where he and his classmates had stopped: "To our astonishment, we saw that the bazaar did not look at all like it usually did: people were shouting and running in fear, the goyim [non-Jews] had taken bagels and baked goods from the shop counters and were even lashing out left and right. At that point we all ran off." The pogrom was led by the police sergeant Borichevskii and the police inspector Artemiev. Eyewitnesses say that Artemiev himself used his sabre to cut to pieces overshoes and other goods in Livshits's shop. After smashing and looting more than thirty shops and stores, the mob, armed with rifles, axes, and crowbars, began smashing windows in Jewish homes. The mob searched the streets for democrats, broke into Jewish homes, and beat the residents. Jews awaited their fate in terror. Yehuda Kom writes: "We gathered in our house, which was located in an inner courtyard. We closed the shutters; the men sat in waiting in the front room, the women and children in another. There were about twenty children, and we were ordered not to make a sound. . . . We hid under the beds and sofas, behind the doors, and kept absolutely still. Trembling, we listened to the roar of the mob looting Jewish property." Yehuda then recounts how the men, after being admonished by his father, the well-respected rabbi Chaim-Shlioma (more about him can be found in subsequent chapters), armed themselves to defend their refuge: some had axes, some crowbars, and others simply picked up stakes. Fortunately for them and their families, the much better armed mob did not enter the house. Evidently, there was resistance in some areas, for shots rang out during the night. The number of victims was relatively small. An old Jew, Abram Arklis, who happened to get in the way of the mob, was killed when he was hit over the head with a plank; seven people were injured. Toward morning, the pogrom subsided.[93]

The self-defense detachment apparently did not venture to take the field, and a representative of the local Bund appealed to Gomel for help by a prearranged telegram. There a decision was taken to send a detachment of twenty men, most of them Bundists but also some Socialist Revolutionaries. Because of the general strike, the strike committee made special arrangements for a train to take the detachment to Rechitsa. At this point the head of the detachment, the well-known and experienced member of the Gomel self-defense organization Leiba Rozhend (nicknamed Stradalets, "The Sufferer"), became careless: he bought tickets for the whole group at the station. In doing so, he aroused the suspicion of one of the police spies who were usually plentiful at railway stations. The quick-witted spy sent a telegram to inform Rechitsa that a self-defense detachment was on its way. The train journey took two hours, and during that time several dozen pogrom thugs commanded by the military director's secretary, Dmitriev, the engineer Kuznetsov, and Police Inspector Artemiev set up an ambush along the route from the station to the center of town. At the same time, they ordered the cabdrivers to leave the station. For some reason, the Rechitsa self-defense detachment was unable to warn the Gomel detachment about this development. When the men from Gomel arrived at the station, they asked about the pogrom; unable to find any cabs, they set off for the town center on foot. They divided into groups of nine and eleven, one group taking the central road, the other using side streets. Their intent was to meet at a designated apartment where they would work out their plan for further action. Neither group suspected anything was afoot, and they fell into the ambush. The pogrom thugs opened heavy fire on

Kazarmennaia Street, beginning of the twentieth century.

them and then ran up and began stabbing them with bayonets and beating the seriously wounded and dead with their rifle butts. According to the account of the defender Gezentsfeig, who miraculously survived, many of his comrades were beaten to death in this way. Medical examination confirmed this. Twenty bayonet wounds were found on the body of Leiba Rozhend, for example. In the end, seven of the defenders were killed and three seriously wounded. The remainder, who had fled from the scene of the carnage, were lightly wounded. Because of the suddenness of the attack and their inexperience, the detachment, armed only with revolvers and bombs, never managed to put up any resistance, and none of their attackers suffered. After this massacre the "patriots" delivered the bodies of their victims to the police. Only then did they discover that several of the victims were not dead but seriously wounded. The pogrom organizers wanted to finish them off, but the police dissuaded them, saying that without medical help they would "finish off on their own." Along with the dead, the three wounded were thrown into the mortuary at the hospital, where, according to different accounts, they remained for six to twenty-four hours without any medical treatment. Then Dr. Nikolai Savinich examined the injured, but he did not even clean their wounds and only bandaged them with some cotton wool. When the wounded were carried to the hospital, the pogrom thugs continued to beat them. The judicial investigator at first refused to send the wounded to Gomel, maintaining that they were under arrest. When the Gomel Bundists learned of the fate of their comrades, they wanted to set off for Rechitsa to liberate them; however, the committee, after lengthy debate, rejected this idea. Only a week later, on instructions of the authorities, did the Rechitsa administration arrange for the return, under guard, of the arrested men to Gomel.[94] The dead were solemnly buried by their comrades.

Among the seven dead Gomel townspeople, two had been born in Rechitsa: Nakhum Rapoport and Iser Vilenskii. It should be noted that the men from Gomel did not come by chance to help Rechitsa during the pogrom. The party organizations of the two towns were closely linked. In the summer of 1903, a few people from Rechitsa had played an active role in Jewish defense during the Gomel pogrom. Yosel Kom, thirty-five years old and brother of the Rechitsa rabbi Chaim-Shlioma, mentioned earlier, was summoned by the Jews of Gomel to help repulse the pogrom mob; for this he was sentenced to five months in prison in 1904.[95] Another Rechitsa man, twenty-nine-year-old Zalman Shekhter, was sentenced at the same time.[96] A third Rechitsa native active in the Gomel defense was Heshel Pasov, who, to avoid a trial, fled to the United States under an assumed name.[97]

The members of the defense group who were killed in Rechitsa, 1905. From Iakov Drapkin, *1905 god v Gomele i Polesskom raione*, in *1905 god v Gomele i Polesskom raione: materialy po istorii sotsial-demokraticheskogo i rabochego dvizheniia v 1893–1906 gg* (Gomel: Gomel'skii rabochii, 1925), 209.

After the vicious murder of members of the self-defense detachment, the participants in the pogrom left the town's Jews alone. Including the old man who had been killed, a total of eight people perished during the Rechitsa pogrom. In Soviet times, two other versions of the number of victims appeared: according to one, thirty people were killed during the Rechitsa pogrom; according to the other, fifty were killed.[98] Seventeen men and seven women received wounds of varying degrees. Forty Jewish families also suffered material losses that, by different estimates made in 1905–1906, totaled from 28,000 to 40,000 rubles.[99] Several days after the pogrom, two representatives of the League for Attaining Full Rights for the Jewish People in Russia were sent to conduct an investigation. These men were the Saint Petersburg lawyer and writer Fëdor Chervinskii (who was Orthodox) and the Gomel doctor Abram Bruk, brother of the Zionist leader and deputy of the First State Duma Dr. Grigorii (Tsvi-Hirsh) Bruk. They were assisted in Rechitsa by the lawyer Feitenberg, who represented the town's Jewish community. After questioning fourteen witnesses to the massacre, they submitted their conclusions to one of the founders and leaders of the League for Attaining

Full Rights for the Jewish People in Russia, the well-known advocate Genrikh Sliozberg. He played an active role in all the major legal cases linked with anti-Semitism in Russia. On the recommendation of Abram Bruk, the Committee for Aid to Victims of the Pogrom paid the families of those killed an average of 4,000 rubles each.[100]

While in Rechitsa, Chervinskii submitted complaints about the activities of the military director Skvortsov, Archpriest Mozharovskii, and Police Inspector Artemiev to the public prosecutor in Minsk and to the prosecutor of the civil court in Vilna, whose jurisdiction included all the provincial civil courts within the Vilna governor-generalship. The prosecutor of the civil court replied that he was preparing to visit Rechitsa. A complaint was also submitted to the chief procurator of the Holy Synod about the activities of the archpriest.[101] In Rechitsa the murder investigation was conducted by an acting investigator and local resi-dent, L. P. Belinskii, who was close to the "patriot" camp. He seized upon the testimony of the organizers of the pogrom, Artemiev and Kuznetsov, who main-tained that the actions of Jewish young people in calling for strikes and the clos-ing of shops had aroused the Christians. They also maintained that the slaughter near the railway station happened because the Christians had to defend them-selves against the armed men from Gomel. Instead of detaining those who carried out the pogrom, Belinskii arrested the members of the self-defense detachment, as noted above. And although he later allowed them to be sent back to Gomel, he initiated a case against them, accusing them of using armed force. Only after the lawyer from Saint Petersburg arrived in town did Belinskii begin investigating the actions of those who had carried out the pogrom. Chervinskii's arrival also had an effect on the Rechitsa Jews who had suffered in the pogrom. They began providing more detailed testimony about the pogrom thugs than they had earlier, when they feared reprisals from Artemiev, who was still in office, and from other policemen. When Chervinskii left, therefore, he gave Feitenberg responsibility for investigating and compiling a list of damages suffered by Rechitsa Jews.[102]

The visits to Rechitsa of various Jewish activists who pressured the local legal authorities to punish the guilty aroused the resentment of the "patriots," above all those involved in the massacre. Their anger, along with the wave of pogroms in Russia that had not yet subsided, created fertile soil for preparations for a new pogrom in the town, set for November 20–21 of that same year. The gover-nor of Minsk, who passed this information to Saint Petersburg at the begin-ning of December, had evidently taken some preventive measures this time, after which—according to his report—calm was restored among the population in Rechitsa.[103]

Because sources are scant, it is difficult to determine how the "patriots" were punished. The general who came from Saint Petersburg to investigate the actions of Rechitsa officials covered for the military director by concluding that the rifles had been issued to help maintain order in the town. And the newspaper *Peterburgskie gubernskie vedomosti* on January 21, 1906, even expressed its thanks to the military director for maintaining order.[104] Apparently the provincial authorities transferred the military director and the police inspector to new posts elsewhere. Their names are not among those on the list of functionaries in Rechitsa compiled several years later. Nikolai Mozharovskii, though, remained in Rechitsa and organized a "secret circle" that was making plans for a new anti-Jewish pogrom. This was noted by the state rabbi of the town, Pinkhas Karasik, in a telegram of June 17, 1907, to the chairman of the council of ministers, Pëtr Stolypin. By that time, the proponents of pogroms had already organized themselves in a section of the Union of the Russian People, with 370 members in Rechitsa and 2,228 members in Rechitsa Uezd. After receiving Karasik's information, Stolypin quickly telegraphed the governor of Minsk with an order for him to take appropriate measures.[105] It seems likely that, as a result of this action, the governor forewarned the supporters of the Black Hundred. In later years, Mozharovskii even advanced up the clerical ladder. By 1914 he was head of the uezd diocesan academic council and became head of the two-year girls' school where he also was the teacher of religion.[106]

Although the Christian population of the town was quite prosperous, as Chervinskii noted in his investigation of anti-Jewish disorders in 1905, Rechitsa was the only place in Minsk Province where a pogrom occurred.[107] On the local level, the reasons for its occurrence were the intense anti-Jewish propaganda of an authoritative figure in the Orthodox Church in Rechitsa, along with the inaction of the local civil powers, who evidently had received no instructions from Minsk. The provincial and town administrations did not restrain either the arbitrary measures of police officials or the activities of an official of the War Ministry who provided armed support to the pogrom's instigators. Thus Rechitsa was included in the list of places where the authorities abetted a pogrom.

The intensification of anti-Semitism in Russia at that time was not a random development. Hundreds of laws and directives that regulated the activity of Jews and significantly restricted their choice of places to live placed the Jewish population in a servile position vis-à-vis the Christians. On the other hand, the modernization of society and the emancipation that took place at the end of the nineteenth and the beginning of the twentieth century had a significant influence on the Jews. Many of them realized that a situation in which they lacked so many

rights needed changing. As a result, ideas about transforming society became popular among Jews. Rechitsa Jews did not stand apart from this process. From the
end of the nineteenth century onward, they participated in the social-democratic
movement, principally in the Bund, a Jewish party that had arisen within the
territory of contemporary Belorussia and Lithuania.

By 1905 the Bund had made the final elaboration of a plan of cultural and
national autonomy for Jews. At the very beginning of the twentieth century, an
independent Bundist organization already existed in Rechitsa.[108] It was closely
linked to the Bund center in Gomel. One of the organizers and leaders of the
Bund in Gomel was a private tutor from Rechitsa, Leiba Dragunskii.[109] Another
active Gomel Bundist, Khramchenko, had also lived in Rechitsa.[110]

By 1902 the activists in the RSDRP (Russian Social-Democratic Workers'
Party), including the Bund, which was then a component of that party, were Iosif
Lenskii, Broider, Brokhina, Vёrtkina, A. Gabov, N. Gabov, Sofia Gabova, Khaikin,
Livshits, and Chaim Spivak. They formed the first social-democratic circle, initially with fifteen to twenty people. By 1903 its membership had grown to a hundred. The organization, in which the Bundists were a majority, held gatherings
twice a week and on Saturdays had rallies in the forest or boat excursions on the
river. A few members—L. Demiakhovskii, Ber, and F. Kozёl—organized small
circles of five to seven people to study political economy.[111] The social-democrats
in the town took the initiative in organizing strikes. Along with May 1, the members of the organization celebrated March 1 each year. This was the anniversary
of the assassination of Alexander II, a ruler revered by most Jews at the time for
expanding their rights and instituting governmental reforms.[112]

Both Bundists and Bolsheviks continued to mark this anniversary even after
the split within the Rechitsa social-democratic organization following the schism
in the RSDRP at its second congress in the summer of 1903. The first group
to split from the Rechitsa organization, in late 1903, was the circle of SRs (Socialist Revolutionaries) that included Breindorf, Leiba Demiakhovskii, A. D. Krupetskii, Nakhum Rapoport, Chaim Spivak, and its leader, Shimon Karasik. By
November 1903 a group of twenty-eight people had coalesced around them.
The town's liberals—the priest Grigorii Lototskii, the pharmacist Iakov Kotsyn,
and the merchant Mordukh Frenkel—supported them. At the same time, an
organization of Zionist workers, Poalei-Tsion, led by M. Kh. Briskin, Bukler, and
M. Shliafer was formed in the town. They worked with the SRs for several years
after they had formed separate organizations in Rechitsa. In 1904 a small group
of Rechitsa Bolsheviks led by Pinkhas Gorelik formed their own cell, which
became part of the Polesia committee.[113]

The Bundists remained the largest organization. At that time, it had about three hundred members, mainly craftsmen and craft workers. They carried on active work, however, and at least fifty people regularly attended their meetings and gatherings. On May 18, 1904, the Bundists organized the first relatively large (by Rechitsa standards) strike, one in which eighty people participated.[114] On the whole, the Bundist organization was a serious power in the strike movement against the owners of tradesmen's shops and large stores, the vast majority of whom were Jews (as will be discussed in detail in the next chapter). The economic damage done to Jewish shop owners, the atheist propaganda of the socialists, and the resentment of the town administration and the Christian population of Rechitsa at the large numbers of Jews involved in the sociopolitical struggle aggravated relations between the town's Jewish elite and the Bundists. Jewish businessmen and religious and community leaders organized their own meetings and insisted that every Jew in Rechitsa refuse to participate in gatherings organized by the socialists and refuse to rent apartments to "democrats." If they did not do so, they were threatened with social boycott (including the withdrawal of aid to the poor and the banning of their children from Talmud-Torah). In a few instances, it seems, these threats were actually carried out, and they achieved the desired result. The Bundists of Rechitsa, commenting on these measures and those of the police, complained: "All this makes our working conditions extremely difficult."[115] Another difficulty for the Bund in Rechitsa was the lack of experienced organizers and propagandists, as well as the lack of party literature.[116]

Under the impact of strikes and walkouts, one group of Jewish business owners made concessions, while another sought the help of the local police, who were carrying on an active struggle against the socialist parties. The Bundists wrote from Rechitsa: "The servants of the tsar . . . show exceptional zeal here in the struggle against 'sedition': they dart about the streets in disguise all night long; they travel on bicycles through the nearby forests; they recruit volunteer spies (teachers from the local school)."[117] All these efforts bore fruit. In November 1903, the police arrested the SR A. D. Krupetskii, who subsequently was exiled to Arkhangelsk Province for three years. Several months later, the police managed to track down one of the political economy circles that had been meeting in the home of Nakhman Gorivodskii on Semionovskaia Street. In January 1904, with the help of a Belorussian provocateur named Pëtr Zinkevich, the police arrested the socialists who had come to a gathering in this house. Another fourteen Bundists and nine SRs were arrested in February of the same year.[118]

Despite these arrests and a campaign by the local "patriots" for a pogrom, by May 1, 1904, the Bundists in Rechitsa had held five meetings attended by twenty-five to eighty people. They printed antimonarchist leaflets on a hectograph, organized strikes, and carried out agitation among Jewish workers.[119] During the 1905 revolution, the Bund in Rechitsa intensified its activity. On March 1, the Bundists organized a meeting on the pogroms in Baku that attracted more than three hundred workers. There were heated arguments at the meeting between the Bundists, on the one hand, and the SRs and the Zionist-socialists, on the other. The Zionists did not have the support of the majority, however, and they walked out of the meeting. The Bundists and the SRs who remained passed a resolution that not only condemned the pogroms but also demanded the overthrow of the monarchy and the convocation of a constituent assembly by universal, equal, direct, and secret ballot.[120]

Several days later, the Bundists organized three strikes. The shortest and most successful of these involved forty-five printers. The owners of the printing shop were forced to improve working conditions, and this raised the Bund's prestige in the town. The strike of employees of a Jewish savings and loan association, organized by the Bund, lasted longer. It was during this strike that the Bundists first came into direct conflict with the elite of the local Jewish community. A quotation from an article published in Geneva in the Bundist newspaper *Poslednie Izvestiia* reveals something of this conflict: "Board members [of the savings and loan association] and its council behave disgracefully. Goldberg, a wealthy bourgeois, and even more, the attorney Vilenkin, try in every way possible to tarnish our organization, calling its members hooligans. . . . Vilenkin poses as a liberal. The strike is not yet over. The employees will most likely emerge victorious."[121] The Jewish elite were no less angered by another strike—of shop clerks—organized by the Bund. It began in the store of one of the major textile merchants, Moshe Shneerson, and then spread to the rest of the stores in the town. The clerks, who worked fourteen hours or more daily, demanded a twelve-hour working day. Without waiting for authorization by the owners, they began closing the stores at nine in the evening. The store owners called a meeting to discuss this matter. The nature of the agreement they reached is unknown, but the fact that some of the owners agreed to meet the demands of the clerks even before the meeting suggests that here too the Bund achieved its aim.[122]

In May 1905, the town's socialist organizations organized a series of May Day events in which both Jewish and non-Jewish workers took part.[123] It is interesting to note that Christian workers in Belorussia respected the Bund and saw it as an organization capable of forcing the owners to make concessions.[124] In 1906–1907, the Bund and other socialist organizations in Rechitsa supported several general strikes that led to the shutdown of industrial enterprises in the town. As a result, the owners had to shorten the working day and provide lunch breaks for the workers.[125] From time to time, the Rechitsa section of the Bund received donations from countrymen who had immigrated to the United States.[126]

Anti-Semitism and Jewish political activity were closely intertwined processes. The growth of one inevitably led to an upsurge in the other. The actions of the tsar and his circle, concerned about the economic gains of Jews and the modernization of Russia connected with them, disturbed the relatively stable state of relations between Jews and Christians at the end of the nineteenth century. This conservative ideological stance, expressed through new restrictive measures against Jews, began a chain reaction that led to a sharp rise in anti-Semitism and in the political engagement of the Jewish population.

In view of the deteriorating social and ethnic relations in the country, Nicholas II was compelled in December 1905 to sign a decree providing various groups of the population, including national minorities, with broad voting rights in elections to the State Duma. Nevertheless, the new law on Duma elections did not give the right to vote to women, students, soldiers, and those below the age of twenty-five. The law stipulated a property qualification and indirect elections. Voters, divided into four groups or curiae (landowners, peasants, townspeople, and workers in enterprises with more than fifty employees), voted separately for electors who then, at provincial congresses, chose the deputies for the Duma. The large number of electors from the landowners' curia guaranteeing them a third of all electors often gave them the decisive vote in the elections for deputies. By providing the landowners in the Duma with representation so disproportionate to their total numbers in the country, the tsar clearly demonstrated to the whole society that he saw them, as previously, as the support for his throne, even though the politically conservative merchant and business class had expanded significantly.

The Jews received equal voting rights under this new law, which was a huge step forward for Russia, where they, as earlier, had been unable to vote in zemstvo and city elections. The vast majority of Jews in Russia belonged to the curia of townspeople. In Rechitsa Uezd the most Jewish voters lived in mestechkos that were far from the center, and the trip to Rechitsa (where the voting took place) and back required more than a little money and time. The majority of voters, who were short of both, were unable to come to choose their electors to the First State Duma. This problem troubled the Rechitsa representative of the League for Attaining Full Rights for the Jewish People in Russia, an organization that made great efforts to elect Jewish deputies to the Duma.[127] It seems likely that it managed to organize some transportation to Rechitsa for some Jewish voters. The results of the voting in Minsk Province show that this organization's efforts were not in vain. Of the twenty electors chosen here by the townspeople's curia, seventeen were Jews. These seventeen electors made an alliance at the provincial congress with a group of progressives (the party of Polish landowners), and they were able to elect to the Duma a representative of the Cadet Party, one of the leaders of the Zionist movement, Shimon Rozenbaum.[128] In the subsequent election to the State Duma, the Jews of Minsk Province did not manage to elect their representative.

Before the voting for the Second State Duma, the senate circulated to the provinces an interpretation aimed at using bureaucratic means to limit the number of Jewish voters.[129] When these measures were applied in Rechitsa, the result was a disproportionately small representation of Jews among those voting for electors. Although Jews comprised 58.7 percent of the town's population, they formed only 42 percent (370 out of 852) of the Rechitsa residents who had the right to vote for electors. This meant that only 5.6 percent of the Jewish population of the town had the right to vote, whereas 10.4 percent of Christians had that right.

A different situation developed in the uezd mestechkos. Because the percentage of Jews was higher there than in the uezd center, and because a large proportion of the Orthodox population voted in the peasants' curia, the percentage of enfranchised mestechko Jews in the townspeople's curia was much higher than in Rechitsa. Their participation in the voting in Rechitsa meant that the Jewish candidate for elector had a much better chance of winning. In the uezd as a whole, 2,050 Jews had the right to vote with the townspeople's curia; this was 70.5 percent of the 2,910 potential voters.[130] This was higher than the proportion of Jewish residents in the mestechkos generally (54.2 percent).[131] But if one considers the other voting curiae in which residents of uezd mestechkos participated, it is evident—from the examples of Loev and Bragin—that the ratio between Jewish and non-Jewish voters in all curiae corresponded approximately to their numbers in the population generally. According to the rules, the townspeople's curia of Rechitsa Uezd was to select only one elector for the Minsk provincial congress that would elect deputies for the Second State Duma. The numerical superiority of Jews allowed them easily to elect their candidate, Aron Vilenkin.[132]

To minimize the influence of Jews and Poles on the results of the election, efforts were made to bring out as many Orthodox citizens as possible to the voting. With that in mind, a preelection committee, under the patronage of the civil powers and the Orthodox clergy, was set up in Minsk. Local branches of this committee were opened across the province, and they were guided by marshals of the nobility, heads of the zemstvos, and the clergy. In Rechitsa, the Black Hundred Union of the Russian People assisted this committee. With its help, the committee could easily bring to the polling stations all Orthodox voters who wished to exercise their right. Committee members freely used anti-Semitic propaganda in their efforts to encourage the Orthodox population to vote. The sections of the League for Attaining Full Rights for the Jewish People in Russia, which opposed these committees, did not have sufficient means to bring Jewish voters from the mestechkos to the uezd centers and to Rechitsa in particular.[133]

Elections for the Third State Duma took place in September–October 1907 in accordance with the new electoral law of June 3, 1907. The government promulgated this law without the Duma's approval, which was against Russian law. The central administration resorted to this tactic in order to form a more conservative and compliant Duma. According to the new law, the townspeople's curia was divided into two parts: one comprised wealthy businessmen and homeowners; the other, the remainder who met the property qualification mentioned earlier. Also, tenants who wished to vote for electors had to present a certificate to the police showing that they lived in a one-family apartment. This measure significantly reduced the number of voters in this category of the townspeople's curia. At the same time, the law changed the number of electors sent to the provincial congresses from the various voters' curiae. As a result of these changes, landowners in European Russia were guaranteed 51 percent of all the electors; peasants, 22 percent; the first townspeople's curia, 13 percent; the second, 11 percent; and the workers' curia, 2 percent. The law also reduced the number of deputies from the fringes of the empire, where a large percentage of the non-Orthodox population lived. The Minister of Internal Affairs was authorized to divide the voters in the two townspeople's curiae by religion in order to reduce the number of Jewish electors. Local administrations assessed the qualifications of Jewish voters much more strictly than those of Orthodox voters. All these measures were introduced to ensure that the vast majority of seats in the Duma would be given to conservatives.[134]

As a result of these measures, the number of people voting for electors in Rechitsa was reduced to 290, that is, by more than half.[135] In all likelihood the proportion of Jews among them was reduced even more. But thanks to the enfranchised Jews from the mestechkos of Rechitsa Uezd, a Jewish elector was chosen by the first townspeople's curia. Once more it was the lawyer Aron Vilenkin.[136] The Jews did not manage to win in the second curia. Here the elector chosen was the town elder Gumskii. On the whole, in Minsk Province the government's measures did significantly reduce the number of Jewish voters. There

were 16 Jews among the 137 electors of Minsk Province for the Second State
Duma, and they all were sent to the provincial electoral congress as part of the
quota of 20 electors from the unicameral townspeople's curia. In the elections
to the Third State Duma, with the same total number of electors from the province, 15 Jews went to the congress as part of the quota of 23 electors from the
bicameral townspeople's curia.[137] Jews represented 11 percent of the electors at
the Minsk electoral congresses for both Dumas, a figure not far below their share
of the province's population (16 percent). This proportion seems satisfactory
for Jews, particularly in the context of the poor representation of peasants and
workers among the electors.

The elections for the Fourth State Duma in 1912 were also conducted in accordance with the law of June 3, 1907. Despite the efforts of the authorities, Jews
were chosen as electors in both townspeople's curiae. In the first curia the elector
was the lumberman and merchant of the second guild Mordukh Frenkel; and in
the second curia, another merchant of the second guild, the chairman of the
mutual aid society, Bentsion Maizus.[138] There were 13 Jews among the 137 electors from Minsk Province for the Fourth State Duma.[139] Thus, while the number
of Jewish electors to the congress from Rechitsa Uezd actually increased, their
overall number across the province continued to decline from election to election.

Another result of these legislative measures restricting the number of Jewish
voters and electors was a decline in the overall numbers of Jewish deputies
elected to the State Duma. There were twelve in the First Duma, four in the Second, two in the Third, and three in the Fourth. The fact that the changes to the
electoral laws had worsened the situation of Jews convinced them that the central
authorities did not intend to give them equal rights. Having lost hope of receiving
equal rights and emancipation from the Pale of Settlement, where keen competition in business and the trades offered no opportunities to attain their desired
level of prosperity, and in the wake of the extensive pogroms of 1905, Jews began
to emigrate in larger numbers. Although emigration from Rechitsa to Palestine
and America had begun as early as the first quarter of the nineteenth century, its
tempo then was meager compared to the huge wave of emigration that began
after the Rechitsa pogrom described earlier.

Although the methods that the government employed to solve the Jewish question in Russia were not noted for their coherence, they did ultimately lead to the
emancipation of the Jews to some degree. As many memoirs attest, those Jews
who assimilated Russian culture but were not baptized as Christians underwent
a difficult internal crisis. In acquiescing to the influence of state educational

requirements either directly or by way of cultural mediators, they alienated themselves in different ways from their own kind, who began to see them as *Epikoyres* (unbelievers, a term with roots going back to the Greek philosopher Epicurus). This became an irretrievable loss for them. Russian society, long in the grip of stereotypes, either absolutely refused to accept them as equals or accepted them with major reservations that were obvious to acculturated Jews. In contrast to other members of Jewish society, they began to feel their legal and cultural abasement more keenly. This situation pushed many of them into political parties.

Although there were few acculturated Jews in Rechitsa, many of the rest started to see them as leaders after the blood slander, the pogrom, and discriminatory elections for the State Duma as well as a successful strike action opposed by the local elite. The growth in political engagement was one of the signs of this development. This trend was particularly marked in October 1913, when the Jews of Rechitsa went on strike to protest the trial of Menachem Beilis, which had begun in Kiev. This action was a part of the general strike within the Pale of Settlement organized by the Bund, and it essentially halted all economic activity in the town. The political sympathies of local Jews were not restricted to the Bund; their spectrum of views was quite wide-ranging. The outbreak of World War I, accompanied by an upsurge of patriotism even within moderate opposition groups in Russian society, internalized many unresolved problems, including the ethnic one, but a few months later these problems burst forth with new force.

Despite the dissatisfaction of Rechitsa Jews with their legal status, especially at the beginning of the twentieth century, the 125 years in the Russian Empire were altogether a period of the greatest personal security for them as well as for Jews in other towns and shtetls throughout the entire period of the Jewish presence in Eastern Europe. Jews felt this very quickly. As far back as 1810, the Russian officer Vladimir Bronevsky, when he found himself in Borisov, noted the following: "The Yids really are sincerely devoted to Russia. They love the emperor and they would not exchange the Russians for any other mentors."[140] This assessment was confirmed during the war with Napoleon in 1812, when the majority of Jews remained loyal to Russia. Although John D. Klier locates the root of this loyalty in Napoleon's unsuccessful Jewish policy, the reason to a great extent can be attributed to the improved economic status of Jews under Russian rule.[141] Also, pillaging by German, Italian, and to a lesser degree French soldiers in Napoleon's army must have left a negative impression.[142]

The economic position of the Jews, very closely connected with their legal status and the economic prosperity of the rest of the population, was sensitive to their fluctuating mood as expressed in the boom-and-bust cycles of the economy.

3

The Economy of the Town in the
Nineteenth and Early Twentieth Centuries

The vigorous economic activity of Jews in the Duchy of Lithuania for the ten
years prior to the second partition of the Polish-Lithuanian Commonwealth continued unabated under Russian rule.[1] Vladimir Bronevskii, writing in 1810 from
Minsk, cited the same old grievances: "The local Yids pestered us so badly with
offers of their services that we had to use threats to get rid of them. Surrounding
us in a crowd or importuning us one by one, they read us a long list of the goods
they could sell us in their shops."[2]

This activity, so offensive to the author, was essentially the dawning of capitalism in the western provinces of Russia. It was based on the important premise
that Jews should be administratively evicted from villages and forced to live in the
towns of the Pale of Settlement. It resulted in a significant increase in the number
of tradesmen's shops and small industrial and commercial enterprises. The most
visible reflection of the economic upturn was the increased trade in the town's
bazaar. Even though the Jewish population sustained sizable financial losses in
the course of this urbanization project—a successful one from the authorities'
standpoint—the population on the whole recovered relatively quickly from
these setbacks. The voluntary migration of Jews from the villages and shtetls to
Rechitsa (discussed in more detailed in the next chapter) in the 1830s and later,
when the wave of administrative evictions had already subsided, shows that they
were attracted by the town's better economic prospects.

At the beginning of the nineteenth century, only 8 percent of town dwellers
(127 people) were classed as tradesmen.[3] In many other towns of Minsk Province
at the time, the tradesman class constituted a larger portion of the population
than in Rechitsa. In Minsk, for example, it was 36 percent; in Slutsk, 30 percent;
in Mozyr, 22 percent; in Polotsk, 17 percent; in Bobruisk, 15 percent; and in

Borisov, 9 percent of the population.[4] The vast majority of tradesmen in Rechitsa were Jews: no more than forty men and youths among these 127 members of the tradesman class (this figure included all family members) could actually have been practicing their trades; according to another available official statistic, there were 32 Jewish tradesmen in Rechitsa at the very beginning of the nineteenth century.[5] Among them were 15 tailors, 4 shoemakers, 3 barbers, 3 cabinetmakers, 2 bookbinders, a wine maker, a glazier, a dyer, a tinsmith, and a carpenter-builder.[6] The sixth census list of 1811 shows 85 Jewish tradesmen in Rechitsa.[7]

Subsequent migration of Jews from the countryside and shtetls into the town, plus the natural increase in population, meant that by the middle of the nineteenth century among the Rechitsa Jews alone there were 66 tradesmen and 227 trade's workers, that is, apprentices. Apprentices at the time were divided among several categories: a *lern-yingl* (literally, "a youth in training," Yiddish) for thirteen to fourteen years and a *poel'* (literally, "a worker," Yiddish), which in their turn were also divided into several subcategories depending on the qualifications of the individual. These figures did not include carpenters, who, along with cabbies, draymen, manual laborers, day laborers, and domestic servants, numbered an additional 102 Jews. It is interesting that, at the time, Christians in many volosts in Rechitsa Uezd did not take up carpentry and did not build their houses; for this they called in Jews or Christians from nearby Chernigov Province.[8] As a result, it seems, a number of carpenters and builders moved into Rechitsa Uezd. According to Valentina Chepko's statistics, from the end of the eighteenth century to the beginning of the 1860s the number of tradesmen in Rechitsa grew by 443 percent, that is, significantly more than in other towns of the province. In comparison, in Pinsk, where a sharp rise in the number of tradesmen was also noted, the increase was 328 percent.[9]

In Rechitsa in the mid-1860s, 30 percent of the 257 tradesmen were employed in the food sector; 15.2 percent made clothing and footwear; 5.5 percent produced household items and tools; 49.4 percent had other specializations that included barbers, clock makers and jewelers, glaziers, and furniture makers. Within Minsk Province, Rechitsa was second only to Minsk in number of workers employed in the food sector.[10] In 1852, as part of a reform in the supervision of trades, a simplified trades' administration was set up in Rechitsa with guilds in which only Jews registered; Christian tradesmen were reluctant to do so, because they did not need to overcome religious restrictions through associations of one sort or another.[11]

Some of the successful tradesmen in Rechitsa apparently entered the third guild of merchants, since only by taking that step could they acquire the legal right to open their own shop.[12] But the bulk of the tradesmen were poor and most often produced their goods at home, by order. In the words of the social anthropologist Illarion Zelenskii, in Minsk Province eight out of ten families practicing trades were "mired in the most terrible poverty."[13]

Over the course of the nineteenth century, the number of tradesmen in Rechitsa increased quite significantly. At the very beginning of the twentieth century, 857 people worked in 205 enterprises.[14] At the beginning of the twentieth century, their numbers grew even more rapidly, rising to 1,227 people in 1907. The vast majority of them were Jews. Evidence indicates that there was very little participation in trades and commerce by gentiles.[15]

The percentage of tradesmen in Rechitsa differed little from those of the eight other uezd towns of Minsk Province. However, Rechitsa Uezd overall had a higher percentage of master craftsmen. As was true for the province as a whole, a particularly high number of them worked in the clothing and household goods sectors.[16] Despite the existence of statistical data, it is difficult to establish how the specialization of Rechitsa tradesmen changed in the period being discussed (from the early 1860s to 1907), since the classification of specializations differs from one source to another. For example, the 1907 statistics most likely include furniture builders in the category of makers of household goods, while in the data for the early 1860s they figure among tradesmen working in other specialties. Nevertheless, one can reasonably assume that over the course of this near half-century, the percentage of tradesmen in the food sector (among whom were many distillers) in Rechitsa in fact declined, while the number of tailors considerably increased. By the end of the nineteenth century, the percentage of tailors in Rechitsa, as throughout the Pale of Settlement, was at its peak. This can be explained, on the one hand, by demand, since factory production, particularly

TABLE 1. Distribution of Rechitsa tradesmen by sector and qualifications
            in 1907

Goods produced	Masters	Journeymen	Apprentices	Total number	Total percentage
Food products	62	54	50	166	13.5
Clothing	146	127	186	459	37.4
Household goods	234	144	160	538	43.8
Other	64	—	—	64	5.2
Total	506	325	396	1,227	100

Source: Compiled from Dokumenty i materialy po istorii Belorussii, 3:125.

in Belorussia, could not meet the demands of the population and, on the other hand, by the relatively low cost of setting up such handmade production. Zalman Abezgauz, one of the few Soviet historians who studies Jewish topics, has calculated that in Minsk Province 80 percent of all those engaged in this and other sectors relating to the production of clothing were Jews.[17]

There were several categories of tailors. Best paid and best known were those who made clothes for the higher levels of town society. They had excellent Singer sewing machines, and their other tailoring equipment was of the highest quality. One such man in Rechitsa was the dressmaker Nokhem Nodelman, whose shop stood on the corner of Preobrazhenskaia and Andreevskaia Streets.[18] A midlevel tailor would serve the corresponding level of the town's population living in his neighborhood, along with his own established clientele. Tailors of both categories were most versatile and could make suits and overcoats, bed linen and curtains with lace and embroidery, dresses, and bridal veils. Tailors of the third category, and they were the majority, worked mainly at remodeling old clothes. They served the poor, who could pay little for the work.[19] Tailors of the first and second categories were better paid but still inadequately, considering their qualifications.

The low compensation of tailors and others tradesmen was a result not only of the population's own lack of resources but also of the keen competition among most of the tradesmen who practiced the same professions and who could not leave the boundaries of the Pale of Settlement. Unable to feed their families by plying their trades, the heads or other members of families sought work in other areas or found a new line of work. Some of them rented gardens and orchards from landowners in the summer. In Rechitsa the families of Mendel Shkolnikov, the butcher Israel-Berka Kaganovich, and the barber Abram Frenkel cultivated such gardens.[20]

Several Jews in Rechitsa bought beeswax and honey from peasants and small landowners and then resold it; as noted earlier, such production and buying had been a tradition there even in the Middle Ages. The Jews shipped wax and honey to Kiev, Pinsk, Gomel, and other towns.[21] At the end of the nineteenth century, Rechitsa Uezd, whose territory had 12,000 beehives, led the province in wild honey farming and apiculture.[22] By 1906, however, the number of hives there had fallen to 7,300.[23] Some Jews raised ducks to sell, particularly for the holidays. The Kazovskii family, for example, did so.[24] Other Jews earned money as servants for wealthy Jewish families. The average wage for such work was meager, however, six rubles a month for men and four rubles for women.[25]

Rechitsa residents and visitors had at their service thirty-nine cabdrivers, forty-six in winter. Two-thirds of them were Jews. The profession of cabdriver is found among Jews in the Polish-Lithuanian Commonwealth as early as the first half of the seventeenth century.[26] At the beginning of the nineteenth century, Jews constituted the majority of cabdrivers in territory that formerly belonged to the Lithuanian duchy. The delivery of ordinary mail in the Pale of Settlement, a responsibility of the state, ended up in their hands. Even on a national level, Jews comprised one-fifth of all cabdrivers in Russia.[27] The town was linked to Minsk and Chernigov by post roads. The first road passed through Gorval', Bobruisk, and Igumen' (after 1923 Cherven'), the second through Kholmech and Loev. Each driver in Rechitsa was a *balagole* ("carriage owner," Yiddish) or a *furman* ("cabdriver" or "wagon driver," Yiddish) who carried passengers and goods outside town, or a cabby proper, whose services were performed within the town limits. They all kept watch for fares near the bazaar, the dock, and the railway station and waited for passengers near the hotels and churches. A cabby took passengers in a one-horse carriage or a droshky called a *lineika*. The carriage was intended for two passengers, the droshky for eight. Passengers in the droshky were seated four on each side, back to back. Town functionaries and their families were regular users of cabs. Rechitsa's young people also liked to "bowl along" in an open droshky. The balagole wagons were covered with heavy canvas stretched over hoops; they were massive and spacious, usually holding up to ten passengers. The wagons often hauled household contents or goods. Depending on the state of the roads, the distance, and the load, the balagoles would harness two or even four horses. Balagoles often kept draft horses. Because of the poor state of the roads and the heavy loads, the wagons moved very slowly.

By the early nineteenth century, Jews had also already taken over almost full responsibility for a related field of activity, the management of state mail services throughout the Pale of Settlement, including Rechitsa. It was granted by contract on a competitive basis. Jews assumed the risk, agreeing to the most onerous terms, and for this reason the government, however reluctantly given its suspicions of Jewish disloyalty and even potential fraudulence, awarded the task to them. Even though individual administrators or officers might quibble about such a state of affairs (it seemed especially ridiculous to them that Jews with *payot* [earlocks] should be wearing the government postal service uniform made of green fabric), on the whole the authorities found the arrangement satisfactory. Even in the midst of the notorious anti-Jewish decrees of 1827, they allowed Jews to continue to occupy these positions in communities where Jews were prohibited from living.[28] At the same time, Jews in 1823 had been prohibited from managing mail services in Vitebsk and Mogilev Provinces, and in 1828 from holding any government positions at all. These measures were introduced gradually while the authorities looked for Christians who could replace the Jews. In other provinces of the Pale of Settlement, Jews continued to handle mail deliveries as previously.[29]

In the first half of the nineteenth century, an important outlet for Rechitsa tradesmen (including food producers) to market their produce was the Saint Nicholas Fair. This fair had taken place in the town since at least the middle of the eighteenth century. There were actually two such fairs yearly, each lasting for the weeks beginning on the two Saint Nicholas Days, May 6 and December 6. For many years, the basic goods sold were fish and salt. The volume of sales was small. In 1828, for example, goods valued at up to 30,000 rubles were offered at this fair.[30] Ten years later the volume of goods brought to the Rechitsa fairs had increased nearly fivefold, reaching the sum of 134,000 rubles. By that time, the fairs went on from May 9 to 21 and from December 6 to 20. A list compiled in 1838 summarizing the results of the previous year's fairs provides an idea of the goods that were in demand in the uezd. The list reveals that goods from Russia were sold at the fair: cotton, silk, blended silk, and other fabrics; metals and metal goods; china and earthenware dishes; bread, fish, livestock, sugar, wax, soap, tobacco, paper, books, flax, and hemp; there were also goods from the Asian countries bordering Russia: tea, cotton cloth, coffee, woolen fabrics, and wool. Apart from these "Asiatic goods," the list has an unspecified category of "goods

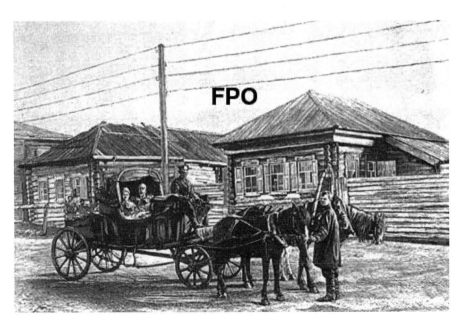

Droshky.

from Persia and Bukhara," which apparently meant carpets, silk fabrics, astrakhan fur, dried fruit, spices, precious items, and other luxury goods.[31]

The colorful description of a fair in the small Belorussian shtetl of Krasnopol'e, written by the researcher Lazar' Rokhlin, is quite applicable to Rechitsa at the end of the 1830s and beginning of the 1840s:

> The outcome of the days of the fair determines the well-being of the inhabitants of the shtetl. People wait eagerly for the fair and prepare for it ahead of time. Well before the fair, the traders in groceries, gold jewelry, manufactured items, and other goods go to Gomel, Mogilev, Moscow, Warsaw, and other cities for supplies. Craftsmen ready their products for sale. Buyers and traders in seeds and grain collect a supply of cash for buying farm produce from peasants. Finally, when the fair days arrive, general haggling is the rule.[32]

Despite the relatively large volume of sales, fairs at the time had only a local significance. In 1837, for example, the vast majority of the 850 people who made purchases at the Rechitsa fair were from the town itself or other places in the uezd. That year goods at a total value of twenty-five thousand rubles were purchased.[33] Apparently most of the merchants, too, were from Rechitsa Uezd.

By the mid-1840s, the importance of trade at fairs had declined in Belorussia, as it had throughout the Russian Empire. Fairs gave way to town and village shops. The decline in trade at fairs in Minsk Province generally between 1837 and 1844 was quite striking, but it was particularly so at the Rechitsa Saint Nicholas Fair, where the volume of business dropped by a factor of nine over that period. The main reason for the decline of the fair's role in trade was the expansion of roads and river transportation from 1840 to 1850. Now there was no need to wait for the fair to buy and sell goods. The peasant could now do it all in one of the nearby mestechkos and towns. As far as wholesale trade was concerned, by the mid-1860s all major dealings at least took place only on the docks, as Zelenskii has pointed out; the fairs were only for minor trading.[34] The status of trade at fairs in the late 1830s and 1840s probably also suffered because of the cholera epidemic that spread over the whole empire at the time and caused more than a million deaths. The severe famines in 1839 and 1843 also had an effect.[35]

The decrease in the volume of trade at fairs in the 1840s in Belorussia was accompanied by an increase in the number of small fairs in the mestechkos. These became links between the cities and the towns, on the one hand, and among the villages, on the other. In Rechitsa Uezd, the number of fairs grew from three in 1837 to five in 1844.[36] The Saint Nicholas Fairs continued to take place in Rechitsa until the late 1880s, and livestock, horses, and grain were sold there.[37] Thus the nature of the fairs had changed. Where they had once catered to the general public, they now became a center for wholesale trade in agricultural products. Tradesmen at the time most often sold their products in their own shops (there was no longer any requirement to enter a merchants' guild in order to open a shop). Those who engaged in certain trades—food producers, blacksmiths, and carpenters, for example—sold their products in the bazaar as well.

The further development of transportation led to an even greater decline in trade at fairs. In 1844 the volume of business at the Rechitsa fair was 5,500 rubles; by the beginning of the twentieth century it had declined to an insignificant sum for the time—3,000 rubles—and had become one of the lowest in Minsk Province.[38] By the beginning of World War I, however, the trade turnover at the Saint Nicholas Fair in Rechitsa had become several times greater, reaching the sum of 8,300 rubles. At that time, the fair took place three times a year, and goods (basically household goods and agricultural produce) were brought in at a value of 20,500 rubles.[39]

The growth of trade at fairs and of other trade generally in Belorussia was hindered by the low purchasing power of the population, something that can be explained by the very limited capacity of peasant households to produce goods for market. The latter was much lower in Belorussia than in the central regions of Russia because a relatively higher percentage of Belorussian peasants continued to be enserfed. Statistics show that in the pre-reform era in the northwestern region only from 1 to 7 percent of the peasants—depending on the productivity of the land—had been transferred from the *barshchina* (labor in lieu of taxes paid to the landowner) to the more progressive quitrent tax, the *obrok*. In the same period, from 23 to 90 percent of the peasants in the central regions of Russia had been transferred to the *obrok*. Also, in the northwestern and southwestern regions, landowners held two-thirds of all the arable land, whereas in the rest of European Russia they owned only a third of such land.[40]

Alexander Shipov, who has studied the Russian economy of the mid-nineteenth century, has noted that the peasants of the Belorussian provinces existed in a state of semistarvation: they used chaff when they baked their bread, something not done in any of the Russian provinces at the time. Shipov attributes the impoverished state of the Belorussian peasants to the territory's very unfavorable natural conditions for agriculture, which required enormous efforts to produce a harvest.[41]

The fact that the peasants were tightly bound by serfdom and the almost total absence of industrial enterprises that followed from these circumstances led to an extraordinarily low cost of labor. Nonetheless, agricultural goods produced there were more expensive than in other provinces.[42] Finding the main reason for this situation is difficult. Possibly, it was because the prices of agricultural products in the region were close to those in neighboring European countries, where it was profitable for local landowners to ship their produce without incurring high transportation costs. Anatolii Liuty's statement that grain was in short supply in Belorussia because it was widely used for making alcohol may quite possibly be true as well.[43]

Belorussian landowners acquired luxury goods abroad, including the latest fashionable items for which demand continually grew within their milieu. Luxury goods, together with the number of serfs one possessed, defined one's place in the hierarchy of landowners. One's authority and status depended heavily on these elements. Accordingly, there was a powerful urge among landowners not to lag behind the fashions of the day. This meant that, on the one hand, they had to find ways of moving from the traditional methods of estate management to a market system and, on the other hand, they continued to extensively exploit peasant labor.

The problem they faced was the inherent limit to the profitability of their estates, a limit defined by natural conditions, the subservience of the peasants, and the peasants' physical capabilities. Landowners could not keep up with the latest western creations in luxury items and novelty goods. The impoverished Belorussian peasants could not manage to pay their tax assessments to the landowner. Their arrears in Vitebsk and Mogilev Provinces in 1853 amounted to the colossal sum of thirty-four million rubles.[44] The situation of peasants in Minsk Province, whose poverty led to the bankruptcy of some landowners, was no better. By 1860 one-quarter of the landowners' estates in this province had been mortgaged. The debts of all the landowners in the territory of Belorussia amounted to about forty-one million rubles by this time.[45] Of course, the value of an estate's production could be increased by introducing new agricultural technologies, but doing so required the landowner to become more heavily involved in estate management. The landowner was not prepared to do this since the considerations of prestige mentioned above meant that he had to pay many social calls, attend balls, and travel to capital cities, resorts, and abroad.

Without the time and often without the desire and the skills to manage his own estate, the landowner passed complete control to intermediaries. In so doing, he made his own well-being dependent on the managerial skills of his overseers. As Adam Teller has argued, by the beginning of the eighteenth century most Jewish entrepreneurs refrained from leasing estates because of tensions with Christian society. They preferred to rent or to manage specific branches of landlords' estates only. By turn landlords to increase its profits wished to give for rent the sectors and not an entire economy.[46] However, reducing of the tension with the Christian population under the Russian rule allowed to Jews to reconsider their attitude toward the leasing. For their part, many Belorussian landowners from the 1830s, overcoming their own religious intolerance and closing their eyes to the "otherness" of Jews, as Yehezkel Kotik recalls, were compelled to transfer management of their estates or lease them to Jews, whose enterprise they highly regarded.[47] On the situation in Minsk Province, Illarion Zelenskii writes: "In the landowner's house and in business, the Jew is the equal of his employer, perhaps even his superior. The landowner scarcely ever makes a business decision without his Jewish agent, who will always settle with you without his principal."[48]

It is interesting to note that even the peasants were more trusting of the Jewish agent when being hired for work. Zelenskii writes: "More than once I chanced to hear that the peasants would never hire themselves out to work for the landowner, no matter how much the wage, until some Cicero in a traditional Jewish *lapserdak* appeared; he needed only to say a few words to the peasants in private, and they would go off to work for the most reasonable wage."[49] Most probably, they believed that the Jew, unlike the landowner, would not cheat them; on the other hand, the Jew had a better understanding of the peasant mentality, and this allowed him to find a common language with them. This is evidenced in the remarks of another writer on conditions in Minsk Province, Nikolai Ianchuk: "If the peasant happens to hear some helpful advice from a landowner or official or to learn some important piece of news, he first goes to some Jewish tavern keeper he knows to verify it."[50] There was a saying in common usage among the peasants at the time: "When trouble's due, go to the Jew" ("Iak beda, to do zhida.")[51] Jewish managers or lessors could quickly improve their standard of living and perfect their entrepreneurial skills on a landowner's estate. On the other hand, the involvement of Jews in rural life promoted the decline of Jewish self-isolation from the Christian population.

As trade in local fairs was supplanted by commerce in the town, the link between the rural area and the mestechko grew stronger. The peasants could now buy all they needed in the mestechko, where they would go when possible on Sundays, except in harvest time. There also came there to sell their own food items, raw materials, and other produce. Lacking the time to become involved in retail sales, which would take them away from running their own farms, the peasants would sell the goods they had brought at wholesale to a middleman in order to return home the same day. In Belorussia, those middlemen were most often

Jews, whom the peasants trusted more than anyone else. Zelenskii writes: "The peasant masses are extremely distrustful of the upper classes. If you try to buy from a peasant some produce he has brought to a bazaar or fair you will probably never come to an agreement about the price; if you send a Jew, the peasant will sell at a price lower than the one you had just offered him yourself."[52] Zelenskii's example vividly characterizes the relationship between the Jews and the peasants, a relationship that can be described as economic symbiosis. Small-scale and even midlevel Jewish intermediaries traveled around the countryside, particularly during harvest time. In later years wholesalers, who were also largely Jewish, would buy up the food products, raw materials, and other peasant produce, especially things being shipped outside the uezd.[53]

The new Polish uprising of 1863–1864 forced the central authorities in this region to rely not on the landowners, three-quarters of whom were Catholics, but on the Orthodox Belorussian peasantry. Even while the uprising was in progress, the tsarist government, in an attempt to win the sympathy of the Orthodox Belorussian peasantry, were compelled in 1863 to issue a decree on the compulsory redemption at reduced prices of peasant lands in the Northwestern Region; they also offered government loans to peasants and ended their obligations to landowners. The urgent necessity to issue this decree came about after the leaders of the uprising declared their intention to transfer land to the peasants on terms more favorable than those provided in the reform of 1861. Other decrees aimed at punishing the rebellious *szlachta* followed in 1863–1865. These proclaimed the economic independence of peasants, their equality before the law in dealings with landowners, and right of peasants to lodge complaints against landowners with appropriate institutions.

The positive results of the measures taken to improve the lot of the Belorussian peasants began to appear only several decades later, particularly after the economic upturn of the 1880s. Over the period from 1860 to 1891, areas under winter crops in Minsk Province increased by 27 percent, spring grains by 24 percent, and potatoes by 56 percent. The economic situation of peasants in Rechitsa Uezd began improving as well. In the 1890s some peasants owned thirty or more head of cattle and a sizable number of smaller livestock. Those who owned fewer than ten head of cattle were considered poor. Such large numbers of cattle could be supported because of the abundant meadows in the uezd. One great benefit for the peasants of the uezd was the opportunity to cut and haul timber to the Dnieper over the winter. About twelve thousand peasants worked at this every year. They were paid a good wage by the standards of the time—from half a ruble to a ruble and a half per day. The money enabled them to replace their agricultural implements and expand their farms. At the end of the nineteenth century, the peasants of Rechitsa Uezd were markedly better off than the other inhabitants of the northwestern region. They and the peasants of Pinsk Uezd were the most prosperous in Minsk Province. The average peasant household in Rechitsa Uezd at the time held a large area of arable land—twenty-two hectares—and the land tax was very low. Just as in Pinsk and Mozyr Uezds, the tax was five rubles a year per *desiatina* (a *desiatina* is roughly the same as a hectare). In comparison with Novogrudok Uezd and some other small areas of Slutsk Uezd, where it was as high as fifty rubles, the tax in Rechitsa was minimal.[54]

The economic situation of the peasants determined the condition of commerce and, accordingly, of the tradesmen; this, in turn, had a direct and fundamental effect on the economic situation of the Jews, who were heavily involved in these sectors. The close link between Jews and commerce requires a more detailed examination of it how it came to develop in the Rechitsa area and the part Jews played in it. To understand the close link between Jews and commerce, we need to examine more closely how trade developed in the Rechitsa area and the role Jews played in that development.

The inclusion of the Belorussian lands in the Russian Empire led to the replacement of the old economic centers by new ones. After annexation by Russia, Rechitsa was no longer the border town that had made it such a good location for trade. It nonetheless maintained its status as an important economic center in Eastern Polesia for many years, thanks to its major navigable water artery. In the first half of the nineteenth century, all the salt consumed in Belorussia came through Rechitsa, from Ukraine up the Dnieper and then via other rivers. In return, potash, tar, and pitch produced in Rechitsa Uezd were sent back to the Ukrainian cities of Odessa, Kremenchug, and Kherson. The most important of the merchants shipping pitch to Ukraine in the mid-1820s was Hirsh Cherniavskii from Rechitsa.[55] But the largest export from the uezd to Ukraine was timber. It is likely that in the early nineteenth century primarily landowners were involved in this trade.[56] In the mid-1820s, Jewish merchants began giving them serious competition. The statistics of cargoes sent via the Dnieper from Rechitsa in the spring and summer of 1827 make this clear: fourteen (52 percent) of the twenty-seven owners of cargoes were Jews.[57]

By the middle of the century, the share of Jewish merchants in the timber trade in the uezd had become even larger. Pavel Shpilevskii, mentioned earlier, traveled through Belorussia at the time. He wrote that the landowners in Minsk Province, with its abundant forests, did not engage in trade since they lacked the substantial capital needed to process the timber on the lands they had purchased; they focused on agriculture. Only the Jewish merchants ventured to buy and market timber along the Berezina, the Dnieper, the Neman, and the Northern Dvina. They preferred to buy pine, since it was the most common timber for general construction and for shipbuilding in particular.[58]

In the timber trade, and in wholesale trade generally, it was most often Jews who, with fewer resources than the landowners, solved their problem by combining their capital, thus creating what amounted to stock corporations whose profits were distributed according to the amounts invested. This prototype of a joint stock corporation in Russia also made provision for joint responsibility and was more flexible and better able to compete than the method used by the landowner entrepreneurs. A group of Jewish entrepreneurs had better chances of obtaining credit from a major consumer (often the state) than did a single person. Operating on credit bore an element of risk, something landowners were often unwilling to assume, given the changeability of the weather, the competitive struggle, and the policies of the administration. Unlike the Jews, who were ever looking for opportunities to enable them to survive, the landowners had a steady income from their estates, and this discouraged them from launching risky ventures.

Although Vladimir Bronevskii, writing in 1810 from Belorussia, states that Jews focused on resales, whereas they needed more education if they wanted to create joint stock companies with joint capital, this was not in fact true.[59] Indeed, Jewish merchants in the eighteenth century often had to create their own capital reserves, for example, for the grain trade or for the import and sale of goods at the Leipzig fair.[60] Jewish merchants in several Belorussian towns continued this practice. The Russian social anthropologist Mikhail Bez-Kornilovich, who visited Shklov in the mid-nineteenth century, was struck by the abundance of foreign goods there as well as the amount of goods produced in Warsaw, Riga, Odessa, and other Russian cities—all of them supplied by Jews. Landlords came there to shop from all over Mogilev Province.[61]

Thus Jews were the most dynamic among the entrepreneurs; their activity stimulated the development of the stock and credit systems within the Russian economy. This happened despite the unfavorable conditions that the state imposed on Jewish entrepreneurs. Jewish merchants of the first guild had to pay dues that, by the standards of the day, were huge: before 1832, 2,200 rubles a year, and subsequently, 1,800 rubles.[62] But even the new, reduced sum was substantial in Russia, considering that members of this guild had to pay the dues when their personal capital had reached 10,000 rubles. Also, beginning in 1831 Jewish merchants were required to pay taxes for impecunious members of the Jewish townspeople (*meshchane*).[63] It was only in 1859 that Jewish merchants of the first guild were allowed to pay the same dues as gentiles; the latter paid 575 rubles per year—500 rubles in state commercial taxes and 75 rubles to the guild. The situation was similar for merchants of the second guild.[64] Other Jewish townspeople were also heavily burdened, in the above-mentioned Zelenskii's view, by the class-based poll tax that each male was required to pay. When real estate taxes were abolished in 1863, conditions for townspeople in Minsk Province tangibly improved.[65]

In Rechitsa Uezd, the competitors in the timber trade were Loev and, particularly, Gorval', which operated from a very convenient location: the point where the Berezina falls into the Dnieper. In the mid-nineteenth century, Gorval's dock had a yearly turnover that was quite high for the time—as much as half a million rubles.[66] The combined turnover of the Rechitsa and the Loev docks was roughly the same.[67] The merchants sent almost all the lumber exported to southern Ukrainian cities through these three docks. Eventually, the most important place for exporting lumber from the uezd became the Rechitsa dock, built in 1890 and having the most modern facilities.[68] This helped attract a railroad, built through the town in the mid-1880s (more on this subject later). It those years, it was largely the Jews who exported timber and wood products from the Rechitsa dock.[69] Christians and some Jews were hired as timber rafters; Jews usually worked as supervisors, managing the teams of raftsmen and traveling with them down the rapids of the Dnieper. Of the people who went downstream with the timber, generally as many as 20 percent were Rechitsa natives.[70]

As for the uezd landowners, in the first half of the nineteenth century their basic income came from the sale of agricultural products and the vodka trade that they carried on through their estate managers or leased out. People of many social levels were involved in the distilling and sale of alcohol. Gavrila Derzhavin, who visited Belorussia in 1800, writes: "Landowners are distilling spirits, as are boyars in mail coats, the Polish gentry, priests, monks of various orders, and Jews."[71] The vodka trade brought in 53 percent of the yearly income of Prince Ivan Paskevich-Erivanskii, the owner of Gomel.[72] In another private holding in eastern Belorussia, Dubrovno County, income from distilling and alcohol sales for the period 1809–1830 grew from 18 to 43 percent relative to other income.[73] Unlike the Russian provinces where distilling was the exclusive privilege of landowners with appropriate state contracts, in Belorussia the landowners of that day had kept the right to distill freely just as they had under the Polish-Lithuanian Commonwealth. Until the 1850s, the landowners paid half a ruble per year for each peasant "soul" they owned for this right; subsequently, the so-called excise tax, which was linked to the volume of alcohol sold, was gradually introduced here as well.[74]

As far as Rechitsa was concerned, the alcohol trade provided almost half of the town's income in the 1820s, as was noted in the preceding chapter. During the first half of the nineteenth century, there were twelve public houses in the town. In the 1840s, Rechitsa residents and visitors—according only to the official statistics—consumed in them four thousand *vedro* (49,200 liters) of wine and vodka for the sum of sixteen thousand rubles.[75] Many taverns were scattered throughout the entire uezd. The owners of most of them were Jews. As previously, taverns were the only places where informal meetings between Jews and the local Christian population could take place; they were unique types of clubs, where everyday local problems and politics in general could be debated. The taverns were important social networks, a place where the Jewish tavern keeper and the Christian client could meet and gain an understanding of a different culture. Grigorii Bogrov vividly describes how peasants in the bar that he kept would not accept his low but fixed prices on vodka. They preferred to bargain about the price instead. They looked with suspicion on the full glasses that his barmaid poured for them and were most indignant when he initially refused to sell them alcohol on credit. By the same time a year later, the peasants were learning to trust him.[76]

Wine and vodka production in the uezd was primarily for export rather than for home consumption, however. In the 1840s, the export of alcoholic beverages in Rechitsa Uezd was second only to the export of lumber. Although the alcohol trade was not as important as the timber trade for Jewish merchants, they played a leading role in it in the uezd during the second half of the nineteenth century. For example, of the eighty thousand vedro (about a million liters) of alcohol exported from Rechitsa Uezd in 1827, 62 percent belonged to Jewish entrepreneurs. The major exporter of strong drink was the Rechitsa businessman Eliyahu Shaikevich.[77] He probably had an official contract for delivering these goods. His son Abram, a member of the first guild of merchants in Rechitsa and holder of the Minsk and Pinsk tax-farming rights, was in the 1830s a major supplier of alcoholic drinks to the state; he also supplied timber and provisions for the army and the navy. With the aim of lowering the cost of the goods he supplied, he helped upgrade river transport, the basic means of transportation in Ukraine and Belorussia at the time. Specifically, he reinforced the canal linking the Dnieper and the Bug. For saving money on his deliveries to the state and for his building contracts for charitable institutions, barracks, and other structures worth tens of thousands of rubles, the provincial authorities even awarded Abram Shaikevich a gold medal of the Order of Saint Anna in 1840. Despite support from the head of the Third Section of the Imperial Chancellery, Count Alexander von Benkendorf, the Council of Ministers refused this request in 1841, citing the emperor's instruction that Jews were not to be rewarded for delivering goods that brought profit to the state treasury.[78]

The denial of this award marked the beginning of a whole chain of misfortunes for the family of Abram Shaikevich. In 1841 he was unable to fulfill his obligations as a tax farmer and lost this lease because he failed to pay excise taxes to the treasury.[79] By March 1845, his debt amounted to 18,000 rubles.[80] In July of that year, the Minsk court ordered the sale for debts of his home in Rechitsa and his father's home in Odessa.[81] In January 1853, Khaia, the wife of his brother, Aizik Shaikevich, was declared insolvent. She lived in Berdiansk but owned real estate in Rechtisa valued at 3,584 rubles, a huge sum in those times. This property was sold for debts.[82] Abram Shaikevich, trying to mend his finances, acquired in the early 1850s some new contracts to deliver a range of food products to the Black Sea fleet. On the whole, there were many Jews among the contractors supplying food, timber, and hemp to the navy. Given the prevailing official anti-Semitism, Jews could win a contract only if they offered the lowest possible prices and reduced the delivery cost. Prices could be reduced through some very agile trading operations—quickly using the credit obtained for some other profitable venture, for example, though this was financially risky. Costs could be reduced by supplying substandard goods, but inspections made this risky.

One particularly notorious inspection by the authorities took place in September and October 1853, on the eve of the Crimean War (1853–1856). It revealed many abuses on the part of contractors for the navy. Abram Shaikevich also came under investigation; although he was listed as previously with the Rechitsa guild of merchants, he now lived full-time in Kremenchug.[83] In Russia at the time all government contractors, whatever their religious faith, resorted to cheating of some kind, at least to conceal their many bribes to the government bureaucrats they relied on for awarding contracts and for prompt payment. Bribery was rampant in all government institutions at the time.[84] It is not known whether Abram Shaikevich was able to prove his innocence or whether he escaped punishment with the help of some bribes. In any case, he was not brought to trial. A few years later he apparently managed to repair his finances to some extent. In January 1855, at his request, the question of the right of Jews to brew beer and mead in their own homes was considered by the Minsk City Council.[85] For some decades thereafter, he carried on small-scale brewing, as is evident from an item in the *Minskie gubernskie vedomosti* in 1877, noting that a portion of the excise tax that had been levied had been returned to him.[86] But his brother's family still had to spend a long time paying off the debts of their father. Thus, in December 1876, their home in Bragin, in Rechitsa Uezd, was sold to pay Eliyahu Shaikevich's debts to the treasury.[87]

Unlike the Shaikeviches, the great majority of Jews involved in distilling and selling alcohol within the Pale of Settlement eked out a miserable living. The governor-general of Volynia, Podole, and Minsk Provinces stated at the beginning of the nineteenth century that the Jews who ran pothouses "did not possess the barest necessities with which to feed their families." Gavrila Derzhavin, who had no particular sympathy for Jews, admitted that the Jews of Belorussia lived "in an extreme of exhaustion and poverty, and this [was] true of the greater part of them."[88] Nevertheless, Jews who kept pothouses were continually subject to persecution since they were seen as responsible for drunkenness among the peasants. The same Derzhavin, in his report in 1800, hypocritically shifted the burden of guilt for the impoverished state of the peasants from the landowners to the Jews.[89] One result of this attitude was the frequent eviction of Jews from the villages. Thus in Minsk Province in 1825, Jews who sold alcohol were evicted from their villages.[90] A short time later, however, the Jews returned to this line of work and continued to do so until 1846, when they were forbidden to sell alcohol in the villages around Minsk.[91]

In the second third of the nineteenth century, the third most important sector of the economy in Rechitsa Uezd became tobacco production. By the middle of the century, Rechitsa had become the largest center of this activity in Belorussia. There were two tobacco factories in Rechitsa, that of the landowner Sigizmund Kenevich and that of the Jew Iosel Borzhovskii; in 1849 they were producing tobacco valued at 3,606 rubles a year.[92] These tobacco factories had a relatively short existence—until the 1860s.[93] Apparently, most of the workers in both factories were Jews since the use of peasant serfs was ineffective. For the serfs, working in factories and large plants was just a variation on barshchina, for which it was only necessary to "put in the time."

Before the abolition of serfdom in Russia, entrepreneurs were in great need of free workers. Jews within the Pale of Settlement became the first hired workers. The strong competition among factories with Jewish workers receiving salaries rather than working off their quitrent to their owners as the peasants did, stimulated the growth of capitalism and the voluntary liberation of some peasants. By the mid-1880s, all fifteen tobacco factories in Minsk Province, along with the five wholesale tobacco warehouses, belonged to Jews.[94] Jews provided the basic workforce in tobacco factories in Rechitsa, as in the rest of the Pale of Settlement. This is evident from the fact that at the end of the nineteenth century, more than three decades after the abolition of serfdom, a third of all workers in tobacco factories in Russia were Jews, although they represented only 4.2 percent of the total population.[95] Obviously it was specifically the free workforce of Jews that also led to the labor-intensive tobacco industry being placed within the Pale of Settlement.

Jews were forced to take on nontraditional work—as workers in industrial enterprises—because of the harshly restrictive laws imposed on them in Russia. The Law of 1804 gave them the right to live only within fifteen of the fifty provinces of the empire. But even in the western provinces where Jews were permitted to live, certain areas were also closed to them. The restriction on living in rural areas was a particularly severe blow to their economic life.

Shut away in the towns and mestechkos of the Pale of Settlement, Jews themselves created a keen competition in two basic spheres of the economy: in the trades and in commerce. The labor intensiveness and often small profits resulting from this competition meant that Christians were not attracted to these spheres. Apart from that, these types of activity were not traditional among Christians, with the exception of a few branches of the trades. In general, Jews at the time dominated commerce in most of the towns and mestechkos throughout the Pale of Settlement. The renowned teacher Nikolai Stolpianskii, describing the ten western provinces, notes: "Trade in the area is entirely in the hands of the Jews and consists in the export abroad of unprocessed foodstuffs and the import from abroad of gold jewelry, small wares, and other goods for local consumption."[96] Of Minsk Province, Illarion Zelenskii writes, with some exaggeration: "All the small trade, along with every other kind, is in the hands of the Jews here. Almost all the shops, with only a very few exceptions; all the roadside taverns and coaching inns, without any exception; almost all the factories, and particularly the distillers and the brewers; all the taverns and workshops—all these businesses belong to the Jews."[97]

The situation was similar particularly in Rechitsa Uezd, as shown in the report of one official to the local administration in 1866.[98] In Rechitsa itself in 1854, evidently, the majority of the forty-four shops in the town belonged to Jews. These included five with quality items (fabrics); twelve bakeries; two chemical shops (dyes, glues, and oils); one hardware shop; one glazier; one pottery shop; and twenty-two small-goods shops.[99]

Most of the retailers in Rechitsa, as was the case throughout Belorussia, were small and midlevel businessmen, since there were very few large-scale merchants of the first and second guilds at that time. In 1798 Belorussia had only six merchants of the first guild, eight of the second guild, and 216 of the third guild. Rechitsa had only merchants of the third guild, and there were but seven of them.[100] It is highly possible that all or almost all of them were Jews, since in 1811 nine Jewish merchants were registered in Rechitsa, and there was very little expansion of the merchant class in the first third of the nineteenth century.[101] This is evident from the fact that in 1833, only 33 people in Rechitsa were registered as belonging to the merchant class; these included women, children, and the aged. But over the next ten years the number of merchants in Rechitsa doubled, numbering 18 in 1843. Only one of them belonged to the first guild, the aforementioned Abram Shaikevich; the remainder belonged to the third guild, and it is likely that a large number of them were Jews. Four of their names are known: Iosel Roginskii and his son Zalman; Nisan and Ekhiel Livshits.[102]

Rechitsa did not differ from the rest of Minsk Province in the number of its merchants: in that same year of 1843 the province had only 7 merchants of the first guild, 12 of the second guild, and 251 of the third guild.[103] In the two decades before the abolition of serfdom, the number of merchants in the Rechitsa guilds continued to grow. This increase is reflected in the number of those registered in the merchant class in the town: from 62 people in 1842 to 303 in 1861. They comprised 6.8 percent of Rechitsa's population in 1861.[104] The increase in the number of merchants in Rechitsa in those years is also shown by the fact that from 1841 to 1861 the number of shops in the town increased from thirty-four to seventy-eight; these included twenty-one shops belonging to guilded merchants; the other fifty-seven were small scale and run by ordinary townspeople. Evidently, all or almost all of the shops in Rechitsa belonged to Jews, since in 1861 95.2 percent of all the shops in Minsk Province were in their hands.[105]

At that time, however, the ability of Belorussian peasant households to market their produce was still limited, and this could only continue to have a negative effect on the situation of Jewish retailers. One contemporary observer described the situation in retail trade as follows: "One can scarcely apply the term 'competition' to the trade by Jews in the northwestern region. The market resembles, rather, an arena where people fight for the opportunity to buy the produce the peasants bring to the town; similar brawls take place when they sell their produce to larger-scale merchants."[106] As a result, food in Rechitsa, particularly bread and potatoes, was expensive.[107] Many Rechitsa Jews thus lived in poverty. According to data from the tenth census (1857), 80 percent of Rechitsa Jews were impoverished. There were even more impoverished Jews in the mestechkos of Rechitsa Uezd—88 percent of the Jewish population.[108] Jewish poverty was responsible for the wretched, run-down look not only of the small mestechkos but even of the uezd towns of Rechtisa, Dokshitsy, Igumen', Mozyr, Borisov, and others. Illarion Zelenskii writes about the particular kind of poverty in these towns and of their "extremely untidy, deserted appearance . . . and their semiragged population whose means of support still remain[ed] a mystery."[109]

The keenly competitive struggle among retailers led to their frequent ruin. The *Minskie gubernskie vedomosti* contains many accounts of such misfortune. In 1876 the house and shop of the Rechitsa native Itsko Gurvich in Bragin was sold at auction because of his bankruptcy.[110] It is possible that Simkha Livshits from Rechitsa met the same fate in 1877, when his property was confiscated for debts.[111] In Rechitsa in 1880, the family home, mill, shops, warehouses, and household goods of the once-prosperous Goldshtein brothers, Berka, Chaim, and Zelik, were sold by the authorities.[112] There are many such examples. The hard times that had fallen on the Jews of Minsk Province are revealed in the reply of an impoverished Belorussian peasant to a question about "Jewish exploitation": "But the Jew is even poorer than I am, and if the Jews were sucking money out of the peasants, then they would have some themselves. But what money does the Jew have? He goes around for a day, maybe two, without anything to eat, and his clothes are all in rags—you can see his naked body!"[113]

Along with the impoverished state of the peasantry, the tax policies instituted in Belorussia retarded the growth of trade. The northwestern region was distinct from central Russia in that the great majority of buildings in its towns were located on leased land. There was practically no vacant land available for construction in the towns and mestechkos. Building lots were held by landowners who imposed various supplementary taxes on lessors, thus slowing the development of trade and industry. These taxes were abolished by law in 1865, as part of the innovations linked with the new policy toward landowners discussed earlier.[114] At the same time, in removing these taxes the authorities were trying to encourage Russians who did not own their own property in the northwestern region to resettle there. As far as the local Jewish and Belorussian populations were concerned, even after the 1860s they continued to have the highest tax on urban property in the empire: 1.13 percent. The policy toward merchants likewise remained unchanged: within Belorussia they paid guild dues of 10 percent of their income, whereas the average for the rest of the empire was only 7 percent.[115]

Burdened by heavy taxes, the merchants sought ways of deceiving the state treasury in order to maintain the profitability of their businesses. Concealing real estate holdings from the tax department was difficult, but it was much easier to hide income from sales from the inspectors who visited periodically to check the inventory and the account books. The memoirs of the well-known Gomel Zionist activist Yehuda-Leiba Kahanovich, who spent his childhood in the shtetl of Gorval' in Rechitsa Uezd, show that local merchants would learn in advance that an inspector was coming, just as happened in the famous play by Nikolai Gogol. Goods were instantly hidden in various houses, and the inspector would see a nearly empty shop with only a few objects for sale. After he received his bribe, the inspector, who knew very well the true state of affairs, would leave, and the shops would be filled once more.[116] Evidently, such a system of concealing income existed throughout Belorussia and even more so in Rechitsa, not far from Gorval'.[117]

The lack of adequate roads also hampered the development of trade in Belorussia. Most of the roads around Rechitsa, as elsewhere in Minsk Province, were simply country tracks. In the spring and autumn, due to the rainy weather, they were almost impassable. There were very few broad, finished roads in Minsk Province. In his yearly report for 1844, the governor describes the grievous state of the province's roads:

> There are 1,400 versts of postal routes, of which a third, built over low-lying areas, can be maintained only with enormous effort; two-thirds of the roads pass over sandy or clay soil. The extremely sandy road in Rechitsa Uezd, which runs for a distance of fifty-seven versts between major posting stations, creates difficulties in the delivery of mail. . . . The postal roads have been divided into sectors whose maintenance in 1844 was the responsibility of local residents, but an exceptionally rainy summer and autumn have inflicted severe damage on roads, dikes, and bridges.[118]

A properly finished road was finally built between Rechitsa and Loev in the 1850s.[119] This project only partially solved the uezd's road problem. Rivers continued to remain the basic mode of transportation, both in Rechitsa Uezd and in the rest of Belorussia. At the beginning of the 1880s, the contractor Kegel began building a railway line from Luninets-Gomel to a station in Rechitsa. Several thousand workers were hired to complete the Rechitsa segment. They were quartered in Rechitsa itself and frequently indulged in thievery and pillaging. Jews suffered most from these depredations. In July 1885, therefore, a decision was made at a session of the Rechitsa Town Council by a majority of Christian votes to urge the provincial governor to hire fifty Cossacks to guard against pillaging workmen, "the cost to be borne exclusively by the [town's] Jews."[120] It should be noted that these workmen had committed violent acts a year earlier, in Gomel, during the building of the first segment of this railway line. They often burned houses in Gomel and threatened to inflict an anti-Jewish pogrom.[121]

In 1886, trains began using the newly built railway line that now linked Rechitsa with the rest of the country.[122] Although the new branch line had one other station in the uezd—at Vasilevichi—many of the mestechkos in the uezd were beyond the range of the railway network. To be sure, the railways built through the towns and mestechkos of Belorussia had a marked influence on their economic situation, helping some but leaving behind those with only river transportation. The improvement in the peasants' standard of living in Rechitsa Uezd in the 1880s, discussed earlier, helped raise the living standard of Rechitsa residents as well. Those registered as townspeople, comprising 89 percent of the town's population, prospered. Along with raising livestock, the townspeople kept vegetable plots and caught fish. The Dnieper was rich in fish at the time; various species such as pike-perch, bream, bass, carp, pike, trout, and even sturgeon and starlet were sold at low prices in fish shops. On the two bazaar days each week—Mondays and Fridays—the town's market, located between Uspenskaia and Preobrazhenskaia Streets near the present-day square, many shops were well stocked with fish. Along with fish, a good deal of farm produce and livestock was brought to the bazaar as well.[123] Most of the fifty shops and stores in Rechitsa were also located on streets adjacent to the market. The growth of retail trade made it necessary to rebuild the bazaar, something that was done more than once, in 1884 and 1891.[124]

The economic situation of Jews in Rechitsa was worse, on average, than that of the Christian population, but it, too, gradually began to improve. Thus in the first half of the 1890s, Jewish shopkeepers opened many new shops and stores

Uspenskaia Street, near the bazaar, end of the nineteenth century.

on Bazaar Square, causing some dissatisfaction within the local administration.[125] On the whole, the administration frequently impeded the economic activities of Rechitsa Jews. In particular, local officials tried to combat the so-called Jewish usury when Jews were buying stores, shops, and other property. For example, in 1893, without the judicial examination required by law, the police even expelled the Erenburg family from the town after an accusation of usury.[126] At the time, both Jews and Christians loaned money at interest since, given the lack of small-scale bank credit in Russia, this was a most profitable way to invest capital. Providing credit was distinguished from illegal usury by the amount of interest charged. The category into which a particular credit transaction fell was determined by the judicial organs; thus these repressive measures exceeded the authority of the civic administration.

Although the bureaucracy was a problem for the entire population, Jews still had greater difficulties because of the tangled complexity of the Russian laws that regulated their activities. Not every official had the expertise to deal with such matters, and few could do so quickly. Local officials believed that "Jewish affairs could be dealt with later." This attitude, apparently, developed in response to the frequent changes in Russian legislation on the Jewish question. Overwhelmed by hundreds of other cases, officials believed—not without some grounds—that during the interval they set aside the "Jewish cases," one or another decree on the Jews might change once more; then they would not have to become involved in the case a second time. Administrative measures directed against restraining the economic activities of the Jews provoked their dissatisfaction and retarded the growth of the town. The police often used the threat of administrative delays to force Jews to give bribes. In 1894 the Jews of Rechitsa lodged a complaint against one policeman who had been extorting money from them.[127] Such a complaint shows only that the policeman had violated the status quo—the unspoken arrangement for levying taxes through bribes.

At harvest time Jewish traders would bring to Rechitsa farm produce and livestock that they had purchased from peasants throughout the uezd. After the harvest had been gathered, the peasants themselves would travel to the town to sell their produce more profitably, to make purchases, and to visit churches. But even at that time the Jews continued to be intermediaries between the town and the countryside. Thus the local correspondent of the *Minskie gubernskie vedomosti*, a man who had no special love for Jews, complained in November 1880 that the peasants who brought farm produce to the Rechitsa bazaar still preferred selling it all to Jews since they believed that a deal with them was more profitable than selling it wholesale themselves.[128]

The Jews' connection with the rural areas did not end here. In Rechitsa, as throughout Minsk Province, basically only Jews rented dairy cattle from the landlords; then they supplied the townspeople with their dairy products. Raphael Mahler maintains that this dairy farming was the only branch of agriculture in Poland in the second half of the eighteenth century.[129] The Jewish tradesmen in Rechitsa, often through their colleagues, the small-scale shopkeepers, supplied villagers with their basic necessities.[130] The evidence shows that Jewish tradesmen enjoyed the respect of the Belorussian peasantry for this reason.[131] Traders, tradesmen, and peasants were closely connected, and a change in the economic situation of one of these groups influenced the standard of living of the rest. For example, the crop failures of 1867 and 1868 in the northwestern region led to famine among the Jews of Belorussia.[132]

Under these circumstances, the Jews became the most economically active segment of the population of Belorussia. For example, in Minsk Province from 1878 to 1880, 98.2 percent of all trading certificates, 70 percent of all trade and manufacturing certificates, and 92.5 percent of the certificates for state contracts and supply of goods to the state were issued to Jews.[133] Jewish business activity contributed to the economic development of both the rural and the urban areas of Belorussia.

Bazaar Square, end of the nineteenth century.

The numerous shops and stores had great importance for Rechitsa's economy at this time. In the mid-1890s, as earlier, the majority of them belonged to Jews. This same situation developed throughout the entire uezd.[134] Against the background of the area's entire trade statistics, the restrictions imposed on Jews earlier in the production and marketing of alcohol did not have an important effect on this situation. After 1866, when Jews were forbidden to sell wine and vodka in the villages, peasant tavern keepers came in to replace them. In some places in Rechitsa Uezd they were front men for Jews, who thus were able to carry on with their former businesses. The Russian administration conducted a ruthless struggle against such activities. Rechitsa Uezd, from at least the middle of the nineteenth century, was the largest center of distilling and brewing in Minsk Province as well as in the entire territory of the Russian Empire.[135] In 1889 the whole province produced alcohol worth 5,300,000 rubles, which comprised 80.6 percent of the value of all goods produced there.[136] Minsk Province had the greatest number of distilleries of all Russian provinces.[137] The "Temporary Regulations" referred to above considerably limited Jews' ability to produce and sell alcohol. The most serious blow to alcohol production by Jews, however, came from the landowners, who set up many distilleries in Minsk Province and exported their production mainly to Ukraine but also to the neighboring Mogilev and Vitebsk Provinces. By the end of the nineteenth century, the Christian population of Rechitsa Uezd had built several dozen such distilleries.[138] The landowner Alexander Gorvat became the biggest alcohol producer in the uezd. He exported not only to neighboring provinces but also abroad. This was the most profitable branch of industry, both within the Pale of Settlement and in Russia generally. The growth of distilleries owned by gentiles led, by the end of the century, to a manifold reduction in Jewish activity in this area. Considering that by 1897 the share of Jews involved in alcohol production in Russia still remained rather high—16.8 percent—one can assume that in the middle of the nineteenth century their share in this production could have been no less that 25 percent.[139] Jews continued to engage in small-scale trade in wine and vodka in the towns. In the 1880s, Jews still owned quite a number of drinking establishments in Rechitsa.[140] But this business too was dealt a blow in 1894–1897, when, on the initiative of finance minister Sergei Witte, a state monopoly on the sale of vodka was introduced. This measure added another 25 percent to the state treasury, but it deprived more than a hundred thousand Jews within the Pale of Settlement of an income, and it deprived the state of excise taxes.[141] Vodka began to be sold in state liquor stores. Thus many Jews were shut out of the wine and vodka industry, one that had been most important for them for several centuries. Although in 1897 Jewish involvement in the alcohol trade in Russia remained quite high—21.1 percent—with the spread of the state monopoly it was certainly reduced.[142] The introduction of the monopoly was aimed not only at enhancing the state treasury but also at depriving the Jews of "an easy way of profiting from the misfortunes of Christians." Generally, their step-by-step removal from the wine and vodka business was connected with the growing opinion in Russia that the Jews were "enchaining" the Orthodox population. In reality, before this "enchainment" in the Pale of Settlement had passed from the hands of Jews to those of the landowners and the state, deaths caused by alcohol were one-third lower there than in the northeastern provinces, where this trade had long been "in Russian hands."[143]

The local administration continued to restrict Jews even after the decisive government measures noted above, for example, regarding the production and sale of wine in the towns. As a result, by the beginning of the twentieth century both taverns in Rechitsa were in the hands of gentiles, and the numerous attempts by Jews to take part in alcohol production were unsuccessful.[144] In March 1914, Bentsion Saf'ian petitioned the administration to allow him to open a factory that would produce wine from raisins. Even though there were no such factories in Rechitsa, he was refused because of fears that raisin wine would lead to a reduction in the consumption of cheap grape wine produced by Christian entrepreneurs.[145]

After encountering such harsh restrictions in one of the most profitable branches of business, that of wine and vodka production, the Jews were forced to develop other branches of trade. Apparently, they very often moved to producing nonalcoholic drinks. As a result, by the end of the nineteenth century the share of Jews in this production amounted to 43.3 percent across the whole of Russia.[146] In Rechitsa, Saf'ian also opened a shop selling soft drinks and mineral waters on the corner of Andreevskii and Preobrazhenskaia Streets.[147]

A large number of the Jewish traders in Rechitsa turned to manufacturing, which in Russia took second place only to the wine and vodka trade. By 1897 the proportion of Jews in manufacturing in Russia had reached 36.5 percent.[148] This proportion was much greater within the Pale of Settlement, of course. As for Rechitsa, at the beginning of the twentieth century it had eight shops and stores that manufactured goods, and all of them belonged to Jews.[149] In all, Rechitsa Jews owned more than forty shops and stores at the time.[150]

Although Jews owned the great majority of commercial businesses and industrial enterprises in Rechitsa, the standard of living of the average Jewish family remained rather low. In 1906, among the 370 Jews in Rechitsa who had the right to vote for the electors in the second State Duma, eight people owned property in the highest category (*sheyne yidn*): Mordukh Zalkind (30,000 rubles); Itska

Gushanskii (11,000 rubles); Shlëma Margolin (3,500 rubles); Vulf Livshits (3,400 rubles); Neukh Rapoport (3,000 rubles); Shimon Frenkel (3,000 rubles); Israel Gutner (3,000 rubles); and David Livshits (2,500 rubles). Twenty-four Jews were considered to be rich (*gvir*)—they owned property valued between 1,000 and 2,499 rubles; there were also forty-three Jews with property valued between 500 and 999 rubles. Even Jews—heads of families—who owned real estate valued between 200 and 499 rubles were regarded as prosperous (*balebatim*). About two hundred families were considered having adequate means. The value of their property was between 40 and 200 rubles.[151] The remainder of the Jewish population of Rechitsa, about 956 households, or 72 percent, (or, according to other statistics, 735 families, or 67 percent) were poor.[152]

Wealthy and well-off Jews, connected by family ties, held a dominant position in many areas of Jewish community life in Rechitsa. Family ties helped them in trade and entrepreneurship. In Rechitsa, as in other places in the Pale of Settlement and beyond it, networks of family ties and letters of recommendation made it easier for Jewish entrepreneurs to find partners, intermediaries, and lenders in other towns and mestechkos. Obtaining credit from private individuals often became the only way for a Jewish entrepreneur, always in need of money, to expand the volume of his business after he had been turned down by a bank. The decision of the bank's accounting and loans committee to refuse credit to a Jew was often guided not by economic expediency but by an attempt to please the local or central administrations, which often had little love for Jews. Therefore, in a country lacking investment funds, and in which Jewish capital stock was limited because of fears that it might be used to acquire real estate, the success of many Jewish entrepreneurial initiatives rested only on credit from private individuals or, as earlier, on the combined capital of several investors.

Thus the Jews in Russia, like the Indian merchants in Southeast Asia and Central Asia, the Italian merchants in western Europe, and the Armenian merchants in the Middle East, created their own commercial networks based on trust and character references. Jewish entrepreneurs valued this network, and it was one of the reasons for their rare conversion to Christianity, which could offer them much greater scope for building a business. As the analyst of Jewish entrepreneurship in Russia Arkadius Kahan has noted, the commercial solidarity of Jewish merchants compensated in many ways for the discrimination they suffered at the hands of the Russian administration.[153]

The most important business centers in this network were the two Russian capitals, Saint Petersburg and Moscow, where many entrepreneurs, whatever their religious faith, tried to relocate. They settled there at the first opportunity, taking

Ruvim and Riva Tsirulnikovs, end of the nineteenth century.

advantage of close contact with banks and highly placed officials in positions to make decisions on many economic questions in Russia. Thus major entrepreneurs like the railway kings the Poliakovs—who originated in the Belorussian mestechko Dubrovno—did not linger in places like Rechitsa or other towns within the Pale of Settlement.

The Jews, as major entrepreneurs and as petty tradesmen and craftsmen, had one significant advantage over their Christian rivals: better communication links. The active involvement of Jews in postal communications and driving for hire, mentioned previously, promoted its development in Russia. In this connection the account of a journey with a Jewish driver from Vilna to Borisov by a Russian civil servant in 1864 is noteworthy. He describes how the coachman, himself a resident of Minsk, did not miss a single tavern, hamlet, or mestechko. He passed on the news from Vilna to people at these locations and received in return all the local news.[154] Leaving their hometowns more frequently than Christians, Jews brought firsthand news with them as well.

With the development of a telegraph network in Russia in the 1860s and 1870s, manufacturers among the Jews quickly appreciated its advantages. In Vitebsk, where Jews played a dominant role in trade, as they did in the other towns of Belorussia, the content of most of the telegrams transmitted in 1865 was commercial in nature.[155] By the late 1870s, a telegraph station had appeared in Rechitsa.[156] Until then, in Minsk Province there had been telegraph stations only in Minsk, Bobruisk, and Pinsk.[157] Unlike telegrams, which were open to the public, access to telephones in the Russian Empire was basically limited to the administrative civil service. Big merchants, factory owners, engineers, doctors, and notary publics were also allowed to use the telephone. In 1910 Rechitsa had an extensive telephone network—eighty versts (about eighty kilometers)—that served 106 subscribers, that is, one telephone for every 113 residents, which was better than in other towns of the province equipped with telephones—Bobruisk, Pinsk, and even Minsk, where there was one telephone for twice as many residents, 225.[158]

By the end of the nineteenth century, Christian industrialists and landlords were setting up different kinds of economic associations for the purpose of competing with Jewish entrepreneurs. The most successful of them was the Agrarian Society with headquarters in Minsk, whose members were drawn primarily from the Polish Catholic nobility. One of its main achievements was the development of direct connections to avoid the need for Jewish intermediaries particularly in the grain trade. The group created additional competition with the Jews later in the meat trade in Minsk.[159] Nevertheless, by Belorussian standards the significance of this economic initiative was minimal.

On the eve of World War I, the Jews in Rechitsa owned almost all the stores: manufacturers, grocery stores, dry goods stores, hardware stores. Stores dealing in the following goods were exclusively in the hands of Jews: flour, rolls and buns, kerosene, wine, wallpaper, tableware, and gold and silver products.[160] A quarter of all Jews who owned stores in Rechitsa were women. The situation was similar throughout the Pale of Settlement, where 28.1 percent of Jewish women were self-supporting. This was a considerably larger percentage than among Christians: 22.8 percent among Ukrainians and 20.9 percent among Belorussians.[161] The conduct of trade by women in shops was not a new phenomenon. A half century before this a researcher in Vilna Province, Captain A. Korev, drew attention to the fact that Jewish women not only helped men in retail trade, but they themselves traded independently.[162]

Some Rechitsa Jews left town to take up small-scale trade. Their profession was called *prosol*. Leiba Pekarovskii became a cattle buyer in nearby villages until 1918, and his income barely allowed him to support the ten members of his family.[163] Vulf Malinkovich traveled around the uezd buying rabbit, fox, and even bearskins from the peasants, which he later sold to town furriers in the shop attached to his home on Shapozhnikova Street. But the money he earned was barely enough to feed his large family.[164] Traveling through the villages was not without its hazards. There were cases in which Jewish traders from Rechitsa were beaten and even murdered. In October 1882 one of the Rechitsa Jews was beaten and had all his belongings stolen (including his clothing) by his peasant partner.[165] At the beginning of the twentieth century a group of peasants once beat and robbed Vulf Malinkovich, after which he gave up traveling and died a few years later.[166]

After the closure of the tobacco factories mentioned earlier, industry in Rechitsa did not begin to recover until the end of the nineteenth century. By the mid-1890s there were several factories in the town. Mordukh Zalkind owned a flour mill, David Gurvich a candle factory, and Hirsh Shchukin owned a brick factory (a second brick factory was owned by the Christian Osip Somovich).[167]

Two sawmills, owned by Mordukh Zalkind and Markus Kagan, mentioned in the introduction, opened in Rechitsa in 1896. In 1904 the first enterprise employed 23 workers, the second, 20; in 1907 they employed 24 and 27 respectively.[168] In that period, 80–85 percent of all factories in Belorussia were such small-scale industrial enterprises employing fewer than 50 workers.[169] Despite the growth of wood-processing enterprises within Belorussia at the time, entrepreneurs continued to export logs to Ukraine along the Dnieper and to other areas by rail.[170] Among the Rechitsa townspeople working in this trade were Jewish timber merchants Bendet Orshanskii, Irma Livshits, Mendel Shklovskii, Zus'

Ioffe, Mendel Albinskii, Zakhar (Skhariia) Kopelian, Bentsion Litvak, Iankel Volfson, Shimon and Pinkhas Frenkel, Berka Miliavskii and his son Aizik, and Aron
and Tsfaniia Raikhenshtein. The most prosperous members of this group hired
4,000–5,000 peasants each season to deliver timber to customers. Most often,
Jewish supervisors from Rechitsa accompanied the timber shipments by rafts
consisting of 150–260 logs and wagons.[171]

Along with the industrial enterprises listed above, at the end of the nineteenth
century Rechitsa also had a creamery and two beer and mead breweries.[172] At the
very beginning of the twentieth century, a plant for the mechanical processing of
wood and a nail factory appeared. By 1904 the largest enterprises in the town were
the Dnieper Match Factory, which belonged to the Shishkin brothers (Mikhail
and Andrei), who were landowners; the sawmills of Moisei Frenkel; the mechanical wood-processing plant of S. Magidson and M. Iunis with 138 workers (which
meant that, by the number of people it employed, it belonged to the category of
midsized enterprises); and also the railway machine shops.[173]

By 1910 the town had six factories employing a total of 363 people. These had
a total production valued at 465,000 rubles.[174] On the eve of World War I the
number of factories in the town had grown to nine; 752 workers now produced
goods at a value of 1.13 million rubles. The most productive enterprise in Rechitsa
was the steam-powered Dnieper Match Factory of the Shishkin brothers. In terms
of its yearly production—worth 186,000 rubles—it was classed as a large factory;
in terms of its workforce of 291, it was considered a midsized enterprise. Although
its management was Jewish, the owners had directed that no Jews be hired as workers.[175] Jews provided the main workforce at the other match factories in Minsk
Province.[176] In Belorussia there were also match factories in Borisov, Mozyr,
Pinsk, Slonim, Gomel, and Koidanov (now Dzerzhinsk in Minsk Oblast). They
all belonged to Jews. In 1905 their owners joined to form the largest syndicate
within Belorussia, one that regulated the prices and the output of matches. By
1913 these factories were producing 10–12 percent of all the matches in Russia,
but by that time the syndicate had come under the control of the V. A. Lapshin
firm from central Russia.[177]

Small-scale enterprises in Rechitsa included the wire and nail factory of the
brothers Vladimir and Boris Rikk (gentiles), which had a yearly production of
barbed wire valued at 76,000 rubles. It employed twenty-eight workers.[178] The
Rikk brothers also owned a sawmill that, like the two Rechitsa sawmills belonging
to Moisei Frenkel, was considered a small-scale enterprise. This factory produced
lumber for military bridging. S. Magidson's plywood factory (it was sometimes
called the mechanical wood-processing plant) also filled orders for the military.

It is most likely that it, like the majority of other plywood factories in Minsk Province on the eve of World War I, had installed a hydraulic press. The Rikk brothers also owned a mill and an alcohol purifying plant in the village of Soltanovo. At the beginning of the twentieth century, they constructed a two-kilometer narrow-gauge railway to link these operations with Rechitsa. In addition to these enterprises, Mordukh Zalkind continued to own a sawmill.[179]

The average wage in the factories increased during the prewar era, and it rose even higher during the war. For example, wages at the Rikk brothers factory rose by 80 percent, reaching forty-five to seventy-seven rubles a month, depending on the worker's qualification. Despite this, workers at the factory were influenced by the agitation of socialist parties against the war. The workers also exploited the difficult situation of a government anxious to avoid social strife on the home front in wartime and to ensure that factories supplied the needs of the military; they began demanding supplementary wage increases and a shift from the piece rate to an hourly wage.[180] The owners of the Rikk factory, along with other factory owners in the town, were unable to persuade the local administration to take stern measures against the strikers and had no choice but to concede to their demands.

Even though there were eight industrial enterprises in Rechitsa in 1916, the town, along with the other towns and mestechkos in Belorussia, lagged behind the general level of industrialization in the country. At a time when the average industrial production within the Russian Empire was 113 rubles per person, in Belorussia it was only 60 rubles.[181] The Rechitsa factories provided work for only a small segment of the population. The majority of Jews worked in commerce and various trades. They had substantial influence on employment statistics in the town. According to data from 1897, the occupations of the residents of Rechitsa fell into the following categories: handcrafts and trades—22.8 percent; commerce—21 percent; transport and communications—9.8 percent; domestic service—9.8 percent; free professions—4.4 percent; other—4.6 percent.[182] Apparently, the situation had not changed drastically even by the eve of the October Revolution.

The authorities were ambivalent about the predominance of Jews in the Belorussian economy. On the one hand, they understood that the economy needed to be developed, but on the other hand, they dreaded the economic influence of the Jews, especially on the peasantry. Ultimately they resolved this dilemma in favor of restrictions inasmuch as the government had a negative evaluation of Jewish influence and in general was afraid of capitalistic sentiments. Hans Rogger has rightly classified this populist discourse as "muzhikophilism."[183]

Despite the legal restrictions that began early in the nineteenth century and continued until the October Revolution in 1917, becoming especially prevalent in the 1880s, on average the economic situation of Rechitsa's Jews improved, although it also fluctuated between boom and bust—prosperity and decline. Meanwhile, for a long time quite a large number of Jews in the town were poverty stricken. They often changed jobs hoping to find an economic niche. Some of them attempted to succeed in other towns or even countries. As we shall see in the next chapter, the economic and legal situations of the Jews in Rechitsa were very closely intertwined with migration processes, which originated in the Jewish family and natural population growth.

4

Demography of the Social-Economic Landscape in the Nineteenth and Early Twentieth Centuries

The main result of the resettlement order issued by Catherine II in 1795 was a 45 percent increase in the number of Jews in Rechitsa between 1789 and 1795. Among the 245 Jews registered in Rechitsa in 1795 were 148 women, that is, 60.4 percent of the Jewish population.[1] Such a sexual imbalance among Jews (among Christians males slightly outnumbered females) suggests that relatively many Jewish men moved their families to Rechitsa while they themselves continued to trade or practice their crafts in rural areas. This situation developed thanks to the flexible attitude of the provincial administration, the body that actually determined if the registration had been completed in the recently conquered region.

Such an arrangement did not suit the central authorities, however. They wanted to use the Jews to increase the population of towns and mestechkos. Thus the Regulations of 1804 on their living and working arrangements included Article 34, which forbade Jews—after 1808—to keep pothouses, taverns, and inns in villages and along main roads and generally to lease property. The same law divided Jews into four categories: merchants; townspeople; manufacturers and tradesmen; and farmers. Everyone possessing capital of more than five hundred rubles at that time, no matter what his occupation, was included in the category of merchants provided that he agreed not to list himself in one of the other three categories. Other artisans, traders and all the homeowners in the towns were listed as townspeople.[2] But once again the central authorities did not manage to achieve their aim completely, since many Jews avoided the law by using fictitious owners and lessees. As a result of new expulsions of Jews from the villages, discussed in chapter 2, the Jewish population of towns and mestechkos increased sharply. The growth of Rechitsa's Jewish population along with the increase of the town's overall population to 1825 is shown in table 2.

The statistics of 1808 show that 179 Jewish males lived in the town; 9 of them were registered as merchants, 125 as townspeople, and 45 as manufacturers and tradesmen.[3] But these figures are low because Jews avoided the census (in Russia they were in revision form until 1897) for fear that additional taxes might be imposed. The leaders of the kahal were particularly interested in concealing the actual number of Jews because they were the intermediaries in the collection of taxes. They imposed taxes based on the incomes of the kahal members and reported the number of individual members to the government. Avoiding the census became a widespread practice among Jews within the Pale of Settlement; thus in 1809 the Senate issued a ukase increasing the penalty for Jews who did so.[4] The sixth enumeration list of 1811, which included only males, showed 283 Jews living in Rechitsa.[5] Considering the figures of subsequent enumeration lists, one can suppose that the ukase on increased penalties did not frighten the Rechitsa kahal and that it again declared low numbers for its membership.

The data of the seventh enumeration list of 1816 appear to be more accurate: they show that 841 Jews were living in Rechitsa—480 males and 361 females.[6] The predominance of males shows again that, despite the actions of the authorities, many of them had been formally compelled to register in Rechitsa while in actuality they continued living with their families in rural villages. Such a sudden statistical growth of the Jewish population in Rechitsa between 1808 and 1816 probably reflects the arrival of Jewish refugees from other areas of Belorussia occupied by Napoleon's army in 1812.[7] It is well known that during this war Rechitsa became the temporary residence of the governor of Minsk Province and the deployment site of the supplies depot of the southern Russian army, which surely intensified the demand for handcraft production and commercial supplies. A large number of Jewish refugees probably had left Rechitsa by the 1820s, after which the proportion of Jews in the overall population dropped to 30–35 percent.

Jewish communities, as noted, were continually trying to show that their population was lower than it actually was. They did so at the end of the eighteenth century and in the first quarter of the nineteenth simply to minimize taxes, but after 1827 they employed the same strategy to reduce the number of recruits that the community had to provide for the army. The Russian administration was aware of this ploy. In 1868, the Rechitsa Uezd police inspector, with the help of deputies of the town duma, verified the data collected during the tenth enumeration in 1857 on the number of Jews in the town. Even though the Jewish community continued to deny concealing several of its members, the police inspector, concerned about Jews being hidden from the military draft, ordered that a fine would be imposed unless the missing members were added to the list within six

TABLE 2. Dynamics of the size of the general and Jewish populations in Rechitsa over 125 years (1789–1914)

Year	Total population	Number of Jews	Percentage of Jews
1789[a]	1,010	134	13.3
1795[b]	1,235	245	19.8
1811[c]	1,865	566	30.4
1816[d]	1,622	841	51.9
1825[e]	2,440	—	—
1839[f]	—	1,421	—
1851[g]	4,715	1,950	41.35
1861[h]	4,504	2,227	49.4
1878[i]	6,492	3,384	52.1
1884[j]	6,615	3,509	53
1893[k]	8,373	4,521	54
1897[l]	9,280	5,334	57.5
1905[m]	11,095	6,522	58.8
1910[n]	12,027	7,064	58.7
1914[o]	12,677	7,499	59.1

Sources:

[a] For sources of this census, see chapter 1.

[b] Petrachenka and Kavalenka, Kameral'noe opisanie rechitskoi okrugi, 239.

[c] Aleksandrov, Di yyidish'e b'ap'elk'erong 'in Myinsk'er gub'erni'e 'in 'anhyyv 19—tan y'arhind'ert, 73. As noted earlier, this enumeration list contains data only on the male population. The number of Jews indicated in table 2 are derived by calculation. On the total population, see Liutyi, Sotsial'no-ekonomicheskoe razvitie gorodov Belorussii, 33.

[d] On the Jewish population, see Aleksandrov, Di yyidish'e b'ap'elk'erong 'in Myinsk'er gub'erni'e 'in 'anhyyv 19—tan y'arhind'ert, 73. The overall population is for 1815 and is taken from Liutyi, Sotsial'no-ekonomicheskoe razvitie gorodov Belorussii, 33.

[e] Belorussiia v epokhu Feodalizma, 3:509–510.

[f] LGIA, f. 378, op. 1840, d. 1209, 3a.–4 (copy in CAHJP, HM2 9757.6).

[g] On the Jewish population, see NIARB, f. 299, op. 2, d. 4379, 37. On the overall population, see Liutyi, Sotsial'no-ekonomicheskoe razvitie gorodov Belorussii, 33.

[h] Stolpianskii, Deviat' gubernii Zapadno-russkogo kraia, 86; NIARB, f. 295, op. 1, d. 501, 97, 99 (copy in CAHJP, HMF 831.35). The figure for overall population includes the military. Without them the total population would be 4,319 (see Zelenskii, Materialy dlia geografii i statistiki Rossii, 2:671). Using that figure, the percentage of Jews would be 51.5.

[i] RGIA, f. 821, op. 8, d. 152, 45a–46 (copy in CAHJP, HM2 7778); Aleksandrov, Di yyidish'e b'ap'elk'erong 'in dyi sht'et 'un sht'etl'ekh fun Vyyasrusland, 355–356.

[j] Alenitsyn, Evreiskoe naselenie i zemlevladenie v iugo-zapadnykh guberniiakh Evropeiskoi Possii, vkhodiashchikh v chertu evreiskoi osedlosti, 26.

[k] Pamiatnaia knizhka Minskoi gubernii na 1894 god (Minsk: Gubernskii statisticheskii komitet, 1893), 3.

[l] Evreiskoe naselenie Rossii po dannym perepisi 1897 g. i po noveishim istochnikam, 48.

[m] Pamiatnaia knizhka Minskoi gubernii na 1906 god (Minsk: Gubernskii statisticheskii komitet, 1905), 108–109.

[n] Pamiatnaia knizhka Minskoi gubernii na 1911 god, 66–67.

[o] Evreiskoe naselenie Rossii po dannym perepisi 1897 g. i po noveishim istochnikam, 48; Aleksandrov, Di yyidish'e b'ap'elk'erong 'in dyi sht'et 'un sht'etl'ekh fun Vyyasrusland, 355–356.

months.[8] And, indeed, this enumeration showed that 1,258 Jews were living in Rechitsa when, as can be seen from table 2, this figure was considerably below their actual number.[9] The uezd police officer from neighboring Mozyr Uezd informed the Minsk military governor that same year of the various tricks to which Jews resorted to understate their numbers.[10] The government had the same problems throughout the entire Pale of Settlement.[11] It is likely that in the last three decades of the nineteenth century the administration managed to carry out a more thorough census of the Jewish population.

In the first half of the nineteenth century, there was one more reason that the census data showed smaller numbers of Jews than there actually were. The administration did not allow Jews registered elsewhere to be included in another community where they may have lived for many years. They were unable to register in their actual place of residence and were considered nonresidents, burdened with all the problems arising from this status when they needed to pay taxes, register births and deaths, submit applications to their place of registry, and so on. When enumeration lists were being compiled, the authorities within the Jewish community—as a rule, the kahal elder, the members of the boards of prayer houses, and members of the town administration—attempted to register a number of nonresident Jews in local Jewish communities to make their lives easier. Russian officials knew about this practice as well and tried to take countermeasures against it. In 1831 the Minsk Treasury became suspicious of the data on the Jews in Rechitsa collected during the eighth revision, in particular the inclusion in the list of Nokhem Vasilevitskii and two children, the infant grandsons of Nokhem Gabaev and Abram Tëmkin. Tëmkin, who had lived in Rechitsa for over ten years, had managed to marry and acquire his own house.[12]

The fact that Jews were not obliged to register girls also undermines the credibility of the statistics. In accordance with Russian laws, a girl was registered in her father's place of residence until marriage, and after marriage in her husband's; only if she became a widow did she acquire independent status as far as registration of residence was concerned. Citizenship was determined on the same principle. If she married a foreigner, a woman in Russia automatically lost her Russian citizenship. This, plus the fact that girls were not called up for military service, weakened the authorities' control over their registration. The view of the demographer Roza Sifman is therefore quite valid: she argues that the census data on Jewish women does not correspond to the actuality, so a general correction of 15 percent should be made to the natural increase of the Jewish population.[13] Nevertheless, the official figures are cited in this study to avoid the confusion that would result from making these corrections. Sifman believes that the corresponding data on the Orthodox and Catholic populations are more reliable than those for Jews, since the registration of the former, done by the clergy, was more closely regulated by the state.[14]

The urbanizing policies of the Russian authorities led to a more than tenfold increase in the Jewish population in Rechitsa in the half-century between 1789 and 1839, that is, almost from the time Rechitsa was absorbed by Russia. What had begun as a forced migration of Jews from the villages and shtetls in the first quarter of the nineteenth century became a voluntary migration, since the economic importance of the towns had increased. Statistical evidence on the Jews in Rechitsa in 1839 shows this continuing urbanization of the Jewish population. In this year the difference between births and deaths was plus thirty-six, so the natural increase amounted to 2.5 percent. But the overall increase of the Jewish population in that same year was 204.[15] Thus the difference between Jews who came to the town and those who left it was 168 persons, that is, the number of Jews there increased by 11.8 percent due to positive migration. This rather high percentage of mechanical (migrational) increase resulted from a population shift primarily from small centers, since Jews from larger centers would not likely be attracted to Rechitsa. In the first third of the nineteenth century, the town's Jewish population began to be a significant minority, one that continued to grow. At the same time, trade and crafts began to develop at a fast pace there, as we have seen. By the 1840s Rechitsa, while remaining an administrative town, took on the features of a Jewish mestechko. This was a collateral result of the urbanization policy carried out by the authorities.

In the quarter century before the reform era, from 1839 to 1863, the rate of growth of the Jewish population of Rechitsa declined, primarily due to negative migration. Despite the steady overall growth of the Jewish population in Rechitsa in this period, Jews from the villages and mestechkos of Rechitsa Uezd, as was shown in the previous chapter, now preferred to move to centers larger than Rechitsa.

The growth of the Jewish population was reflected in the statistics of the overall population of Rechitsa. A particularly rapid increase in the overall population occurred in the second quarter of the nineteenth century, when the town's growth, as shown in table 2, was 193 percent, that is, an almost twofold increase. In the third quarter of this century, the rate of growth slowed. The lack of complete statistics does not allow us to establish which years in this period showed a particularly large increase, but the statistics on Jews show that the sharp growth in their numbers continued only to the beginning of the 1840s. In the third quarter of this century, the rate of growth slowed. But in the last quarter of the nineteenth century, the population again began expanding, and the result was an absolute growth in the overall population of Rechitsa of 185 percent, that is, an increase of more than one and a half times.

The Belorussian historian Zakhar Shybeka, in studying the economic demographics of the towns of Belorussia from 1863 to 1913, has quite logically—taking into account regional historical processes—divided these fifty years into three periods: from 1863 to 1885; from 1885 to 1897; and from 1897 to 1913. According to his statistics, the urban population of all Belorussia grew on average by 41.8 percent during the first period, while the population of Rechitsa grew by 35.8 percent, that is, on average by 1.7 percent per year.[16] As shown in table 2, the Jewish population of Rechitsa over approximately the same period (from 1861 to 1884) grew by almost the same amount: 36.5 percent, or 1.6 percent per year.

The relative growth of the overall population in the whole of Rechitsa Uezd, even over the rather lengthy period from 1857 to 1884, was considerably less than in Rechitsa itself. It increased by 16 percent in all. Within this context, the increase of the Jewish population in the whole uezd—46 percent—appears significant. As a result, the proportion of Jews within the overall population of the uezd over the same period grew from 10.9 percent in 1857 to 17.1 percent in 1884.[17] Thus in the first period noted above (1863 to 1885), the dynamics of growth in the Jewish population within Rechitsa Uezd slightly outpaced the corresponding growth index of the Jewish population of Rechitsa town. By contrast, the growth rate of the overall population in the uezd lagged considerably behind that of Rechitsa itself.

The growth in the population of the town led to an increase in the number of residents packed into a single house because construction of a new dwelling required significant time. The density of the town's population rose from 5.9 people per house in 1811 to 8.4 in 1854.[18] But in the course of the previous decade, it had decreased to seven residents.[19] Then in the course of four decades the density of the population rose again to the level of 7.7 inhabitants squeezed into one house in 1904. That notwithstanding, Rechitsa was distinguished from other town in Minsk Province by its low population density, which is explained by the low price of timber in Rechitsa Uezd. On average nearly twice as many persons (15.2) lived in each house in Minsk.[20]

The relative growth of the overall population of Rechitsa Uezd in the period 1863–1885 was almost two times less than the average growth of the urban and rural populations of Belorussia, which was 32.7 percent.[21] In turn, the growth of Belorussian cities and towns over this period lagged behind the average growth of cities and towns in European Russia by 8.6 percent. Zakhar Shybeka attributes this tendency to the movement of Jews from the mestechkos and towns of the Belorussian provinces to cities within Russia. The towns of Belorussia, in his view, attracted mainly peasants and landowners.[22] In reality, however, it was only an insignificant portion of the Jewish population that was able to leave the Pale of Settlement due to the strict restraints then in force regarding Jewish places of residence. Therefore, the most important factor responsible for the reduction of the population within Belorussia at the time was the epidemics that took so many lives.

The cholera epidemic of 1866, which took some three million lives in Europe, hit Belorussia particularly hard. Evidently, many fewer of Belorussia's inhabitants died during the typhus epidemic that gripped Rechitsa Uezd in 1878–1879.[23] Outbreaks of cholera continued in Belorussia in subsequent years as well. For example, in 1894, 331 people died of it in Minsk Province alone (mainly in Pinsk and Lakhva). Altogether in this year, 4,520 people in the province died of infectious diseases; the fewest victims were in Rechitsa—only eight people.[24]

The opening of the railway line through Rechitsa led to a rapid growth of the town's population during the next period (1885–1897). While the population of Belorussian towns and cities grew on average by only 8 percent over these twelve years, in Rechitsa the population increase was 24.7 percent. In 1890, for example, Rechitsa had the largest yearly gain in population of all the towns in Minsk Province, 2.4 percent.[25] Among the forty-five other towns in Belorussia, Rechitsa held eighth place in growth rate during this period.[26]

The Jewish population of Rechitsa grew at an even faster rate during this period, by 34 percent, that is, an increase of 2.8 percent per year. Thus, as table 3 shows, in this period the town's overall growth (in Shybeka's second period, 1885–1897), comprising both natural and mechanical (migrational) increases, was the highest of all the years between 1816 and 1914. This great increase was caused above all by the migration of Jews into Rechitsa. A particularly large Jewish migration here took place in the 1890s; its peak year was 1894, when Rechitsa's Jewish population grew by 5.2 percent. That year also set a record for the growth of Rechitsa's overall population, which expanded even more than the town's Jewish population—by 6.4 percent.

Rechitsa Uezd as a whole presents a different picture during 1885–1897. While the total population of the uezd increased by 50 percent, its Jewish population grew at a rate almost the same as that of Rechitsa itself, 33.6 percent. After the turbulent growth of the mid-1880s, which created a sizable increase of the non-Jewish population, the proportion of Jews within the overall population of the uezd began to decline: in 1878 it was 11.4 percent; in 1884, 17.1 percent;

in 1897, 12.9 percent; in 1905, 9.8 percent; and in 1914, 8.7 percent.[27] The reason for this was the increased migration of Jews from the many tiny mestechkos of the uezd into Rechitsa, Gomel, and Rogachev as well as outside the Pale of Settlement.

In 1902, when the number of inhabitants in Rechitsa rose above ten thousand, the town moved from the category of small to that of midsized. In 1913, toward the end of the third period, the town's population reached thirteen thousand, an increase of almost 28 percent since 1897. But this was still less than the average growth of the other Belorussian towns, which was 33.4 percent during that period.[28] The reason was most likely the departure from Rechitsa of a large number of Jews, as can be seen in their comparatively small relative increase in numbers between 1897 and 1914—28.9 percent, or 1.7 percent per year. On the basis of indicators of yearly increase in the town's Jewish population, this period can be divided into two time segments: from 1898 to 1905, that is, when it comprised 2.4 percent; and from 1906 to 1914, when it dropped to 1.4 percent.

Thus, after a prolonged period of growth, the peak of which came between 1889 and 1896, the yearly increase of Rechitsa's Jewish population in the prewar decade returned to the level of the first two-thirds of the nineteenth century. In Rechitsa Uezd the yearly increase of the Jewish population declined much more sharply; it equaled only half of Rechitsa's Jewish population itself during the prewar years.

Over fifty years (1863–1913), the overall population of the town increased by 2.9 times, slightly exceeding the average indicator for the growth of Belorussian towns (2.8 times). Over that same period, Belorussia's rural population increased by almost 2.7 times.[29] Although the growth of Rechitsa's population over the period was the average of that of the forty-five other Belorussian towns, in terms of growth rate it was sixteenth. The reason for this lay in the different rates at which towns developed. In the 1870s, inhabitants of towns and mestechkos that lay outside the railway network began migrating to places where there

TABLE 3. Rates of yearly Increase in the Jewish population of Rechitsa and Rechitsa Uezd (in percentages)

Years	Rechitsa	Rechitsa uezd
1816–1860	1.4	—
1861–1884	1.6	1.7
1885–1897	2.6	2.6
1898–1905	2.4	1.5
1906–1914	1.4	0.7

was a railway. Clear preference was given to rail centers. Thus Jews, merchants, and tradesmen from the mestechkos of Rechitsa Uezd sought better earnings by migrating to Rechitsa and even more to Gomel, where two economically important railway lines, the Polesia (1882) and the Libava-Romny (1873) intersected. Until the 1850s, Gomel remained in the hands of private owners, and they, according to Valentina Chepko, developed the local economy more effectively than the state could have done.[30] Thus the number of people registered there as merchants grew from 32 in 1833 to 597 in 1861, an increase of 18.6 times over three decades.[31] One significant factor in this growth was the transit trade in grain with Ukraine.[32] The town grew even more when the two railway lines mentioned above were built through it. Gomel's economic growth attracted both Jews and non-Jews from the mestechkos and villages of southeastern Belorussia. The following facts provide a vivid demonstration of the large proportion of migrants in Gomel's Jewish population at the very beginning of the twentieth century: among the 36 people who supported various opposition parties and who were convicted of participation in the self-defense movement during the pogrom of 1903, only 11 (less than one-third!) belonged to the local community of townspeople, while almost all the others were registered in midsized and small mestechkos in eastern Belorussia.[33] In that same year there were even fewer Gomel townspeople among the members of the Bund committee—7 out of 31, that is, 22.6 percent![34] Even among the Jews registered as Gomel townspeople, some were probably natives of other centers or children of migrants whose social status was on average lower than that of Gomel natives, a factor that led to their membership in the Bund. Thanks to migration, Gomel's population over a half century—from 1863 to 1913—increased eightfold.

During that same period the population of another town in eastern Polesia—Rogachev—increased by almost the same factor. This growth was promoted by the fact that in the mid-nineteenth century the dock of this small mestechko was the focal point of all the timber trade between Mogilev Province and Ukraine.[35] In 1873, after the Libava-Romny railway line was built through nearby Zhlobin, and then in 1902, when the Vitebsk-Zhlobin railway line was extended through Rogachev itself, the town grew even more, surpassing Rechitsa's population by the beginning of twentieth century. The close proximity of fast-growing Rogachev and, particularly, of Gomel slowed Rechitsa's economic and cultural growth since enterprising merchants, the intelligentsia, and young people moved to these towns.

According to Shybeka's study, from 1885 to 1913 the rate of urbanization of the towns of southern Belorussia (Gomel, Mozyr, Pinsk, Rogachev, and Rechitsa) significantly outpaced those of the other Belorussian regions.[36] But Shybeka's division of all Belorussian towns into western, northern, eastern, southern, and central is questionable. Gomel and Rogachev could just as easily be considered part of eastern Belorussia, while Pinsk could be included in the western part. It seems that the division should be made along the lines of the contemporary division into oblasts, which would better correspond to the historical-cultural and economic character of the regions. Thus, with the exclusion of Pinsk—which should be regarded as part of southwestern Belorussia to correspond to the borders of today's Brest Oblast—the four other towns in today's Gomel Oblast mentioned above are part of southeastern Belorussia. In terms of the rate of urbanization between 1885 and 1913 (a rate largely determined by Gomel and Rogachev), this region outpaced the other parts of Belorussia even more than did the region defined by Shybeka as southern.

The large growth in the overall population of Rechitsa in the first quarter of the nineteenth century, as shown in table 2, occurred because of migration from the mestechkos of the uezd. This flow continued in the second half of that century, but because of factors mentioned above, part of both the Jewish and the gentile population had already left Rechitsa itself. At that time the outflow of Rechitsa's Jewish population to large economic centers was greater than the influx from the shtetls. On the whole, such a migratory process was typical for all areas of the Pale of Settlement. It was a part of the general process of urbanization that was evident throughout the Russian Empire.

Aside from this migration, the overall increase in the proportion of Jews in Rechitsa's population over the period under examination was, as can be seen in table 2, basically a result of a greater natural population increase among Jews. An exception is the decline in the proportion of Jews in the town's population between 1905 and 1910. This occurred because of the increase in Jewish emigration abroad and because of their migration beyond the Pale of Settlement made possible by a certain easing of the Russian government's restrictive policies toward some elements of its own population.

The most important development stimulating outward migration came in 1865, when Jews who had completed training in certain approved trade schools and who were working at their chosen specialty were given permission to leave the Pale of Settlement. As a result, between 1870 and 1890 some Jewish tradesmen settled in Central Russia and an even greater number in Siberia, the Turkestan, and the Caucasus. Some of them, along with Jewish merchants who had received legislative benefits upon leaving the Pale of Settlement in 1859, settled in Moscow. Jews from Minsk Province, including some from Rechitsa, also settled in

Moscow as well as in the other economic and cultural center, Kiev.[37] Many of them, however, had to return from Moscow or move elsewhere during the expulsions of 1891–1892. Elsewhere the threat of expulsion to their former places of registration constantly hung over these Jews until World War I. They often had to prove their rights to residence in the places to which they had migrated.

As for Jewish emigration abroad, statistical evidence shows that it peaked between 1905 and 1907, while in Rechitsa it peaked in 1906 and 1907.[38] In these two post-pogrom years, more than a quarter of all the 887 Jews who emigrated from Rechitsa to the United States came through the American port of Ellis Island. Rechitsa Jews arriving in the United States evidently also used other ports during these years.

Although figures on emigration to other countries from 1907 to 1910 are far from complete, seventy-one Jews are recorded as receiving emigration documents through the Rechitsa branch of the Emigration Society that opened in August 1907. This branch was run by Aron Vilenkin and Iakov Kotsyn, who were succeeded a few years later by Mordukh Frenkel and Alexander Agranovich.[39]

TABLE 4.   Statistics on Immigration of Rechitsa Jews through the port of Ellis Island (1903–1923)

Year	Numbers	Proportion of total arrivals for all years (%)
1903	16	1.8
1904	60	6.8
1905	40	4.5
1906	119	13.5
1907	112	12.7
1908	67	7.6
1909	55	6.2
1910	68	7.7
1911	91	10.3
1912	50	5.6
1913	84	9.5
1914	61	6.9
1915–1921	—	—
1922	13	1.5
1923	51	5.8
Total	887	100

Source: Calculated from the database at http://www.jewishgen.org/databases/EIDB/ellisjw.html.

Evidently, many Rechitsa Jews completed their emigration documents through the Minsk and other branches of this society as well.[40]

Statistics on Jewish emigrants who went abroad from Minsk Province in 1909 certify that 75 percent of them went to the United States (including 60 percent to New York), 12 percent to Palestine, 4.2 percent to Europe, 3.2 percent to Canada, 1.8 percent to Argentina, and 1 percent to South Africa.[41] Statistics for Gomel paint a somewhat different picture—and these can certainly be applied to Rechitsa as well—79 percent of Jewish emigrants in 1910 were bound for the United States; 8 percent for Canada; 7.7 percent for Argentina; 2.7 percent for Palestine; and 2.6 percent for other countries.[42] Projecting from the statistics for immigration through Ellis Island, one can estimate that about 130 Jews from Rechitsa (0.18 percent from their total population) emigrated abroad in that same year of 1910.

As to the age groups of Jewish immigrants to various countries, like those of the group bound for the United States, one-third were young people between sixteen and twenty-two. Among all Rechitsa emigrants, 76.7 percent were below the age of thirty. Only a very few were over the age of fifty.

People from Rechitsa kept in contact in their new homes, at least in the United States and Erets-Israel.[43] In particular, the organization in Chicago in May 1927 of the Rechitsa Society for Aid to Education and Collective Recreation chaired by Solomon Goldshteyn testifies to the maintenance of links in that city. The honorary president was Max Malisov and the treasurer Charles Pozin. Until World War II, that is, as long as it remained possible, the society supported all the charitable organizations in Rechitsa along with some individual families. An educational committee led by Iakob Katz organized lectures and concerts by

TABLE 5. Ages of Jewish immigrants from Rechitsa arriving in the United States via Ellis Island (1903–1923)

Age group	Numbers	Proportion of total arrivals for all years (%)
0–9	167	18.9
10–19	260	29.4
20–29	251	28.4
30–39	109	12.3
40–49	69	7.8
50–65	29	3.3
Total	885	100

Source: Calculated from the database at http://www.jewishgen.org/databases/EIDB/ellisjw.html.

immigrants from Rechitsa. In those years a special section, no. 65, called the "Rechitzer," was set aside in the Waldheim Jewish Cemetery in Chicago.[44]

The founding of community immigrant associations in the United States and Canada for Russian Jews from the same hometowns or mestechkos was a common occurrence. These immigrant associations included the Shklover Benevolent Association, the Turover Aid Society, the Minsker Ladies Benevolent Society, the Independent Minsker Aid Society, the Hlusker Benevolent Society, and many others. They were social-economic networks, the aim of which was mutual aid, help in finding links in a new country, setting aside a separate section in the Jewish cemetery, the promotion of collective assistance for relatives in the Russian Empire, and an exchange of information about their native community.[45]

Formally, the authorities in Russia did not place obstacles in the way of Jewish emigration, but neither did they encourage it. At the same time, migration of Jews into the Russian Empire was severely restricted, and during the reigns of autocratic rulers it was completely closed. In accordance with the Regulations of 1892, Jews, unlike other emigrants from Russia, were forbidden to return to their former homeland. At the same time, it was made easier for Jews, considered undesirable citizens, to leave the country than it was for others.[46]

The industrial surge and the growth of monopolies in the Russian Empire between 1908 and 1912 had a negative impact on the work of Jewish craftsmen

The gate of the Waldheim Jewish Cemetery in Chicago. Courtesy of Bill Schechter.

and tradespeople. The considerable growth of the Jewish population has affected their work even more because it sharpened the competition between them. For a quarter century, from 1872 to 1897, the number of Jews in all of Minsk Province increased from 148,356 to 345,031; that is 232.6 percent.[47] Only these reasons can explain the steady growth of Jewish emigration on a national scale beginning in 1910. It reached a peak in 1913, when 51,500 Jews emigrated from the country. Over the first seven months of 1914, 45,000 Jews managed to emigrate, but the outbreak of the war interrupted this process, precipitated by the increasing awareness among Jews of their ethnic inequality.[48] The rate of emigration from Rechitsa, as shown in table 4, was somewhat different. Its new peak came in 1911, but in 1913 and the first half of 1914 it was also quite significant. Out of 1,523 Jews responding to inquiries who left Minsk Province in 1909, 62.6 percent gave economic reasons for emigration, and 32.5 percent gave family reasons.[49] It appears, however, that a significant number of the latter group in fact may have departed for economic reasons. This follows from common emigrant patterns. Often the a husband moved first. When things had come right in a new place, he could invite his wife and children, and in some cases brothers and sisters. Brothers and sisters were invited to emigrate by early moved unmarried family member as well.

Despite Jewish emigration abroad, the proportion of Jews in Rechitsa, as already mentioned, continued to grow steadily in the second half of the nineteenth and the beginning of the twentieth century. This growth reduced the proportion of the Christian population in the town, in which the Orthodox faith predominated.

As can be seen from table 6, the proportion of the Orthodox population over the period fell by almost 10 percent. In 1854 the Orthodox population included 2.6 percent Old Believers, comprising 1.24 percent of the total population of the

TABLE 6. Changes in the religious composition of the population of Rechitsa from 1854 to 1910 (%)

Religion	1854[a]	1910[b]
Orthodox	49.4	39.2
Catholic	7.0	2.0
Protestant	0.02	0.1
Jewish	43.4	58.7
Total	100	100

Sources:
[a] NIARB, f. 21, op. 1, d. 1, 395–396.
[b] Goroda Rossii v 1910 godu, 92–93.

town. The figures for 1910 contain no separate data on the Old Believers, so it is impossible to trace any change in their proportion of the town's population. The proportion of Protestants, particularly Lutherans, grew significantly over this period. The proportion of Catholics generally declined. On the whole, there were fewer Catholics in Rechitsa than in other uezd towns in Minsk Province.[50]

The religious composition shown here scarcely changed during the prewar years.[51] In 1915, after the resettlement to Rechitsa of thousands of Jewish refugees evicted from the war front (discussed in next chapter), he proportion of Jews in the town's population increased even more, reaching approximately 63 percent.

Unlike ordinary migration processes, it is more complicated to expose the demography of Jewish families, given the limited research devoted to it and the exceptional lack of attention given it in the sources. Only recently have important articles appeared in which one or another aspect of this question has been examined, and I use them as relevant material in the agenda of the present study. Studies on this topic published in Russia before 1917 suffer from several important defects. Jewish historians relied on a narrow foundation of source examination in the basic correspondence of 1897, whereas non-Jewish researchers, still in the thrall of negative prejudices that influenced their view of Jews, presented their studies to the public in a tendentious manner. The contention that "Jews marry too soon" and one that flows from it, "Jews are very fertile," are two basic stereotypical views that have endured for a long time in the Russian bureaucracy. Russian bureaucracy even went so far as to ascribe to Jews a fabricated birthrate that was twice that of Christians.[52] The first of these views was partially correct when the aforementioned Russian officer Bronevskii met the Jews he writes about in 1810. Following a visit to mestechko Koidanov, he was billeted at a Jew's house, which prompted the following observations, "My host sells wine, liqueurs, and outstanding mead [*medovukha*]; I could not drink a full wineglass of the last one, it was so strong. Not since Lemberg have I drunk such good coffee. It is brewed in mugs served to me by a sweet Yid daughter twelve years old and already an engaged bride to be."[53] Two years later Christoph Ludwig von Yelin, an officer in Napoleon's army saw a Jewish couple in Belorussia. The husband was fourteen and the wife twelve years old. They took turns living first with her parents, then with his.[54] The fact that both officers singled out these cases even though they saw many Jews there (as indicated by their differing generalizations) is evidence that such marriages nevertheless were not a very widespread phenomenon.

This conclusion is confirmed in Jacob Goldberg's study of the ages when Jewish women married in the towns and villages of central Poland's rural uezds. According to Goldberg, at the end of the eighteenth century 11.3 percent of the women in towns married between the ages of fifteen and nineteen, and 32.1 percent did so in villages. By the time they reached twenty-five to twenty-nine years of age, 95.8 percent of the women in towns and 92.8 percent in villages were married. By the time men were twenty years old, 20 percent in the towns and 10.9 percent in villages were married.[55] Although Goldberg could not find statistical data on marriages of women younger than fifteen, it would not be wrong to assume on the basis of the data shown here that their number did not exceed 5 percent in towns and 2 percent in villages.

Here we are talking about the tradition known by the Yiddish word *kest*. Aside from this patronization of a young family, the tradition of early marriages, which may have its origins in the early modern period, might then have been a means for parents to safeguard their children from forced conversion to Christianity as preadolescents.[56] At least that is how Bukharan Jews reacted to the forced conversion and abduction of their sons and daughters by Muslims at that time in Central Asia.[57]

In Russia, when Jewish girls were no longer threatened with abduction for conversions, the number of early marriages gradually decreased. Contributing to this was the publication of a special law in 1835 prohibiting marriages for Jews and Muslims if the groom was younger than seventeen and the bride younger than sixteen. Until the early 1840s, however, Jews often evaded this law by using false papers to marry off their children several years earlier than was permitted.[58] It is therefore possible that in the first two-thirds of the nineteenth century the proportion of marriages among Jews in the lower range of authorized ages actually increased in comparison with the number during the Polish-Lithuanian Commonwealth. In 1867 61 percent of women and 43 percent of men were already married by the time they were twenty years of age. Shaul Stampfer, following the lead of Sara Rabinowitsch-Margolin, tracks the subsequent rise in the age at marriage in the Russian Empire from then until 1902. In this period of time the proportion of men and women younger than twenty among all married people again decreased, to 24 percent among women and 5 percent among men.[59]

The statistics they cite show a breakdown in the exemplary age-defined marriage model in the 1875–1885 period. This breakdown likely resulted from the introduction in 1874 of the universal military obligation, with its six-year service requirement. Furthermore, most of the Jews inducted into the army were single, which one can deduce from the statement by Iohanan Petrovskii-Shtern that the percentage of married men among Christians was significantly greater.[60] Nevertheless, the new rules of universal military obligation have been reflected in marriage patterns of the Gentile population as well. As Boris Mironov has argued, after 1874 there was a tendency among eighteen- to twenty-year-old Orthodox men not to marry, instead marrying after their military service, when they were twenty-four or twenty-five. Similarly, the marriage age of Orthodox women shifted from sixteen to eighteen years old to twenty-one to twenty-two years old.[61]

By the end of the nineteenth century, the marriage age among Jews was the highest among all the religious confessions in Russia. As was the case generally in Russia, Jews in Rechitsa married much later than did the members of other religious groups. The proportion of Jewish women in Russia who married below the age of twenty-one was 25.2 percent, the lowest among the figures provided in the 1897 census. By contrast, 60.8 percent of Orthodox women in this age group were married. Among Muslims the figure was 53.3 percent. Although only 5.9 percent of Jewish males in this age group in Russia were married, in the empire as a whole, 38.8 percent of Orthodox and 9.9 percent of Muslims were married. Only Catholics and Armenians married later than Jews: 4.6 percent and 3.6 percent respectively were married by the age of twenty-one.[62]

The marriage age among Jews early in the twentieth century continued to rise. Marriage records kept by the official state rabbi of Minsk for 1912 (table 7) permits the development of age-related models and models for marriages conducted at this time. It is difficult to imagine that the situation in Rechitsa could be different, especially since among couples getting married in Minsk we find Jews registered in Rechitsa and other small towns of the province.

As these data clearly show, by their twenties only 9.6 percent of Jewish women were married, whereas among men very few were married. Moreover, only one woman aged sixteen was included in the sixteen-to-nineteen age group, and the

TABLE 7. Age at marriage among Jews in Minsk, 1912 (in percentages)

Age	Female	Male
16–19	9.6	2.1
20–24	46.5	25.7
25–29	29.9	40.7
30–34	7.0	18.7
35–39	3.7	3.7
40–44	0.7	2.8
45–49	0.5	0.9
50–older	2.1	5.4
Total	100	100

Source: Calculations are based on CAHJP, RU16.

ages of the others were higher. If there had been efforts at this time, as earlier, to raise the marriage age, they would have favored the lowest authorized ages. Since this was not the case, this information should be considered trustworthy. In 16.8 percent of all marriages the brides and grooms were the same age, and in 34 percent the bride was older. In general the age difference was no greater than five years, and only in three marriages was it ten years or higher. In ten anomalous cases the difference was eighteen years and higher. Beginning with age fifty and to a striking degree after thirty-five, there were remarriages at least in the case of one of the parties. I shall return to the question of remarriages later.

Closely linked with statistics on age at marriage are the marriage rates for Jews and Christians. This linkage can be seen in statistics for Minsk Province in 1889.[63] Across the province in that year there was one marriage for every 910 one Orthodox residents and only one per 175 Jews. At the same time, in Minsk, which as the provincial center exhibited a different marriage pattern than elsewhere in the province, there was one marriage for almost the same number of Orthodox and Jewish residents—125 and 132 respectively. In the province's other ten uezd centers, including Rechitsa (the Jewish and Christian populations in these centers were rather large), the picture differs sharply from that in Minsk and from the provincial average. In these ten towns there was only one marriage for every 228 Orthodox residents, while the figure was one per 142 among the Jews. In Rechitsa there was one marriage per 160 Orthodox residents and one per 112 Jews.[64] Thus the rate of marriages among Jews in the big towns was considerably higher than that of the Orthodox, while in small towns, shtetls, and villages the situation was the reverse. In a place where almost everyone knew everyone else, society definitely put a great deal of pressure on young women not to "turn into old maids."

In the second half of the 1860s the Jews of the Russian Empire registered marriages most often in June and August, whereas Orthodox Christians tended to marry in January and especially in February.[65] These distinctive features were preserved on a national scale even fifty years later in the Russian Empire.[66] And indeed, peasants most often married in January and February, during the period between religious fasts, when the Orthodox population was permitted to eat meat. This custom was linked to the wish for children to be born in late autumn, since the peasant family needed women to help with the harvest.[67] On the other hand, in wintertime, after the harvest had been gathered and the money earned from it was available, peasants could rest until field work began in spring and so could celebrate weddings. In the Minsk and neighboring Mogilev Provinces, Orthodox Christians celebrated most of their marriages in these months, but the Jews of the region conducted themselves altogether differently from their coreligionists elsewhere in the Russian Empire. Most marriages of Jews in Minsk Province in 1867 were held not in the summer but in March (11 percent) and September (9.9 percent), and in Mogilev Province in March (13.6 percent) and January (11.3).[68]

The divorce rate among the Jewish population—where women enjoyed higher status in the family than did women of the Orthodox and Muslim populations— was also higher. Administrative records confirm the high proportion of divorces among the Jewish population. In 1839 20 percent of marriages in Rechitsa ended in divorce, and in other locations of Rechitsa Uezd the number came to 66.7 percent. This fact suggests that in the Uezd it was possible for Jews to divorce out-side Rechitsa. In the entire Minsk Province 40.4 percent of marriages ended in divorce, in the Minsk metropolitan area excluding the city 33 percent, and in Minsk itself a still larger proportion, 62.5 percent.[69] At the same time, however, such an excessively high divorce rate gives reason to question the completeness of the official registration of marriages at that time. It is likely that some were not recorded in the special community registration books of the rabbis as the law of 1835 stipulated. Arguing in favor of this conjecture is the disinclination of Jews to participate in censuses, discussed earlier. In Minsk, with its large population as well as the numbers of Jews living in nearby villages, it was easier for Minsk's Jews to avoid the official registration of their marriages in the rabbinical books. The existence of illegal marriages among Jews is confirmed by several sources dealing with other regions.[70] Although the procedure for divorce is easier for Jews than for Orthodox, Catholics, and Muslims, in comparison with marriages it has re-mained much more complicated to the present day and always requires written registration. Not all rabbis were able to complete this procedure; thus a couple might go to another town, usually to a big city, to have the divorce duly registered. Therefore, the proportion of divorces in these cities was higher .In Rechitsa in 1862, there were three divorces for fourteen marriages (17.6 percent), and in 1874, six divorces for thirty-nine marriages (13.3 percent).[71] There were many more divorces at that time in Ukraine. In 1862 38.7 percent of the marriages in Berdichev ended in divorce. Although in 1868 this percentage decreased some-what, it still remained quite high: 30.4 percent.[72]

Chaeran Freeze notes a large proportion of divorces in Ukraine in comparison with Belorussia and Lithuania, which she attributes to the different attitude re-garding marriage on the part of "southerners"—Hasidic Jews—and "northern-ers," Misnagid Jews.[73] Because from the middle of the nineteenth century Hasidic Jews were also predominant in Belorussia, it seems that the explanation lies in the different mentalities of Litvak and Ukrainian Jews, which I have discussed in the first chapter.

In Moscow, according to the data presented by Kh. Braude, for the decade of 1871–1880 the divorce rate totaled 21 percent.[74] Even this relatively low level of divorces for Jews in Russia seemed large to Braude; he attributes it to the fictitious marriages that couples claimed to secure the right to live in Moscow. In reality, according to Russian laws a man could not acquire the right to live in any locality if his mother, daughter, or wife was a legal resident there. To the contrary, a wife lost her previous right of residence if she married a man from another locality. Because the social-economic activity of a man at that time in Russia, as was the case everywhere, greatly outstripped that of women, it was almost impossible to have a fictitious marriage in Moscow.

The records of the official state rabbi of this uezd for 1912 help to establish the percentage of divorces in the Jewish population of Minsk Uezd more than seventy years later, after the data cited above.[75] In this uezd, including Minsk, 67 occurred, thus totaling 31.3 percent of 214 marriages performed there in that year. During that period the number of divorces declined quite noticeably there. Thus it might mistakenly occur to someone that the Haskalah ("Jewish enlightenment," Hebrew) movement had no effect on divorces. Rather it led to parents paying much greater attention to the wishes of children regarding their future partners in life. The increase in the age at marriage discussed above gave young people the opportunity to design a package of preferences and formal requests for their future chosen one. All of this made for stronger marriages. In Rechitsa, where in any event the divorce rate was low, there was hardly any significant decrease at all.

In the absence of sources it is difficult to understand completely the reasons for the divorces. The available official data from Minsk for 1857 reveal that out of forty-two divorces among Jews, eight (19 percent) occurred because of childlessness, and the rest (81 percent) because of mutual dislike.[76] In Minsk in 1880 mutual dislike was given as the reason for all forty-five cases of divorce that year.[77] It is most likely that the changes in mentality that took place at this time did not permit some couples to indicate the actual reason for the divorce. The same thing evidently occurred in Minsk and in 1912, when the same reason was given for all divorces.[78] Chaeran Freeze also cites several statistical lists with the reasons for the divorces given, but these relate to Vilna. They give more details: most divorces there in 1837–1838 (24 percent) occurred because the spouse found it impossible to support his family. And although dislike occupies the second position among reasons given—19.6 percent—obviously it could have been combined under "mutual dislike" with the 11.3 percent that ascribed the divorce to wife beating. Although childlessness played a minor role there among the other reasons (only 10.5 percent), this category could have been expanded to include "illness of spouse" and "inability to have children."[79] In 1845 the majority of divorced people (30.8 percent) in Vilna gave "lack of means of existence" as their reason for divorce. Mutual dislike took second place with 23.4 percent. An absence of children was the reason given for divorce in only 8.4 percent of the cases.[80]

Freeze analyzes these and other reasons for divorce in detail.[81] Divorces stemming from army conscription need to be added to the list, as suggested by her statistics for Vilna in 1837–1836, which indicate that 45 percent of the men were divorced between the ages of thirteen and twenty-five. And by 1860 this rate even increased slightly, comprising 47.5 percent.[82] One of the first Russian Jewish writers, Grigorii Bogrov, describes how his father in the latter 1820s was divorced from his wife because of the debts he owed prior to being conscripted for military service. This took place by decision of the leaders of the kahal. In this tale, which underwent literary revision, the rabbis even maintain that they had such a rule— to send debtors in default to the army.[83]

Yet another stereotypical view accepted without proof by prerevolutionary researchers is the supposition that Christians in Russia more frequently remarried than did Jews.[84] Indeed, according to the data cited by Shaul Stampfer for 1867, 1885, and 1910 about the western provinces of Russia, in comparison with Orthodox, Protestant, and Catholic Christians, the remarriage rate among Jews was always higher.[85] At this point he observes that in contrast to Christian men, whose remarriages were more frequently with a woman who had not previously been married, both spouses in a Jewish remarriage were more likely to have been married before.

This was also the case in Minsk Province. In 1867 87.3 percent of Orthodox men who remarried wed a woman who had not previously been married; among Jews in the region 80.6 percent of remarriages were of such character. Regarding the incidence of remarriage for just one of the spouses as a percentage of all marriages, in Minsk Province they constituted 22.7 percent for Orthodox Christians and 30.3 percent for Jews.[86] Information on marriages among Jews gathered in 1912 by the Minsk official state rabbi yields virtually the same rate of remarriages: 30.4 percent.

Widowers predominate among the people who remarry: 18.3 percent of all marriages in 1912. This gives us reason to postulate that marriages ended more frequently as a result of the death of one of the spouses than as a result of divorce. This should be all the more valid for the nineteenth century, when mortality from epidemics was higher. Given the large proportion of widowers who remarried

TABLE 8. Marriages and remarriage among Jews in Minsk Uezd, 1912 (in percentages)

Groom	Bride		
	First marriage	Divorced	Widow
First marriage	69.6	1.4	0.9
Divorced	5.6	3.7	0.5
Widower	9.8	5.2	3.3

Source: Calculations are based on CAHJP, RU16

and the fact that men took the initiative in remarriages, one may also conclude that the small percentage of widows among women getting married argues that these widowers preferred not widows but rather young girls and then divorcees.

These Minsk statistics cannot be considered as urban statistics because the official rabbi was also obliged to register marriages in nearby mestechkos. The proportion of these external marriages was even higher than half between all his recorded marriages in 1912. Therefore, the average level for a model of marriage behavior is also completely applicable to an average Belorussian town such as Rechitsa.

Over the course of forty years, from 1874 to 1914, some changes took place in the sex ratio of the whole population in Rechitsa. In 1874, women comprised 52.2 percent of the population; in 1914, their proportion had dropped to 46.7 percent.[87] This slight reduction in the proportion of women took place despite the introduction of universal military service for men and the greater mobility of the male population. Evidently, the increase in the proportion of women in the town was compensated for by the higher number of male births. In 1874 male babies accounted for 54 percent of the total 189 births in Rechitsa.[88] This increase in the number of male births in the town resulted from the increase in the Jewish population, within which, as we know, higher numbers of males were born than among the Slavs.[89] Therefore, the proportion of boys among all Jewish infants should have been even higher in 1874. This confirms the existing data for Rechitsa in 1862, which show that of the 129 children born in Jewish families, 56.6 percent were male.[90]

An analysis of masculine names shows that in Rechitsa between 1860 and 1870, the most common names given were Iankel or Iakov (6.5 percent); Movsha or Moshe (6.5 percent); Mordukh (6.2 percent); Itsik or Itska (5.6 percent); Aron (5.6 percent); Berka (5.4 percent); and Zalman (5.1 percent). Unlike Minsk, where Abram was the most common name (11 percent), in Rechitsa it was given to only 4.6 percent of boys. Other common names in Minsk were Iankel or Iakov (10.6 percent) and Aron (10 percent).[91] As these data show, the range of names among Jews in Rechitsa was broader. The lack of any list of female names from Rechitsa at the beginning of the twentieth century does not allow for a comparison with an existing list from Minsk: there the commonest names for girls were Rivka (6.7 percent), Sarah (6.5 percent), and Leah (6 percent).[92]

In this same period there were even greater changes in the natural increase of Rechitsa's Jewish population, changes that, like the migratory processes, directly influenced the overall population increase, the data for which are shown in table 3. As indicated earlier, in 1839 the rate of natural increase among Rechitsa Jews was 2.5 percent; in 1862, 2.4 percent; in 1864, 2.1 percent; and in 1865, 2.9 percent.[93] The statistics for births and deaths in subsequent years are available only for the general population, so one cannot calculate the natural increase among the Jews, but they do make it possible to follow its tendency in Rechitsa, where, from the 1870s onward, Jews began to make up the majority of the population. In 1874 there were 72 deaths in Rechitsa and, as mentioned, 189 births.[94] As a result, the overall natural increase was almost 2.3 percent. In 1885 there were 161 deaths and 275 births (1.8 percent of them illegitimate) in the town; as a result, the general rate of natural increase was much less, only 1.7 percent.[95] It continued to fall by degrees in the years that followed. In 1913 there were 185 deaths in Rechitsa and 351 births (1.7 percent of them illegitimate); as a result the rate of natural increase of the overall population was only 1.3 percent.[96] This is a rather low general natural increase for the time. For example, in 1913 in neighboring Mozyr it was 1.7 percent and in Borisov, 1.4 percent.[97]

I shall now return to everyday matters. The accepted belief before the end of the nineteenth century was that the natural increase of the Jewish population was greater than that of Christians, and the stereotypical view was one of "the high fertility of the Jews." As Chaeran Freeze has shown, beginning in the 1860s the number of Jewish births steadily declined, from highest in comparison with other ethnic groups to the lowest at the end of the century.[98] This decline was compensated for by a relatively lower rate of infant mortality.[99] For example, in Vilna Province, according to the statistical data for 1846–1858, 20 percent of children born to Jews did not survive to their first birthday. For the Orthodox the figure was 25.1 percent and for Catholics 19.3 percent.[100]

Analyzing the reasons for the lower child mortality figures for Jews, David Ransel explains in his study that Jewish newlyweds lived with the parents of the bride, whose mother was able to provide essential help to her daughter. He also notes that Jewish children were generally born in winter, while Orthodox children were usually born in summer, when they had a greater risk of infection by harmful bacteria.[101]

Actually, the number of newlyweds who moved in with the parents of the bride was fairly small. Rich households considered it a mark of prestige for a daughter to marry a young Talmud scholar with a promising future, after which the young couple would move in with the bride's family. On the other hand, as the memoirs of Yehezkel Kotik and Polina Vengerova show, in the Russian Empire newlywed couples also moved in with the parents of the groom.[102] The writer Bogrov describes how in the mid-1830s during negotiations with the father of the bride, the matchmaker, extolling the fine qualities of the groom, would speak of the readiness of the young man's father to allow the couple to live in his house for ten years after the marriage.[103] Moreover, Bogrov himself, almost ten years earlier, had spent the first year of his marriage living with his in-laws in their home.[104]

The selection of a place for the newlyweds to live was not mandatory at that time. In certain cases they moved in with the parents of the groom, in other cases with the parents of the bride, and in still other cases they lived apart from their parents. Several memoirs recount newlyweds taking up residence with the groom's parents.[105] In 1924, Litman Turovskii wrote in his diary that formerly in Rechitsa newlyweds settled as a rule either with the groom's parents or with those of the bride.[106] This was possible largely because a Jewish family was not as patriarchal as a Slavic family of the time. Regarding the above-mentioned kest tradition, the rich people who benefited from it had renounced the practice of marrying off their daughters to budding scholars by the end of the nineteenth century.[107] The economic growth of the final decades of this century and the desire to take advantage of it by receiving a general education, which I shall treat in the next chapter, changed the concept of the ideal son-in-law in the eyes of the rich.

The tradition of moving in with the wife's parents was more highly developed in Soviet times, when women were expected to work. This new norm led to a decline in the birthrate and as a result the number of family members was reduced; also, the woman needed her non-working mother to help look after the children, and she felt she could rely on her more than on her mother-in-law.

On the scale of the whole empire, one can agree with Ransel regarding the period of the highest birthrates for both Orthodox and Jewish couples. However, it is more legitimate to compare their fertility by provinces in the Pale of Settlement. While births to Jews in Minsk Province and adjacent Mogilev Province occurred most often in the month of January in 1867, for Orthodox families of these same provinces most births did not occur in the summer but in the same month of January (corresponding to 10.8 percent and 12.9 percent of all births), and the fewest babies arrived in October (corresponding to 9.9 percent and 9.4 percent of all births). In the adjoining Kiev Province, most births among Jews were in January, whereas births to Orthodox parents occurred mostly in October (10.8 percent), September (10.5 percent), and January (10.4 percent).[108] Wanting to make the best use of their female workforce at harvest time, the peasants planned for the birth of children in the fall or winter.[109]

Whether the survival of infants depended on the time of year in which they were born is definitely a relevant factor. But in contrast to the seasonal fluctuation suggested by David Ransel, physician and demographer Ivan Iastrzhembskii considers that mortality among Jews was highest during the growth periods in January, July, March, and especially February according to the mortality of children up to one year of age in 1878 in the Kherson Uezd. In the other months it was 50–75 percent lower. Mortality among Orthodox infants in the summer months exceeded that of the winter months by 10 percent and in the other seasons was lower.[110]

Evidently under the circumstances of Belorussia with its cool summers, both Jewish and Christian infants died more frequently from respiratory diseases than from the summertime multiplication of microbes. The fact that summertime mortality of infants was significantly lower in the southern Russian provinces than in the northern ones shows that an increased chance of infection in summer was not a defining factor in infant deaths in Russia generally.[111]

Although Ransel writes that the Jews, unlike the Christians, much less frequently used a baby's dummy (this small cloth bag filled with flour or bread paste was a source of bacteria), Jewish mothers did indeed use exactly this same kind of dummy.[112] However, Jewish mothers did not replace breast-feeding with a dummy. The Jewish mother normally found time to breast-feed and care for her child in the course of normal household work; the Orthodox mother, busy with farm labor, often left her child until evening in the care of older children and with a dummy filled with food of little nourishment such as leftover porridge, cottage cheese, blancmange, or kvass. The Orthodox mother would sometimes take the infant with her to the field, where it would remain a long time without any care.[113] The need to be away from home for field work forced the Orthodox mothers to resort to artificial feeding, often with inappropriate or stale food.[114] According to statistical surveys carried out in Kazan Province, Tatar mothers traditionally breast-fed their children at least until the age of one, and the level of infant mortality among them was 1.5 times lower than among the Orthodox.[115] In Russia, Jewish and Bashkir mothers also fed their children breast milk for a long time, and their rate of infant mortality was much lower than that of the Orthodox.[116]

Belorussian townspeople. Courtesy of Evgeny Kovalevsky.

Thus it appears that the prolonged period of breast-feeding was the basic reason for the lower rate of infant mortality among Jews, by comparison with the Orthodox population in Russia generally and in Rechitsa Uezd in particular. One must agree with Ransel's argument that the Orthodox population had a lower standard of personal hygiene than did the Jews, and that this also influenced their higher infant mortality. The Jews more often observed the rules of hygiene prescribed by religion and made more frequent use of qualified medical assistance.[117]

Overall statistics show that Jewish women sought medical help more frequently than did gentile women. Among gentiles, Orthodox women in the countryside particularly rarely sought medical help, especially from midwives. In the whole of Minsk Province in 1911, only 2,909 women giving birth (3 percent of the total number in the province) consulted the Zemstvo midwives who looked after rural areas, not including mestechkos. Furthermore, Orthodox peasant women comprised 73.5 percent of that number; Jewish women, 15.9 percent; Catholics (the source not quite correctly calls these "Polish women"), 10 percent; and Muslims, 0.5 percent.[118] At the same time, the zemstvo midwife was scarcely overburdened with work. On average, she looked after forty-six deliveries a year across the province—less than one delivery per week.[119] This situation was evidently typical for all provinces in the Russian Empire having an Orthodox majority. Even in the central Moscow Province, one of the most advanced places in Russia in terms of medical services, only 2 percent of deliveries at the turn of the century were overseen by midwives; the remainder were assisted by untrained "wise women."[120]

In contrast to the Jews, the Orthodox population, living largely in isolated villages, had fewer opportunities to consult a midwife, much less a specialist in women's or children's diseases. Across the whole broad extent of Rechitsa Uezd, there were only seven zemstvo doctors, including two in Rechitsa. Given the lack of good roads, traveling to the doctor or calling him to a village took too much time. The nearest doctor might be away visiting another patient, or the peasant would put off seeking medical help until the last moment in hope that "things would sort themselves out"; thus help for the patient often came too late. Doctors were not overworked: a doctor in Rechitsa Uezd in 1903 saw on average 411 patients per year, that is, a total of 1.1 patients per day.[121] These statistics show that the distance to the midwife's location was the deciding factor in whether she would be consulted. In rural areas 87 percent of all the midwife-assisted deliveries were done by a midwife who lived no farther than ten versts (one verst is 1,067 meters) away; 8.2 percent when the distance was between ten and twenty versts; 4.4 percent when it was more than twenty versts.[122] On the other hand, the

higher level of education of the Jews in comparison with the Orthodox population generally, and in particular in comparison with the rural population, also
influenced their greater readiness to seek medical help. Peasants often mistrusted
medical people, including midwives.[123] The local Orthodox population was much
more inclined to put their faith in the spells and charms of "wise women" that
superstition held could help a sick person or woman about to give birth. On the
whole, the peasants had much more faith in the "wise woman."[124] To some extent,
this preference developed because the zemstvo midwives were not always successful. In Minsk Province in 1911, among the deliveries mentioned that took
place with the help of midwives, 2.2 percent of the mothers died and 11.4 percent
of the babies were stillborn.[125] Evidently, the level of qualification of midwives in
the mestechkos was higher since it was paid for, and the midwives delivered more
babies and thus undoubtedly had more experience.

It was not uncommon for medical assistants to help with deliveries in rural
areas, although they were located only in the larger villages. There were seventeen medical assistants in Rechitsa Uezd in 1903. Seven of them were attached
to hospitals, which meant that they were not sent out on calls to patients. The
medical assistants were much busier than the doctors. In that same year, medical
assistants (including those attached to hospitals) saw on average 1,324 patients,
that is, 3.6 per day.[126] Although this profession was widespread in Russia, the
medical assistant's professional skills and ability to help a woman giving birth
could not match those of a doctor or a midwife.

Within the towns the Jews and the Orthodox sought medical attention at
roughly the same rate. On the whole, in the towns and large mestechkos the
Orthodox population more frequently resorted to medical help and practiced
better hygiene. The dependence of marriages on seasonal work did not apply
here either. Town and mestechko residents did not need families as large as the
peasants, since they usually had no need of extra hands to help with the work.
Accordingly, in the towns and large mestechkos the natural increase of the Jewish
and the Orthodox populations was roughly the same.[127] At the beginning of the
twentieth century this was also true of Rechitsa, where between 1910 and 1914
the overall population grew by 5.13 percent, that is, 1.2 percent per year on average. The yearly increase in the Jewish population, as shown in table 3, was exactly
the same.

On the whole, in the first quarter of the nineteenth century, statistics show that
the Jewish and Orthodox populations in Rechitsa expanded much more due to
migration than to natural increase. In the following period, until the 1870s, the

number of people coming to Rechitsa was equal to the number migrating from it, and the population expanded primarily due to natural increase. By the early 1870s, more Jews began leaving Rechitsa than coming to it. In 1874 the natural increase among Rechitsa Jews was about 2.3 percent, significantly higher than the average yearly increase in the number of Rechitsa Jews over this period, which was about 1.6 percent. The difference came from the negative balance of migration. Subsequently, until 1917, migration continued to cause the growth rate of Jews in the town to lag behind the yearly rate of natural increase. Jewish migration from Rechitsa, closely linked to the growth of the town's economy, in turn had a negative impact on the growth rate of Rechitsa's overall population.

In these years the changes to the law on military obligations of Jews as well as rising levels of prosperity and education influenced their marriage pattern and rate of natural increase. In the period under consideration, over a stretch of 125 years the percentage of Jews in the population of Rechitsa increased from 20 percent to 59 percent. Such a significant growth exerted a monumental cultural effect on the character of the town. In an inverse relationship to the strengthening of the Jewish character of Rechitsa, the rights of Jews in town self-government steadily shrank. This contradiction was reflected not only in social-ethnic conflict, as shown in chapter 2, but the conflict also had a profound effect on the public life and attitudes of Rechitsa Jews.

5

Prerevolutionary Jewish Social Life and Education

At the very end of the eighteenth century, Hasidism spread through Minsk Province, and its followers gradually displaced the Misnagidim.[1] Hasidism came to Rechitsa at this time as well, and the two tendencies were in conflict there during the first third of the nineteenth century. By the 1830s, Hasidism had become the dominant religious tendency among the Rechitsa Jews. The chief rabbi in the town at that time was Vulf Strashinskii.[2]

All of the *shechita* (literally, "the ritual slaughter of animals and fowl in accordance with religious prescriptions," Hebrew) in the town passed into the hands of Hasidic *shoychets* (a *shoychet* is "a person who performs shechita"). Apart from this, the Hasidic shoychets used smooth, polished knives for the shechita, and these had to be regularly presented to the Hasidic rabbis for inspection. The Hasidic leaders encouraged such a system in order to make the shoychets, who had to use the new knives, more dependent than was the case under the Misnagidim. These smooth knives, as well as special clothing, had a symbolic character whose aim most likely was to demonstrate the spread of Hasidism and so exert some psychological influence on the "Jewish street." Although the Misnagid leadership attempted to resist these symbols, they could do nothing since the symbols did not run contrary to the halacha (normative aspect of Judaism that regulates the everyday life of Jews). The struggle for control of the shechita was also important because everywhere it comprised one of the basic sources of income from religious services. With time, and with the stabilization of relations between the Hasidim and the Misnagidim, the conflict over the selection of knives for the shechita subsided as well.[3]

The discord between the Misnagidim and the Hasidim in Minsk Province at the end of the 1830s attracted the attention of the province administration. At the time, this province had some mestechkos with an overwhelming majority of Hasidim, other mestechkos and towns where the Misnagid tendency was dominant (Slutsk), and yet others where the numbers of Misnagidim and Hasidim were roughly equal (Bobruisk).[4] In compliance with the instructions of the central administration, the governor gathered information about the Hasidic Jews, who despite being known as fanatical sectarians, were noted for their loyalty to Russia and their nonparticipation in the Polish rebellion.[5]

A decade later, however, authorities, low-appreciating their success in the acculturation of Jews and their nurture of *grazhdanstvennost'*, by which was meant primarily an imperial patriotism, came to the conclusion that all the fault of the negative impact of Chassidic teachings. Il'ia Bibikov, governor-general of Vilna Province and the official in charge of the Belorussian provinces, again asked that information about fanaticism of Hasidic Jews be collected. Therefore, in 1853 a new governor of Minsk Province issued instructions for collecting material on the various religious rituals of the Jews and on their adherence to one or another tendency. He directed uezd administrations to send information on the Jewish Skakuny or Kitaevtsy sects that might be in their area. These were the names given in the territory of Belorussia at that time for the Hasidim because of their swaying during prayer and their men's suits made from *kitaika* (a type of cotton fabric). The Rechitsa administration passed this question to Nokhem Pinskii (1810–?), who had been the town rabbi since 1851. Concerned that this inquiry might lead to repressive measures, Pinskii cautiously replied that the Rechitsa Jewish community adhered to Hasidic rituals that had existed since time immemorial. As to the Hasidim's differences from the Misnagidim, who had long been acknowledged by the administration, the rabbi evasively wrote that they lay only in the name and in some minor differences in the words pronounced during prayer.[6] Nevertheless, this answer was not heeded, as was evident from the report of the governor of Minsk Province stating that the "Kitaevtsy" were "stubborn and malicious—and in their manner of thinking [were] irreconcilable foes of Christianity. Their actions [were] harmful not only to Christianity but even to their own coreligionists."[7] The last sentence provides some basis for wondering whether adherents of the Misnagid movement might not also have applied this same characterization to the Hasidim. Fortunately for the Hasidim other information about them gathered by the administration was more complimentary; as a result Bibikov did not agree with his Minsk subordinate.[8]

On the other hand, the *maskils* (literally, "enlightened," Hebrew; an enlightened Jew, follower of the Haskalah rationalistic movement mentioned earlier) also had unflattering things to say about the Hasidim at that time. Thus Grigorii Bogrov, himself the offspring of a Hasidic family in Poltava, venerated the high morality exhibited by the Misnagidim and considered the Hasidim, especially the Polish ones, to be ignoramuses. He made exceptions for one category of the latter—the righteous ones—among the Belorussian Hasidim, about whom he had the Chabad movement in mind. But in Bogrov's view they were less pure than the Polish Hasidim.[9]

Before Rechitsa was appended to Russia at the end of the eighteenth century, there were two Jewish *beis midrash* ("study house," Yiddish) in existence there.[10] In the Russian Empire the number of Jewish religious institutions allowed was determined by rules specifying that a town having up to eighty private Jewish houses might open one synagogue; with every additional thirty houses, one more house of prayer could be opened, although it had to be located a sufficient distance from any Orthodox church. Within these guidelines, Rechitsa had one synagogue and three houses of prayer in the 1830s.[11] These were managed by religious boards of several officials—a Jewish scholar (*uchënyi evrei*), an elder (or *gabe* in Yiddish, *gabai* in Hebrew), a treasurer, and in the synagogues a rabbi as well. In the middle of the nineteenth century, the latter post was held by the aforementioned Nokhem Pinskii. Unlike the Orthodox churches, which received subsidies from the state for their maintenance, Jewish religious institutions existed entirely through the support of members of the Jewish community.

The main source of income for the synagogues or houses of prayer was payment for the best front seats in them. These places were paid for by the *gvir* (well-to-do members of the community) a year in advance and were reserved for them. There were, however, also free places for poor people and soldiers. The Jewish community considered possession of one of the best places to be very prestigious. Thus merchants were prepared to pay dearly for them, the more so because synagogues and houses of prayer were the social centers of the mestechkos; it was here that Jews made agreements about transactions, shared information on prices, discussed the latest laws, and also kept an eye out for potential brides and grooms for their children. Additional sources of income for synagogues and houses of prayer were the *aliya* payment for standing on the bimah (an elevated place in the synagogue on which stands a table for reading the Torah scroll) to read the prayers aloud (often the aliya was sold at auction)—and the sale of *etrog* (an essential item for the Sukkot holiday), which were obtained from abroad. In 1852 the Rechitsa congregants collected two hundred rubles for the four institutions of prayer, including thirty-nine rubles for the synagogue.[12] By 1861 the number of houses of prayer had increased to five, which reflected the numerical growth of the Jewish population of the city.[13]

The spiritual rabbis' (*dukhovnyi ravvin*) sources of income were fees for circumcisions and weddings and taxes on the purchase of yeast and paschal wine. Money from the sale of candles and from the collection box would sometimes come their way. As Shlyoma Zaltsman writes, it was customary to give the rabbi presents on holidays; this was a particular practice of wealthy Jews who had lived for a long time in nearby villages where they rented out land.[14]

In 1857 a new law was promulgated in Russia stating that the only people eligible to hold the post of rabbi were those who had completed studies at the rabbinical colleges set up by the state in Vilna and Zhitomir (these existed from 1844 to 1873) or who had a general secondary and higher education. As a result, these posts gradually became occupied by a new generation of rabbis who had completed preparation at such educational institutions but who lacked any authority among the Jews. At that time Jews regarded rabbinical colleges as hotbeds of atheism; therefore many pious parents were categorically opposed to their children studying in them. Natan Golubov, the member of Narodnaia Volia mentioned in chapter 2, ran away from home in the early 1860s to the Zhitomir rabbinical college. All his father's efforts to have his son returned to Rechitsa from this "den of unbelief" were unsuccessful.[15] The Jewish communities' refusal to accept these rabbis led in 1873 to the transformation of the Zhitomir and Vilna colleges into Jewish teachers' colleges.

According to law, a general meeting of Jewish men of property over the age of twenty-five, registered as local urban dwellers in towns and mestechkos which the Ministry of Internal Affairs had permitted to have a rabbi, was to select a candidate for the post; the candidate had to be a graduate of one of the state-approved educational institutions. The local administration would send their representative to these elections and then confirm the candidacy of the person elected by the Jews for a three-year term. It often happened that those opposed to the rabbi elected by the majority—a rabbi who came to be called "the state rabbi" (*kazënnyi ravvin*)—would submit complaints to the local administration about violations of the voting procedure, bribery of the voters, unjust compilation of the voters' lists, or the insufficient educational qualifications of the chosen candidate. They would appeal the result and request new elections that would exclude the chosen candidate. The other members of the religious board—the treasurer, the elders, and the scholar—were chosen at the same time. Spiritual rabbis often served as scholars in the synagogues.

The Russian administration assigned the state rabbis the function of bureaucrats who were to maintain the register of births and promote official policies within the Jewish community. In the last quarter of the nineteenth century, the authorities did not require them to have a Jewish religious education; they merely needed a knowledge of Russian and a secondary education. Not many people who possessed a secondary education were prepared to take on the ill-paid post of a state rabbi, however. The authorities therefore quite often resorted to a compromise (as in the case of Karasik, which will be discussed later), since finding a candidate who was acceptable to both the Jewish community and the Russian administration was not an easy task. The Russian authorities and the Jewish community made different demands on the state rabbi. The administration wanted to appoint a maskil, who would foster the acculturation of the Jewish population, whereas the Jewish leadership in the small towns and shtetls—and it was they who determined the choice of a candidate—tried to maintain the old, accustomed way of life and alleviate anti-Jewish legislation by granting various benefits or by "closing the eyes" of a bureaucrat to some infringement of the law. Therefore, they sought a state rabbi who could be a shtadlan (see chapter 1) at the local level.

In all likelihood, the first state rabbi in Rechitsa was Kalman Tauber (1841–1901), who had graduated from the Vilna rabbinical college not long before he took his post in 1866. He enjoyed the support of the administration, which came in no small degree from his active participation in the social life of the town and the province. He was a member of a number of societies and committees. Tauber proved his worth particularly through his efforts as a member of the province's statistical committee.[16] He spoke Russian well and urged the Rechitsa Jews to master it.[17] Through Tauber's help another house of prayer was opened in Rechitsa in 1874.[18]

Despite the support of the local administration, in 1883 Kalman Tauber lost the election for the post of state rabbi to Pinkhas Karasik, after which he left for Vilna.[19] In 1887 he headed the Vilna yeshiva Ramailes, following the departure of the previous director, Rabbi Shmuel Isar, after the authorities insisted on the teaching of Russian and general subjects there. Kalman Tauber agreed to teach these subjects, along with Jewish ones. Also, in the autumn of that same year he invited the teacher Isaak Katsenelson to the yeshiva to teach general subjects. Tauber plunged into his responsibilities for the yeshiva, thereby earning the respect of both the authorities and the local Jewish community. Nonetheless, the Vilna yeshiva, attended by 120 to 200 students, experienced constant material difficulties. Thanks only to the personal authority of Kalman Tauber did it manage to survive on donations, which came mainly from the Jewish intelligentsia of the city.[20] To some degree, this support was also an acknowledgment of his profound knowledge of the Talmud, a requirement for holding such a post in Vilna, the main center of Russian Jewish scholarship. Kalman Tauber founded the Takharat Nefesh synagogue in Vilna and was its elder.[21]

At this time Pinkhas Karasik won the respect of Rechitsa residents as director of the Rechitsa Jewish college, a position he assumed in 1880. By 1889 Karasik had managed to have two more houses of prayer opened in the town, and the number of Jewish religious buildings in Rechitsa increased to eight. Some Jewish residents were dissatisfied with Karasik and tried to find an alternative to him at every rabbinical election. In 1893 they managed to gain a majority of votes in favor of Tauber as state rabbi, but when Tauber came to Rechitsa and learned that he would receive a very low salary—only two hundred rubles—from the community, he turned down the post he had been offered.[22] This provoked the displeasure not only of the residents of Rechitsa but of the provincial authorities as well, who did not consider Karasik a suitable state rabbi. They found a formal cause for replacing him: the lack of sufficient educational qualifications. For a few years after these elections, there was a protracted correspondence between the governor of Minsk, the Ministry of Internal Affairs, and the Rechitsa Uezd police officer, who described Karasik, the only remaining candidate for the post, in positive terms. The Minsk director of public schools and the Rechitsa Town Council also spoke positively of Karasik. Karasik's loss of the state rabbi position coincided with the closure of the college in Rechitsa; with ten children, he was left in material difficulties. Only in 1895 was the case at last resolved in his favor: because no one with sufficient education was willing to accept the post of state rabbi in Rechitsa, the Ministry of Internal Affairs, following the practice of the time when positive appraisals were given by local leaders, permitted Karasik once more to offer himself as a candidate for the position. Thereafter, the administration organized a new election in which Pinkhas Karasik won a decisive victory over the Zionist Israel-Barukh Sosnovskii.[23]

Pinkhas Karasik, who held the post of state rabbi until the October Revolution of 1917, was quite active. In 1896, after four years of petitioning, he obtained permission to organize a Jewish school. As noted earlier, in 1907 he took measures to avoid the repetition of a pogrom in Rechitsa. In 1908, in an attempt to ease the situation of couples that had been separated due to migration abroad, Karasik approached the Rabbinical Commission through the provincial administration with a proposal that divorces completed outside the country be made valid in Russia once they had been verified by the appropriate Russian consular officials.[24]

Although the state rabbis were a valuable intermediary link between the Jews and the administration—something that is evident from many intercessions and petitions—the spiritual rabbis enjoyed much more authority within the Jewish community. Although they were not certified as rabbis by the local administration, they had authority in religious circles. Generally, they had certifications issued by well-known rabbis.

Toward the middle of the nineteenth century, Nison Feigin became a spiritual rabbi in Rechitsa. The existing houses of prayer were insufficient, so he gathered his followers for prayer in his own home, which was the Russian law forbade. When the administration learned of this, they began an investigation. The outcome is not known, but evidently the punishment was not severe. Rabbi Feigin lived a long life. At the age of ninety he still found the strength to attend synagogue. According to the recollections of his contemporaries, Nison Feigin once organized a wedding at which some three hundred people danced the Jewish *freylekhs* at one time.[25] A small orchestra, consisting of three musicians playing the violin, the harp, and the flute, was usually invited to a wedding.[26] Additional musicians—a clarinet and another violin—would be summoned for a big wedding. Very often Jews from nearby shtetls played at weddings in Rechitsa.[27]

In the 1860s, Menakhem-Tovia of Piriatin became a spiritual rabbi in Rechitsa. He was a student of the third Chabad tsadik Menakhem-Mendel Shneerson (known as Tsemakh Tsedek), the grandson of Shneur-Zalman of Liady.[28] His arrival exacerbated a struggle between Chabad and several other Hasidic movements that predominated in Rechitsa before.[29]

The Chabad movement became even stronger in Rechitsa with the arrival in 1880 of the *admor* (tsadik, the head of a Hasidic house) Sholom-Dov-Ber Shneerson (1840?–1908), grandson of Tsemakh Tsedek. Before his move to Rechitsa, Sholom-Dov-Ber studied under his father, tsadik Yehuda-Leib (1811–1866), the founder of the Kopys' branch of Chabad, and after his death under his elder brother, Shlomo-Zalman of Kopys' (1830–1900), the only tsadik who supported the Palestinophile movement. Sholom-Dov-Ber Shneerson founded a Chabad yeshiva in the town immediately after his arrival, and by the end of the nineteenth century he had transformed Rechitsa into one of the most important centers of Chabad Hasidism. After the death of his brother Shlomo-Zalman in 1900, Sholom-Dov-Ber became the head of this branch of the Shneersons, the most active part of the Chabad movement at this time.[30]

Chabad is commonly identified with Lubavitch Hasidism. This view is a product of the transmission of Chabad's history by representatives of the prevailing Lubavitch branch of the movement early in the twentieth century. This model of interpreting the development of a doctrine is usually chosen by its followers to prove the direct descent of the current teaching from the philosophical conception of its legendary founder. In the course of doing so, "incorrect" teachings are removed. Using the same pattern, adherents of Leninism made it the direct heir of Marxism. In the light of this grotesque analogy, it is easy to understand how a model for developing a process of succession offers broad opportunities for creating a cult not only of the legendary founder but also for a later practical embodiment of his ideas.

In reality the Lubavitch branch was not the most authoritative in Chabad until the end of the nineteenth century only because its founder Shmuel (1834–1882) was almost twenty years younger than the three other tsadiks, his brothers, the most authoritative of which was Yehuda-Leib. Only after the death of the sons of the founder of the Kopys' dynasty in Chabad did leadership pass to the Lubavitch branch headed by the other Sholom-Dov-Ber Shneerson (1860–1920), the cousin of the Rechitsa tsadik. In 1897 he also founded a yeshiva called Tomchei Temimim. It became popular among the adherents of Chabad and therefore added to the authority of the Lubavitch tsadik, whose charismatic practices surpassed the analogous practices of his Rechitsa namesake.

Regarding the Rechitsa tsadik, the many "responses" (*sheelot ve-tshuvot*, "questions and answers," Hebrew) testify to his great authority and activity during this period. His correspondence in 1885 with four other well-known Chabad rabbis on the question of the first ablution of a girl in the *mikvah* show that even then he enjoyed great respect among the rabbis.[31] Unfortunately, his responses, scattered in various archives, were not assembled into a single collection as were the responses of other respected rabbis.

The well-known religious writer and philosopher Hillel Tseitlin (1871–1942) considered Sholom-Dov-Ber Shneerson to be one of the greatest men of his time.[32] Tseitlin, having heard his sermons in Rechitsa over the course of a year, described their effect on him as follows: "At first his talks seemed to produce no influence over me. But not long after I left Rechitsa I suddenly became enflamed. After that moment—and I was then thirteen years old—I spent half a year literally immersed in eternity. . . . My thoughts were constantly directed toward the divine, scarcely without interruption, even for a second."[33]

Rabbi Shneerson enjoyed immense authority among the Hasidim in Rechitsa as well as far beyond it. Thousands of his followers gathered in Rechitsa for his funeral in 1908. According to legend—probably an exaggerated one—a velvet carpet was spread on the road from his home on Uspenskaia Street right to the Jewish Cemetery. Until 1922 the cemetery was located on an elevation between the Kozlov and the Shchukin Marshes (the latter name derives from the owner of the brick factory mentioned earlier). This cemetery reputedly had some very old tombs. Judging from the old topography of the town, it might well have existed here since the Middle Ages. When the old Jewish Cemetery was closed and a new one opened, the remains of Rabbi Sholom-Dov-Ber Shneerson were transferred to the new site. During the years of Nazi occupation, his tombstone was destroyed, most likely by machine-gun fire when Jews were executed near the grave (see chapter 7). A new tombstone was erected only in 1960.

Sholom-Dov-Ber had four sons and a daughter. His eldest son, Shneur-Zalman Shneerson of Rechitsa (died 1928), married the daughter of Fishel Braitman, a merchant from Kamenets-Podolsk, and went to live with his father-in-law. There he continued his study of the Talmud and made an attempt to become a trader. After the failure of his enterprise he had to return to Rechitsa. A year later, with the help of his father, he received the post of a rabbi in Repki, and several years later he became a rabbi in Gomel. In Kamenets-Podolsk he had two sons. The first of them, Isaac (1881–1969), completed his religious education and was authorized by formal rabbinic certification (*smikha le-rabanut*) as a spiritual rabbi. From 1906 onward he served as a state rabbi in Gorodnia, Chernigov Province, and from 1908 in Chernigov. He immigrated to France after 1917 and there became an entrepreneur. He was a member of the French resistance from 1940 to 1944, and was the initiator of the creation of the Paris memorial "To the Unknown Jewish Martyr" in 1956. In 1968, not long before his death, he published a book in Paris in Yiddish, *The Life and Struggle of Jews in Tsarist Russia, 1905–1917*.[34]

His brother, Yehoshua-Fishel (1887–1958), received an excellent religious education as a child but gradually began to abandon religion in his youth. He wrote in his autobiography of submitting his application to take his high school examinations in order to obtain his school-leaving certificate:

> I at last became convinced that the all-embracing Talmud could not offer me very much by way of an outlook on life, and that its philosophy was bound in a veil of mysticism that was impenetrable for a youth. Without anyone to guide me, I plunged eagerly into the history of philosophy. But here I discovered a new world where almost everything was hidden from me behind a cover of ignorance, and I was lost in an endless ocean of various systems and tendencies. The teacher in the high school program advised me to study. When my parents learned of my intention, they were more than a little distressed since they feared I might abandon the Talmud, in which I was making enormous progress. Wishing to obtain their permission, when I had just turned sixteen I received a diploma with the title of

spiritual rabbi [*smikha le-rabanut*] from the chief rabbi of the uezd, who called me "a brilliant expert in the Talmud." Then my parents, pleased with my extraordinary success, allowed me to begin studying subjects in general education. I began my studies with my usual energy.[35]

Most probably, after he had passed the final examinations, he was unable to enroll in a university in Russia due to the percentage quota and so went to Berlin to study. From 1915 onward he was a doctor of psychology and psychiatry. In 1917 he became an assistant to Vladimir Bekhterev. In 1920 he founded and headed the world's first Faculty of Teaching Methods in Medicine at Kiev University. Yehoshua-Fishel Shneerson left for Warsaw in 1921 and moved to Berlin in 1922 and to the United States in 1927. He organized centers for psychological treatment of children in those countries. In addition to editing psychological journals, he wrote several books on psychology (including a study of the psychological treatment of Jewish children who had suffered from pogroms in Russia) in German and several novels in Yiddish. In 1933 he returned to Warsaw, and in 1937 was repatriated to Erets-Israel.[36] He published a collection of stories in 1954, among them his recollections of his 1905 visit to his well-known grandfather in Rechitsa, when he witnessed the pogrom that took place there.[37]

The second son of Sholom-Dov-Ber Shneerson, Chaim-Ishiyahu (1865–1921), became a rabbi in Parichi in 1894 and then in Romny in 1900. The other two sons lived in Rechitsa. Yehuda-Leib was a rabbi, and Moshe, apart from his religious studies, became a manufacturer, as was noted.[38] None of them was able to become Sholom-Dov-Ber's successor in Rechitsa, and the Shneersons' yeshiva ceased to exist. The Kopys' branch was headed by Sholom-Dov-Ber's younger brother, Rabbi Shmaria-Noakh Shneerson, who founded his own Hasidic house in Bobruisk as early as 1901. When he died in 1923, the Kopys' strain of Chabad ceased to exist, and its followers joined the Lubavitch branch.

As Shaul Stampfer has argued, a communal rabbi had disappeared in the majority of large Jewish communities by the end of of the nineteenth century.[39] However, in towns and mestechkos of Belarus where the number of Jews did not exceed twenty thousand, such as Turov, Samokhvalovichi, and Luban', the pattern of a dominant spiritual rabbi continued to exist.[40] With regard to Rechitsa, published after the death of Sholom-Dov-Ber Shneerson ad in the Hebrew newspaper Hazman on searching a new rabbi, who could "manage the community," even more clearly states on maintenance of communal rabbi.[41]

A record in the announcement that in addition to fees from individuals for mentioned above ritual services, the Rechitsa community was going to pay to a new rabbi 2,000 rubles annually, that is the amount in ten times more than was paid to state rabbi, clear indicates on the attitude to these positions from the community leaders. Similar ads about search of communal rabbi were published by Libava (today Liepāja, Latvia) community in 1905, Slutsk community in 1912 Nova Basan' (today in Ukraine) community in 1913.[42]

On the other hand, in these years as in the past, there were marginal rabbis in Rechitsa whose ritual services were paid directly by their followers, who preferred to pay a rabbi who most appealed to them rather than a communal rabbi appointed by local elite. In contrast to the communal rabbi, who lived on the salary he earned from the community and for which he was supposed to provide a definite list of services, each member of the community paid "his own" rabbi, which served to bring Hasidic Jews closer to their own tsadik. Also, the new system was more flexible in that it gave Jews the right to choose "their own" rabbi. That in turn indirectly influenced the amount paid for each concrete service.

The Hasidic house established in Rechitsa by Sholom-Dov-Ber Shneerson did not replace completely but applied strong pressure on the former Hasidic center that had existed there and that was headed by members of the large and well-known Kom family. The most striking member of that family was Rabbi Chaim-Shlioma Kom (1859–1932), son of the Lubavitcher Hasid Shimon-Zimel. In 1899 Kom published the first of his four books of responses. Included among those who approved the edition were the rabbinical scholars and at a different time the heads of the Volozhin yeshiva Chaim (Halevi) Soloveichik and Rafael Shapiro, as well as another authoritative scholar, Rafael-Mordechai Barishanskii.

In 1904 Kom left for Moscow, where, over eight years, he was a private teacher, a bibliographer, and an educator of children in the home of the wealthy entrepreneur and famous Jewish benefactor Yeshua-Zelik Persits. This post could be obtained only after one passed an oral examination that, in cases like this, was usually given by rabbis whom the potential employer regarded as authoritative; the examination would take place only after the candidate had provided detailed and positive letters of recommendation. Persits's house was a Jewish social and religious center, and well-known rabbis, scholars, and writers often stayed there. It was here that Chaim-Shlioma wrote his last book, *Khaei Shlioma*, which contains his interpretations and commentaries on Jewish religious literature as well has his responses to the Jewish religious tradition. However, he managed to publish this book only several decades later, in Jerusalem.[43]

During his stay in Moscow Chaim-Shlioma maintained his links with the Jews of Rechitsa. Evidence for this comes from a question addressed to him by the respected rabbi from Lomzhi after the pogrom in Rechitsa and published in the

ספר

ויבן שלמה

כולל שני חלקים

חלק שני	חלק ראשון
הגהות ובאורים נכונים על פמ"ג	כולל חדושים ובאורים בגמרא פי'
רש"י ותוס' על כמה מסכתות	ילדי. להרחיב דבריו הק
אשר הלכות ציוד אשר	תם על י"אוה
ולהגעיטם לחקך הקורא ע"פ מקרים	תגני ה' ברהבני לחדש מדעתי.
אמתים .	

כל אלה חוברו מאתי הצעיר

חיים שלמה בי' שמעון זיסל קאם

יליד רעציצע (פלך מינסק)

ברדיטשוב

בדפוס של חיים יעקב שעפטעיל

שנת תרנ"ט לפ"ק

ВАИВЕНЪ СОЛОМА

РАЗН. КОМЕНТАР. КЪ ТАЛМУДУ и ЗАКОН. ЕВР.

Соч. С. Кома.

Бердичевъ Лито-типографія Я. Г. Шефтеля.

1899

Title page of Chaim.-Shlioma Kom's first book.

aforementioned book: "Who should replace the window glass, the owner or the tenant?" The answer was laconic: in the case of a dwelling, the tenant should replace the glass; the owner should replace the window frames. Chaim-Shlioma corresponded with many rabbis, including Chaim-Ishiyahu and Shneur-Zalman Shneerson. However, Chaim-Shlioma Kom managed to gain major influence in the town only after the death of Sholom-Dov-Ber. In 1913 Chaim-Shlioma returned from Moscow to Rechitsa, where his family had remained for all those years. After his arrival he founded his own yeshiva and became the head of the religious court (*beit din rabani*).[44]

I was unable to find additional sources with information about the activity of this court, which is a result of the unofficial character of its activity. The authorities could learn about the activity of such courts only from complaints submitted to it, but even then the head of the court could present an order in the form of advice on how to regulate a conflict; for this reason, they normally were not submitted for separate case management. The Russian historian Sergei Bershadskii writes about the continued activity of the Jewish religious court, despite the official embargo placed upon it.[45] The Minsk Provincial Committee on Jewish Affairs debated the functions of these courts in 1881. Although a majority of the members of the committee (as usual, no more than 10 percent of them were Jews) expressed lack of confidence in the courts, the committee refrained from applying prohibitory measures to them. In the course of the discussion, the curious proposal of the delegate of the Minsk city duma, Sigismund Sventsitskii, to legalize the court with a precise definition of its functions and its subordination to the state judicial system was not supported.[46]

The central government had a negative view of the Jewish religious courts since it regarded their activity as an assault on their own judicial prerogatives. Very few items of information reached it, however, because in such cases and in many similar ones local authorities were afraid that reports up the chain of command would be investigated with possibly unpleasant consequences for them. Therefore, they preferred to settle such conflicts on the spot using oral testimony. Aside from suits, only memoirs and diaries kept by members of the court could have shed light on this activity, but extremely few of these have been found. A similar situation involving the presence of only very rare sources pertaining to the religious courts is characteristic of many towns in Belorussia and Ukraine even though they are known to have existed in the nineteenth century, for example, in Dubrovno, Igumen', Ostroh, and Shklov.

Evidence of the existence of *beit din rabbani* in many places is provided by the preservation until the 1870s of the custom of payments for hazaka, mentioned earlier.[47] Upon the abolition of kahals in Russia, which I shall discuss later, hazaka continued to be one of the sources of unofficial income for rabbis. Such a lengthy retention of this custom under circumstances in which Jews were losing their autonomy could remain the case as long as Jews continued to respect the *beit din rabbani*. Given the restrictions placed on leaseholding by the "Temporary Regulations" mentioned earlier, hazaka had evidently disappeared completely.

Nevertheless, the loss of autonomy by Jews in the Russian Empire, as Shaul Stampfer has argued, led to the gradual decline of the legal authority of the rabbinate dating from the early years of the nineteenth century.[48] This began with the abolition by Russian authorities of the position of chief rabbi of the voivodship and in particular of Minsk Voivodship at the end of the eighteenth century.[49]

During the absence of Chaim-Shliomo Kom from Rechitsa, Shimon Lazarev (1885–1934) emerged as a spiritual rabbi in 1910–1912. He was born in Priluki, received a good religious education in Ekaterinoslav (now Dnepropetrovsk), and then became an entrepreneur. After a few years he suddenly gave up his business and returned to study in a yeshiva. Lazarev soon became a shoychet in Ekaterinoslav and continued to study under well-known rabbis. In 1909 he became a spiritual rabbi in the mestechko of Uvarovichi in Gomel Uezd. He then moved to Rechitsa, where he wrote a book of responses.[50] Along with the other Chabad rabbis of Rechitsa, he supported the Zionist idea and donated funds to assist settlers in Palestine. Lazarev was one of the organizers of the underground heders, yeshivas, and the mutual aid society in Leningrad, for which he was convicted by the Soviet authorities in 1930; he died in prison three years later.[51]

At approximately the same time that Lazarev moved to Rechitsa, Rabbi Avraam-Dov-Ber Reinin arrived from Velizh in Vitebsk Province. He became the principal spiritual authority in the town. In 1913 in his capacity as rabbi of Rechitsa, he also published the book of responses titled *Bat ain*. No well-known scholars among the rabbis approved it as they had for Kom.

According to official figures, Rechitsa had a synagogue and eight Jewish houses of prayer in 1912.[52] Apart from these, in 1910 Rechitsa also had the minyan (literally, "an assembly of no less than ten male Jews who gather for common prayer") of Zalman Sandler, which most probably was unknown to the authorities. By 1912 another unofficial minyan had opened in the town, that of Shmuel-Iakov Dantsig.

One of the houses of prayer, Beis-midrash de-ashkenazim, belonged to the Misnagidim, a small number of whom had always lived in Rechitsa. They were under the spiritual leadership of rabbi Shmuel Kikoin, who died in 1898.[53] It should be noted that in terms of its number of Misnagidim, Rechitsa Uezd did not stand out among many other southeastern counties of Belorussia. Misnagidim predominated, on the other hand, a little to the north, in the center, and in eastern Mogilev Province according to data from the early 1880s. Thus in Mogilev 65.8 percent of all synagogues of various types belonged to them, as did 66.6 percent in Cherikov Uezd, 77.3 percent in Klimovichi Uezd, and 80.8 percent in Mstislav Uezd.[54]

During World War I this movement experienced a certain regeneration in Rechitsa with the arrival there of refugees from western Belorussia and, specifically, of followers of Rabbi Iosif Uziel Gurovich (1846–1920), who was called the Elder of Novogrudok. In 1914 he arrived in Gomel from the area then overtaken by the war front with a Misnagid yeshiva he had established in Novogrudok. This yeshiva belonged to the *Baalei musar* (members of a moralistic movement *musar*—in Hebrew, *musar* means "morals"). Rabbi Gurovich was one of the most active followers of this spiritual and ethical movement. It had arisen in the mid-nineteenth century among the Misnagidim, and its aim was the religious, moral, and ascetic training of the personality. This movement had to withstand Hasidism, on the one hand, and Haskalah (enlightenment) and the assimilation linked with it on the other. Two types of "Lithuanian" yeshivas arose within the framework of this movement: first, the Slobodka and the Novogrudok, in which the discussion of ethical problems occupied an important place. The second type of yeshiva, whose model became the *Baalei musar* of Rabbi Gurovich, differed from the first in its special techniques of psychological self-therapy aimed at freeing the person from characteristic flaws of human nature such as vanity and the lust for money.

Study in the yeshiva quickly resumed in one of the synagogues of Gomel. The Elder of Novogrudok would send out his graduates to spread the teachings and to organize small yeshivas in many places, including the mestechkos and the towns of southeastern Belorussia: Rechitsa, Rogachev, Bragin, Mozyr, Khoiniki, Poddobrianka, and Iurovichi.[55] Rabbi Gurovich was trying to create a network of Misnagid education that would compete with the Chabad movement. After the death of this famous rabbi the Gomel center, *Baalei musar* continued, despite organizational problems, to support the small Rechitsa yeshiva until its leaders decided to immigrate to Poland in 1922.[56] It is possible that the Rechitsa members of the movement also fled abroad at that same time.

EDUCATION

All Jewish boys in Rechitsa received a religious education in traditional heders, of which there were five in the mid-nineteenth century. By the end of the century, that number had doubled. Boys usually began studies at the age of five.[57] There were several levels of heders. Children would begin in a heder where they learned to read the prayer book in Hebrew; then they would continue in a higher-level heder where they studied the Torah (Pentateuch). In heders of the highest level, the children learned about the Talmud.[58] Writing in Hebrew was not a part of the heder program, so parents who wished to give their child a higher level of education would arrange with a melamed (a teacher in a heder) for additional lessons that were paid for separately. Studies usually lasted from 9:00 a.m. to 8:00 p.m., with a lunch break from 1:00 to 3:00 p.m. Children went home for lunch but had breakfast in the heder itself. July and August were holiday months for the students.

The majority of the heders in Rechitsa were housed in rented rooms in private homes and only rarely in the homes of the melameds themselves. In the mid-nineteenth century all five of the Rechitsa heders were concentrated on two streets, Polevaia and Proboinaia (later Uspenskaia Street). The level of instruction in the heders was often not very high. At the end of the century, the melameds received from 120 to 260 rubles per year, depending on their qualifications and the demand. There were usually five to ten pupils in a heder. Parents paid on average 2 rubles a month for each pupil. Heders with better-qualified and more prestigious melameds who could devote more attention to the children were rather scarce. When their child enrolled for study, the parents would come to an agreement about the terms. Most important for them in the choice of a melamed were two mutually dependent factors—the melamed's knowledge and the size of the fees. When they sent their child to study with a melamed, the majority of parents did not know or were unable to evaluate the level of his knowledge and so trusted the recommendations of rabbis or the experience of their friends and relatives. There was great competition among melameds of all levels. More than a few Rechitsa melameds who were unable to organize a heder in the town set themselves up in other Belorussian mestechkos and towns.[59]

Girls were taught by *shraybers* (a shrayber is a "scribe") who either came to their homes or who taught groups of girls in their own homes. Much less time was given to the education of girls in families with very low incomes. Although schooling was not mandatory, as early as the mid-1830s—as the memoirs of Grigorii Bogrov in the episode of the marriage proposal illustrate—it was a definite minus if the bride was illiterate.[60] With the passage of time, under the influence of Haskalah, attitudes regarding the education of girls became more serious.

At the beginning of the twentieth century, parents paid the shrayber about three rubles a year for teaching each girl.[61] According to the findings of Shaul

Stampfer, girls mastered grammar much more quickly than boys did. One of the main reasons for this was that girls learned to read in Yiddish, a language they had understood since childhood; boys, on the other hand, learned in Hebrew, a language they did not know at all. Thus, girls could move rather quickly to reading independently in the considerable literature that existed in Yiddish. They could also quickly master Yiddish because vowels were indicated in the text, whereas Hebrew texts usually indicated only a small number of vowels. The curriculum for girls included prayers, reading and writing in Yiddish, the books *Nachlas tsevi* (a treatise on ethics in Yiddish) and *Tsenah urenah* (a collection of midrashim for women in Yiddish). Apart from these studies, girls learned handcrafts. Girls, unlike boys, were not physically punished by their teachers.[62]

In the 1880s, through the efforts of the Jewish community, a Talmud Torah was opened in Rechitsa. Unlike the heders, which required payment of fees, schools of this type were supported by the community, and children of poor families could receive a free primary religious education in them. The Talmud Torahs often barely eked out an existence: children huddled together in small rooms that were unsuitable for schools; teaching was at a low level, since teachers' salaries were tiny. The Talmud Torah in Rechitsa differed favorably from such struggling examples. In 1903 it had its own separate building and a good teacher. The school's interior, however, was not well appointed, a problem that was even discussed in the Yiddish newspaper *Der Fraind*.[63] In spite of the financial difficulties it encountered, this Talmud Torah continued to exist until the early 1920s. During the 1890s, when the number of heders in the whole of Minsk Province grew from 90 to 523 because of the increase of the Jewish population, several dozen new heders were opened in Rechitsa as well. Nevertheless by 1913 the total number of heders in the province had declined to 471.[64]

A heder education usually ended when the child was between nine and twelve.[65] Very few children continued their studies in a beit-midrash. Until the end of the nineteenth century, the completion of the heder marked the end not only of the religious education of most children but also of their education generally. There were several reasons for this. In the mestechkos and even in the larger towns, most families kept to the tradition of limiting education only to religious instruction. This was due primarily to the limited financial means of many parents, particularly up to the last quarter of the nineteenth century. There were also very few schools within the Pale of Settlement at the time, particularly in the mestechkos.

The authorities looked askance at heders. With no opportunities to prohibit them, beginning in the 1840s they made various attempts to affect them negatively. This effort was manifested in the introduction of regulations concerning cleanliness in heders, verification that melameds possessed certificates issued by committees of Jewish institutions, instructions that they follow special guidelines devised by the Department of Public Education, and the imposition of certain obligations on state rabbis (1856 law) to compile data concerning melameds and how much they were paid, lists of pupils, and information about where the heder was located and in what condition.

Sometimes special provincial committees on Jewish affairs even adopted decisions to prohibit instruction in heders and yeshivas or to prosecute melameds who violated this order. Such a decision was reached unanimously by the Minsk Provincial Committee in 1881. Osip Gurvich, who held the position of "learned Jew" on the governor's staff, made a significant contribution to the passage of this ordinance. Perceived as a representative "of the Jews," he made statements, such as, "Among Jews there is not even one halfway reasonable person who would not want the destruction of the heders," that deluded the other thirty, Christian members of the committee.[66] The embargo was not confirmed by the minister of internal affairs in the first place for fear that Jews would "swarm" into public educational institutions and crowd out Christian children, who, in the opinion of the bureaucrats, developed more slowly.

As far back as the time of the Polish uprising of 1863–1864, Mikhail Murav'ëv, the governor-general of the Northwestern Territory, which comprised Minsk Province, forbade Jews to speak Polish and ordered them on pain of fines to teach their sons Russian. In 1865 he had imposed responsibility for the fulfillment of these instructions on rabbis and the members of the committee on Jewish affairs and had ordered them to collect the candle tax (discussed below), which would be used to finance the payment of teachers.[67] It got even to enforced by the police concentration of children to state schools in Russian for Jews.[68] Succeed to Murav'ëv—Konstantin von Kaufman tried in June 1866 to limit the Yiddish press in the Northwestern Territory.[69] Apparently their orders were canceled in 1867–1868 the pressure of Russification policies in this region weakened.

These orders, as well as the initiative Gurvich, were nothing but a clumsy attempt to expand quite a thin layer of loyal people in the border region through the acculturation of the Jews. Encouraged by the loyalty of the Jews during the Polish uprising,[70] the authorities sought to accelerate the nurture of the Jews' grazhdanstvennost', seeing the inevitability of a future war with Germany. The authorities saw in Yiddish the German cultural influence on the Jews. As shown by Michael Dolbilov, fighting against Germanization of Jews was one of the cornerstones of the Jewish policy in the Northwest Territory.[71]

The atmosphere of Russification permitted local maskil Leiba Rubin in the early 1870s to open a private Jewish two-year school for boys that offered instruction in Russian.[72] Jewish religion and Hebrew were taught there as well as Russian and the four arithmetical functions of mathematics. Despite the opening of this school, the town still did not have enough educational institutions generally and ones for Jews in particular, and this had an impact on the level of Jewish education. For example, in 1926 among the Jewish population of Rechitsa born in the years 1857–1876, the percentage of those able to read and write Yiddish and Russian was 76.5 for men and 42.5 for women. In Rogachev the literacy figures for Jews born in the same period were 76 percent and 43.8 percent respectively. In the much larger city of Gomel the literacy rate was higher: 81.5 percent for men and 50.6 percent for women.[73]

Literacy among the non-Jewish population of Rechitsa was even lower than that of the Jews—65 percent for men and 30 percent for women.[74] Against this background seems implausible the data of the 1897 census, according to which among Jews in Rechitsa literate were the 42.9 percent of men and 22.6 percent of women, and among Orthodoxes were 41.9 percent of men and 18.8 percent of women.[75]

The problem with education in Rechitsa was not an exception. The situation was the same throughout the whole General-Governorship of Vilna, where for every 10,000 Jews only 14.7 Jewish children were enrolled in school. There were even fewer students among the Orthodox and the Catholics, 5.5 and 10.2 students, respectively, while among the Lutherans there were twice as many, 31.3 students.[76]

Rubin made the case for the need to open a trade school for low-income Jews in the Great Synagogue in 1880 during prayers on the twenty-fifth anniversary of the reign of Alexander II.[77] A year later the correspondent for the newspaper *Russkii evrei* described the situation of education in Rechitsa in somber tones: "Education among the Jewish community in Rechitsa is today in a truly regrettable state. One cannot find here a single Jew with an acceptable level of education, a fact that, of course, is a result not only of the lack of any state-sponsored educational institution, but also the lack of private, experienced tutors. On the other hand, Rechitsa abounds in Orthodox Jews who consider it a sin to promote the intellectual development and the moral improvement of their contemporaries."[78]

The private Jewish school was in continual financial difficulties. In 1879–1880 it was supported by the community, which provided, with permission of the administration, 150 rubles from the collection for candles.[79] In 1880 the aforementioned Pinkhas Karasik was appointed by order of the Vilna School Division as head of this school. He had qualified as a teacher after completing the Rechitsa Uezd school. Karasik remained head of the school until 1893, when it was temporarily closed due to lack of funds.[80] In 1892 he and a group of Jews had tried to get permission to teach girls in this school in order to avoid its closure. The provincial education bureaucrats at first ignored his request and petitions. Only in August 1895 did the new director of public education for Minsk Province, Nikolai Akoronko, agree to the admission of girls, to be taught separately, and on the condition that the community be entirely responsible for providing some 350–400 rubles of support each year and that the education be provided free. Then the general meeting of the Jewish community and the mayor, Alexander Batagovskii, concerned to renew teaching in the school, had to agree to provide this money from the collection box, an event that will be discussed later.[81] Thanks to this measure, the teaching of boys recommenced in November 1895.[82]

The section for girls, run by the teacher Sara Gershenzon, was opened almost a year later, in September 1896. Since there were no other schools for girls in the town, a large number of girls—110—enrolled here. Because the schools could not accept all those who wished to enroll, the school authorities, headed by Karasik, directed on September 22 that more than 40 girls from the most prosperous families should be excluded; they believed that these families could provide for educating their daughters in other cities—Minsk, Kiev, or Gomel. That same day a committee of several Jews made the selection, and the girls were excluded. In his article on this selection, the correspondent of the *Minsk Listok* noted that "this was a division of the poor into those who were simply impoverished and those who were desperately impoverished."[83] When one considers the self-interest of the school authorities precisely in abandoning the children of rich parents, this decision of the community leaders speaks even more persuasively of the philosophical change in the minds of the local elite in favor of the just reorganization of society. Such rethinking most probably occurred under the influence of public opinion in the ranks of the Russian intelligentsia. The Jewish community had no opportunity to receive aid for this school from the town authorities. In 1896 the Town Council spent only 1,325 rubles on education, that is, 6.4 percent of the town's expenditures, and all the money went to the church parish school.[84]

As a result of the development of a system of public elementary schools in the Pale of Settlement by the end of the nineteenth century and Jewish parents' changing attitudes about educating their daughters, the percentage of girls in schools outpaced that of boys. The 1897 census shows that girls comprised 54 percent of all Jewish pupils in primary schools. Girls did not form a majority in primary schools among any other ethnic group in Russia.[85] At the beginning of the twentieth century, this sexual imbalance in primary schools became even more pronounced, in view of the exclusion of Jewish girls from the percentage norms and due to a new attitude among the Jewish population toward general education. Of course, this change affected boys as well, but in their case the parents remained more conservative and gave priority to the heder and the beit-midrash. Also, in many families the boys, unlike girls, were sent off as apprentices by the age of thirteen or fourteen.

Only the Jewish elite could give their children a complete heder education, which meant that at thirteen they could independently begin to study complex Talmudic texts. But it is difficult to call study in a beit-midrash completely independent inasmuch as an atmosphere of collective study of difficult passages of the Talmud was the rule there; novices therefore listened intently to the opinion of older authoritative students and were always able to double-check their work with them. These are exactly the circumstances where adherence to one or another religious movement would take root.

The substandard level of teaching in the Rechitsa heders and the aspirations of parents to provide their boys with a general education induced Israel-Yehuda Adler (1870–1948), a social activist and innovative pedagogue, to open a Reform heder (*cheder metukan*) there in 1900. Iakov Rivenzon, a member of the Society for the Support of Ancient Hebrew (Tomkhei sfat ever), which had opened in Rechitsa in that same year, was the first teacher in the heder. Along with religious subjects, the children in this school studied Hebrew by the "Hebrew in Hebrew" system, and Russian, mathematics, and the geography and history of Palestine.[86] The idea of creating a Reform heder came from the Zionist intelligentsia and was intended to embody the symbiosis of a high-level, traditional Jewish education and a general education appropriate for the demands of the era. Moshe Frank maintains that it was the first experiment in creating such a school in Russia, and it was done before Adler opened a Reform heder in Pinsk in 1900, a school that became widely known for its successes. In 1901 Adler opened a similar heder in Gomel. After Reform heders had spread in Belorussia, they began appearing in many other places within the Russian Empire. At the same time, such schools were often resisted by rabbis and melameds.[87] The rabbis of Rechitsa, as mentioned earlier, had traditionally sympathized with the Zionist idea, and they also recognized the need for Jewish schools on a higher level. They were not opposed to the opening of the Reform heder. For example, Pinkhas, the grandson of Rabbi Sholom-Dov-Ber Shneerson, studied in the Rechitsa Reform heder. Isaac (1898–?), the son of Tsvi Bykhovskii, one of those very close to the Rechitsa rabbi

Sholom-Dov-Ber Shneerson, also graduated from this Reform heder.[88] Iakov-Pinkhas, one of the sons of Rabbi Chaim-Shlioma Kom, head of another Chabad center in Rechitsa, also studied there.[89]

In 1903, when Moshe Frank (at that time his last name was Raykhenshtein) at the age of five went to study in the Reform heder, it was called in the town *Die metoda* or *Lapitskis metoda*. It had become, in fact, a different heder, in a different building, and with different teachers. It had opened in 1901–1902 to replace its predecessor and continued to exist until 1918. Over those years, Mendel Lapitskii and the aforementioned Israel-Barukh Sosnovskii ran it and taught in it. Initially, the teacher M. Shkliar, who had come from Gomel with Adler's recommendation, taught in this heder for several years; he later returned to Gomel, however. According to Frank's memoirs, all the teachers had formerly studied in yeshivas, but Lapitskii and Shkliar were Zionists and members of the intelligentsia of a new type, while Sosnovskii was part of the older generation. They all avoided speaking Yiddish. The children who began their studies in the Reform heder found themselves in an unfamiliar atmosphere where the teachers and the older pupils spoke only Hebrew. At first all the students were supposed to wear a flat, Lithuanian yarmulke with sharp corners and deep red in color, although after several years they were permitted to wear regular caps. Jewish holidays were celebrated in the heder, and to honor them the children often put on theatrical performances. Israel-Yeguda Adler, who continued to look after this heder until his departure for Palestine in 1904, was invited to one of these amateur performances held in the home of Pesakh-Leiba Gurovich. In later years the new teachers Zalman Vilenskii and I. L'vovich began working there. The Reform heder in Rechitsa was distinct from Adler's Gomel heder in that children there were not taught Russian and the other general subjects necessary for admission to a gymnasium.

The popularity of the Reform cheder aroused hostile feelings among melameds and private teachers. In 1914 several of them wrote the chief inspector of educational institutions in the province to complain that a new heder was sowing seeds of sedition among the pupils. The official, however, considered the complaint and realized that professional rivalry had prompted it.[90]

For preparation in Russian and the other general subjects, the Rechitsa Jews sought private tutors for their children. The study of the shtetl Krasnopol'e, mentioned earlier, describes a situation in education that likely differed little from the one in Rechitsa; it shows that private tutors often had no diplomas, and the subjects they offered were by no means complex. They would teach the children to read and write Russian and to master the four basic rules of arithmetic. These tutors earned a meager wage for their efforts: Lazar Rokhlin, author of the study, writes that it varied "between the limits of fifty kopecks to five rubles per month; three rubles a month was considered good compensation, and a whole family could usually study for five rubles."[91]

One may assume that in Rechitsa and in the mestechkos of Eastern Europe as a whole only a few were able to write more than their given name and surname. A greater number of children acquired the ability to read Hebrew by attending the elementary grades of heders, but because they lacked opportunities to apply this knowledge in everyday life, even these skills were forgotten. Pavel Chubinskii may be right in reporting that in Lithuania and Belorussia 20–25 percent of the Jewish population knew Hebrew, whereas in Ukraine the figure was 15–20 percent.[92] Surely a greater number of Jews could read Yiddish, which they studied outside the school system.

The educational situation among Christians was even worse than the system of heders that was so severely criticized by contemporaries. Church parish schools gave their pupils a very weak elementary education. The most advanced educational institution in Rechitsa for many years was the parish school with a two-year cycle of schooling; it had existed there at least since the first decade of the nineteenth century. In the early 1860s the children there had received, apart from Scripture lessons, instruction in mathematics, geography, spelling, penmanship, draftsmanship, and drawing.[93]

In the mid-1860s, along with thirty Orthodox pupils, six Catholics, and one Lutheran, seven Jews were enrolled in this school.[94] In the 1870s a women's section was opened there, and girls studied alternately with boys. Although there were significantly fewer Jewish children there than Christians, the Christian parents wanted only the Jews to bear the cost of renting accommodations for the school. Jewish parents naturally resisted that situation; therefore in 1879 the school was forced to close temporarily because of lack of funds. In the mid-1880s an attempt was made to reopen it, but material problems led to its rapid closing.[95]

By the end of the nineteenth century, there were several primary church-parish schools in the town but only a single one-year active public school.[96] The lack of schools had negative consequences for the townspeople. There were not enough schools anywhere in the territory of Belorussia. There were no higher educational institutions there that could graduate qualified teachers, doctors, lawyers, and so on. As a result, many midsized Belorussian towns and mestechkos had scarcely any intelligentsia, particularly an intelligentsia that could provide teachers. Rechitsa was one such place.[97] Also, a teaching position had little attraction in Russia because it was poorly paid—300–400 rubles per year, at a time when a doctor or an agronomist could earn 1,000–1,500 rubles and an engineer 2,000 rubles a year.[98]

Concerned about the low level of education in Rechitsa, the province's inspector of public schools encouraged the opening there in 1900 of a three-year boys' Pushkin Public School in a house rented from Shlëma Margolin. In 1901 81 pupils were enrolled there; in 1907, 198; and in 1915, 168.[99] A series of prosperous Jews attempted to have their children educated there, but given a general state policy of restricting the admission of Jews to public educational institutions, the school's administration accepted only a few of them. In 1904 the school's first class graduated, and among them was only one Jew, Shmaia Gorelik. In 1905 the Ministry of Public Education at last opened a nonclassical secondary school on Rechitsa's central thoroughfare, Uspenskaia Street (in Soviet times the Kalinin Movie Theater was housed in this building). There were three teachers on staff. Apart from Russian, the children learned German and French, and there were many Jewish students.

The government, which had previously urged the Jews to accept broader, general education, now seemed unprepared for their acculturation. The authorities regarded Jews—not without some basis—as more receptive to revolutionary ideas because of the restrictions on their legal status; they were concerned that

The Pushkin School, early twentieth century.

the Jews might spread revolutionary ideas among the other students in secular schools. In an effort to avoid this, the government in 1887 introduced *numerus clausus* (restrictive quotas) on secondary and higher educational institutions for men. Jews were not the only ones faced with restrictive quotas. In that same year of 1887, the authorities promulgated a law popularly called the "law of the cook's children." This law provided for reducing the number of children of "coachmen, servants, cooks, laundrywomen, small shopkeepers, and similar people" admitted to secondary schools since, from the viewpoint of the minister of education, Ivan Delianov, giving such people an education would lead to "dissatisfaction with their usual way of life and animosity toward the inequality that exist[ed] and [was] an inevitable product of the nature of things."[100] Although the stated measure, directed against Jews, did not affect women's educational institutions, some of them instituted restrictions on their own if they already had enough female Christian entrants. In 1914 the admission of Jewish girls to the Vitebsk high school was halted.[101]

Restrictive measures toward Jews in the area of education had several significant results: (1) They made a secondary education even more attractive for them, thus fostering their acculturation. (2) A rather significant portion of Jewish young people who did not pass the harsh selection process and could not overcome the notorious quota system in Russia went abroad for their higher education. They returned infected by revolutionary ideas whose spread could not be impeded in Russia by any police measures. (3) Many secondary and higher educational institutions within the Pale of Settlement either closed their doors because of insufficient numbers of non-Jewish students or where compelled to lower standards for admission and for performance generally, a fact that had a negative effect on the level of study.

The aforementioned high school in Rechitsa did not function for long because of the 10 percent quota on the admission of Jewish children in boys' secondary schools within the Pale of Settlement. This quota, imposed in Russia in 1887 by a special decree, had initially not been introduced in Rechitsa, and the high school was able to begin operating. When it was imposed in 1911, there were not enough Christian children enrolled in the school and it closed.[102]

In 1906 Elizaveta Gavrilova opened, at her own expense, a primary school for girls in Rechitsa. In 1908 it received the status of *progymnasium* and in 1911 of women's gymnasium.[103] The opening of this classical high school became possible thanks to the fact that the quota for women's schools was not widespread. On the eve of World War I, thirteen teachers taught 300 students there. Almost two-thirds of them (161, or 63.5 percent) were Jews; 86, or 28.5 percent, were

Orthodox; 18 (6 percent) were Catholics; and the remainder Muslims or Old Believers. Some 11 percent of the girls were daughters of nobles or civil servants. The school's yearly budget was 24,000 rubles, and it was enhanced by school fees and donations.[104]

Another secondary school in Rechitsa was the higher primary school that opened about the same time; its administrator was Evstafii Oldekop. Other lower schools were operating in Rechitsa at this time: there were four one-year parish schools; a two-year parish school; an introductory trade school; a private, one-year Jewish school; and a private two-year Jewish school.[105] In all, there were 1,243 students in Rechitsa schools at the time, comprising 10 percent of the town's residents. Within Minsk Province this indicator was higher only in Igumen'.[106] A boys' gymnasium was opened in Rechitsa only in 1916, using the resources of a school relocated there from Lida.[107]

The quota system and insufficient state funding retarded the development of a Jewish and, most probably, of a Belorussian intelligentsia, and it had an impact on general secondary education in Rechitsa as well. The restrictive measures did not permit the creation of a system of secondary schools for boys. The town had a particularly acute need for a boys' gymnasium—a secondary school of the highest level that could prepare young people for admission to a university. Such a gymnasium had been opened in neighboring Mozyr as early as 1859.[108] In general the outflow of young people with great potential, both Jewish and gentile, had a negative effect on the level of culture both in Rechitsa and in many other mestechkos within the Pale of Settlement.

At the same time, the efforts of the most advanced members of Jewish society and the Ministry of Education promoted the growth of primary education among the Jewish and the gentile populations of Rechitsa at the beginning of the twentieth century. According to statistics for 1926, the share of literate people among the Jewish population born between 1897 and 1906 had grown to 96 percent of the men and 93 percent of the women.[109] These figures show, among other things, that the widespread view of a significant difference in literacy between men and women is mistaken. A study of the educational level of Minsk tradesmen offers further support: the study indicates that at the beginning of the twentieth century the proportion of illiterates among women was higher than that among men by 6 to 10 percent.[110] Among the gentile population in the same age group, the proportion of literates, compared with the figures cited earlier for those born between 1857 and 1876, was even greater—94 percent among men and 82 percent among women. It must be kept in mind, of course, that a portion of the illiterate population learned to read and write later, in postrevolutionary times.

The increase of the number of literate girls over the last quarter of the nineteenth century was not the result of an abstract recognition of the value of an education but rather a way to ensure the attainment of practical goals. These goals included the ability to conduct commercial business deals in Russian, given the growth of economic activity among Jews, with the concomitant need to communicate with the authorities; the demand for news and the rapidly growing requirements of correspondence among themselves also spurred the desire for education. The growth of written sales correspondence was stimulated by the sharply increasing migration of Jews within the Russian Empire. The documents of the chancery of the governor-general of Turkestan that I have investigated contain many copies of letters exchanged for various reasons by Jews in the Pale of Settlement and the new Russian colony (for example, the need to learn how to enable the illegal immigration of friends and relatives to Turkestan) that were of interest to the censors.

A reflection of the growing need for Jews to compose business letters, documents, and wills was a publication by Abram Paperna in Warsaw in 1875: "The Russian-Jewish Letter Book."[111] This is the first compendium of its kind in Russia consisting of models of documents and business letters; to enable a complete understanding of its contents it provides translations into Hebrew in almost all cases. Although anyone, including non-Jews, could use the models, the translations nevertheless show that the author, who completed studies at a state Jewish institution, was oriented to a definite circle of readers.

In addition to serving business and communication purposes among Jews within the Pale of Settlement and beyond its borders, correspondence was the only way to connect with relatives who had emigrated abroad. The letters of the Rapoport sisters, one of whom stayed in Kholmech in Rechitsa Uezd while the other immigrated to the United States, exemplify the epistolary excellence that could be attained by Jewish women in both Yiddish and Russian.[112] The new Jewish approach to education, and in particular to the education of women, can possibly be attributed to the increased economic activity of townspeople and the rural population in the last quarter of the nineteenth century.

Until the end of the nineteenth century, only a small portion of the Jewish population of Rechitsa spoke Russian. With time, this portion increased, particularly among young people, since the rapid economic growth of the town and all of Belorussia in the last third of the nineteenth century demanded a good knowledge of the Russian language. According to Moshe Frank, it was impossible to find work in Rechitsa not only as a bookkeeper or a salesman but even as a simple shop assistant without knowing Russian. The opening of general, nonreligious schools in Rechitsa at the beginning of the twentieth century encouraged the process of Russification of the Jewish population, which had become particularly strong in the town on the eve of World War I.[113]

THE JEWISH COMMUNITY AND SOCIAL MOVEMENTS

Until the 1820s the Jewish kahal itself was in charge of the collection box, an inner-community tax levied primarily on the sale of kosher meat.[114] This tax had been introduced by Jewish kahals within the Polish-Lithuanian Commonwealth in the second half of the seventeenth century when, as a result of Cossack, Russian, and Swedish invasions, the Jews had become impoverished and deeply in debt to the state treasury for taxes. After the accession of the Polish-Lithuanian Commonwealth to Russia, this collection box remained in effect, although the Jews no longer able had control over it. In accordance with the new demands of the Russian authorities, "the box" was to be used not only for the maintenance of synagogues, religious officials, and charities but, first and without fail, for the needs of the town: public lighting, improving and cleaning the town, and paying salaries to city officials. Thus the tax itself had to be increased. The kahals were responsible for keeping records of income to and expenditures from the collection boxes; the Russian administration checked these records.

Through its close connection with the shechita, the collection box caused an increase in the price of meat, something that was already beyond the means of many. The situation in Rechitsa differed little from the one that G. Natanson found in one of the uezd towns of the Northwestern region in 1879. Without naming the mestechko, the author writes that of a thousand Jewish families in it, only thirty to forty ate meat each day; two to three hundred would have meat on Saturdays. The remainder would eat meat only on holidays, and then the special money to pay for it—*basar aniim* (literally, "meat for the poor")—was usually collected from prosperous families.[115] Another contemporary, describing the situation of Jews in Minsk Province, wrote in 1880 that because of the collection-box tax, meat could be eaten only on Saturdays and poultry even more rarely. As a result, a saying even emerged that "a Jew eats a chicken only when he is sick or the chicken is sick."[116] Natanson himself concluded that the sickly condition of Jewish draftees was the result of the impoverished state of the Jewish population, made even more difficult by the heavy burden of requisitions for the collection boxes.[117]

In towns, where the overall sum of the collection box was significant, the right of collecting it from the community, in accordance with the 1825 law, was leased to Jews for a four-year term at a substantial sum. So it was that in Rechitsa and the neighboring shtetl of Iurovichi, the right for collections for kosher meat for the period 1840–1843 was given jointly to the aforementioned Nison Feigin and his uncle, Leiba Feigin. Nison was the grandson of the well-known tsadik Shender of Iurovichi and son of the important merchant, rabbi, and social activist Litman (Motel) Feigin. The latter was quite a popular figure in the Jewish community, since he tried to use his many connections in government circles in the early 1830s to ease the lot of the Jews. He often wrote to chief of gendarmes and executive director of the Third Section Count Alexander von Benkendorf and to Nicholas I, acting in fact as a shtadlan.[118]

The sums paid by the Feigins to the state treasury for the right to control the collection box were 3,850 rubles for Rechitsa and 415 rubles for Yurovichi. The rights for collections for kosher meat in other mestechkos in Rechitsa Uezd in those years were leased to the Rechitsa merchants of the third guild: Zalman Frenkel in Kholmech (690 rubles), Loev (2,230 rubles), and Kholui (300 rubles); and Beniamin Ravikovich in Bragin (3,760 rubles) and Khoiniki (1,290 rubles).[119]

The descendants of the entrepreneur-shtadlan turned out to be poor businessmen, however. The Feigins never considered that the overwhelming majority of Rechitsa Jews were impoverished, as noted, and rarely bought meat. Nison Feigin was unable to pay off the entire cost of leasing the collection rights in Rechitsa, and as a result, the administration launched a legal action against him. After a prolonged investigation, in August 1855 his house, furniture, and other household utensils were sold at public auction to clear his debt.[120]

No one could be found who was bold enough to pay such a high cost for the rights to collect fees for kosher meat in Rechitsa, and in 1857 the authorities were compelled to reduce the price to 2,510 rubles, that is, to 2 rubles for every Jew registered in the tenth census. But even that sum was substantial for the poor Rechitsa Jews. In the mestechkos of the uezd the collection-box tax was not quite half that. In 1857, 535 rubles in candle taxes (a tax on candles for Jewish education) were collected from the Jews of Rechitsa, that is, an additional 0.42 rubles per person). In the mestechkos of the uezd, the proceeds from this tax were also lower.[121]

Impoverishment due to high taxes, together with other restrictions (the most important of which economically was the ban on ownership of property in rural areas and, accordingly, the difficulty of becoming an entrepreneur) and the keen competition in crafts and trade, forced a small number of Rechitsa Jews to convert to Christianity in the second half of the 1840s and the 1850s.[122] Without doubt, conversions to Christianity also took place earlier: in 1835, for example, David Pisarenko became an Orthodox Christian after moving to the nearby village of

Zaspa.[123] Such cases were rare, however. The gradual liberalization in lawmaking that began in the 1860s allowed the average Jew some hope for improvement in his legal rights. On the other hand, the rise in the standard of living after the abolition of serfdom, as discussed earlier, somewhat blunted the keenness of competition among Jews; this led to a decline in numbers of those converting to Christianity.

Those newly converted to Christianity treated their Israelite brethren in different ways. Some remained sympathetic and offered help; others completely isolated themselves from them; a third group took a uniformly hostile attitude. Most often, the latter was a reaction to the attitude of Jews to the newly converted and their condemnation of baptism as treachery. But sometimes there was general hostility in the community toward a certain Jew even before his baptism, usually because he had informed on someone, been deceitful, or behaved scandalously. In such cases, baptism was a natural response to the ostracism of the Jewish community, since a Jewish boycott meant the virtual loss of the opportunity to carry on a trade or a craft in a mestechko and the denial of social assistance. The majority of the newly converted themselves broke their link with the Jewish community. With this in mind, they would often change their place of residence, and in their new homes they would break off contact with the Jewish community. Most often, it was the members of the intelligentsia—who had become Christians in order to overcome barriers in their choice of profession, job, or place of residence—who remained helpful and compassionate toward their Israelite brethren. They often contributed to Jewish educational institutions or Jewish charities in their new place of residence or in the community from which they had come.

For the majority of Jewish communities in the Pale of Settlement, charitable aid was important because of the poverty in which the people lived, at least until the last quarter of the nineteenth century; therefore, as a rule, they did not refuse it, even when it came from a convert. As noted, until almost the end of the nineteenth century many Jewish families in Rechitsa were, if not impoverished, at least not living well, and this had an impact on the nature of charity in the town. It meant donating money to the poor and paying for burials through the Chevra kadisha burial society. At the same time, sometimes through the initiative of the administration, the town council, or leaders of the Jewish community, Rechitsa Jews would donate money for some special purpose: help for widows and orphans who had been deprived of their breadwinner or for an impoverished newlywed couple; aid to a family whose house had burned down, and so on. For example, in 1839 the military administration approached the townspeople with an appeal for aid to the residents of the mestechko David-Gorodok, who had lost their homes thorough fire. The principal donors were a few landowners and the wealthy Jews Aizik Shaikevich, B. Rafalovich, Zelik Livshits, and Abram Rabinovich.[124] In 1855, during the Crimean War, the Rechitsa Jewish traders Zalman Brokhin, Nokhem Gabaev, Zalman Roginskii, the Livshitses, and others donated money for the heroes of the defense of Sevastopol.[125] When a fire in 1895 in mestechko Loev burned eighty-five Jewish homes, Rechitsa's Jews sent food to victims.[126]

The authorities were reluctant to agree to the requests of Rechitsa Jews when they concerned intracommunity activities. Thus, in 1898, when the Jews wanted official recognition for the burial society Chevra kadisha, which had existed in the town from time immemorial, the Department of Religious Affairs of Foreign Creeds, which dealt with Jewish religious questions in Russia, refused their request. This decision was influenced in no small degree by the town police chief, who, guided by the principle "always say no," even when the issue was only a funeral service, informed his superiors that the petitioners were poor people, a number of them "unreliable."[127] The appeal of Rechitsa Jews to the administration on the same question in 1901 was likewise rejected.[128] Nevertheless, the community continued to exist semiofficially.[129] It was possible thanks to the positive outlook of the town administration, whose interest lay in the preservation of public order even at the cost violating legality.

Organized charities became more common toward the end of the nineteenth century, as the standard of living of Rechitsa Jews rose. Aside from Chevra kadisha, about a dozen other Jewish charitable societies appeared in Rechitsa. The Rechitsa Society for Aid and Relief to the Poor held the central place among them. By 1900 its budget had reached a considerable sum—5,133 rubles. The most important among its various funds was the Passover allowance, to which even poor Jewish families contributed as best they could. This fund's committee would then decide who would receive the money for the holiday. To avoid humiliating the poor families by a handout, no one in the town except the members of the committee knew which families received support. This kind of charity was called *matan be seter* (a secret gift). It was an unwritten rule that the donation be concealed even from many members of the family who received it. In Rechitsa, as in other Belorussian mestechkos and towns, donations were also collected by individual, public-spirited people. These were usually elderly "intercessors"—men or rather women (*gabaites*)—who canvassed Jewish homes to collect alms (*a nedovo*) for the poor. In Yiddish this ancient form of Jewish charity work was called *gein in gaboes* (to gather alms for another).[130]

In 1898 in Rechitsa, official registration was obtained for the charitable society Linat ha-tsedek, which had been founded several years earlier by Hirsh Izraelit. The society provided comprehensive care for those who were sick and indigent and cheap firewood for all the poor. At the end of 1899, it obtained the agreement of the authorities to open a hospital for the poor. The society lacked the means to complete this project, however.[131] Instead of a hospital, the society opened an outpatient clinic, which in 1913 accepted 975 patients.[132]

By no means could everyone in town donate a significant sum; therefore small sums were welcomed. Many families whose income was below average kept a piggy bank at home to collect money for donations, *pushke*. Aside from the fulfillment by all Jews of Saint Paul's prescription in Galatians for rich residents to help the poor, the donation, or more accurately its size, codified the internal social hierarchy. By participating in many general town charitable activities, the Jewish elite improved the impression it made on the local administration, to which it, too, had to turn for the resolution of residential and economic problems. Such participation had a beneficial effect on interethnic contacts, to some degree diminishing the accumulated tension, which was greatly needed in the average Belorussian township. In its own turn the Christian intelligentsia of the town contributed aid, for example, to those in neighboring mestechkos who had been made homeless in a fire, with the understanding that most of the population there were Jews.

Furthermore, the geographic expansion of the dispersed settlement of Jews in the Russian Empire at the end of the nineteenth century was accompanied by the development of interregional commercial relations among them. At this time Russian Jewish newspapers began to publish lists with the names of contributors to various charitable projects. Even if such publications were not on the same footing with letters of recommendation among businessmen, they at least added to the potential partners of the interregional authority.

Prominent religious and social figures headed the committees of these charitable organizations. For example, Rabbi Sholom-Dov-Ber Shneerson organized the sale of groceries and firewood at prices within reach of poor Jews.[133] With the agreement of the administration, community leaders allocated money from the collection box to support the poor. In 1886, for example, 1,120 rubles from the collection box were used for this purpose.[134] Despite this assistance, the poorest elements of society remained in need, and therefore a Jewish Mutual Credit Society was founded in Rechitsa. In 1912–1913 it had 418 members.[135]

At the very beginning of World War I, a Committee for Assistance to Soldiers was organized in Rechitsa. Two Jewish representatives were invited to join, and they worked actively in it. Rechitsa Jews made generous donations to this committee. Jewish women and girls helped make underclothes for soldiers. Nevertheless, the attitude of Jews toward the committee remained hostile. The Jewish community then had to organize its own separate women's committee attached to the Linat ha-tsedek Society. Jews of the town contributed what was a large sum for those times—more than 400 rubles—to support the society. In addition to this, an amateur troupe staged the play *Iakov the Blacksmith*, the proceeds from which (about 300 rubles) also went to this fund. The money collected paid for five hundred pairs of underwear and the same number of tobacco pouches with presents for soldiers. These items were all sent to the army in the name of the Jews. A total sum of 1,300 rubles was collected for families of Jews whose breadwinners had been called up into the army. Jews of the town also donated money to the Russian committee to aid those called up for service.[136]

In 1914, after the government had begun to evict Jews from the area of the front lines due to unfounded accusations of their disloyalty and espionage activities, many towns in the eastern part of the Pale of Settlement were filled with thousands of hungry refugees. Because of the drafting of men into the army and the destabilization of the economy, however, these same towns had increasing numbers of their own impoverished residents. Therefore, streams of Jewish refugees poured into the so-called inner Russian provinces, despite hundreds of state prohibitions and circulars. The Russian administration, which for almost a century and a half had kept the Jews confined, unexpectedly discovered that its very own measures had led to the virtual abolition of the Pale of Settlement. Powerless to detain the Jewish refugees within the Pale of Settlement, it was compelled to face facts. The government did not officially legalize this abolition, though it did send out appropriate secret circulars to provincial governors. This was done to avoid attracting the attention of the political right and out of concern for an even more massive flight of Jews beyond the limits of the Pale of Settlement. The "quiet" form—by circular—of making known this decision, relieved the tsar from having to approve a decree on the issue, one that had the potential to collapse the enormous structure of Russian laws concerning Jews.

As early as February 1915, the first party of Jewish refugees arrived in Rechitsa. They were given accommodation in houses of prayer. To provide support for them, collection cups were immediately passed around the town, raising one thousand rubles. A Rechitsa resident commented in Jewish newspaper *Novyi Voskhod*:

> This sum, a huge one for our poor town, surpassed all expectations. Our own impoverished mass of Jews was particularly responsive. Those who made the

collections tell touching stories: when they appeared with their cups in the poor area of the town, a commotion ensued. People came running; some borrowed from their neighbors and with tears in their eyes would bring their little contributions. Poor children tossed in the last kopecks they had been given for breakfast in the heder. A decision was made that the collectors would not go to the homes of gentiles, though they would ask for money from people they met on the street. Very few of these responded, and those who did, did so reluctantly.[137]

Within a month, a special committee had been organized in Rechitsa to help Jewish refugees, the numbers of which reached a thousand within a year. The most pressing problem was that of living space. Overcrowding in the houses of prayer caused a rapid spread of infectious diseases. Although the committee quickly managed to find housing for all but four families and paid for the rental and heating of rooms and separate apartments, conditions remained very difficult. The committee was helped in providing food for the Jewish refugees by the All-Russian Union of Zemstvos, which contributed 408 rations per day beginning in October 1915. The committee itself also gave money for food for the neediest families and supplied the refugees with clothing, linens, and footwear. It managed to arrange for a reduction in the price of prescription medicines for refugees and for lower payments for visits to medical assistants and doctors. A boarding school was opened for 40 to 45 refugee children from needy families; here they were fed and provided with clothing. They could also get schooling, though lessons were conducted mainly in Hebrew with a few in Yiddish. A private four-year primary school was opened on Kazarmennaia Street in October 1916 for 150 children. Because the authorities had requisitioned part of the school building, the children had to attend classes in two shifts. The three teachers taught Hebrew, Yiddish, and Russian, as well as arithmetic and natural history (in Hebrew). Children received free textbooks, and school supplies were sold at reduced prices. Refugee children also attended other schools in the town: 19 in heders; 11 in the nonreligious primary school; and 7 in the Talmud Torah. The Rechitsa Committee for Aid to Jewish Refugees paid the full cost of their schooling and was also responsible for all the organizational work. In addition to the help from the Jews of Rechitsa and the Union of Zemstvos, the committee received significant support from the Tatiana Committee, which in 1916 provided 450 rubles and goods valued at 2,000 rubles. Despite this assistance, the refugees felt that the aid was insufficient and longed to return to their homes as soon as possible.[138] Nevertheless, a number of the refugees took up permanent residence in the town after the war ended.

The leaders of the Rechitsa community during the war did not ignore their own local needy people. In 1916 the Women's Jewish Committee allocated some minor assistance to all Jewish families who had members on active service.[139]

The members of the Women's Committee belonged to the relatively small circle of intelligentsia that had grown up in Rechitsa at the end of the nineteenth century. At its center stood the aforementioned members of the numerous local town and Jewish social organizations—representatives of a new generation. At that time, only a small number of Rechitsa residents participated in national

Aron and Feiga Atlas, early twentieth century. Courtesy of Anna Atlas.

Jewish social movements, something that was typical of small towns and shtetls. Nevertheless, with each passing year a larger number of Rechitsa Jews became involved in them.

The Zionist idea appealed to a number of Rechitsa Jews. After the creation in 1900 of the Society for the Support of the Ancient Jewish Language, mentioned earlier, and of the Reform heder, Hebrew began to be more widely studied in the town. It ceased to be regarded there only as the language of the Torah. Even earlier, in the late 1890s, a Zionist circle was established in Rechitsa. From 1895 to 1916, within the framework of the Society for Mutual Aid to Jewish Farmers and Tradesmen in Syria and Palestine, it raised several thousand rubles through the Rechitsa synagogues for the development of agricultural work and craftsmanship in Palestine. The money was also used to buy land for Jewish colonies, for the Jaffa gymnasium, and for the Jerusalem Misgav-Ladakh Hospital. In 1902 one of the two representatives of this society in Rechitsa was Rabbi Chaim-Shlioma Kom, who was a proponent of the idea of religious Zionism. With the beginning of the world war in 1914, supporting the settlers' movement and the organizations in Palestine became more complicated, since the Ottoman Empire, which possessed that area, had entered the war against Russia. Nevertheless, the society found ways to send money via third countries.[140] Members of the Zionist circle were active. They organized meetings and the so-called Palestine Week to publicize their ideas, and they sponsored lectures. The lecturers were given by members of the circle as well as Zionists from other cities. Shortly before 1917, several lectures were given by Zakharii Moglin from Gomel, who was shot in 1937 as the son-in-law of Leo Trotsky.[141]

In 1906 the Rechitsa lawyer Aron Vilenkin worked with the Union for Attaining Equal Rights for the Jewish People. In 1909 he was also a member of the Jewish Historical and Ethnographical Society. On the eve of World War I, Rabbi Chaim-Shlioma Kom founded a section of the "Mizrakhi" Zionist religious movement in Rechitsa.[142]

Even in the late 1880s, Zionist youth had begun to seek ways to migrate to Erets-Israel. Some of them did so individually, by going to Odessa and from there by ship to the port of Jaffa. This is how the follower of Lubavitch Hasidism Levi-Isaac Ashbel arrived from Rechitsa. With this aim in mind, some Rechitsa residents joined Zionist organizations in Rechitsa and other towns. In order to learn a profession appropriate for Erets-Israel, Bendet (Berka) Orshanskii and his wife, Genia Bakst, went from Rechitsa to Ekaterinoslav, where he joined the Bilu organization. (This Jewish youth organization had arisen in 1882. Its name came from the first letters of the words of the Bible verse, *Bet I'akov lekhu ve-nelkha*: "House of Jacob! Arise and go!"—Exodus 2:5). In 1890 they and their children left for Palestine, where they worked as farmers in the Gedera agricultural colony. There Bendet Orshanskii raised wheat and grapes, mostly American and French varieties. His nine thousand grapevines brought him about 1,200 francs in income each year. This money allowed him to pay off the loan he had taken in the 1890s from the aforementioned Society for Mutual Aid to Jewish Farmers and Tradesmen in Syria and Palestine. That same society made many nonrepayable loans to settlers, including Orshanskii. A powerfully built man, Bendet Orshanskii often helped to defend the settlements from marauding bands of Arabs and to

Shmuel Pekarovskii, 1908. Courtesy of Michael Baker.

track them down and recover what they had stolen. In 1900 the Rechitsa native Iakov-Iosef Koparovskii joined him in Gedera.[143]

In 1909 the Rechitsa native, Iosif Sosnovskii (1871–1930) left for Erets-Israel along with his family. He had previously been a merchant who worked in Irkutsk supplying cattle and horses to the army. Iosif Sosnovskii became one of the first residents in the settlement of Kfar-Saba.[144] The first wedding celebrated in the settlement was that of his son, Chaim, in 1911.

One of the sons of the aforementioned Yehuda-Leiba Shneerson, Pinkhas (1893–1975), left for Odessa in 1906, after he had completed study in the Rechitsa Reform Cheder; in Odessa he taught in a trade school. There he became acquainted with Zionists, and in 1908 arrived in Erets-Israel, where he worked in Jewish settlements and took part in confrontations with Arab bands. Because of his height, his comrades nicknamed him Pinkhas the Eucalyptus. In the battle for Tel-Khai in 1920 he took over command from the mortally wounded Iosif Trumpeldor and showed himself to be a bold leader. In the 1930s and 40s, Pinkhas Shneerson held various administrative posts.[145]

Nevertheless, the people of Rechitsa, like the people of many similar towns and mestechkos, were not heavily involved in the many Jewish social organizations that existed at the time. This can be explained by the fact that the town lacked any institutions of higher education and did not have enough secondary schools. The most capable among the Jewish youth, motivated by a desire to study, left Rechitsa and moved to cities with universities.

Rechitsa was only slightly affected by the "war" between Misnagid and Hasidic Jews because of the substantial predominance of the latter in the town in the first half of the nineteenth century. To a large extent this manifested itself as a spirit struggle among Hasidim, outwardly the representatives of the various tendencies within Chabad, but in fact it was a striving by the local elite to acquire greater authority. Clashes between candidates for the position of state rabbi occupied the same ground. The authorities wanted to wangle the appointment of a maskil to this post, but the community could not pay him commensurate with his education, and they also feared the initiatives he might take to reform the traditional way of life in the town. In the 1880s, however, the greater part of the local elite itself began to support the idea of a Jewish school of a new type, where religious education would be combined with general education subject matter. In a parallel move the local Jewish elite began to devote more time in a different way to philanthropy. Not only their emancipation but also the growth of general prosperity influenced this trend.

The February Revolution of 1917, which extended equal rights to Jews, gave them unique opportunities for social and community construction on the path to the national cultural autonomy that Dubnov had dreamed of. These plans were not destined to come to fruition, however, because the new change of power involved a cataclysm not only for Jewish public institutions but for the entire Jewish way of life.

6

Between Revolution and War, 1917—1941

POLITICAL POWER AND THE JEWS

The February Revolution brought the Jews equal rights and democratic freedoms that they had not previously enjoyed. Inspired by these new opportunities, the Jews, and the young generation and intelligentsia in particular, plunged euphorically into establishing Jewish social and communal organizations and began participating more actively in political movements outside their own community. The Jews of Rechitsa also joined in this general movement. Their political sympathies became apparent in the elections to the town duma in 1917, which elected ten Jews: two general Zionists; two representatives of Tseirei-Zion (literally, "The Youth of Zion"); three Bundists (the Gabov brothers and Briskin); one member of the Zionist Socialist Workers Party; and two others who were leaders of non-Jewish socialist parties. One of the Zionists elected to the Rechitsa duma became its secretary, another a member of its board. Non-Jewish socialist parties participated in the elections: the Socialist Revolutionaries (the right wing of the Rechitsa section of this party was headed by Efim Spivak); the Bolsheviks (by that time there were no Jews in the party leadership); the Social Democrats (headed by Leiba Papernyi); and the People's Socialists (headed by Dr. David Kagan).[1]

Although Jews were leaders of three of the four extranational socialist parties participating in the elections, Jews themselves were not broadly represented in them. Nevertheless, Jewish voters actively supported these parties. This is the only explanation for the fact that in the town duma (with a total of twenty-seven councillors) Jews held only 37 percent of the posts even though they had a slight numerical majority in the population of Rechitsa. And the Jews were every bit as politically active as the rest of the population. By way of comparison: in Vitebsk, where Jews constituted roughly half of the population, they elected 52 percent of all councillors.[2] Thus the election results in Rechitsa reveal that the majority of local Jews considered social problems, not national ones, their priority.

Conservative circles in the town were displeased by the granting of equal rights to Jews and by the election results themselves, even though they provided only modest Jewish representation. They expressed their views by breaking windows in some Jewish homes and looting several Jewish shops. The high-school teacher Kovaliuk called for an anti-Jewish pogrom. By the end of October, after he had been deported by the Soviet of Soldiers' and Workers' Deputies, the atmosphere in the town became less tense.[3]

On October 26, 1917, the day after the October coup (the news of this event, which was to have such a dramatic effect on the fate of Russia's Jewish and non-Jewish populations, had not yet reached the town), the large Kupechskaia Synagogue was the scene of a ceremonial session of the Zionist organization dedicated to the declaration of the English lord Arthur James Balfour that created a Jewish national home in Palestine. Two Zionists from Gomel, Azarkh and Leikin, came specially to participate. The building was filled to overflowing with people inspired by the prospect of creating a Jewish state that lay before them. During this wave of enthusiasm preparations for the first communal elections to the VES (All-Russian Jewish Congress) took place in Rechitsa. At the beginning of December 1917, a meeting of delegates from all Jewish parties was held to discuss the elections. After heated debates, in which the Bundists and the Zionist-Socialists were attacked by the delegates of Tseirei-Zion, an electoral committee of seven was formed.[4] Through the efforts of the committee, elections were organized at the very end of December 1917; 1,819 voters participated. The results of the election to the Jewish town commune were as follows: four United Socialists (287 votes); four representatives of the bloc of religious parties, Akhdus (291 votes); five Bundists (403 votes); three nonparty members (146 votes); one nonparty workers' representative (80 votes); two independent Zionists (161 votes); five representatives of Zionist organizations, primarily Zionist-Socialists and members of Tseirei-Zion (412 votes). None of the thirty-nine members of the Union of Tenants was elected. In all, twenty-three people were elected as members of the community council.[5] Because the Zionists received slightly fewer votes than the Socialists, it was vital for both groups to win the support of the four nonparty members and the four backers of the religious party Akhdus if they were to solve the problems of the community. After power shifted to the Soviets, the competence of community organs of self-government was significantly reduced, but they did not survive for long even in this capacity. As early as April

1919 a special decree for their liquidation was signed. The Soviets had no intention of sharing power with anyone.

The reasons for the gains of socialist parties on the "Jewish street" were the victory of the Bolsheviks in Rechitsa and their strong-arm methods of struggle with opposition. The change of power in the town took place on October 30, 1917, by the Julian calendar (November 12, 1917, by the Gregorian calendar, adopted in Russia in February 1918). The events of October evidently aroused more alarm than joy among the overwhelming majority of the Jewish population since there were few supporters of the Bolsheviks and Left SRs among them, and no one knew the practical plans the new government had, particularly regarding everyone's greatest concern: economic issues.

Over the course of three weeks, the Bolsheviks set up a military-revolutionary committee in the town, reorganized the police (the militia), and removed town councillors they did not approve of in order to form a more "compliant" town duma. But they found even a duma of that sort to be an impediment since it had been elected by democratic means and also created the illusion of dual power in the town. Therefore, in January 1918 the chairman of the Executive Committee of the Rechitsa Town Soviet, N. E. Shcherbitov, sent a memorandum to the People's Commissariat of Internal Affairs in which he pointed out the necessity for liquidating town dumas and zemstvos. In the wake of this, in mid-February the Executive Committee of the Rechitsa Soviet closed the town duma and the zemstvo assembly. But the Bolsheviks soon lost their grasp on power. By the end of February 1918, the town was taken by the Germans.[6]

Under the terms of the Treaty of Brest-Litovsk between Russia and Germany, signed on March 3, 1918, southern Belorussia, including Rechitsa Uezd, was attached to Hetmanate Ukraine. Soon Ukraine sent in detachments of irregular troops, the Haidamaks, who worked closely with the Germans. The German authorities maintained order in Rechitsa, stopping potential outrages against the Jews instigated either by the Haidamaks or the local Orthodox population. At the same time, the German authorities put an end to Bolshevik Party activities in the area.

The Bolsheviks set up an underground committee in Rechitsa headed by L. Kh. Vasilevitskii. In June 1918, on the initiative of the chairman of the Polesia Party committee, S. T. Khavkin, who had come to Rechitsa, an underground party committee was chosen that consisted entirely of Jews: G. Kazovskii, N. Abramovich, Z. Malinkovich, Z. Albinskii, and L. Kh. Vasilevitskii (chairman and, simultaneously, head of the revolutionary committee). The committee, which worked from the home of Zakhar Malinkovich, printed and distributed leaflets, carried out agitation among the workers and German soldiers, and collected weapons for partisans. The Polish socialist Feliks Kon and the Red Army commander Evgeny Mitskevich came to Rechitsa in May 1918 to provide organizational assistance to the committee.[7] Kon later became a Soviet political figure, Mitskevich an NKVD (People's Commissariat of Internal Affairs, 1934–1946) agent who worked among White émigrés in Western Europe, Japan, and the United States.

The impact of the revolutionary events in Germany in November led to the breakdown of discipline among German troops, something that Soviet Russia immediately used to its advantage when it violated the Brest agreement and began an offensive across the whole front. The Red Army regained Rechitsa in mid-December 1918. At the end of February 1919, a uezd committee of the party was chosen in Rechitsa that, along with its secretary Bukshtein, included L. Kh. Vasilevitskii and Ia. P. Mitskevich. The latter was at the same time the chairman of the town soviet.[8]

Tranquility did not last long. On the night of March 25/26, 1919, the local guard company of 125 men under the former officers Solodukho, Volskii, Metelskii, and Berzin, joined the Gomel uprising of M. Strekopytov and rose up against Soviet power in Rechitsa. After putting down a feeble resistance, the rebels arrested communists and looted their apartments. Nine communists were executed, including four Jews. Criminal and political prisoners were released from prison. The rebels destroyed the buildings of the revolutionary committee, the military committee, the extraordinary committee, and the justice department. They abandoned the town in haste, since units of the Red Army were approaching. Before leaving the insurrectionists also looted the apartments of many local residents, particularly those of Jews. By April 1, 1919, Rechitsa had been liberated, and the rebels had withdrawn to Vasilevichi, where, together with some of Strekopytov's detachments, they organized an anti-Jewish pogrom.[9] Playing on the anti-Semitic sentiments that had grown stronger among the local population during the war, these detachments operated under the slogan "Down with the War. We Will Not Defend the Yids."[10] Tit Nazarenko became secretary of the newly chosen uezd committee of the party.

Power in the town changed hands once more on May 8, 1920, when the Polesia Formation of the Polish Army, under the command of Władysław Sikorski, entered Rechitsa and threatened the Fifty-Seventh Rifle Division of the Red Army with encirclement. The Poles blocked the tracks around the railway station so that the Red Army troop trains could not move eastward. At that point two armored trains broke through the barriers and drove off the Polish infantry with machine-gun fire. They disassembled the barriers, allowing the division to cross the bridge over the Dnieper. In the area of Volch'ia Gora, Rechitsa home-guard volunteers—communists and members of the Komsomol—covered the retreat of Red Army troops through the town. Many of the volunteers perished.[11]

In Rechitsa town the Poles refrained from the anti-Jewish pogroms they had organized in villages in Rechitsa Uezd. In Kholmech many Jews were drowned in the Dnieper, and most of the Jews found in the suburb of Rovnoe, including eighteen children, were killed.[12] In the neighboring uezd, Mozyr, the entire Jewish population was robbed, thirty-two Jews were killed, and some three hundred Jewish women were raped. In the village of Skrigalovo in Mozyr Uezd, the whole of the Jewish population was also robbed by the Poles (120 head of cattle were taken away, as were all of the tradesmen's tools), and fifteen Jews were killed. In the village of Petrikov in the same uezd, the entire Jewish population was robbed, many homes were burned, forty-five Jews were killed, and as many as a hundred Jewish women were raped.[13]

In Rechitsa the Poles sent Jews to forced labor, picking up young people on the streets for that purpose.[14] Because their front was so extended, the Poles did not manage to hang on to Rechitsa and other areas of southern Belorussia for long. On July 19, 1920, in the course of the summer counteroffensive by troops on the western front commanded by Mikhail Tukhachevskii, Rechitsa was liberated.[15] According to the recollections of an eyewitness, David Rubinoff, Polish soldiers in Rechitsa treated the Jews worse than the Germans did. The behavior of the Red Army troops varied. As Rubinoff recollects, one of them threw him off a ferry into the Dnieper during a crossing, while another jumped in and saved him.[16] Comparing the treatment of Rechitsa's Jewish population by the various regimes in power between 1917 and 1920, one is led to conclude that the most tolerant were the German authorities. This proper regard for the Jews was appreciated, and because of it a number of them, even two decades later in the summer of 1941, flatly refused to leave their town.

Meanwhile, the idea arose in Poland of creating two autonomous eastern cantons as buffers with Soviet Russia: a Lithuanian canton with its capital in Kaunas and a Belarusian Lithuania with Minsk as its capital. This buffer was supposed to be a stage in the restoration of the Polish-Lithuanian Commonwealth.[17] In order to realize the Belorussian part of this idea, which was especially close to the heart of Józef Piłsudski, in the spring of 1920 the People's Volunteer Belorussian Division of Stanislaw Bulak-Bulakovich, formed in the region of Brest with Polish support, had entered Polesia, where it operated mainly by raiding the headquarters and the supply trains of the Reds. But by the summer its forces had grown to twenty thousand bayonets and sabers. In September of that year,

Bulak-Bulakovich managed to capture even Pinsk with these forces. Throughout the area of their operations, Bulak-Bulakovich's forces organized bloody anti-Jewish pogroms. In Rechitsa Uezd the killings were particularly numerous in Khoiniki, Kalinkovichi, Iurovichi, Vasilevichi, and also in the Jewish colony of Sitnia. Those Jews left alive fled from here and from neighboring Mozyr Uezd to Rechitsa. But in mid-November Bulak-Bulakovich's forces were approaching Rechitsa as well, creating panic among the Jews and malicious joy among the Christian population.[18] At the same time, several Jewish homes were plundered at night by retreating Red Army men.[19] A detachment of volunteer home guards was raised to defend Rechitsa. This detachment, together with the regular troops that had advanced more closely, inflicted a defeat on the insurgent forces in the days after November 20, 1920.[20] The aforementioned Zakhar Malinkovich, who had sided with the Bolsheviks even during his service in the tsarist army in 1916, fought with this detachment.[21]

In January 1921 the band of Galak (Ivan Vasilchikov), numbering some seventy people, arrived in Rechitsa Uezd from the Chernigov region. Here, with the addition of deserters, criminals, Bulak-Bulakovich's troops, and others opposed to the Soviet regime, the band's numbers had grown to 800. Taking care not to become involved in a clash with a large military formation, the band regularly raided and robbed small settled areas. Galak explained his operations to the peasants as follows: "A dark cloud had come over us, a dark force, the Yids and the commissars, and we all know they are plunderers."[22] That same year the bandits organized an anti-Jewish pogrom in Kholmech and killed twenty-three Jews. In the village of Ruchaevka, also in Rechitsa Uezd, there were only two children left alive after a bandit raid; the other forty-five had been killed. A report on Galak's activities stated: "He directs his malice primarily toward Jews. Everywhere he appears he organizes vicious Jewish pogroms. He slaughters old men of eighty and nursing infants."[23] According to information from the former tsarist general I. Danilov, who was serving with the Red Army in Gomel, that same year bandits had attacked the railroad station in Khoiniki. Thirty-two Jews and communists were identified in the group that was captured, and right there in front of the others, were killed with crowbars.[24] Near Loev two big steamboats going down the Dnieper were stopped by the bandits. After being screened, seventy-two people, all of them communists and Jews, were taken off and killed.[25] Many Jews from surrounding areas fled to Rechitsa to escape the bandits and then took up residence there.[26]

A special detachment headed by Evgeny Mitskevich was organized in the uezd to wage a struggle against this band. This force, however, was insufficient.

Grigory (Hirsh) Mikhailovskii was specially dispatched from the Gomel Cheka Section for the Struggle against Banditry as head of the Rechitsa Criminal Investigation Section.[27] He could not surround Galak for a long time, and he was difficult to catch. Mikhailovskii changed tactics by infiltrating three communists into the gang. Galak unmasked two of them, but the third one even succeeded in becoming his orderly. When the opportunity came, the orderly killed Galak.[28] Mikhailovskii was then able to wipe out the gang almost completely in March 1921. The bandits took their revenge on Mikhailovskii. In 1924, when he was chief of the Gomel provincial criminal investigation unit, they tracked him down and brutally killed him.[29]

As many as several hundred Jews from Rechitsa served in the ranks of the Red Army in the campaigns against bandits and the White movement during the civil war. It is quite possible that some Rechitsa Jews also sided with the opponents of Soviet power, particularly with those generals such as Baron Pëtr Vrangel who were tolerant to Jews. After 1917 some of the Jews of Rechitsa were deprived of their property, of course, and many lost their livelihoods. Still, it would seem that the majority of the Jews who were dissatisfied with the new order preferred to emigrate from Rechitsa abroad since they had little faith in the victory of the opposition in Russia or they were concerned about renewed bloodshed. Aside from émigrés motivated by those factors, some Jews who left Rechitsa to go abroad did so mainly because they were unable to carry on their political activity. For that reason in the autumn of 1921 members of Hekhaluts ("pioneer" in Hebrew), Naftali Slobodskii, Leib Zilber and Yehuda Kom, son of the rabbi mentioned above, fled abroad.[30]

When he emigrated, Yehuda Kom took with him a diary that, despite its brevity, is of great interest as a unique document that provides a picture of the activities of the Rechitsa section of Hekhaluts. We learn from his diary that at the end of August 1918 this party celebrated the Week of Erets-Israel in the town. Sometime after October 20 in that same year, a lecture on Erets-Israel was given at a party meeting and a theatrical presentation was made, the proceeds from which went to the party treasury. The Central Committee of Hekhaluts sent newspapers and brochures on beekeeping, horticulture, and animal husbandry to local party members. To mark the festival of Tu Bishvat on February 25, 1919, a theatrical performance to raise funds for the party took place with great success. In that same period the Repatriation Commission of the Rechitsa section organized a cooperative group Akhuza ("land tenure," in Hebrew) among middle-class residents of the town to teach them about agriculture and prepare them for subsequent emigration to Erets-Israel. Unfortunately, the fate of this group, which was to be repatriated during the celebration of Pesakh in April of that same year, is unknown. The Rechitsa section of Hekhaluts, which occupied several apartments in the town, had a number of other commissions, sections, and circles. Its drama circle enjoyed particular popularity in the town.[31]

In February 1920 a new working commune called Hekhaluts was formed on the initiative of the central bureau of Hekhaluts in Moscow. A plot of land some eight kilometers from Rechitsa was leased in order to train commune members. Yehuda Kom, the author of the diary, enrolled in this group. The plot of land was an abandoned and dilapidated estate. The settlers had already ploughed the soil and sown their winter crops when a group of peasants arrived to stake their claim on this land. Though the inhabitants of the village had been unable to work this land themselves, they demanded that the strangers leave the estate and threatened them with violence. Later they organized a pogrom at night. Only thanks to the former steward of the estate, who hid the settlers in his cellar, did they escape physical harm.[32] For this reason, in the summer of 1921 the group prepared to leave for the Nikolaev region in Ukraine for training in agriculture. But it was most likely because of the growing threat that emigration would be halted that in October 1921 the group left for Vilna, at that time a Polish city.[33] According to another member of the group, Noakh Gantman, Rechitsa at the time was generally considered a center of the Halutsim movement.[34] A nucleus of nine people comprised the leadership of the organization in the town. At the same time, they were all members of Tseirei-Zion and Maccabee.

After the delegates to the third Hekhaluts conference in 1922, including the Rechitsa native Yehuda Kaganovich, were temporarily arrested, the right wing of the organization, unwilling to renounce Zionist activity, went underground and formed the National-Labor Hekhaluts, while the left wing accepted the authorities' conditions permitting the new Hekhaluts only to promote agricultural work among the Jews. The NKVD supported the idea of a legal Hekhaluts. In 1923 it even approved the statutes of the new Hekhaluts, after changing its title to the All-Russian Labor Organization Hekhaluts. Nonetheless, the new Hekhaluts became the target for attacks from the Evsektsiia (Jewish Section of the Russian Communist Party [Bolsheviks], from 1925 All-Russian Communist Party [Bolsheviks]) that was striving for complete ideological control over the Jewish population. But it was not until 1928 that its opponents managed to close the legal Hekhaluts.[35] In the years 1923–1925 the Histadrut, the trade-union organization of Erets-Israel, attempted to reconcile the legal and the illegal Hekhaluts. Some noted political figures from Erets-Israel who had come to the USSR served as intermediaries: David Ben-Gurion and Yehuda Kopelovich and, in 1925, David

Remez and Levi Eshkol. Success eluded them, however. It was Yehuda Kagan-ovich specifically who had the final word in this schism: in 1923, at a joint session of representatives of fragmented Hekhaluts and in the course of a heated discus-sion, he fired a shot over the head of his leftist opponent Yehoshua Altshuller. After that, the possibility of a merger could not even be discussed.[36]

Aside from Hekhaluts there were other semilegal Zionist organizations active in Rechitsa: the youth organization Ha-Shomer ha-tsair ("young guard," banned in 1927); the sports association Maccabee; and the Zionist Socialist Party. Ha-Shomer ha-tsair was the largest group in the town, with a membership of about one hundred. It was headed by Sene-Khaia Gorevaia, known by her party aliases of Yaffa and Nadia. One of the most active members was Riva Zelichonok, whose apartment was used for the organization's meetings. On the night of February 5–6, 1925, they were both among the thirty members of Ha-Shomer ha-tsair who were arrested in Gomel Province.[37] A few weeks later, on March 1, 1925, several more rank-and-file members of this organization were arrested in Rechitsa, in-cluding Eli Goldovskii and Roza Budovskaia, both born in 1908. There were held in prison for only a few weeks; soon their parents sent the young people out of Rechitsa to relatives. Sene-Khaia Gorevaia and Riva Zelichonok were sentenced to exile in Kirghizia for three years, the usual measure taken against Zionists. The authorities, well aware that Zionists would continue their struggle even after they had been released from prison, offered a number of them voluntary emigration from the country after their full term of punishment had been served. Officially, this appeared to be the positive result of intercession by Ekaterina Peshkova, the wife of Maxim Gorky. In fact, she had made such a request, but her influence in the upper echelons of power was not strong enough to have had any signifi-cant effect on an issue such as this. Incidentally, among the several dozen Zionists who immigrated to Erets-Israel in this way were Sene-Khaia Gorevaia and Riva Zelichonok.[38] The Rechitsa native Moshe Bareslavskii, who had been arrested in Moscow, was also among them. After these arrests the Rechitsa Ha-Shomer ha-tsair was left without leaders, and in that same year, 1926, its members ap-proached the so-called Northwestern Uezd Headquarters of this party to request help in reorganization.[39]

For several years after the 1917 revolution, the Jewish representatives of the socialist parties entered the town soviet along with the Bolsheviks and so enjoyed some influence in Rechitsa. In January 1920, however, despite the votes of the electors and in violation of one of the basic principles of democracy—free elections—the Bolsheviks at the Second Provincial Congress of Soviets made the decision to expel the socialists from all organs of power.[40] In the wake of this decision, in February 1920, the Zionists, and specifically the Tseirei-Zion faction, were also expelled.[41] Soon the orchestra of the Tseirei-Zion party with its thirty musicians, a group that had enjoyed great popularity in Rechitsa, ceased to exist.[42]

The Bundist youth organization Yugnt-Bund, which had great influence on Jewish youth, was also active in Rechitsa until the beginning of the 1920s.[43] Sessions of the Bund that were organized during this time attracted a large audience.[44] But with the appearance in Rechitsa in May 1919 of the Komsomol organization led by Pëtr Patiuk, this influence began to fade. In 1920, at its twelfth conference in Moscow, the Bund split into two parties, the Social Democratic Bund and the Communist Bund. The rightists left the conference, while the leftist majority, including the delegate from Rechitsa, stayed on and passed a pro-Bolshevik resolution.[45] But not all the Bundists in Rechitsa agreed with their delegate. The Social Democratic Bund in Rechitsa was headed by the doctor Ber Levinson, a Bund member since 1901. At the end of 1922, during the mass arrests of the opposition Social Democrats, he was arrested and exiled to Orenburg Province.[46]

By 1923 the Jewish parties, including the left and the right Bund, had been closed or had voluntarily ended their activities; the only exceptions were the new Hekhaluts and the Maccabee, which had been recognized as useful for popularizing physical training and sports among the Jews.[47] Many of the Jewish young people in Rechitsa joined the Komsomol. The sharp changes in social and economic life motivated young people to take an active part in this process. At the same time, some of those who joined the Komsomol held on to their Jewish traditions secretly. Young people were attracted to the Komsomol by its fashionable paraphernalia (posters, red kerchiefs, blue blouses, a new vocabulary, etc.), the sense of belonging to a special group, and the possibility of having some influence on urban life through this organization. Komsomol membership allowed youth an unprecedented possibility of replacing the older generation in organs of town power. Apart from that attraction, membership in the Komsomol to some extent neutralized one's nonproletarian origins in the eyes of the authorities.

"Unsuitable" social origins or working in commerce were the reasons for the expulsion of 102 people, most of them Jews, from the town Komsomol cell during the general purge that took place in May 1920.[48] Despite this and other purges, the responsible positions in the town Komsomol organization were held almost exclusively by Jews Dvornikov and Rapoport joined the town Komsomol committee. Mikhail Malikin was elected member of the bureau and deputy secretary of the Rechitsa Uezd committee as well as to the Supervisory Section for Work among Worker and Peasant Youth. From 1922 to 1925 Natan Vargavtik headed the accounting section of the uezd committee of the Komsomol and in 1927 had become an instructor in the party organization.[49] Apart from them, there were many other Jewish activists in Rechitsa at the beginning of the 1920s, as is evident from the photograph of members of the plenum of the Komsomol uezd committee. In the 1920s Jews constituted 45 percent of first- and second-level schools of the Komsomol organization.[50]

A relatively large number of Jews in Rechitsa were among the first to join the ranks of the Bolshevik Party immediately after the October Revolution. But in the spring of 1920 there was also a party purge there; as a result 116 of the 218 party members (53 percent) were expelled.[51] In general it was Jews who were "purged," since many of them could not boast of having worker or peasant origins. Yet other groups of Jews in Rechitsa lost their party cards during the massive purge in the summer of 1921; generally, these were former members of the Social

Members of the uezd Committee of the Komsomol, Rechitsa, 1922. Standing, from left to right: Pinskii, Mikhail Malikin, Sofia (Sara) Finkelberg, Iosif Resin, Bliumkin, Natan Vargavtik. Seated on chairs: Z. Albinskii, P. Mosin, Ivan Murashko, S. Kaganovich, Vilenskii. Front row: E. Kaganovich, Iakov Lipov, F. Malikina. Courtesy of Rechitsa Regional Museum.

Democratic parties.[52] Nevertheless, after these party purges in Rechitsa many Jews still remained in the ranks of the communists, unlike the situation in neighboring Mozyr.[53]

In the first convocation of the Rechitsa Uezd party school in December 1921, 56 percent of the participants were Jews.[54] In the years that followed, many of them left Rechitsa, while other Jews were accepted into the party less frequently than were Belorussians. This was a reflection of the campaign for *korenizatsiia* (native roots) taking place in the USSR.[55] But the proportion of Jews in the Communist Party was scarcely lower here than the average for the BSSR (Belorussian Soviet Socialist Republic), where the percentage, according to materials from the party census of 1927, was 26.8 percent of full members and 18.6 percent of candidate members. In neighboring Soviet republics, the proportion of Jews as full and candidate party members was much lower: 2.7 percent and 1.4 percent, respectively, in the Russian Republic; and 13.1 percent and 10 percent, respectively, in the Ukrainian Republic.[56] As early as 1927 the proportion of Jews in the Communist Party was reduced by one-third. This reduction was the result, on the one hand, of further party purges and strict checking of the social origins of the candidates and, on the other hand, of the departure of Jews to other areas. It is appropriate at this point to mention the communist Shmaryaha (Alexander) Malinkovich (brother of Zakhar Malinkovich), who left to study at the Academy of Political Economy in Moscow, which trained the so-called Red professors. In Moscow he sided with the Trotskyites, something indicating that he was probably unable to complete his studies. In 1925, during the suppression of the Trotskyites, he was either exiled to Kazakhstan or, with foresight, went there voluntarily. In any case, he returned to Moscow in the 1930s and worked as a humble economist. From there he went to the front, and during the battles in the northern Caucasus in 1942 he shot himself when his unit became surrounded. While in Moscow at the beginning of the 1920s and then in Kazakhstan, he had maintained contact with his childhood friend the aforementioned Zionist Moshe Bareslavskii. Some years later Bareslavskii mistakenly (see chap. 7) decided that Shmaryaha Malinkovich had been executed by the Soviet authorities.[57]

One's social origins could be a serious obstacle not just for admission to the party but for the granting of civil liberties as well. In Rechitsa by the mid-1920s among 6,721 people of voting age (eighteen and older), 6,154 had the right to vote, while the remainder (8.5 percent) were had been deprived of voting rights.[58] Without doubt, among those deprived of voting rights in Rechitsa, as in other areas of the Belorussian Republic, the overwhelming majority were Jews. This is corroborated by the results of the 1926 elections to the town soviet. Ninety-five deputies were elected, forty-one (43.2 percent) of whom were Belorussians; thirty-two (33.7 percent) were Jews; twenty (21 percent) were Russians; two (2.1 percent) were Ukrainians.[59] Although the deputies were not representatives of ethnic groups, both the Jews and the non-Jews in Rechitsa at the time and later continued to maintain a dichotomous division between "ours" and "theirs." Thus in 1928, during the voting on the application of a Jewish worker to be admitted to the party, the votes at a session of the bureau of the party cell at the M. P. Tomsky Sawmill were divided along ethnic lines.[60] Therefore, there can be no doubt that, considering the proportion of Jews in Rechitsa in 1926 (44.6 percent), and at least equal political involvement among Jews and gentiles, many Jews were unable to participate in the these elections to the town soviet because they were *lishentsy* (disenfranchised persons). A total of 69 percent of the voters took part in these elections, something that testifies to the increase in voters' interest; a year earlier, in 1925, only 42 percent of those having the right to vote participated in them.[61] By all appearances, the increase in the percentage of voters was achieved through a stronger campaign of agitation.

A holiday meeting of Komsomol members in Rechitsa, May 1, 1924. Courtesy of Rechitsa Regional Museum.

The largest proportion of deputies elected at the time were Belorussians. This, as well as the increase in the numbers of Belorussians in the population of Rechitsa, resulted from official promotion of a new form of nationalism that would strengthen the Belorussianization of the republic among the Slavic population of the BSSR who did not yet clearly distinguish themselves by ethnicity. Formerly the Belorussians would refer to themselves as "local people." As far as Rechitsa was concerned, in 1919 the Slavic population opposed the incorporation of the town into the Belorussian Republic.[62] As a result, in April 1919 Rechitsa Uezd was included in the newly created Gomel Guberniia as part of the RSFSR (Russian Soviet Federated Socialist Republic).[63]

In the mid-1920s the central authorities decided to compensate the BSSR for the loss of its western territories by transferring to it from the RSFSR several okrugs with a Belorussian-speaking population. After a survey of the ethnic composition of the territories bordering the BSSR, the okrugs (which were introduced in 1924) of Rechitsa and Gomel were turned over to it. Subsequently, Rechitsa Okrug was abolished and a new Rechitsa raion, encompassing a rather small territory, became a part of Gomel Okrug. A review of republican boundaries in 1931 led to some expansion of Rechitsa Raion.[64]

Even before Rechitsa was incorporated into the BSSR, the chairman of the Central Executive Committee of the BSSR, Alexander Cherviakov (who held this post from 1920 to 1937), visited Rechitsa to campaign for incorporation. When he spoke to the residents of a factory region with a Russian-language population who were largely opposed to joining the BSSR, he promised to continue to allow them to deal with state institutions in Russian and to provide for the teaching of Russian in the local school.[65] Nonetheless, the majority of workers in Rechitsa remained opposed to the transfer of the town to the BSSR.[66] Even in rural areas of Rechitsa Raion the population, according to the census of 1920, gravitated toward the Russian rather than the Belorussian language, 83.7 percent compared to 11.6 percent. At the same time, 45.1 percent of the population referred to themselves as Belorussians.[67] According to the census of 1926, 90 percent of Belorussians in Rechitsa Raion knew how to read and write Russian, a figure twice as high as that of the republic generally.[68] Therefore, after the annexation of the raion the authorities intensified the Belorussification campaign, which had begun as early as 1924. In contrast to such efforts in other republics, the Soviet localization program in Belorussia was especially complicated because in Soviet terms Belorussians nationalism was still in the "diaper stage." In this connection the organizers of that campaign considered the Belorussian language threatened by Russian and Polish, though not by Yiddish. They rightly regarded Jewish youth as potential proponents of Russification and were even pleased at the campaign for Yiddish that was being carried out in parallel by the Evsektsiia in the USSR generally and in the BSSR in particular.[69]

To help promote the use of Yiddish in Rechitsa, a chamber of the Jewish court was opened in April 1927 to which Jews could submit legal actions in their everyday language. Many Jews took advantage of this. In May alone of that year forty-five cases were heard there, thirty-four of them civil and eleven criminal. Through the efforts of the local representatives of the Evsektsiia of the town soviet, the militia and the taxation office began accepting statements in Yiddish.[70] The Evsektsiia had to create textbooks and competent journalism in Yiddish. In general in the 1920s the Evsektsiia played a valuable role in the development of culture in Yiddish and the Yiddishization of the Jewish population. The demonstration of an official policy of pluralism in the national question and specifically in language issues was reflected in the change of signs on government institutions in Rechitsa. In the second half of the 1920s they appeared in four languages: Belorussian, Russian, Polish, and Yiddish; in the 1930s, with a change in language policy and an end to the fostering of languages of nationalities living outside their territory, these four languages were replaced by two, Belorussian and Russian. The Yiddish sign over the popular kosher coffee house on Lenina Street remained in place longer than any others.

The authorities' efforts directed against national dissociation produced some results. Interfaith marriages began taking place, something that was not permissible before the revolution, when a mixed marriage was allowed only when the Jewish partner converted to one of the Christian denominations.[71] The first interfaith marriage in Rechitsa took place at the beginning of the 1920s between the militiaman Nikolai Dorofeev and the Jewess Liuba (her last name is unknown); it became the talk of the town in Rechitsa.[72] In the BSSR in 1926 the proportion of marriages between Jewish women and gentiles in the town reached an unprecedented level: 4.3 percent. The proportion of marriages between Jewish men and gentiles was a good deal lower, 1.8 percent. The number of mixed marriages in towns and cities of the Ukrainian Republic was twice as high. In cities of the European part of the RSFSR, every fourth Jew married a non-Jew, and every sixth Jewess married a non-Jew.[73] Such a large difference in the number of mixed marriages in the BSSR and the European part of the RSFSR was connected with a certain shortage of Jewish brides outside the borders of the former Pale of Settlement and the shortage of Jewish grooms within it. Marriages between Jewish men and gentile women continued in Rechitsa to the end of the 1920s. The number of such marriages grew through the 1930s, but they were still not common.[74] Interfaith marriages became possible under the conditions of sudden acculturation that both Jews and gentiles experienced in the 1920s.

Despite some successes that the authorities achieved in their ethnic policy, overcoming long-established prejudices proved to be very difficult. Thus in 1928 one Russian worker at the M. P. Tomsky Sawmill made a written request to leave the Komsomol for the following reason: "I am leaving the Komsomol because the Yids are in power."[75] He gathered several workers together and told them, "All the Yids have gone off to the holiday center, and the party cell isn't taking any measures against this."[76] Classifying this worker's behavior as anti-Semitism, the secretary of the party cell who reported these facts in a memorandum also pointed out that not only were there anti-Semitic incidents at the sawmill but also ones reflecting Jewish nationalism.[77] In Rechitsa at the time, the issue of allowing Jews to speak in Yiddish at general meetings of various enterprises was being resolved. The Belorussian authorities preferred to have Yiddish and not Russian serve as a second language at meetings. This was entirely suitable to the representatives in the Evsektsiia. The problem came from Russian-speaking workers who opposed Yiddish. As far as the Jewish workers were concerned, the majority preferred to use Russian in order to be understood by everyone present and also to avoid irritating the Russian workers.[78] At the same time, some of the Jews who spoke did so in Yiddish on principle, asserting their right to speak in their native language. Thus the director of the Rechitsa Jewish School, Sara Bychkova, gave her report in Yiddish at a townwide pedagogical conference in 1928.[79] Incidents such as these provided communists of other nationalities the grounds for accusing Jews of nationalism.

In connection with this situation, the Jewish Bureau in Rechitsa had to undertake interethnic work among Jewish workers and become more active in promoting Belorussification. When it passed such a resolution in 1928, the Jewish Bureau included in it a clause on attracting Jewish workers to groups learning Belorussian.[80] This was more a propaganda measure intended as "insurance" against possible accusations. In actuality Jewish workers, just like Russian workers, had no desire to learn Belorussian.

Although the campaign for korenizatsiia was not particularly successful in the republic as a whole, in Rechitsa Belorussian was introduced successfully in schools, largely thanks to the considerable pedagogical talents of two teachers sent from Minsk.[81] Belorussification was pursued as a policy with special rapidity among the cadres, as a comparison of the ethnic composition of the Rechitsa town soviet in 1926 and in 1929 clearly shows. Over that period the proportion of Jews there decreased from 33.7 percent to 28.1 percent even though their proportion of all residents had scarcely declined. The proportion of Russians decreased even more, from 21 percent to 8.9 percent. At the same time, the proportion of Belorussians increased significantly, from 43.2 percent to 57.9 percent.[82] Without doubt the reduction in the proportion of Russians in the Rechitsa soviet occurred as a result of their own reconsideration of their ethnic self-identification. Despite the reduction in the proportion of Jews and Russians in the Soviet, in 1929 they still comprised a large percentage of those in management positions—38.1 percent and 14.3 percent respectively.[83] At the same time, precisely one-third of all managers were Belorussians, a figure that corresponded to their share of the population of the town. All this shows the artificiality of the incorporation of Belorussians into the town soviet. The share of Jews in management positions in the Rechitsa town soviet was somewhat higher than that in the republic generally. According to the statistics available for 1927, Jews comprised 30.6 percent of all members of town soviets in the BSSR.[84]

In the years that followed, even though Jews lost their former level of representation in local organs of power, they remained an influential part of the apparatus. The presence of Jews within the town administration is attested by the participation of the Rechitsa delegate N. Galperin to the Twelfth Congress of Soviets of the BSSR in 1935.[85] Also, the secretary of the Town Committee of the Komsomol from 1937 to 1941 was Isaak Maskalik, who held the post of cadre secretary in the Rechitsa Raion committee of the party until the beginning of the war.[86] During that period in Rechitsa, as in other towns in the BSSR, Jews continued to be appointed from time to time to fill vacancies even in formally unelected positions. Thus in 1937 Abram Frenkel was assigned as a judge in the second division (the town was divided into two divisions); he continued to fill that post until 1938, dealing with criminal cases. In 1939 the post of chairman of the Raion Executive Committee was held by Abram Fridliand.

THE ECONOMY

Though it may seem paradoxical, even though Jews, because of their limited rights in comparison with other ethnic groups, provided a large number of leaders to parties opposing the tsarist regime, there was perhaps no other ethnic group in Russia whose socioeconomic status declined so drastically after October 1917. This happened largely because of the state's subsequent monopolization of trade, an area where the proportion of Jews significantly exceeded that of other ethnic groups in Russia. The situation that unfolded sharpened the economic conflict between the state and the tradesmen, the other major area in which Jews were prominent. A great number of Jewish families were in a catastrophic situation until the end of the 1920s. The chairman of the Evsektsiia, Shimon Dimanshtein, noted in 1926: "The majority of Jews did not even gain from the revolution; they lost. If we compare the general situation of Jews in mestechkos before the revolution and now, we see that 15–20 percent have now improved their situation, 30 percent have remained in the same situation, and 50 percent are in a worse situation. The largest group of Jews made livings from handcrafts and trade; now this is no longer in their hands."[87] In reality the proportion of those who had improved or maintained their situation was a good deal lower. The majority of Jews were forced to look for employment in other areas, a difficult task because of the restrictions placed on them as people formerly engaged in trade. Changing employment took time and energy for rrequalification, training, and job seeking. These efforts began to bear fruit only in the second half of the 1920s, when the average economic level of Jews gradually began to rise. The proportion of Jews among doctors, engineers, teachers, lawyers, and other professions requiring higher education quickly began to increase. By that time those with such professional qualifications in the USSR could work only within the state sector. This was an area to which, before 1917, Jews with higher education had only limited access; those with only secondary or primary education had, in practice, no access at all. This situation changed during the years of Soviet power.

The abolition of the legal and free market destroyed the traditional Jewish family structure. A man could no longer feed his family, and a woman had to look for a job. Formerly she had been able to help out in the family shop or work at home or in a workshop at whatever handcraft her skills permitted, even while giving priority to her domestic duties; now, however, working in the state sector made these obligations secondary. By the mid-1930s 36 percent of the Jews in the BSSR who were employed in the state sector were women, and the vast majority of them (81.4 percent) were employed as workers.[88] Considering that the situation in Rechitsa at that time was similar, one can conclude that the changes in the Jewish family structure in Rechitsa were radical. Thus, ten years earlier, in 1926, only 13.7 percent of Jewish women in Rechitsa worked outside the home; over the whole raion only 11.5 percent did so. That figure shows that Rechitsa and the raion had passed well beyond similar administrative units in Gomel Province.[89] This process also took place within other ethnic groups, of course, but there it happened gradually. Slavic peasant households did not experience immediate significant changes following 1917. As far as urban areas were concerned, the proportion of male workers in gentile families was much higher than that in Jewish families. The new regime was more cognizant of workers since it saw them as a source of support; therefore the decline in their standard of living took place gradually. Even taking that into account, however, workers remained the best-paid social group (apart from bureaucrats) during the entire existence of the USSR. Therefore, this relative prosperity allowed the workers' wives to remain without jobs for some time.

In Rechitsa after the February Revolution of 1917, factory committees and soviets were formed that demanded factory owners shift their workers and other employees to an eight-hour workday and increase their wages. These demands were accompanied by strikes. In July 1917 the plywood factory and sawmill that had been taken over by Kaplan and Livshits went on strike. The first strike involved 150 workers, the second 60. The factory owners, crushed by taxes, were compelled to make concessions to avoid closing down.[90] These factories apparently were soon nationalized. They ceased working when military operations were in progress. It was only in 1921–1922 that the town authorities managed to get the plywood factory, the match factory, and the tannery working again, along with the wire and nail factory "Gvozd'," which had been established in 1918.[91] In 1923, 103 Jews worked at the "Dnieper" match factory, 14 percent of all the workers.[92] In 1924 this factory and three like it (in Malyi Vyshkov, Novozybkov, and Novobelitsa) were merged to form the Polesia Match Corporation.

The civil war and the breakdown of the former economic mechanism of the country led, in 1919, to a famine that affected the residents of Rechitsa.[93] Litman Turovskii wrote in his diary of the difficult food-supply situation that existed in Rechitsa at the time: "There are illnesses. . . . People are dying, and the living walk about looking like skeletons."[94] Although by 1920 the new regime had basically managed to deal with its external and internal enemies, the economic devastation had a powerful influence on the living standard of the population and provided fodder for the voices of opposition within the state, an opposition that threatened to grow into a nationwide rebellion. Under such conditions the Soviet regime in 1921 had little choice but to move to a new economic policy (NEP). Its positive results were not long in coming. Many former entrepreneurs were quite quick to reestablish trade and small industry in Russia. The English communist Ralph Fox, who visited Russia in 1923, writes: "This was the zenith of the NEP, and all of Russia was like America at the beginning of the [18]40s. . . . People were in a fever to enrich themselves and to restore what the revolution had taken away, and money was being made so quickly that foreign analysts began to think that Russia was developing into a major modern industrial state."[95] The Jews of Rechitsa took an active part in this process. Hotels owned by the Krymskii sisters, Motl Grande, Frenkels, the Cherniavskiis, Riabkins, and the Porotskiis opened once again. Abram Eventov built a bakery, and Kreina Tëmkina ran a delicatessen on the corner of Kalinin and Kooperativnaia Streets. Chaim Berkman continued as a trader and owner of a hardware store that had existed since before the revolution. The Orshanskiis, the Sheftels, the Pertsovskiis, and Khaia Shklovskaia opened dry-goods stores at this time. Many small shops opened, particularly at the new market. The market was virtually empty on Saturdays since the Jewish owners, as previously, did not work in their shops on Saturday. Goods and food products from towns in Belorussia and Russia were brought to the traditional fairs in Rechitsa.[96] The tannery and some wood-processing plants were in private hands at that time.[97]

In all there were 258 traders in the town in 1922, the overwhelming majority of whom, as before 1917, were Jews. Among them were 116 grocers (45 percent), 49 haberdashers (19 percent), 21 dry-goods merchants (8.1 percent), and 14 butchers (5.4 percent).[98] There were also sellers of bread, vegetables, fish, and food products, and traders in livestock, metal and tar products, stationery, perfume, and dishes. Six Jews owned cafeterias and teahouses; seven had warehouses for the wholesale trade.[99]

A session of the bureau of the Komsomol cell in the Dnieper factory in the mid-1920s. Seated, from left to right: Sonia Rabinovich, Isaak Shustin, Bruk (secretary), Mamed Ovsei, Pavel Chizhik. Standing, from left to right: Fania Frenkel and Pasha Zlatkina. Courtesy of Rechitsa Regional Museum.

At that time there were 169 registered artisans or, as they were called in those years, handcraftsmen (*kustari*) in Rechitsa. The majority of them were Jews. They included seventy-eight shoemakers (46 percent); twenty-three tailors (13.6 percent); thirteen blacksmiths (7.7 percent); eight barbers (4.7 percent); seven each of millers and hatters (4.1 percent); and five carpenters (3 percent).[100] The remainder were locksmiths and bakers, four of each; watchmakers and dyers, three of each; two each of soap makers, tinsmiths, glaziers, confectioners, and carters (evidently, owners of heavy wagons). There was also one wheelwright, one jeweler, and one photographer.[101]

Tanners, most of whom were shoemakers, comprised the most common trade in the BSSR among Jewish handcraftsmen, comprising 25.6 percent of the total. This was somewhat more than those in the sewing trades (primarily tailors and hatters), who comprised 25.2 percent. In Rechitsa, as in other places, there were many shoemakers among the handcraftsmen; for this reason Gomel Province held the leading place in the tanning trade but had fewer tailors and hatters (a total of 17.7 percent).[102] When one compares the distribution of jobs by specialization in Rechitsa with that of the republic generally, one can see that the proportion of metalworkers (blacksmiths, locksmiths, and tinsmiths) among Jewish handcraftsmen was roughly the same (11.2 percent in Rechitsa, 12 percent for the republic as a whole), while the proportion of those in the food, forest, and construction industries was several times smaller.[103]

A society of handcraftsmen was organized in Rechitsa in 1923. Under the leadership of David Rudoi, its first concern was setting up a savings and loan association. Its membership expanded quickly. In 1925 the membership numbered some 300 handcraftsmen; by 1927 the figure had grown to 521. The state bank extended small credits to the association that were immensely helpful in enabling owners of small businesses to survive as the NEP progressed. As a social safeguard, the society of handcraftsmen also established a mutual aid fund.[104] By 1928 the majority of members had lost interest in the society because it had become short of funds and its tax assessment had increased; they had also been refused the status of members of trade unions. Nonetheless, the society managed to organize four workers' cooperatives—for hatters, shoemakers, tailors, and bakers. Most of their members were Jews. The board of administration submitted a complaint to the Evsektsiia over its lack of support. The board wished to receive support in the form of reduced taxes and the granting of benefits for recruiting new independent handcraftsmen to the society. The majority of handcraftsmen in 1928 paid an income tax of 20 to 50 rubles, but the taxes of some were more than 100 and even 1,000 rubles. One of the tanners, for example, paid income tax of 1,382 rubles; a baker paid 279 rubles; and a soap maker 115 rubles.[105] The tax-rate schedule in the USSR in the 1920s was determined not as much by income as by the officially defined type of work of the taxpayer and its relationship to private property.[106]

According to the data from 1926, 476 handcraftsmen in the towns of Rechitsa Raion had officially registered their trades. As was the case over the whole of Gomel Province, almost half of these (48 percent) continued to practice the traditional "Jewish" professions of tailor, hatter, or shoemaker.[107] At the same time and in the 1930s, many Jews in Rechitsa practiced other trades as well. They were millers, butchers, saddle makers, cabdrivers, barbers, watchmakers, locksmiths, stove makers, bricklayers, tinsmiths, blacksmiths, glaziers, and carpenters. The latter, united in the workers' cooperative, had a separate trade union and management office where the language was Yiddish. The craftsmen fulfilled the orders of private individuals as well as those for collective farms both in the town and in the villages around it.

About 70–80 percent of all the tradesmen in Rechitsa at the time were Jews. As for the proportion of Jews in various other trades, the available scattered data for the town show that their percentage scarcely differed from that of the distribution across the republic generally, according to which for the whole BSSR in 1927, Jews comprised 91 percent of all those in the sewing trades (which included both tailors and hatters), 70 percent of the tanners (mainly shoemakers), 73 percent of printers, 45 percent of those in the food industry (from 1924 to 1927 the proportion of Jews here doubled, a fact explained by the availability of jobs in this area during a time of continued food shortages throughout country), 37.6 percent of those in the building trades, 35.5 percent of woodworkers (primarily carpenters), 32 percent of textile workers, and 31.6 percent of metalworkers.[108]

As far back as early 1921, the authorities resorted to the gradual smothering of the NEP by taxation. A vivid firsthand account of this period is given by a Jewish trader in Gomel:

I opened the business in October [1921]; I paid three million for the right to retail merchandise for one month—they would not accept more since it had been announced that no one knew what the price was going to be in the next month. In November I paid six million, in December ten, in January fifteen, and just now I got a notice that I have to hand over thirty million to them. In addition to the state fees, there's no telling how much I paid on the orders of the provincial executive committee when there were "weeks" of various kinds. Now I don't have thirty million, but I still could get it and pay it to them if only I could be sure that next month the price would not go up again.[109]

He concludes further: "You can't run a normal business under the Soviets, you can only speculate, and that's the trap I ended up in."[110] "Weeks" was the name given to nonrecurrent, specifically directed taxation measures on a provincial scale. Thus "weeks" were organized in Rechitsa for "aid to the starving in the Volga region," "improving the material circumstances of Red Army veterans," "schools," and so on.

The further intensification of the tax burden continued, an exception being the period from the spring of 1925 to the autumn of 1926.[111] After the NEP was finally abolished in 1928, the authorities in Rechitsa nationalized the homes of prosperous Jews. The Khazanovskii family's building on the corner of Soviet-skaia and Lunacharskaia Streets that housed their hairdressing shop and their apartment above it was taken away from them; Girsh Vasilevitskii lost his house on the corner of Vygonnaia Street. The Maizus family house on the corner of Uritskaia Street, noted for its beautiful decorative wooden mosaics on the ceilings, was seized (subsequently a school was opened here). The house of the timber merchant Mendel Ioffe on the same street was converted to a children's home, and Pesia Golberg's house was used for the town executive committee. Houses were also seized from Pinkhas Goldberg (Lunacharskaia Street), Khaia Shklovskaia (Lenina Street), and from the factory owner Chaim Kaplan (Soviet-skaia Street). Also, the hotels mentioned earlier that had been opened by Jews were nationalized. After their campaign of nationalizing private property, the authorities in 1930 began another campaign, popularly referred to as "the yellow fever," of confiscating gold from the population. The apartments of former trades-people and manufacturers were searched; they were imprisoned and demands were made on their relatives to bring gold and valuables to ransom them. At that time many prosperous families moved away to live in places where they were not known.[112]

The ending of the NEP was a heavy blow to both the traders and the artisans. In the second half of the 1920s, the whole area of handcraft work experienced a crisis because of the lack of raw materials.[113] In Rechitsa as in other places, therefore, the number of handcraftsmen was reduced, as was the number of workers' cooperatives. The problem of earning one's daily bread became even more acute for the Jewish population. Even in the relatively problem-free time of the NEP, there were, according to the incomplete official figures, 704 unemployed people in Rechitsa.[114] In general Rechitsa differed from the other towns of Gomel Province particularly by the large number of dependents for every employed Jew. In Gomel in 1926 there were 1.8 unemployed for every employed Jew, but in Rechitsa the figure was almost 2.5; this can be explained, above all, by the lack of jobs there.[115] In order to feed themselves, the Rechitsa Jews began more intensively working the small plots of land that, as noted earlier, belonged to almost every home. But this was not enough to solve the problems of poverty and unemployment under the generally impoverished conditions of the entire population. When a labor exchange was opened in Rechitsa in February 1927, 982 people registered. Each day the exchange found jobs for 8–9 percent of the unemployed and provided free meals. After six months, however, the exchange in Rechitsa was closed due to lack of funds.[116] The actual unemployment figures were significantly higher than the official ones. According to the study by Gennadii Kostyrchenko, Jews in the mestechkos, as social pariahs, were often refused registration as unemployed. According to his figures, in 1928 72 percent of Jews in all the Belorussian mestechkos were unemployed.[117]

To feed their families and get rid of the lishentsy status some Rechitsa Jews decided to take up agriculture, an activity that was then being strongly advocated by the Evsektsiia. With that in mind, several dozen families from Rechitsa resettled in the Crimea in 1924–1925; this trend was particularly strong in 1926, when twenty-seven families (153 people) moved there. They became part of the Jewish agricultural settlements in Dzhankoi Raion in the Crimea: ten families (59 people) settled in Nay-Land-Arbeter; eight (52 people) in Frai-Arbet; nine (42 people) in Krymer Blum.[118]

In 1927 the Rechitsa section of OZET (The Society for Disposition of Land to Jewish Workers) led by the member of the raion committee of the party, Khusidman, organized the second major resettlement of Jews from Rechitsa in which another twenty families left to take up agricultural work on collective farms in Ukraine and primarily in the Crimea.[119] Among these one small group of families chose to work and live in the Jewish agricultural settlement of Iudendorf in Larindorf Raion, and the majority of Rechitsa's expatriates settled in the so-called third section of Kurman Raion (both of these raions are in the Crimea), which later received the place-name Fraidorf. It consisted of two streets—Rechitskaia and Gorvalskaia with twenty-two and eighteen houses respectively. This Jewish settlement received considerable aid from American Agro-Joint. In 1929 the economies of the settlers were collectivized into the P. G. Smidovich kolkhoz.[120] The head of the settlement, the immigrant from Rechitsa Solomon (Shlema) Surpin, was declared to be against collectivization. For this and also for his acquaintance with Lev Trotsky, the authorities attempted to arrest him in 1929, but Surpin was warned in advance and had time to leave the Crimea.[121]

There was no resettlement from Rechitsa to Ukraine or the Crimea in 1928.[122] At the beginning of the 1930s, the last group of Jewish settlers set off from Rechitsa to the Crimea. They remained living on the Jewish P. G. Smidovich Collective Farm, established in 1925 by a group from Gomel Province that may have included some families from Rechitsa. The collective farm came under the jurisdiction of the Rottendorf Jewish Village Soviet. The introduction of the kolkhoz system forced several of them to move to Simferopol in the second half of the 1930s.[123]

Apart from these resettlers, in Rechitsa itself about a dozen families (forty-four people) in October 1928 established an agricultural collective named Roiter Oktiaber (Red October), which was granted a parcel of forty-one hectares of land not far from the town. But only one-fifth of this land could be cultivated during the first year because of the almost total lack of ploughs, seeders, and other machinery for working the land. Overall, this farm owned only three horses, seven cows, and three goats.[124]

As a result of resettlements, by 1931 a quarter million Jews, comprising 9 percent of the Jewish population of the country, were involved in agriculture in the USSR. This was an enormous jump; before 1917 the percentage of Jews involved in agriculture was low due to the power of tradition, on the one hand, and restrictions on the right to own land outside the limits of towns and mestechkos, on the other hand. Subsequently, however, due to collectivization, the increase in taxes, the anti-kulak campaign, the famine in Ukraine in 1933–1934, the cut in aid from the American Jewish organization Agro-Joint, and the growth of industry in the USSR, many Jews abandoned their colonies. According to information published by the well-known economist B. D. Brutskus in the Paris Jewish newspaper *Rassvet*, as early as 1929 one-third of all Jewish farmers in the Crimea were forced to abandon their farms because of "extreme measures in expropriating produce and the anti-kulak campaign."[125] The Israeli historian Mordechai Altshuler states that by 1939 the majority of Jews in the USSR had given up agriculture.[126]

In addition to resettling Jews from Rechitsa to collective farms in the Crimea, the local OZET in the early 1930s began organizing the relocation of families to the Jewish Autonomous Region in Birobidzhan. The number of those wishing to build Jewish autonomy there turned out to be much lower than those willing to take up agriculture in the Crimea, however, since the Jews of Rechitsa, as noted at the beginning of this chapter, had scant interest in the national idea and were primarily concerned with social problems. The result was that two families from Rechitsa arrived there at the beginning of February 1932 and another eight in April of the same year.[127] It is quite likely that a few families left Rechitsa for Birobidzhan in other years, but on the whole such resettlement was insignificant.[128]

As early as 1931, the Rechitsa section of OZET was criticized for its shortcomings in selling lottery tickets for the organization and for failing to sign up anyone for resettlement to Birobidzhan in that year.[129]

During the first years of Soviet power in Rechitsa, as in other towns, traders and resellers appeared who earned large profits thanks to the vacuum in retail sales; because of this they were labeled speculators. Yet because of the low buying power of the population and persecution by government representatives—many of whom demanded bribes from the speculators—the speculators had scant opportunity to become wealthy. Before the elimination of bread rationing in 1935 and of other food products later, the speculators and the black market they had created played a huge role in the life of any town or mestechko. Although the ration cards ensured that the population was provided, at least to some extent, with food, such essential items as tea, tobacco, sugar, salt, matches, kerosene, and often milk could be purchased only on the black market. Rechitsa residents used the black market to buy bread as well, since it was often in short supply in the state's network of stores.[130] On the black market one could buy high-quality products made by handcraftsmen—clothing, shoes, hats—as well as factory-made items that came from retail stores ("through the back door") or directly from the factories through the connivance of managers or from ordinary pilferers. The speculators or middlemen in Rechitsa, as in other places in the former Pale of Settlement, included a good many Jews, whose practical skills at trade and entrepreneurship were most useful for this new career. Still, their proportion was not significant among the Jews as a whole, since many of them were afraid to undertake an illegal activity. Speculation was one means of survival under conditions of economic destitution. After the end of rationing, the role of the black market decreased, but when there were regular shortages of products it continued to play an important role in the economy of the town.

Another place where Soviet citizens could acquire scarce products in the 1930s, though only for foreign currency or precious metals, was the chain of Torgsin (literally, "trade with foreigners") stores. They opened in 1931 and continued to function until the beginning of 1936. Initially the plan was for Torgsin stores to sell goods only to foreigners, but subsequently they began serving Soviet citizens as well. This turned out to be a rather successful enterprise that did much to cover the expenses of purchasing industrial equipment from abroad.[131] The Torgsin in Rechitsa, housed in the former hairdressing shop of the Khazanovskiis, began playing a role of some importance in the economic life of the town, as it did in other towns. Once it had opened, the Jews of Rechitsa acquired a legal channel for using the foreign currency that they had received from abroad in the

1920s, mainly from the United States. It is estimated that about 20 percent of families received some such support at that time, and about 10–13 percent in the first half of the 1930s.[132] The reduction was due to the Great Depression. The reduction could have been even greater, but the reception by Torgsins foreign currency from the citizens in early 1930s became for them an encouraging sign of the authorities, and more Soviet Jews began to seek assistance from their foreign relatives. Apart from Torgsin the inhabitants of Rechitsa were also served by fifty-two stores and thirty-nine vendors' kiosks. Between 70 and 80 percent of these were located on the three central streets.[133]

Thanks largely to the taxes collected from private enterprises operating during the NEP years, the local authorities in Rechitsa were able to build an electrical generating station and open a clothing factory that in 1923 employed 103 Jews, some 14 percent of the workforce.[134] By 1925 there were already seven industrial enterprises operating in Rechitsa. By 1927 a new building for the match factory (the former "Dnieper" factory) had been erected and renamed "Ten Years of October;" the old building became a part of the expanded plywood factory. In 1929 346 Jews—22 percent of the workforce—were employed in the match factory. Between 1927 and 1940 a factory making tanning extracts, a shipyard, a starch factory, a flax mill, a bakery, and a distillery were built in Rechitsa.[135] The opening of these enterprises helped in some measure to solve the problem of job placement in the town.

It is appropriate to note here that in the mid-1920s the authorities in the USSR realized that they could not eradicate drunkenness by cutting back on state production of alcohol because of the relative ease of producing it at home. Therefore, the state again returned to intensive alcohol production, the economic sector that had been most profitable in the former Russian empire. As a result, from 1923 to 1927 the growth in the production of spirits in the BSSR broke all records. It increased by a factor of forty-four! By way of comparison: the manufacture of bricks, the item holding second place for growth of output in the republic, increased by twenty-one times.[136]

In the mid-1930s, a number of workers' cooperatives whose members were largely Jews were active in the town. Thirteen tailors worked in the sewing cooperative "Kooperator." The head of production was Naum Goldshtein, and the chairmen of the board were, at various times, Basia Malinkovich and Ehiel Fishman. Somewhat larger was the shoemakers' cooperative "Obedinenie," in which thirty-six shoemakers worked. The chairman of the board was Zelik Dobrushkin. Everyone spoke Yiddish at board meetings, but the minutes of the meetings were translated into Russian.[137] Velvel Mikhlin became president of the shoemakers'

The Chertok family, 1930s.

cooperative on the eve of the war. The largest cooperative was that of the cab-drivers, with forty-seven members, including thirty-six owners of heavy wagons.[138] In addition to these, a small tinsmiths' cooperative, whose chairman was Chaim Kaganovich, and the "Red October" rope makers' cooperative, whose chairman was Pinkhas Gorivodskii, functioned in the town until the very end of the 1930s.[139] In 1936 Zelik Dobrushkin was appointed chairman of the revived cooperative "Kharchevnik," which produced fruit drinks, ice cream, confectionary products, wine, sausage, and other food products. Meer Zelichonok was head of production, and the overseers of the shops were Lazar Spivak and Isaak Livshits.[140] In 1938 Zelichonok became chairman of this cooperative. Most of the tradespeople had a small yearly income for those times—from 1,200 to 3,500 rubles.[141]

The large number of lishentsy in the country who had been deprived of their rights frustrated the authorities' wish to proclaim their successes; thus in 1930 the lishentsy status of several categories of the population was canceled. As a result, the disproportionately high percentage of Jews among the lishentsy was somewhat reduced, bringing their proportion closer to that of the overall population of the country. Those citizens who remained in the category of lishentsy lost their rights to housing, medical services, and ration cards. The Constitution of 1936 abolished the status of lishentsy, although social origin continued to play an important role in one's acceptance for study or for work as well as for appointment to administrative or party posts.

As people with experience in business and with higher or secondary education, Jews in the 1920s and 1930s were more often appointed to posts as managers, administrators, or directors in the state sector than were people from the rest of the population.[142] As the most educated part of the population, Jews in general comprised a large percentage of white-collar workers not only in Rechitsa but across the whole BSSR. In 1927 they comprised 49.3 percent of all white-collar workers in central state economic institutions, 42.1 percent in legal institutions, 24.8 percent in administrative institutions, and 10.1 percent in agricultural institutions.[143] As for the bodies subordinate to the area authorities—and these were the majority of the Rechitsa administrative institutions—Jews comprised 19.1 percent of the topmost levels and 22.3 percent of all other white-collar workers.[144] In 1928 17 percent of the entire adult Jewish population of the Belorussian Republic were white-collar workers; 26.4 percent were handcraftsmen; 16.7 percent, workers; 13.1 percent, peasants; 10.2 percent, traders; 7 percent, unemployed; 1.1 percent, military; and the remaining 5 percent, uncategorized.[145] In Rechitsa the proportion of handcraftsmen, workers, traders, and unemployed was somewhat higher, evidently because of the relative lack of peasants. In Rechitsa the proportion of Jews in the militia (the police) in 1927 was 6 percent.[146] From the end of the 1920s, the proportion of Jews among civil servants began gradually to decline because of Belorussianization, but by the mid-1930s Jews represented almost one-quarter, according to the findings of the American historian Salo Baron.[147]

By 1941 the economic situation of the Jewish population had improved somewhat by comparison with the situation at the end of the 1920s. Nonetheless, it left much to be desired, and accordingly Jews as earlier looked for ways to supplement their incomes. The most important of these was the keeping of domestic cattle and poultry. Every Jewish family in Rechitsa at this time kept an average of six to eight domestic fowl (primarily chickens), and every third family had a cow (occasionally a bull calf); 30–40 percent of families kept pigs, and half of these owners had several head. At the time only a few families kept two cows because this required a considerable investment of money as well as time to care for them. A cow was considered something very valuable: one cost between twenty-five and thirty thousand rubles, an amount equivalent to the cost of an apartment with about thirty-five square meters of living space. Less than half of

Jewish families lived in apartments having greater floor space than this. A pig, though it cost four times less, was also rather valuable. Therefore, Jewish families, including those who maintained religious traditions, would buy piglets that they would raise and then sell. Only a few Jews—every twelfth family—kept goats. Every fifth Jewish family owned a horse. A few families kept bees, an activity that, as already noted, had been widespread there from time immemorial.[148]

Among the 604 representatives of Jewish families who completed questionnaires in Rechitsa in 1945 in order to receive compensation from Germany for damage done during the war (later this information was summarized and included in a memorandum presented by the USSR at the Nuremburg trials), about 41 percent indicated that they had owned plots of land before the war on which they grew mainly potatoes, vegetables, greens, and fruit. According to these questionnaires, the area of the plots (not including land used for housing) that belonged to Jews ranged from two to forty *sotki* (a *sotka* was a plot of land ten meters square). The largest plots of land in the first half on 1941 were owned by Mordukh Brants and Vulf Malinkovich. On the basis of the figures recorded, which showed that the income from a single sotka ranged on average from 1,000 to 1,500 rubles per year, the income of the owners of these large plots was quite significant, from 25,000 to 30,000 rubles annually.[149]

It is very likely that the figures on income from the plots was exaggerated in order to qualify for greater compensation since, unlike the area of the plot, the income from it was something that the administration was unable to verify. But an exaggeration like this could not have been too great or it would have glaringly obvious. Even taking a 30 percent correction into account and so lowering the maximum income per sotka to 700 to 1,100 rubles a year, and assuming that the

TABLE 9. Distribution of plots of land belonging to Jewish families by area

Plot area, sotka	Number of plots	Proportion of total (%)
2–5	119	48.2
6–10	74	30
11–15	30	12.1
16–20	12	4.9
21–25	6	2.4
26 and above	6	2.4
Total	247	100

Source: Calculated from questionnaires completed by Rechitsa homeowners (1941); GARF, f. 7021, op. 85, d. 247–251, 263 (copy in YVA, JM 23638–23639).

average size of plot owned by Jews was 8.5 sotki, the average income of garden plots in Rechitsa was a large sum, from 6,000 to 9,400 rubles per year.[150]

The income from garden plots seems particularly high in comparison with the salaries received at the beginning of the war by those who completed the questionnaire. Of the 604 people questioned, 231 indicated their monthly income (understood as salaries, pensions, and benefits) in the questionnaires. It is difficult to determine why the others did not state their monthly incomes, even though the questionnaire was also intended for compensation for the loss of income during the period of wartime evacuation. Possibly a number of the women—and it was specifically women who for the most part filled out the questionnaires in April 1945 since many of their husbands had not yet returned from the front or had died in battle—had not worked before the war. A part of those questioned might have considered their prewar incomes as insignificant by comparison with the value of the property they had lost. At the same time, it seems improbable that those who did not complete the questionnaires had, during their evacuation, received wages higher than those that they had had in Rechitsa. The data in the questionnaires testify to the great differences in the incomes of Rechitsa residents in the prewar years. They ranged from 150 to 1,500 rubles per month. On average the incomes of those surveyed were from 350 to 400 rubles per month, or 4,200 to 4,800 rubles per year.[151]

Because these figures do not take into account the incomes of the many men who were killed during the war or who had not yet been demobilized from the army and do not include the incomes of those who were not heads of families, the

TABLE 10. Monthly incomes of Jews

Incomes (in rubles)	Number of people stating their income	Proportion of total (%)
up to 300	74	32
301–500	93	40.3
501–700	34	14.7
701–1000	21	9
1001 and higher	9	3.9
Total	231	100

Source: Calculated from the questionnaires of Rechitsa homeowners (1941): GARF, f. 7021, op. 85, d. 247–257, 263 (copy in YVA, JM 23638–23639). Town authorities knew the prewar incomes of the population; thus it is likely that those who completed the questionnaires were afraid to exaggerate them. My surveys of people who stated their prewar incomes confirm the accuracy of the information provided in 1945.

average prewar monthly income indicated does not fully reflect the actual situation. Nonetheless, the data testify that the average income from garden plots was no less and was even somewhat higher than the yearly income of an adult member of a Jewish family. The cost of a single domestic animal (discussed above) was also more than this income. Therefore, in single-parent families and in families where not all the adult members worked, the net income earned by those who owned garden plots and domestic animals could comprise as much as 70 percent of the family budget.

Some of the questionnaires also contain information about the living space of Jewish families. Although some isolated families had large houses (among them was Berka Press, whose home at 27 Chapaeva Street had an area of 116 square meters), these data testify to the poor living conditions of the majority of the Jewish population. When several related families lived at the same address, the questionnaire indicated the living space that was conventionally divided among them (not always into equal parts).[152]

As can be seen by the data in the table, Jewish families lived in rather cramped conditions. It must be kept in mind that considerable space (from four to five square meters) in the houses of Rechitsa was taken up by the stove on which food was prepared up to the 1960s. The furniture in many homes was of the same type: a bed raised high off the floor and covered with blankets; an old chest of drawers; a cabinet; a small shelf of books; a large dining table; a sideboard or buffet with a range of glasses, wineglasses, pitchers, vases, and various figurines. An invariable feature of the kitchen was the washstand with water supplied by buckets from a kolonka (street hydrant). At night the windows of almost all the houses were covered by shutters and the outside gate was barred shut.

TABLE 11. Amount of living space of Jewish families in the first half of 1941

Living space (square meters)	Number of families	Proportion of the total (%)
up to 30	150	54.5
31–50	82	29.8
51–80	35	12.7
above 80	7	2.5
Total	274	100

Source: Calculated from the questionnaires of Rechitsa homeowners (1941): GARF, f. 7021, op. 85, d. 247–257, 263 (copy in YVA, JM 23638–23639). The table has been compiled based only on the 274 questionnaires in which the amount of living space was indicated. It seems reasonable to assume that the majority of the Jews in Rechitsa lived under similar conditions.

Tsiva Khvoinitskii, 1920s.

Living in cramped, congested conditions was most likely typical for all families in Rechitsa, Jews and gentiles alike. Nonetheless, in the 1930s the housing
situation of the Jewish population evidently improved more than that of the gentiles. Although the number of houses in the town had grown to 1,951 by 1922,
a one-third increase over 1910, there remained 7.7 inhabitants per house, as earlier.[153] In later years the construction of houses was barely able to outstrip the
growth of the population, though the ethnic composition of the population
changed at the same time. This occurred because the migration of Jewish young
people was greater than that of gentiles in the 1920s and 1930s. As a result by
1941 the Jews in Rechitsa occupied 33.6 percent of all the houses in the town,
comprising, at the same time, only one-quarter of all the inhabitants of the town,
as can be seen in table 12.[154]

At the beginning of the 1920s Jews owned the overwhelming majority of the
houses on the central streets: Bazarnaia Street; First and Second Kladbishchenskaia Streets; Lugovaia; Preobrazhenskaia; Aleksandrovskaia; Andreevskaia; Vladimirskaia; Vokzalnaia; Vygonnaia; Kazarmennaia; Sapozhnitskaia; and Uspenskaia

Streets. By the beginning of the 1940s, however, a Jewish majority remained only on the following streets: 91 percent of the homes on Proletarskaia (formerly Sapozhnitskaia); 82.4 percent on October Square (formerly Bazarnaia Square); 70.7 percent on Tankovaia (formerly Second Kladbishchenskaia); 64.3 percent on Uritskaia (formerly Vladimirskaia); 67.4 percent on Lenina (formerly Preobrazhenskaia); 59.3 percent on Kalinina (formerly Aleksandrovskaia); 57.5 percent on Kooperativnaia (formerly Kazarmennaia). Jews also occupied a sizable number of houses, some 43.7 percent, on the main street, Sovietskaia (formerly Uspenskaia), as well as on one of the prettiest streets, Naberezhnaia (43.6 percent), where they had not been a majority before the revolution.[155]

Unlike these streets and the town center generally, the industrial area was considered "Russian" by the early 1940s. Former peasants who had settled in Rechitsa in the 1930s because of collectivization lived there and in other areas on the outskirts. In those years Rechitsa absorbed several adjoining settlements: Novy Svet, Dachny, Il'icha Settlement. By the end of the 1930s, the total length of town streets was 100.6 kilometers.[156]

Some elements of the Orthodox population disapproved of the fact that Jewish houses, more spacious than their own, were located in the center of the town and that the status of the Jews had changed (particularly since they began receiving

The Smilovitskii family, 1929. Courtesy of Leonid Smilovitsky.

positions within the bureaucracy); during the time of the Russian Empire they had become accustomed to regarding Jews as officially sanctioned social pariahs. It is clear that the economic and the related actual legal status of wealthy and well-off traders even before 1917 was relatively high, but at that time their status was determined by the amount of capital they held. The change of power in 1917 led not only to a leveling of the economic status of all ethnic groups but also to a publicly proclaimed legal equality, the full measure of which, as pointed out earlier, did not extend to the many Jews who had been deprived of their rights. The gradual abolition of lishentsy status allowed every Jew to realize fully his or her capacities in government service as well, a field that had been forbidden to Jews before 1917 by a number of special decrees. The efficiency, readiness to learn, and mobility of many Jews advanced their careers to levels previously inconceivable in Russia. When Jews emerged as administrators and economic managers at various levels, however, the non-Jewish population was antagonized and blamed them for the government's socioeconomic failures across the country as a whole and for the costs of the new order within cities or specific enterprises.

The Soviet authorities themselves—as paradoxical as it may seem—inherited from the tsarist regime a dichotomous view of the population they ruled, and of Jews in particular, as "useful" and "useless." A minor change was made in terminology. In Soviet times the population began to be divided into "working" and "nonworking." Just as before the October coup, the borders between these extreme definitions were drawn arbitrarily, depending on the outlook of local bureaucrats and the shifts in the internal policies of the central authorities. However, if before 1917 such an approach merely codified the relationship to various social strata and its application caused only hypothetical changes in socio-legal status, in the 1920s and 1930s the transfer from one category to the other meant an actual and sudden change in this status.

DEMOGRAPHICS

Social upheavals and new career possibilities produced major effects on the demographic situation within the Jewish population. As noted, the birthrate among Jews in Rechitsa declined noticeably between the 1860s and the beginning of the twentieth century. By 1920 it had fallen to 18 births per thousand residents, compared with 58 per thousand in 1861.[157] The general mobilization of men between eighteen and forty (and in practice from the age of seventeen) to fight in the civil war that began in the summer of 1918 could not but have had an influence on the drop in the 1920 birthrate among Jews.[158] Most likely the birthrate among Jews increased after the demobilization of those soldiers who had survived, although only insignificantly. In any case, it began to lag even further behind the birthrate of the remainder of the population, which rose in the first half of the 1920s. There were 45 births for every thousand Russians living in the European territory of the USSR in those years, 42 per thousand Belorussians, and only 24 per thousand Jews.[159] Jews in the BSSR had almost exactly the same birthrate: 24.5 per thousand.[160] Of course, it was the rural population that created a higher birthrate among the non-Jewish population, but even among urbanites the birthrate among non-Jews was higher. As for Rechitsa, as a small city the correlation of the birthrate here between Jews and non-Jews did not differ markedly from that of the republic generally.

Between 1926 and 1935 the birthrate within the BSSR steadily declined. In Buda-Koshelevsk Raion, which bordered on Rechitsa Raion in Gomel region, official statistics reveal that in 1934 only 21.3 percent of pregnancies resulted in births.[161] The large number of abortions in the country induced the government to make them illegal in 1936. As a result, in the period 1936–1938 the birthrate in the country and in the BSSR in particular began to rise.[162] Beginning in 1939, however, because of the worsening economic situation in the USSR, it again began to drop. Trends in the birthrate among the Rechitsa population and among the Jews in particular were probably similar. The general decline in the birthrate across the country led to an even greater decline in births among Jews.

From 1917 to 1920, as can be seen from table 12, the total population of Rechitsa declined by 5,231, that is, by 30 percent. This was the largest decline in population in all the towns of Gomel Province.[163] This occurred not only because of the mobilization of men, however, since over this period the proportion of the male population in the town even rose by 2.3 percent after the demobilization and the release of prisoners captured during World War I.[164] Although their return did improve the demographic situation in Rechitsa, it did so only marginally.

A major reason for the population decline after the October Revolution was the slowing of economic migration into Rechitsa by Jews from surrounding areas. Although the pogroms in the raion in 1919–1921 led Jewish refugees to seek the protection of the strong garrison in Rechitsa (nearly one thousand Jews arrived from Kholmec alone), the political and economic situation in the town made them apprehensive.[165] Accordingly, some of them, even before the end of the civil war, migrated farther to more heavily populated centers of Soviet Russia (mainly to Gomel) or abroad. For the same reasons, during those years part of Rechitsa's native population, Jews and gentiles, migrated out of the town.

After the general stabilization of the situation, some Rechitsa natives who had migrated returned to the town, thanks to which its overall population rose by

2,591 people, that is, by 15 percent, between 1920 and 1923.[166] The growth of population from 1920 to 1923 occurred, despite the spread of two epidemics— typhus and measles—in Gomel Guberniia.[167] In Rechitsa itself in 1920, typhus (the *sypniak*) was evidently responsible for the deaths of several hundred people.[168] Two years later the situation in Rechitsa Raion had improved, at least if one overlooks the problem of scurvy, an illness that was more prevalent there than anywhere else in the province. In Rechitsa itself in 1922, 180 people died from epidemic diseases; these accounted for 12 percent of all deaths, a relatively low figure for those times. In eight of the eleven towns in Gomel Province, the situation was worse.[169]

Almost a fifth of the Rechitsa residents who returned home between 1920 and 1923 were demobilized soldiers. As a result the proportion of males in the Rechitsa population grew from 45.6 percent in 1920 to 49.4 percent in 1923.[170] In 1920 the percentages of males in the Jewish and the non-Jewish populations were the same, a fact that testifies to the equal proportions of ethnic groups that served in the army.[171] In the period from 1920 to 1926, the proportion of males among the Jewish population grew slightly from 45.7 percent to 46.42 percent.[172] The census of 1926 shows that there was a sexual imbalance in the 16–19, the 20–24, and the 24–29 age groups in both the Jewish population and the population as a whole.[173] Jewish males comprised, respectively, 46 percent, 39 percent, and 40 percent in each of these groups, while in other age groups the difference was insignificant. The situation was substantially different for non-Jewish males in these same age groups—42 percent, 45 percent, and 50.5 percent respectively. There was a difference between the proportion of Jewish and non-Jewish males in other age groups, but it was much less.

In the 16–19 age group the increased proportion of males among Jews can be explained, as noted in chapter 4, by the large number of male children born among them. The smaller percentage of male Jews in the remaining two age groups examined can be attributed to their greater mobility: they left Rechitsa to earn more money or to study. Young Jews from Rechitsa and other Belorussian centers, as well as from the former Pale of Settlement generally, most often migrated outside the republic and most commonly to the Russian Republic, resulting in a significant prevalence of males among the Jewish population there.[174] Jewish males from Rechitsa also migrated to Ukraine. This can be determined from the place of residence indicated in the list of those repressed,[175] and in particular, by those who were between the ages of twenty and twenty-nine in 1926.

The migration of Rechitsa Jews abroad also continued until the mid-1920s. The USSR at that time allowed persons between the ages of seventeen and fifty-five to leave only with special permission. Those who were leaving had to have the agreement of the receiving country.[176] All emigrants went first to Poland and from there traveled to Erets-Israel, Western Europe, or the United States, although a certain number of them remained in Poland. Relying only on official figures, one can determine that over the course of almost a year and a half, from August 1922 to the end of 1923, 2,928 Jews left Gomel Province.[177] In the first years after the revolution, the flow of refugees was small, but it grew from 1919 to 1923. In 1923, however, the Polish government passed a decree on returning refugees back to Russia, after which emigration declined. At the same time, the illegal Jewish emigration was apparently no less than the legal one.[178] After the mid-1920s it became a very complicated matter to leave the country.[179] The total number of Jewish emigrants from Rechitsa abroad from 1917 to 1925 can be estimated as between 1,000 and 1,500 persons.

Thus, because of these migrations, particularly of young men, and the drop in the birthrate, the proportion of Jews in the Rechitsa population declined. According to the census of 1920, Jews made up 52 percent of the population, while ethnic minorities, in declining order, were Russians, 44.15 percent; Belorussians, 2.2 percent; Poles, less than 1 percent. One must agree with Viktor Pichukov and Mikhail Starovoitov, who have calculated that the number of Belorussians (276 in total) had been understated in favor of the Russians.[180] This was a necessary measure for the authorities to justify the inclusion of Gomel Province into the RSFSR. By 1926, although the proportion of Jews in Rechitsa had declined to

TABLE 12. Statistics of the general and the Jewish populations of Rechitsa,
          1917–1939

Year	Total population	Number of Jews included	Percentage of Jews
1917[a]	17,594	—	—
1920[b]	12,363	6,439	52
1923[c]	15,139	7,428	49.2
1926[d]	16,559	7,386	44.6
1939[e]	29,796	7.237	24.3

Sources:
[a] *Biulleten' gomel'skogo gubernskogo statisticheskogo biuro,* 2:13.
[b] Ibid.; Pichukov and Starovoitov, *Gomel'shchina mnogonatsional'naia,* 149–150.
[c] Binshtok, *Evrei v Gomel'skoi oblasti,* 82.
[d] *Yidn in V.S.S.R.,* 9.
[e] *Vsesoiuznaia perepis' naseleniia 1939 goda, Gomel'skaia oblast',* CAHJP, RU 537.22, table 27.

44.6 percent (see table 12), they continued to form a relative majority by comparison with the Belorussians (33.7 percent) and the Russians (18.3 percent).[181]

In total, over the twelve years between 1914 and 1926, the proportion of Jews in Rechitsa declined from 59.1 percent to 44.6 percent. During that period their number in the town increased by 113 in all and this even despite the fact that the birthrate, which had declined between 1915 and 1920, had returned to its prewar level.[182]

The proportion of Jews within the entire population of Rechitsa Raion remained, even up to World War I, among the lowest in all of Minsk Guberniia, 8.7 percent. It was lower only in the Borisov (5.9 percent) and Minsk Raions (8.3 percent); at the same time their average proportion across the province was 9.3 percent.[183] By 1926 in Rechitsa Okrug the proportion of Jews had become the lowest in the BSSR, 6.9 percent, while the average across the republic was 8.2 percent.[184] After Rechitsa Raion had been formed, the proportion of Jews there, together with that in Rechitsa town, had reached 8.73 percent by 1939.[185] This growth resulted from the reduction of the rural area that came under the jurisdiction of Rechitsa.

The death rate of Jews in Rechitsa Raion in the 1920s and 1930s (particularly among infants) was lower than that of the surrounding non-Jewish population. As in earlier years this factor had an influence on the proportion of Jews in the raion population as a whole. The reasons for this, as was the case before 1917, were better sanitation and a more favorable seasonal prevalence of infant births. At the beginning of the 1930s, however, conditions among the peasantry deteriorated because of famine and the epidemics linked to it; bodies weakened by hunger are, as we know, much more susceptible to disease. This crisis resulted from the campaign for collectivization of the rural economy. Peasants who fled to the cities to escape collectivization and famine spread the epidemics there. Epidemics swept over the USSR in 1932–1933. They touched Rechitsa as well, particularly epidemics of typhoid fever, measles, and diphtheria. In the mid-1930s the rate of infant mortality in the country improved somewhat but began to increase again toward the end of the decade. In Rechitsa infant mortality increased from 88.4 per thousand persons in 1937 to 141.3 in the first eleven months of 1938, an increase of 160 percent.[186] Without doubt the increase in infant mortality in these years touched the Jewish population as well.

Toward the end of the 1930s, child mortality increased as well. According to the statistics for the BSSR over the period 1936–1938, the incidence among children of such serious illnesses as measles, whooping cough, typhus, diphtheria, and scarlet fever grew exponentially.[187] The large number of deaths among children of four and younger is attested in surveys taken among Jews who migrated from

Rechitsa. In many families only 25–50 percent of children in this age group survived. From 1934 to 1939 the death rate in Rechitsa, including that of children, very likely declined as it did in the USSR generally, though it rose again in 1940.[188]

In Rechitsa in the 1930s Jews continued to marry later than the rest of the population, as shown by the statistics from mestechkos in Gomel Oblast. In the 20–29 age group the number of married Jewish and non-Jewish women was the same, 62 percent; the proportion of married Jewish men—56 percent—was higher than that of Belorussian men (49 percent) and Russians (39.3 percent). This gap among married men was significantly smaller in the 30–39 age group; the figure remained almost the same among women. In older age groups, because of the their longer lifespan Jews had more married people than did the rest of the population. The difference among women in the 50–59 age group is striking: 67 percent of Jewish women were married; for Belorussians the figure was 56.4 percent; for Russians, 49.7 percent. It would not be wrong to assume that this imbalance was largely due to the higher death rate of the non-Jewish male population caused primarily by their traditional predilection for alcohol.[189] Although this predilection applied to women to a lesser degree, the drop in numbers of the non-Jewish population in this age group was considerably sharper than among Jews.[190] Because of the longer lifespan of Jews and the larger migration of Jewish young people from Rechitsa, the average age of the Jewish population here was five to ten years higher than that of the rest of the population.

From the mid-1920s Jewish migration from the mestechkos of the southeastern BSSR was to (in declining order) Leningrad, Moscow, Kiev, Minsk, Kharkov, and other cities.[191] According to questionnaires completed for the Holocaust Martyrs' and Heroes' Remembrance Authority, Yad Vashem, in Jerusalem (we will return to this questionnaire later), 3.5 times more Jewish natives of Rechitsa migrated to Leningrad than to Moscow. This was linked with the traditional attraction of Belorussian Jewry, unlike that of Ukraine, to the northern capital. These same questionnaires filled out by 632 Jews born in Rechitsa in various years show that by June 1941, two-thirds of them remained in the town and the rest had migrated, primarily in the 1920s and 1930s. The departure of the Jewish population by the end of the 1930s reduced their numbers in Rechitsa to 24.3 percent of the overall population (see table 12). Not since the beginning of the nineteenth century did Rechitsa have such a low percentage of Jews. The Jews again became a minority in the town, though a significant one. Evidently as a result of the shift in ethnic policy within the territory of the BSSR that led to a change in the way the local Slavic population identified itself, the proportion of Russians in Rechitsa declined to 11.2 percent, while that of Belorussians grew to 59 percent.

Also, the proportion of Ukrainians in the town had almost doubled since the last census. In 1939 they made up 4 percent of the population, due to their flight here during the famine of 1933–1934.[192]

The Jewish population of Rechitsa increased somewhat in the autumn of 1939, that is, after the census had been taken, because of the arrival of refugees who fled from Polish territories after the Molotov-Ribbentrop Pact with Germany. At that time, some five hundred refugees, the overwhelming majority of them Jews, arrived in Rechitsa. About a hundred of these people were given jobs in the match factory; a similar number of refugees were sent to labor camps, mainly in the Urals and Siberia, in 1940; and some moved to the Ukraine and to Russia.[193] Taking into account as well the migration from the town over the two years that followed the 1939 census, the overall Jewish population of Rechitsa by June 22, 1941, can be estimated as 7,500.

By comparison with the Jewish population of Rechitsa, which had declined from 1913 to 1939 by several hundred people, the overall population of the town over this near quarter century had grown by 56.4 percent, while the relative growth of the population was 229 percent. The overall population of Gomel over this period grew by only 27.8 percent, while its relative growth was 138.5 percent. The population of Rogachev, a town whose economy had formerly rivaled Rechitsa's, not only did not increase but actually declined by 30.7 percent.[194]

RELIGION

In ending restrictions on religious belief, the February Revolution enabled religious life to flourish. The number of synagogues in the town increased. The new authorities did not attempt to control the lives of believers, and as a result the institution of state-appointed rabbis essentially ended. The Bolsheviks, who came to power in October 1917, regarded religion as a harmful alternative ideology that they tried to combat in various ways. The beginning of this struggle was the decree of January 23, 1918, on the separation of the state and religion. Judaism, which in tsarist times existed only as a tolerated religion, was not closely connected with the state; therefore such traditional Jewish religious institutions as the rabbinate, the heder, and the synagogue were not directly damaged to any degree, at least initially. In general, in these early years the authorities were busy maintaining their grip on power and had neither the forces nor the means for a total struggle with religion. This was an item put on the agenda for a later date, the beginning of the 1920s. The primary role in the struggle with the Jewish religion was assigned to the Evsektsiia of the Central Committee of the All-Russian Communist Party (Bolsheviks), which, through its branches in many towns with a Jewish population, could ensure that local authorities carried out one or another of the antireligious resolutions and initiate the struggle.

The decree by the VTsIK (the All-Union Central Executive Committee) of February 23, 1922, on the confiscation of church valuables marked an intensification of the persecution of the church. The reason and the justification for this decree was the famine that had gripped Russian, particularly in the Volga area, since 1921.[195] The nationalization of synagogue utensils and synagogues was part of this campaign. Unlike the churches the synagogues in Eastern Europe were impoverished, apart from those in large cities, where wealthy members of the community donated rich utensils to the synagogues and thus consolidated their authority among the congregants. There was nothing, therefore, to nationalize, with the exception, perhaps, of some silver candlesticks, the crowns for the Torah (*keter Tora*), medallions from the Torah scroll (*Tora-schild*), pointers for reading, and incense boxes (*bsamim*). In the majority of synagogues, which as a rule were small ones, these utensils were made of simple metals. The confiscation in Rechitsa, carried out with some help from the Evsektsiia, amounted to no more than twelve pounds (about five kilograms) of silver from all the synagogues.[196] Authorities everywhere were disappointed with the insignificant quantity of silver valuables in the synagogues, particularly given the widespread opinion in Russia of the wealth of Jewish kahals. In neighboring Gomel this disappointment was expressed by the direct accusation that rabbis were hiding the synagogue utensils, which may have been the case. It may well be that this disappointment later became one of the reasons that more synagogues were nationalized than churches. Another reason may have been the large number of Jews among the local authorities who were wary of being accused of sympathy for "their" religion and thus took an uncompromising attitude toward Jewish synagogues. At the beginning of the 1920s, a noisy campaign, headed by the Evsektsiia, preceded the closure of synagogues in the BSSR. This found expression in antireligious newspaper propaganda and in public trials, real or mock, of heders, *shameses* ("synagogue beadles," Yiddish), rabbis, and melameds. In Rechitsa, as in other places, the Evsektsiia organized provocative antireligious demonstrations in times of traditional holidays; these often ended in verbal abuse and arguments, if not in fights. Such confrontations heightened the conflict between generations and hastened the destruction of the Jewish community in the mestechkos. In 1923, during this campaign, a synagogue building was nationalized for the first time.[197]

In 1923–1924 the authorities began changing their tactics in the struggle with religion: now it took the form of atheist propaganda.[198] For example, on the eve of the Jewish New Year and the fast of Yom Kippur (the Day of Atonement), in the autumn of 1928, the Evsektsiia carried out a regular antireligious campaign designed for those particular days.[199] The authorities used the initiative "from below" to carry out their antireligious measures. As early as 1925, the Evsektsiia had initiated, through the handcraftsmen's society, the transfer to that society of the building housing the Kopys' Synagogue on Lunacharskaia Street. After remodeling, the Avrom Merezhin Club (Merezhin was one of the functionaries of the Evsektsiia) was opened here.[200] Over the next few years, the premises of three more synagogues were taken over in the same way. The buildings were transformed into a town sports hall, a club for construction workers, the House of Pioneers, and even an apartment building.

One component of the new campaign against religion that began in early 1929 and continued to 1932 was the closure of houses of prayer, among them synagogues. This campaign was preceded by the forced declaration, organized by the authorities in 1928, in which Soviet rabbis announced to the West that the Jewish religion was not being persecuted in the USSR. Among the signers of the declaration were the Rechitsa rabbis Avraam Roginskii and Hirsh Reinin.[201] In the wake of this, through the period 1929–1932, came the closure of more than half of the synagogues that were still active within the territory of the BSSR.[202] Through the summer of 1929, a real struggle broke out in Rechitsa over the building that had housed the largest synagogue, the High Synagogue, on Sovietskaia Street, one of the four synagogues that was left for Jews by that time. Formally, several hundred handcraftsmen from various cooperatives had demanded that the authorities nationalize this building.[203] Because religious believers actively opposed this measure, the authorities hesitated. Thus, in that same year, the Evsektsiia initiated new demands—from four hundred handcraftsmen and almost as many workers in the "Dnieper" factory—to hand over the building for their use.[204] Finally, on January 15, 1930, at the height of collectivization, the authorities decided to nationalize the building. Their decision had a propagandistic nature that can be seen in its wording: "in consideration of the insistent demands of workers from a number of major enterprises, demands that had been drawn up in resolutions of general meetings of more than 5,000 people."[205] Given the size of the Rechitsa population, including children, and the overall number of workers in the town's factories, this figure seems highly elevated. Also, it was the Jewish women and the elderly workers who were religious. The correspondent of the Yiddish newspaper *Oktiabr* noted this in his story lamenting their continued loyalty to kosher meat.[206] Another correspondent noted the same thing in his report about the large number of Jewish women who gathered in the synagogue to hear a *magid* ("preacher," Hebrew) who had come to Rechitsa.[207]

The members of a tradesmen's cooperative behaved less aggressively toward religion. In 1925, during the reading of a report on the topic "Where did Pesakh come from?," they began defending the Jewish religion, which provoked terrible displeasure from the Evsektsiia. The result was the creation of a commission to check on the activity of this cooperative.[208]

At the beginning of the 1930s, the struggle against religion became the prerogative of the NKVD. Fear of persecution from this body had a greater effect on active adherents to Judaism than did the measures of the Evsektsiia, which was closed in 1930 as part of the abolition of national sections within the party.[209]

During another wave of closures of churches and synagogues organized in 1937–1938 in the USSR generally and in the BSSR in particular, the Rechitsa authorities deprived believers of yet another synagogue.[210] This was the Old Lubavitch Synagogue on the corner of Proletarskaia and Kalinina Streets. This time the authorities had even less regard for the population and so did not even notify the believers beforehand. Thanks only to decisive action by Jews from nearby homes, the Torah scrolls were rescued from the synagogue at the last moment. After a remodeling, the authorities opened a children's technical center there; after the war it housed a dermatovenerology dispensary.[211]

In the 1920s the majority of Rechitsa's Jewish population remained traditional believers. Many of those in organized cooperatives would find various pretexts not to work on the Sabbath and particular on Jewish holidays. The management of the cooperatives had to respect the attachment of their workers to Judaism and did so by taking a lenient attitude to these "acts of truancy." Moreover, managers of cooperatives were, as a rule, compelled to hide such facts as best they could from members of the Evsektsiia. Handcraftsmen who were not in organized cooperatives found it easier to observe Jewish traditions, something that became an important argument against their enrolling in cooperatives.[212] It is a revealing fact that during these years, managers of cooperatives and even workers' committees in various enterprises took part in the organized sale of kosher meat to Jewish workers. Though they clearly found this activity burdensome, they had to do it because of pressure from religious workers, women above all.[213]

A few rabbis remained in Rechitsa after the October Revolution. The most striking of these was Chaim-Shlioma Kom. He continued to head the yeshiva for several years after the revolution, but because of economic difficulties and pressure from the authorities, he had to close it at the beginning of the 1920s. At that time, he was regarded as the chief rabbi of the town, and as earlier, he headed the Rechitsa rabbinical court.[214] He nonetheless evidently endured material difficulties even more severe than those of other rabbis and people holding religious posts (i.e., the *klei kodesh*, literally, the "sacred vessels," Hebrew), and he was compelled to seek additional sources of income. Specifically, Rabbi Kom's family took up raising geese in order to feed themselves. In a letter written in Hebrew to his son in Erets-Israel at the end of 1923, he dwelled in detail on the economic problems of rabbis in the mestechkos:

> Have you forgotten how the people of our town have behaved since times long passed? Even in peaceful times, they cried out that the rabbis' requisitions were taking away their livelihood. This was even more so in years that were not peaceful and after the wealthy and prosperous had been cast down utterly and their places taken by others, coarser by nature. The collection for boxes, the collection for candles have been reduced to nothing, and after them the other collections have been abandoned one after the other, including the Hanukkah and the Purim; many also no longer pay at weddings; and now that there are no loans or debts that can be recalled, religious ceremonies scarcely exist since they have been forbidden by the authorities. Nothing remains for the rabbis but to ask someone in authority to collect donations from the congregants for them.[215]

In addition to all this, the authorities imposed higher taxes on the rabbis. In another letter to his son, Rabbi Kom lamented that they had taken 9 rubles from him, and two weeks later he was told that this had covered only part of the tax.[216] The rabbi's taxes indeed seem high, considering that for 1.5 rubles one could buy a *pood* (sixteen kilograms) of rye flour in Rechitsa at the time, while a pound (400 grams) of nonkosher beef cost 22 kopeks.[217]

Under such circumstances Chaim-Shlioma Kom had little choice but to immigrate to Jerusalem in 1924, where he became the rabbi of one of the town's divisions.[218] After his departure the most authoritative rabbi in the town was Abraam Poginskii, who in December 1925 registered the Rechitsa congregation under the name "Adas Israel" with the authorities in Gomel. Its president was Barukh Porotskii.[219] During their trip to Gomel they visited Rabbi Shneur-Zalman Shneerson, a former resident of Rechitsa with whom they had always maintained a close relationship. They discussed the question of organizing an all-union congress of religious communities in Leningrad. At the same time, rabbis and leaders of religious communities in Gomel, Rechitsa, Novozybkov, Mglin, Starodub, Klintsy, Klimov, and Unecha had gathered in Gomel for a general meeting. This became known to the authorities, and all the participants in this meeting were arrested.[220] They were released shortly thereafter.

At the instigation of the Evsektsiia, on April 23, 1921, the People's Commissariat of Education accepted a resolution on the closure of yeshivas and heders.[221] This resolution could not be enforced, however, either because local authorities did not have the financial resources or they did not want to spend them on increasing the number of alternative secular schools. The Evsektsiia, therefore, had to press for ways to carry out the resolution by passing additional, local decrees. In the BSSR such a decree was issued in August 1922. Thereafter religious educational institutions began to be closed or, more commonly, to begin operating illegally. The official closing of the heder in which David Rubinoff and some twenty other children aged five to eight studied is indelibly stamped in his memory. The heder, located on Kooperativnaia Street (now Koneva Street), was invaded by four soldiers: "They looked tough and frightening. They humiliated the teacher by cutting off his beard and told the terrified children that the melamed was a liar and that God did not exist."[222] As a result the majority of heders began to operate illegally, after dividing themselves into smaller units.[223] This process was accompanied by a reduction in the number of students, a drop in the level of instruction. and a lowering of the payment to the melamed, something that Rabbi Chaim-Shlioma Kom lamented in his letter mentioned above.[224]

The measures taken by the authorities against the rabbis, the synagogues, and religious schools bore fruit. According to one study, by 1930 only 23.6 percent of the Jewish population remained believers; the figure was somewhat higher for Russians and Belorussians—28.5 percent. Among Poles, however, 44.1 percent maintained their belief.[225] Among Jews the men were more religious than the women, who represented 63 percent of all believers.[226] It is very likely that these same figures applied to Rechitsa as well.

Rabbis Avraam Roginskii and Hirsh Reinin responded to the decline in religiousness in the Jewish population of Rechitsa. In 1929 they spoke out against the violation of Sabbath rest by Jewish workers. Their comments found a response in the town, since the rabbis continued to have influence not only among workers but also among the intelligentsia.[227] Aside from these rabbis, the names of a few more people who held religious positions in Rechitsa in the 1920s and 1930s are also known. Hirsh Tëmkin was the gabbai in the Rogove Synagogue in the first half of the 1920s.[228] The duties of shoychet and mohel in the 1930s were carried out by Heshel Pinskii; other shoychets were Israel Malinkovich, Ziama Pinskii, Hershel Tsivlin, and Aron Khavin, who had moved to Rechitsa from Kholmech in 1933.[229] In the 1930s, on Rechnaia Street, in a bathhouse near the Dnieper there was a *mikvah*. This mikvah continued to exist after the war until the bathhouse was closed at the beginning of the 1950s. In the 1920s and the beginning of the 1930s, there was a Jewish hospice in Rechitsa. One of the handcraftsmen's societies had its own medical center. It is appropriate to mention here the midwife Kaletskii, who served the Jewish population in the 1920s and through whose hands passed the majority of the infants born at this time. Leah Fain-shmidt was another Jewish midwife.[230]

The shift of Jews from private business and trades to state organizations and enterprises in the 1920s made it practically impossible for them to observe the Sabbath rest as well as several other prohibitions of the Jewish yearly calendar cycle. As a result of the persecution of heders and synagogues, Jews were deprived of the opportunity to pray and study the Torah collectively and openly. The closure of mikvahs and the persecution of shoychets and mohels made it more difficult to observe a number of Jewish religious rituals. A broad campaign of anti-religious propaganda, directed particularly at youth, took place across the whole country. Given such conditions, the majority of Jewish youth in Rechitsa began to lose touch with Jewish traditions. The Catholic and the Orthodox churches in Soviet Russia suffered scarcely less persecution. The Catholic church in Rechitsa was confiscated in 1932, and the Orthodox Uspenskii Cathedral in 1935.[231]

EDUCATION AND CULTURE

Changes of no less importance occurred after 1917 in the areas of education and culture. According to the 1926 census, 89.5 percent of the Jews in Rechitsa indicated that Yiddish was their first language.[232] The vast majority of the rest of the population declared Russian as their first language. The people of Rechitsa had a much stronger connection to Yiddish than was typical in urban centers (68 percent) in the USSR, and the figures for the town itself were closer to the demographic indicators for those populated areas defined as rural (94 percent).[233] These data reveal the low level of assimilation in the town. The census materials for 1939 contained no data for first language in Rechitsa. Such information was provided only for the urban and rural populations of the entire Gomel Oblast, and it showed that only 47.7 percent in the towns and 61.3 percent in rural areas (what is meant here, in fact, are the mestechkos, since the language environment was limited due to the small number of Jews in villages) declared Yiddish as their first language.[234] Considering that the percentage of Yiddish speakers in previous years in Rechitsa was close to that in the shtetls, we may assume that in 1939 in Rechitsa about 57 percent of Jews had kept to Yiddish, while the remainder considered Russian their first language.

As noted earlier, Hebrew was not alien to the people of Rechitsa, particularly those who moved in Zionist circles. Evidence of this comes from the fact that in mid-February 1920 Yehuda Kom gave a lecture in Hebrew on the poet Yehuda-Leib Gordon to a general meeting of Hekhaluts.[235] At the beginning of the 1920s, the Evsektsiia began an active struggle against Hebrew and the members of the

Zionist parties, particularly because this issue concerned the politics of staffing in the field of education. In 1923 all personnel in the three children's homes located in the town were dismissed; they had been members of various Zionist parties. In their place were appointed unqualified workers who had, however, completed a party school and therefore had the "correct" point of view.[236]

In Rechitsa Raion in 1923, 40 percent of school-age children of all ethnicities were not attending state schools.[237] Evidently among them were many Jews who were studying in heders. On the one hand, there were not enough state schools; on the other hand, there was still a strong attachment to religion among the population. By my estimate some 60 percent of Jewish children were studying in heders at the beginning of the 1920s. The rapid growth of state schools and the efforts of the Evsektsiia in persecuting melameds and carrying out antireligious agitation pressured parents and led to some decline in the number of children in underground heders over the first half of the 1920s. An increase in the proportion of boys in state schools in Rechitsa leads to this conclusion. In 1925 boys comprised 53.1 percent of all pupils in the town in grades 1 to 4, while the proportion in grades 5 to 7 was 47.5 percent.[238]

According to figures for the same year, the town had nine primary schools (grades 1 to 4), two middle schools (grades 5 to 7), and two seven-year schools (grades 1 to 7).[239] One-quarter of the teachers in these schools were Jews, a proportion considerably below that of the republic generally, where seven out of every ten teachers were Jews.[240] Most likely the situation in Rechitsa changed little until the late 1930s.

Among the schools mentioned there were two in which teaching was done in Yiddish—a four-year school and a seven-year school that opened in Rechitsa in the early 1920s. In 1923, 280 children were enrolled in them.[241] By 1929—after these schools had been combined into one seven-year institution—the number of children studying in Yiddish had increased by 31 percent and totaled 406.[242] Since there were 1,181 Jewish children of school age (from seven to thirteen) in Rechitsa that year, the proportion of Jewish children attending schools with instruction in Yiddish was 34.4 percent.[243] Another 285 Jewish children (24.1 percent) attended schools where the language was Russian or Belorussian.[244] Although twelve years had passed since the revolution, the remaining 490 Jewish children, 41.5 percent of all those in school, were attending heders or were not going to school at all. In the entire BSSR and the Ukrainian Republic, the proportion of Jewish children who were not attending Soviet schools at this time is estimated to be rather smaller, 34 percent.[245] However, if one keeps in mind the increase in the proportion of Jewish children attending schools with instruction in Yiddish within the republic, the situation in Rechitsa in 1929 appears close to the average for the BSSR.

Arkadii Zeltser notes that the illegal heders continued to exist in significant numbers until the mid-1930s, after which the NKVD took much tougher measures against them.[246] By that time probably no more heders existed in Rechitsa. Illegal heders, for example, were run by Israel-Barukh Sosnovskii and Mendel Lapitskii only until the beginning of the 1930s. Children would study in heders after their day in a state school. The melameds Aizik Fradkin and Israel Malinkovich taught a few children even until the war.[247]

In 1929, 58.8 percent of all Jewish children studying in state schools attended the Rechitsa school with instruction in Yiddish. This is somewhat higher than the average suggested by the American historian Zvi Halevy for the whole BSSR. He calculated that in 1929, 56 percent of all Jewish children studying in state schools in the BSSR attended the Yiddish school.[248] The Rechitsa Yiddish school was popular because of its high standards and its material resources, which were greater than those of other schools thanks to the American Jewish charitable society Joint.[249] The end of this aid in the early 1930s and, even more, the impossibility of continuing education in Yiddish after finishing the school led to a decline in the number of children attending the Yiddish school in Rechitsa. Even earlier, however, a number of the older pupils found Yiddish instruction to be a burden.[250]

The surveys I have taken among Rechitsa natives show that Jewish families who maintained their religion did not always enroll their children in Yiddish schools once study in a heder had become impossible. The opposite was more often the case, since the antireligious, anti-Jewish propaganda in the so-called Jewish school was stronger.[251] Religious parents preferred to send their children to a "Russian" school, where a pupil's absence for a Jewish holiday was not as obvious. Generally, the children who had grown up in a Yiddish-language milieu were sent to the Yiddish school. Families in which the parents (or at least one of them) spoke Russian to the children and used Yiddish mainly for speaking to each other preferred Russian or Belorussian schools for practical considerations. The situation was quite different in the 1920s and even at the beginning of the 1930s in small mestechkos with a predominantly Jewish population, where scarcely anyone in the older generation had a fluent knowledge of Russian.

Before its merger with the seven-year school, the director of the four-year Yiddish school in Rechitsa was Moishe Parkhovnik; the seven-year school's director was Mikhel Erenburg (at the beginning of the 1930s this institution became the Iakov Sverdlov ten-year school).[252] In 1935 the school was remodeled; physics and chemistry rooms were provided. A so-called grade 0 was added to the school to prepare children for grade 1.[253]

By the beginning of the 1930s, it had become obvious to the central authorities that the Evsektsiia's efforts at spreading Soviet propaganda among the Jewish population in a language they understood had not proven to be of much value. The Jews themselves realized that an education in Yiddish limited opportunities for more-advanced study and for finding work; they began studying Russian much more willingly and became interested in reading materials in Russian. The popularity of Yiddish schools had declined even more by the mid-1930s. Accordingly, the authorities, who generally followed a pragmatic policy on language in the field of education, closed all the Yiddish schools in the BSSR in September 1938.[254] The Rechitsa Yiddish school switched its language of instruction to Belorussian. There was no obvious negative reaction to that move. M. Tsimberg, who had been an inspector in the National Minorities' Section of the Raion People's Commissariat of Education, was appointed director of what in essence was a newly created Belorussian seven-year school (in the same building).[255] In Rechitsa, as in other centers, the pupils and the teachers in Yiddish schools were distributed among other town schools where the language was Russian or Belorussian. Being transferred in this way could not help but have an effect on the progress of Jewish pupils, but because the level of instruction in the Yiddish schools was higher than the average in the town, many of them adapted relatively quickly to the new conditions of study.[256] Meir Chakhotskii, who was transferred to School no. 3, where the language was Belorussian, even received a letter of commendation at the end of the 1938–1939 school year.

In 1929 a pedagogical technical-vocational school that served mainly to prepare teachers for primary grades was opened in Rechitsa.[257] Many of its students were Jews. By 1935 there was one secondary school, two seven-year schools, and six primary schools in the town.[258] An eighteen-month school for nurses was opened in 1937.[259] In all, by the beginning of the war there were thirteen primary and high schools in Rechitsa (with a total of 5,874 pupils and 206 teachers), as well as a pedagogical institute and a school for nurses.[260]

All of Rechitsa's educational institutions had many Jews on their teaching staff, but the lack of complete figures makes it impossible to determine the exact percentage. Riva Finkelberg was in charge of preschool education in the Rechitsa Section of the Ministry of Education. On the eve of the war with Germany, she and her husband, M. Tsimberg, were sent to Western Belorussia to set up a Soviet system of education.[261] Contrary to their banning of Yiddish-language instruction in schools in Eastern Belorussia, the authorities introduced it in western areas at the end of 1939. Thus, by the beginning of 1940 there were eighteen such schools in Pinsk Province, and in Baranovichi as many as forty-six.[262] The reason for this policy, inconsistent though it may seem at first glance, was the attempt to give children a rapid, ideologically tinged education in a language they understood. Doing this in another language that was understood in this area—Polish—seemed wrong at a time when the USSR was moving toward chauvinism as a national policy. By opening Yiddish schools, the authorities again demonstrated their pragmatism in the field of education.

By 1926 the average literacy rate in the Jewish population of Rechitsa, including infants, was 70.3 percent, while it was 64.2 percent among non-Jews.[263] The data for the Jewish population are very close to the average for Jews in urban areas in the BSSR, 69.1 percent.[264] By 1939 the proportion of literate people in Gomel Oblast in the 9–19 age group had practically equaled that of other nationalities, reaching almost 99 percent, while the proportion of Jewish literates in the 20–49 age group in towns was several points higher; in rural areas (95.4 percent literate among Jews) they were ahead of Russians by 1.8 percent and Belorussians by 18 percent.[265] According to this same census, for every thousand people with higher education in Gomel Oblast there were 15.4 Jews, 14.2 Russians, and only 2 Belorussians.[266]

In 1926 a section with instruction in Yiddish was opened at a school for working youth in Rechitsa; at the same time, however, as can be seen by the statistics quoted earlier for books that were read, the view of Yiddish as a language without many prospects was growing stronger. Therefore, the very idea of a section with instruction in Yiddish led to concerns that it would be difficult to find people willing to study in it. These fears were not realized. There were twenty-two students (thirteen party members, nine not), which was sufficient for the section to open. In his report on this, the correspondent of the Minsk Yiddish newspaper *Oktiabr* noted with satisfaction that none of the students in the new section was older than twenty-two.[267]

As mentioned, Rechitsa in the 1920s had three small Jewish children's homes that housed altogether about ninety children, mainly those who had been orphaned because of pogroms in nearby mestechkos. The teachers spoke Yiddish to the children. In 1928 two children's homes were amalgamated. For preschoolers there was a kindergarten, also in Yiddish, attached to these homes.[268] In 1939 the language used in the children's homes became Belorussian.[269]

The installation of electrical service in the town in 1921 made a deep impression on the inhabitants of Rechitsa. David Rubinoff, mentioned earlier, recalled the day on which his aunt Rosa Sverdlova's apartment—one of the few that was

Jewish kindergarten, 1930. Courtesy of Leonid Smilovitsky.

equipped with electricity—was first lit up by a single bulb (more than one was not allowed). Many people gathered to look at this "miracle," and all of them were enchanted; he, as an eight-year-old nephew, had the privilege of staying to gaze upon the light bulb for a long time.[270] By the early 1930s there were already three electric generating stations operating in Rechitsa.[271] By the end of the 1930s, 77 percent of the streets were illuminated.[272] The population viewed electrification of the town less as inevitable progress and more as the triumph of the new order. Radio had a no less powerful effect on the population. Radio became known in Rechitsa at the very beginning of the 1930s, when local amateurs began assembling their own radio receivers, which became an object of pride for their owners.[273] The general public of Rechitsa came to know radio in 1936–1937, when loudspeakers (or "plates," as they were then called) were hung on lampposts. Another innovation in the town in the 1930s was the appearance of passenger buses that traveled along two routes.[274]

A House of Culture was set up in the now nationalized building of the Uspenskii Cathedral after it had been extensively renovated (at a cost of 760,000 rubles). The first floor was equipped as a nine-hundred-seat auditorium with a balcony and a mechanized stage; the second story housed the town library and a small meeting hall. Two lobbies were added, and the overall usable space was expanded threefold.

The authorities carried out widespread propaganda campaigns on behalf of the new order by various means. The cinema and the press had a special place in this process. The authorities, therefore, made considerable efforts to publish and distribute newspapers in national languages, including Yiddish. In cases where it was difficult to establish a separate newspaper in a minority language in an area with a large concentration of speakers, other print media would include articles, columns, or whole pages in the language concerned. Thus the regional Rechitsa newspaper *Rechitskaia Pravda* (later renamed *Zaria Kommuny*) published material in Yiddish from time to time.

The local press in the former Pale of Settlement devoted a particularly large amount of space to conditions in the mestechkos and in general to their modernization. This news was reported to readers in Rechitsa as well. In the 1920s the authorities repaired abandoned buildings and roads, and in the 1930s, they paved several central streets. By the end of the 1930s, more than half of Bazaar Square had been paved as well. The majority of streets remained unpaved, however, and in spring and summer they were impassable because of puddles and mud.

Local authorities tried to use newspapers to familiarize the population with the new realities of life, but the effect produced was not entirely the one desired: the local residents began to realize that living this "exuberant new life" was possible only if one moved away to a big town. Jewish youth fled Rechitsa to continue their educations in Moscow, Minsk, Kiev, and particularly Leningrad, a city that people in Rechitsa had traditionally preferred as a center for education. The young people who left Rechitsa almost always went to their relatives or friends in the big cities, counting on them for help in establishing themselves in a new place.[275] After completing studies in a university or an institute, a small number of them—several dozen—continued their education and went on to receive scholarly degrees. The majority of young specialists remained in the cities where they had studied. A smaller number of them returned to the BSSR to work, mainly in Minsk, Gomel, and Vitebsk. Only an insignificant few young people returned to work in Rechitsa. But even this led to a fivefold increase in the number of Jews with higher education there between the mid-1920s and the end of the 1930s.[276]

Young people in the mestechkos were attracted to the new centers by the social life—the clubs, which the authorities held up as an alternative to the synagogues. In Rechitsa the central role in social and cultural influence on the Jewish population was the Handcraftsmen's Club. In 1926 a music circle and two drama circles (in Yiddish and in Russian) were opened there. They put on concerts and plays, and there was also a library. Most likely, the library patrons were mainly Jews since there were more of them among the handcraftsmen, and the number of literate people was higher among the Jews than among the rest of the population. In the mid-1920s Rechitsa Jews, first and foremost children and young people (and without doubt they were the most ardent readers), preferred books in Russian. Thus in 1926, 19,500 books were checked out of this library; of these, books in Hebrew and Yiddish made up 13 percent; in Belorussian, 1.33 percent; and the remainder, by all appearances, were in Russian.[277] Periodicals in Yiddish and in Russian could be found here, although there were none in Hebrew; in those years no periodicals in Hebrew were published in the USSR.

According to the figures for 1927, Yiddish newspaper subscriptions in Rechitsa were as follows: *D'er 'Emes*, twenty-eight subscribers; *Yunger Arbeter*, thirty-three; *Yunger Pioner*, six. For magazines: *Shtern*, ten; *Yungvald*, ten.[278] Among the subscribers were social organizations, as well as members of the party and the Komsomol, who were obliged to subscribe to these publications by the local bureau of the Evsektsiia. The number of subscribers in towns and shtetls testifies to the success of the work of local representatives of the Evsektsiia. These data, however, should not be regarded as indicators of the number of Jews who regularly read in Yiddish. Most Rechitsa Jews preferred not to subscribe to Yiddish periodicals but rather to read and examine them in the library or on newsstands on the street. A few people in Rechitsa read literature only in Yiddish and ignored Soviet propagandistic periodicals. They had the opportunity to buy poetry and prose published in Yiddish in the USSR at the time in the Rechitsa section of the Shul un bukh Publishing House. In 1927 that publishing house sold books (including social and political journalism and textbooks) to a value of 1,500 rubles, a sizable sum, particularly considering the difficult economic situation of that time.[279]

In the 1920s and 1930s, the so-called Worker's Club was housed in the two-story building of the former Kupecheskii (Merchant's) Synagogue on the corner of Lenina and Kalinina Streets (after the war the Prosecutor's Office took over this building). The club offered its building for use as an amateur theater. The directors were the former professional actor Moisei Bliankman and the hairdresser Iona Kanevskii. The amateur actors were mainly craftspeople and artisans from Rechitsa, the most prominent among them being Iankel Kravchenko, Moshe Sverdlov, and the Unegovskii sisters. They performed plays by Sholem Aleichem, Peretz, Ansky, and Kushnirov and also ones from the repertoire of the Belorussian State Jewish Theater in Minsk. The plays *Holiday in Kasrilovka, Herschel Ostropoler, The Recruit, Heder, The Deaf Man, The Song of Songs, The Sorceress, Wandering Stars, Two Hundred Thousand, Tevye the Milkman, Hirsh Lekkert,* and others enjoyed success. Jewish theatrical troupes from Ukraine (including that of Iakov Guzik) also performed here. They put on the plays *The Dybbuk*, *The Sorceress*, *Spring*, and others.[280] Sometimes movies, or as they were called for many years in Rechitsa and other mestechkos, "pictures," were shown here.

Lenin's slogan about the importance of the cinema was taken to heart by Stalin, so it was no accident that Rechitsa's most important cultural center was the M. I. Kalinin Movie Theater. Each new film was an event in the town, one that the authorities used to propagandize the triumph of the new order over the old life of the town. Once in 1935, when the film broke during a showing and the audience began to express its indignation, the club manager announced: "Go to your rabbi and complain."[281]

THE REPRESSIONS

To suppress potential opposition and dissatisfaction, the Soviet state apparatus carried out widespread political repression from the 1920s to the mid-1950s. Members of various ethnic groups within the BSSR fell victim to these measures; however, the percentage of Jews among all those repressed was somewhat higher than their proportion of the general population. According to evidence compiled by Vladimir Adamushko, that proportion during the years of repression in the republic amounted to 8.93 percent, while the 1939 census (chosen here because the major wave of the repressions came at the end of the 1930s) showed that Jews comprised 6.7 percent of the population.[282]

If we assume that the proportion of Jews who were immediately executed corresponded to their proportion that was sent to labor camps and colonies, then this proportion, according to Adamushko, fundamentally differs from the corresponding proportion for the country as a whole, as indicated in the collective study "Victims of the Soviet Penal System in the Pre-war Years." According to it, the proportion of Jews in corrective labor camps in 1939 was 1.5 percent, that is, less than the percentage of Jews in the population of the USSR generally, which was about 1.8 percent in 1939.[283] However, such a low percentage of Jews imprisoned in camps is not consistent with their high proportion among white-collar workers and casts doubt on the accuracy of these statistics even in the eyes of the authors, who state in a footnote that the data evidently derive from declarations of ethnicity made by the arrested people themselves.[284] It is understandable that under conditions of ever-increasing anti-Semitism, a large number of imprisoned Jews preferred to conceal their ethnicity.

The research of the demographer Viktor Zemskov, one of the authors of the collective work mentioned above, reveals indirectly that the proportion of repressed Jews was in fact significantly higher within the country as a whole. His figures on the composition by ethnicity of deportees, the exiled, and the banished on January 1, 1953, show that Jews made up 5.1 percent.[285] Although several Jewish cultural figures exiled in the early 1950s would now be included in this figure, their numbers were not large and would not have significantly altered the proportion of Jews who had been serving out their sentences since the end of the 1930s. On the other hand, a number of collaborationists, representatives of banished nations, and former Soviet prisoners of war liberated from German captivity would now be included. Therefore, the percentage of Jews among deportees, the exiled, and the banished for the whole USSR should have been higher in 1939 than in 1953. Perhaps the actual percentage of Jewish prisoners in Soviet camps in 1939 was also similar to the percentage of Jews among deportees, the exiled, and the banished.

Archival sources of the NKVD also confirm Vladimir Adamushko's findings. The proportion of Zionists and Bundists alone comprised 8.8 percent of the 2,750 people repressed during the devastation of the so-called anti-Soviet underground in the BSSR in 1937–1938. The proportion of Jews among all those repressed might have been as high as 15 percent, considering that many of them were among the Trotskyites and Zinovievites arrested at the same time.[286]

The figures cited by Adamushko show yet again the zeal with which the Belorussian authorities began throwing Jews, above all those from the intelligentsia and the bureaucracy, under the steamroller of "the great terror." The actions of the republic's authorities in the struggle with party and cultural figures linked with Yiddish culture (including many members of the Evsektsiia) were particularly conspicuous.

Given their generally high percentage among bureaucrats, as noted earlier, a good many Jews were among Stalin's elite of terror. In Rechitsa, for example, the head of the town OGPU (Joint State Political Directorate under the Council of People's Commissars of the USSR) at the beginning of 1933 was Pinkhas Simanovskii (1901–1940), and from October 1934 to January 1935 the head of the raion section of the NKVD (NKVD replaced OGPU in 1934) was Zalman Kaufman (1900–1939).[287] From May until November 1938 this section was headed by Isaac Volovik (1905–1939).[288] Samuil Shlifenson (1903–1939), the region head of the UNKVD, zealously carried out orders from above for arrests in Gomel Oblast, including Rechitsa, from 1936 to 1938.[289] All four were themselves swallowed up by the machinery of repression during Lavrenty Beria's purge of the apparatus of bureaucrats who had served his predecessor, Nikolai Ezhov, and who were supposedly disloyal to him personally. One result of Beria's rise to power was that Jews in the leadership of the NKVD were among the first to suffer. In 1934 they made up 38.9 percent of the leadership, more than any other national group. Of these, 92 percent had joined the "organs" mainly between 1917 and 1921, during the time of euphoria at the long-awaited reorganization of society. As a result by 1941 Jews made up 6.4 percent of the leadership of the "organs."[290] In the course of this purge of personnel, Vladimir Shvartsev and Dmitrii Gusev were appointed to head, respectively, the Rechitsa Raion section and the Gomel region UNKVD.[291]

As for the non-Jewish members of the punitive organs, they were heavily infected by everyday anti-Semitism. All this predetermined the high percentage of Jews repressed in the BSSR, where their proportion as a whole and specifically within the urban population, which suffered the most, was high.

The absence of complete statistical data do not allow for tracking the repressions in Rechitsa along national lines, but there is no basis for believing that the proportion of Jews repressed in Rechitsa was markedly different from that of the republic. It has been possible to establish the names of more than fifty Jews in Rechitsa who were repressed.[292] Among them are three Rechitsa natives and nineteen nonnatives arrested in Rechitsa, and thirty-five Rechitsa natives arrested in other places. These figures are undoubtedly incomplete, but even they will allow for some analysis. Those repressed between 1922 and 1950 can be divided into four age groups: 17 to 27 (21 percent of the total); 28 to 37 (21 percent); 38 to 47 (41 percent); 48 to 57 (17 percent). Thus, two-fifths of those repressed came from the third age group. If one takes only the years 1937–1938, then this age group becomes even larger (47 percent), whereas the victims of repression in the 1920s were mainly young people. The surge in repressions in 1937–1938 within the third age group occurred because it included workers who had attained positions of some note in society and who thereby found themselves in a group of increased risk: they were the ones most often denounced, and their "errors" were plain for all to see. As far as the geography of repression is concerned, those Jews who left Rechitsa for large cities had increased chances of falling victim largely because many of them were now at the peak of their careers. For example, of the fifteen Jewish men who were repressed and who had been born in the town in the period 1897–1906 (and so were between the ages of twenty and twenty-nine in 1926, that is, in the two age groups examined in the "Demographics" section), nine were arrested in major cities in the RSFSR, four in the Ukrainian Republic, one in Rechitsa itself, and one more in Minsk.

The numbers of those repressed in 1937–1938 might have been even higher had it not been for the appointment of Lavrenty Beria as People's Commissar of

Internal Affairs in 1938. To demonstrate the beginning of some liberalism in
Stalin's internal policy, Beria immediately ordered the release of thousands of
people being held for investigation in Soviet prisons. In Rechitsa a group of prisoners, including some Jews, who had been charged with espionage during the
period when Nikolai Ezhov was in charge of the NKVD were now released from
prison. The Rechitsa native Simkha Gurevich was arrested in Perm at the very
end of 1937, but on Beria's orders his case was quashed in July 1938 on the
grounds of the absence of criminal activity. In Minsk this change of power
touched another former Rechitsa resident, Iosif Resin.

Iosif Resin, the business manager of the corporation LesBel (Belorussian
Wood), as well as all members of its management in Minsk, in December 1937
were accused of subversive activities, described as "disruption of logging, injuri-
ous development of wood and disorganization of the timber industry in BSSR."
The report "About Blasting Work in the Corporation LesBel (on December 15,
1937)," prepared for the secretary of Central Committee of the Communist Party
of the Belorussian Volkov, alleged extensive mismanagement: oak had been used
as firewood (Rechitsa and Gomel), an alder and an oak had been used for the
manufacturing of barrels (Klichev's timber enterprise); there had been bad planning, an absence of mechanization at logging sites, the loss of horses; a corruption
of the methods of the Stakhanov movement, a disregard for safety techniques,
and an increase in worksite accidents. According to the report, "latent bribery"
had been discovered in the corporation; directors of the timber enterprises,
under the pretext of the payment of expenses for the recruitment of labor, had
paid considerable amounts to communist secretaries of raion committees and
to secretaries of executive committees. In the course of the investigation, Iosif
Resin was identified as the head of a harmful organization, connected with the
anti-Soviet underground of Trotskyites. Branches of the organization were discovered in timber mills in Rechitsa and Borisov.[293] Participants in the "United
Anti-Soviet Underground" were accused of causing the failure of the development of the Soviet food-processing industry, which was based on local resources.
Investigators explained the arrests as primarily due to the failures in the processing of vegetables and berries.[294] Nevertheless, Beria, at the beginning of 1939,
decided to halt the case and to liberate all these prisoners.

Rechitsa's Iosif Resin provided an occasion for the Gomel management of the
NKVD to instigate a search for anti-Soviet groups in the town. There was the fabricated "Rechitsa Affair," as it was called, in October 1938, when the republican
NKVD arrested the first secretary of the raion committee of the party, Ryzhov;
the chairman of the Raion Executive Committee, Fridliand (mentioned earlier);
his deputy, Domaratskii; the head of the Raion Agricultural Section, Kozlovskii;

the Raion procurement commissioner, Ostrovskii; and the head of the Financial Section of the Raion Executive Committee, Kupreichik.

All were accused of "wrecking" and counterrevolutionary activities as well as connivance in the seizure of collective farm lands by independent farmers. The investigator Voronkov, who personally beat those arrested, managed to extort confessions from all of them. The prosecutor for special cases in the Gomel Oblast prosecutor's office, A. Ia. Vulfin, who reviewed these cases at the beginning of 1939, made a courageous decision: to acquit and release the leadership of Rechitsa Raion; the judicial organs, however, were powerless before the steel of the machinery of repression. The new people's commissar of internal affairs of Belorussia, Lavrenty Tsanava (who held this post from 1938 to 1941), saw this as a good opportunity to demonstrate his vigilance, something for which he might receive, at worst, a slap on the wrist. In January 1940 he sent memoranda to the NKVD of the USSR, the Central Committee of the All-Russian Communist Party (Bolshevik) and the Central Committee of the Communist Party (Bolshevik) of Belorussia in which he accused the Gomel court of negligence in its examination of the "Rechitsa Affair." Thereupon, the Central Committee of the BSSR spent six months examining the case and, fearing a direct confrontation with one of Beria's men, in June 1940 directed the prosecutor's office to reexamine the case. The members of the "Ryzhov Group" were arrested once again, and their final fate is unknown.[295] Maybe they were finally acquitted or sent to labor camps. It is likely that Abraham Fridliand, whom I mention in postwar Rechitsa chapter, is the same person who concluded the "Rechitsa Affair."

Things did not turn out so well for Vulfin either. As early as mid-February 1939, at a session of the Bureau of the Central Committee of the Belorussian Communist Party, he was criticized for his "lack of vigilance," something instigated, evidently, by the NKVD in order to punish a refractory prosecutor. He had to write an explanatory report addressed to the first secretary of the Central Committee of the Belorussian Communist Party, Panteleimon Ponomarenko.[296]

Apart from imposing exile, imprisonment, and execution, the USSR in those years also would dismiss people from their jobs, expel their children from the Komsomol, and give reprimands according to the party line; these were elements in the work of a single repressive machine. The party member Chaim Iashchin, who worked in Rechitsa in 1938 at one of the town's enterprises, received a party reprimand because he knew of the existence of "a counterrevolutionary Trotskyite group" but failed to report it to the party organization.[297]

The measure and the type of punishment were determined to a large extent by "connections," not only on the highest level but on the local level as well. One of the problematic cases that the judge Abram Frenkel, mentioned earlier, had to decide was that of the chairman of the town food services (a Jew) and two of his deputies (a Jew and a Russian). Because they had allowed the free sale of kerosene, which was in very short supply, and because this led to a huge queue in front of the store and an ensuing brawl, they were arrested in 1938 and initially accused of economic counterrevolution. The NKVD, however, did not find corpus delicti and passed the case to the regular judicial authorities with the suggestion that the accused be tried for abusing their authority. Unexpectedly for the "organs," Frenkel, in a trial that shook the whole town, acquitted all the accused. The judge, fearing the consequences, went the next day to the secretary of the town committee of the party, a Belorussian who, like Frenkel, was a native of the village of Savichi, near Kalinkovichi. The secretary confided to him that he had responded to the NKVD's recommendation to arrest the judge by saying, "We can arrest him at any time, but I need to look into the whole affair." After which he told Frenkel, "I know your family, and you're not an enemy of the people."[298]

After a nine-month period (from February until October 1917) of democracy and community building, the Jews in Soviet Russia began a partially grandiose experiment on the path of constructing a classless society. The Bolshevik vision of this experiment excluded any form of ideological competition on the part of other parties, religions, ethnic-communal organizations, or even philanthropic associations. This model of the state also involved the elimination of the formerly prosperous layers of the population through physical annihilation or reeducation in labor camps. All tradespeople were relegated en masse to the affluent sectors of the population, regardless of their former level of income. Because prior to the revolution trade and crafts were the two principal occupations of Jews, their weight among the "superfluous" members of the new society was disproportionately heavy in comparison with that of other ethnic nationalities. In exchange, Jews obtained the opportunity to acquire an education and communicate with bureaucrats in their native language; they were also relieved of the burden of anti-Jewish legal discrimination. Many Jews took advantage of their newly acquired opportunities to occupy positions as state employees, only to discover that this had become a new source of common, everyday anti-Semitism.

Jews, like all other people in the USSR, were forced to come to terms with the new regime and seek out opportunities if only to survive. One of the most effective methods of escaping from a sector of the population subjected to discrimination was migration, to large cites and collective farms. In new places it was easier to conceal a person's membership among the so-called deprived. Many of the Jews who remained in Rechitsa were involved in the new system of education in the Yiddish language. Some were people from the poorer strata of the population with a lower degree of acculturation who stayed in the town, but others were Jews with a greater commitment to Yiddish who migrated to Rechitsa from shtetls.

When compared with the prerevolutionary period, the economic situation of Jews in Rechitsa in the period under review worsened. About two-thirds of them could barely make ends meet. However, the situation of non-Jewish towns-people overall was even worse. In contrast to the Jews, who largely migrated out of Rechitsa, the non-Jewish residents more painfully felt the housing crisis. The economic situation improved somewhat by the mid-1930s.

With the consolidation of Soviet power, Stalin began to search for new sources of support for his rule, and he thought it possible to begin a new struggle with potentially dangerous elements of the population. The campaign of repressions of 1937–1938 marked the final shift to Russian chauvinism that in the first half of the 1930s had been marked by Stalin's reprisals against the national intelligentsia of the Jews, as well as that of the Belorussians, the Ukrainians, the Kazakhs, the Uzbeks, and many other ethnic groups. Almost all the members of the Evsektsiia and the active proponents of korenizatsiia in their own republics were repressed. Those who supported the Latinization of the languages of the peoples of the USSR, and particularly those who called for the Latinization of Russian, met the same fate. An active process of changing languages to the Cyrillic alphabet began. This all meant, in reality, that Stalin had begun to fear that his policy of "nativi-zation" was leading to the strengthening of nationalist sentiments in the USSR. The centrifugal force of those sentiments was something that, in his view, inter-nationalism would be powerless to halt. Fearing the threat of the disintegration of the USSR along national lines, Stalin saw more solid support for his regime in the development of Russian chauvinism, that is, by shifting his nationalities' pol-icy in the same direction as that used by the Russian authorities even before the October Revolution. This Stalinist discourse gained an even stronger foothold during the war with Germany, which by no means bypassed Rechitsa.

7

Under German Occupation, 1941–1943

Rechitsa suffered less from German bombardment than many of the other towns in Belorussia at the beginning of the war. But the first bomb was dropped on the town as early as the evening of June 22, 1941, from a reconnaissance aircraft attracted by the closely situated railway and automobile bridges across the Dnieper. The bomb burst near the town's center; no one was killed and nothing was damaged, but it clearly signaled that the war had begun.[1] A few days later another German bomb directly hit the cafeteria where soldiers of the Tenth Motorized Rifle Battalion of the NKVD, guarding the railway bridge across the Dnieper, were eating. Eighteen of them were killed.[2] We know of only one Jewish family killed during the bombing before the actual battles to capture the town began.[3]

In the two and a half years before the war, the Soviet authorities, bound by the nonaggression treaty with Germany, gave out no information about the Nazi attitude toward the Jews. Once the war began, the issue of genocide was not ignored in anti-German propaganda, but neither was it widely disseminated. The authorities were rightly concerned that information in the Soviet mass media on anti-Jewish genocide could confirm one of the basic tenets of the German propaganda spread in Soviet territory, that Germany was waging its war against the Jews. Thus information on this in Russian-language newspapers appeared in the form of brief comments in the back pages. Yiddish newspapers, which many Jews in Eastern Belorussia still read, devoted much more attention to the issue of persecution of Jews in Germany and in occupied territory.[4] The response to this information was mixed. Through the years of Soviet power, Jews, like other Soviet citizens, had developed a mistrust of newspapers, regarding them primarily as a means of propaganda and not as a source of information.[5]

It is also true that when the war began the Soviet authorities still did not know that the Germans' treatment of Jews in the Soviet territory they occupied was much harsher than in the countries they had subjugated earlier. Such information began to arrive in late July 1941.[6] The authorities did not raise the issue of Hitler's genocide of Jews widely and publicly until the end of August, the day after Rechitsa's occupation, when Jews were no longer able to flee from there or from the rest of Belorussia, now also occupied. On August 24, 1941, a Jewish anti-fascist rally was held in Moscow. The speakers included People's Artist Solomon Mikhoels, Professor Pëtr Kapitsa, the film director Sergei Eisenstein, the poet and translator Samuil Marshak, the writer Il'ia Erenburg, journalist and editor Shakne Epshtein, and others.[7] Calling the rally "Jewish" was a decision taken, if not by Stalin himself, then at least with his personal approval, and it shows that the leader temporarily abandoned his own definition of a nation, one that had not included the Jewish people. In an attempt to mobilize "his own" Jews and, even more, "foreign" Jews in the struggle against the Nazis, Stalin went even further by sanctioning an appeal in the press that began with words that would have been inconceivable in the prewar years: "Jewish brethren throughout the world!" This language was reminiscent of his famous "Brothers and sisters!" appeal at the beginning of the war. The speakers at the anti-fascist rally, along with Jews well known in the USSR and abroad, issued an open letter to their brethren in which they spoke not only of the heroism of Soviet Jewish warriors, the need for aid to the USSR, and the importance of an economic and political boycott of Germany, but also presented facts about the Jewish genocide that was being carried out by German occupying forces.[8]

But even then the State Defense Committee did not issue any directives, even secret ones, on evacuating the Jewish population.[9] In the light of the widespread anti-Jewish propaganda the Germans spread in both occupied and unoccupied territories by leaflets, agents, and rumors, such a directive could have served as grounds for confirming the view that "Bolshevik power was wielded by the Yids" and so have given rise to an even harsher attitude toward both the Jews and the authorities. On the other hand, the authorities had already discredited themselves in the eyes of some of the population because they had been unprepared for war and made a chaotic retreat in its early days.

As early as June 24, officials of the Central Committee of the Communist Party (Bolshevik) of Belorussia and the Council of Ministers of the BSSR had fled with their families from Minsk toward Moscow. Not only had they failed to organize any evacuation of the population and factories from the eastern regions of the BSSR; they had not even informed the local authorities of their departure.

Several ministers fled without even alerting their own departments.[10] To be fair, it should be noted that the authorities of the Lithuanian and Latvian republics behaved in similar fashion.[11] Panic and anarchy spread through Minsk after the flight of the republic's authorities.[12] Various organizations seized motor transport from one another. There were incidents in which vehicles used for transporting children were taken from kindergartens.[13] By July 7, 1941, a large part of the central Belorussian apparatus and of many ministries—171 people, or 466 including their family members—had arrived in Moscow.[14] The report of Moscow's Police Directorate on the flight of senior Belorussian officials states that "the families of some responsible personnel took a large assortment of property with them, including various carpets, etc. Meanwhile, a line of workers and their families [including children] from these same institutions were following the same route toward Moscow on foot. They begged to be taken into the vehicles, but their requests were denied."[15]

The mood of panic among the authorities of the republic infected the local authorities in a number of towns in the still unoccupied parts of Belorussia. In Rechitsa on June 23, three days after the oblast authorities had announced the evacuation of the civilian population, no one remained in the state institutions. Secret documents were burned, and unclassified ones were thrown into the courtyard of the Raion Executive Committee. The first secretary of the Rechitsa Raion Committee of the party, Alexander Kuteinikov, and the chairman of the Executive Committee of the town soviet, Vasilii Kostroma, hastened to areas in the rear along with their families. Their actions, along with the complete disorganization of this first wave of evacuation, increased the panic among the population. The public prosecutor for Rechitsa Raion, Trashchenko, informed Moscow of this and also wrote: "A number of people—women and children without any food—set off on foot for unknown destinations; others waited on the dock but returned in the evening."[16] Trashchenko remained at his post and was able to prevent wide-scale looting in Rechitsa Raion.[17] In July 1941 the new prosecutor, G. Safonov, also reported on these events in Rechitsa to the Central Committee of the All-Union Communist Party (Bolshevik). He added that according to the latest information he had received, the executive employees in Rechitsa had returned to the raion on July 10.[18] The authorities in neighboring Mozyr behaved even worse. In accordance with an outdated but still unrevoked decree of the Bureau of the Central Committee of the Belorussian Communist Party of June 23 on the "halting of further movement of evacuees" and on the prohibition on the use of motor vehicles "for individual evacuation," the Mozyr authorities evacuated themselves and their families after issuing an order banning departures from the town.[19]

The Belorussian authorities who had come to Moscow under the circumstances just described now had to quickly pull themselves out of their awkward position. At that time Stalin gave that sort of behavior short shrift. The Central Committee of the Belorussian Communist Party and the republic's Council of Ministers chose Gomel in mid-July 1941 as their abode and hastily returned to Belorussia. There the Belorussian authorities quite quickly set about organizing the resistance and the evacuation. To help in this endeavor, they also sent back to eastern Belorussia the group of local authorities that had already managed to flee.[20] As a result, given some time and the availability of railway transport, the authorities evacuated many industrial enterprises, including some small ones, from there and from Gomel Oblast in particular.[21]

The desire of the republic's authorities to increase the number of those evacuated, indicated in their subsequent reports to the national administration, was the reason that local officials in eastern Belorussia particularly urged Jews to leave, because others would be reluctant to abandon their homes. It seems in late July and the first half of August during the agitation Belarusian officials used the data about executions of Jews in the occupied areas. According to information uncovered by Mordechai Altshuler, a Belorussian Komsomol leader in El'sk, a mestechko not far from Rechitsa, went to the homes of Jews, persuading them to flee.[22] In nearby Kalinkovichi the local authorities responded favorably to requests from Jews for assistance with transportation.[23] And in neighboring Khoiniki someone even used the announcement system in the railway station to urge Jewish young people to flee because Jews would all be killed when the Germans arrived.[24] In Gomel the local authorities allocated vehicles to take anyone wishing to leave to the railway station. Moreover, the police made daily rounds of apartments to "remind" the population to take advantage of this.[25] Although it is hardly likely that Jewish apartments were singled out, during talks with Jewish residents the issue of the German attitude toward Jews would have been raised. It is possible that such arguments were used by the local authorities of Turov and Zhlobin who, according to Ben-Zion Pinchuk, also called on the population to be evacuated.[26]

The Rechitsa authorities who returned also deserve credit. According to Leonid Smilovitsky, the local authorities in Rechitsa made the rounds of Jewish homes to persuade them to leave. Those involved included Vasilii Kostroma, chairman of the Raion Executive Committee; Zelik Dobrushkin, party political instructor in Rechitsa Raion and chairman of the Evacuation Committee; and Sara Rabinovich, chairman of the town's Council for Education.[27] For the evacuation of the civilian population, the authorities in Rechitsa provided *teplushki*—heated freight cars—which were used mainly for taking people from all regions eastward. To board the train one had to present a pass from the town authorities showing permission to leave. Passes were issued, as a rule, with a minimum of formalities; their purpose was only to determine the place of evacuation. At the same time, the authorities did not control or regulate the boarding, and the departure of trains was often known only a short time in advance. A more organized evacuation of industrial factories and workers was also under way. They were sent off in special railway cars or entire trains. Between June 3 and June 11, the authorities evacuated the workers and the equipment of the nail factory (six cars) and the match factory (eight cars) from Rechitsa.[28] Such trains often only changed locomotives over the course of their journey, so the enterprise traveled to its planned new location with only a few stops along the way. It was much more difficult for people to leave the mestechkos and villages located far from the railway. The success of their flight eastward depended on the use of horse-drawn carts and motor transport to bring them to the nearest railway station.

In 1939 many people in Rechitsa had seen the films *Professor Mamlok*, based on the play by Friedrich Wolf, and *The Oppenheim Family*, based on the novel by Lion Feuchtwanger. These films gave them an idea of how the Nazis treated Jews.[29] Also, several Polish Jews who appeared in Rechitsa after crossing the new Soviet-German border in late 1939 and the first half of 1940 told of victimization, forced labor, and sporadic executions.[30] In September and October 1939 the German authorities forcibly deported many Jews to Soviet territory. Subsequently, they often did not prevent Jews from crossing the border independently, although they did not neglect the opportunity to rob them while doing so. The refugees faced difficulties with Soviet border guards, who were increasingly less inclined to admit them to Soviet territory. Jews were sometimes forced to return, but on their return journey they were fired upon by the Germans, who did not want to allow them back. In general during this period Germany tried to rid itself of Jews by deportation to other countries, not by total annihilation. The Polish Jews who came to Rechitsa could not have known the Nazis' plans for East European Jewry.

In their own propaganda directed at the Slavic population of Belorussia, the Germans insisted that they were struggling only with the communists and the Jews and that destroying these groups would give the local population a better life. Leaflets making such statements were dropped from aircraft, over Bobruisk specifically.[31]

Jews in the USSR were confronted with a truly complex dilemma: to flee or to remain in their homes. They did not want to abandon their property and apartments (on the whole, these fears were eventually justified), and they had hopes that the Germans would do no harm to ordinary Jews—tradespeople, office workers, and pensioners. Such optimistic ideas were spread by those who recalled the relatively peaceful German occupation of Rechitsa in 1918 and also by those who had been in Germany as prisoners of war during World War I.[32]

As the front line drew closer, the majority of Rechitsa Jews decided to be evacuated, however. This decision was encouraged emotionally, to some extent, by the relatively large number of Jewish refugees—inhabitants of Pinsk, Minsk, and, principally, of Polesia Oblast—who passed through Rechitsa going toward Gomel. The streams of Jewish refugees, in trains, trucks, carts, and on foot, helped spread a mood of panic in the town.[33] Looking at them and at the deserted homes of Jews who had already left Rechitsa in the first weeks of the war, most of the many Jews who remained also decided on evacuation. The availability of rail and river transport, the local authorities' support for evacuation, and the delayed occupation of Rechitsa because the German's principal offensive had come farther north suggest that the many inhabitants of Rechitsa who wanted to be evacuated were able to do so. Who, then, remained in Rechitsa? The most detailed list of Jews who perished in Rechitsa (see below) shows that those who stayed in the town were mainly not of working age: people below the age of fifteen and those aged fifty-six and older.

The elderly were the most reluctant to abandon their homes, fearing the difficulties of evacuation and establishing themselves in a new location. A further complication arose because their sons had been called up into the army, and some of their daughters were living elsewhere, in areas with which communication had been disrupted after the German invasion. Some of the elderly were seriously ill. Daughters with children or daughters-in-law often remained with elderly people who flatly refused to be evacuated. The large percentage of children who perished, given the relatively small percentage of women victims in the

TABLE 13. Age groups of Jews (male and female) who perished in Rechitsa in 1941 (%)

Age	0–15	16–25	26–35	36–45	46–55	56–65	65 and older	Total
Males	34	4.9	5.4	10.3	8.6	20	16.8	100
Females	25.8	7.6	12.2	12.2	9.1	19	14	100
Both Sexes	28.9	6.6	9.5	11.5	9	19.32	15.3	100

Source: The table was compiled from an analysis of data on victims in the materials of the Extraordinary State Commission to Investigate Atrocities Committed by German Fascist Invaders. See YVA, M 33/476, 21–61; YVA, JM 20006, 21–61.

26–45 cohort, suggests that mothers with several children did not leave. For understandable reasons they feared being left homeless and without work. At the same time, many women of working age, in the 46–55 cohort and without young children, also left Rechitsa. Even more women in the 16–25 cohort, most of them without children or with only one child, were also evacuated. As can be seen from tables 13 and 15, a number of men of draft age remained in the town, probably because of illness. It is also possible that these men were soldiers who had managed to escape and make their way home after being surrounded by the Germans. In the 16–25 and 26–25 cohorts, as can be seen in table 14, there were, respectively, nine and ten such men. In any case the lowest percentage of male victims came in these age groups. At the same time, it should not be forgotten that there were fewer adult men than women in Rechitsa, as noted earlier. This was due both to their greater mobility and to casualties during the civil war.

In July 1941 the first group of Jews left the town by barges down the Dnieper. After passing Kiev they arrived in southern Ukraine, the northern Caucasus, and the Stavropol region. From these places many Rechitsa residents did not manage to be evacuated farther eastward in time and were killed in bombing raids or during the German occupation. Some of the people from Rechitsa who left the town by barge at the end of July were forced to return because of the rapid German advance in the south. Rechitsa Jews also evacuated by train toward Briansk, mainly in late July and the first half of August. This route proved to be more reliable than by barge.

Leaving by train was complicated due to the damage done to the bridge across the Dnieper at the beginning of July 1941. Although this was partially repaired by July 13, the train could move across the bridge only at very slow speed.[34] By mid-August evacuation had become possible only southward, via Loev, and then eastward through Ukraine. Several groups of refugees left the town on August 20–22, on the eve of occupation. Because of the general confusion and the lack of information, most of them chose the wrong direction and were killed. The family of Samuil and Sosha Seletskii left Rechitsa by cart, going north along the road to Ozershchina. A few local residents armed with axes, crowbars, and pitchforks attacked them while en route. The Jews were slaughtered, and their murderers buried their pillaged bodies near the site of the attack.[35] At that time in a similar manner some inhabitants of the village of Bronnoe slew and plundered several Jewish families (Shmuel Frenkel's, with five people, including a three-year-old child; Mania Erenburg with her year-old son, and others)—about twenty people in all—who had fled from Rechitsa in horse-drawn carts. After the war the sister of Shmuel Frenkel, Ester-Frada Koparovskaia, discovered the details of the incident, and several of the murderers were sent to prison. They were amnestied after Stalin's death in March 1953.[36]

As early as the end of June 1941, the local authorities, acting on instructions of the republic's leadership, formed what was called a Destroyer Battalion of 150 men in three companies. A Jew and party member, Makar Turchinskii (1924–1984), was designated as its commander. Pëtr Kalinin, secretary of the Central Committee of the Belorussian Communist Part and head of the Belorussian staff of the partisan movement, wrote of him in his memoirs: "Strong-willed, bold, and decisive, from the first day he demanded the strictest observance of military discipline from his troops."[37] But these qualities were no substitute for lack of military experience. This was already evident in the poor organization of the two-week course of training. At the end of the course one company was sent to prepare TNT for antitank mines whose wooden cases were being made at the local plywood factory. Another company was boarded on an armored tanker from the Dnieper flotilla, whose vessels were sent upriver and then into the Berezina River. This rather ineffectual landing comprising mainly small boats was easily crushed by the Germans near the mestechko of Parichi. As the front line drew nearer, the two companies that remained in Rechitsa were thrown into the battle to protect the town. One of the companies took up a defensive position along the road to the village of Ozershchina. They put up a valiant defense until July 10, eliminating eight armored vehicles, a tank, a tracked reconnaissance vehicle, and seven enemy machine guns from action. In August 1941 the one surviving company was sent to guard the bridge.[38] Some troops from this company were killed during the bombardment and defense of the bridge, when the Germans approached after bypassing Rechitsa on the side of the railway station.

Although four regiments of the 143rd Rifle Division had been stationed in Rechitsa on the eve of the war, they were probably shifted closer to the front in the first month. There were no other major concentrations of troops near the town as the enemy approached. The enemy's striking forces advanced some distance away from Rechitsa and linked up farther to the east, near Gomel. The last of the town's defenders barely managed to avoid capture, having crossed to the other bank of the Dnieper on a pontoon bridge while under fire from mortars and aircraft. Pontoons burst, and many soldiers drowned. The remnants of the Destroyer Battalion withdrew to Loev, where one of the companies, under fire and with losses, miraculously managed to cross the river on a pontoon bridge. The other company perished along with the battalion commander.[39]

As noted, Rechitsa was occupied on August 23. It was included in the Zhitomir Gebietskommissariat of the Reichskommissariat of Ukraine. A section of the

Gestapo, commanded by Georg Galunder, was established in the town, along with a section of the Security Service (SD). There were also local security and civil police, secret field police (GFP), and a raion field gendarmerie headed by Commandant Fischer, a guard section attached to the commandant's office, and a detachment of SS troops.[40] The new authorities immediately set about restoring the town's industry and economy. The town's waterworks and its soap and match factories were put back in order.[41]

Two weeks after the occupation, the Nazi authorities ordered the Jewish population to sew five-pointed yellow stars on each sleeve and write the word *Jude* on their backs in chalk. They were forbidden to appear in public places.[42] Trial materials from the case of "Atrocities Committed by German-Fascist Criminals" begun in Minsk in February 1946 show that Corporal Heinz Fischer, a communications specialist, set off on a motorcycle with a driver in October 1941. He was carrying a package from the radio station on the opposite bank of the Dnieper to Rechitsa, where the divisional headquarters was located. The two Germans came across nine people, four of them children, who were preparing to cross the Dnieper. After they had checked the fugitives' documents and ascertained that they were Jews, the Germans shot them.[43] The Dobrushkin family and some relatives (seven people in all) made a successful escape at the beginning of September 1941. Miraculously, they managed to make their way out of Rechitsa, pass on foot through the enemy's rear areas, and cross the front line into Orel Oblast.[44]

In this period the Germans and the *Polizei* in Rechitsa often executed Jews individually or in small groups. Before being executed the Jews were subjected to public humiliation, a widespread practice in the occupied territories. In the first days of Rechitsa's occupation, Zelda Bliumkin was ordered to drown her three children in the Dnieper. When she refused, she was drowned along with them. The Germans ordered Iudka Smilovitskii to be harnessed to a sled in place of a horse and tried to force his wife, Khaia, to lash him on with a whip. When she refused, Iudka was shot while his wife and whole family looked on. Khaia herself was sent to the Rechitsa prison. The next day their five-year-old son, Lëva, tried to pass his mother a food parcel through the fence and was shot by a guard from the watch tower. Seventy-year-old Basia Smilovitskaia was locked in a cellar where the Germans watched her die. Khana Shpilevskaia was tied to a moving motorcycle. When she fell, exhausted, she was dragged along the ground for some time, while the soldiers and the Polizei laughed, and then beaten to death. The Germans picked up an old Jew. A rope was tied to his neck, and every so often he was lowered into a well. A group of Jews were brought to witness this, and then they were executed. Sheindel Resin found hiding places in various villages, but she was caught and brought to Rechitsa. She was harnessed to a cart and made to haul water from the river and to eat hay. Then she was executed. The Germans did the same with Aron Atlas. They tied his wife, Fania Atlas, by her hair to a horse-drawn cart, dragged her along the street, and then executed her. The same was done to Shlëma Gutiontov. Sixty-year-old Mikhul Kazovskii was forced to haul his paralyzed wife, Mariasia, in a barrel of water; then, after being savagely beaten, he was executed. Peasants hid the tailor Leiba Genin in the villages, but after someone reported this to the Germans he was captured, harnessed to a cart to haul water, and then executed. In September 1941 a German soldier demonstrated his marksmanship by shooting from some distance Lëva Atamchuk, who was fishing. Atamchuk, however, was not killed because he was a Jew. A Belorussian might just as easily have been the victim. The Germans set up a firing range in the Jewish cemetery and practiced shooting at the gravestones, many of which were destroyed.[45]

At the same time, there were some cases in which the Germans provided assistance. Thus in September 1941 the German civil engineer who was supervising the reconstruction of the bridge across the Dnieper not only allowed the group of Jews mentioned earlier—the Dobrushkin family and their relatives who were fleeing from Rechitsa—to cross but even carried a child across a particularly dangerous area.[46]

About ten days after the town's occupation, Israel Malinkovich, the former melamed mentioned earlier, was summoned to the commandant's office (located in School no. 6). Malinkovich had been a bookkeeper until the war began. He was ordered to compile a list of the Jews who remained. The Germans chose him since they assumed that this "rabbi" would be well acquainted with all the Jewish residents and would cooperate because of grievances over the Soviet regime's persecution of the Jewish religion.[47] According to the account of Ekaterina Matveeva, Malinkovich did compile such a list. Nevertheless—as many witnesses testify—he was killed before the creation of the ghetto and the mass executions. It would have seemed that his efforts might have led the new authorities to appoint him head of the Judenrat or elder. Such figures were normally used to make assignments, levy contributions, and resolve other issues, even in places with fewer Jews than Rechitsa. Immediately after the occupied territories were liberated, the Soviet authorities labeled such people "fascist collaborators."

In keeping with the Stalinist approach, everyone confined to a ghetto and all those in concentration or prisoner-of-war camps were expected to perish rather than cooperate in any way with the Germans. The Soviet organs of state security seemed scarcely aware of the absurdity of attaching the label of "fascist collabo-rator" to a Jew whose physical existence within occupied territory had no place in the Nazis' plans, despite any services he may have rendered them. In any case, in many places in the occupied territory of the USSR the heads of the *Judenrats* or the Jewish elders behaved properly toward other prisoners. When both the Polizei and his own wife tried to send Iosif Kulik, elder of the Brailov ghetto (Ukraine), back to the ghetto from the place of execution, Kulik chose to be killed because his own activities—organizing work details and collecting contri-butions (before asking for contributions from others he offered all the valuables that he himself owned)—had failed to avert the mass execution of Jews.[48]

As for Rechitsa, Malinkovich was likely executed for nonpayment of the com-pulsory contributions that the Germans normally imposed on the Jewish popu-lation. Nothing is known about the appointment of a new elder. Most probably, no one was assigned to the post, and the functions of the elder were carried out entirely by the Polizei. They assigned Jews to various kinds of physical labor; women, specifically, were to sweep Sovietskaia Street, sections of which they allotted among themselves.[49]

At the beginning of September, more than 200 Jewish men of working age—between fifteen and fifty—were driven into a building in the industrial area on the pretext of being sent to work rebuilding the bridge across the Dnieper. Then the Germans and the Polizei executed them at a spot two kilometers to the west of Rechitsa, near the cemetery. Several days later, on orders of the authori-ties, peasants buried the corpses in antitank ditches. According to the official report of Einsatzkommando 7b (the special SS detachment created to annihilate the Jewish population within the territory of the BSSR), 216 persons were exe-cuted.[50] Because reports of such detachments often understated the number of victims, it is worth noting the testimony of Ekaterina Matveeva in 1968 (by that time she had changed her last name to Liakutina). She claims that more than 300 were killed during this action, most of them men but a few women as well.[51]

Alexander Meyer, the new commandant who came to Rechitsa, declared that he would not assume command in the town until all the Jews had been exe-cuted.[52] It is also possible that this statement was made by the burgomaster of the Rechitsa and Loev Raions, Karl Gerhardt.[53] He was killed by the partisans at the beginning of 1943.[54]

Early in the third week of November 1941, the Jews, in accordance with an order that had been posted throughout the town, went to the House of Culture; from there they were sent to two two-story buildings on the grounds of the for-mer prison in the industrial area, at the corner of Frunze and Sovietskaia Streets.

(According to other accounts, these buildings housed the dormitory of the match factory.) Here the Germans set up a ghetto, fencing off the territory with barbed wire to a height of about two meters. To enter or leave one had to pass through a guardhouse. The prisoners were held in exceptionally cramped conditions, with about forty persons per room; thus they had no choice but to stand. It was less crowded only during the day, when people capable of work were taken away to do labor. The ghetto was carefully patrolled by the Polizei.[55] Prisoners of war, communists, and activists were also imprisoned here. They were executed on the morning of November 25.[56]

By December 12 the Germans and the Polizei had rounded up and brought to the ghetto those Jews who had not appeared as ordered. At the same time, Jews discovered in neighboring villages were also brought to Rechitsa. Iakov Gutarov testified that his grandfather and grandmother, who were in a small village near Rechitsa, were rounded up along with other Jews and brought to the town, where later they were all executed. He himself, along with his mother and Khana Streshinskaia, managed to escape and hide.[57] According to documents from the ChGK (the accepted abbreviation for the Extraordinary State Commission to Investigate Atrocities Committed by German Fascist Invaders), at 4:00 p.m. one day in the third week of November 1941, seven trucks drew up to the ghetto. The prisoners were told that they were being taken to a state collective farm to harvest cabbage and carrots. Forty to forty-seven people were loaded into each truck; they were then taken outside the town or to an antitank ditch near the tuberculosis sanatorium dug by the townspeople during their defensive operations in July 1941. People were unloaded in groups of fifteen or twenty and made to stand in the antitank ditch. After their earrings, rings, bracelets, and other jewelry had been taken away, they were shot with submachine guns. A few of the younger people managed to run away, but they were killed by rifle fire. According to one of the witnesses, before being executed twelve-year-old Boris Smilovitskii managed to shout, "Bandits, fascists, you may spill our blood, but the Red Army will still conquer and take revenge for us!" One of the Polizei then shot him with his submachine gun. About three hundred Jews were executed during this action.[58]

Until approximately December 10, the Germans and the Polizei took groups of Jews every day to be executed. Maia Iastrebinskaia, who somehow managed to survive, testified before the ChGK that her mother and other relatives were arrested on November 16 and shot on November 29. She herself witnessed the execution of the Shklover, Vasilevitskii, Kaganovich, Gurarie, and Kogelman families on that same day.[59] Ivan Kopanskii gave detailed testimony to the commission that in November 1941 the Jewish Kutikov and Korokin families were arrested and then shot and buried near the nail factory. The large Pugach family, arrested by the Germans at the same time, were shot near the village of Ozershchina. He also testified that the doctor Vikendeeva was arrested in December of that year and shot near the nail factory.[60] At the end of November 1941, Elizaveta Bobchonok saw a truck taking Jews from the prison on Sovietskaia Street to the icehouse near Ozershchina to be executed. At the beginning of December of that year, she witnessed eighty Jews being taken to that same place in two trips made by a single truck.[61] Larisa Borodich does not give the date of her family's arrest in her testimony, but she writes that her grandfather had been arrested earlier. She notes that groups of Jews were being sent off every night for execution.[62]

We know from the testimony of Olga Fukson, contained in materials of the ChGK, that at the beginning of December 1941 the Germans and the Polizei selected a few Jewish families and individual persons (about twenty people in all), loaded them into a truck, and took them south of the town to the village of Bronnoe or somewhere nearby and apparently executed them.[63]

Sometime between December 15 and 18, 1941, several prisoners in the ghetto were taken in three trucks to the antitank ditches located two kilometers south of the town on the road to the distillery. Despite the cold, the victims were forced to undress completely. They were made to stand facing the ditch and then were executed by submachine-gun and machine-gun fire. The Germans took babes in arms from their mothers, tossed them in the air, and fired at them.[64] Leiba Riabenkii, who was paralyzed and unable to climb into the truck on his own, was thrown in on a pitchfork. Many of the victims cursed their oppressors as they were being led to execution. Khava-Seina Rudnitskii shouted: "Stalin will win!"[65] It was probably during this action that Malvina Gribovskaia's Jewish daughter-in-law was executed. In her testimony of November 20, 1943—that is, immediately after Rechitsa's liberation—she stated that her daughter-in-law Genia (neé Shustina) and other Jews were taken out of the prison (local residents, apparently, were not very familiar with the term "ghetto" and unaccustomed to using it to describe a single or several buildings) in three trucks to a location some five kilometers outside the town and executed. Although Gribovskaia confused the dates when she stated that her daughter-in-law was picked up at the beginning of December and then spent six weeks under arrest in the ghetto, we can suppose that the young woman was arrested early in the third week of November and remained in the ghetto until mid-December.[66] In any case, Gribovskaia would have surely remembered marking the New Year with her grandsons at a time when their mother had been executed. The Polizei did not arrest and execute such children from mixed marriages (Gribovskaia's son was serving in the Red

Army), a fact that distinguishes Rechitsa favorably from many other areas under occupation.[67] Since the Nazis considered Slavic blood inferior, such children in Eastern Europe were usually exterminated.[68] In "Aryan" countries, they were subject to "reeducation."

Several days later, sometime around December 20, the ghetto was completely liquidated. This was the last and the largest action, in which more than five hundred people perished. The prisoners were led to a large pit that they had previously been forced to dig. One German gendarme moved along the line, smashing the victims' heads with a wooden club and pushing them into the pit; a second finished them off with a shot. After the action the gendarmes left, and the pit, almost filled, was covered with earth by the police. The arrests and executions were carried out mainly by a special German punishment detachment (probably a subunit of the Einsatzgruppe) working from a building on 82 Lunacharskaia Street.[69]

Apart from the execution sites of Rechitsa Jews mentioned above, a few other sites are known: one was near the nail factory; another was in the Jewish cemetery near the grave of Sholom-Dov-Ber Shneerson, mentioned earlier, on the foundation of the former stone synagogue.[70]

Evidently, a selection process preceded the executions, the usual procedure in other places within the occupied territory of the USSR and in Belorussia in particular. Left alive were those who had "essential" professions, that is, basically artisans and their families. But they too were eventually executed along with other prisoners incapable of working but who had been temporarily spared to do various kinds of labor.

Perhaps the greatest problem in the study of the Nazi genocide in Rechitsa is determining the number of victims. According to the report of the ChGK, based on the testimony of Ekaterina Matveeva (November 1943), 785 Jewish families, or 3,000 people, were executed in Rechitsa. These figures on the Holocaust in Rechitsa, which appear in all the historiography, assume approximately 4 people per family, which is unlikely. Appended to the report was a list of people executed in Rechitsa compiled from interviews done immediately after the liberation. Of the 631 people on the list, 443 were Jews.

Questionnaires done by the Yad Vashem Holocaust Martyrs' and Heroes' Remembrance Authority in Jerusalem make it possible to compile another list of Jews who perished in Rechitsa.[71] After eliminating about two dozen duplicates and even triplicates completed by different people about the same persons, they show the total number of victims (based on information available as of March 30, 2005) reaching 266. A comparison of the two lists reveals forty three names that

TABLE 14. Numbers and proportions of males among Jews who perished in
          Rechitsa in 1941, by age group

Age	Numbers killed	Males killed (Number)	Males killed (Proportion, %)
0–15	128	62	48.4
16–25	29	9	31
26–35	42	10	23.8
36–45	51	19	37.2
46–55	40	16	40
56–65	85	36	42.3
65 and older	68	31	45.6
Total	443	183	41.3

Source: The table has been compiled from an analysis of the list of those killed in the materials of the Extraordinary State Commission to Investigate Atrocities Committed by German Fascist Invaders. See YVA, M 33/476, 21–61; YVA, JM 20006, 21–61.

appear in both. With that taken into account, the total number of Jews who perished and whose names are known is 666. Based on that, and taking into account that many Rechitsa Jews who managed to evacuate in time or had been called up into the army, one can estimate the number of Jews who perished in Rechitsa during the war at 1,300 to 1,400. This comprises 18 percent of the total prewar Jewish population, a figure that seems entirely realistic.

This figure nearly coincides with the one stated by Ekaterina Matveeva in her new testimony given during an investigation by the KGB in February 1968. The investigation was done at the request of the People's Republic of Poland, where former Senior Lieutenant Fischer was on trial. Although the two sets of testimonies were made a quarter of a century apart, the new statements of the witnesses appear to be more reliable. According to them, some 1,300 Jews perished in Rechitsa, comprising about 400 incomplete families.[72] Ekaterina's mother, Olga Fukson, provided the investigator with almost the same information.[73]

Some interesting supplementary information was provided in that same year by the witness Il'ia Kolotsei:

I saw the police taking Jews in carts to the large apartment buildings owned by the "Ten Years of October" factory; it was 250 meters from my home. These buildings were surrounded by barbed wire to a height of about two meters and they were called a "ghetto." Jews were ordered to sew white and yellow strips of cloth on their clothing, and they were marched off to work. For two weeks the Jews were digging a huge pit near the ghetto toilets while being guarded by police. . . . I saw ten Jews hauling a cart with a water barrel out of the ghetto. A German soldier was sitting on the barrel and beating with a stick those who were not pulling hard enough. . . . One time [this was after the large-scale execution at the antitank ditch in November] they chased the Jews out of these two buildings and formed them into a column. They were mostly teenagers and young children. Many of the women were carrying babies. Standing near the pit that the Jews had dug were two German gendarmes wearing the skull and crossbones emblem and metal chains on their chests.

The witness goes on to state that one of the gendarmes used a wooden club to smash the heads of the Jews one after the other while the second finished them all off by shooting. "The pit was filled to the top with corpses. The gendarmes left after that, and the police covered the corpses with earth and then went away."[74]

Another witness in this investigation, Daria Seleverstova, spoke about the liquidation of the ghetto: "During the execution I could see from my house how they brought a Jewish woman with two children up to the pit. The gendarme tried to take away her baby, but she didn't let him and jumped into the pit herself, still holding the baby. Her eight-year-old boy was clinging to his mother's skirt, and the gendarme threw him into the pit alive. I fainted from seeing such horrible things. By evening the pit was filled to the top with corpses—more than 500 Jews."[75]

To return to the activity of the ChGK in Rechitsa, it should be noted that the commission began work on November 20, 1943, two days after the liberation, and finished in April 1945. Initially the investigation was conducted by military men, lawyers, and medical experts, but in later stages it was composed mainly of town leaders and community representatives, which underlined its civil status. During the final stage Viktor Polovinko (probably a person designated by the republican authorities) became its chairman; its members were local leaders (the chairman of the executive committee, the chairman of the town soviet, the raion prosecutor), a medical expert, an archpriest, and other community figures.[76] Most likely the figures in the testimony of Olga Fukson and her daughter Ekaterina Matveeva on the number of victims were provided by members of the ChGK. Considering that mother and daughter were in the same crowded room in the ghetto, while Jews were continually being brought in and then quickly executed in groups, they would not have been able to keep a tally of the overall number of prisoners. As for the members of the Rechitsa commission, they wished in this way to exaggerate the scale of human losses in view of the forthcoming trial of

Nazi war criminals. Commissions acted this way in a number of other cities in the USSR.[77] In any case the tragedy in Rechitsa and in other places is in no way diminished by determining that the number of Jews executed was actually somewhat smaller than believed.

The later testimony of Ekaterina Matveeva-Liakutina, that there were four hundred Jewish families in Rechitsa during the occupation, was something she had learned from Israel Malinkovich.[78] Most likely it is on the basis of this information that the figure of 1,300 Jewish victims was derived, a figure that is entirely legitimate, considering that due to the war many families who remained in Rechitsa were incomplete.

Among the Jews who perished in Rechitsa were evidently several dozen refugees from places west of the town who did not manage to travel farther east. We know, for instance, of David Vernik from Brest. Several relatives of Alexander Dobrushkin also came from there to Rechitsa. Very likely the majority of such refugees were not included in Israel Malinkovich's list; the same is true of Jews from nearby villages.

The attitude of the local population toward the annihilation of the Jews was ambiguous. Some risked their lives trying to save Jews; others sold them out to the Germans in hopes of a reward or of appropriating the victim's property. In May 1942 Burgomaster Karl Gerhardt issued Directive no. 65, ordering the population to turn in phonograph records they had taken from Jews. This shows that literally everything was plundered.[79] Apart from the incident of unorganized violence against Jews in neighboring villages mentioned earlier, there were cases of murder in Rechitsa itself. Iankel Rozhavskii was killed by a neighbor when he tried to flee the town on the day it was occupied.[80] Immediately after the occupation, Sara-Rasha Sherman was killed by her neighbor, a member of the Polizei. An inhabitant of Rechitsa, Garai, killed an old man, David Kravtsov, with the aim of seizing his cow and household goods; this took place before the mass executions described above.[81] After Sosnovskii's son Chaim and husband Iosif were executed, a neighbor woman arrived and told her that she wanted to take the things that Sosnovskii "wouldn't be needing anymore." Sosnovskii tried to resist, but during the struggle she was stabbed with a pitchfork.[82] Iosif Malinkovich, who escaped while being marched under guard to execution, was killed in his own yard by a neighbor.[83] A man armed with two knives broke into the Dobrushkins' home, forced the family into another room, threw the bedcovers to the floor, and began piling their belongings onto them. Thanks only to the help of some acquaintances, who had been promised many of these belongings, did they manage to take the robber away to the commandant's office.[84] One sentence in

Malvina Gribovskaia's testimony to the ChGK, mentioned earlier, gives an idea of the attitude of some local people toward the Jews. Her half-Jewish grandsons lived with her during the occupation, and she told the commission: "I am happy now that the Red Army has come because I won't be taunted with being a Jew, even though I'm a Belorussian by nationality."[85]

In the towns and mestechkos of Belorussia, there were often not enough local Polizei prepared to take part in the liquidation of the Jewish population, so the Germans sent them from Ukraine or Lithuania. In Rechitsa, which was subordinate to the Zhitomir Gebietskomissariat, the German authorities had no difficulty with the Polizei, who were generally chosen from local residents and, when necessary, sent in from Ukraine. In Rechitsa, as in other places, even a few Soviet functionaries went to serve in the police.[86] People who had been frustrated in their prewar social positions found that police service offered new status and the opportunity to exercise their power over others and to rob them. It exempted them from being sent to forced labor in Germany, although it did not save them from the risks connected with serving in the police. In Belorussia and Ukraine the German and local police often got drunk before actions to liquidate Jews or other segments of the population.[87] The same thing probably happened before the executions in Rechitsa. Among the Polizei, Melnikov and Iakov Kruk showed particular zeal in persecuting Jews.

A number of the Rechitsa Polizei received their punishment immediately after the liberation. Six gallows were set up in the central square next to the former office of the commandant. Partisans from the brigade of Il'ia Kozhar used them to hang the Hitlerites and Polizei who had been found hiding in cellars. To the chest of each person hanged was attached a placard listing the crimes he had committed against the civilian population.[88] But many of the Rechitsa Polizei managed to escape vengeance, some within the USSR, others abroad. Relying only on official statistics, we know that 120 people linked with the occupying regime in one way or another fled Rechitsa Raion with the Germans.[89] Even greater numbers of former Polizei in the eastern oblasts of Belorussia, and evidently in Rechitsa Raion as well, left with the Red Army immediately after the territory had been liberated and so escaped arrest.[90]

One result of the efforts of the Rechitsa Polizei, apparently, was the deaths of no fewer than ten Jews who had gone into hiding. Neighbors were concealing seven-year-old Khana Mnuskin, but someone informed and the Polizei shot her. The Belorussian Anna Zakrevskaia hid five-year-old Abram Vasilevitskii in a pit that she herself had dug under her barn; this eventually became known to one of the Polizei, who then shot the boy himself.[91] The Kovalevskii family hid

Dvoira Melamed and her daughter and grandson, but through the carelessness of neighbors the Polizei found out and executed the three of them.[92] Other such incidents were mentioned earlier.

Apparently, ten to fifteen Jews who were in Rechitsa when the occupation occurred or who arrived very shortly thereafter still managed to save themselves. This could not have happened without the help of the gentile population, who themselves faced the death penalty for concealing Jews. Only a few of the names of those saved are known. Khaia Kofman managed to survive in the village of Zhmurovka thanks to the accordionist A. Goroshko, who was well known there. Grigorii Slavin, married to a gentile, was saved in the village of Kazazaevka. Several Jewish children were hidden by an elderly woman, Elizaveta Gavrilova, in her barn. A few of their friends helped them survive.[93]

The story of Ita (Gita) Shustina (mentioned in the previous chapter) is a dramatic one. She had married a gentile who had gone to serve at the front in the early days of the war. Thanks to her neighbors, she and her three small children managed to escape being put into the ghetto. On the advice of her neighbors, Ita and her children were baptized by the local priest, who then hung crosses around their necks. Nevertheless, sometime later and after many Jews had been executed, Ita Shustina herself was sent to the ghetto. But fate was kinder to her than to her distant relative, Genia Gribovskaia (Shustina), mentioned earlier. The neighbors appealed to the burgomaster, "strengthening their case" with some presents. He informed the Germans that Ita was Russian. This was confirmed by the head of the prison, Korzhevskii. For this reason the Germans soon took her from the ghetto to the commandant's office for her case to be examined. From their hiding place the children watched their mother, completely naked, being taken there by a deliberately long route. At the commandant's office she was interrogated for a long time and then released thanks to a German-language teacher, Nina Kartovich, who headed the commandant's translation section during the occupation. After that, Ita and the children, fearing that the Germans might still find out that she was Jewish, left for the village of Kazazaevka a few kilometers from Rechitsa. One of the local people hid her in a cellar there. After his neighbors threatened to turn in Ita and the children, this man took them to various villages nearby and found them temporary hiding places.[94]

Only one girl, Larisa Uretskii (her married name was Borodich), managed to escape directly from the ghetto itself. One night her mother pushed this eleven-year-old girl under the barbed wire to the outside and told her to run to Lidia Nazarova. The Polizei fired at Larisa but missed. She was unable to stay long with the Nazarovs since the Polizei who had sent the seven members of the Uretskii family to the ghetto lived next door. The girl wandered about her native town in tears, afraid to tell any of the passers-by that she had escaped from the ghetto. She was taken in by Elena Bogdanova, who knew her family. She hid Larisa in her own home at 60 Vygonnaia Street and with her friends, the Gorshkovs, the Ferentsevs, the Kozorezovs, and the Stankeviches. She even managed to hide Larisa in the home of the burgomaster, but only his wife and the servants were aware of it. Bogdanova, along with Maksim Iankov, was a liaison person for the Voroshilov Partisan Detachment. Larisa Uretskaia had to spend her nights in nearby villages, staying in abandoned homes and buildings where she went hungry and froze. Larisa spent a year and a half moving from place to place in this way. Finally, Bogdanova, who knew where the girl was hiding, collected her in early May 1943 and took her to her partisan detachment. There Larisa helped with the cooking and washing and risked her life going to the villages to get milk for the wounded. At the end of October 1943, as the Soviet front lines drew nearer, she was transferred to a rear area by airplane along with several dozen wounded. She spent some time in a children's home there and then returned to Rechitsa and lived with Elena Bogdanova for several years more. Il'ia Erenburg briefly recounted this tale to readers of his 1944 story, "One Person's Victory" ("Pobeda cheloveka").[95]

Olga Fukson and her daughter Ekaterina (born 1926), mentioned earlier as witnesses for the ChGK, had both been wounded during the execution of other Jews; an unidentified old man helped them climb out from under the pile of corpses. They stayed in Rechitsa for about two weeks while their wounds healed; then, in fear of the Polizei, they left for Vasilevichi in Polesia Oblast, her native town. There they settled in the home of some relatives who had fled. Olga spoke Belorussian and was fluent in German. Although they had not known her earlier, the residents of neighboring houses—S. Sopot, N. Brel, and E. Shulga—took the risk of signing her statement that she was a native of the German colony who had run away from the train of carts used to deport members of the collective farm. The burgomaster, Karl Ionus, accepted her statement and even took her on as a housekeeper. Olga used the liaison man, Sopot, to pass on to the partisans any information she picked up in the burgomaster's house. She taught her daughter German, and when the Germans were present would tell her of Germany's imminent victory and the return of their exiled relatives from Siberia. After the war Olga Fukson and her daughter returned to Rechitsa.[96]

The best known among those who saved Rechitsa Jews is Olga Anishchenko. She was an underground liaison person and in her apartment at 1 Naberezhnaia Street she hid nineteen-year-old Maria Rokhlin. Her neighbor, Luka Koziaev, informed the police, however, and Maria was arrested. Sometime later the girl managed to escape. For a brief time she was hidden by others in Rechitsa, and then she made her way out of the town and reached the Frunze Partisan Detachment.[97] This probably happened no earlier than the second half of 1942, since until then there were few partisans in Belorussia, and Jews from the ghetto had essentially no one whom they could join. Only a few of the Jews who fled to the forest could survive on their own, hiding in dugouts, through the harsh winter of 1941–1942. By the spring of 1942, the vast majority of the Jewish population in eastern Belorussia had been wiped out. But even those Jews who did manage to escape and find their way to the partisans in 1942 often found the commanders unwilling to accept them into their detachments. Sometimes this was due to anti-Semitism, sometimes to the wish not to burden the detachment with extra "baggage" in the form of the elderly, women, and children. There were cases of partisans killing Jews they encountered in the forest. However, such partisans dealt harshly with the gentile population as well. Probably all the partisans forcibly confiscated provisions from peasants who refused to give them, since that was what enabled them to survive. Yet some of them were essentially bandits who masked themselves as partisans, and they found the forest merely a cover for their real intentions of looting and hiding from active military combat on any side. Such people often stole valuables from both Jews and gentiles and raped women.[98] After the middle of 1942, when the partisan movement was placed under central control, the attitude of the detachments toward Jews changed somewhat.[99]

Some of the Jews who escaped from Rechitsa did make their way to the forest, found partisans, and were taken into their detachments. Subsequently, many of them were killed in battle. Among the partisans who survived to victory day, Makar Turchinskii, mentioned earlier, was particularly well known. He organized the first partisan detachment in the raion. He was the commissar of the Voroshilov Partisan Detachment, and in April 1943, after this detachment was transformed into a brigade of the same name, he commanded the Frunze Detachment of this brigade. For his actions he was made an honorary citizen of Rechitsa after the war.[100] Other Jews also served in the Voroshilov Brigade. Among them were Samuil Shulman (killed in April 1943), Boris Shmidov (killed in May 1943), and Izrail Dubrovskii (killed in October 1943). Commissar Solomon Egudkin, as well as Bronya Zolotukhina, Viktor Shitman, and Iakov Antenberg, also fought in the Voroshilov Detachment of this brigade until the Red Army arrived.[101]

Some of the Jews who fled to the forest from Rechitsa fell into the hands of the Germans and the Polizei in late 1941 and early 1942 and were executed. Among them was a family of refugees from Byten (Brest Oblast) who found themselves in the town on the eve of war and were killed in February 1943.[102] Their fate was shared by Rechitsa Jews who were captured while already serving as partisans. Fifteen-year-old Iakov Gutarov, mentioned earlier, joined the Shchors Partisan Detachment, one that permitted families, but when part of the forest was block-aded by a punitive squad in October 1942, he and other detachment members were taken prisoner and sent to the Khoiniki and later the Mozyr concentration camp. He was assigned to heavy construction work but miraculously survived.[103]

Apart from the incidents in which Jews were saved by the Slavic population of Rechitsa, there were cases in which the persecuted were helped with food or clothing. For example, the wife of Dr. Chapurnoi left some potatoes on the porch of the Dobrushkin home, after which she hurriedly left, fearing she might be seen.[104] Help was more often given to Jews by those connected in some way to the partisans. These links had grown much stronger by the summer of 1942, despite the fact that the local population faced the harshest punishments at the least sus-picion of aiding the partisans. Documents of the ChGK show that old people, women, and children in Rechitsa were shot for helping the partisans. There were several such actions. The Germans shot one group of twenty-five in August 1942 in an antitank ditch on the edge of the town; another group of as many as three hundred was executed in November–December 1942 in the cellar of 105 Vokzal-naia Street.[105]

More than a few Rechitsa Jews who left the town between 1925 and 1940 per-ished in their new places of residence. Four basic groups can be identified among them, according to the place in which they were killed: (1) in other towns and mestechkos of eastern Belorussia (mostly in Minsk, Vitebsk, and Parichi—at least twenty in all; (2) in western Belorussian (mostly in Brest—at least twenty); (3) in Ukraine, including Kiev (at least ten), and in Russia, including Leningrad (dur-ing the blockade, at least fifteen) and the Crimea, then part of Russia (at least ten); and (4) in Poland (at least twenty, including at least ten in Auschwitz and Treblinka).

In November 1943 Rechitsa was liberated during the campaign that became known in history of the war as the Gomel-Rechitsa Offensive. Marshal Konstan-tin Rokosovskii wrote the following about the liberation of the town: "Troops of the Forty-Eighth Army also operated successfully, advancing along the west bank of the Dnieper toward Rechitsa. Batov made a bold decision: two rifle divi-sions and two tank brigades of M. F. Panov's corps had surged ahead, and Batov turned them into the rear area of the Hitlerites who were in defensive positions in Rechitsa. Because the enemy was not expecting such a strike, the town was lib-erated with only small losses to our forces."[106]

Army general Pavel Batov himself described these events later:

Rechitsa was not within the area of attack of the 65th Army. But a favorable situation was created for a deep maneuver and strike at the town from the rear, because
D. I. Samarskii's corps had managed to move all its divisions across the Dnieper.
It would have been inexcusable to let such an opportunity slip by. . . . Two brigades
of the Guards Don Tank Corps, working with the 37th Guards and 162nd Siberian
Divisions, struck at Rechitsa from the northwest, broke through to the town, and
joined battle in the streets. A rifle corps from the 48th Army advanced from the
east. It pinned down substantial numbers of the enemy who had been designated
to defend the town. We captured Rechitsa almost without losses, did not allow the
enemy to destroy the town, seized a great deal of enemy equipment, and took many
prisoners. The battle for Rechitsa was an example of mutual support by troops
from two different armies whose joint efforts liberated the town. Even more, this
battle provides an example of mutual support of regular and partisan troops in the
offensive.[107]

It should be added that the "pinning down of the enemy" by the Forty-Eighth
Army in the Rechitsa area was achieved largely due to the accurate fire by the
First Guards Artillery Division, commanded by the Jew Arkadii Volchek, who
had been promoted to major general only two months earlier.[108] The major panic
that the artillery barrage caused among the Germans gave rise to a popular saying
at the time: "In Rechitsa the fascists are running like rabbits" (*Fashisty v Rechitse
ot strakha mechutsia*).

More-detailed information is provided by the memoirs of Evgenii Galota, one
of the participants in the battle and, at the time, a sergeant in command of an
artillery gun crew. Toward evening on November 16, a striking force of an
artillery, an infantry, and a tank division was formed to carry out the assault on
Rechitsa. The attack caught the Germans by surprise. They responded with
machine-gun fire, but this had little effect against tanks and artillery. At 4:00 a.m.
on November 18, 1943, the Red Army troops broke through to Rechitsa. The
only serious resistance came in the area of the railway station from troops cover-
ing the German retreat. They fought for an hour and a half and then surrendered.
The Germans even abandoned their staff cars on the streets. Local residents were
particularly puzzled by the new Soviet uniforms with shoulder boards. Witnesses
recall that they did not realize who had taken the town. Once they understood,
their joy was boundless. People offered soldiers whatever food and drink they
had. Galota recalls that when a column of prisoners who had been "defending"
the railway station was marched past, "Misha, a scout from our battery, spotted
them and grabbed his submachine gun: a week before he had discovered that the

Germans had killed his whole family—his wife and two small children. We were barely able to hold him back."[109]

The percentage of Jews who went to war was rather higher than that of the general population that remained in the occupied territories, and there were objective reasons for this. Jewish males who had been evacuated and who were in an age group not previously eligible for call-up were now drafted. Gentiles in the same age group remained in occupied territory, and many of them were not drafted into the Red Army even after the liberation. Some men, particularly in rural areas, had avoided the draft even before the occupation by hiding in the forests or with friends.[110] Jewish soldiers at the front rarely surrendered and generally tried to avoid capture, since they knew that the Germans would execute them. About 27 percent of all Jews who served did so as volunteers, a statistically higher percentage of volunteers than other ethnic groups.[111] Keen motivation explains the disproportionately high percentage of Jews, relative to their overall numbers, who were awarded medals or designated Heroes of the Soviet Union. At the same time, according to Aron Shneer's research, it must be kept in mind that due to the increase in both social and official anti-Semitism in wartime, some Jews were not given these awards, sometimes despite the recommendation of their commanders.[112] In some cases, they received a lower grade award than they deserved, as happened with Rechitsa resident Chaim Dubrovskii. But in other cases, the highest authority even increased the level of rewards offered to Jewish soldiers by their commanders. This happened with Rechitsa natives Isaak Mnuskin and David Mendelson (twice). In some cases, deprived by orders war cripple Jews were awarded after the war thanks to initiatives of local Military Registration Offices. In Rechitsa it's happened with Naum Komissarov in 1947 and Aron Chertok in 1950—not the most favorable year to the Soviet Jews. It's happened in other places as well, for instance in Stalinabad (today Dushanbe) in 1946 with Nison Abramov and in Kovel in 1949 with Rechitsa former resident Isaak-Meer Rapoport.[113]

Analysis of the database on the awarded Jewish battle-veterans shows that a considerable part of them conceal their ethnicity for fear of anti-Semitism. A random sample of fifty questionnaires of Rechitsa residents designed for the front shows that 11 (22 percent) hid their Jewish identity. And this despite the fact that the awards clearly show their courage. Among them ten declared himself Belarus and one an Armenian. Obviously some part of the Jewish war veterans could not hide their identity because of unambiguous Jewish first and last names.

By my own count of the names published in the general lists in the book *Memory* (*Pamiat'*) dedicated to Rechitsa (although the authors do not cite their source, it was most probably data from the Military Registration Office), 399 Jews were killed in battle, comprising 37 percent of the total fallen soldiers of all ethnicities who were born or lived in the town before the war.[114] This is significantly higher than the proportion of Jews within the general population which, according to table 12, was 24.3 percent in 1939.

If one considers all the Jews and gentiles born in Rechitsa who were killed in battle, then the proportion of Jews among them is even higher, since before the war many Jews, as discussed, moved to other places, often farther east from Rechitsa. In such places there was a greater likelihood of their being sent to the front than there was in Rechitsa itself. On the other hand, if we take the year 1926 as an example, we must keep in mind that in that year Jews made up a slightly higher percentage of all births in the town. Also, very few Jews who were taken prisoner, as distinct from the gentiles, returned home.

The Memorial Book of Jewish Warriors Who Fell in the Battle against Nazism makes it possible to add to the list of Rechitsa natives who were killed at the front.[115] Here are found the names of 190 Jews born in Rechitsa. A third source that enables the list of fallen Jews to be expanded is the questionnaires of the Yad Vashem National Institute of Remembrance of Victims of Nazism and Heroes of the Resistance in Jerusalem. These show that 213 Jewish natives of Rechitsa were killed in battle. Comparing all three sources, we can derive a general list of 635 Jews from Rechitsa who were killed in battle, and this is still incomplete. The overall number of Jewish natives of Rechitsa who were killed in battle is at least 800. A good many other Jews who lived in Rechitsa before the war but who were born elsewhere were also killed. There are 55 such names in the Rechitsa *Memory* list, 47 in the questionnaires.[116] The combined list thus includes 102 names, evidently considerably less than their actual number.

More than three dozen Jewish families lost two or more of their members at the front.[117] Among the 635 Jewish natives of Rechitsa who died in the war and whose names we have been able to discover, 103 (16.2 percent) were officers. Among these officers, 17.5 percent served on the military-political staff, that is, they were political instructors or commissars of various ranks. There were only a few senior officers among those killed, something that evidently reflects the proportion of them among Rechitsa natives who served in the military. In 1941 Battalion Commander (the rank corresponds to that of major) Abram Graiver was listed as missing. As noted earlier, Battalion Commissar Zakhar Malinkovich shot himself when his unit became surrounded during the battles in the northern Caucasus in 1942. Major Nison Tarakhovskii, head of a section of SMERSH, was also listed as missing in 1942. In 1943 Major David Margolin, a propagandist from a section of the political directorate of the Leningrad Front, died of wounds. Lieutenant Colonel Boris Goldin was killed during the liberation of Poland in 1944. In October 1941 Military Technician First Class (the rank corresponds to that of colonel) Chaim Linovich was listed as missing. Supply Technician First Class (the rank corresponds to that of colonel) Polina Margolina was listed as missing in 1943.

Considering that overall statistics show that 40 percent of all the Jews serving in the regular forces died in battle, as prisoners of war, or were listed as missing, we may confidently assume, on the basis of the number of Jews native to Rechitsa who died in battle, that some two thousand Jews born in the town went to war.[118]

A list with the birth dates of 404 Rechitsa Jewish natives who fell in the war makes it possible to examine their age characteristics. Males born between 1919 and 1921 and in the first half of 1922 were called up for military service even before the war began. Together they made up 11.9 percent of those on the list. They were serving in the regular army when the war began and were the ones who absorbed its first shock. By decree men born between 1905 and 1918 inclusively were called up for service by June 23, 1941. Among the Rechitsa Jews in the 1905–1914 birth years who were called up, the death toll varied slightly between 12 and 18 for each year of birth. Casualties among the drafted Rechitsa Jews born between 1915 and 1918 were only half of this—from 6 to 10 persons in each year of birth. This was a direct result of the low birth rate during World War I (1914–1918).

TABLE 15. Age characteristics of Jewish Rechitsa natives fell in battles of the war, by year of birth

Year of birth	Death toll (numbers)	Death toll (percentage)	Average the fallen per year of birth (numbers)
1890–1896	18	4.4	2.6
1897–1904	81	20	10.1
1905–1914	161	40	16
1915–1918	32	7.9	8
1919–June 1922	48	11.9	13.7
July 1922–1923	37	9.1	24.6
1924–1927	27	6.7	6.8
Total 1890–1927	404	100	10.9

Source: The table has been compiled from an analysis and comparison of the lists, mentioned in chapter 7.

Between August and October 1941, depending on the distance from the front, young people born in the second half of 1922 and in 1923 were called up for service. They suffered the greatest losses: thirteen and twenty-four persons respectively, comprising 9.1 percent of the entire list. Some of them were called up or enlisted voluntarily (i.e., before the decree was issued) before the occupation of Rechitsa. Many of them perished in the Destroyer Battalion mentioned earlier (sixteen- and seventeen-year-old youths were taken here, along with volunteers from older age groups who at that time were exempt from the draft). The largest part of them, no less then three-quarters of the cohort of the second half of 1922 and in 1923, had left Rechitsa to live elsewhere before the war began or had managed to be evacuated. Poorly trained, they were thrown into the "meat grinder" of the fiercest battles, while those soldiers who had been drafted before the war began and had evaded the German encirclement were reequipped, had their wounds treated, and were reverified by the NKVD. By comparison with the 1923 cohort, the 1924 cohort (those called up in 1942), had losses only half as great, twelve persons. As for those Jews from the 1925–1927 cohort, depending on the year in which they were drafted (the 1927 cohort was drafted in the autumn of 1944), they spent relatively less time at war, and as a result their overall losses comprised 3.7 percent of those on the list.

In Rechitsa in the first half of August 1941, before the occupation, the authorities managed also to draft those born between 1890 and 1904 and those who had not managed to be evacuated. Others were drafted from the places to which they had been evacuated. Typically, those in the 1897–1904 cohort suffered losses of between six and sixteen persons per year, a somewhat higher figure than those from the 1890–1896 cohort, which varied from zero to five persons per year. Of course, among those from the cohorts of the 1890s were relatively many who were not called for army service for reasons of health or because they had remained in occupied territory. It must be kept in mind that among them, just as among the other cohorts, were people who had been exempted. At the same time, among those in the different age groups exempted for various reasons, there were many who volunteered to go to the front. We can assume that the statistics presented here are typical for all other Jews from Rechitsa who fell in battle.

The veterans who returned from the war became the most active segment of the Jewish population. Military medals and orders to some extent gave a de facto right to do many things that before the war would have elicited administrative or even legal sanctions. In 1946, on the personal initiative of the veteran Chaim Gumennik, the remains of some of the Jews who had been executed in the antitank ditch on the grounds of the tuberculosis sanatorium were exhumed. Tsaler Vasilevitskii and Avraam Dovzhik helped in this effort. The latter recalls:

> The corpses lay no more than fifty centimeters deep. The stench was horrible. . . . [I] saw children's heads; I scraped my shovel across and uncovered some long black hair from which fell an aluminum comb. There was the head of a red-haired child and little feet in sandals. . . . I placed all these remains in bedsheets and canvas and in old sacks and carried them to a box that was set on a cart. A sledgehammer was also lying there. A Russian man who was present at the excavation and showed us where to dig came up and said that this sledgehammer had been used to finish them off.[119]

This group of Jews intended to go on collecting the remains the next day, but the chairman of the town's Executive Committee arrived with the police and forbade them from continuing, promising to erect a general monument on this spot. The monument was later set up not far away, near the tuberculosis sanatorium on Frunze Street.[120]

The box of remains that they had managed to collect before being stopped was taken to the Jewish cemetery. There they were reburied, with prayers, in a common grave. In 1946, with money collected from Jewish homes, a brick monument with an inscription on a steel plate was erected here. At roughly the same time, monuments were erected to the Lurye brothers, whose bodies had been identified, as well as to the five who were killed at the corner of Chapaeva and Vokzalnaia Streets: Khatskel Kagan, Hillel Resin, Shmuel Chertok, Avraam Serebrianny, and Moishe Pinskii.[121] Another monument was set up half a kilometer from the town, on the road to Ozershchina where, as noted, Jews were executed and where, nearby, other Rechitsa residents who had somehow run afoul of the Germans were later killed.[122] A common marble monument to Jewish victims of Nazism to replace the older brick one was built in 1994 from donations by Rechitsa natives in Israel. Its inscription reads, "3000, for what?"

The questionnaires of the Yad Vashem Institute provide a more permanent commemoration of those who perished than does the monument. In all 752 questionnaires were compiled concerning those Rechitsa Jews who are still missing, who died while in evacuation or of wounds in hospital, who were killed in Rechitsa or in other places during the occupation, or who died in battle. Among them, as noted earlier, are 266 questionnaires about those who perished in Rechitsa—35.4 percent of the actual numbers of those killed as determined above. This is a low percentage, considering that four-fifths of Rechitsa Jews managed to survive.

The occupation of areas across the whole of the former Pale of Settlement, where Jews had lived for hundreds of years, caused irreparable damage to the traditional way of life of the Jewish mestechkos. Many of them either disappeared or were left without any Jewish population. After the war Jews, who once had comprised the vast majority of the population of the small mestechkos of Belorussia, became only an insignificant portion of the inhabitants. Under such conditions they rapidly assimilated. Although Jews remained an important minority in the larger mestechkos like Rechitsa, they had lost their former positions in social and community life and ceased to influence its character.

Their lack of information about the Nazis' feelings about Jews and the progress made by the rapidly advancing German army deep into the territory of the USSR did not give all the Jews time to escape from Rechitsa or to select the right direction to go when they did escape. At the same time, the fact that Rechitsa was the last Belorussian town to be occupied by the Germans provided a unique opportunity for about 80 percent of the prewar Jewish population of the town to escape to the east or enlist in the army. The majority of the people who stayed behind comprised the weakest segments of the population, the elderly and mothers with many children. With good reason they feared trying to live without means of subsistence away from Rechitsa. Affecting their choice was the army's call-up of husbands and adult sons born in the years 1890–1918 as well as volunteers. Approximately eight hundred Jews born in Rechitsa died at the front or to a much lesser extent in partisan detachments. A particularly large number of soldiers died who were born in the second half of 1922 or in 1923.

Although Rechitsa was under enemy occupation for a relatively short time, twenty-seven months, almost all the Jews who stayed during the occupation were killed in the ghetto that existed for about a month, and a small fraction of that number perished in the surrounding forests. Some of the surrounding local population helped the Jews, while others handed them over to the Germans, counting on a reward. Most of the local non-Jewish population, however, simply stayed out of sight during the "solution of the Jewish question." They were afraid of bringing retribution down on their heads, for in Eastern Europe, unlike Western, capital punishment was the certain reward for hiding Jews. This position did not exclude compassion for the Jews, as eyewitness testimony about the massacres of Jews demonstrated at the end of 1943.

Starting in late July 1941, Soviet authorities received information about the Nazis' annihilation of Jews in Belorussian territory. The central leadership did not reveal this to the public, fearing that it would, on the one hand, inflame anti-Semitic and anti-government sentiments and, on the other, arouse panic among the Jews of the USSR. The authorities of the Belorussian SSR had a somewhat different outlook on this question. After hastily fleeing Minsk, they tried to rehabilitate themselves in the eyes of Stalin from mid-July to mid-August by their active work in evacuating industrial enterprises and people from the unoccupied southeastern section of Belorussia. Because many of the people did not want to leave, the bureaucrats put special emphasis on agitating for the Jews to evacuate, at the same time communicating a limited amount of information about the Nazis' attitude toward them.

Throughout the German occupation, however, the resistance network set up by the authorities did not receive any directives about saving the Jews of the region. Jews were only reluctantly accepted by partisan detachments, especially if they could not fight. At the same time, individual leaders of the resistance helped Jews, but this emanated from their own conception of their duty.

Nazi wartime propaganda and then the formation in the USSR of a new intrapolitical discourse, a component of which was state anti-Semitism and the growth of widespread anti-Semitism based on conflicts over the return of expropriated Jewish property, all contributed to changes for the worse in attitudes toward the Jews in the postwar years.

8

From Liberation to the Collapse
of the USSR, 1943–1991

Economic Life

By the end of 1943, almost immediately after liberation, some though not all of Rechitsa's Jewish residents began gradually returning from evacuation.[1] For the majority of Jewish refugees, the several years spent in evacuation were an arduous trial. It was especially difficult for families with children, invalids, and the elderly. Families with members capable of working survived much more easily. But even they earned two times less in evacuation that they had in Rechitsa before the war.[2] Many refugees found themselves in the severe climatic conditions of Central Asia, the far north, and Siberia to which they were unaccustomed. Food shortages, the lack of properly heated accommodation, and in the hot regions of Central Asia, the absence of a clean environment contributed to the spread of diseases, some of which were of epidemic proportions. According to the Yad Vashem questionnaires, a particularly high number of the Rechitsa natives who died during their evacuation—as many as one-quarter—lived in Uzbekistan.[3]

At the same time, some people from Rechitsa managed better in their new places of residence. Thus some of them chose not to return to Rechitsa after its liberation. There were other reasons for this as well. Some of the refugees had lost all they owned in Rechitsa. Others had lost their close friends and did not want to return to a town where everything reminded them of those who had perished. In such cases, as a rule, there were also grudges against gentile residents who had not done enough to save their Jewish neighbors or who had even served in the police. The destruction, the shortage of food, and the typhus epidemic that broke out in Belorussia and in Rechitsa Raion in particular after liberation also stood in the way of returning.[4] Often there were several reasons for people not to return.

On the other hand, after the war some Jewish families that had not formerly lived in Rechitsa settled in the town. In general, they had formerly lived in neighboring shtetls—Kalinkovichi, Kholmech, Gorval', and others. Some former residents of Gomel, which had been badly damaged, came when they found that they were unable to return to their own homes or had found them destroyed. They came to Rechitsa in hope of finding at least some form of accommodation.

In any case, in the few years immediately following the liberation, at least five thousand people—Jews and gentiles—came to the town. A large part of the population returned to Rechitsa from evacuation in the summer of 1944: over the first two weeks of June alone some 1,500 people arrived in the town.[5] And this took place despite the fact that special permission from the local authorities was then needed to return to the liberated areas of Belorussia.[6] Most probably, evacuees continued to return here at least at the same rate after this restriction was lifted in September 1944 and all former inhabitants of Belorussia were given special passes to allow them to return.[7] Available statistics on the population of Rechitsa show its stable growth from 19,300 in May 1945 to 25,300 in April 1946. In November of that year, however, the population fell to 19,400.[8] The drop in population was caused in part by the difficult economic situation in the town due to war damage and by the food shortages and disease noted earlier. The unprecedented and sudden growth of the population after liberation aggravated the situation. The number of people in Rechitsa, estimated at about 15,000 when the town was liberated in the autumn of 1943, had, by the spring of 1945, increased by 40 percent over eighteen months. Apart from the return of refugees and discharged soldiers, this growth resulted from the arrival of people who had been sent to work in Germany during the occupation. By February 1947 the population of Rechitsa had stabilized at 20,200.[9] Rechitsa, however, reached its prewar population level only toward the end of the 1950s (see table 16). Beginning in 1950, the country's death rate, including the rate of infant mortality, declined, which contributed to the rise in Rechitsa's population.[10] Infant mortality in Rechitsa had dropped sharply as early as 1948, when it was 4.5 percent; in the previous year, by contrast, it had reached 7.7 percent.[11] At that same time, the death rate among adults in Rechitsa also began to decline, basically as a result of improvements in medical services and the end of the postwar epidemics that had broken out there.[12]

The improvements in medical services and public health were due to the actions of the local authorities, who made special efforts to attract doctors to Rechitsa. The number of doctors there had declined by 200 percent from that of the prewar years.[13] The republic's authorities, who had begun collecting information on the locations of doctors and teachers from Belorussia as early as the spring of 1942, were very helpful in this undertaking.[14] For example, the Belo-russian Ministry of Education sent three telegrams to the Rechitsa teacher Maria Rubinchik in her place of evacuation inviting her to come to Minsk.[15] Similar efforts were made to attract doctors and nurses. Thus between 1944 and 1948 the number of doctors and nurses in Rechitsa more than doubled.[16] Although by the late 1940s the town's authorities had still not managed to find a neuropathologist and an oculist, the number of doctors and nurses in Rechitsa exceeded that of the prewar years.[17]

The families of Jewish evacuees coming to Rechitsa, both natives and new set-tlers, usually found themselves in a difficult economic situation. The men of many families had been killed during the war. There was not enough work, living accommodations, or food. Valuables had already been sold while people were in evacuation. The bread ration that local authorities allowed evacuees who were working or hospitalized was 500 grams; orphans received 400 grams; depend-ents, 300 grams.[18] These were small rations, but due to frequent interruptions in the flour supply, the evacuees often did not receive even that much. Statistics from the town's Executive Committee for 1946 show that 827 schoolchildren in Rechitsa, most of them apparently evacuees, were going hungry.[19] Some of the town's functionaries were unable to help the evacuees; others did not try to, preferring to ignore their problems. On the whole, the general population gave a cool welcome to the returning Jews. Although there were instances of neighbors and friends warmly welcoming the returning refugees, other residents met the Jewish evacuees with hostility. Khana Minevich, who arrived in Rechitsa at the beginning of 1944, was struck by this attitude and wrote to Maria Rubinchik in her place of evacuation to tell her not to return.[20]

This negative attitude to Jews was linked to some degree with the success of the anti-Semitic propaganda to which the local population had been subjected during the occupation.[21] Primarily, however, it was linked to the issue of the return of Jewish property, above all, of houses and apartments, both private and state owned. Former owners of the latter found it particularly difficult to have them returned. Although the Christian population returned some housing and house-hold goods voluntarily, some was returned only after legal action or an appeal to the town's administration; some, for various reasons, was never returned. Pëtr Portnoi and Izrail Chechik had their houses returned unconditionally, but many of their household goods had disappeared.[22] A woman from the partisan move-ment had settled into the Mikhalevskiis' house on Kalinina Street immediately after the liberation, but she returned the house when asked by the returning refugees.[23] The household goods of Vulf Malinkovich, Meir Dvorkin, and Aron

Atlas were lost forever to looters.[24] The house of the father of the Sheinkman brothers was returned after legal action.[25] The house of Leiba Gutiontov had been taken over by the family of a convicted member of the former collaborator Polizei, but the family was able to repossess it with help from the court.[26] Through legal action Abram Gluskin managed to have his grandfather's home on Naberezhnaia Street, seized during the war, returned.[27] Isaak Volfson also managed to have his home, seized by local peasants, returned to him through the court.[28] Judge Gorelik in Rechitsa assisted Jews in the return of their property. Given the imperfections of the legal system, however, the rights of the powerful often prevailed. The Rechitsa authorities preferred to involve themselves as little as possible in this process to avoid exacerbating interethnic tensions. It was easier for a demobilized soldier to have his home returned that it was for the elderly or a widow with children. It was particularly difficult to have property returned that had been confiscated by state representatives. Seina-Ita Frenkel, who returned to Rechitsa in 1944, found her house on Kalinina Street occupied by a policeman. After being pressured by neighbors, he provided one room to the refugee but did all he could to force the woman to move out, even threatening her with a pistol. Seina-Ita had to resort to the court, which made a decision in her favor only in 1946. When he moved out, the policeman took all her household goods with him.[29] Tsipa Kaganovich, a war widow with two small children, had a much sadder ending to her struggle to reclaim her home on Proletarskaia Street. In 1945, after she had moved in following a court decision in her favor, she was shot in her own home. The local authorities tried to hush up the affair, even though it roused the anger of the town's entire Jewish population.[30]

Such behavior by the authorities was not specific to the circumstances of the re-emigration of the Jewish population of Rechitsa: the situation was the same in other liberated areas of Belorussia and Ukraine.[31] The former front-line officer M. I. Dargolts wrote to Stalin in November 1945 about the indifference of the authorities in Kamenets-Podolsk to the problem of providing facilities for reevacuated Jews and returning their apartments. In his words one of the bureaucrats, the chairman of the Housing Authority, even stated: "If you hadn't gone away, your apartments would not have been lost."[32] In some places in Belorussia, Jewish functionaries who helped return property to reevacuated people were disciplined and even removed from their posts.[33] Jews in Kiev found themselves in a particularly difficult situation. Those who were unable to prove that they had resided there until the war were expelled from the town.[34]

While many Jewish homes in Rechitsa had been seized for living space, more than a few had been torn down to be used for building materials. This happened to the homes of 274 Jewish families, that is, 15–17 percent of all the houses that belonged to Jews in early 1941. Of the families who fell victim to this, four-fifths suffered partial losses—from 25 percent to 90 percent—while the others lost their dwellings completely.[35] Sometimes houses were burned down after being plundered to cover the tracks of the marauders. Considering that the town suffered practically no damage from bombing or during its liberation, this was apparently what happened to the houses of Hillel and Chaim Levin.[36] During the war or immediately after liberation, local residents and neighboring peasants dismantled the home of Aron-Shleime Faktorovich and carted it away, along with its contents.[37] The same was done to the state-owned homes of Iakov Shustin and Zusia Kaganovich.[38] All abandoned houses belonging to Jews were looted.[39]

The shortage of living accommodations for those reevacuated to Rechitsa and the connivance of the local authorities in the arbitrary seizure of dwellings brought criticism from the Executive Committee of the Gomel Oblast Soviet of Deputies. Its chairman, Pëtr Kovalchuk, wrote in August 1945 of the arbitrary measures being taken in Rechitsa: "Many townspeople are without apartments, and there is a no order of priority in the assignment of available living space. The decree of the Council of Peoples' Commissars of the USSR on the return of living accommodations to owners returning from evacuation is being blatantly violated. Many communal apartment buildings have not been occupied and are being pulled apart piece by piece."[40]

The collaborationism of part of the local population, the three years of anti-Jewish propaganda by the Nazis, and the seizure of Jewish property and the struggle to have it returned had all helped heighten tensions between Jews and gentiles across the traditional area of Jewish settlement generally and in Rechitsa specifically. Frustrated at being forced to return property they had seized to its true owners, some local people who had prospered during the war played up rumors of Jewish cowardice at the front and of the wholesale flight of Jews to Tashkent.[41] This was a way that some gentiles used to absolve themselves before the authorities, at least to some degree, from the taint of having to write "lived in occupied territory" when filling out various forms. Postwar anti-Semitism was not a feature of Rechitsa alone. In the oblast center of Gomel, where very few acceptable living accommodations remained because of the war, it was even stronger. In 1945 an investigator on the Gomel railway, Grigorii Kaganovich, was beaten to death by some air force men who were passengers. They had first subjected him to anti-Semitic taunts and then stripped his body and threw it on the tracks of the Gomel-Uvarovichi line. This case, like others, was hushed up by the authorities.[42]

In neighboring Ukraine, where the attitude toward Jews was even worse, beating and taunting Jews was common in the postwar years. In Dargolts's letter to Stalin, mentioned above, he writes: "A terrible, unbridled, boundless anti-Semitism reigns in Kamenets-Podolsk, and local organizations do nothing to combat it. . . . The word 'Yid' is heard regularly, at every turn, as are such expressions as 'The Jews did not go to war' and 'The medals Jews wear have been bought for money.' There have been more than a few cases of public brawls brought on by this."[43] According to a report by the authorities, Jewish children returning to Dneperopetrovsk Oblast from evacuation were harassed by Russian and Ukrainian children who had remained in occupied territory.[44] In Krivoy Rog the air force veteran Semën Fridzon returned to his former apartment in June 1944 and found it had been seized after the execution of his wife and children. The new tenants raised a cry: "The Jews have come back and are beating the Russians." A crowd from the nearby bazaar came running in response to this. Fridzon was badly beaten, to shouts of "Five mine shafts weren't enough for the Jews; all the mines should be filled with them."[45] When the woman who managed the communal apartments tried to stop the violence, the mob turned on her with shouts of "This communist is here to defend the Jews. Beat her, beat her."[46] In Kiev one such excess led to a pogrom. Two demobilized Ukrainian soldiers, acting on anti-Semitic impulses, badly beat Lieutenant Iosif Rozenshetin in Kiev on September 4, 1945. He was dressed in civilian clothes at the time. Although he tried at first to tell his attackers that he was a member of the People's Commissariat of State Security of Ukraine, in reply he only heard, "Ah, one of the Tashkent partisans." After he fled to his home and changed into his uniform, the lieutenant returned and tried to take his attackers to the police. When they resisted, Rozenshtein shot them. The funeral procession on September 7 passed through the central streets toward the Jewish bazaar. Along the way it grew to a mob of three hundred. The mob viciously beat about a hundred Jews they encountered along the way and threw stones at them. Among the thirty-six Jews who were admitted to hospital afterward, five died that same day.[47] In the wake of this incident, all the troops of the Kiev garrison were placed on alert. According to the eyewitness account of Fridrikh Valler, a Rechitsa native then enrolled in the Kiev Artillery Academy, when the cadets were called out for the emergency, the Jews were ordered to fall out and then dispatched as sentries in the academy buildings; the others were sent to the town to restore order.[48] But even the postwar situation in Ukraine cannot in compare with that of the Jews in Poland when they returned, largely from Soviet Central Asia. Between 1945 and 1948, with the connivance of the new authorities, several thousand Jews were killed by Poles.[49]

Although the Soviet authorities also considered the Kiev pogrom and the postwar situation in Belorussia and Ukraine as a sign of dissatisfaction with the regime, they, like the Polish authorities, did not want to further irritate the Slavic population, already exhausted by the war, by taking repressive measures. They decided, therefore, to limit their response simply to explanatory work within party organizations. According to the recollections of Basia Malinkovich, as passed on by her son, while she was the secretary of the party organization in a small garment plant in Ust-Kamenogorsk she was summoned to the Eastern Kazakhstan Oblast Committee of the party. There she and the other secretaries heard a confidential letter from the party's Central Committee read aloud. The letter dealt with the outbreaks of anti-Semitism and of the contribution of Jews to victory in the war as well as to science and culture.[50] The fact that this document was distributed throughout the country testifies to the broad wave of anti-Semitism in the USSR. The authorities refrained from a mass public campaign against anti-Semitism since they did not to incur disfavor among the population or renounce their own policy of state anti-Semitism, which they had elaborated on the eve of the war.

Though the local authorities in the recently liberated Belorussia and Ukraine took the passive attitude of an observer regarding the return of property to Jews, they did show preference to gentiles when placing people in jobs. According to Dargolts's letter, Jews in Kamenets-Podolsk who had formerly been in managerial positions were not accepted back to work after they returned from the front.[51] In Rechitsa the policy of the authorities toward Jews was expressed through the limited numbers of them accepted in state institutions and enterprises; this continued until the early 1950s.[52] Evidently the local authorities took this position without any direct instructions from Moscow but simply as a result of sensing the growing anti-Jewish mood within the central echelons of power toward the end of the war.[53] Nonetheless, these actions by local bureaucrats can well be classified as state anti-Semitism since the central authorities knew of them and could easily have stopped what was happening.

Local authorities showed special concern for the families of Belorussians arriving in the BSSR in the autumn of 1944 as part of the agreement with Poland on population exchange. There were fifteen such families in Gomel Oblast. They were given housing and jobs in industrial enterprises.[54] This preference was part of the central authorities' attempt to win the sympathy of former Polish citizens for purposes of propagandizing the Soviet system among the people of Poland.

In such difficult conditions of gaining employment, Rechitsa Jews were forced to find jobs in other cities and accept work for which they were unqualified. In 1945, Sara-Pesia and Eva Lifshits, Iulia Gorbatsevich, Mania Liubinskaia, Musia

Fridman, Rakhel Sorkina, and Raia Romanovskaia had to take on the heavy "men's" work of rafting timber. Twenty-five people had to accept work for which they were unqualified in the nail factory (hardware plant) and the "Ten Years of October" match factory. Among them were fourteen Jews. But they were pleased even to have such jobs.[55]

Of much greater practical benefit was the restoration of a prewar form of work—the artel, or cooperative. Unlike the state enterprises, in which the authorities designated directors because of their reliable backgrounds (social origins, party service, ethnicity, etc.), the artels were run by people with good organizational skills and practical experience in business and commerce. Often they had prewar experience in managing smaller state or social organizations. The authorities probably kept these things in mind when confirming the elected chairmen, although even that was not an essential condition, since serious reasons were needed for rejecting a candidate. Particularly after the purges of the late 1930s and the war, there remained few workers with managerial experience who would not have spent time in occupied territory and who would have had a "spotless" curriculum vitae. Sometimes even service with the partisans was not enough to ensure proper rehabilitation, since the authorities knew that a number of bandits had joined partisan detachments on the eve of liberation.

In short time the Jews managed to organize themselves into artels and get production moving. The artels could operate with more mobility and flexibility than the state enterprises, which were held back by an inflexible bureaucratic structure and administrative responsibility. The shoemakers' "Union" (Obedinenie) artel, employing more than a hundred people, held top place among the newly revived artels, just as it had earlier. From 1944 to 1951 it was headed by Rona and Velvel Mikhlin, and then, to the end of the 1950s, by Iosif Cherniavskii. Elia Malikin was head of one of the artel's workshops. Other artels, revived or newly established after the war, were "The Cooperator" (Kooperator), for tailors; "The Red Cabinetmaker" (Krasny mebelshchik), for cabinetmakers (and later a house-building combine) and fine-furniture makers (its chairmen until 1948 were Itska Portnoi and then Mikhail Livshits); "The Red Transport Worker" (Krasnyi transportnik); "Metal Handicraft" (Kustarny metal), for tinsmiths and blacksmiths; "The Red Warrior" (Krasnyi boets), for physically handicapped people (its chairman was A. Merman); "Food Worker" (Kharchevik), for food products workers (Meer Zelichionok); "Collective Labor" (Kolletkivny trud), for shoemakers (president, Sofia Kazovskii); "Red October" (Krasnyi Oktiabr), for rope makers (twelve people employed, name of president unknown); "Dawn" (Rassvet), for wheelwrights (chairman, Izrail Kofman).[56]

It is difficult to exaggerate the significance of the artels in providing jobs in Rechitsa for Jews and the population generally. In 1946 they employed from 850 to 900 workers, while the six factories in the town had fewer than 600. As for output, the nine artels and the Town Industrial Combine (director, Mikhail Zakhar'in) had a yearly output of goods valued at 7.7 million rubles, while the production of the six factories was valued at 1.7 million rubles.[57] Thus the town economy at this time was essentially based on artel production. These artels had almost equal significance for Rechitsa Raion as well. With the help of the artels the peasants, who had been deprived of their supply of goods for two years, could now meet their needs for footwear, clothing, household goods, and so on.

Wages in the artels were low, and this forced the Jews, who, as noted, had lost practically all their property during the war, to look for supplementary sources of income, not only to feed their families but also to acquire clothing and house-hold goods. The most widespread way of doing this was to bring other family members into the artel, including youths of twelve and older. Jews more rarely resorted to black-market speculation in order to feed their families. For example, in Bobruisk at this time several Jewish families bought up cakes of yeast stolen from the bread-making plant, cut them in sections, and sold them at retail in the market.[58] Jews in Rechitsa, living in conditions of chronic shortages of goods, found similar forms of income for themselves. Some shoemakers and tailors provided goods unofficially, either to order or for sale, that were made from mate-rial stolen at work or bought on the black market. Generally, one could also find other scarce goods, such as soap, soda, sugar, and felt boots, on the black market. Immediately after the war demobilized soldiers returning home through Rechitsa would sell "trophy" goods: watches, gramophones, cameras, radios, fashionable European clothing, and other luxury items. In the late 1940s, goods began ap-pearing on the black market via dealers within the state trade network or were brought in especially from Moscow and Leningrad. One Rechitsa trader in such goods named Chaim Goman was arrested and convicted in 1948.[59]

Apart from the tax on income from the artels, the other major source for enhancing the town and regional treasuries after the war, just as it had been before the war, was the sale of alcohol. The letter of the chairman of the Gomel Oblast Executive Committee to the chairman of the Rechitsa Raion Executive Committee in 1948 is symptomatic. Given that Rechitsa lacked the funds to pay its medical personnel and teachers, his letter directs his colleague to place wine and vodka products under monopoly control and expand their sale; at the same time, it forbids the sale of alcohol by the glass in all retail and dining establish-ments apart from cafeterias.[60] Alcohol remained an important and irreplaceable source of state income throughout the whole country as well. Nonetheless, for ideological reasons this issue was not discussed in the USSR.

New industrial enterprises were built in the town in the postwar years: a plywood and furniture combine and factories that produced spare parts and sewer pipes and extracted tannic acid. Oil began to be produced in Rechitsa Raion in 1964. These developments solved, to some extent at least, the problem of jobs and salaries. Later there appeared plants and factories to repair ships and produce hardware, clay pipes, reinforced concrete (two plants), thermoplastics, ceramic decorative pieces, beer, canned food and wines, butter and powdered milk, hydrolyzed yeast, bread, and linen, as well as a weaving association, four pharmacies, and two hospitals.[61]

The artels, which the population had long accepted as Jewish enterprises, were unable to compete with state enterprises and bear the burden of taxes and ceased to exist. The "Union" shoemaking artel held out until 1960 and then was transformed into a household goods combine. I. Cherniavskii headed it until 1965. In 1960 the rope-making artel was likewise transformed into the "Red October" weaving mill with almost five hundred workers. The "Red Cabinet Maker" artel lasted until the early 1970s and then merged with the town furniture combine.

The closing of the artels in fact marked the end of the era of Jewish craftsmanship. Some Jews, of course, did continue working at municipal Dom bytovogo obsluzhivaniia (Center for everyday services) for many more years as watchmakers, jewelers, tailors, or barbers.

Artisans and their families preserved their commitment to Judaism longer than did other social groups. The greatest surge in interest in the Jewish tradition over the Soviet period in the USSR generally and in Rechitsa specifically was seen immediately after the liberation.

Religious Life

Jewish religious life began to revive in the town after the war even though the synagogue buildings had not been returned to the members. Tsodik (Tsidikiia) Karasik (1859–1952), a man of advanced years, became the rabbi.[62] Crushed by the losses of so many relatives and friends, as well as by the difficult economic situation, many elderly Jews in the town began to turn to religion. The Jews had been united by the commonality of their fate as a nation. The enthusiasm of earlier years, brought on by the speed of modernization, changed to disillusionment with Soviet internationalism. To a much greater degree than earlier, the minyans became not only meetings with a quorum of ten or more adult males for common prayer but also centers of Jewish communal fellowship.[63]

In the 1945 report of P. Maslov, representative for Belorussia on the Council for Religious Affairs of the Council of People's Commissars of the USSR, Rechitsa was named as one of six towns and mestechkos in Belorussia where believers were most actively gathering in illegal minyans.[64] The report goes on to state that such minyans in Minsk and Gomel Oblasts were organized by Rabbi B. E. Rozentsvain, so it is possible that the minyan in Rechitsa, in the home of Chaim Gumennik at 54 Lenina Street, was also organized with his help. Jews attempted to legalize their gatherings for prayer, but the Executive Committee decision of May 15, 1946, rejected their plea under the pretext of that the town lacked available accommodation. In October 1947 the authorities demanded that Gumennik sign a declaration that his home would cease being used for religious gatherings. After that, the minyan began meeting in the apartment of Mendel Zaks at 16 Lunacharskaia Street. Another group of religious Jews met in the apartment of Khasia Feigina at 25 Karl Marx Street, opposite the fire station. Although the authorities compelled her to sign a similar declaration, the minyan continued to meet secretly in her home.[65]

Despite the precautions taken by religious Jews, the authorities knew of the minyans' gatherings. The deputy head of the town KGB, Riumtsov, attempted to get sanctions from the deputy chairman of the Town Executive Committee, Tarkhanov, against to people mentioned; Tarkhanov, for some reason, took no such measures. In January 1949, Luganskii, the deputy representative for Belorussia on the Council for Religious Affairs of the Council of Ministers of the USSR, came to Rechitsa. He had learned of the two minyans, and he demanded that the chairman of the town Soviet, Mikhail Iurchenko, fine Karasik, Zaks, and Feigin, which was apparently, was done.[66] Generally, heavy fines were the weapon that the administration used everywhere in the struggle against Jewish prayer, but these measures did not stop all the religious believers in Rechitsa. At the end of the 1940s and the beginning of the 1950s, the most active among them, apart from those mentioned above, were Naum and Genokh Zasenskii, Lev Gurevich, Chaim Palei, the Pikovskii brothers, Ziama Gorelik, Lazar and Meir Dvorkin, and Iankel Puperman. Information from the administration shows that in Rechitsa in 1954 the two illegal minyans continued to meet as previously.[67] On the Jewish New Year on September 28–29, 1954 (the year 5715 by the Jewish calendar), forty to fifty people were present in one minyan, at 23 Karl Marx Street.[68]

The Council of Religious Affairs in Belorussia, mentioned above, generally frowned on the registration of minyans, that is, the virtual legalization of synagogues. Thus by the early 1950s, there were only two synagogues in the republic: in Minsk and in the shtetl of Kalinkovichi, not far from Rechitsa.[69] At the same time, there were many more in other republics with sizable Jewish populations: twenty-nine in Russia, forty in Ukraine, twenty-five in Georgia, and eleven in Moldavia.[70]

Under conditions of religious persecution, the minyans had to change their meeting places regularly. The religious institutions of the Baptists in Rechitsa and Rechitsa Raion were suppressed in the same way or even more severely.[71] As distinct from these religious groups, the policy toward the Orthodox Church during the war underwent changes; in November 1943 the Council of People's Commissars adopted Resolution 1325, "On the Procedure for Opening Churches."[72] In the wake of this resolution, 510 new Orthodox churches were opened in the USSR in 1945 alone.[73]

The issue of opening a church was also taken up at the session of the Rechitsa Executive Committee on June 6, 1946. As noted earlier, the Uspenskii Cathedral building was confiscated in 1935, and after major renovations costing 760,000 rubles, a House of Culture was opened in it. The first floor of the building housed a theater with nine hundred seats, a balcony, and a mechanized stage; the second floor was the town library and a small meeting hall. Two foyers were also added; the result was a threefold increase in the building's usable space. The building was again used as a church during the German occupation. After the liberation, because there was no other building of its size, the Executive Committee asked the Council of Ministers of the BSSR to return it to the town as a place where mass cultural events could take place. The committee proposed that the House of Officers at 72 Second Polevaia Street be used to house the church.[74] Evidently this was a response to a directive from Minsk to return a number of church buildings. As a result of talks with the Council of Ministers of the BSSR, in April 1948 the Executive Committee adopted a resolution on providing the Orthodox community, "in place of the House of Socialist Culture, illegally occupied by the community during the German occupation" with the building of the Food and Industry Retail at 57 Kooperativnaia Street. The Food and Industry Retail was given twenty-four hours to vacate the building.[75]

The opening of Orthodox churches showed the local population that changes had taken place "at the top" with regard to religion. This development could not but raise hopes among Rechitsa Jews for a rather more liberal approach by the authorities toward their religion as well. Such a change, however, did not materialize. The only help that the authorities gave the Jews of Rechitsa (as a community) in the postwar period was to repair the enclosure around the cemetery. By April 1946 the Jews had restored the cemetery, badly damaged during the occupation, to order and had begun to rebuild the enclosure; the town authorities provided the necessary building materials. After this work had dragged on for a long time, the Executive Committee decided in September 1948 to give the local municipal services three weeks to build enclosures around both the Jewish and the Orthodox cemeteries. Municipal services were also directed to continue to maintain these cemeteries in proper condition.[76]

The proclamation in 1948 of the State of Israel and the Arab aggression toward it led to an upsurge of ethnic feeling among Soviet Jews.[77] The formation of the State of Israel aroused lively interest in Rechitsa. The issue of Israel was discussed with particular excitement in the minyan on Lenina Street headed by Isaak Komissarchik. Members of this religious group expressed their willingness to volunteer for service in the war in Palestine if the authorities consented or to provide material aid to the young Jewish state.[78] In general the minyans and synagogues were the only institutions in the USSR at the time that united Jews on the basis of national identity. Many Jews who had attended synagogues or minyans from time to time now came not primarily to satisfy their religious needs but for contact with others of the same ethnicity. At the same time, the postwar upsurge of national consciousness was not reflected in an increased attraction to Yiddish. To the contrary, having improved their knowledge of Russian while in evacuation or serving at the front, the vast majority of parents after the war were motivated by practical considerations and spoke to their preschool and school-age children only in Russian.

After Stalin's death in March 1953, Belorussian Jews found new hope that the attitude toward Judaism would change. Thus Jews in several Belorussian towns submitted requests for the opening of synagogues as early as the second half of 1953.[79] The general policy on religion changed little, however, and all the requests of the Belorussian Jewish communities were evidently refused. At the same time, after Stalin's death the authorities used less-harsh methods to combat religion generally and Judaism in particular. According to Leonid Smilovitsky, the result of these changes was a sharp growth in the number of people attending synagogues and participating in minyans in Belorussia.[80] By the autumn of 1953 there were sixty people participating in prayers in the two minyans of Rechitsa.[81] Subsequently, the number of minyans grew as well, to at least four. In 1956 these were located at 54 Lenina Street, in the home of Chaim Gumennik; at 92 Lenina Street, in the home of Movsha Olbinskii; at 84 Proletarskaia Street, in the home of Zalman Mnushkin; and at 48 Karl Marx Street, in the home of Eli Ioffe and Nakhman Vasilevitskii. The faithful, almost all of them elderly, would gather there on Saturdays and on religious holidays.[82]

No fewer than fifty people gathered in each apartment for the Jewish New Year on September 6 and 7, 1956 (the year 5717 by the Jewish calendar). At this time Chaim Gumennik, evidently unaware of whom he was dealing with, confidentially told the representative of the Council on Religious Affairs during a gathering of the minyan that there were about four hundred religious Jews in Rechitsa, 60 percent of them women, none of them young people, and only a few of middle age.[83] According to Gumennik, Hirsh Pinskii (the shoychet Heshel Pinskii, 1898–1956, mentioned earlier) had taken on the duties of their rabbi, and the shoychet had been David Glukhovskii, who had recently passed away. A few Rechitsa Jews who wanted to have their infants circumcised had it done in Kalinkovichi and Bobruisk.[84] The same source states that despite the negative attitude of the authorities, Rechitsa Jews did not despair and hoped for the return of the buildings that had housed their two former synagogues.[85]

In the 1950s and 1960s, most of the older generation maintained Jewish traditions and, specifically, observed *kashrut*, followed religious prescriptions at Pesakh and Yom Kippur, and marked the Jewish holidays. They kept special chinaware for their holiday tables. Those who were still working, however, were unable to observe the Sabbath.[86] In the 1950s and 1960s, minyans gathered in the apartment of Heshel Pinskii (until his death) on the corner of Lenina and Aviatsionnaia Streets; at the home of Movsha Olbinskii on Lenina Street; at the Levins' home on the corner of Lenina and Kutuzova Streets; at the Livshits's on Michurina Street; in another home on Kalinina Street; and in several more. Money was donated for various purposes of the religious community and in memory of deceased relatives.[87] Some of the town's Jews, worried about the authorities, did not attend the minyans and said their prayers on their own at home. The Yom Kippur fast was the only religious tradition observed by the Rechitsa seamstress Rakhel Raiskaia. The bookkeeper Noakh Ladin, who did not attend a minyan, circumcised his children himself. The spread of circumcision in Rechitsa, as in Belorussia generally, irritated the authorities since it showed that the Jewish population continued to observe in secret religious rituals that had still not been eradicated. Thus the authorities fought against the mohels and the shoychets, the baking of matzo, and the existence of mikvahs, believing that after the closure of Jewish religious institutions—the heders and the synagogues—the final stage of the struggle with the Jewish religious tradition had arrived. The circumcision of infants was done in Rechitsa at that time by the mohel and shoychet Shmuel-Gershon Sorkin from Gomel.[88] It is also possible that circumcisions were done by the shoychet and melamed Yehuda Pinskii

(1897–1966), who had been invited to Rechitsa from Bragin in the early 1950s. He was a close friend of Iosif-Itskhak Shneerson, the sixth Chabad tsadik.[89]

In the 1970s the number of religious Jews in Rechitsa declined, and only one minyan remained. In one instance the minyan was planning to meet in the home of Genia Levin at 49 Karl Marx Street. In the night, however, unidentified persons smashed the shutters, broke the windows and made their way into the porch. This invasion was accompanied by curses and threats to destroy the "Yids' synagogue." In those same years this minyan would also gather in the home of Dora and Lena Kapustin on the same street. The actual organizer of the minyan was the manager of a food store Grigorii Ovetskii. At the beginning of the 1980s the minyan gathered in the basement of this store.

Because of the persecutions, organizers of the minyan would change the apartments in which it gathered. When the police, who often were acting on information from an informer, discovered a prayer meeting, they would usually draft a report and have the owner of the apartment brought to trial; the others present were let off with threats. The authorities also compiled lists of Jews who baked matzo. Matzo was usually baked at night. Until the second half of the 1970s, much of it was baked in the home of Ester-Frada Koparovskaia, located at the intersection of Kalinina and Lunacharskaia Streets. Matzo was also baked in the home of Khonia Rumanovskii.[90] Under pressure from the authorities, Jewish religious life in Rechitsa was slowly dying, until it finally ended in 1986 along with the collapse of the religious community.[91] In the early 1990s, however, in the era of perestroika in the USSR, a minyan was again organized in Rechitsa.

SOCIAL AND CULTURAL LIFE

By the middle of the war, state anti-Semitism had grown even stronger, and it was expressed through the dismissal of Jews, particularly those in managerial positions, from publishing houses and scientific research and cultural institutions.[92] After the war this policy not only continued but spread, in Belorussia in particular, to employees of administrative and judicial bodies.[93] Initially these dismissals were not widely publicized, but by 1947 some ideological justification had to be offered for this purge, and one was found. The authorities began to explain the dismissal of Jews from their posts as a vital part of the struggle with the "rootless cosmopolitans" who were in thrall to the West. A hypertrophied form of Russian national culture and the writings of Lenin and Stalin were held up to oppose such ideals. Thus the Rechitsa native Boris Korman (1922–1983), who was a senior lecturer in the Faculty of Russian Literature at the Stalinabad Pedagogical Institute was removed from his post in 1949 and accused of cosmopolitanism for his criticism of a report studded with citations from the leaders. More often, however, the personnel departments used other formulaic statements when giving the reason for the dismissal of a Jew: "released from his post as having been compromised" or "released from his post for obstruction of managerial personnel."[94] In Rechitsa in those years, "farsighted" managers began quietly dismissing Jewish office workers.[95]

The culmination of this campaign was the "case of the doctor-poisoners" in 1952–1953. The harsh and lawless methods used against the Jewish intelligentsia even gave rise to rumors at the time of the imminent deportation of Jews to the Far East.[96] In Rechitsa the "case of the doctor-poisoners" led to increased hostility toward all Jews.[97] On January 13, 1953, a small crowd even gathered in the town square shouting anti-Semitic slogans and calls for a pogrom.[98] The local detachment of the KGB began collecting compromising materials on Pëtr Ratnev, a surgeon in the town hospital, to be used for his eventual arrest.[99] Because of Stalin's death, this did not occur. State anti-Semitism did not die with Stalin, however. Rather, it became an integral part of Soviet domestic policy.

In the mid-1960s, with the further growth of state anti-Semitism in the USSR, even "rank-and-file" Jews began to be subject to greater discrimination. Under the

Komsomol members, 1946. Courtesy of Boris Kaganovitch.

circumstances of formal equality, guaranteed by the constitution, such discrimination rested on secret directives. Entry of Jews into educational institutions, the
party, and jobs was limited, as was travel abroad, the chance of advancement at
work, and the award of bonuses and honorific titles. Even in the schools Jewish
students who were candidates for medals had their marks lowered.[100] Correspondence with relatives abroad was recorded by the KGB, which from time
to time punished or warned those who had stepped across the line. Ida Kaplan
was removed as director of a night school for receiving parcels from abroad. Of
course, these prescriptions applied not only to Jews, but considering that most
Jews in Belorussia maintained links with people abroad, Jews and gentiles alike
saw these measures as specifically anti-Jewish. State anti-Semitism stimulated
hostility toward Jews in daily life. This animosity had always existed in the country, and its degree depended on the tolerance of the population in one or another
area; it could even differ from one region to another. As for Rechitsa, everyday
anti-Semitism was expressed primarily in personal insults, sometimes public
ones. But on the whole, from the mid-1940s to the 1960s, Jews in Rechitsa suffered more from state anti-Semitism that that of everyday life. Under such conditions some people began altering the entry on ethnicity in their passports and
changing Jewish first names and patronymics and sometimes even last names to
ones that sounded more "melodious." The majority of Jews changed their first
names and patronymics without any registration, but there were some who did
officially register the change. At the same time, other Jews continued to give their
children Jewish names, something probably intended to honor tradition or protest the growing anti-Semitism.

A clear indication of everyday anti-Semitism was the destruction of gravestones in the Rechitsa Jewish Cemetery that began in the 1950s. Not infrequently,
soldiers fired at Jewish gravestones (a military unit was located nearby). Some of
the gravestones remained disfigured; others were restored by a stonemason who
looked after the carving of Hebrew inscriptions in the stones until the 1960s.[101]
The town authorities sometimes made repairs to the cemetery, but this was most
often covered by contributions from Rechitsa Jews. When the town authorities
placed a swine market near the cemetery in the 1970s, the Jews saw it as mockery
of their traditions. Subsequently, some garages were built there. At the same time
the owners of the cars seized some of the cemetery land without authorization.
On January 15, 1990, hooligans destroyed about thirty graves in the Jewish cemetery. Several more such attacks followed, though the greatest damage was done
on the night of February 9–10, 1999, when thirty-five monuments were damaged
and seven totally destroyed. The obelisk commemorating victims of the Nazi

genocide was broken in half. This act of vandalism was widely publicized in the rest of the world. It is mentioned in all reports of international organizations defending human rights. Another thirteen Jewish gravestones were damaged in Rechitsa in February 2003. Yet another of these acts of vandalism in the cemetery was committed on the night of April 7–8, 2005, when twenty-nine gravestones were smashed. In November of the same year, ten graves were badly damaged.[102] On the night of May 26–27, 2011, fourteen gravestones and a monument to the victims of the Holocaust were vandalized.

Between the 1930s and the 1950s, a number of Jewish families remained traditional, something reflected not only in religious tradition but also in family lifestyle. Some Jewish families in Rechitsa had five or more children during these years. Archives of the town administration show that mothers of such families received medals from the government. Emoluments of this kind as well as disbursements of cash benefits to the mothers of many children began to be utilized in the USSR in 1944 to make up for population losses by stimulating fertility.[103]

In the 1950s and 1960s Rechitsa was a town of wooden buildings spread over a large area with its old center not far from the Dnieper and with relatively broad and quiet streets. Ancient poplars here and there raised their majestic branches over the rooftops; dahlias and asters bloomed in front gardens. Rechitsa came to

A group of children, 1948. Courtesy of Boris Kaganovitch.

life in summer. Emanuel Bogdanov gives a vivid, if somewhat idealized description of Rechitsa's atmosphere in those years:

> The scent of blooming chestnuts, acacias, and a variety of flowers fills the air with an intoxicating aroma, particularly on warm, quiet summer evenings. The people of Rechitsa stroll along the broad sidewalks on the central streets. Packs of young people flit among the strollers. The music of a waltz or tango can be heard in the distance. This is the band playing in the park on the Dnieper. Pairs of dancers circle endlessly on the famous dance floor there, watched with eager curiosity by children and old people standing on the foot bridge above the dancers. The elderly, recalling their youth, seek out their children among the dancers. Perhaps they are also picking out future mates for their own offspring. "There's no better place in the world than Rechitsa" was a line from a song of those years.[104]

The sharp drop in the Jewish population in the 1960s and 1970s meant that the minyan lost its role as an informal center of Jewish national fellowship available to all. Such fellowship, to some extent, continued among the fifty or more active elderly Jews, both men and women, who passed on "Jewish" news in Yiddish from person to person. Well known among this group was the glazier Aba Gelzin. The apartments of about two dozen of these people, where in the course of the day visitors would pass by to exchange information, served as Jewish information centers of a sort. In a period when the existence of a Jewish community in the town was vanishing, even the beggar woman Tsilimonikha, who regularly made the rounds of Jewish apartments and homes looking for handouts, was a kind of connecting link.

Visiting Jews ran into one another on the central streets of the town, where they could meet during their evening walks. Jewish grandmothers were particularly energetic during this time in introducing girls and young men. Young people themselves also socialized in the so-called Jewish crowds that existed in the town in the 1970s; these became much larger in the summer. What held these groups together, aside from distant family connections, was a common mentality that differed somewhat from that of the rest of the population, both in Rechitsa and beyond it.

Despite the state's repressive measures toward Jews that have been mentioned, after the liberation and until the early 1970s, several dozen Jews still held responsible positions in Rechitsa, mainly in the administrative and economic areas. The reason for such "liberalism" was the shortage of appropriate personnel within the rest of the population.[105] As previously, the lack of competent managerial-level personnel with appropriate education and "untainted" by time spent within occupied territory meant that Jews had to be assigned to responsible positions. Also, the non-Jewish population suffered in large measure from alcoholism, which was an obstacle to such appointments. For example, in September 1945 the communist Sima Khaitovich was appointed as director of the Kalinin movie theater. She replaced Evgenii Turutin, who had been dismissed for "systematic drunkenness and rude treatment of patrons."[106] Aside from her, other Jews held managerial-level jobs from the mid-1940s to the beginning of the 1970s: Zakhar Malinkin was the director of a weaving organization; Boris Trebukh the director of a construction enterprise and head of a section in the Town Soviet; Abram Fridliand the director of an industrial complex; Leonid Streshinkii the director of a linen mill; Anna Chauskii (Levin) the director of a clothing factory; Simkha Revzin, and then his son Ilia, the manager of the dock; Mikhail Zakhar'in the head of production in the plywood and furniture combine; Isaak Maskalik at various times the director of a milk plant and director of a food combine; Boris (Borukh) Gluskin the chairman of a fishermen's artel; Shimon Belzer the director of a tannin-extracting plant; Maria Rubin the head of the tuberculosis sanatorium; and Pëtr Ratnev the head and chief surgeon of a hospital.

In terms of the republic as a whole, the proportion of Jews in managerial-level jobs in the second half of the 1940s remained rather high, from 5 to 6 percent.[107] Occasionally, due both to problems finding appropriate personnel in Belorussia and for the sake of ethnic representation, Jews even held elected posts. In Rechitsa, for example, Sima Khaitovich was a deputy of the town soviet in the mid-1940s, while the people's judge at the time was Semën Lozovik. In February 1948 a session of the Gomel Oblast Soviet elected him deputy chairman of the Gomel Oblast Court.[108]

Jews also worked in various spheres of the town economy and in medical services. As before the war, they made up a large share (as much as 50 percent) of the town's lawyers. But the percentage of Jews among teachers was very likely even greater. Between the 1940s and 1960s there were as many as fifty Jewish teachers in Rechitsa.[109]

In the 1950s there were five high schools and two seven-year schools in Rechitsa, along with a boarding school and a medical college. Nine Jews taught in the medical college, comprising 45 percent of the entire teaching staff. The activities of the town's cultural organizations gradually returned to normal. In 1948–1949 Moisei Bliankman (1896–1968) once again organized a theatrical company in Rechitsa. Vera Pevtsov (Vikhno) was featured in his productions. The company staged Sholem Aleichem's plays *Wandering Stars* and *Stempeniu*. From 1947

Jewish girls, 1950s.
Courtesy of Boris
Kaganovitch.

to the mid-1960s, Anis (Nosun) Finkelberg served as director of the town's
House of Culture. During his tenure he organized a song-and-dance ensemble
that he took to the International Youth and Student Festival in Moscow in 1960.
Finkelberg was at last honored by being awarded the title Distinguished Artist of
Belorussia, even though he had previously been removed from his post several
times because he was a non-party Jew and then brought back because he was a
professional.[110]

Everyday anti-Semitism reared its head in Rechitsa in the 1970s and 1980s.
This was due in part to anti-Israeli propaganda and in part to the arrival of large
numbers of new residents who had come to work in the oil industry. These
people brought their prejudice toward Jews with them. It was also a reaction to
their poor living conditions as compared with long-time residents, a large number of whom were Jews. The new arrivals settled mainly in the town's new raions.

In general the presence of an "alien" population helped inflame xenophobia, displayed in the 1970s in the mass conflicts between groups of the town's young people who faced off in struggles over territory.

The growth of everyday anti-Semitism led many Rechitsa Jews to see the disadvantages of their place of residence. Migration within the country sometimes enabled them to find a place with a lower level of anti-Semitism, but it was impossible to hide from state anti-Semitism. From the late 1960s onward, anti-Semitism and economic backwardness helped motivate some Jews to try to leave the country. As mentioned, emigration out of Rechitsa had begun in the early years of Soviet power. This wave of emigration ended in the mid-1920s. Most probably, only a few isolated individuals from Rechitsa left the country between the later 1940s and the 1960s. In the early 1970s the authorities allowed limited numbers to leave, and this continued until the mid-1980s. Over this period it is estimated that several dozen families left the town for the United States, Canada, Israel, and other countries.[111] A number of families waited a long time for official permission to leave and so became what were called "refuseniks." They lost their jobs, their family members were expelled from schools, and the KGB applied psychological pressure on them through "chats," interrogations, and arrests. In Moscow the Rechitsa native Artur Neiman became one of them; he was denied permission to emigrate for more than ten years.[112]

The people of Rechitsa will remember for the rest of their lives April 26, 1986, the day that a radioactive cloud from the exploding generating unit in the Chernobyl (Ukraine) nuclear power station 120 kilometers away reached the town. Under these conditions, leaving the town for another region without help from the state was very difficult because of the problem of finding living accommodations. Nevertheless, many residents, including Jews and particularly those with children, temporarily left the town to stay with relatives in other cities of the USSR. Rechitsa became deserted, but within a year or two some of the residents had to return. At the end of the 1980s, as the Iron Curtain began to open, emigration from the town proceeded at a rapid rate. Rechitsa Jews left for the United States, Israel, Australia, and later Germany. Several people from Rechitsa eventually moved from Israel to Canada.

Concurrent with the emigration, Jewish national organizations began springing up in Rechitsa, as they did across the former USSR. In November 1989 a Jewish cultural club, "Ami" (My People), opened. Its first chairman was Lev Rutman. Rimma Khazanovskaia, Naum Ladin, and Sara Levin worked with him in founding the club and as organizers; in 1992 Levin became its new chairperson. The club was located in the "Neftianik" Palace of Technology and was involved in spreading knowledge about Israel and information on the history and traditions of the Jewish people. From 1993 onward the Jewish holidays were also celebrated here as was Victory Day. On several occasions during 1993–1994, the club's activists organized volunteer Sundays for repairing and tidying the cemetery. During those years the club was officially registered with the authorities. After 1996 the club undertook charitable activities. In the mid-1990s an *ulpan* for Hebrew and a Hebrew Sunday school began operating in Rechitsa.[113] The club was headed by Alla Shkop from 1997 to 2006.

Many Rechitsa Jews found it difficult to leave their native town, despite the fact that, architecturally, it had long since lost its character as a mestechko and had transformed into a provincial town with typically multistory buildings. Economic backwardness and widespread alcoholism among the population intensified the depressing picture of local life.[114] After taking up permanent residence in other countries, Rechitsa Jews frequently return to the town—to visit the cemetery, to wander along its old streets, and to meet friends. Their interest in local news and in political developments in the republic shows that they are still

TABLE 16. Statistics for the general and Jewish populations of Rechitsa (1959–2000)

Year	Total population	Including Jews (number)	Including Jews (percent)
1939	29,796	7,237	24.3
1947	20,251	3,800	18.8
1959	30,602	4,000	13
1970	48,393	3,123	6.5
1979	60,327	2,594	4.3
1989	69,427	1,904	2.7
1996	71,500	450	0.6
2000	71,900	294	0.4

Source: Smilovitsky, *Katastrofa evreev v Belorussii*, 275. Official information on the number of Jews in Rechitsa was also received from Sara Levin in her letter of April 26, 1997, and from Arkadii Mikhalevskii in an interview on October 14, 2000. Data on Jews for 1947 and 1959 are estimated on the basis of the censuses of 1939 and 1970 and information on wartime deaths and migration during the war and the postwar period. These data do not include the children of mixed marriages, whose numbers increased beginning in the 1960s. However, in these years, given the growing anti-Semitism, the vast majority of them were most likely not registered as Jews during the census. It can be presumed that a certain number of Jews "by passport," that is, those whose parents were both Jewish, also declared themselves as non-Jews. Considering this and the accepted practice among Jews of declaring their nationality based on that of their mother, the official statistics on Jews from the censuses of 1970, 1979, and 1989 can be quite legitimately increased at least by 10%.

drawn to their native town. Many former Rechitsa natives maintain their links with one another. The most effective means of preserving their self-identification are the meetings of expatriates. These take place yearly in Israel, on the first Saturday in May in the forest of Ben-Shemen, with as many as two thousand people in attendance. There are sporadic meetings in the United States, mainly in New York, where about a hundred people gather.

Following the war some Jewish refugees did not return to Rechitsa. They either succumbed to starvation and sickness, or they did not want to leave their new homes. Those who came back had to repossess their former homes, which more often than not had been expropriated by their new occupants. Most of them reclaimed their dwellings, by court action or voluntary surrender of the occupants. A few homes had been destroyed or dismantled for construction materials, and the returning refugees had to look for other accommodations. The housing problem and the lack of jobs and food strengthened the growth of grassroots anti-Semitism in postwar Rechitsa. Helping this along was the revival of state anti-Semitism in the USSR.

The Holocaust, postwar anti-Semitism, and the creation of the state of Israel led in their turn to the rebirth of Jewish self-awareness. One of its manifestations was a return to religion by some of the population. Because Jews in overcrowded professions were cheated out of work elsewhere, they formed handicraft cooperatives (artels). These artels maintained jobs under the circumstances of an acute shortage of goods, and their productivity contributed considerable value to the local and neighboring population as well as to the town's economy. All the industrial plants in Rechitsa were severely challenged in terms of earning power in the first postwar decade.

The migration of Jewish young people out of Rechitsa continued in 1950–1970, delivering a death blow to the Jewish character of the town. In addition to moving to the big cities, Jews began to emigrate abroad as well, and this trend grew to mass proportions in the 1980–1990s. Migration did not allow an opportunity for the regeneration of Jewish religious and community life, which had commenced early in the 1990s during major changes in the political regime. The history of almost four hundred years of the presence of Jews in Rechitsa had come to an end.

Conclusion

The tolerance toward Jews in the Grand Duchy of Lithuanian and the broad range of economic opportunities that opened up in the sixteenth and the first half of the seventeenth centuries encouraged them to settle in the duchy's eastern counties. Jews settled in Rechitsa as well at the turn of the sixteenth century. But in the mid-seventeenth century, the Jewish community in Rechitsa, as in other mestechkos of eastern Belorussia, became victims of the Khmelnitsky campaigns and the invasion of Muscovite troops. The situation stabilized in the last third of the seventeenth century, and the Jewish communities began to revive, though they were unable to recover economically from this war in the autonomous Lithuanian duchy. The economic decline of the Polish-Lithuanian Commonwealth in the eighteenth century brought hard times to the Jewish communities. The result, at least in the territory of Rechitsa Uezd, was the continued de-urbanization of the Jewish population. The tax system based on collective responsibility that existed in the Grand Duchy of Lithuania and in Poland led to a division of East European Jewry into subethnic groups with distinctive languages, mentalities, and cultures. In particular a community that came to be called "Litvaks" developed within the territory of contemporary Belorussia and the Baltic countries.

After the area was absorbed into the Russian Empire, the authorities maintained the former system of community responsibility for payment of taxes for more than half a century. This, as well as the responsibility of providing recruits for the army, encouraged Jewish communities to remain isolated from the remainder of the population. The growth of Hasidism within the territories annexed by Russia undermined the isolation of the Jewish communities and the subethnic groups. Adherence to one or another religious tendency or to Hasidism had become, by the mid-nineteenth century, of greater significance than membership in a community or a subethnic group. Attachment to one's own rabbi, particularly within the Hasidic groups, simultaneously both encouraged and discouraged migration, depending on how far away the rabbi lived. The abolition of the kahal system in 1844 weakened the Jews' link to their community. Modernization of Russian society led to the growth of Jews' economic migration and contributed to the process of destroying the Jewish communities' organizations.

Parallel with this change ran the process of emancipation. With each decade the number of young people aspiring to study general, nonreligious, subjects and the Russian language grew significantly, although their numbers within the overall Jewish population remained small for a long time. Jewish emancipation as a product of both the modernization of society and the intensification of legal restrictions promoted the growth of national self-consciousness; this, in turn, led to the struggle for social and national reorganization or to immigration to Erets-Israel. At the end of the nineteenth century, this development found expression in the participation by the broad masses of Jews in opposition socialist and Zionist organizations. The Muslims, another non-Russian group within the Russian Empire whose legal rights were infringed, underwent a similar process, although to a lesser extent. The most emancipated among them who, due to a series of historical causes, lived along the Volga River—the Tatar and the Bashkir intelligentsia—created the Jadid movement, which had national and socialist goals similar to those of the Jews.

Despite the general improvement in the economic circumstances of Jews immediately after the affiliation of Rechitsa with Russia, many of them were poor. Their situation began to improve in the 1870s, thanks in no small way to the reforms of Alexander II. The reforms he initiated also led to the alleviation of the legal standing of Jews. But this process of alleviation slowed in the final years of his reign and especially when his son Alexander III came to the throne. The weak rule of Nicholas II, combined with his marked anti-Jewish bias, led to a broad wave of pogroms in Russia, a wave that touched Rechitsa in October 1905. For this reason, Jewish emigration from Rechitsa, and from Russia in general, increased. The Jews who remained in Russia began playing a more active role in opposition movements. This engagement was encouraged by the results of elections to the state dumas, which showed that the authorities had no intention of offering equal rights to the Jews, despite their expanded role in the economy at the beginning of the twentieth century. The growth of emigration and politicization among the Jews was also influenced by the increase in the Jewish population within the Pale of Settlement, a result of a lower death rate than that of the remainder of the population. Some Jews no longer found it possible to provide for themselves independently in Rechitsa. At the end of the nineteenth century, the Jewish population in the town began to devote more attention to charitable activities. This was encouraged by the actions and personal example of Tzadik Sholom-Dov-Ber Shneerson. At that time Rechitsa had become one of the most important centers of Hasidism in Russia. The growth of the Jewish intelligentsia, thanks to the increased numbers of educational institutions in Rechitsa, both Jewish and general, also affected the increase in charitable activity in the town. A special place in Jewish education in the town at the beginning of the twentieth century was held by the Heder Metukan, founded by proponents of Zionism to replace the traditional heder.

The February Revolution of 1917 opened unprecedented possibilities for the Jewish population in both local and community self-government. The new freedoms led to hitherto unseen political activity among the Jews within existing All-Russian (notably the Cadets) and Jewish political parties. With the consolidation of the Bolshevik regime, however, such activity became possible only within the framework of the ruling party, which provided both the formal ruling and the administrative structures. Jewish youths who had not emigrated before the early 1920s actively joined the Bolshevik Party or the Komsomol, influenced by the romantic Bolshevik idea of reorganizing the world and moved by new career possibilities. The limitations of the town somewhat restricted these possibilities, and many young people made the decision to leave Rechitsa.

In many respects the town retained its traditional way of life, although the authorities, through the Jewish Section, waged a campaign against the Jewish religion and the religious system of education. On the other hand, the Jewish Section did a great deal to promote the growth of Yiddish in the USSR. A system of preschool and primary- and secondary-school education in Yiddish was in place in Rechitsa until 1939. The end of the New Economic Policy in 1927–1928 led to the impoverishment of the population. Many Jewish families in particular were given the status of "deprivees," which limited their possibilities for jobs, education, social support, and so on. Difficult material circumstances became a reason for economic migration, beginning in the second half of the 1920s. This process continued into the 1930s. It "aged" the mestechkos and hastened the collapse of Jewish communities, small ones in particular. As a result of migration, the proportion of Jews among the overall population in Rechitsa was reduced from one-half to one-quarter during the 1920s and 1930s. Migration was generally to large cities, where there were greater possibilities for self-fulfillment.

Some members of the Jewish population were able to establish themselves in Rechitsa, thanks in particular to the system of tradesmen's artels. Jews also comprised a large proportion of civil servants and administrative-economic managers in the town. Even among them, however, salaries were small, and they were even smaller among the tradesmen and handcraftsmen, who had to buy raw materials and sell their goods on the black market in order to survive. A great help to many families in Rechitsa was the garden plot, the income from which often exceeded the wage of an adult member of the family. Many Jews had to keep domestic animals and poultry.

Both in Rechitsa and beyond it, Rechitsa Jewish natives fell victim to the Stalinist repressions, which peaked in 1937–1938, when about two-thirds of those repressed during the years of Soviet power were annihilated. Particularly hard hit by the repressions were Jews in the 38–47 age group, that is, those who had achieved a certain position in Soviet society. They comprised two-fifths of all those repressed and almost half in the years 1937 and 1938. It is likely that in Belorussia and in Rechitsa as well, the proportion of Jews repressed was somewhat higher than the proportion of Jews within the overall population.

Because Rechitsa was not immediately occupied by the Germans, about 82 percent of its Jewish residents managed to flee to the east or to be called up into the army. The local authorities helped in the evacuation of Rechitsa residents and even carried on a publicity campaign to urge the Jewish population to leave. Among the Jews who remained in the town were many elderly people and mothers with several small children, since they feared they would be unable to establish themselves in a new area. When the Germans came, these people were subjected to mockery and violence. Beginning in the third week of November 1941, groups of Jews were confined to a ghetto, from which they were regularly taken to be executed. By that time no Jews remained living in Rechitsa legally. While the ghetto was in existence, more than two dozen Jews tried to hide, but many of them were picked up and executed.

Regarding the "final solution," some gentiles in Rechitsa worked with the Germans, some of them remained neutral, but others helped the Jews by providing refuge, clothing, or food. A large number of the Jews who survived went to the partisans. Not all of them survived to see the liberation of Rechitsa in November 1943. Jews also took part in the capture of the town. On the whole the proportion of Jewish Rechitsa natives in the Red Army was higher than that of their gentile fellow townspeople, since more Jews had migrated east of Rechitsa in the 1920s and 1930s and in the first months after the war began; mobilization was also carried out in a more organized fashion in the rear areas. More than thirty Jewish families in Rechitsa lost two or more family members during the war. In all no fewer than eight hundred Jewish Rechitsa natives perished at the front.

About 16 percent of them were officers. Losses among those born in the second half of 1922 and in 1923 were particularly high. A good many Jews who were living in Rechitsa until the war but who were natives of other towns also perished.

The German occupation and the mass genocide of 1941–1942 dealt an enormous blow to the mestechkos of the former Pale of Settlement. The majority of Belorussian, Ukrainian, and Baltic Jewish communities were destroyed. Jewish life was maintained only in the larger mestechkos and towns like Rechitsa, where the Jews returned after the war. Their places of residence could scarcely be called mestechkos anymore, however, since they had lost their Jewish character permanently.

Between 10 and 20 percent of Jewish refugees from Rechitsa died from illnesses and hunger in the places to which they had been evacuated. Some of them managed to establish themselves successfully in their new places and preferred not to return, the more so since all the homes of Jewish refugees in Rechitsa had either been taken over by gentiles or had been torn down for building materials. Still a large number of the Jews preferred to return to Rechitsa. Some of them managed to reclaim their homes, while others had to go through the courts to achieve this. State-owned apartments and houses were not returned to the majority of Jewish refugees. The re-evacuation of the Jewish population and the problem returning Jewish property gave rise to an increase in anti-Semitism in Rechitsa. In this regard the situation was even worse in neighboring Ukraine. The influence of anti-Semitic propaganda, to which the local population had been subjected under the German occupation, made itself felt. Soviet power suppressed any disorders that arose from national hostility, but it did nothing to combat anti-Semitism.

During this period the USSR held to a course of state chauvinism that meant hostility toward the Jews as a disloyal element. Jews returning from the front and from evacuation found it difficult to reestablish themselves in their jobs. Only because of the shortage of qualified personnel in Rechitsa did some Jews (particularly after the death of Stalin in 1953) manage to find work within the state sector, including managerial positions. For many other Jews, work in tradesmen's artels again became the way out of their difficult economic situation, just as it had been in the 1920s and 1930s. The artels continued to exist until the 1960s, when they were either transformed into state enterprises or merged with already existing enterprises of the same or related nature.

In the postwar years the Soviet authorities gradually stifled any manifestations of Jewish life. Although the regime had followed a liberal policy toward the Orthodox Church during the war years as part of its program of reviving Russian chauvinism, its attitude toward the Jewish religion and toward Jews generally not only did not improve but grew even harsher within Belorussia. This was particularly true in the western regions, where the authorities, taking advantage of the extermination of the Jews, obstructed the return of surviving synagogues and the reconstitution of communities. In eastern Belorussia, where, because of its distance from the front, relatively large numbers of Jews had managed to flee and survive, the commonality of their fate during the years of the Holocaust had brought Jews together; one sign of this was a revival of interest in religion. The authorities, however, blocked this route because they did not want a revival of Judaism, even in a form they could control. Thus the Judaism in the postwar years, in Rechitsa and in the former large and medium-size mestechkos, could only smolder after going underground. By the end of the 1970s, with the emigration abroad of those Jews most dedicated to religion, Jewish life in Rechitsa had almost completely died out. Having passed through the surge of Jewish religiosity and social activism in the 1990s (a manifestation of which was the erection of a monument to Jews who had been executed), Jewish life in Rechitsa at the beginning of the new millennium had almost ended. The vast majority of Jews had either been repatriated to Israel or had emigrated to the United States, Germany, or other countries. Thus the almost four-hundred-year history of this once populous Jewish community, which had known periods of florescence and decline and had been closely linked with the general situation in Rechitsa and the whole of southeastern Belorussia, came to an end.

Notes

INTRODUCTION

1. See his memoirs compiled from the diaries he kept: Dubnov, *Kniga zhizni*, 1:343–344.

2. Ibid., 1:344–345.

3. Ibid., 1:39–40, 177, 206, 298, 342–343. Dubnov deliberately does not mention Vera's last name in his memoirs. When he told Kagan about this in a letter to him from Riga in 1934, Dubnov wrote that he thought it necessary to omit the details of his romance with Vera Gurovich. He also wrote that privately he still called this trip to Rechitsa a "midsummer night's dream." Dubnov wanted to send her a copy of his memoirs and asked his old friend to give him Vera's address. Letter of June 4, 1934, AJNUL, ARC 4° 1068, d. 123.

4. Kahanovich, Homel, 196–197, 221; Tadger, *Entsyiklopedyiah le-halutsey ha-Yishuv ve-bonav*, 3:1114–1116; ibid., 15:4796; Aizik Ramba, *Ha-Z'azu'a be-mishpoha 'Erezyisraelit yad'uh, M'aariv*, August 4, 1967, 19.

5. Dubnov, *Kniga zhizni*, 1:344–345; Dubnova-Erlikh, *Zhizn' i tvorchestvo S. M. Dubnova*, 103.

6. Dubnov, *Kniga zhizni*, 1:350.

7. Hakohen, *'Olami*, 3:100–103.

8. Dubnov, *Kniga zhizni*, 1:362–363.

9. *Agrot Ahad Ha'am*, 2:336–373; *Ahad Ha'am*, 161–174. At the time, Ahad Ha'am was editor of the journal *Ha-Shiloakh* and head of the Akhiasaf publishing house.

10. Hakohen, *'Olami*, 3:100–103, 106.

11. Dubnov, *Kniga zhizni* , 1:362–363. Later, M. G. Kagan's daughter Roza (Shoshana) married Shlomo Ginsberg (Ginosar), the son of Ahad Ha'am, whom she had met in Rechitsa. She was the first woman lawyer in Israel. Kagan's other daughter, Khana, married Artur Rupin, a leading figure in the Zionist movement and initiator of sociological studies of the Jewish people. His son David was the first Israeli ambassador to Burma and a member of the Knesset's Commission on Foreign Affairs and Security. See Dubnov, *Kniga zhizni* , 1:363; Tadger, *Entsyiklopedyiah le-halutsey ha-Yishuv ve-bonav*, 3:1116; Ramba, *Ha-Z'azu'a*

be-mishpoha 'Erezyisraelit yad'uh, 19. Three and a half decades later, when a correspondence began between Dubnov and Roza Ginsberg, he recalled these meetings in Rechitsa with her and her father. Bischitzky, Simon Dubnow an Rosa Ginzberg, 370–372.

12. Hakohen, 'Olami, 3:106–107.

13. Ibid., 3:109–110.

14. Ibid., 3:364–365.

15. Letter of July 29, 1901, AJNUL, ARC 4° 1068, f. 123.

16. Dubnov, Kniga zhizni, 1:379.

17. TsDIAK, f. 442, op. 1, d. 7890, 48–119 (a copy held in CAHJP, HM2 8969 was consulted by the author). For example, the presence of these features led to Krasnopol'e (Zhitomir region) and Shershinets (Odessa region) being called mestechkos, while Golosokov (Odessa region) was denied this status. Ibid., 62, 112–113a. There were even earlier changes of status during the Russian period. For example, Aleksandrovka village in Chernigov province was converted to a mestechko in 1794, with the right to regulate its own trade and markets. Etnograficheskii sbornik, 313.

18. Vol'tke, Mestechki.

19. Cf., for example, Goldberg, Ha-hevra ha-Yahudit ba-mamlekhet Polin-Lit'a; Hundert, Jews in Poland-Lithonia in the Eighteenth Century.

20. Weinryb, Jews of Poland, 46–47.

21. Fishman, Russia's First Modern Jews.

22. Nadav, Jews of Pinsk, 1506 to 1880.

23. Smilovitsky, Evrei v Turove.

24. Zeltser, Evrei sovetskoi provintsii.

25. For a general background the recently published work of the Belorussian researcher on mestechkos, Ina Sorkin, is noteworthy; see I. Sorkin, Miastechki Belarusi u kantsy XVIII—pershai palove XIX st.

26. Klier, Russia Gathers Her Jews, 7, 44.

27. The system of making decisions on Jewish cases is examined in detail in my study of Bukharan Jews. Russian laws on this topic were unique in several particulars. Kaganovitch, Attitude of the Czarist Administration to the Bukharan Jews.

28. Wrangel, Vospominaniia, 118.

CHAPTER 1. RECHITSA AND THE JEWS UNDER THE POLISH-LITHUANIAN COMMONWEALTH IN THE SEVENTEENTH AND EIGHTEENTH CENTURIES

1. Shpilevskii, Puteshestvie po Polesiu i Belorusskomu kraiu, 125.

2. Dubnov, Kniga zhizni, 1:342.

3. On the tribal settlement in Belorussia and its historiography, see Picheta, Belorussiia i Litva XV–XVI, 611–616. Another viewpoint maintains that the Dregovichi formed the majority here; see Kukharenko, Poles'e i ego mesto v protsese etnogeneza slavian, 44–45.

4. Patriarshaia ili Nikonovskaia letopis', Polnoe sobranie russkikh letopisei, 10:67; Gustynskaia letopis', Polnoe sobranie russkikh letopisei, 40:113.

5. Ocherki po arkheologii Belorussii, 2:130.

6. Pashuto, Obrazovanie Litovskogo gosudarstva, 268–269.

7. Tikhomirov, Spiski russkikh gorodov, dal'nikh i blizhnikh," 218, 223–224. It is curious to find among the Lithuanian towns mentioned the name Jerusalem, whose location Mikhail Tikhomirov was unable to determine (242).

8. Picheta, *Belorussiia i Litva XV–XVI*, 532–533, 538–539, 548.

9. Snyder, *Reconstruction of Nations*, 17–18.

10. Picheta, *Belorussiia i Litva XV–XVI*, 529.

11. Liubavskii, *Ocherk istorii Litovsko-Russkago gosudarstva do Liublinskoi unii vkliuchitel'no*, 117–118. Sergei Bershadskii, a Russian researcher on Lithuanian Jews, argues that the privileges associated with Vitautas were based on Ottokar II of Bohemia privileges granted to Jews in Prague (1254), but with certain changes. Bershadskii, *Litovskie evrei*, 211–226.

12. *Statut Vialikaha Kniastva Litouskaha 1588*, 315–316.

13. Liubavskii, *Ocherk istorii Litovsko-Russkago gosudarstva do Liublinskoi unii vkliuchitel'no*, 119–120.

14. Ibid., 269–270, 274.

15. *Belorussiia v epokhu Feodalizma (sbornik dokumentov)*, 1:111–112; *Ocherki po arkheologii Belorussii*, 130.

16. Kaganovitch, *Rechitsa v srednevekovyi period*, 32.

17. *Pamiatnaia knizhka Minskoi gubernii na 1911 god* (Minsk: Gubernskii statisticheskii komitet, 1910), 80.

18. Liubavskii, *Ocherk istorii Litovsko-Russkago gosudarstva do Liublinskoi unii vkliuchitel'no*, 203–204.

19. *Pamiatnaia knizhka Minskoi gubernii na 1911 god*, 80.

20. *Pamiatniki diplomaticheskikh snoshenii drevnei Rossii s derzhavami inostrannymi*, 35:698–703, 861; *Litovskaia metrika*, 1:1015, 1092, 117 (index); Tkachëÿ, *Rechickiia umatsavanni*.

21. Zelenskii, *Materialy dlia geografii i statistiki Rossii*, 1:30; Picheta, *Belorussiia i Litva XV–XVI*, 566.

22. *Evreinovskaia letopis'*, 236.

23. *Regesty i nadpisi*, 1:105. On Jan Abraham Ezofowicz Rebrikovich, see Bershadskii, *Avram Ezofovich Rebrikovich, podskarbii zemskii, chlen Rady Velikogo Kniazhestva Litovskogo*.

24. Bershadskii, *Litovskie evrei*, 180–182; Vishnitser, *Obshchii ocherk*, 36.

25. *Regesty i nadpisi*, 1:395, 472–474.

26. See the complaint of Lithuanian Jews to King Stefan Batory (1533–1586) in 1578 about the attempts to try them under Magdeburg, not the king's laws: *Regesty i nadpisi*, 1:273.

27. *Akty, otnosiashchiesia k istorii Iuzhnoi i Zapadnoi Rossii*, 1:133–134.

28. Zelenskii, *Materialy dlia geografii i statistiki Rossii*, 1:30.

29. Snyder, *Reconstruction of Nations*, 106.

30. Sergii, *Opisanie Markovogo monastyria*, 14–15.

31. Iakov Marash, *Ocherki istorii ekspansii katolicheskoi tserkvi v Belorussii 18 veka*, 226.

32. *Barkulabovskaia letopis'*, 186–187, 189.

33. Jelski, *Rzeczyca*, 134; *Zhivopisnaia Rossiia*, 381; *Historyia Belaruskai SSR*, 1:199, 247–248.

34. *Pamiats'*, 1:37.

35. *Barkulabovskaia letopis'*, 182.

36. Zakhoder, *Kaspiiskii svod svedenii o Vostochnoi Evrope*, 2:110–112.

37. Pryzhov, *Istoriia kabakov v Rossiĭ v sviazi s istoriĭei russkago naroda*, 150–151.

38. Shiper, Rasselenie evreev v Pol'she i Litve ot drevneishikh vremën do kontsa XVIII veka, ii (explanatory text to the maps); Marek, Administrativnoe delenie evreiskih poselenii v Litovski oblasti, 208.

39. On the move of Christians from the western part of the Duchy to its eastern voivod-ships see, Picheta, *Belorussiia i Litva XV–XVI*, 124, 140.

40. On this reform see Picheta, *Belorussiia i Litva XV–XVI*, 140.

41. Liubavskii, *Ocherk istorii Litovsko-Russkago gosudarstva do Liublinskoi unii vkliuchi-tel'no*, 304.

42. Kopysskii, *Ekonomicheskoe razvitie gorodov Belorussii*, 50.

43. Ibid., 27, 50–51.

44. Vishnitser, *Obshchii ocherk*, 67.

45. Baron, *Russian Jews under Tsars and Soviets*, 124.

46. *Letopis' samovidtsa po novootkrytym spiskam*, 4–5. For preconceived notions about the Jews in this and other Ukrainian writings of this epoch, see Kohut, Khmelnytsky Uprising.

47. Antonovich, *Monografii po istorii Zapadnoi i Iugo-Zapadnoi Rossii*, 1:188–192; Shkandrij, *Jews in Ukrainian Literature*, 16. It would be an oversimplification to label the position of these Ukrainian historians as anti-Semitic inasmuch as in 1858, when the polemics on the Jewish question appeared in the literary journalistic press, they expressed themselves in favor of ceasing the vilification of Jews, and they expressed the hope that equality before the law would lead to lessening the hatred of Jews toward Christians. Pis'mo of Kostomarov, Kulish, et al.

48. Vishnitser, *Obshchii ocherk*, 67–69; Dubnow, *History of the Jews in Russia and Poland*, 1:141–142.

49. Ettinger, Jewish Participation in the Settlement of Ukraine; and in greater detail, Ettinger, *Beyn Polin le-Rusia*, 124–142. Following the example of his predecessors, Ettinger there, too, singles out the participation of Jews in leasing and buyouts. However, in the dozen examples he cites, more than half of the towns were far removed from the epicenter of the uprising in Zaporozhe and the Kiev region. These were towns in Volynia and even in Poland (Chelm, Bielsk). Then rearranging the total statistics regarding tenant farming in Ukraine, Ettinger conjectures that most of these farms belonged to Jews. It follows without any proof from the writings of Salo Baron, who also cites total statistics regarding the impor-tant role of the leasing of real estate in ten uezds of Ukraine.Then he supposes that Jews were leaseholders. Salo Baron, *Social and Religious History of the Jews*, 16:270–273. At the same time, it is possible to agree that Jews were preeminent in Volynian tax sales. Berkowski, Struktury administracyjne komór celnych i mytnych na Wołyniu od XVI do połowy XVII wieku. It is clear from the list he cites that Jews did not account for 78 percent of them, as the author maintains on p. 327; rather, it was no more than 65 percent.

50. *Torgivlia na Ukraïni, XIV—seredina XVII stolittia*.

51. *Regesty i nadpisi*, 1:336, 350, 356, 368.

52. Floria, Novye svidetel'stva ob otnoshenii naseleniia Ukrainy k evreiam pervoi poloviny XVII v.

53. Shafonskii, *Chernigovskago namestnichestva topograficheskoe opisanie s kratkim geograficheskim i istoricheskim opisaniem Maloi Rossii, sochinennoe v Chernigove 1786 goda*, 60.

54. *Regesty i nadpisi*, 1:416.

55. Documents of the seventeenth and eighteenth centuries contain many reports about Orthodox tavern owners in Ukraine. The first statistical example of this, however, relates to 1765. In that year in the small Ukrainian town of Glukhov, where Jews were forbidden to live, there were 166 (!) taverns. Baron, *Social and Religious History of the Jews*, 269.

56. Bershadskii, *Litovskie evrei*, 395.

57. *Akty, otnosiashchiesia k istorii Zapadnoi Rossii*, 5:78–83.

58. Ibid., 5:83–84.

59. Baron, *Social and Religious History of the Jews*, 299.

60. Hanover, *Abyss of Despair (Yeven metzulah)*, 36.

61. Stampfer, What Actually Happened to the Jews of Ukraine in 1648?

62. Hanover, *Abyss of Despair*, 36–38.

63. *Regesty i nadpisi*, 1:398–399.

64. Ibid., 370–371. Somewhat later that same year, the Russian tsar sent an embassy to Warsaw to congratulate Władysław IV Vasa on the occasion of his wedding. Despite the tsar's instructions not to allow Jews to enter Russia, his envoys yielded to the pressure of the magnates and agreed that Jews could travel just to the cities of Svinesk (Riazan region) and Viaz'ma (Smolensk region) to conduct trade (373).

65. Klier, Russia Gathers Her Jews, 25–27.

66. *Khronologicheskii ukazatel' materialov dlia istorii inorodtsev Evropeiskoi Rossii.*

67. *Regesty i nadpisi*, 1:398.

68. *Belorussiia v epokhu Feodalizma*, 2:27; *Pamiats'*, 1:41; *Istoriia Belorusskoi SSSR*, 1:141.

69. *Evreiskie khroniki XVII stoletiia*, 113.

70. Because of the ideological narrative in the Russian Empire, this history offers the following explanation without any kind of documentary support: "In the period of the Cossack wars, Rechitsa took the side of Khmelnitsky in 1648 and subsequently suffered severely at the hands of the troops of Hetman Radziwill, who was loyal to the crown." *Gorodskie poseleniia v Rossiiskoi Imperii*, 3:109.

71. *Belorussiia v epokhu Feodalizma*, 2:38–40, 42–43; *Istoriia Belorusskoi SSSR*, 1:149–150, 153.

72. *Belorussiia v epokhu Feodalizma*, 2:44–45, 46–47; Kotłubaj, *Życie Janusza Radziwiłła*, 140–148. On the Orthodox detachment, see Charopka, Rechytsa ў kazatska-selianskai vaine 1648–1651 gadoў na Belarusi, 86.

73. Kotłubaj, *Życie Janusza Radziwiłła*, 149–155; *Istoriia Belorusskoi SSSR*, 1:152–153.

74. Charopka, Rechytsa ў kazatska-selianskai vaine 1648–1651 gadoў na Belarusi, 87–88.

75. Ibid., 88–89; Kotłubaj, *Życie Janusza Radziwiłła*, 163–171.

76. Sahanovich, *Neviadomaia vaina, 1654–1667*, 5–15.

77. *Belorussiia v epokhu Feodalizma,* 2:67–68, 102–103; Sahanovich, *Neviadomaia vaina, 1654–1667,* 19; *Zbor pomnikau historyi i kul'tury Belarusi,* 313.

78. Vishnitser, *Obshchii ocherk,* 74.

79. *Regesty i nadpisi,* 1:459–460. In view of the devastation of the Jews who survived in Stary Bykhov and, no doubt, in order to attract new Jewish settlers, in 1669 they were absolved by the king from paying taxes for twenty years (491).

80. Cited from Sahanovich, *Neviadomaia vaina, 1654–1667,* 17. On the anti-Jewish pogroms during this war see also Shiper, *Rasselenie evreev v Pol'she i Litve ot drevneishikh vremën do kontsa XVIII veka,* 112. Similar actions against Jews in this war were not exceptions to the behavior of the Muscovite forces. A hundred years earlier, in 1563 during the Livonian war, Ivan the Terrible, after capturing Polotsk, offered the Jews the opportunity to be baptized; those who refused were, by his order, drowned in the river along with their wives and children. *Regesty i nadpisi,* 1:233.

81. Sahanovich, *Neviadomaia vaina, 1654–1667,* 25.

82. *Regesty i nadpisi,* 1:438–439. According to the statements of Bishop Orest, no fewer than nine-tenths of them later went back to Judaism.

83. Cited from Sahanovich, *Neviadomaia vaina, 1654–1667,* 28.

84. *Regesty i nadpisi,* 1:437.

85. Ibid., 1:436–437.

86. Rospis' zhidom', *Opisanie dokumentov i bumag, khraniashchikhsia v Moskovskom arhive ministerstva iustitsii,* 4:408.

87. *Regesty i nadpisi,* 1:434.

88. *Belorussiia v epokhu Feodalizma,* 2:103; Sahanovich, *Neviadomaia vaina, 1654–1667,* 28–31.

89. There is still no commonly held view among historians that recognizes Russian serfdom in the seventeenth and eighteenth centuries as a form of slavery. Some believe that it had no parallels to the situation in European countries during the existence of serfdom there and is best defined as slavery. See, for example, Blum, *Lord and Peasant in Russia,* 271–276, 608–613. Others argue that since the peasant had a house and household goods and could dispose freely of the fruits of his labor on the land allotted for his use, his situation was not that of a slave. See, for example, Pipes, *Russia under the Old Regime,* 148–154.

90. Sahanovich, *Neviadomaia vaina, 1654–1667,* 74.

91. Ibid., 46, 73–82.

92. Vakar, *Belorussia,* 63.

93. Sahanovich, *Neviadomaia vaina, 1654–1667,* 75–77.

94. Ibid., 124.

95. *Regesty i nadpisi,* 1:480, 485, 510. On the failure of Muscovy to observe this article of the agreement in respecting captives and Belorussians who were simply kidnapped, see Sahanovich, *Neviadomaia vaina, 1654–1667,* 126–128.

96. Gessen, *Evrei v Moskovskom gosudarstve XV–XVII vv.,* 246–252; Kunin, *Evrei v Moskovskom gosudarstve XV–XVII vv.,* 306–309.

97. Minaev, *Sviedieniia o stranakh po verkhov'iam Amu-Dar'i po 1878 god,* 223–225.

98. *Russko-indiiskie otnosheniia v XVII veke,* 278.

99. Jelski, Rzeczyca,133.

100. Sahanovich, *Neviadomaia vaina, 1654–1667*, 149.

101. Bartoszewicz, *Studja historyczne i literackie*, 2:28; Egorov, *Gradostroitel'stvo Belorus-sii*, 77–78.

102. *Istoriia Belorusskoi SSSR*, 1:180.

103. *Regesty i nadpisi*, 2:86–87.

104. Doÿnar, Stan darog i darozhnykh kamunikatsyi Rechytskaga paveta, 221.

105. *Starozytna Polska*, 4:692, 695; Aleksandrov, Rechitskii povet in y'or 1789, 55.

106. *Akty o evreiakh, izdannye Vilenskoi Arkheograficheskoi komissiei dlia razbora drevnikh aktov*, 29:380–384; 406–408, 411–416, 427–429.

107. Balaban, Obshchii ocherk politicheskoi i sotsial'noi istorii evreev v Pol'she i Litve, 183.

108. *Akty, otnosiashchiesia k istorii Iuzhnoi i Zapadnoi Rossii*, 1:107–109.

109. *Russko-evreiskii arkhiv*, 2:45.

110. *Akty, otnosiashchiesia k istorii Iuzhnoi i Zapadnoi Rossii*, 1:201–205.

111. Guldon and Wijaczka, Accusation of Ritual Murder in Poland, 139.

112. Marek, Administrativnoe delenie evreiskih poselenii v Litovski oblasti, 208.

113. *Yahadut Lita*, 1:54.

114. Vishnitser and Shiper, Ekonomicheskii byt, 278–281.

115. Nadav, *Jews of Pinsk*, 259–260.

116. Bershadskii, *Litovskie evrei*, 40.

117. Vishnitser and Shiper, Ekonomicheskii byt, 281; Shiper, Podatnoe oblozhenie evreev, 311–316.

118. *Yahadut Lita*, 1:58, 163; Korobkov, Statistika evreiskogo naseleniia Pol'shi i Litvy vo vtoroi polovine XVIII veka, 554.

119. Mahler, Ha-Yehudim be-Polin erev ha-tkufat ha-khalukot, 243; Nadav, *Jews of Pinsk*, 247; Stampfer, 1764 Census of Polish Jewry, 42–57.

120. *Regesty i nadpisi*, 2:182–183.

121. Bez-Kornilovich, *Istoricheskie mesta o primechatel'nykh mestakh v Belorussii*, 158.

122. Vishnitser, Evrei-remeslenniki i tsekhovaia organizatsiia ikh, 288–290; Gekker, Evrei v pol'skikh gorodakh vo vtoroi polovine XVIII veka, 195–199; Rosman, *Lord's Jews*, 52–53, 64–85; Teller, *Kesef, koakh ve-hashp'ah*, 54.

123. Bez-Kornilovich, *Istoricheskie mesta o primechatel'nykh mestakh v Belorussii*, 158; Fishman, *Russia's First Modern Jews*.

124. Hundert, *Jews in Poland-Lithuania in the Eighteenth Century*, 108–109.

125. Gessen, *Evrei v Rossii*, 292, 296.

126. Shiper, *Podatnoe oblozhenie evreev*, 315.

127. On these, see Mahler, Ha-Yehudim be-Polin erev ha-tkufat ha-khalukot, 255–256.

128. *Oblastnoi pinkos Vaada glavnykh obshchin Litvy*, 1:4; Balaban, Obshchii ocherk politicheskoi i sotsial'noi istorii evreev v Pol'she i Litve, 183; Lederhendler, Did Russian Jewry Exist prior to 1917?, 17–18.

129. *Pinkas kehylot Lit'a*, 11; Zajka, Self-Perception of Lithuanian-Belarusian Jewry, 21, 24, 28–29.

130. Zaltsman, 'Ayarati, 106–107.

131. Vengerova, *Vospominaniia babushki*, 211–212.

132. Kotik, *Zikhronotav shel Yihzk'el Kotik*, 2:73–75. On the contempt toward Litvaks in Poland, see Zaltsman, 'Ayarati, 28, 39. Zaltsman also writes of asceticism and industriousness as distinguishing traits of the Litvaks (27). A page later he adds that even in modern times a Polish Hasid is proud if he manages to became related to a Litvak.

133. Zajka, Self-Perception of Lithuanian-Belarusian Jewry, 28.

134. Kotik, *Zikhronotav shel Yihzk'el Kotik*, 2:70.

135. Weeks, *Nation and State in Late Imperial Russia*, 166–168.

136. Zaltsman, 'Ayarati, 27.

137. Ben-Ammi [Rabinovich], Detstvo, 18. In fact, the wearing of sidelocks had been forbidden everywhere in Russia since 1852. Evidently, the local authorities in Ukraine enforced this ban with a good deal of lenience.

138. Ibid., 18–20.

139. Balter, Davar al yoshvyi Lyt'a, 213.

140. Kh. Tsybukmakher, Byt evreiskikh zemledel'tsev, *Rassvet*, April 24, 1880, 654–656.

141. Shimon Yehuda Stanislavskii, Mikhtavei sofrim: Ekaterinaslav, *Ha-Yom*, March 3, 1886, 1.

142. Samoilov, Provintsial'noe evreistvo, 19.

143. Zaltsman, 'Ayarati, 29.

144. Dovnar-Zapol'skii, *Issledovaniia i stat'i*, 279. In the same place the author writes of the restraint of the Belorussian population as its distinctive trait when compared with the Russian (Great Russian in the text) population. It is possible that the Litvaks also owe this trait to them.

145. For these and many other differences, cf. Sandler, Idish, 367–368; Katz, *Words on Fire*, 146–151.

146. On the differences in dress, see Zajka, Self-Perception of Lithuanian-Belarusian Jewry, 28.

147. Vengerova, *Vospominaniia babushki*, 202–205, 220.

148. Ibid., 232.

149. Zaltsman, 'Ayarati, 52–58.

150. Chubinskii, *Trudy Etnografichesko-statisticheskoi ekspeditsii v Zapadno-Russkii krai*, 7:33.

151. As early as 1815, however, the most respected Litvak rabbis gathered at a congress in Minsk to discuss the issue of Jewish colonization of Kherson Province. Shaul Stampfer writes that this was an unofficial body that acted in place of the Lithuanian Vaad, which had been dissolved fifty years earlier. See Stampfer, *Ha-Yeshivah ha-Lita'it be-hithavutah*, 33.

152. Klier, Traditions of the Commonwealth, 15.

153. Nathans, *Beyond the Pale*, 3, 335.

154. *Sbornik dokumentov, kasaushchikhsia administrativnogo ustroistva Severo-Zapadnogo kraia pri imperatritse Ekaterine II (1792–1796)*, l, 132.

155. *Istoriia Belorusskoi SSSR*, 1:178. On the fact that Rechitsa and Bobruisk, two towns in Rechitsa Powiat that had formerly had Magdeburg Rights, lost them in 1793, see *Sbornik dokumentov*, 1903, l, 132.

156. Aleksandrov, *Rechitskii povet*, 48–55. Aleksandrov's figures on the total population differ from those of Liutyi, who shows that in 1786, 1,729 people lived in Rechitsa and 2,080 in Bobruisk. See Liutyi, *Sotsial'no-ekonomicheskoe razvitie gorodov Belorussii*, 33.

157. Aleksandrov, Rechitskii povet in y'or 1789, 55.

158. Perepis' evreev v Malorossii v 1736 g., 400–407, 526–536; *Regesty i nadpisi*, 3:213–215.

159. Shiper, Rasselenie evreev v Pol'she i Litve ot drevneishikh vremën do kontsa XVIII veka, 131.

160. Mahler, Ha-Yehudim be-Polin erev ha-tkufat ha-khalukot, 252–259; Gessen, *Istoriia evreiskogo naroda v Rossii*, 1:39. Among these restrictions can be included the issuance in 1766 of a document by the town of Nevel (at that time, part of the Grand Duchy of Lithuania, today in Pskov Oblast) forbidding Jews to trade on Sundays, to build synagogues, and to be in the town during Christian processions. See *Regesty i nadpisi*, 3:153–154.

161. Coxe, *Travels in Poland, Russia, Sweden and Denemark*, 237.

CHAPTER 2. UNDER RUSSIAN RULE, 1793–1917

1. *Sbornik dokumentov, kasaushchikhsia administrativnogo ustroistva Severo-Zapadnogo kraia pri imperatritse Ekaterine II*, xxxv, xxxviii, 137, 140, 143–144, 149–150, 162–164, 166, 195, 199–200.

2. Ibid., xxxv, 141–142, 148, 152, 155, 159, 180–181, 185–187, 197–198.

3. *Regesty i nadpisi*, 3:205–206; Gessen, *Istoriia evreiskogo naroda v Rossii*, 1:49–55.

4. NIARB, f. 295, op. 1, d. 501, 4 (copy in CAHJP, HMF 831.52).

5. *Khronologicheskii ukazatel' materialov dlia istorii inorodtsev Evropeiskoi Rossii*, 192.

6. Gessen, *Evrei v Rossii*, 289–297.

7. Ibid., 323–337; Liutyi, *Sotsial'no-ekonomicheskoe razvitie gorodov Belorussii*, 42–45.

8. On the measures of the Russian administration, see Bez-Kornilovich, *Istoricheskie mesta o primechatel'nykh mestakh v Belorussii*, 280. On the devotion of Belorussians to Polish culture and the conversion, see Vladimirov, O polozhenii pravoslaviia v Severo-Zapadnom krae; Dolbilov, *Russkii krai: Chuzhaia vera*, 379.

9. *Pamiats'*, 1:54–55. The official, evidently trying to pass the desirable for the actual, also wrote that after the abolition of serfdom, the peasants wanted to reject everything Polish and Catholic and turn to Russian culture and Orthodoxy. In actuality, though such a turn did happen slowly in the second half of the nineteenth century, Polish influence was very palpable even at the end of that century.

10. Vakar, *Belorussia*, 13, 74.

11. *Pamiats'*, 1:49.

12. *Istoriia Belorusskoi SSSR*, 1:244, 253.

13. Rybtsevich, *Gorod Rechitsa*, 3–4. Archpriest Iosif Rybtsevich writes in his study (which is difficult to treat as a more or less objective source because of its furious anti-Polish stance) that the monastery was closed because the monks were converting the local Orthodox people to Catholicism. A town park was later laid out on the site of the monastery.

14. See, for example, Bez-Kornilovich, *Istoricheskie mesta o primechatel'nykh mestakh v Belorussii*, 280; Dovnar-Zapol'skii, *Issledovaniia i stat'i*, 336.

15. Weeks, *Nation and State in Late Imperial Russia*, 73–74, 122.

16. Dovnar-Zapol'skii, *Issledovaniia i stat'i*, 279.

17. Ibid., 336.

18. Ianchuk, *Po Minskoi gubernii*, 25.

19. See, for example, *Trudy gubernskih komissii po evreiskomu voprosu*, vol. 1, sec. 6.

20. Noska, Pravoslavnoe hramostroitel'stvo v Rechitse, 2:100–101. This information differs from that provided by the Rechitsa Archpriest Iosif Rybtsevich, a man who moved in "Black Hundred" circles. He blames another contractor, a Rechitsa Jew named Gets, who supposedly disappeared after the collapse of the structure. See Rybtsevich, *Gorod Rechitsa*, 7.

21. Noska, Pravoslavnoe hramostroitel'stvo v Rechitse, 100–101.

22. Rybtsevich, *Gorod Rechitsa*, 7.

23. Chepko, *Goroda Belorussii v pervoi polovine XIX veka*, 116.

24. In the early 1860s Catholics comprised 87 percent of the uezd nobility. Calculated from Zelenskii, *Materialy dlia geografii i statistiki Rossii*, 1:415.

25. Ibid., 1:550.

26. Stolpianskii, *Deviat' gubernii Zapadno-russkogo kraia*, xiii.

27. Jelski, *Rzeczyca*, 134.

28. NIARB, f. 299, op. 5, d. 291.

29. Liutyi, *Sotsial'no-ekonomicheskoe razvitie gorodov Belorussii*, 20; Gusev, *Zakony o evreiakh'*, 12–13.

30. LSHA, f. 378, op. 1840, d. 1209, 1–5 (copy in CAHJP, HM2 9757.5); *Pamiatnaia knizhka Minskoi gubernii na 1866 god* (Minsk: Minskii gubernskii statisticheskii komitet, 1866), 204; Gessen, *Evrei v Rossii*, 228–234, 239–240, 256–257.

31. Hence the assertion by John Klier that in 1803 the decree of Catherine II was annulled and the action of the Lithuanian Statute concerning Jews was reinstated. Klier, *Russia Gathers Her Jews*, 151–152.

32. *Khronologicheskii ukazatel' materialov dlia istorii inorodtsev Evropeiskoi Rossii*, 194.

33. Klier, *Russia Gathers Her Jews*, 63–65, 115; Kappeler, *The Russian Empire*, 91.

34. Gessen, *Evrei v Rossii*, 256–260.

35. Ibid., 241, 251–252, 257–258; Gusev, *Zakony o evreiakh'*, 12–13.

36. CAHJP, HMF 831.30, 54–55, 68.

37. *Adres-kalendar' Vilenskogo general-gubernatora na 1868 god*, 565; *Pamiatnaia knizhka Minskoi gubernii na 1880 god* (Minsk: Gubernskii statisticheskii komitet, 1879), 280; Vilenskii, Izraelit, and Livshits, Iz Rechitsy.

38. NIARB, f. 145, op. 2, d. 682.

39. Gessen, *Evrei v Rossii*, 259.

40. Ibid., 260, 284.

41. Ibid., 284–288.

42. On the tolerant relationship, see *Minskie gubernskie vedomosti* 45 (1880), 9. I am grateful to A. Bell for providing this information.

43. *Gorodovoe polozhenie*, 2:159–178; Pazhitnov, *Gorodskoe i zemskoe samoupravlenie*, 39–42; *Goroda Rossii v 1910 godu*, 163.

44. Shybeka, *Garady Belarusi*, 69, 219–220.

45. *Pamiatnaia knizhka Minskoi gubernii na 1896 god* (Minsk: Gubernskii statisticheskii komitet, 1895), 80; *Pamiatnaia knizhka Minskoi gubernii na 1915 god* (Minsk: Gubernskii statisticheskii komitet, 1914), 206–208.

46. Jelski, Rzeczyca, 134; *Belorussiia v epokhu Feodalizma*, 3:509–510.

47. *Pamiatnaia knizhka Minskoi gubernii na 1915 god*, 215.

48. Ibid., 516; Chepko, *Goroda Belorussii v pervoi polovine XIX veka*, 106.

49. For the statistical data, see Chepko, *Goroda Belorussii v pervoi polovine XIX veka*, 105.

50. *Belorussiia v epokhu Feodalizma*, 3:541.

51. Zelenskii, *Materialy dlia geografii i statistiki Rossii*, 2:674; *Trudy gubernskogo statisticheskogo komiteta*, 1:425.

52. Jelski, Rzeczyca, 133; Boris Umetskii, *Rechitsa*, 8.

53. *Dokumenty i materialy po istorii Belorussii*, 3:165.

54. NIARB, f. 705, op. 1. d. 14, 230, letter from Maria Rubinchik, April 12, 2001; Smilovitsky, *Katastrofa evreev v Belorussii*, 261–262. The stone houses of the Shklovskiis and the Agranoviches, according to a letter from Lev Agranovich of January 28, 2002, actually belonged to their relative Irma Livshits.

55. *Goroda Rossii v 1910 godu*, 107, 111, 116–117; interview with M. S. Rubinchik, January 1, 2001.

56. Golubov, *Institut ubezhishcha u drevnikh evreev v sviazi s ugolovnym i gosudarstvennym pravom Moiseia i Talmuda i sravnitel'no s institutami ubezhishch u drevnikh grekov, rimlian, v srednevekovoi i novoi Evrope*.

57. Dayan, *Yehudim be-tnu'at-hkhofesh shel' Russia*; Svatikov, *Evrei v russkom osvoboditel'nom dvizhenii*, 80, 147.

58. Svatikov, *Evrei v russkom osvoboditel'nom dvizhenii*, 92–94; Polonsky, *Jews in Poland and Russia*, 1:433–434.

59. Barskii, *Voinskaia povinnost' evreev*, ; Pozner, *Armia v Rossii*; Petrovskii-Shtern, *Evrei v Russkoi Armii*, 114–137, 149–166, 416.

60. On administrative abuses and anti-Semitism, see Gessen, *Istoriia evreiskogo naroda v Rossii*, 2:35.

61. Natanson, *Neskol'ko slov o korobochnom sbore i ob otnoshenii ego k otbyvaniu voinskoi povinnosti*.

62. Jews comprised 4.37 percent of those serving; they made up 4.16 percent of the population. See Gepshtein, *Ekonomicheskaia struktura evreiskogo naseleniia Rossii*, 20–21. For more details on the percentage of Jews in the army, see Petrovskii-Shtern, *Evrei v Russkoi Armii*, 194–196.

63. Korngol'd, *Russkie evrei na voine 1877–1878*, 227–228; Pozner, *Armia v Rossii*, 164–167.

64. I am grateful to Donald Girshgorn for this information.

65. Dubnov, *Kniga zhizni*, 3:161; Pozner, *Armia v Rossii*, 167–168; Petrovskii-Shtern, *Evrei v Russkoi Armii*, 324. Vannovskii's anti-Jewish activity in government was so marked that the publishers of the *Jewish Encyclopedia* that appeared in 1908–1913 even found it necessary to include a special article about him. See Braginskii, *Vannovskii Pëtr Semënovich*.

66. RGAVMF, f. 1345, op. 1, d. 99, 26 (copy in CAHJP, HM2 8452). This same directive limited the share of other national minorities (understood in Russia as non-Slavic peoples) to 30 percent among officers and clerks (with the exclusion of the Caucasian and Turkestan military provinces).

67. Usov, *Evrei v armii*, 143, 151, 155, 161.

68. Tadger, *Entsyiklopedyiah le-halutsey ha-Yishuv ve-bonav*, 14:4507; interview with Raisa Genina, October 10, 2001; letter from Aron Kaganovich, March 25, 1995; account of Boris Erenburg, March 12, 2004; letter from Fridrikh Valler, August 10, 2001; interview with Iakov Shustin, February 14, 2005.

69. See tables 2 and 12.

70. Vilenskii, Izraelit, and Livshits, *Iz Rechitsy*.

71. CAHJP, HM2 9074, 21.

72. *Trudy gubernskih komissii po evreiskomu voprosu*, vol. 1, sec. 6, 90. As for the findings of these commissions, see Löwe, *Tsars and the Jews*, 66–70.

73. Urusov, *Zapiski gubernatora*, 299.

74. *Trudy gubernskih komissii po evreiskomu voprosu*, vol. 1 sec. 6, 85.

75. NIARB, f. 299, op. 2, d. 16755, 1–5; d. 17315; 1–23a; d. 18028, 1–20; f. 333, op. 9, d. 261, 317a.

76. Bukhbinder, *Istoriia evreiskogo rabochego dvizheniia v Rossii po neizdannym arkhivnym materialam*, 278.

77. Smilovitsky, *Evrei Belorusii*, 25.

78. *Dokumenty i materialy po istorii Belorussii*, 3:416–417.

79. *Pamiats'*, 1:68.

80. *Dokumenty i materialy po istorii Belorussii*, 3:612.

81. Stepanov, *Chernaia sotnia v Rossii*, 52.

82. Lopukhin, *Otryvki iz vospominanii*, 86–87.

83. CAHJP, P 10, 11. For evidence that in the years 1905 to 1907 within the territory of contemporary Belorussia the attitude toward Jews, despite their great concentration and significant role in the economy, was neutral rather than hostile, see also the study of Ol'ga Bukhovets, which examines about seven hundred various complaints by the Christian population of the area to the authorities during that time. See Bukhovets, *Evrei v narodnom soznanii*.

84. *Poslednie Izvestiia*, May 05, 1905, 4.

85. S. Ia. Mishpat Retsitsa, *Hatsfirah*, December 29, 1904, 3.

86. Compare the detailed reasoning of Hans Rogger on this topic: Rogger, *Jewish Policies*, 40–55, esp. 50. In 1903–1905 Shcheglovitov occupied the post of chief prosecutor of the Criminal Appeals Department of the Senate and therefore was not in a position to influence Murav'ëv's decision to stage the trial in Rechitsa.

87. On Saint Nicholas's Church and Mozharovskii's official positions see Jelski, *Rzeczyca*, 134; *Pamiatnaia knizhka Minskoi gubernii na 1915 god*, 212–213. On the pre-pogrom situation in the town, see RGIA, f. 1565, op. 1, d. 19, 35; d. 20, 8, 20–23; CAHJP, P 10, 10, 17; *Voskhod*, October 27, 1905, 39; *Khronika evreiskoi zhizni*, October 28, 1905, 23; Motzkin, *Die Judenpogrome in Russland*, 2:465–467; Gorfunkel', *1905 god v Rechitse—gorode i uezde*; Smilovitsky, *Pogrom in Rechitsa*, 70.

88. Ben-Tsafon, Hadashot, *Hazman*, June 2, 1905, 3; Hadashot be-Israel, *Hashkafa*, June 20, 1905, 5.

89. On Saint Nicholas's Church and Mozharovskii's official positions see Jelski, Rzeczyca, 134; *Pamiatnaia knizhka Minskoi gubernii na 1915 god*, 212–213. On the pre-pogrom situation in the town, see RGIA, f. 1565, op. 1, d. 19, 35; d. 20, 8, 20–23; CAHJP, P 10, 10, 17; *Voskhod*, October 27, 1905, 39; *Khronika evreiskoi zhizni*, October 28, 1905, 23; Motzkin, *Die Judenpogrome in Russland*, 2:465–467; Gorfunkel', 1905 god v Rechitse—gorode i uezde; Smilovitsky, Pogrom in Rechitsa, 70.

90. Relying of family history, Aron Kaganovich told me about this in an interview on May 6, 2000. Aron Kaganovich's mother and her parents hid in the village of Soltanovo, some seven kilometers from Rechitsa.

91. CAHJP, P 10, 17.

92. Gorfunkel', 1905 god v Rechitse—gorode i uezde, 25; *Revoliutsionnoe dvizhenie v Belorussii 1905–1907 gg.*, 357.

93. RGIA, f. 1565, op. 1, d. 19, 35; d. 20, 8–9, 22–23, 117; GARF, f. 533, op. 1, d. 448, 14–16, 47–50 (copy in CAHJP, HMF 235); CAHJP, P 10, 11, 17; *Voskhod*, October 27, 1905, 39; November 11, 1905, 67; *Khronika evreiskoi zhizni*, October 28, 1905, 23; Motzkin, *Die Judenpogrome in Russland*, 2:465–467; Shumatskii, *Revoliutsinnaia provintsiia*, 36; Y. Kom, *Shoresh ve-'Anaf*, 141–142; *Sefer gvura*, 3:186–190; Stepanov, *Chernaia sotnia v Rossii*, 58, 71; Smilovitsky, Pogrom in Rechitsa, 70–71; Glushakov, Otriad samooborony v Gomele, 70.

94. Ibid.; Drapkin, 1905 god v Gomele i Polesskom raione, 200–203.

95. *Gomel'skii protsess*, 15, 42, 1074–1075, 1146; Delo o besporiadkakh v Gomele, 36.

96. Kahanovich, Homel, supplement to 207.

97. Letter from Donald Girshgorn, July 16, 2001. Heshel Pasov changed his name to Izya.

98. Gorfunkel', 1905 god v Rechitse—gorode i uezde, 23–24; Rechitsa, *Encyclopedia Judaica*, 14:1432.

99. CAHJP, P 10, 17, 23; Motzkin, *Die Judenpogrome in Russland*, 465–467; Stepanov, *Chernaia sotnia v Rossii*, 71. According to other accounts, fifteen people were wounded. See R.D. Oktiabr'skie pogromy v tsifrakh.

100. RGIA, f. 1565, op. 1, d. 18, 36–37a; d. 19, 35; d. 20, 8–9, 22, 117; CAHJP, P 10, 17.

101. CAHJP, P 10, 11, 17; Smilovitsky, Pogrom in Rechitsa, 75.

102. RGIA, f. 1565, op. 1, d. 20, 20–21; CAHJP, P 10, 11, 17.

103. *Revoliutsionnoe dvizhenie v Belorussii 1905–1907 gg.*, 357.

104. CAHJP, P 10, 17.

105. Smilovitsky, Pogrom in Rechitsa, 78–79; Lipetski, Saiuz ruskaga naroda.

106. *Pamiatnaia knizhka Minskoi gubernii na 1915 god*, 212–213.

107. RGIA, f. 1565, op. 1, d. 19, 35; CAHJP, P 10, 11, 17. On the prosperity of the Ortho-dox population of Rechitsa, see also the discussion later in this chapter.

108. Bukhbinder, *Istoriia evreiskogo rabochego dvizheniia v Rossii po neizdannym arkhiv-nym materialam*, 278.

109. CAHJP, HM2 7574, 16, 346; *Bund v Belorussii 1897–1921*, 113–115.

110. *Bund v Belorussii 1897–1921*, 77.

111. Gorfunkel', 1905 god v Rechitse—gorode i uezde, 23–24.

112. Regarding the assassination, see *Poslednie Izvestiia*, April 30, 1903, 4; May 25, 1903, 4; March 21, 1904, 3; May 5, 1905, 4. For Alexander II's expansion of Jewish rights, see Po povodu tsarskogo iubileia 19-go fevralia, *Russkii evrei*, February 20, 1880, 281–287; Vengerova, *Vospominaniia babushki*, 281–283.

113. Gorfunkel', 1905 god v Rechitse—gorode i uezde, 23–24. Given this fact, Boris Umetskii's statement, repeated in the *Pamiats'* collection, that a RSDRP (b) organization was formed in Rechitsa only in 1917 seems to be mistaken. See Umetskii, *Rechitsa*, 20; *Pamiats'*, 1:73. At the same time, it may well be that this Rechitsa cell did not exist for long.

114. *Poslednie Izvestiia*, March 21, 1904, 3; May 05, 1904, 2; August 29, 1904, 4; Bukhbinder, *Istoriia evreiskogo rabochego dvizheniia v Rossii po neizdannym arkhivnym materialam*, 278; Gorfunkel', 1905 god v Rechitse—gorode i uezde, 23–24.

115. *Poslednie Izvestiia*, August 29, 1904, 4. On Talmud-Torah and other schools, see chap. 5.

116. *Poslednie Izvestiia*, August 29, 1904, 4; May 5, 1905, 4.

117. *Poslednie Izvestiia*, August 29, 1904, 4.

118. *Poslednie Izvestiia*, July 19, 1904, 8; Gorfunkel', 1905 god v Rechitse—gorode i uezde, 23–24.

119. *Poslednie Izvestiia*, May 5, 1904, 2; August 29, 1904, 4; Bukhbinder, *Istoriia evreiskogo rabochego dvizheniia v Rossii po neizdannym arkhivnym materialam*, 278.

120. *Poslednie Izvestiia*, May 5, 1905, 4.

121. Ibid.

122. Ibid.

123. *Revoliutsionnoe dvizhenie v Belorussii 1905–1907*, 163; Savitski, Rechytskaia arganizatsyia RSDRP (b).

124. *Bund v Belorussii 1897–1921*, 219.

125. Gorfunkel', 1905 god v Rechitse—gorode i uezde, 30.

126. *Folkszeitung*, July 17, 1907, 4. I am grateful to Vladimir Levin for providing this source.

127. RGIA, f. 1565, op. 1, d. 263, 12.

128. Levin, Yehudey Rusiah veshalosh hadumot har'ishonot, 18, 90.

129. Ibid., 29; Braginskii and Lozinskii, Duma Gosudarstvennaia, 373.

130. *Evreiskii izbiratel'*, January 23, 1907, 18; RGIA, f. 1565, op. 1, d. 263, 1 (copy in CAHJP, HM2 7949, 93).

131. Calculated from data from the 1897 census: Rechitsa, in *Evreiskaia entsiklopediia*.

132. I am grateful to Vladimir Levin for providing this information.

133. RGIA, f. 1565, op. 1, d. 244, 11; d. 263, 1–2.

134. Braginskii and Lozinskii, Duma Gosudarstvennaia, 373; Levin, Yehudey Rusiah veshalosh hadumot har'ishonot, 49–51.

135. *Goroda Rossii v 1910 godu*, 163.

136. Rechitsa, *Rassvet*, October 6, 1907, 38.

137. Levin, Yehudey Rusiah veshalosh hadumot har'ishonot, 92, 97.

138. Rechitsa, *Rassvet*, October 12, 1912, 24. I am grateful to Vladimir Levin for providing more-precise information on the Jewish electors from Rechitsa Uezd.

139. Levin, *Yehudey Rusiah veshalosh hadumot har'ishonot*, 100.

140. Bronevskii, *Puteshestvie ot Triesta do Sankt Peterburga v 1810 godu*, 2:225–226.

141. Klier, *Rossia sobiraet svoikh evreev*, 269–271.

142. *Materialy dlia geografii i statistiki Rossii*, 3:775–778.

CHAPTER 3. THE ECONOMY OF THE TOWN IN THE
NINETEENTH AND EARLY TWENTIETH CENTURIES

1. For a description of this activity, see the quoted passage from William Coxe at the end of chapter 1.

2. Bronevskii, *Puteshestvie ot Triesta do Sankt Peterburga v 1810 godu*, 2:201.

3. Chepko, *Goroda Belorussii v pervoi polovine XIX veka*, 19. It is most likely that nearly the same number of townspeople were practicing trades there unofficially.

4. Ibid.

5. Aleksandrov, Di yyidish'e b'ap'elk'erong 'in Myinsk'er gub'erni'e 'in 'anhyyv 19—tan y'arhind'ert, 73.

6. Ibid.

7. Ibid.

8. *Pamiats'*, 1:55.

9. Chepko, *Goroda Belorussii v pervoi polovine XIX veka*, 21.

10. Ibid., 25–27.

11. NIARB, f. 295, op. 1, d. 1202, 32a–35a, 54–54 (copy in CAHJP, HMF 831.30).

12. Chepko, *Goroda Belorussii v pervoi polovine XIX veka*, 35.

13. Zelenskii, . *Materialy dlia geografii i statistiki Rossii*, 2:277.

14. *Zbor pomnikau historyi i kul'tury Belarusi*, 313; *Dokumenty i materialy po istorii Belorussii*, 3:121.

15. Frank, Haḥeder hametukan beRecitsa, 87.

16. Ibid.

17. Abezgauz, *Rabochii klass Belorussii v nachale XX veka 1900–1913*, 86.

18. Interview with Maria Rubinchik, August 25, 2001.

19. Interview with Raisa Genina, October 10, 2001.

20. Interview with Ida Kaganovich, April 23, 2000; interview with Maria Rubinchik, March 2, 2002.

21. *Pamiatnaia knizhka Minskoi gubernii na 1896 god*, 38.

22. Ibid.

23. *Pamiatnaia knizhka Minskoi gubernii na 1908 god* (Minsk: Gubernskii statisticheskii komitet, 1907), 76.

24. Interview with Iosif Kazovskii, February 12, 2004.

25. *Dokumenty i materialy po istorii Belorussii*, 3:95.

26. Baron, *Social and Religious History of the Jews*, 16:233.

27. Gepshtein, *Ekonomicheskaia struktura evreiskogo naseleniia Rossii*, 22–23.

28. *Khronologicheskii ukazatel' materialov dlia istorii inorodtsev Evropeiskoi Rossii*, 201.

29. *Materialy dlia geografii i statistiki Rossii*, 3:185–187.

30. *Belorussiia v epokhu Feodalizma*, 3:429.

31. Ibid., 3:453.

32. Rokhlin, *Miestechko Krasnopol'e Mogilevskoi gubernii*, 12.

33. *Belorussiia v epokhu Feodalizma*, 3:450–453.

34. Zelenskii, *Materialy dlia geografii i statistiki Rossii*, 2:380.

35. *Naselenie Rossii v XX veke*, 1:399.

36. *Belorussiia v epokhu Feodalizma*, 3:450–453, 481–483.

37. Jelski, *Rzeczyca*, 134–135.

38. For 1844 statistics, see Zelenskii, *Materialy dlia geografii i statistiki Rossii*, 2:380; for early twentieth-century data, see *Dokumenty i materialy po istorii Belorussii*, 3:138.

39. *Obzor Minskoi gubernii za 1913 god*, 23.

40. Fëdorov, *Sotsial'no-ekonomicheskoe razvitie Rossii* (pervaia polovina XIX veka), 9, 12.

41. Shipov, *Khlopchato-bumazhnaia promyshlennost' i vazhnost' eë znacheniia v Rossii*, 2:83, 88.

42. Ibid. Richard Pipes believes that the natural conditions in Lithuania, Belorussia and Russia's central regions generally made it very difficult to achieve surpluses in agricultural production. See Pipes, *Russia under the Old Regime*, 6–8.

43. Liutyi, *Sotsial'no-ekonomicheskoe razvitie gorodov Belorussii*, 98.

44. Fridman, *Otmena krepostnogo prava v Belorussii*, 28.

45. Ibid., 21–22.

46. Teller, *Hape'ilut hakalkalit shel hayehudim bePolin bemahatsit hasheniyah shel hame'ah ha17 uveme'ah ha18*, 216–218.

47. Kotik, *Zikhronotav shel Yihzk'el Kotik*, 1:96–110, 321–322. In the first decades after the Russian conquest some Jews leased entire estates (see: Sobolevskaia, *Iudei v belorusskikh vladeniiakh Radzivilov v kontse 18–nachale 19 vekov*, 33–34), but apparently these still were few. Otherwise their involvement in this area of business in the 1830s would not be represented as a phenomenon by Kotik.

48. Zelenskii, *Materialy dlia geografii i statistiki Rossii*, 2:377.

49. Zelenskii, *Materialy dlia geografii i statistiki Rossii*, 2:377.

50. Ianchuk, *Po Minskoi gubernii*, 25. I am grateful to Dmitrii Tolochko for providing this source.

51. Ibid., 23.

52. Zelenskii, *Materialy dlia geografii i statistiki Rossii*, 2:377.

53. Ibid., 2:378.

54. *Stoletie Minskoi gubernii*, 89; *Pamiatnaia knizhka Minskoi gubernii na 1896 god*, 41; *Svod zakonov Rossiiskoi imperii*, vol. 5, ed. A. F. Volkov and Iu. D. Filippov, 2nd ed. (Saint Petersburg: Obshchestvennaia pol'za, 1899), 87–145.

55. *Belorussiia v epokhu Feodalizma*, 3:420.

56. *Pamiats'*, 1:49.

57. *Belorussiia v epokhu Feodalizma*, 3:418–420. The lack of statistics on the value of cargoes makes it impossible to compare the volume of trade by Jews and Gentiles.

58. Shpilevskii, *Puteshestvie po Polesiu i Belorusskomu kraiu*, 126–127.

59. Bronevskii, *Puteshestvie ot Triesta do Sankt Peterburga v 1810 godu*, 2:226.

60. Hundert, *Jews in Poland-Lithuania in the Eighteenth Century*, 34–35.

61. Bez-Kornilovich, *Istoricheskie mesta o primechatel'nykh mestakh v Belorussii*, 209–210.

62. *Polnyi khronologicheskii sbornik zakonov i polozhenii*, 377–378.

63. *Khronologicheskii ukazatel' materialov dlia istorii inorodtsev Evropeiskoi Rossii*, 209.

64. TsGARUz, f. 1, op. 17, d. 966, 5.

65. Zelenskii, *Materialy dlia geografii i statistiki Rossii*, 2:277–278.

66. Stolpianskii, *Deviat' gubernii Zapadno-russkogo kraia*, 86; *Zhivopisnaia Rossiia*, 381.

67. Zelenskii, *Materialy dlia geografii i statistiki Rossii*, 2:374.

68. *Zbor pomnikau historyi i kul'tury Belarusi*, 313.

69. Jelski, *Rzeczyca*, 134.

70. Chepko, *Goroda Belorussii v pervoi polovine XIX veka*, 111.

71. Cited from Gessen, *Evrei v Rossii*, 293.

72. Liutyi, *Sotsial'no-ekonomicheskoe razvitie gorodov Belorussii*, 98.

73. Bolbas, *Razvitie promyshlennosti v Belorussii, 1795–1861 gg.*, 11.

74. Ibid., 102–104.

75. NIARB, f. 21, op. 1, d.1, 401.

76. Bogrov, *Zapiski evreia*, 391–395.

77. *Belorussiia v epokhu Feodalizma*, 3:418–419.

78. CAHJP, RU, d. 360, 1–5, 16–29.

79. Ibid., 24–25.

80. *Minskie gubernskie vedomosti* 3 (1845), attachment; 26 (1845), attachment.

81. Ibid., 7 (1845), attachment.

82. Ibid., 5 (1853), 61.

83. Ibid., 43 (1853), 476.

84. Yehezkel Kotik has provided a good description of the system of bribery in Russia, using the example of Kamenets, a shtetl in northwestern Belorussia. See Kotik, *Zikhronotav shel Yihzk'el Kotik*, 1:156, 176–178, 269, 274.

85. *Minskie gubernskie vedomosti* 17 (1855), 90.

86. Ibid., 10 (1877), 109.

87. Ibid., 48 (1876), 759.

88. Gessen, *Evrei v Rossii*, 110. On Derzhavin's hostility toward the Jews, see 46–71.

89. Gessen, *Istoriia evreiskogo naroda v Rossii*, 1:133–134.

90. RGIA, f. 1216, op. 1824, d. 325.

91. *Voenno-statisticheskoe obozrenie Rossiiskoi imperii*, 33.

92. Bolbas, *Razvitie promyshlennosti v Belorussii, 1795–1861 gg.*, 252.

93. Chepko, *Goroda Belorussii v pervoi polovine XIX veka*, 59.

94. Subbotin, *V cherte evreiskoi osedlosti*, 2:21.

95. Gepshtein, *Ekonomicheskaia struktura evreiskogo naseleniia Rossii*, 20–21.

96. Stolpianskii, *Deviat' gubernii Zapadno-russkogo kraia*, xv.

97. Zelenskii, *Materialy dlia geografii i statistiki Rossii*, 2:376.

98. *Pamiats'*, 1:55.

99. NIARB, f. 21, op. 1, d. 1, 402. I am grateful to Leonid Smilovitsky for this material.

100. Liutyi, *Sotsial'no-ekonomicheskoe razvitie gorodov Belorussii*, 115.

101. Aleksandrov, Di yyidish'e b'ap'elk'erong 'in Myinsk'er gub'erni'e 'in 'anhyyv 19—tan y'arhind'ert, 73.

102. *Belorussiia v epokhu Feodalizma*, 3:479. Zalman Roginskii remained a merchant of the third guild, at least until the end of the 1850s. See *Minskie gubernskie vedomosti* 28 (1860), 257.

103. *Belorussiia v epokhu Feodalizma*, 3:479.

104. Chepko, *Goroda Belorussii v pervoi polovine XIX veka*, 63; NIARB, f. 21, op. 1, d. 11, 347, 350, 352.

105. Chepko, *Goroda Belorussii v pervoi polovine XIX veka*, 97; Zelenskii, *Materialy dlia geografii i statistiki Rossii*, 2:382–383.

106. Mozeszon O., Material'noe polozhenie evreiskoi massy v Severo-Zapadnom krae, 611.

107. *Rassvet*, February 1, 1880, 179.

108. *Minski gubernskie vedomosti* 30 (1885), 3.

109. Zelenskii, *Materialy dlia geografii i statistiki Rossii*, 2:680.

110. *Minski gubernskie vedomosti* 4 (1876), 4.

111. Ibid., 11 (1877), 22.

112. Ibid., 32 (1880), 481.

113. Ianchuk, *Po Minskoi gubernii*, 23.

114. Shybeka, *Garady Belarusi*, 26–28.

115. Ibid., 24.

116. Kahanovich, *MiHomel 'ad Tel-Aviv*, 16.

117. See above, on the discussion of bribery in the memoirs of Yehezkel Kotik.

118. *Belorussiia v epokhu Feodalizma*, 3:480.

119. Shpilevskii, *Puteshestvie po Polesiu i Belorusskomu kraiu*, 126.

120. *Minskie gubernskie vedomosti* 27 (1885), 3.

121. Amitin, Homel.

122. *Pamiats'*, 52. During construction of the railway, the Rechitsa Town Council made special pleas to the central authorities to route the line specifically through their town. See Aliakseichanka, Rechytsa ў drugoi palove XIX st., 258.

123. Jelski, Rzeczyca, 134; *Goroda Rossii v 1910 godu*, 86–87; *Pamiats'*, 1:63; interview with Maria Rubinchik, January 1, 2001; letter from Avraam Dovzhik, September 28, 2001.

124. Jelski, Rzeczyca, 134; Aliakseichanka, Rechytsa ў drugoi palove XIX st., 260.

125. NIARB, f. 295, op. 1, vol. 2, d. 5617, 1–52.

126. Ibid., d. 5224, 1–12.

127. Ibid., d. 5977, 1–11.

128. *Minskie gubernskie vedomosti* 44 (1880), 766.

129. Mahler, Hayehudim be-Polin erev ha-tkufat ha-khalukot, 251.

130. Rechitsa, *Entsiklopedicheskii slovar'*, 489, Gessen, *Evrei v Rossii*, 330–331; Shybeka, *Garady Belarusi*, 34.

131. Ianchuk, *Po Minskoi gubernii*, 24.

132. Nakhmanovich, *Evreiskaia politika Tsarskogo pravitel'stva v 1870-kh gg.*, 10.

133. Lozinskii, *Sotsial'nye korni antisemitizma v srednie veka i v novoe vremia*, 188.

134. *Vsia Rossiia na 1895*, 616; interview with Maria Rubinchik, August 25, 2001.

135. Zelenskii, *Materialy dlia geografii i statistiki Rossii*, 2:264–266.

136. Abezgauz, *Razvitie promyshlennosti i formirovanie proletariata Belorussii vo vtoroi polovine 19 veka*, 44. Considering that quite a significant amount of the wine and vodka production was concealed from the excise administration, the actual value of production was even higher.

137. Zelenskii, *Materialy dlia geografii i statistiki Rossii*, 2:263.

138. Subbotin, *V cherte evreiskoi osedlosti*, 2:21–22; *Vsia Rossiia na 1895*, 617; Vol'tke, *Vinnye promysly*, 611; *Pamiats'*, 1:52, 55–56.

139. Gepshtein, *Ekonomicheskaia struktura evreiskogo naseleniia Rossii*, 20–21.

140. *Minskie gubernskie vedomosti* 44 (1880), 766.

141. Vol'tke, *Vinnye promysly*, 614; Ignat'ev, *S.Iu. Vitte—diplomat*, 103.

142. Gepshtein, *Ekonomicheskaia struktura evreiskogo naseleniia Rossii*, 20–21.

143. Lozinskii, *Sotsial'nye korni antisemitizma v srednie veka i v novoe vremia*, 187.

144. *Vsia Rossiia na 1912*, 1574.

145. Ibid.; RGIA, f. 821, op. 8, d. 37, 128 (copy in CAHJP, HM2 9050.4).

146. Gepshtein, *Ekonomicheskaia struktura evreiskogo naseleniia Rossii*, 20–21.

147. Interview with Maria Rubinchik, March 2, 2002.

148. Gepshtein, *Ekonomicheskaia struktura evreiskogo naseleniia Rossii*, 22–23.

149. *Vsia Rossiia na 1902*, 808.

150. This conclusion can be reached from the data collected in Rechitsa on the damage done to thirty-three stores and shops during the pogrom of 1905. At the same time, archival documents give no indication (as in a number of other towns) of the fact that all the Jewish retail establishments were wrecked. See CAHJP, P, d. 10, 17, 23; Motzkin, *Die Judenpogrome in Russland*, 2:465–467.

151. List of voters for electors from Rechitsa Uezd to the Second State Duma, 1906. http://www.jewishgen.org/databases/Belarus/DumaVoterLists.htm (accessed September 11, 2011).

152. The number of families in Rechitsa was calculated based on the typical composition of a Jewish family, meaning five persons living under one roof. The commonly accepted view of the average number of members in a Jewish family differs from the data provided by Zelenskii, which admittedly comes from an earlier time, the 1860s. It shows that six persons lived in Jewish houses in the towns of Minsk Province (and Rechitsa was listed as a town), compared with five among Christians (Zelenskii, *Materialy dlia geografii i statistiki Rossii*, 1:478). On the fact that the vast majority of Rechitsa Jews were regarded as poor, see also *Pamiats'*, 1:54.

153. Kahan, *Hyozmot hayhudit be-Rusyah hats'aryt*, 399.

154. Zakhar'in, *Vospominaniia o sluzhbe v Belorussii*, 553.

155. *Pamiatnaia knizhka Vitebskoi gubernii na 1865 g.*, ed. Alexander Sementovskii (Saint Petersburg: Vitebskii gubernskii statisticheskii komitet, 1865), 256.

156. *Pamiatnaia knizhka Minskoi gubernii na 1880 god*, 282.

157. *Adres-kalendar' Vilenskogo general-gubernatora na 1868 god*, 530–531.

158. *Goroda Rossii v 1910 godu*, 103.

159. Voinilovich, *Vospominaniia*, 1:83–106.

160. *Vsia Rossiia na 1912*, 1574.

161. Gepshtein, *Ekonomicheskaia struktura evreiskogo naseleniia Rossii*, 19.

162. *Materialy dlia geografii i statistiki Rossii*, 3:417.

163. Interview with Roza Dvorkina, October 1, 2002.

164. Letter from Fridrikh Valler, August 10, 2001.

165. *Hamelits*, December 12, 1882, 927.

166. Ibid.

167. Regarding Zalkind, see NIARB, f. 299, op. 5, d. 308. I am grateful to Leonid Smilovitsky for the opportunity to consult this material. For Gurvich and Shchukin, see *Vsia Rossiia na 1895*, 616.

168. *Vsia Rossiia na 1902*, 808; *Adresnaia kniga fabrichno-zavodskoi i remeslennoi promyshlennosti vsei Rossii*, 22.

169. Abezgauz, *Rabochii klass Belorussii v nachale XX veka 1900–1913* , 17.

170. *Zbor pomnikau historyi i kul'tury Belarusi*, 313.

171. NIARB, f. 295, op. 1, vol. 2, d. 4743, 1–14; Jelski, Rzeczyca, 134; Frank, Haḥeder hametukan beRecitsa, 96; Kom, Bereshet hanyitsul, 172.

172. *Zbor pomnikau historyi i kul'tury Belarusi*, 313.

173. *Dokumenty i materialy po istorii Belorussii*, 3:58–59.

174. *Vsia Rossiia na 1912*, 101.

175. *Delo pomoshchi*, February 25, 1917, 33.

176. Abezgauz, *Rabochii klass Belorussii v nachale XX veka 1900–1913*, 82.

177. V. Sekhovich, Iz spichki vozgoritsia plamia . . . , *Belorusskaia delovaia gazeta*, July 12, 2005, 12; Abezgauz, *Rabochii klass Belorussii v nachale XX veka 1900–1913*, 20, 35, 39.

178. *Obzor Minskoi gubernii za 1913 god*, 20, 72.

179. *Dokumenty i materialy po istorii Belorussii*, 3:815–816.

180. Ibid., 863; NIARB, f. 295, op. 1, vol. 2, d. 9270a.

181. Abezgauz, *Rabochii klass Belorussii v nachale XX veka 1900–1913*, 38.

182. Shybeka, *Garady Belarusi*, 223–224.

183. Rogger, *Jewish Policies*, 58.

CHAPTER 4. DEMOGRAPHY OF THE SOCIAL-ECONOMIC LANDSCAPE
IN THE NINETEENTH AND EARLY TWENTIETH CENTURIES

1. Petrachenka and Kavalenka, Kameral'noe opisanie rechitskoi okrugi, 239.

2. Gessen, *Istoriia evreiskogo naroda v Rossii*, 1:56.

3. Aleksandrov, Fun myinsk'er 'arkhyiion, 763.

4. Liutyi, *Sotsial'no-ekonomicheskoe razvitie gorodov Belorussii*, 27.

5. Aleksandrov, Di yyidish'e b'ap'elk'erong 'in Myinsk'er gub'erni'e 'in 'anhyyv 19—tan y'arhind'ert, 73.

6. Ibid.

7. The requisitions and pillaging by Napoleon's army to which the Jews in occupied towns were subjected could have influenced this migration. On this, see Liutyi, *Sotsial'no-ekonomicheskoe razvitie gorodov Belorussii*, 81, 93–94.

8. NIARB, f. 295, op. 1, d. 1858, 12 (copy in CAHJP, HMF 831.38).

9. *Minskie gubernskie vedomosti* 30 (1885), 3.

10. NIARB, f. 295, op. 1, d. 1858, 23 (copy in CAHJP, HMF 831.38). On the understated figures in this census of Jews in Minsk Province, see also Zelenskii, *Materialy dlia geografii i statistiki Rossii*, 1:465.

11. Avrutin, *Jews and the Imperial State*), 29–31.

12. NIARB, f. 295, op. 1, d. 501, 4–5 (copy in CAHJP, HMF 831.27).

13. Sifman, Dinamika chislennosti naseleniia Rossii za 1897–1914, 71–72.

14. Ibid., 70–71.

15. Calculated from LSHA, f. 378, op. 1840, d. 1209, 2 (copy in CAHJP, HM2 9757.6).

16. Ibid.

17. Zelenskii, *Materialy dlia geografii i statistiki Rossii*, 467; Alenitsyn, *Evreiskoe naselenie i zemlevladenie v iugo-zapadnykh guberniiakh Evropeiskoi Possii, vkhodiashchikh v chertu evreiskoi osedlosti*, 26.

18. Calculated from NIARB, f. 295, op. 1, d. 501, 97, 99 (copy in CAHJP, HMF 831.35); Aleksandrov, Di yyidish'e b'ap'elk'erong 'in Myinsk'er gub'erni'e 'in 'anhyyv 19—tan y'arhind'ert, 73; *Belorussiia v epokhu Feodalizma*, 3:541; *Pamiats'*, 1:49, 57;

19. Zelenskii, *Materialy dlia geografii i statistiki Rossii*, 2:674.

20. Calculated from *Dokumenty i materialy po istorii Belorussii*, 3:165.

21. *Dokumenty i materialy po istorii Belorussii*, 3:302.

22. Shybeka, *Garady Belarusi*, 58–59.

23. I was told of the deaths of the wife and two children of Israel-Pinkhas Levin in Rechitsa and Kholmech during this epidemic by Ella Bark in an interview on July 4, 2002.

24. *Pamiatnaia knizhka Minskoi gubernii na 1896 god*, 20–21. This same source notes that in 1893 there were even more cases of cholera in the province. Ibid., 22.

25. *Pamiatnaia knizhka Minskoi gubernii na 1891 god* (Minsk: Gubernskii statisticheskii komitet, 1890), 199.

26. Calculated from Shybeka, *Garady Belarusi*, 219–220.

27. Alenitsyn, *Evreiskoe naselenie i zemlevladenie v iugo-zapadnykh guberniiakh Evropeiskoi Possii, vkhodiashchikh v chertu evreiskoi osedlosti*, 26; Aleksandrov, Di yyidish'e b'ap'elk'erong 'in dyi sht'et 'un sht'etl'ekh fun Vyyasrusland, 355–356.

28. Shybeka, *Garady Belarusi*, 59, 219–220.

29. Ibid. This increase occurred despite the large emigration of peasants from Belorussia to America. A large group of these were peasants who had lost their farms in 1912. According to accounts—perhaps somewhat exaggerated—in the newspaper *Russkaia molva*, 100,000 people left at that time. See *Russkaia molva*, May 16, 1913, 3.

30. Chepko, *Goroda Belorussii v pervoi polovine XIX veka*, 45.

31. Ibid., 63. It is significant that in 1842 Gomel had only 30 shops, i.e., several fewer than Rechitsa; by 1861 their number had grown to 195, more than three times more than Rechitsa.

32. Ibid., 78.

33. Kahanovich, Homel, attachment to 207.

34. *Bund v Belorussii 1897–1921*, 79–82.

35. Chepko, *Goroda Belorussii v pervoi polovine XIX veka*, 88.

36. Shybeka, *Garady Belarusi*, 220, 223.

37. Ibid., 255, 257. On the migration of Jews, particularly merchants, from Pinsk to Ukraine, see also Nadav, *Jews of Pinsk*, 392–394. For an example of the migration of Jews from Rechitsa to Kiev, see Tadger, *Entsyiklopedyiah le-halutsey ha-Yishuv ve-bonav*, 11:3815.

38. *Otchiot o deiatel'nosti informatsionnogo biuro dlia emigrantov za 1907 g.*, 27, 32; Sudarskii, *Ekonomicheskoe polozhenie evreiskogo mestechka*, 12.

39. *Otchiot o deiatel'nosti informatsionnogo biuro dlia emigrantov za 1907*, 39, 67; *Otchet dlia okazaniia pomoshchi evreiam-pereselentsam za 1909 g.*, 32; *Otchet o deiatel'nosti po uporiadocheniiu evreiskoi emigratsii za 1910 g.*, 9, 50.

40. *Otchet o deiatel'nosti po uporiadocheniiu evreiskoi emigratsii za 1910 g.*, 6–7.

41. Ibid., 5.

42. *Evreiskoe obozrenie*, May 27, 1910, 49. According to the Regulations of 1892, Jews, unlike other emigrants, could not return to Russia.

43. Frank, *Haḥeder hametukan beRecitsa*, 90–91.

44. Sorkin, *Bridges to an American city*, 313. (I am obliged to Bill Schechter for this source and for information on the cemetery and some of the photos). The book mistakenly states that this refers to Rezhitsa (renamed Rezekne after 1917), but the list of members of the organizing committee leaves no doubt that these people came from Rechitsa. The Waldheim Jewish Cemetery also has another special section, no. 241, for Jews from Rechitsa.

45. For more details about the functions of these societies, see Soyer, *Jewish Immigrant Associations*.

46. Kabuzan, *Emigratsiia i reemigratsiia v Rossii v XVIII—nachale XX veka*, 178–179.

47. *Pamiatnaia knizhka Minskoi gubernii na 1892 god* (Minsk: Gubernskii statisticheskii komitet, 1891), 159; *Pervaia vseobshchaia perepis' naseleniia Rossiiskoi Imperii 1897*, 1–3.

48. Bezhenstvo i emigratsiia, *Rassvet*, June 10, 1922, 16–17.

49. *Otchet dlia okazaniia pomoshchi evreiam-pereselentsam za 1909 g.*, 6.

50. Ibid. In Minsk in 1852 Catholics made up 75.2 percent of the Christian population. Many Catholics lived in the shtetls of Minsk Province: in Novogrudok (59.4 percent); Pinsk (56.3 percent); and Borisov (39.2 percent). See Chepko, *Goroda Belorussii v pervoi polovine XIX veka*, 128.

51. *Evreiskoe naselenie Rossii po dannym perepisi 1897 g. i po noveishim istochnikam*, 44; *Obzor Minskoi gubernii za 1913 god*, 53; NIARB, f. 295, op. 1, d. 2576, 7 (copy in CAHJP, HMF 831.42).

52. *Protokol zasedaniia otdeleniia statistiki severo-zapadnogo otdela imperatorskogo Russkogo Geograficheskogo obshchestva ot 2 dekabria 1872 g.*, 128; Chubinskii, *Trudy Etnografichesko-statisticheskoi ekspeditsii v Zapadno-Russkii krai*, 7:3, 14, 22. See *Trudy gubernskih komissii po evreiskomu voprosu*, vol. 1, sec. 1, 87.

53. Bronevskii, *Puteshestvie ot Triesta do Sankt Peterburga v 1810 godu*, 2:186.

54. Pozner, *Evrei Litvy i Belorussii 125 let tomu nazad*, 81.

55. Goldberg, *Ha-hevra ha-Yahudit ba-mamlekhet Polin-Lit'a*, 211.

56. See, for example, the account of the abduction of a Jewish girl in Brest in 1780. *Akty izdavaemye Vilenskoi Arkheograficheskoi komissiei*, 5:128–129. On the creation of a network of convents in the Lithuanian Duchy in 1737, the aim of which was to convert 500 Jewish women to Christianity, see Hundert, *Jews in Poland-Lithuania in the Eighteenth Century*, 67. On the conversion of Jews and a bull from the pope in Rome against their compulsory conversion, see Teter, Jewish Conversions to Catholicism.

57. I explore this topic in an article about the status of women in the Bukharan-Jewish community of the modern era, which I am now preparing for publication.

58. Bogrov, *Zapiski evreia*, 240.

59. Stampfer, *Families, Rabbis and Education*, 23.

60. Petrovskii-Shtern, *Evrei v Russkoi Armii*, 221.

61. Mironov, Traditsionnoe demograficheskoe povedenie krest'ian v XIX–nachale XX v, 92.

62. Shabad, Naselenie Rossii, 543–544.

63. All calculations are based on data provided in *Pamiatnaia knizhka Minskoi gubernii na 1891 god*, 204–205.

64. *Naselenie Rossii v XX veke*, 1:49.

65. Dvizhenie rossiiskogo naseleniia za 1867, 456–457, 394–395; Dvizhenie rossiiskogo naseleniia za 1870, 62–63, 76.

66. Shabad, Naselenie Rossii, 543–544.

67. *Naselenie Rossii v XX veke*, 1:62.

68. Dvizhenie rossiiskogo naseleniia za 1867, 376–377, 394–395.

69. LSHA, f. 378, op. 1840, d. 1209, 2 (copy in CAHJP, HM2 9757.6).

70. Freeze, *Jewish Marriage and Divorce*, 124–128.

71. NIARB, f. 295, op. 1, d. 1405, 97, 99 (copy in CAHJP, HMF 831.35); d. 2576, 7 (copy in CAHJP, HMF 831.42); LSHA, f. 378, op. 1840, d. 1209, 2 (copy in CAHJP, HM2 9757.6). Available data show that ninety weddings took place within the town in 1913. See *Obzor Minskoi gubernii za 1913 god*, 72.

72. Calculated according to Stampfer, *Families, Rabbis and Education*, 46. The divorce rate among Odessa Jews was almost the same as in Berdichev (calculated according to the same source).

73. Freeze, *Jewish Marriage and Divorce*, 154.

74. Braude, Materialy po estestvennomu dvizheniiu evreiskogo naseleniia v Moskve za 48 let, 377.

75. Calculated in accordance with CAHJP, RU 16 and RU 17. The census of the Russian Empire conducted in 1897 reflects not the number of divorces but only the number of divorced people in the country. Therefore, it is impossible to make use of it for a comparative analysis. After all, people did remarry.

76. *Trudy gubernskih komissii po evreiskomu voprosu*, vol. 1, sec. 6, 39.

77. Ibid., 40.

78. CAHJP, RU 16 and RU 17.

79. Freeze, *Jewish Marriage and Divorce*, 151.

80. Ibid., 152.

81. Ibid., 163–190.

82. Ibid., 159–160.

83. Bogrov, *Zapiski evreia*, 18–24.

84. Protokol zasedaniia otdeleniia statistiki severo-zapadnogo otdela imperatorskogo Russkogo Geograficheskogo obshchestva ot 26 Marta 1873 g., 188.

85. Stampfer, *Families, Rabbis and Education*, 58.

86. Calculated according to Dvizhenie rossiiskogo naseleniia za 1867, 376–377, 394–395.

87. *Evreiskoe naselenie Rossii po dannym perepisi 1897 g. i po noveishim istochnikam*, 44; *Obzor Minskoi gubernii za 1913 god*, 53; NIARB, f. 295, op. 1, d. 2576, 7 (copy in CAHJP, HMF 831.42).

88. NIARB, f. 295, op. 1, d. 2576, 7 (copy in CAHJP, HMF 831.42).

89. See, for example, V.R., Iz mira antropologicheskoi statistiki, 77. At the end of the nineteenth century, 949 girls were born for every 1,000 boys among the Orthodox, while among the Jews the figure was 811. See Shabad, Naselenie Rossii, 544.

90. NIARB, f. 295, op. 1, d. 1405, 97, 99 (copy in CAHJP, HMF 831.35).

91. Calculated from the list of voters for electors from Rechitsa Uezd to the Second State Duma, 1906 (from a list of 370 names), in Kniga zapisei brakov evreev v Minske za 1912 g., CAHJP, RU 16 (from a list of 1,400 names).

92. Calculated from Kniga zapisei brakov evreev v Minske za 1912 g., CAHJP, RU 16 (from a list of 450 names).

93. Calculated from NIARB, f. 295, op. 1, d. 1405, 97, 99 (copy in CAHJP, HMF 831.35); *Trudy gubernskogo statisticheskogo komiteta*, 428.

94. NIARB, f. 295, op. 1, d. 2576, 7 (copy in CAHJP, HMF 831.42).

95. Alenitsyn, *Evreiskoe naselenie i zemlevladenie v iugo-zapadnykh guberniiakh Evropeiskoi Rossii, vkhodiashchikh v chertu evreiskoi osedlosti*, 26; Jelski, Rzeczyca, 134.

96. *Obzor Minskoi gubernii za 1913 god*, 72.

97. Ibid.

98. Freeze, *Jewish Marriage and Divorce*, 58–60.

99. Shabad, Naselenie Rossii, 545.

100. *Materialy dlia geografii i statistiki Rossii*, 3:345–347.

101. Ransel, Kul'tura detorozhdeniia u belorusskih, evreiskih i tatarskikh zhenshchin na territorii Belarusi kontsa XIX—nachala XX vekov, 76, 80.

102. Kotik, *Zikhronotav shel Yihzk'el Kotik*, 1:332–333; Vengerova, *Vospominaniia babushki*, 206.

103. Bogrov, *Zapiski evreia*, 119.

104. Ibid., 252–253.

105. Kotik, *Zikhronotav shel Yihzk'el Kotik*, 1:332–333; Vengerova, *Vospominaniia babushki*, 206.

106. YVA, O33/6606 (diary of Litman Turovskii), 144–145.

107. Stampfer, *Families, Rabbis and Education*, 226, 299.

108. Calculated per Dvizhenie rossiiskogo naseleniia za 1867, 16–17, 34–35.

109. *Naselenie Rossii v XX veke*, 1:62. In this connection, the assertion by the prerevolutionary demographers Sokolov and Grebenshchikov that the highest number of births among the Orthodox occurred in summer seems erroneous. See Sokolov and Grebenshchikov. *Smertnost' v Rossii i bor'ba s neiu*, http://www.gvinfo.ru/node/31 (accessed September 12, 2011).

110. Iastrzhembskii, *Opyt statisticheskogo dvizheniia naseleniia Khersonskoi gubernii: Khersonskii uezd*, 21–22.

111. Sokolov and Grebenshchikov, *Smertnost' v Rossii i bor'ba s neiu*.

112. Vengerova, *Vospominaniia babushki*, 227–228. Cf. Ransel, *Village Mothers*, 36–38.

113. *Naselenie Rossii v XX veke*, 1:64; Sokolov and Grebenshchikov, *Smertnost' v Rossii i bor'ba s neiu*. These authors assert that during the time of field work, Orthodox mothers would leave their infants under the care of eight- to ten-year-old children for three or four days each week. These children often would not manage to change the infants regularly, yet another cause of the spread of infections.

114. Sokolov and Grebenshchikov, *Smertnost' v Rossii i bor'ba s neiu*; Ransel, *Village Mothers*, 37.

115. Sokolov and Grebenshchikov, *Smertnost' v Rossii i bor'ba s neiu*.

116. Ibid. On the prolonged period of breast-feeding by Jewish mothers, see also Ransel, *Village Mothers*, 36.

117. Ransel, *Village Mothers*, 22. Polina Vengerova writes that the cholera epidemic that rolled across Belorussia in 1855 affected Christians more than Jews because the latter had better hygiene. Vengerova, *Vospominaniia babushki*, 240.

118. *Meditsinskii otchiot po Minskoi gubernii za 1911 g.*, 44.

119. Ibid.

120. *Naselenie Rossii v XX veke*, 1:63.

121. Calculated from *Naselenie Rossii v XX veke*, 1:7.

122. Ibid., 44.

123. The medical report cited notes in regard to Minsk Province that some of the midwives had not been at work for long and still had not managed to win the trust of the rural population. Thus there were fewer than average consultations with them. Ibid.

124. Dovnar-Zapol'skii, *Issledovaniia i stat'i*, 295.

125. *Naselenie Rossii v XX veke*, 1:44.

126. Calculated from *Naselenie Rossii v XX veke*, 1:7.

127. Leshchinskii, Dvizhenie evreiskogo naseleniia v Rossii, 144.

Chapter 5. Prerevolutionary Jewish Social Life and Education

1. Gessen, *Evrei v Rossii*, 157–158.

2. LSHA, f. 378, op. 1849, d. 1320, 1–2 (copy in CAHJP, HM2 9780.8).

3. Shmeruk, Mashm'euta haḥevratit shel' hashḥitah hahasidit; Stampfer, *Families, Rabbis and Education*, 346–352.

4. *Bobroysk*, 46.

5. Agranovskii, "Skakuny" i "kitaiovtsy"—hasidskoe dvizhenie v Litve glazami pravitel'stvennykh chinovnikov, 334–336.

6. NIARB, f. 295, op. 1, d. 501, 96 (copy in CAHJP, HMF 831.27). See appendix 1, the list of Jews who signed this reply along with the rabbi.

7. Agranovskii, "Skakuny" i "kitaiovtsy"—hasidskoe dvizhenie v Litve glazami pravitel'stvennykh chinovnikov, 340.

8. Ibid.

9. Bogrov, *Zapiski evreia*, 4–5.

10. Petrachenka and Kavalenka, Kameral'noe opisanie rechitskoi okrugi, 239.

11. LSHA, f. 378, op. 1840, d. 1209, 3a–4 (copy in CAHJP, HM2 9757.6).

12. CAHJP, HM2 7771, 60a; NIARB, f. 295, op. 1, d. 501, 96 (copy in CAHJP, HMF 831.7).

13. Stolpianskii, *Deviat' gubernii Zapadno-russkogo kraia*, 86; NIARB, f. 295, op. 1, d. 1409, 97–99.

14. Zaltsman, 'Ayarati, 31.

15. Shafir, Moi vospominaniia, 107.

16. *Pamiatnaia knizhka Minskoi gubernii na 1880 god*, 74, 287.

17. Attachment in Russian to *Hakarmel*, March 10, 1886, 110–111.

18. NIARB, f. 295, op. 1, d. 2576, 7 (copy in CAHJP, HMF 831.42).

19. RGIA, f. 821, op. 8, d. 123, 81, 93 (copy in CAHJP, HM2 7772).

20. Tauber, *Svedeniia o sostoianii eshibota "Ramailes" v g. Vilne, zavedyvaemogo ravvinom K. Tauberom; Pamiatnaia knizhka Vilenskoi gubernii na 1893 god* (Vilno: Vilenskii gubernskii statisticheskii komitet, 1893), 164; Kats, 'Al' 'itonim ve'anashyim, 67.

21. *Yahadut Lita*, 3:169.

22. RGIA, f. 821, op. 8, d. 458, 102–103; d. 123, 81, 93–98, 107–107a, 118 (copy in CAHJP, HM2 7944, d. 7772); f. 1290, op. 4, d. 574, 192a; Jelski, Rzeczyca, 134. Kalman Tauber died in 1901. Semen, Vilna, *Hamelits*, June 3, 1901, 3; *Yahadut Lita*, 3:169. Therefore, Ben-Tsiyon Kats's statement that he was still alive in 1908 is incorrect. Kats, 'Al' 'itonim ve'anashyim, 67.

23. RGIA, f. 821, op. 8, d. 123, 81, 93–94a, 97–98, 107–107a, 118 (copy in CAHJP, HM2 8277); *Hamelits*, August 10, 1895, 2; September 1, 1895, 3.

24. CAHJP, HMF 831.25, 7; Kahanovich, Homel, 260.

25. Ibid.

26. Kahanovich, *MiHomel 'ad Tel-Aviv*, 17.

27. Ibid.

28. Piriatin, 543; Al'fasi, *Ha-Hasidut*, 228.

29. *Hamelits*, February 21, 1871, 43–44.

30. Slonim, Toldot mishpahat ha-rav mi-Ladi, 82; Kahanovich, Homel, 253; Rechitsa, *Encyclopedia Judaica*; Al'fasi, *Ha-Hasidut*, 80; N. Fridman, *Otsar ha-rabanim*, 377; Helman, *Sefer Beit Rabi*, 249–250.

31. *Yagdil' Tora* 8, nos. 1–6 (1983–1984), 110–127.

32. Tseitlin, Korotko o sebe, 79–80; Frank, Haḥeder hametukan beRecitsa, 96.

33. Tseitlin, Korotko o sebe, 79–80.

34. Heilperin, *Sefer ha-Tseitsaim*, 291.

35. Udler and Dodina, Evrei Brianska vchera i segodnia, 2002.

36. Slonim, *Toldot mishpahat ha-rav mi-Ladi*, 136–137; following Slonim, Heilperin, *Sefer ha-Tseitsaim*, 291–292. Yehoshua-Fishel's date of birth indicated in both sources— 1895—is incorrect. See his book: Schneerson, *Die katastrophale Zeit und die heranwachsende Generation.*

37. The present study used the second edition of this book: F. Shneerson, *Sipurey hatglut hasyidyim*, 199–228.

38. Gotlib, *Sefer Ohole-shem*, 104–105; Al'fasi, *Ha-Hasidut*, 80, 226, 230; N. Fridman, *Otsar ha-rabanim*, 377; Helman, *Sefer Beit Rabi*, 249–250; I. Shneerson, *Lebn un kamf fun Yidn in tsarishn Rusland 1905–1917*, 33–35. Information on Shneur-Zalman's two sons can be found in the final chapter of this book. Moshe's only son, Pinkhas, who was born in Rechitsa in 1895, moved to Berdichev after the 1917 revolution. There, in September 1941, he was executed along with other Jews. See Testimony of Eva Khodorova, November 20, 1989, Hall of Names, Yad Vashem Museum.

39. Stampfer, *Families, Rabbis and Education*, 285–295.

40. About Turov and Samokhvalovichi see Smilovitsky, *Evrei v Turove*, 77–78. About Liuban' see *Toldot anshei shem*, 2:72; Liuban, 206–224.

41. *Hazman*, July 14, 1909, 4.

42. *Hazman*, June 20, 1905, 4; *Hazman*, November 3, 1912, 1; *Hazman*, May 26, 1913, 4.

43. Ch. Kom, *Hyaye Shlioma*, 96; Tadger, *Entsyiklopedyiah le-halutsey ha-Yishuv ve-bonav*, 16:5002–5003; Y. Kom, *Shoresh ve-'Anaf*, 142, 209–210; Frank, *Reshyimot bekatseh h'et*, 154; Abraham Grinbaum, *Rabane Berit ha-mo'atsot ben milhamot ha-'olam*, 48.

44. Ch. Kom, *Hyaye Shlioma*, 96; Tadger, *Entsyiklopedyiah le-halutsey ha-Yishuv ve-bonav*, 16:5002–5003; Y. Kom, *Shoresh ve-'Anaf*, 142, 209–210; Frank, *Reshyimot bekatseh h'et*, 154; Grinbaum, *Rabane Berit ha-mo'atsot ben milhamot ha-'olam*, 48.

45. Bershadskii, *Litovskie evrei*, 62.

46. *Trudy gubernskih komissii po evreiskomu voprosu*, vol. 1 sec. 6, 10–12, 17, 19.

47. Chubinskii, *Trudy Etnografichesko-statisticheskoi ekspeditsii v Zapadno-Russkii krai*, 7:12–13.

48. Stampfer, *Families, Rabbis and Education*, 318.

49. Aizenshtadt, *Rabaney Minsk va-hakhameha*, 23.

50. Gotlib, *Sefer Ohole-shem*, 378–379.

51. N. Fridman, *Otsar ha-rabanim*, 411; Osipova, *Khasidy "spasaia narod svoi . . . ,"*53–57, 193.

52. *Goroda Rossii v 1910 godu*, 121, 126–127; NIARB, f. 299, op. 2, d. 16713, 51; d. 17275, 251.

53. *Hamelits*, June 16, 1898, 4.

54. Dembovetskii, *Opyt opisaniia Mogilëvskoi gubernii*, 1:713.

55. Nakrich, *Yeshivat Beyt Yosef Denovrodok*, 256.

56. Ibid., 262–265.

57. LSHA, f. 567, op. 6, d. 527, 202–203 (copy in CAHJP, HM2 9790.14); NIARB, f. 458, op. 1, d. 9, 60–60a; Frank, *Reshyimot bekatseh h'et*, 153; *Trudy gubernskih komissii po evreiskomu voprosu*, vol. 1, sec. 6, 27.

58. Chubinskii, *Trudy Etnografichesko-statisticheskoi ekspeditsii v Zapadno-Russkii krai*, 7:80–81. For more details on the instructional program in heders, see Stampfer, *Families, Rabbis and Education*, 153–156.

59. CAHJP, HMF 831.46; HMF 831.49; RU, d. 181; LSHA, f. 567, op. 6, d. 527, 202–203 (copy in CAHJP, HM2 9790.14).

60. Bogrov, *Zapiski evreia*, 120.

61. Rokhlin, *Miestechko Krasnopol'e Mogilevskoi gubernii*, 23–25.

62. Stampfer, *Families, Rabbis and Education*, 169, 176–179.

63. Even Zahav, R'etshyits'a; Talmud-Tora, *D'er Fraind*. I am grateful to Isaac Len for translating these articles from Yiddish.

64. *Pamiatnaia knizhka Minskoi gubernii na 1902 god* (Minsk: Gubernskii statisticheskii komitet, 1901), 141; *Obzor Minskoi gubernii za 1913 god*, 72.

65. Frank, Reshyimot bekatseh h'et, 153. The evidence cited by Frank relates to the early nineteenth century. The lists of pupils in Rechitsa's heders for 1857 do not mention a single pupil older than ten years of age. See the list in Kaganovitch, *Rechitsa: Istoriia evreiskogo mestechka Iugo-Vostochnoi Belorussii*, 387–388.

66. *Trudy gubernskih komissii po evreiskomu voprosu*, vol. 1, sec. 6, 34–36.

67. Predpisanie nachal'nika severo-zapadnogo kraia ob izuchenii evreiami russkogo iazyka.

68. Dolbilov, *Russkii krai: Chuzhaia vera*, 560.

69. Staliūnas, *Making Russians*, 212.

70. About such a view of Russian authorities on Jewish position see Klier, *Imperial Russia's Jewish Question, 1855–1881*, 147–148, 184.

71. Dolbilov, *Russkii krai: Chuzhaia vera*, 551–559, 716–717.

72. NIARB, f. 295, op. 1, d. 2576, 7 (copy in CAHJP, HMF 831.42); *Pamiatnaia knizhka Minskoi gubernii na 1880 god*, 285.

73. *Yidn in V.S.S.R.*, 21, 45–46.

74. Ibid.

75. Calculated from *Pervaia vseobshchaia perepis' naseleniia Rossiiskoi Imperii 1897*, 109–111. On the issue that this census registered as literate mainly those who were able to read Russian, see Shabad, Gramotnost' evreev v Rossii, 756–757.

76. Kaufman, Uchatsia li evrei, 271.

77. *Rassvet*, March 3, 1880, 375.

78. Nam pishut iz Rechitsy.

79. TsDIAK, f. 442, op. 548, d. 66, 32, 35 (copy in CAHJP, HM2, d. 8357.4).

80. RGIA, f. 821, op. 8, d. 123, 93–94a, 97–98.

81. *Nedel'naia Khronika Voskhoda*, September 17, 1895, 1044; NIARB, f. 458, op. 1, d. 167, 83.

82. NIARB, f. 458, op. 1, d. 171.

83. See the reprint from this paper, *Nedel'naia Khronika Voskhoda*, October 6, 1896, 1035.

84. NIARB, f. 458, op. 1, d. 156, 1–14, 83, 167.

85. L.V., Nachal'noe obrazovanie u evreev, *Evreiskie vesti* 5 (1916), 14–15.

86. I. Berer, R'etshyits'a, *Hamelits*, January 25, 1901, 2; Even Zahav, R'etshyits'a; Frank, Haḥeder hametukan beRecitsa, 85. For more on Adler, see Tadger, *Entsyiklopedyiah le-halutsey ha-Yishuv ve-bonav*, 2:1040–1042, 3:1535.

87. Kahanovich, Homel, 199; N.O., Gomel'skoi Talmud-Tore, *Rassvet*, January 4, 1905, 45; Frank, Haḥeder hametukan beRecitsa, 85–87. On the heder in Pinsk, see Shokhat, Toldot kehilat Pinsk 1881–1941, 86–87.

88. Subsequently, Isaac Bykhovskii studied in the Kiev yeshiva. In 1912 he moved to Erets-Israel and from there set off to Italy to study medicine. After he complete his medical studies, he opened a private clinic in Petakh-Tikva and participated actively in various social organizations (he founded an ambulance service there and was the chair of its board of trustees for more than twenty years). Tadger, *Entsyiklopedyiah le-halutsey ha-Yishuv ve-bonav*, 11:3815.

89. Frank, Haḥeder hametukan beRecitsa, 93.

90. S., Retsitsa, *Hatsfirah*, January 10, 1914, 4.

91. Rokhlin, *Miestechko Krasnopol'e Mogilevskoi gubernii*, 21–22.

92. Chubinskii, *Trudy Etnografichesko-statisticheskoi ekspeditsii v Zapadno-Russkii krai*, 7:19.

93. Zelenskii, *Materialy dlia geografii i statistiki Rossii*, 2:425; *Adres-kalendar' Vilenskogo general-gubernatora na 1868 god*, 540.

94. *Pamiatnaia knizhka Vilenskogo general-gubernatorstva na 1868 god* (Vilno: Vilenskii gubernskii statisticheskii komitet, 1868), 298.

95. Jelski, Rzeczyca, 134; *Pamiatnaia knizhka Minskoi gubernii na 1880 god*, 285; Nam pishut iz Rechitsy.

96. NIARB, f. 458, op. 1, d. 188.

97. Frank, Haḥeder hametukan beRecitsa, 87.

98. Bel'skii, Zemskaia biurokratiia.

99. Andrei Samusik, Navuchal'nyia ўstanovy Rechytsy ў XIX—pachatku XX stagoddziaў, 265.

100. TsGARUz, f. 47, op. 1, d. 260, 60–61.

101. Stupakevich, *Zhenskoe obrazovanie v Belarusi*, 45. For the introduction of the *numerus clausus* in Russia and its consequences for Jews, see Nathans, *Beyond the Pale*, 262–282.

102. *Rassvet*, April 17, 1911, 29; Rechitsa, *Nedel'naia Khronika Voskhoda*, April 8, 1911, 24.

103. Samusik, Navuchal'nyia ўstanovy Rechytsy ў XIX—pachatku XX stagoddziaў, 266.

104. *Obzor Minskoi gubernii za 1913 god*, 72.

105. *Pamiatnaia knizhka Minskoi gubernii na 1915 god*, 210.

106. *Goroda Rossii v 1910 godu*, 155.

107. Samusik, Navuchal'nyia ўstanovy Rechytsy ў XIX—pachatku XX stagoddziaў, 267.

108. Zelenskii, *Materialy dlia geografii i statistiki Rossii*, 2:417.

109. *Yidn in V.S.S.R.*, 46.

110. Ginzburg, Minsk, 88.

111. Paperna, *Russko-evreiskii pis'movnik*.

112. *Bessie's Letters.*

113. Frank, Reshyimot bekatseh h'et, 153.

114. Kosher meat is meat obtained from the shechita. Since Jews ate only kosher meat, Christians within the Pale of Settlement were able to buy treyf (nonkosher meat) very cheaply. Treyf included meat from animals that had been sick as well as parts of the carcass that were accepted as kosher but from which the sciatic nerve had not been removed.

115. Natanson, Neskol'ko slov o korobochnom sbore i ob otnoshenii ego k otbyvaniu voinskoi povinnosti, 226.

116. Katsenel'bogen, Evrei Minskoi gubernii, 807.

117. Natanson, Neskol'ko slov o korobochnom sbore i ob otnoshenii ego k otbyvaniu voinskoi povinnosti, 226–227.

118. Gessen, Zabytyi obshchestvennyi deiatel'.

119. *Minskie gubernskie vedomosti* 35 (1839), 411. In 1845, Beniamin Ravikovich and his father, Mordukh, sustained major losses due to the bankruptcy of their debtors, the Butovich family, who were landowners. See *Minskie gubernskie vedomosti* 42 (1853), 470.

120. *Minskie gubernskie vedomosti* 23 (1855), 118; Kahanovich, Homel, 260. Even earlier, at the end of the 1840s, Litman Feigin's business went bankrupt. See Gessen, Zabytyi obshchestvennyi deiatel'.

121. *Minskie gubernskie vedomosti* 30 (1885), 3.

122. NIARB, f. 136, op. 1, d. 15697; d. 20994; d. 24017; d. 25206; d. 25591.

123. Ibid., d. 10937.

124. NIARB, f. 295, op. 1, d. 237, 158–159.

125. *Minskie gubernskie vedomosti* 51 (1855), 279.

126. *Hamelits,* July 10, 1895, 3.

127. NIARB, f. 295, op. 1, d. 6482. 3–19a. I am grateful to Mikhael Passof for this document.

128. RGIA, f. 821, op. 8, d. 261, 40a–41ob (copy in CAHJP, HM2 7776.2).

129. NIARB, f. 295, op. 1, d. 6482, 3–19a.

130. *Pamiatnaia knizhka Minskoi gubernii na 1902 god,* 134; *Ustav Rechickogo evreiskogo obshchestva podaianiia pomoshchi i posobiia bednym; Even Zahav;* Rokhlin, *Miestechko Krasnopol'e Mogilevskoi gubernii,* 82; *Otchiot Rechitskogo evreiskogo obshchestva podaianiia pomoshchi i posobiia bednym za 1914–1915 gody.*

131. Chaim Shlomo Mogilevskii, R'etsyits'a, *Hatsfirah,* November 19, 1897, 1272; Ish Yehudi, M'ir R'etsyits'a, *Hatsfirah,* December 2, 1900, 953; R'etsyits'a, *Hatsfirah,* January 10, 1900, 1251; *Even Zahav.*

132. Abramenko, Iz istorii zdravokhraneniia Rechitskogo uezda, 124; *Obzor Minskoi gubernii za 1913 god,* 53.

133. *Rassvet,* January 30, 1880, 179.

134. RGIA, f. 821, op. 8, d. 152, 45a–46 (copy in CAHJP, HM2 7778).

135. *Rassvet,* February 15, 1913, 33.

136. Nelson, Rechitsa, *Novyi Voskhod,* March 13, 1915, 66–67; V Rechitse, *Rassvet,* April 5, 1915, 38.

137. Nelson, Rechitsa.

138. Rechitsa, *Delo pomoshchi*, February 25, 1917, 33–35; *Evreiskaia nedelia*, June 21, 1915, 31.

139. Rechitsa, *Delo pomoshchi*, 33–35.

140. RGIA, f. 1565, op. 1, d. 85, 22; Kaganovitch, *Rechitsa*, 204, appendix 5.

141. Barsella, Bor'ba za iskhod v 20-kh gg. nashego veka, 69–70; Barsella, Polgoda sredi bukharskikh evreev, 58.

142. Y. Kom, *Shoresh ve-'Anaf*, 209–210.

143. Kaganovitch, *Rechitsa*, 206; Tadger, *Entsyiklopedyiah le-halutsey ha-Yishuv ve-bonav*, 2:659; letter from Kherut Shlomov, Janary 25, 2001.

144. Karol' and Linman, *Sefer Bet ha-kevarot ha-yashan be-Tel Aviv*, 245.

145. Slonim, 138–139; Tadger, *Entsyiklopedyiah le-halutsey ha-Yishuv ve-bonav*, 4:1808–1809; Frank, Haḥeder hametukan beRecitsa, 96.

CHAPTER 6. BETWEEN REVOLUTION AND WAR, 1917–1941

1. *Rassvet*, February 13, 1917, 29–30; August 20, 1917, 30; Ginzburg, Rechitsa; *Pamiats'*, 2:73–74.

2. Zeltser, *Evrei sovetskoi provintsii*, 31.

3. *Belorussiia v period podgotovki sotsialisticheskoi revoliutsii (fevral'-oktiabr' 1917 g.)*, 1:421; Ginzburg, Rechitsa.

4. Ginzburg, Rechitsa.

5. Rechitsa, *Rassvet*, January 24, 1918, 27.

6. *Dokumenty i materialy po istorii Belorussii*, 4:285–286; Umetskii, *Rechitsa*, 22–23; *Zbor pomnikau historyi i kul'tury Belarusi*, 313.

7. Umetskii, *Rechitsa*, 26; *Pamiats'*, 2:93; letter from Fridrikh Valler, June 17, 2001.

8. Umetskii, *Rechitsa*, 32.

9. *Pamiats'*, 2:96, 101; *Revoliutsionnye komitety BSSR*, 133–34; *Zbor pomnikau historyi i kul'tury Belarusi*, 27; Umetskii, *Rechitsa*, 31. A memorial to victims of the uprising has been erected on Sovietskaia Street.

10. GAOOGO, f. 52, op. 1, d. 30, 3, 39. I am obliged to Dmitry Tolochko (Gomel) for providing this material.

11. Kholostiakov, *Vechnyi ogon'*, 12–13; Umetskii, *Rechitsa*, 34–35; Drogovoz, *Kreposti na kolësakh*, 147–148.

12. YVA, O33/6606 (diary of Litman Turovskii), 136–137.

13. *Evreiskie pogromy 1918–1921 gg.*, 26, 55.

14. Y. Kom, *Shoresh ve-'Anaf*, 212.

15. Umetskii, *Rechitsa*, 36.

16. Interview by Penny Rubinoff with her father, David Rubinoff, November 16, 2003. I am obliged to her for kindly allowing me to use this interview.

17. Snyder, *Reconstruction of Nations*, 64, 68.

18. Y. Kom, *Shoresh ve-'Anaf*, 15–16.

19. Ibid.

20. CAHJP, HM2 9499.9; *Materialy ob antievreiskikh pogromakh*, 1:73–74; Ioffe and Mel'tser, *Dzhoint v Belarusi*, 10–14; Pichukov and Starovoitov, *Gomel'shchina mnogonatsional'naia*, 151–152.

21. Interview with Iosif Kazovskii, September 23, 2000; letter from Fridrikh Valler, June 17, 2001. After the end of World War I, Zakhar Malinkovich studied at the Sverdlov Industrial Academy in the same class as Stalin's wife, Nadezhda Allilueva. Stalin himself lectured to this group of students. In later years Malinkovich managed a salt mine in Orenburg Province; worked in the People's Commissariat of Forest Industry; and later headed the Chief Directorate of Paper and Cellulose Industry. In 1938 he arrived in Rechitsa with a driver and car, an M-1 ("Emka") designated for his use; the car was awaiting him on the station platform. For Jewish Rechitsa this was a notable event. In 1942 Malinkovich, then commissar of a rifle battalion, found himself surrounded, and he shot himself to avoid being taken prisoner by the Germans.

22. GAOOGO, f. 52, op. 1, d. 13, 39.

23. Ibid.

24. Danilov, Vospominaniia o podnevol'noi sluzhbe u bol'shevikov, 209.

25. Ibid., 207–208.

26. Interview with Maria Rubinchik, June 15, 2004.

27. Raiskii and Gershanok, Evrei Gomelia v period NEPa, 79. In 1924, when Mikhailovskii was head of the Gomel Province Criminal Investigation Section, he was tracked down by bandits and brutally murdered.

28. Danilov, Vospominaniia o podnevol'noi sluzhbe u bol'shevikov, 209.

29. CAHJP, HM2 9499.9; Raiskii and Gershanok, Evrei Gomelia v period NEPa, 79.

30. Y. Kom, *Derekh vedrakhim*, 113.

31. Ibid., 109–110.

32. Ibid., 111–113; *My nachinali eshchë v Rossii*, 327–328.

33. Y. Kom, *Derekh vedrakhim*, 111–113.

34. *My nachinali eshchë v Rossii*, 327. In 1923, Noakh Gantman himself left for Erets-Israel, where he became one of the founders and leaders of the Ramat ha-Sharon settlement. See Tadger, *Entsyiklopedyiah le-halutsey ha-Yishuv ve-bonav*, 14:4507.

35. Pines, Stranichka istorii; Kostyrchenko, *Tainaia politika Stalina*, 75.

36. *My nachinali eshcië v Rossii*, 51–59, 286.

37. *Ha-Shomer ha-tsair*, no. 1 (July 1926), 22–23; Minova, Problema antisemitizma v mezhnatsional'nykh otnosheniiakh na Gomel'shchine v 20–30-e gody XX veka, 157; Raiskii, *Sud'by liudskie*, 11–12.

38. Frank, Haḥeder hametukan beRecitsa, 91.

39. Raiskii, *Sud'by liudskie*, 11–12.

40. *Pamiats'*, 2:129.

41. Y. Kom, *Derekh vedrakhim*, 111.

42. Ibid., 110.

43. Umetskii, *Rechitsa*, 30.

44. Interview with Iosif Kazovskii, September 23, 2000.

45. *Bund v Belorussii 1897–1921*, 511; Altshuler, *Ha-Yevsektsiyah bi-Brit-ha-Mo'etsot*, 82–87; Gelbard, *Sofo shel'o ktḥyilato*, 153–164.

46. AKGBGO, f. 1, d. 18932, 215–216. I am grateful to Leonid Smilovitsky for making this document available.

47. El', Pis'mo iz Moskvy, 11; Baron, *Russian Jews under Tsars and Soviets*, 289; Kostyr-chenko, *Tainaia politika Stalina*, 75–76.

48. *Pamiats'*, 1:129.

49. Ibid.; Umetskii, *Rechitsa*, 30; Smilovitsky, *Katastrofa evreev v Belorissii*, 263.

50. Pushkin, Natsiianal'nyia menshastsi ў gramadska-palitychnym i kul'turnym zhytstsi Rechytskaga raëna 20-kh gg., 119.

51. *Pamiats'*, 2:129.

52. On this purge, see Altshuler, *Ha-Yevsektsiyah bi-Brit-ha-Mo'etsot*, 108–110.

53. On the mass expulsion from the party of Jews in Mozyr in 1921, see Altshuler, *Ha-Yevsektsiyah bi-Brit-ha-Mo'etsot*, 113.

54. Materials of the Rechitsa Museum of History and Regional Studies. In 1921 the secretary of the RKSM (Russian Communist Union of Youth) cell of the Rechitsa Uezd printing plant, Yakov Lipov, and two other young communists were sent to the submarine warfare school of the Red Navy as part of the military call-up.

55. Altshuler, *Ha-Yevsektsiyah bi-Brit-ha-Mo'etsot*, 177.

56. *Materialy po evreiskoi demografii i ekonomike*, 4:28.

57. Letter from Fridrikh Valler, June 17, 2001; Barsella, Bor'ba za iskhod v 20-kh gg. nashego veka, 67; Barsella, Polgoda sredi bukharskikh evreev, 57–58.

58. M. Rudoi, Di 'Ersht'e zytsung fun-nyi'ym r'at, *D'er 'Emes*, February 5, 1926, 4.

59. Ibid.

60. GAOOGO, f. 451, op. 1, d. 27, 1–2. This situation was typical not only of Rechitsa. For additional examples of voting for "our" candidates in other Belorussian villages, see Zeltser, *Evrei sovetskoi provintsii*, 216.

61. Rudoi, Di 'Ersht'e zytsung fun-nyi'ym r'at.

62. Starovoitov, Osobennosti osushchestvleniia politiki belorusizatsii v Rechitskom regione,156.

63. *Zbor pomnikau historyi i kul'tury Belarusi*, 27.

64. Starovoitov, Osobennosti osushchestvleniia politiki belorusizatsii v Rechitskom regione, 157.

65. Letter from Fridrikh Valler, June 17, 2001.

66. Pichukov and Starovoitov, *Gomel'shchina mnogonatsional'naia*, 182.

67. *Biulleten' gomel'skogo gubernskogo statisticheskogo biuro*, 5/6:3–4, 113. More than likely these results were conditioned by the lack of any explanation of the issues to the population or to a slanted question about native language on the query.

68. Starovoitov, Osobennosti osushchestvleniia politiki belorusizatsii v Rechitskom regione, 160–164.

69. Altshuler, *Ha-Yevsektsiyah bi-Brit-ha-Mo'etsot, 1918–1930*, 322–323.

70. GAOOGO, f. 451, op. 1a, d. 55, 19; d. 84, 59–60; d. 95, 15; Y. K'otyk, 'Aunz'er yyidy-ish'e g'eryikht-k'am'er, *Oktiabr*, June 18, 1927, 4.

71. Only one directive, from 1817, existed in Russian legislation that permitted the conversion of a gentile to Judaism. It concerned only Kalmyk women who had been sold against their will and brought into to Russia from abroad. Only they were allowed to convert to Judaism before being married to Jews in Siberia. See RGIA, f. 1151, op. 1, d. 20, 18. We

have no information about the number of Kalmyk women who were converted to Judiasm in this way; however, the very existence of such a directive suggests that these were not isolated occurrences.

72. Interview with Maria Rubinchik, June 15, 2004. Rabbi Chaim-Shlioma Kom expressed his indignation over mixed marriages in Rechitsa in a letter to his son in Erets-Israel in 1924. Y. Kom, *Shoresh ve-'Anaf,* 218.

73. *Materialy po evreiskoi demografii i ekonomike,* 4:21.

74. YVA, M33, d. 477, 8; letter from Pesia Royhavskii, January 14, 2001; interview with Tamara Kuz'minich, August 7, 2005 (I am obliged to Alla Shkop for this source).

75. GAOOGO, f. 451, op. 1, d. 27, 1–2.

76. Ibid.

77. Ibid.

78. Ibid., 29–30.

79. After she made her report, the Belorussian teacher Makhnach proposed to those present that speeches be made in a commonly understood language, Russian; he was subsequently removed from his post for Russian chauvinism. See Kandybovich, *Razgrom natsyianal'naga rukhu ў Belarusi.* There were still other cases of Jews putting the legal equality of Yiddish on the back burner in Belorussia, for instance, at the Minshvei factory in Minsk. Bemporad, Yiddish Experiment in Soviet Minsk, 95–96.

80. GAOOGO, f. 451, op. 1, d. 84, 59–60.

81. Starovoitov, Osobennosti osushchestvleniia politiki belorusizatsii v Rechitskom regione, 164–165; Bemporad, Yiddish Experiment in Soviet Minsk, 95.

82. On statistics for 1929, see Pushkin, Natsiianal'nyia menshastsi ў gramadska-palitychnym i kul'turnym zhytstsi Rechytskaga raëna 20-kh gg., 119.

83. Ibid.

84. *Prakticheskoe razreshenie natsional'nogo voprosa v BSSR,* 1:32.

85. Abramenko, Iz istorii zdravokhraneniia Rechitskogo uezda, 125.

86. Interview with Sveta Maskalik, December 21, 2006; *Belarus' v pervye mesiatsy Velikoi Otechestvennoi voiny, 22 iiunia—avgust 1941 g.,* 346.

87. Cited from Kostyrchenko, *Tainaia politika Stalina,* 88.

88. Zinger, Evreiskaia zhenshchina v narodnom khoziaistve Belorusskoi i Ukrainskoi SSR, 30.

89. Calculated in Binshtok, Evrei v Gomel'skoi oblasti, 83.

90. *Belorussiia v period podgotovki sotsialisticheskoi revoliutsii,* 1:509, 528–529, 616–617; *Dokumenty i materialy po istorii Belorussii,* 4:50, 137–139.

91. Savinskaia and Aleinikova, Rechitsa v 20-e gg. XX veka, 142, 144.

92. Rechitsa, *D'er 'Emes,* February 22, 1923, 4.

93. Y. Kom, *Derekh vedrakhim,* 110–111.

94. YVA, O33/6606 (diary of Litman Turovskii), 129.

95. Fox, *People of Steppes,* 77.

96. Interview with Maria Rubinchik, January 1, 2001; Umetskii, *Rechitsa,* 44. Eventov's son immigrated to Israel, where he became a professor. On the five hotels that existed in the town in 1922, see Savinskaia and Aleinikova, Rechitsa v 20-e gg. XX veka, 142–143.

97. Savinskaia and Aleinikova, Rechitsa v 20-e gg. XX veka, 143.

98. Calculated from Savinskaia and Aleinikova, Rechitsa v 20-e gg. XX veka, 142–143. That the tradesmen were predominantly Jewish follows from the 1928 report of Alexander Khatskevich showing that they constituted 89.2 percent within the BSSR. See Khatskevich, Vyniki raboty siarod natsyianal'nykh menshas'tsiai ỹ BSSR (1928), 83.

99. Savinskaia and Aleinikova, Rechitsa v 20-e gg. XX veka, 142–143.

100. Ibid. At the same time, millers can only be arbitrarily called tradesmen since part of their activity is entrepreneurial.

101. Ibid.

102. Zinger, Evreiskoe naselenie v Sovetskom Soiuze, 59–60.

103. Ibid.

104. M. Tsinberg, G'elebt 'ain kh'eshben-g'esht'arben 'ain r'ekh'enung, D'er 'Emes, August 21, 1925, 4; Savinskaia and Aleinikova, Rechitsa v 20-e gg. XX veka, 147.

105. Savinskaia and Aleinikova, Rechitsa v 20-e gg. XX veka, 147–148.

106. Zeltser, Evrei sovetskoi provintsii: Vitebsk i mestechki, 1917–1941, 81.

107. Biulleten' gomel'skogo gubernskogo statisticheskogo biuro, 5/6:32.

108. Prakticheskoe razreshenie natsional'nogo voprosa v BSSR, 1:21.

109. Cited by Danilov, Vospominaniia o podnevol'noi sluzhbe u bol'shevikov, 228–229.

110. Ibid.

111. Zeltser, Evrei sovetskoi provintsii: Vitebsk i mestechki, 1917–1941, 80–81.

112. Interview with Maria Rubinchik, January 1, 2001.

113. Zinger, Evreiskoe naselenie v Sovetskom Soiuze, 3.

114. Savinskaia and Aleinikova, Rechitsa v 20-e gg. XX veka, 148.

115. Binshtok, Evrei v Gomel'skoi oblasti, 83–84.

116. Savinskaia and Aleinikova, Rechitsa v 20-e gg. XX veka, 149.

117. Kostyrchenko, Tainaia politika Stalina, 101.

118. Evreiskii krest'ianin, 2:236; Materialy po evreiskoi demografii i ekonomike, 4:25.

119. Rechitsa, Tribuna evreiskoi sovetskoi obshchestvennosti 4–5 (1927), 36; Materialy po evreiskoi demografii i ekonomike, 4:25. Over the second half of the 1920s, the membership of the regional organization of OZET expanded from 80 to 230 people. The Rechitsa organization was divided into five cells along territorial lines. See Bialyi, OZET v Rechitse.

120. Pëtr Germagenovich Smidovich, a native of Rogachev in Gomel Province and an aristocrat by origins, was from 1923 to 1935 the chairman of the Committee for Disposition of Land to Jewish Workers (KomZET), under the Presidium of the Soviet of Nationalities of the USSR. At the same time, he held senior administrative positions in the All-Russian Central Executive Committee of the USSR.

121. Surpina, Chto ia znaiu i pomniu.

122. Materialy po evreiskoi demografii i ekonomike, 4:25.

123. Interview with Sonia Kaganovich, May 5, 2003. These families managed to leave the town before it was occupied by the Germans. After the war they returned to the former Jewish kolkhoz that had now lost its ethnoreligious identity.

124. Yidn in V.S.S.R., 132–133. I am obliged to Aviv Shashar-Izakson for help in translating this text from Yiddish.

125. A.G., V Sovetskoi Rossii, 12. On the anti-kulak campaign on Jewish collective farms, see also L.B., Kollektivizatsiia i evrei, Rassvet, July 22, 1930, 14–15.

126. Altshuler, Soviet Jewry, 31–34.

127. Birobidzhan, Tribuna evreiskoi sovetskoi obshchestvennosti 10–11 (1932), 33; Rechitsa, Tribuna evreiskoi sovetskoi obshchestvennosti 8 (1932), 11.

128. Interview with Raisa Kofman, November 1, 2004.

129. Rechitsa, Tribuna evreiskoi sovetskoi obshchestvennosti 16 (1931), 8.

130. On the shortage of bread in Gomel Raion in 1927 and 1937, see: Pamiat': Gomel', 1:336–337.

131. Osokina, Zoloto dlia industrializatsii, 546–548.

132. Even in the small Ukrainian shtetls of Mezherov and Dashov, 17 percent of families received money transfers in 1928 (Aizkis, Sanitarno-bytovoe obsluzhivanie evreiskogo mestechka, 90). It is likely that the people of Rechitsa received more assistance since, on the one hand, in a town people were better informed and this influenced the level of emigration, and on the other hand, those who came from shtetls and had become dispersed among American cities had fewer opportunities to set up charitable organizations to help their countrymen than did those who came from midsized and large places. The Rechitsa association of expatriates in Chicago is discussed in chap. 4. It is possible that there were similar organizations in other American cities as well.

133. Aleinikova and Savinskaia, Sotsial'no-ekonomicheskoe razvitie Rechitsy v 1930-e gody, 333.

134. Regarding the electrical generation station, see Pamiats', 2:128. On the clothing factory, see Rechitsa, D'er 'Emes.

135. Yidn in V.S.S.R., 125; Zbor pomnikau historyi i kul'tury Belarusi, 313; Umetskii, Rechitsa, 40.

136. Promyshlennost' BSSR v diagramakh i tablitsakh, 15.

137. Aleinikova and Savinskaia, Sotsial'no-ekonomicheskoe razvitie Rechitsy v 1930-e gody, 332; letter from Fridrikh Valler, June 17, 2001; Dobrushkin, Istoriia odnoi sem'i), 2 (I am obliged to Asia Astoshinskaia for this source).

138. Aleinikova and Savinskaia, Sotsial'no-ekonomicheskoe razvitie Rechitsy v 1930-e gody, 332.

139. Letter from Maria Rubinchik, April 12, 2001.

140. Dobrushkin, Istoriia odnoi sem'i, 2.

141. Aleinikova and Savinskaia, Sotsial'no-ekonomicheskoe razvitie Rechitsy v 1930-e gody, 332.

142. ZGAR, f. 342, op. 1, d. 4, 130. I am obliged to Leonid Smilovitsky for copies of materials from this archive.

143. Khatskevich, Vyniki raboty na praviadzen'i belarusizatsyi ў BSSR (1927), 64.

144. Ibid.

145. Ibid., 82.

146. Prakticheskoe razreshenie natsional'nogo voprosa v BSSR, 1:13.

147. Baron, Russian Jews under Tsars and Soviets, 217.

148. Calculated from questionnaires completed by Rechitsa homeowners (1941), GARF, f. 7021, op. 85, d. 247–251, 263 (copy in YVA, JM23638–23639).

149. Ibid.

150. Ibid.

151. Calculated from the questionnaires of Rechitsa homeowners (1941), GARF, f. 7021, op. 85, d. 247–257, 263 (copy in YVA, JM23638–23639).

152. Ibid.

153. Savinskaia and Aleinikova, Rechitsa v 20-e gg. XX veka, 141.

154. Jewish occupancy rate calculated by the list and the questionnaires of Rechitsa homeowners for 1941, GARF, f. 7021, op. 85. d. 247–51, 263 (copy in YVA, JM23638–23639).

155. Calculated from the sources cited in the preceding note. Apart from those streets mentioned in the text, several others were also given new, standardized names: Andreevskaia became Lunacharskaia; First Kladbishchenskaia, Aviatsionnaia; Mikhailovskaia, Karl Marx; Semenovskaia, Chapaeva. After the war Kooperativnaia Street was again renamed, becoming Koneva Street, in honor of the marshal who had served in Rechitsa in the 1930s. Only four streets kept their prerevolutionary names: Naberezhnaia, Vygonnaia, Lugovaia, and Vokzalnaia (the latter two were renamed only in 1983). See interview with Maria Rubinchik, June 15, 2004; letter from Avraam Dovzhik, September 28, 2001.

156. Aleinikova and Savinskaia, Sotsial'no-ekonomicheskoe razvitie Rechitsy v 1930-e gody, 333.

157. Calculated from NARB, f. 295, op. 1, d. 1405, 97, 99 (copy in CAHJP, HMF 831.35) and consideration of the data on migration from Rechitsa from 1920 to 1926 (*Yidn in V.S.S.R.*, 46).

158. YVA, O33/6606, 124–126.

159. Zinger, *Evreiskoe naselenie v Sovetskom Soiuze*, 26.

160. Calculated from *Yidn in V.S.S.R.*, 46.

161. Abramenko, *Zdravoohranenie BSSR—stanovlenie sovetskoi sistemy*, 158.

162. Ibid., 153.

163. *Biulleten' gomel'skogo gubernskogo statisticheskogo biuro*, 1:15.

164. Ibid., 1:13.

165. *Kniga pogromov*, 674.

166. *Biulleten' gomel'skogo gubernskogo statisticheskogo biuro*, 1:15.

167. Ibid., 1:21.

168. Dobrushkin, *Istoriia odnoi sem'i*, 2. Typhus was responsible for 800,000 deaths across the country in 1920. See *Naselenie Rossii v XX veke*, 102.

169. *Biulleten' gomel'skogo gubernskogo statisticheskogo biuro*, 1:21.

170. Ibid., 1:13.

171. Pichukov and Starovoitov, *Gomel'shchina mnogonatsional'naia*, 149–150.

172. Ibid., 195.

173. *Yidn in V.S.S.R.*, 46.

174. Zinger, *Evreiskoe naselenie v Sovetskom Soiuze*, 21.

175. Appendix 7 in Kaganovitch, *Rechitsa: Istoriia evreiskogo mestechka Iugo-Vostochnoi Belorussii*, 392–397.

176. Bezhenstvo i emigratsiia, *Rassvet*, January 14, 1923, 16.

177. Raiskii and Gershanok, Evrei Gomelia v period NEPa, 73–74. On the emigration of young people from Rechitsa in the mid-1920s (including Liubov' Farbman and El'iakim Rubinshtein), see interview with Maria Rubinchik, March 29, 2002.

178. *My nachinali eshchë v Rossii*, 387–391.

179. Ibid., 391–393.

180. Pichukov and Starovoitov, *Gomel'shchina mnogonatsional'naia*, 34, 149–150.

181. Ibid., 195.

182. *Yidn in V.S.S.R.*, 46.

183. Aleksandrov, Di yyidish'e b'ap'elk'erong 'in dyi sht'et 'un sht'etl'ekh fun Vyyasrus-land, 355–356.

184. Zinger, *Evreiskoe naselenie v Sovetskom Soiuze*, 10.

185. Vsesoiuznaia perepis' naseleniia 1939 goda, Gomel'skaia oblast', CAHJP, RU537.22, table 27.

186. Abramenko, *Zdravoohranenie BSSR—stanovlenie sovetskoi sistemy*, 161.

187. Ibid.

188. On the death rate in the USSR in these years, see Isupov, *Demograficheskie katastrofy i krizisy v Rossii v pervoi polovine XX veka*, 109–114, 126–127.

189. About Belorussians' traditional predilection for alcohol, see Dovnar-Zapol'ski, *Issledovaniia i stat'i*, 278.

190. On the number of married persons by age and ethnicity, see Vsesoiuznaia perepis' naseleniia 1939 goda, Gomelskaia oblast', CAHJP, RU537.22, table 9. For statistics on marriages by religious affiliation, see Leshchinskii, Dvizhenie evreiskogo naseleniia v Rossii, 144.

191. Khatskevich, Vyniki raboty siarod natsyianal'nykh menshas'tsiai ў BSSR (1928), 89; Pichukov and Starovoitov, 101.

192. For Ukrainian population data, see Vsesoiuznaia perepis' naseleniia 1939 goda, Gomel'skaia oblast', CAHJP, RU537.22, table 27. Regarding impact of the famine of 1933–1934, see interview with Maria Rubinchik, October 23, 2006. Many of these refugees immediately died of exhaustion and malnutrition in Rechitsa and surrounding villages, though a number of them managed to survive. On the flight of Ukrainians from Ukraine to Belorussia generally, see *Naselenie Rossii v XX veke*, 1:266.

193. Regarding the refugees' employment in the match factory, see Tolochko, Faktor ob'edineniia Belarusi osen'iu 1939 g. v istorii Rechitskogo raiona, 172. The assumption about those sent to labor camps or moving elsewhere is based on data for Gomel Oblast taken from the internal memorandum of Lavrentii Tsanava. See Ioffe and Selemenev, Jewish Refugees from Poland in Belorussia.

194. The population of Rogachev in 1913 was indicated earlier; for the 1939 figures see Vsesoiuznaia perepis' naseleniia 1939 goda, Gomel'skaia oblast', CAHJP, RU537.22, table 27.

195. Krivova, Vlast' i tserkov' v 1922–1925 gg.

196. Minova, *Problema antisemitizma v mezhnatsional'nykh otnosheniiakh na Gom-el'shchine v 20–30-e gody XX veka*, 154, with reference to GAOOGO, f. 2, op. 1, d. 154, 11a.

197. *Archivy Kremlia*, 1:401.

198. Altshuler, *Ha-Yevsektsiyah bi-Brit-ha-Mo'etsot*, 299–300.

199. GAOOGO, f. 451, op. 1, d. 27, 27–28.

200. Tsinberg, G'elebt 'ain kh'eshben-g'esht'arben 'ain r'ekh'enung; M. Tsinberg, Myit 'ayin fus 'af ts'en 'y'aryiden, *D'er 'Emes*, May 16, 1926, 3.

201. *Oktiabr*, March 9, 1928, 3. I am obliged to Arkadii Zeltser for this material and for his translation.

202. For more details on this campaign, see Zeltser, *Evrei sovetskoi provintsii*, 253–260.

203. NARB, f. 4, op. 10, d. 117, 32; f. 750, op. 1, d. 567, 11; Tsinberg, G'elebt 'ain kh'eshben-g'esht'arben 'ain r'ekh'enung.

204. N'at'e, 'Af v'em'en h'at 'a vyrkung r'etshyts'er kl'eryk'al, *Oktiabr*, June 1, 1929, 3.

205. NARB, f. 6, op. 1, d. 2209, 11; Minova, *Problema antisemitizma v mezhnatsion-al'nykh otnosheniiakh na Gomel'shchine v 20–30-e gody XX veka*, 155.

206. N'at'e, 'Af v'em'en h'at 'a vyrkung r'etshyts'er kl'eryk'al.

207. Pinkes, Der vyib'ersh'er m'agyd 'ain R'etshyts'e, *Oktiabr*, April 15, 1927, 2.

208. Tsinberg, G'elebt 'ain kh'eshben-g'esht'arben 'ain r'ekh'enung.

209. Altshuler, *Ha-Yevsektsiyah bi-Brit-ha-Mo'etsot*, 303.

210. Zeltser, *Evrei sovetskoi provintsii*, 264.

211. Letter from Fridrikh Valler, June 17, 2001.

212. Iodfat, *M'eamad hdat hyhudit bebryt-hamu'etsot vemilhamah bah beshnot hash-loshym*, 36.

213. N'at'e, 'Af v'em'en h'at 'a vyrkung r'etshyts'er kl'eryk'al.

214. Y. Kom, *Shoresh ve-'Anaf*, 224, 230; Y. Kom, *Derekh vedrakhim*, 110–111.

215. Y. Kom, *Shoresh ve-'Anaf*, 217.

216. Ibid., 218.

217. *Biulleten' gomel'skogo gubernskogo statisticheskogo biuro*, 5/6:49.

218. Y. Kom, *Shoresh ve-'Anaf*, 210–211; Grinbaum, *Rabane Berit ha-mo'atsot ben mil-hamot ha-'olam*, 48.

219. Beizer, and Karasev, Debate about a Congress of Jewish Religious Communities, 168–171.

220. Ibid., 145–146.

221. Kostyrchenko, *Tainaia politika Stalina*, 68.

222. Interview by Penny Rubinoff with her father, David Rubinoff, November 16, 2003. The renaming of the street in 1973, for the thirtieth anniversary of the liberation of the town, was done in tribute to Marshal I. S. Konev, who lived here in 1935–1936, when he commanded the Thirty-Seventh Rifle Division headquartered in Rechitsa.

223. V Rossii i na Ukraine, *Rassvet*, September 29, 1922, 23–24.

224. Y. Kom, *Shoresh ve-'Anaf*, 217.

225. Volfson, *Suchasnaia religiinas'ts'*, 94.

226. Ibid., 99.

227. N'at'e, 'Af v'em'en h'at 'a vyrkung r'etshyts'er kl'eryk'al.

228. Interview with Maria Rubinchik, January 1, 2001; Umetskii, *Rechitsa*, 44.

229. Letter from Sara Ber and Mikhail Balte, April 05, 2001; interviews with Anna and Iakov Khavin, October 14, 2000; with Iosif Kazovskii, September 23, 2000; with Maria Rubinchik, March 2, 2002; and with Leonid Belugin, February 8, 2006.

230. Interview with Maria Rubinchik, March 2, 2002; Tsinberg, Myit 'ayin fus 'af ts'en 'y'aryiden; Smilovitsky, *Katastrofa evreev v Belorussii*, 272.

231. ZGAR, f. 342, op. 1, d. 6, 258. After its steeple had been taken down, the Catholic church was used as a warehouse. As for the Orthodox cathedral, in 1941 the church council, taking advantage of German occupation of the town, reclaimed the building as a church and maintained it until 1948. For more detail on this, see chap. 8.

232. *Yidn in V.S.S.R.*, 9.

233. Zinger, Rodnoi iazyk evreiskogo naseleniia SSSR, 9.

234. Vsesoiuznaia perepis' naseleniia 1939, Gomel'skaia oblast', CAHJP, RU537.22, table 13.

235. Y. Kom, *Derekh vedrakhim*, 111.

236. M. Lyiz'ers, R'etsh'yts'e, *D'er 'Emes*, July 21, 1923, 4.

237. Zeliankova, Dasiagnenni i prablemy shkol'nai spravy ў Rechytskim pavetse, 136.

238. *Biulleten' gomel'skogo gubernskogo statisticheskogo biuro*, 4:2.

239. Ibid.

240. *Biulleten' gomel'skogo gubernskogo statisticheskogo biuro*, 5/6:17, 120; *Materialy po evreiskoi demografii i ekonomike*, vol. 3, table 4.

241. Lyiz'ers, R'etsh'yts'e.

242. Kofman and Gorivodskii, R'etshyts'e, *Oktiabr*, August 14, 1935, 3.

243. *Yidn in V.S.S.R.*, 46.

244. Zeltser, *Evrei sovetskoi provintsii*, 259–260.

245. Altshuler, *Ha-Yevsektsiyah bi-Brit-ha-Mo'etsot*, 326.

246. Zeltser, *Evrei sovetskoi provintsii*, 259–260.

247. Interviews with Ania and Iakov Khavin, October 14, 2000; with Iosif Kazovskii, September 23, 2000; with Maria Rubinchik, August 25, 2001, and March 2, 2002.

248. Halevy, *Jewish Schools under Czarism and Communism*, 176.

249. See the information from the Jewish Section of the People's Commissariat of Education on the Jewish school in Rechitsa in 1925: TsGAOR of Ukraine, f. 166, op. 6, d. 829, 23 (copy in CAHJP, HM2 7311). On aid from Joint, see Ioffe and Mel'tser, *Dzhoint v Belarusi*, 6, 59, 64.

250. GAOOGO, f. 451, op. 1a, d. 95, 15.

251. This is attested by the resolution of the session of the Jewish Bureau in Rechitsa in 1928: GAOOGO, f. 451, op. 1, d. 84, 59–60.

252. Kofman and Gorivodskii, R'etshyts'e, *Oktiabr*, August 14, 1935, 3; interview with Maria Rubinchik, August 25, 2001; letter from Lazar Dvorkin, June 28, 2001; Smilovitsky, *Katastrofa evreev v Belorussii*, 263. Zalman Litmanovich Vilenskii (1859–1941), as noted earlier, was a teacher in the Reformed heder. At the end of 1941, he was executed by the Nazis in Rechitsa. See YVA, JM20006, 22. In general it was quite common to find former

teachers from the Reformed heders teaching Yiddish in Soviet schools. See Altshuler, *Ha-Yevsektsiyah bi-Brit-ha-Mo'etsot*, 318.

253. Kofman and Gorivodskii, R'etshyts'e, *Oktiabr*, August 14, 1935, 3.

254. Iatskevich, Adukatsyia natsyianal'nykh menshastsei na Belarusi ў 1920–1990 gg.; Selemenev and Zeltser, Liquidation of Yiddish Schools, 77–78. In the field of education the authorities were pragmatic not only in their linguistic policy but also in the question of staffing. In Kazakhstan in 1938, for example, more than 1,500 teachers were dismissed after being accused of "wrecking" activity (some of them were arrested), of "ambiguous social origins," and of being related to "enemies of the people." When the People's Commissariat of Education of the republic then faced a drastic shortage of teachers, many of these cases were reexamined. See *Istoriia Kazakhstana*, 176–180.

255. Smilovitsky, *Katastrofa evreev v Belorussii*, 263; letter from Lazar Dvorkin, June 7, 2001; letter from Sara Ber and Mikhail Balte, April 5, 2001.

256. Letter from Raisa Ioffe, June 20, 1998.

257. *Biulleten' gomel'skogo gubernskogo statisticheskogo biuro*, 4:4; *Zbor pomnikau historyi i kul'tury Belarusi*, 313.

258. Umetskii, *Rechitsa*, 42. In 1936 Tikhon Kiselev graduated from this technical-vocational school. From 1956 to 1959 he held the post of second secretary, and from 1980 until his death in 1983 of first secretary, of the Central Committee of the Communist Party of Belorussia. From 1959 to 1978 he was chairman of the Council of Ministers of the BSSR.

259. *Pamiats'*, 2:135.

260. Smilovitsky, Voskresnaia shkola v Rechitse, 172.

261. Smilovitsky, *Katastrofa evreev v Belorussii*, 263.

262. Kostyrchenko, *Tainaia politika Stalina*, 191.

263. Calculated from *Yidn in V.S.S.R.*, 46.

264. Zinger, Gramotnost' evreiskogo naseleniia SSSR, 6.

265. Vsesoiuznaia perepis' Naselenie 1939 goda, Gomel'skaia oblast', CAHJP, RU537.22, table 14.

266. Ibid., table 15.

267. Antsevitsh, H. R'etshyits'er p'olit-shulen, *Oktiabr*, January 9, 1927, 5; H. Shapiro, 'Unz'er p'olit-shul', *Oktiabr*, January 27, 1927, 3.

268. GAOOGO, f. 451, op. 1, d. 84, 59–60; M. Tsinberg, M. Di byildung-'arb'et R'etshyits'er kryin, *Oktiabr*, January 20, 1927, 3.

269. Smilovitsky, Voskresnaia shkola v Rechitse, 172.

270. Interview by Penny Rubinoff with her father, David Rubinoff, November 16, 2003.

271. Aleinikova and Savinskaia, Sotsial'no-ekonomicheskoe razvitie Rechitsy v 1930-e gody, 333.

272. Ibid.

273. Interview with Maria Rubinchik, April 24, 2003.

274. ZGAR, f. 342, op. 1, d. 6, 258.

275. Interview with Iosif and Khaia (Olbinskaia) Kazovskaia, February 12, 2004.

276. Calculated from the statements of eyewitnesses.

277. Sh. Goldovskii, R'etshyits'er ts'entr'al'er 'arb-klub, *Oktiabr*, April 17, 1927, 3.

278. GAOOGO, f. 451, op. 1, d. 27, 6.

279. Ibid.

280. Interviews with Maria Rubinchik, January 1, 2001, April 24, 2003, and June 15, 2004.

281. Ibid.

282. Adamushka, *Palitychnya represii 20-50-ykh hadou na Belarusi*, 11-12; *Distribution of the Jewish Population of the USSR 1939*, 11.

283. Getty, Rittersporn, and Zemskov, *Victims of the Soviet Penal System*, 1028; also calculated from *GULAG*, 416-417. For the percentage of Jews in the USSR in 1939, see *Distribution of the Jewish Population of the USSR 1939*, 9.

284. Getty, Rittersporn, and Zemskov, *Victims of the Soviet Penal System*, 1029. The Israeli historian Mordechai Altshuler does not agree with this qualification. See Altshuler, *Soviet Jewry on the Eve of the Holocaust*, 195.

285. Zemskov, *Zakliuchënnye, spetsposelentsy, ssyl'noposelentsy, ssyl'nye i vyslannye*, 160-161.

286. Adamushko, *Palitychnyia represii 20-50-ykh hadou na Belarusi*, 54; *Istoriia Belarusi v dokumentakh i materialakh*, 494.

287. *Pamiats'*, 2:150-151; Petrov and Skorkin, *Kto rukovodil NKVD*, 228.

288. Ramanava, *Novaia historyia inkvizitsyi ÿ dakumentakh*, 364-365.

289. Petrov and Skorkin, *Kto rukovodil NKVD*, 451; NARB, f. 4, op. 21, d. 1718, 19-20.

290. Zeltser, *Jews in the Upper Ranks of the NKVD*, 71-72, 80-87.

291. NARB, f. 4, op. 3, d. 676, 27.

292. Kaganovitch, *Rechitsa: Istoriia evreiskogo mestechka Iugo-Vostochnoi Belorussii*, 392-397.

293. Prot'ko, Delo "Ob'edinënnogo antisovetskogo shpionsko-vreditel'skogo podpol'ia v BSSR," 133-134.

294. Ibid. Stakhanov's movement was an integral part of "heroes production," workers, record-breakers, first in industry, then in different fields of the Soviet economy. See Fitzpatrick, *Everyday Stalinism*, 74.

295. Velikii, Rechitskoe delo 1939 g.; NARB, f. 4, op. 21, d. 1718, 200.

296. NARB, f. 4, op. 21, d. 1718, 200.

297. GAOOGO, f. 702, op. 1, d. 29, 51.

298. Interview with Abram Frenkel', August 16, 2004.

CHAPTER 7. UNDER GERMAN OCCUPATION, 1941-1943

1. Galeznik, *Zapiski o voine*.

2. *Vechernii Minsk*, June 19, 1998, 5.

3. This was the five-member Polsman family. On the bombing of the town in July 1941, see: Dobrushkin, *Istoriia odnoi sem'i*, 4.

4. Altshuler, Ha-pynuy vehamenusaḥ shel' yehudim miBeylorussiyah ha-mizrahyt bi-tkufat ha-Sho'ah, yuny-'ogust 1941, 129-131.

5. Ibid., 132-133.

6. For details on this information, see note 3 in Kaganovitch, Jewish Refugees and Soviet Authorities, 85-86.

7. Miting predstavitelei evreiskogo naroda, *Vecherniaia Moskva*, August 25, 1941, 3.

8. "Brat'ia evrei vo vsëm mire!," *Vecherniia Moskva*, August 25, 1941, 3. Similar forms of address began to be widely used in the mass media with respect to other ethnic groups as well. See, for example, *Krasnaia Zvezda*, January 15, 1943, 4; June 10, 1943, 3; August 8, 1943, 3. As early as 1942 the authorities had detailed information about the mass genocide of the Jewish population, not only within the territory of the USSR but in other countries as well. This is attested by substantial articles in the most important newspapers: *Krasnaia Zvezda*, May 26, 1942, 3; December 19, 1942, 1; *Izvestiia*, December 19, 1942, 1; December 20, 1942, 4.

9. Not a single such directive has been uncovered in the formerly classified archive materials of the Evacuation Committee. The Rechitsa native Iosif Kazovskii, who served during the war in various posts in the Ministry of Transport, including that of deputy head of the Bureau of Military Transport, knows nothing of any special evacuation of the Jewish population. See interview with Iosif Kazovskii, February 12, 2004.

10. GARF, f. A259, op. 40, d. 3032, 19–20 (copy in YVA, JM24.678).

11. Ibid.

12. I. Voronkova, Voina obrushilas' na Minsk bombardirovkami, *Vechernii Minsk*, June 20, 1997, 5.

13. Altshuler, Ha-Pynuy vehamenusaḥ shel' yehudim miBeylorussiyah ha-mizrahyt bi-tkufat ha-Sho'ah, 136–137.

14. GARF, f. A259, op. 40, d. 3032, 19–20 (copy in YVA, JM24.678).

15. Ibid.

16. Zhirnov, Proverka strakhom, 72–73.

17. *Belarus' v pervye mesiatsy Velikoi Otechestvennoi voiny*, 167.

18. Zhirnov, Proverka strakhom, 72–73.

19. *Belarus' v pervye mesiatsy Velikoi Otechestvennoi voiny*, 14–15; Zhirnov, Proverka strakhom, 72–73.

20. *Belarus' v pervye mesiatsy Velikoi Otechestvennoi voiny*, 19, 24.

21. Ibid., 19–28, 36–74.

22. Altshuler, Ha-Pynuy vehamenusaḥ shel' yehudim miBeylorussiyah ha-mizrahyt bi-tkufat ha-Sho'ah, 143.

23. Ibid., 142–143.

24. Letter from Fridrikh Valler, June 17, 2001.

25. Altshuler, Ha-Pynuy vehamenusaḥ shel' yehudim miBeylorussiyah ha-mizrahyt bi-tkufat ha-Sho'ah, 142–143; *Belarus' v pervye mesiatsy Velikoi Otechestvennoi voiny*, 251.

26. Pinchuk, *Yehudey Bryit-Hamu'atsot mul' paney ha-Shu'a*, 108.

27. Dobrushkin, *Istoriia odnoi sem'i*, 4; Smilovitsky, *Katastrofa evreev v Belorussii*, 264. Company Commander Captain Zelik Dobrushkin was killed not far from Rechitsa during the liberation of Rogachev. See *Kniga pamiati voinov-evreev, pavshikh v boiakh s natsizmom*, 1:449

28. Dobrushkin, *Istoriia odnoi sem'i*, 4; interview with Abram Frenkel, August 16, 2004.

29. Here and subsequently I consciously avoid using the term "fascism" that was widely used in the USSR and in the countries created after its collapse since in reality it was only

German Nazism that envisaged the physical annihilation of separate nations and entire races. Lion Feuchtwanger's novel *The Oppenheim Family* was republished in the USSR about ten times between 1935 and 1938. Zelda Rozhavskaia states (October 17, 2001) that her decision to be evacuated was due in large measure to reading this book.

30. Interview with Sofia Burzhinskaia, July 25, 2004. For more general information on the spread of such information among Soviet Jews by Polish Jews, see Altshuler, *Ha-Pynuy vehamenusaḥ shel' yehudim miBeylorussiyah ha-mizrahyt bi-tkufat ha-Sho'ah*, 129–130, 132.

31. Ibid., 131–133.

32. Dobrushkin, *Istoriia odnoi sem'i*, 4; Smilovitsky, *Katastrofa evreev v Belorussii*, 264. Aron Atlas, Israel Malinkovich, Israel Pekarovskii, Lev Gurevich, and others expressed such views.

33. Dobrushkin, *Istoriia odnoi sem'i*, 3.

34. *Belarus' v pervye mesiatsy Velikoi Otechestvennoi voiny*, 181; letter from Avraam Dovzhik, September 28, 2001; interview with Fima Sheinkman, March 17, 2003.

35. Attestation of Eugenie Gorelik, Hall of Names of the Yad Vashem Holocaust Martyrs' and Heroes' Remembrance Authority in Jerusalem.

36. Letter from Avraam Dovzhik, September 28, 2001.

37. Kalinin, *Partizanskaia respublika* , 21.

38. Ibid.; *Belarus' v pervye mesiatsy Velikoi Otechestvennoi voiny*, 181.

39. Galeznik, *Zapiski o voine*.

40. YVA, JM20006, 12–13; Umetskii, *Rechitsa*, 48–49; Smilovitsky, *Katastrofa evreev v Belorussii*, 265.

41. YVA, JM1322, 3–4.

42. Ibid., JM20006, 75a–76.

43. Ibid., M41/2433, 98, 169, 230, 248.

44. Dobrushkin, *Istoriia odnoi sem'i*, 9–11.

45. On the firing range in the cemetery, see Dobrushkin, *Istoriia odnoi sem'i*, 9.

46. Ibid., 11.

47. The same reasoning was applied when appointing religious figures as Jewish elders or heads of the *Judenrat* in other occupied areas of the USSR as well. In towns where there were no religious leaders or in larger cities, the occupiers often placed respected teachers or doctors in these posts. By contrast, Jews in official positions—who were usually party members—were quickly liquidated.

48. *Pinkas ha-kehilot*, 1:411; *Chernaia kniga*, 65–66.

49. Dobrushkin, *Istoriia odnoi sem'i*, 9.

50. YVA, JM20006, 3, 77–770b; *Einsatzgruppen Reports*, 180.

51. AKGBGO, f. 1, d. 234, vol. 4, 4–7. I am grateful to Leonid Smilovitsky for providing me with materials on this case.

52. YVA, JM20006, 74a, 78a.

53. Ibid., 12a–13; Dobrushkin, *Istoriia odnoi sem'i*, 12.

54. Umetskii, *Rechitsa*, 48–49.

55. A. Dvornik, Poslednii svidetel', *Aviv* 7 (1998), 2; letter from Avraam Dovzhik, September 28, 2001; attestation by Tamara Kuzminich, August 7, 2005.

56. YVA, JM20006, 1–2, 74–75a. There were Jews among them as well (15).

57. Page of testimony of Iakov Gutarov, June 15, 2001.

58. AKGBGO, f. 1, d. 234, vol. 4, 4–7, 14–17; YVA, JM20006, 2, 78a. The Germans frequently executed Jews in antitank ditches. See Altshuler, Unique Features of the Holocaust, 177.

59. YVA, JM20006, 90–90a.

60. YVA, JM20005, 95a.

61. YVA, JM20005, 104–104a.

62. Letter from Larisa Borodich to the Rechitsa Regional Executive Committee, August 10, 1996. I am obliged to Alla Shkop for giving me the opportunity to see this letter. An excerpt from it can be found in *Dniaprovets*, April 21, 2005, 2.

63. YVA, JM20006, 2, 78a.

64. Ibid., 78–78a.

65. Letter from Izrael Rogachevskii, January 16, 2001; letter from Pesia Rozhavskii, January 14, 2001.

66. YVA, M33/477, 8–10.

67. Ibid.

68. Altshuler, Unique Features of the Holocaust, 180.

69. YVA, JM20005, 95.

70. Ibid., 106; interview with Maria Rubinchik, January 1, 2001.

71. The questionnaires were officially called "Pages of Testimony by Witnesses," which does not accurately reflect the connection between the authors and the victims, since they were completed mainly by friends and relatives and not by witnesses.

72. AKGBGO, f. 1, d. 234, vol. 4, 4–7, 14–17.

73. Ibid., 14–17.

74. Ibid., 8–9.

75. Ibid., 11–13.

76. The fact that an archpriest was included is significant and shows the changed attitude of the authorities toward the Orthodox religion (on this, see next chapter).

77. Feferman, Soviet Investigation of Nazi Crimes in the USSR, 593–598.

78. AKGBGO, d. 234, vol. 4, 4–7.

79. YVA, JM11218/14, 1.

80. Letter from Samuil Rozhavskii, December 31, 2000.

81. Smilovitsky, Bor'ba evreev Belorussii za vozvrat imushchestva i zhilishch v pervoe poslevoennoe desiatiletie 1944–1954, 173.

82. Dobrushkin, *Istoriia odnoi sem'i*, 9.

83. Testimony of Fridrikh Valler, Hall of Names of the Yad Vashem Holocaust Martyrs' and Heroes' Remembrance Authority in Jerusalem.

84. Dobrushkin, *Istoriia odnoi sem'i*, 10.

85. YVA, M33/477, 10.

86. Dobrushkin, *Istoriia odnoi sem'i*, 4.

87. Altshuler, Unique Features of the Holocaust, 176.

88. Chernyshëv, *Dorogami voiny*, 102.

89. *Pamiats'*, 2:215.

90. *Osvobozhdënnaia Belarus'*, 64.

91. Interview with Sofia Burzhinskii (Zaionchik), February 15, 2002.

92. Letter from Faina Vinnnik, April 22, 1998.

93. Letter from Izrail Rogachevskii, January 16, 2001; letter from Pesia Rozhavskii, January 14, 2001; interview with Maria Rubinchik, March 2, 2002.

94. Attestation by Tamara Kuz'minich, August 7, 2005.

95. Erenburg, *Voina*, 3:399–402. For details on how this girl was saved, see Dvornik, Poslednii svidetel'. Recently, the Yad Vashem National Institute of Remembrance of Victims of Nazism and Heroes of the Resistance in Jerusalem awarded Elena Bodganov (posthumously) the title of Righteous among the Nations (Archive of the Section of the Righteous, Yad Vashem, 10601). I am grateful to Katia Gusarov, a staff member of this institute, and to Alla Shkop, former chair of the Rechitsa Jewish community, for assisting me in with this.

96. One of the witnesses, Stepan Sopot, who had also saved a Jewish soldier during the occupation, was in 1997 awarded the title of Righteous among the Nations by the Yad Vashem National Institute of Remembrance of Victims of Nazism and Heroes of the Resistance in Jerusalem (Archive of the Section of the Righteous, Yad Vashem, A-7831).

97. Photocopy of Maria Rokhlin's (her married name was Aizenshpis) statement to the Moscow authorities, August 5, 1952 (Archive of the Section of the Righteous, Yad Vashem, A-7719). Although her reason for writing this statement is not precisely known, its tone clearly indicates a desire to testify to the loyalty of Olga Anishchenko. It is clear from the statement that the authorities were accusing Olga of the crime of teaching school for several months during the occupation. Maria explained this by Olga's need to earn money for food and to avoid being sent to Germany for forced labor. According to the testimony of Semën Kofman, Maria regarded Olga Anishchenko as her second mother, and when she went away to Moscow after the war, she helped Olga's family through these hungry postwar years by sending them food parcels. In the mid-1960s Rokhlin came to Rechitsa to meet members of the partisan brigade and to tell her story to local schoolchildren. See letter from Semion Kofman in the Section of the Righteous, Yad Vashem (Ibid.). Through his initiative, in 1997 Yad Vashem awarded Olga Anishchenko (posthumously) the title of Righteous among the Nations and bestowed on her honorary Israeli citizenship.

98. Interview with former partisan Mikhail Astashinskii, March 12, 2001; *Leksykon Hagvurah*, 1:11–13, 104–107, 152–153.

99. Altshulerr, Unique Features of the Holocaust, 183. But even in the spring of 1944, Jewish partisans in some detachments in Belorussia still were subject to anti-Semitism. See *Vstali my plechom k plechu . . .* , 155.

100. *Pamiats*, 2:226–227, 240–241.

101. Ibid., 240–241, 340; *Vsenarodnoe partizanskoe dvizhenie v Belorussii v gody Velikoi Otechestvennoi voiny*, 2:376. Several people from Rechitsa fought with the partisans in other areas. For example, Vladimir Stolberg served in the Crimea after his regiment had been cut off near Alushta in the autumn of 1941. See AISJR, f. 11728.

102. Attestation of David Abramovich, Hall of Names of the Yad Vashem Holocaust Martyrs' and Heroes' Remembrance Authority in Jerusalem.

103. Letter from Iakov Gutarov, March 21, 2004, to the Conference on Jewish Material Claims against Germany in Jerusalem.

104. Dobrushkin, *Istoriia odnoi sem'i*, 11.

105. YVA, M33/477, 2–5.

106. Rokossovskii, *Soldatskii dolg*, 313.

107. Batov, *V pokhodakh i boiakh*, 361. German documents on the defense of Rechitsa and Rechitsa Region by the Second Army confirm the creation of a strong defensive position and the redeployment of troops there; they also confirm the Germans' surprise at the Red Army's attack in this area. See YVA, JM5022–5023. Along with the German troops in Rechitsa was a small detachment of Italians. See *Vsenarodnoe partizanskoe dvizhenie v Belorussii v gody Velikoi Otechestvennoi voiny*, 2:286–287.

108. Sverdlov, *Evrei—generally vooruzhënnykh sil SSSR*, 60.

109. *Sovetskaia Belorussiia*, November 18, 2003, 5.

110. *Belarus' v pervye mesiatsy Velikoi Otechestvennoi voiny*, 187–188.

111. Shneer, *Plen*, 2:27.

112. Ibid., 2:38–49.

113. TsAMO, f. 33, op. 686196, d. 1221, d. 5572; ibid., op. 687572, d. 1128; ibid., op. 744807, d. 986; ibid., op. 744808, d. 682, d. 1271; ibid., op. 744809, d. 412.

114. *Pamiats'*, 2:72–93.

115. *Kniga pamiati voinov-evreev, pavshikh v boiakh s natsizmom*, vols. 1–7.

116. See list: Kaganovitch, *Rechitsa: Istoriia evreiskogo mestechka Iugo-Vostochnoi Belorussii*, 318–319.

117. Ibid., vol. 2, 76; *Kniga pamiati voinov-evreev, pavshikh v boiakh s natsizmom*, 1:19, 67; questionnaires of the Hall of Names of the Yad Vashem National Institute of Remembrance of Victims of Nazism and Heroes of the Resistance in Jerusalem.

118. Shneer, *Plen*, 2:28–29.

119. Letter from Avraam Dovzhik, September 28, 2001.

120. Ibid.

121. Ibid.; interview with Roza Dvorkin, October 1, 2002; letter from Maria Rubinchik, April 12, 2001.

122. *Zbor pomnikau historyi i kul'tury Belarusi*, 316. In 2008 the grandson of one of the victims, former vice mayor of Moscow Vladimir Resin, built them a new monument at his own expense.

CHAPTER 8. FROM LIBERATION TO THE COLLAPSE OF THE USSR, 1943–1991

1. On the return of Semën Kofman and other Jews to Rechitsa at the end of 1943, see his letter in Archive of the Section of the Righteous of the Yad Vashem Holocaust Martyrs' and Heroes' Remembrance Authority, Jerusalem, A-7719.

2. As the questionnaires of 1945 mentioned earlier show, the average wage of Rechitsa residents in evacuation was reduced by 60–70 percent. GARF, f. 7021, op. 85, d. 247–251, 263 (copy in YVA, JM23638–23639). This is confirmed by the information from Yosef

Litvak that the average wage of those evacuated was 300 rubles (Litvak, *Plytym Yehudym miPolyin leBryt haMu'atsot 1939–1946*, 143), whereas before the war Jews in Rechitsa earned on average 350–400 rubles (see chap. 6).

3. I am now in the process of preparing a study of living conditions in Central Asia during the war and, in particular, on the high death rate among Jewish refugees there. Some results of this research are in Kaganovitch, Jewish Refugees and Soviet Authorities during World War II. As for the Jews of Rechitsa, it is a telling fact that half of Abram Levin's six children (one son was fighting at the front) who were evacuated to Uzbekistan and later to Kazakhstan died there of diseases (letter from Sara Levin, March 25, 2001).

4. As can be seen from the appeal of the chairman of the Council of People's Commissars of the BSSR, Panteleimon Ponomarenko, to Viacheslav Molotov and Georgii Malenkov in February 1944, the Germans, before retreating, dispersed among neighboring villages patients ill with typhus whom they had collected earlier from Orel, Briansk, and Gomel Oblasts and had placed in the Rechitsa Typhus Hospital. As a result of this and the widespread typhus epidemic in eastern Belorussia, 72 percent of the inhabitants of the village of Novyi Barsuk in Rechitsa Raion, for example, became infected. See *Osvobozhdionnaia Belarus'*, 41. In Gomel Oblast and the now partially liberated Polesia Oblast, there were 6,540 households with typhus (42). The fact that the army command, despite the heavy battles in which it was engaged, sent twenty-seven medical detachments in early 1944 to assist the civil authorities in combating the epidemic testifies to its scale (44). In his appeal Ponomarenko asked that another seven hundred doctors be returned to Belorussia as part of a reevacuation (45).

5. ZGAR, f. 342, op. 1, d. 2, 159.

6. *Osvobozhdionnaia Belarus'*, 189.

7. Ibid.

8. ZGAR, f. 342, op. 1, d. 4, 71.

9. Ibid.

10. Isupov, *Demograficheskie katastrofy i krizisy v Rossii v pervoi polovine XX veka*, 229.

11. GAOOGO, f. 342, op. 1, d. 11, 115.

12. Ibid., 105.

13. Ibid.

14. Olekhnovich, *Ekonomika Belorussii v usloviiakh Velikoi Otechestvennoi voiny*, 9.

15. When she arrived in Minsk, M. S. Rubinchik was urgently requested to go to western Belorussia to become head of a high school, but she preferred to return to Rechitsa. There she was joyously welcomed by the town's education department. The Rechitsa authorities replaced teachers who had taught in schools during the occupation by returning evacuees, who were largely Jews. This became a source of interethnic tension. See *Osvobozhdionnaia Belarus'*, 66; interview with Maria Rubinchik, August 7, 2006. See also the investigation of the case of Olga Anishchenko in chap. 7. Beginning in the 1950s, "collaborationist teachers" were again hired to work in their professions.

16. GAOOGO, f. 342, op. 1, d. 11, 105.

17. Ibid.

18. ZGAR, f. 342, op. 1, d. 2, 103, 145, 151.

19. Ibid., 185.

20. Interview with Maria Rubinchik, August 7, 2006.

21. Testimony to the success of Nazi propaganda in the occupied territories of eastern Belorussia is the fact that after the liberation many peasants did not want to work at restoring and registering in the collective farms. See *Osvobozhdionnaia Belarus'*, 64–65. The self-identification of the inhabitants of Belorussia also changed. This is evident from the letter of the head of the Political Directorate of the First Belorussian Front, S. F. Galadzhaev to the aforementioned P. K. Ponomarenko in June 1944. Here Galadzhaev states that the majority of the inhabitants of the liberated areas did not call the Red Army troops "ours" but referred to them as "Russians" or "Reds" (82).

22. Interview with Bat'ia Shchukin, October 11, 2001; Smilovitsky, Bor'ba evreev Belorussii za vozvrat imushchestva i zhilishch v pervoe poslevoennoe desiatiletie, 169–170.

23. Interview with Arkadii Mikhalevskii, August 30, 2001.

24. Letter from Fridrikh Valler, June 17, 2001; Letter from Lazar Dvorkin, June 28, 2001; Letter from Anna Atlas, November 27, 2001.

25. Interview with Fima Sheinkman, March 17, 2003.

26. Interview with Roza Gordon, June 22, 2001.

27. Legal resolution of the action of Abram Gluskin, 1944. I am grateful to Zinaida Gluskin for allowing me to see this document.

28. Letter from Isaak Volfson, August 30, 1998.

29. Letter from Maria Rubinchik, April 12, 2001; Smilovitsky, Bor'ba evreev Belorussii za vozvrat imushchestva i zhilishch v pervoe poslevoennoe desiatiletie, 175.

30. Smilovitsky, Bor'ba evreev Belorussii za vozvrat imushchestva i zhilishch v pervoe poslevoennoe desiatiletie, 175.

31. Altshuler, Antisemitism in Ukraine, 82–83; Kostyrchenko, *Tainaia politika Stalina*, 440–441; Mitsel', *Evrei Ukrainy v 1943–1953 gg.*, 20–33; Smilovitsky, Bor'ba evreev Belorussii za vozvrat imushchestva i zhilishch v pervoe poslevoennoe desiatiletie, 175–176.

32. YVA, M37/1319, 3. The local authorities prepared a document showing that legal actions by Jews in 1945 had a 94 percent favorable outcome in cases of the return of apartments and 64 percent in the return of property (to specific persons). But these statistics were evidently the result of the energetic measures taken by local authorities immediately after they received a copy of Dargolt's letter (6–7).

33. Smilovitsky, Bor'ba evreev Belorussii za vozvrat imushchestva i zhilishch v pervoe poslevoennoe desiatiletie, 175–176.

34. Gutin, *Kor 'Ony*, 247–250.

35. GARF, f. 7021, op. 85, d. 247–251, 263 (copy in YVA, JM23638–23639).

36. Regarding war-related damage, see letter from Liubov' Tsirkin (Graiver), February 20, 2001. Zalman Atlas, who spent some time in Rechitsa during his leave from the front in early January 1944, informed his sisters of the same thing in a letter. I am grateful to his daughter, Anna Atlas, for allowing me to see this letter. For the fate of Levin houses, see letter of Iosif Levin, March 3, 2005.

37. Interview with Roza Dvorkin, October 10, 2002.

38. Interviews with Iakov Shustin, February 14, 2005, and Aron Kaganovich, March 8, 2006.

39. GARF, f. 7021, op. 85, d. 247–251, 263 (copy in YVA, JM23638–23639).

40. ZGAR, f. 342, op. 1, d. 3, 151.

41. On these rumors in Rechitsa, see letter from Zlata Chechik, March 3, 1998; letter from Faina Vinnik, April 22, 1998; letter from Sofia Zherebovich, June 20, 1999; letter of Liubov' Tsirkin, September 11, 1999.

42. Interview with Raia Strashinskii (niece of the victim), May 31, 1999.

43. YVA, M37/1319, 2.

44. Ibid., M37/1332, 4.

45. Ibid., 3.

46. Ibid., 4.

47. YVA, M37/196, 6–8; Mitsel', *Evrei Ukrainy v 1943–1953 gg.*, 34, 38–41, 54–55, 63–66; Kostyrchenko, *Tainaia politika Stalina*, 354–356. Rozenshtein was arrested and, after a three-week investigation, was executed.

48. Letter from Fridrikh Valler, June 17, 2001. After being demobilized and studying in an institute, Valler worked as a hydrometeorologist. For twenty years he held the post of director of the Astrakhan Area Hydrometeorological Observatory.

49. Litvak, *Plytym Yehudym miPolyin leBryt haMu'atsot*, 248–251.

50. Letter from Fridrikh Valler, June 17, 2001.

51. YVA, M37/1319, 2.

52. Letter of Samuil Rozhavskii, December 31, 2000; letter of Sof'ia Ezerskii, February 12, 2002; interview with Arkadii Mikhalevskii, October 14, 2000.

53. Kostyrchenko, *Tainaia politika Stalina*, 246–275.

54. *Osvobozhdionnaia Belarus'*, 236–237.

55. ZGAR, f. 342, op. 1, d. 4, 57; interview with David Turovskii, March 21, 2005.

56. ZGAR, f. 342, op. 1, d. 4, 30–34; d. 2, 159; letter from Avraam Dovzhik, September 28, 2001.

57. Calculated from *Pamiats'*, 2:214–215.

58. Interview with Alexander Simanovskii, April 27, 2005.

59. Interview with Lev Dobrushkin, December 28, 2006.

60. ZGAR, f. 342, op. 1, d. 12, 187.

61. *Zbor pomnikau historyi i kul'tury Belarusi*, 314.

62. CAHJP, RU154, 8.

63. Ro'i, *Jewish Religion in the Soviet Union*, 269.

64. CAHJP, RU153, 142; GARF, f. 6991, op. 3, d. 30, 83–84 (copy in YVA, JM11268).

65. CAHJP, RU154, 8; ZGAR, f. 342, op. 1, d. 6, 94.

66. Ibid.

67. GAOOGO, f. 144, op. 61, d. 73, 100–101.

68. Ibid.

69. CAHJP, RU154, 80.

70. Beizer, *Nashe nasledstvo*, 42.

71. CAHJP, RU154, 9–11. Aside from the Baptists, a community of evangelical Christians was organized in Rechitsa after the war (CAHJP, RU152, 244).

72. With reference to GARF, f. 6991, op. 2, d. 1, 26–27, see Tsekhanskaia, Rossia.

73. With reference to GARF, f. 6991, op. 1, d. 2, 14, see Tsekhanskaia, Rossia.

74. ZGAR, f. 342, op. 1, d. 6, 258.

75. Ibid., d. 14, 161.

76. Ibid., d. 6, op. 94; d. 14, 384.

77. Kostyrchenko, *Tainaia politika Stalina*, 388–405.

78. Smilovitsky, Jewish Religious Leadership in Belorussia, 111.

79. Ibid., 114.

80. Ibid.

81. Ibid.

82. GAOOGO, f. 144, op. 69, d. 159, 144–145.

83. Ibid.

84. Ibid.

85. Ibid.

86. Interviews with Roza Dvorkin, October 1, 2002; Raisa Genina, October 10, 2001; Tsilia Ruzina (Korbinskaia), April 16, 2004; Maria Rubinchik, March 2, 2002; Avraam Dovzhik, October 15, 2003.

87. Interview with Arkadii Mikhalevskii, October 14, 2000.

88. Rothenberg, *Jewish Religion in the Soviet Union*, 159.

89. *Vosemnadtsat'*, 182; Grinbaum, *Rabane Berit ha-mo'atsot ben milhamot ha-'olam*, 45.

90. Letter from Sarra Ber and Mikhail Balte, April 5, 2001; interviews with Arkadii Mikhalevskii, August 30, 2001, Tsilia Ruzin (Kobrinskii), April 16, 2004, and Maria Rubinchik, June 15, 2004; Altshuler, *Yahadut ba-makhbesh ha-Sovyeti*, 287.

91. Letter from Sara Levin, April 26, 1997.

92. Kostyrchenko, *Tainaia politika Stalina*, 242–275.

93. Leizerov, Natsional'nyi sostav partiinogo, gosudarstvennogo, hoziaistvennogo apparata v Belarusi, 101–103; interview with Abram Frenkel, August 16, 2004.

94. Such were the formulas used in the dismissal, respectively, of Pavel Kogan, director of the Azovstal Metallurgical Factory in Mariupol in 1950 and of Mikhail Belotserkovskii, director of the Frunze Machine Building Factory in 1952 (YVA, M37/361, 19–20).

95. Letter from Sofia Zherebovich, June 20, 1999.

96. Gennadii Kostyrchenko has proved the groundlessness of this myth in his study *Tainaia politika Stalina*, 671–685.

97. Letter from Sof'ia Zherebovich, June 20, 1999.

98. Smilovitskii, *Katastrofa evreev v Belorussii*, 270.

99. Interview with Tsilia Ruzin (Korbinskii), April 16, 2004.

100. On such manifestations of anti-Semitism in Rechitsa, see interviews with Arkadii Mikhalevskii, August 30, 2001, and Maria Rubinchik, June 15, 2004; letter from Sof'ia Zherebovich, June 20, 1999; letter from Sofia Ezerskii, February 12, 2002; Smilovitskii, *Katastrofa evreev v Belorussii*, 271–272.

101. Interview with Maria Rubinchik, March 2, 2002.

102. Interview with Alla Shkop, May 10, 2005; *Gomel'skaia prauda*, November 10, 2005, 2.

103. ZGAR, f. 342, op. 1, d. 4, 37, 126, 137, 182, 187; d. 6, 54, 88, 93; d. 7, 49, 88.

104. Mendelson, *Skvoz' dymku snov-vospominanii*, 252–253.

105. On the shortage of leadership personnel even in the party, Komsomol, and economic organizations in Eastern Belorussia in 1944, *Osvobozhdionnaia Belarus'*, 76–77.

106. ZGAR, f. 342, op. 1, d. 4, 130, 176.

107. Smilovitsky, Evrei Belorussii v pervoe poslevoennoe desiatiletie, 216.

108. ZGAR, f. 342, op. 1, d. 4, 176; d. 12, 26.

109. Ibid., d. 14, 350.

110. ZGAR, f. 342, op. 1, d. 10, 49; letter from Rita Rozental', May 19, 2001. Finkelberg's son, Arnol'd Sviatogorov (Finkel'berg) became a well-known composer in folk genres in Ukraine. At the end of the 1980s he was the musical director of the Kiev Jewish Theatre "Mazel tov."

111. Interview with Eugeny and Sima Vesiolyi, November 15, 2004; letter from Iosif Levin, March 3, 2005.

112. Interview with Maria Rubinchik, June 15, 2004.

113. Letter of Sara Levin, April 26, 1997.

114. The rate of fatal alcohol poisoning rate increased 6.8 times in Belarus between 1970 and 2005. Razvodovsky, All-Cause Mortality and Fatal Alcohol Poisoning in Belarus, 563.

Bibliography

ARCHIVAL SOURCES

AISJR—Archive of the Institute for Study of the Jewish Resistance, Kibbutz Beit Lokhamei
ha-getaot, Israel

AJNUL—Manuscript Archive of the Jewish National and University Library, Jerusalem
Fond ARC 4° 1068

AKGBGO—KGB archive of Gomel Oblast, Gomel
Fond 1

CAHJP—Central Archive of the History of the Jewish People, Jerusalem
Fonds HM2, HMF, INV, P, RU

GAOOGO—State Archive of Social Associations (formerly, Regional Archive of Communist Party) of Gomel Oblast, Gomel
Fonds 144, 702

GARF—State Archive of the Russian Federation, Moscow
Fonds 533, 7021

LSHA—Lithuanian State Historical Archive, Vilnius
Fonds 378, 567

NARB—National Archive of the Republic of Belarus, Minsk
Fonds 4, 6, 255, 750

NIARB—National Historical Archive of the Republic of Belarus, Minsk
Fonds 21, 136, 145, 255, 295, 299, 333, 458, 705

RGAVMF—Russian State Naval Archive, Saint Petersburg
Fond 1345

RGIA—Russian State Historical Archive, Saint Petersburg
Fonds 821, 1216, 1290, 1565

TsAMO—Central Archive of the Ministry of Defence of the Russian Federation, Podol'sk
Fond 33

TsDIAK—Central State Historical Archives of Ukraine, Kiev
Fond 442

TsGAOR of Ukraine—Central State Archive of the October Revolution and Socialist Construction of Ukraine, Kiev
Fond 166
TsGARUz—Central State Archive of the Republic of Uzbekistan, Tashkent
Fond 1
YVA—Yad Vashem Archives, Jerusalem
Fonds JM, M33, M37, O33
ZGAR—Local State Archive of the Rechitsa, Gomel Region
Fond 342

NEWSPAPERS AND PERIODICALS

Belorusskaia delovaia gazeta (Minsk)
Dniaprovets (Rechitsa)
Gomel'skaia prauda (Gomel)
Evreiskaia nedelia (Moscow)
Evreiskii izbiratel' (Saint Petersburg)
Evreiskoe obozrenie (Saint Petersburg)
Gomel'skaia prauda (Gomel)
Ha-Shomer ha-tsair (Lvov)
Izvestiia (Moscow)
Khronika evreiskoi zhizni (Saint Petersburg)
Krasnaia Zvezda (Moscow)
Minskie gubernskie vedomosti (Minsk)
Nedel'naia Khronika Voskhoda (Saint Petersburg)
Novyi Voskhod (Saint Petersburg)
Poslednie Izvestiia (Geneva)
Rassvet (Saint Petersburg)
Russkaia molva (Saint Petersburg)
Russkii evrei (Saint Petersburg)
Russkoe prilozhenie k Hakarmel (Vilna)
Sovetskaia Belorussiia (Minsk)
Tribuna evreiskoi sovetskoi obshchestvennosti (Moscow)
Vechernii Minsk (Minsk)
Voskhod (Saint Petersburg)
אקטיאבר *Oktiabr* (Minsk)
הזמן *Hazman* (Vilna)
המליץ *Hamelits* (until 1871 Odessa, then Saint Petersburg)
מעריב *Maariv* (Tel Aviv)
העולם *Haolam* (London)
עמעס *D'er 'Emes* (Moscow)
פאלקסצייטונג *Folkszeitung* (Vilna)
דער פריינד *Der Fraind* (Saint Petersburg)
צייטשריפט *Tsaitshrift* (Minsk)
הצפירה *Hatsfirah* (Warsaw)

Books and Articles

Abezgauz, Zalman. *Rabochii klass Belorussii v nachale XX veka 1900–1913.* Minsk: Nauka i Tekhnika, 1977.

———. *Razvitie promyshlennosti i formirovanie proletariata Belorussii vo vtoroi polovine 19 veka.* Minsk: Nauka i Tekhnika, 1971.

Abramenko, Mikhail. Iz istorii zdravokhraneniia Rechitskogo uezda. In *Chatsvёrtyia mizhnarodnyia doўnaraўskiia chytanni,* vol. 2, edited by Valentina Lebedzeva and others, 122–126. Gomel: Gomel University, 2004.

———. *Zdravoohranenie BSSR—stanovlenie sovetskoi sistemy (1917–1941 gg.).* Gomel: GGMU, 2005.

Adamushka, Vladimir. *Palitychnyia represii 20–50-ykh hadou na Belarusi.* Minsk: "Belarus," 1994.

Adres-kalendar' Vilenskogo general-gubernatora na 1868 god. Edited by Alexander Sementovskii. Vitebsk: Vitebskii statisticheskij komitet, 1868.

Adresnaia kniga fabrichno-zavodskoi i remeslennoi promyshlennosti vsei Rossii. Edited by Aleksander Pogozhev. Saint Petersburg: Kalmanson, 1907.

Agranovskii, Genrikh. "Skakun" i "kitaiovtsy"—hasidskoe dvizhenie v Litve glazami pravitel'stvennykh chinovnikov. *Vestnik evreiskogo universiteta v Moskve* 9 (2004): 331–344.

Agrot Ahad Ha'am. Vol. 2. Edited by Aryeh Simon. Tel Aviv: Davir, 1956.

A. G. V Sovetskoi Rossii. "Kollektivizatsiia i evreiskie sel'skokhoziaistvennye poseleniia": Beseda s prof. B. D. Brutskusom. *Rassvet,* May 4, 1930, 12–13.

Ahad Ha'am: Mikhtavim be-inyene Erets-Yisirael (1926–1891). Edited by Shulmit Leskov. Jerusalem: Yad Yitshak Ben-Tsevi, 2000.

Aizenshtadt, Ben-Tsion. *Rabaney Minsk va-hakhameha: Sefer ha-zikaron.* Vilna: Bi-defus haalmanah veha-ahim Rom, 1898.

Aizkis, I. G. Sanitarno-bytovoe obsluzhivanie evreiskogo mestechka. *Voprosy biologii i patalogii evreev* 3, pt. 2 (1930): 75–98.

Akty izdavaemye Vilenskoi Arkheograficheskoi komissiei. Vol. 5. Edited by Iakov Golovadskii (Akty Brestskogo i Grodnenskogo gorodskikh sudov). Vilna: Arkheograficheskaia komissiia, 1871.

Akty o evreiakh, izdannye Vilenskoi Arkheograficheskoi komissiei dlia razbora drevnikh aktov. Vol. 29. Vilna: Arkheograficheskaia komissiia, 1902.

Akty, otnosiashchiesia k istorii Iuzhnoi i Zapadnoi Rossii. Vol. 1, *1361–1598.* Edited by Nikolai Kostomarov. Saint Petersburg: Arkheograficheskaia komissiia, 1863.

Akty, otnosiashchiesia k istorii Zapadnoi Rossii. Vol. 5, *1633–1699.* Edited by Ioan Grigorovich. Saint Petersburg: Arkheograficheskaia komissiia, 1853.

Aleinikova, Maryia, and Maryna Savinskaia. Sotsial'no-ekonomicheskoe razvitie Rechitsy v 1930-e gody. In *Piatyia mizhnarodnyia doўnaraўskiia chytanni,* edited by Valentina Lebedzeva and others, 331–335. Gomel: Gomel University, 2005.

Aleksandrov, Hillel. Di yyidish'e b'ap'elk'erong 'in dyi sht'et 'un sht'etl'ekh fun Vyyasrusland. *Tsaitshrift* 2–3 (1928): 309–378.

———. Di yyidish'e b'ap'elk'erong 'in Myinsk'er gub'erni'e 'in 'anhyyv 19—tan y'arhind'ert. *Tsaitshrift* 4 (1930): 67–88.

———. Fun myinsk'er 'arkhyiion. *Tsaitshrift* 2–3 (1928): 763–777.

———. Rechitskii povet in y'or 1789. *Tsaitshrift* 4 (1930): 48–66.

Alenitsyn, Vladimir. *Evreiskoe naselenie i zemlevladenie v iugo-zapadnykh guberniiakh Evropeiskoi Possii, vkhodiashchikh v chertu evreiskoi osedlosti: Statisticheskii vremennik Rossiiskoi imperii.* Seriia 3, vypusk 2. Saint Petersburg: Thentral'nyi stat. komissiia Ministerstva vnutrennikh del, 1884.

Al'fasi, Yitshak. *Ha-Hasidut.* Tel Aviv: Sifriyat Ma'ariv, 1974.

Aliakseichanka, Genadz'. Rechytsa ў drugoi palove XIX st.: Munitsypal'nae samakiravanne i razvitstse gorada. In *Piatyia mizhnarodnyia doўnaraўskiia chytanni,* edited by Valentina Lebedzeva and others, 255–262. Gomel: Gomel University, 2005.

Altshuler, Mordechai. Antisemitism in Ukraine toward the End of World War II. In *Bitter Legacy: Confronting the Holocaust in the USSR,* edited by Zvi Gitelman, 77–90. Bloomington: Indiana University Press, 1997.

———. Ha-Pynuy vehamenusaḥ shel' yehudim miBeylorussiyah ha-mizrahyt bi-tkufat ha-Sho'ah, yuny-'ogust 1941. *Yahadut Zmaneynu* 3 (1986): 119–158.

———. *Ha-Yevsektsiyah bi-Brit-ha-Mo'etsot, 1918–1930: Ben le'umiyut le-komunizm.* Tel Aviv: Ha-Makhon le-Yahadut zemanenu, ha-Universitah ha-'Ivrit bi-Yerushalayim, 1980.

———. *Soviet Jewry on the Eve of the Holocaust.* Jerusalem: Centre for Research of East European Jewry, Hebrew University of Jerusalem and Yad Vashem, 1998.

———. The Unique Features of the Holocaust in the Soviet Union. In *Jews and Jewish Life in Russia and the Soviet Union,* edited by Yaacov Ro'I, 171–188. London: Frank Cass, 1995.

———. *Yahadut ba-makhbesh ha-Sovyeti: Ben dat le-zehut Yehudit bi-Verit ha-Mo'atsot, 1941– 1964.* Jerusalem: Merkaz Zalman Shazar le-toldot Yisìra'el, 2007.

Amitin, A.-L. Homel. *Hamelits* (July 21, 1884): 881–882.

Antonovich, Vladimir. *Monografii po istorii Zapadnoi i Iugo-Zapadnoi Rossii.* Kiev: Tipografiia E. Ia. Fëdorova, 1885.

Archivy Kremlia. Edited by Nikolai Pokrovskii and Stanislav Petrov. Vol. 1, *Politbiuro i tserkov'.* Moscow: ROSSPEN, 1997.

Arkhiv Iugo-Zapadnoi Rossii. Pt. 6 (akty ob ekonomicheskikh i iuridicheskikh otnosheniiakh krest'ian v 16–18 vekakh), vol. 1. Edited by Ivan Novitskii. Kiev: Komissiia dlia razbora drevnikh aktov, vysochaishe utverzhdënnaia pri Kievskom, Podol'skom i Volynskom general-gubernatore, 1876.

Avrutin, Eugene M. *Jews and the Imperial State: Identification Politics in Tsarist Russia.* Ithaca, N.Y.: Cornell University Press, 2010.

Balaban, Meir. Obshchii ocherk politicheskoi i sotsial'noi istorii evreev v Pol'she i Litve. In *Istoriia evreiskogo naroda,* vol. 11, pt. 1, edited by Alexander Braudo and others, 161–180. Moscow: Mir, 1914.

Balter, Gershon. Davar al yoshvyi Lyt'a. *Hamelits* 29 (1868): 213–214.

Barkulabovskaia letopis'. In *Polnoe sobranie russkikh letopisei,* vol. 32, edited by Nikolai Ulashchik, 174–192. Moscow: Nauka, 1975.

Baron, Salo. *The Russian Jews under Tsars and Soviets.* New York: Macmillan, 1987.

———. *Social and Religious History of the Jews.* Vol. 16, *Late Middle Ages and Era of European Expansion (1200–1650): Poland-Lithuania.* New York: Columbia University Press, 1976.

Barsella, Moshe. Bor'ba za iskhod v 20-kh gg. nashego veka. *Menora* 14 (1977): 65–74.

———. Polgoda sredi bukharskikh evreev. *Menora* 26 (1985): 55–58.

Barskii, A. Voinskaia povinnost' evreev. *Rassvet*, August 8, 1880, 1345–1349.

Bartoszewicz, Julian. *Studja historyczne i literackie.* Vol. 2. Krakow: Nakladem Kazimierza Bartoszewicza, 1881.

Batov, Pavel. *V pokhodakh i boiakh.* Moscow: Golos, 2000.

Beizer, Mikhail. *Nashe nasledstvo: Sinagogi SNG v proshlom i nastoiashchem.* Moscow: Gesharim, 2002.

Beizer, Mikhail, and Anatolii Karasev. A Debate about a Congress of Jewish Religious Communities in the USSR, 1925–1926. *Jews in Russia and Eastern Europe* 1, no. 50 (2003): 138–174.

Belorussiia v epokhu Feodalizma (sbornik dokumentov). Vols. 1–3. Edited by Anatolii Azarov and Valentina Chepko. Minsk: Akademiia nauk BSSR, 1960–1961.

Belorussiia v period podgotovki sotsialisticheskoi revoliutsii (fevral'-oktiabr' 1917 g.). Vol. 1. Edited by Timofei Gorbunov. Minsk: Gosizdat BSSR, 1957.

Belarus' v pervye mesiatsy Velikoi Otechestvennoi voiny, 22 iiunia—avgust 1941 g.: Dokumenty i materialy. Edited by Vladimir Adamushka and others. Minsk: NARB, 2006.

Bel'skii, A. Zemskaia biurokratiia. *Obrazovanie* 2 (1905): sec. 2, 5.

Bemporad, Elissa. The Yiddish Experiment in Soviet Minsk. *East European Jewish Affairs* 37, no. 1 (2007): 91–107.

Ben-Ammi [Rabinovich], Mordechai. Detstvo. *Knizhki Voskhoda* 9 (1904): 13–32.

Berkowski, Władysław. Struktury administracyjne komór celnych i mytnych na Wołyniu od XVI do połowy XVII wieku. In *Nad społeczeństwem staropolskim: Kultura—Instytucje—Gospodarka w XVI–XVIII stuleciu*, vol. 1, edited by Karol Łopatecki and Wojciech Walczak, 321–338. Bialystok: Osìrodek Badanì Europy Sìrodkowo-Wschodniej, 2007.

Bershadskii, Sergei. *Avram Ezofovich Rebrikovich, podskarbii zemskii, chlen Rady Velikogo Kniazhestva Litovskogo.* Kiev: Tip. G. T. Korchak-Novitskago, 1888.

———. *Litovskie evrei: Istoriia ikh iuridicheskago i obshchestvennago polozheniia v Litve ot Vitovta do Liublinskoii uniii, 1388–1569.* Saint Petersburg: Tipografiia M. M. Stasiulevicha, 1883.

Bessie's Letters: Correspondence from Russia to Bessie Rapaport Schechter, 1913–1935. Edited by Bill Schechter. Brookline, Mass.: privately published, 1998.

Bez-Kornilovich, Mikhail. *Istoricheskie mesta o primechatel'nykh mestakh v Belorussii.* Saint Petersburg: Tipografiia III otd. Sobstv. E. I. V. Kantseliarii, 1855.

Bialyi, Iosif. OZET v Rechitse. *Tribuna evreiskoi sovetskoi obshchestvennosti* 8 (1928): 20.

Binshtok, Veniamin. Evrei v Gomel'skoi oblasti. In *Voprosy biologii i patologii evreev*, 1:81–86. Leningrad: Prakticheskaia meditsina, 1926.

Bischitzky, Vera. Simon Dubnow an Rosa Ginzberg: Briefe und Postarten aus Riga 1937–1941. *Judaica: Beiträge zum Verstehen des Judentums* 66 (2010): 366–393.

Biulleten' gomel'skogo gubernskogo statisticheskogo biuro. Vols. 1–6. Rechitsa: Gomel'skoe gub. Stst. biuro, 1923–1926.

Blum, Jerome. *Lord and Peasant in Russia: From the 9th to the 19th Century.* Princeton, N.J.: Princeton University Press, 1961.

Bobroysk: Sefer zikaron li-kehilat Bobroysk u-venoteha. Edited by Yehuda Slutsky. Tel Aviv: Hotsa'at tarbut ve-hinukh, 1967.

Bogrov, Grigorii. *Zapiski evreia.* Saint Petersburg: Tipografiia V. Tushnova, 1874.

Bolbas, Maksim. *Razvitie promyshlennosti v Belorussii, 1795–1861 gg.* Minsk: Nauka i tekhnika, 1966.

Braginskii, M. Vannovskii Pëtr Semënovich. In *Evreiskaia entsiklopediia,* vol. 5, edited by Semën Dubnov and others, 302. Saint Petersburg: Brokgauz-Efron, 1908–1913.

Braginskii, M., and S. Lozinskii. Duma Gosudarstvennaia. In *Evreiskaia entsiklopediia,* vol. 7, edited by Semën Dubnov and others, 369–375. Saint Petersburg: Brokgauz-Efron, 1908–1913.

Braude, Kh. B. Materialy po estestvennomu dvizheniiu evreiskogo naseleniia v Moskve za 48 let (1870–1917). In *Evrei v Moskve: Sbornik materialov,* edited by Iurii Snopov and Artur Klempert, 374–379. Jerusalem: Gesharim, 2003.

Bronevskii, Vladimir. *Puteshestvie ot Triesta do Sankt Peterburga v 1810 godu.* Vols. 1–2. Moscow: A. S. Shiriaev, 1828.

Bukhbinder, Naum. *Istoriia evreiskogo rabochego dvizheniia v Rossii po neizdannym arkhivnym materialam.* Leningrad: Akademicheskoe izd-vo, 1925.

Bukhovets, Olga. Evrei v narodnom soznanii (opyt izucheniia na primere Belorussii v XX veke). In *Pravo na svobodu: Materialy Mezhdunarodnoi konferentsii,* edited by N. I. Basovskaia, 81–103 Moscow: RGGU, 2000.

Bund v Belorussii 1897–1921: Dokumenty i materialy. Edited by Eduard Savitskii. Minsk: BenNIIDAD, 1997.

Charopka, Stanislav. Rechytsa ў kazatska-selianskai vaine 1648–1651 gadoў na Belarusi. In *Chatsvërtyia mizhnarodnyia doўnaraўskiia chytanni,* vol. 2, edited by Valentina Lebedzeva and others, 81–90. Gomel: Gomel University, 2004.

Chepko, Valentina. *Goroda Belorussii v pervoi polovine XIX veka.* Minsk: BGU, 1981.

Chernaia kniga: O zlodeiskom povsemestnom ubiistve evreev nemetsko-fashistskimi zakhvatchikami vo vremenno-okkupirovannykh raionakh Sovetskogo Soiuza i v lageriakh unichtozheniia Pol'shi vo vremia voiny. Edited by Il'ia Erenburg and Vasily Grossman. Kiev: MIP "Oberig," 1991.

Chernyshëv, Aleksei. *Dorogami voiny: Vospominaniia o Velikoi otechestvennoi voine, 1941–1945.* Tambov: Tambovpoligrafizdat, 2004.

Chubinskii, Pavel. *Trudy Etnografichesko-statisticheskoi ekspeditsii v Zapadno-Russkii krai.* Vol. 7. Saint Petersburg: Imperatorskoe Russkoe geograficheskoe obshchestvo, 1872.

Coxe, William. *Travels in Poland, Russia, Sweden and Denmark.* London, 1802. Reprint, New York: Arno Press and New York Times, 1970.

Danilov, I. Vospominaniia o podnevol'noi sluzhbe u bol'shevikov. *Arkhiv russkoi revoliutsii* 16 (1925).

Dayan, Moshe. Yehudim be-tnu'at-hkhofesh shel' Russia. *Haolam* (November 21, 1935): 713–714.

Delo o besporiadkakh v Gomele. *Voskhod,* October 21, 1904, 27–40.

Dembovetskii, Alexander. *Opyt opisaniia Mogilëvskoi gubernii.* Vol. 1. Mogilev: Gubenskii statisticheskii komitet, 1882.

Distribution of the Jewish Population of the USSR 1939. Edited by Mordechai Altshuler. Jerusalem: Hebrew University of Jerusalem, 1993.

Dobrushkin, Lev. *Istoriia odnoi sem'i.* New York: privately published, 1998.

Dokumenty i materialy po istorii Belorussii. Vols. 3–4. Edited by Vladimir Pertsev. Minsk: Akademiia nauk BSSR, 1953–1954.

Dolbilov, Mikhail. *Russkii krai: Chuzhaia vera: etnokonfessional'naia politika imperii v Litve i Belorussii pri Aleksandre II.* Moscow: Novoe literaturnoe obozrenie, 2010.

Dovnar-Zapol'skii, Mitrofan. *Issledovaniia i stat'i.* Kiev: Izdanie A. P. Sapunova, 1909.

Doÿnar, Aliaksandr. Stan darog i darozhnykh kamunikatsyi Rechytskaga paveta (1765–1766 gg.). In *Piatyia mizhnarodnyia doÿnaraÿskiia chytanni,* edited by Valentina Lebedzeva and others, 220–225. Gomel: Gomel University, 2005.

Drapkin, Iakov. 1905 god v Gomele i Polesskom raione. In *1905 god v Gomele i Polesskom raione: materialy po istorii sotsial-demokraticheskogo i rabochego dvizheniia v 1893–1906 gg.,* 65–245. Gomel: Gomel'skii rabochii, 1925.

Drogovoz, Igor'. *Kreposti na kolësakh: Istoriia bronepoezdov.* Minsk: Kharvest, 2002.

Dubnov, Semën. *Kniga zhizni: Vospominaniia i razmyshleniia.* Vols. 1–3. Riga: Jaunātnes Grāmata, 1934–1938.

Dubnova-Erlikh, Sofiia. *Zhizn' i tvorchestvo S. M. Dubnova.* New York: Komitet imeni S. M. Dubnova, 1950.

Dubnow, Simon. *History of the Jews in Russia and Poland.* Vol. 1. Philadelphia: Jewish Publication Society, 1946.

Dvizhenie rossiiskogo naseleniia za 1867. Statisticheskii vremennik Rossiiskoi imperii, vol. 8. Saint Petersburg: Tsentral'nyi statisticheskii komitet MVD, 1872.

Dvizhenie rossiiskogo naseleniia za 1870. Statisticheskii vremennik Rossiiskoi imperii, vol. 14. Saint Petersburg: Tsentral'nyi statisticheskii komitet MVD, 1879.

Egorov, Iurii. *Gradostroitel'stvo Belorussii.* Moscow: Gos. izd-vo lit-ry po stroitel'stvu i arhitekture, 1954.

The Einsatzgruppen Reports: Selections from the Dispatches of the Nazi Death Squads' Campaign against the Jews, July 1941–January 1943. Edited by Yitzhak Arad, Shmuel Krakowski, and Shmuel Spector. New York: Holocaust Library, 1989.

El', A. Pis'mo iz Moskvy. *Rassvet,* June 18, 1922, 10–11.

Erenburg, Il'ia. *Voina.* Vol. 3. Moscow: Gosudarstvennoe izd-vo khudozhestvennoi literatury, 1944.

Etnograficheskii sbornik. 1st ed. Saint Petersburg: Biblioteka Sankt-Peterburgskogo blagorodnogo sobraniia, 1853.

Ettinger, Shmuel. *Beyn Polin le-Rusia.* Jerusalem: Zalman Shazar Center for Jewish History and Bialik Institute, 1994.

———. Jewish Participation in the Settlement of Ukraine in the Sixteenth and Seventeenth Centuries. In *Ukrainian-Jewish Relations in Historical Perspective,* edited by Howard Aster and Peter J. Potichnyj, 23–30. Edmonton: Canadian Institute of Ukraine Study Press University of Alberta, 1990.

Even Zahav, B. I. R'etshyits'a. *Der Fraind* (January 19, 1903): 4.

Evreinovskaia letopis'. In *Polnoe sobranie russkikh letopisei,* vol. 35, edited by Nikolai Ulashchik, 214–238. Moscow: Nauka, 1980.

Evreiskie khroniki XVII stoletiia. Edited and translated by Saul Borovoi. Moscow: Gesharim, 1997.

Evreiskie pogromy 1918–1921 gg. Edited by Zalman Ostrovkii. Moscow: Shkola i kniga, 1926.

Evreiskii krest'ianin: Sbornik, vol. 2. Moscow: Tsentr. pravleniia Ozet, 1926.

Evreiskoe naselenie Rossii po dannym perepisi 1897 g. i po noveishim istochnikam. Edited by P. Klingin. Petrograd: Kadima, 1917.

Fëdorov, V. A. Sotsial'no-ekonomicheskoe razvitie Rossii (pervaia polovina XIX veka). In *Istoriia SSSR, XIX—nachalo XX veka,* edited by Ivan Fedosov, 4–29. Moscow: Vysshaia shkola, 1987.

Feferman, Kiril. Soviet Investigation of Nazi Crimes in the USSR: Documenting the Holocaust. *Journal of Genocide Research* 5, no. 4 (2003): 587–602.

Fishman, David. *Russia's First Modern Jews: The Jews of Shklov.* New York: New York University Press, 1995.

Fitzpatrick, Sheila. *Everyday Stalinism: Ordinary Life in Extraordinary Times; Soviet Russia in the 1930s.* New York: Oxford University Press, 1999.

Floria, Boris. Novye svidetel'stva ob otnoshenii naseleniia Ukrainy k evreiam pervoi poloviny XVII v. In *Evreiskoe naselenie v Tsentral'noi, Vostochnoi i Iugo-Vostochnoi Evrope: Srednie veka—Novoe vremia,* edited by Gennadii Litavrin, 136–138. Moscow: Nauka, 1994.

Fox, Ralph. *The People of the Steppes.* Boston: Houghton Mifflin, 1925.

Frank, Moshe. Haḥeder hametukan beRecitsa. *He-'Avar* 16 (1969): 85–96.

———. Reshyimot bekatseh h'et. In *Kom, Derekh vedrakhim,* 153–155.

Freeze, Chaeran. *Jewish Marriage and Divorce in Imperial Russia.* Waltham, Mass.: Brandeis University Press, 2002.

Fridman, M. B. *Otmena krepostnogo prava v Belorussii.* Moscow: Izdatel'stvo Belgosuniversiteta im. V. I. Lenina, 1958.

Fridman, Natan Tsvi. *Otsar ha-rabanim: Tekufat ha-rabanut (4730–5730).* Bnei Brak: Agudat otsar ha-rabanim, 1975.

Galeznik, Boris. *Zapiski o voine.* Krasnyi Yar: B. Galeznik, 1999. http://kokshetau.online.kz/history/galeznik-war.htm.

Gekker, Elena. Evrei v pol'skikh gorodakh vo vtoroi polovine XVIII veka. *Evreiskaia Starina* 6 (1913): 184–200.

Gelbard, Arye. *Sofo shel'o ktḥyilato: Katso shel' ha"bund" harusyi.* Tel Aviv: University, Diaspora Research Institute, 1995.

Gepshtein, Solomon. *Ekonomicheskaia struktura evreiskogo naseleniia Rossii.* Saint Petersburg: Vostok, 1906.

Gessen, Iulii. Evrei v Moskovskom gosudarstve XV–XVII vv. In *Moskva evreiskaia,* edited by Konstantin Burmistrov, 227–262. Moscow: Dom evreiskoi knigi, 2003.

———. *Evrei v Rossii.* Saint Petersburg: Tipo-litogr. A. G. Rozena, 1906.

———. *Istoriia evreiskogo naroda v Rossii.* Vols. 1–2. Moscow: Evreiskii Universitet v Moskve, 1993.

———. Zabytyi obshchestvennyi deiatel': Zapiska kuptsa Feigina na imia imperatora Nikolaia. *Evreiskaia starina* 4 (1911): 394–402.

Getty, Arch, T. Rittersporn Gábor, and Viktor Zemskov. *Victims of the Soviet Penal System in the Pre-War Years: A First Approach on the Basis of Archival Evidence.* American Historical Review 98, no. 4 (1993): 1017–1049.

Ginzburg, A. Minsk. In *Evreiskaia entsiklopediia*, vol. 11, edited by Semën Dubnov and others, 87–89. Saint Petersburg: Brokgauz-Efron, 1908–1913.

Ginzburg, M. Rechitsa (Minskoi gubernii). *Rassvet* 1 (1918): 31.

Glushakov, Iurii. Otriad samooborony v Gomele. In *Evrei Belarusi*, vol. 5, edited by Inna Gerasimova, 57–78. Minsk: Chetyre chetverti, 2000.

Goldberg, Y'akov. *Ha-hevra ha-Yahudit ba-mamlekhet Polin-Lit'a.* Jerusalem: Zalman Shazar, 1999.

Golubov, Natan. *Institut ubezhishcha u drevnikh evreev v sviazi s ugolovnym i gosudarstvennym pravom Moiseia i Talmuda i sravnitel'no s institutami ubezhishch u drevnikh grekov, rimlian, v srednevekovoi i novoi Evrope.* Saint Petersburg: Tip. G. Pinesa i I. Tsederbauma, 1884.

Gomel'skii protsess: Po protokolam zashchitnikov i otchetam, pechatavshimsia v zhurnalakh "Pravo" i "Voskhod" i gazetakh "Kievskie Otkliki." Edited by B. Kraver. Saint Petersburg: Obshchestvennaia Polza, 1907.

Gorfunkel', Z. 1905 god v Rechitse—gorode i uezde. *Polesskii kommunar* 23 (1925): 23–24.

Goroda Rossii v 1910 godu. Saint Petersburg: Tsentral'nyi statisticheskii komitet, 1914.

Gorodovoe polozhenie (1892). In *Svod zakonov Rossiiskoi imperii*, vol. 2, edited by Aleksandr Volkov, 159–181. Saint Petersburg: Obshchestvennaia pol'za, 1899.

Gorodskie poseleniia v Rossiiskoi Imperii. Vol. 3. Saint Petersburg: Tipografiia K. Vulfa, 1863.

Gotlib, Shmuel' Nakh. *Sefer Ohole-shem.* Pinsk: Tip. M. Glouberman, 1912.

Grinbaum, Abraham. *Rabane Berit ha-mo'atsot ben milhamot ha-'olam, 1917–1939.* Jerusalem: Ha-Merkaz le-heker ule-ti'ud Yahadut Mizrah Eropah, 1994.

GULAG: Glavnoe upravlenie lagerei, 1917–1960. Edited by A. P. Kokurin and N. V. Petrov. Moscow: Mezhdunarodnyi fond "Demokratiia," 2000.

Guldon, Zenon, and Jacek Wijaczka. Accusation of Ritual Murder in Poland, 1500–1800. *Polin* 10 (1987): 99–140.

Gusev, A. N. *Zakony o evreiakh': Sbornik' izvlechenii iz' svoda zakonov rossiiskoi imperii deistvuiushchikh o evreiakh postanovlenii.* Kharkov: Izd. knizhnago magazina V. i A. Biriukovykh, 1889.

Gustynskaia letopis'. In *Polnoe sobranie russkikh letopisei*, vol. 40. Edited by Vladimir Kuchkin. Saint Petersburg: Dmitrii Bulanin, 2003.

Gutin, Ysrael. *Kor 'Ony: Reshymot dmuyiot, zikhronot.* Tel Aviv: 'Aked, 1979.

Hakohen, Mordecai Ben Hillel. *'Olami.* Vol. 3. Jerusalem: Ha-poalim, 1927.

Halevy, Zvi. *Jewish Schools under Czarism and Communism: A Struggle for Cultural Identity.* New York: Springer, 1976.

Hanover, Nathan. *Abyss of Despair (Yeven metzulah): The Famous 17th Century Chronicle Depicting Jewish Life in Russia and Poland during the Chmielnicki Massacre of 1648–1649.* Translated by Abraham J. Mesch. New Brunswick, N.J.: Transaction Books, 2009.

Heilperin, Shmuel Eliezer. *Sefer ha-Tseitsaim: 'Ilan 'Yohas'yn le-tseitsei hod kh"k rabeinu hagadol kadosh ha-kadashim mofat dorot ha-'ahronim hagaon h'akki moran rabi Shn'yur Zalman mi-L'iydy neshmato 'eden.* Jerusalem: s.n., 1980.

Helman, Chaim Meir. *Sefer Beit Rabi.* Tel Aviv: Sfaryim, 1978.

Historyia Belaruskai SSR. Vol. 1. Edited by Illarion Ignatenko. Minsk: Navuka i tekhnika, 1972.

Hundert, Gershon David. *Jews in Poland-Lithuania in the Eighteenth Century.* Berkeley: University of California Press, 2006.

Ianchuk, Nikolai. *Po Minskoi gubernii: Zametki iz poezdki v 1886 godu.* Moscow: Tipografiia A. Levinson i Ko., 1889.

Iastrzhembskii, Ivan. *Opyt statisticheskogo dvizheniia naseleniia Khersonskoi gubernii: Khersonskii uezd.* Kherson: Khersonskaia gubernskaia zemskaia uprava, 1882.

Iatskevich, Siargei. Adukatsyia natsyianal'nykh menshastsei na Belarusi ў 1920–1990 gg. *Bialoruskie Zeszyty Historyczne* 10 (1998): 68–81.

Ignat'ev, Anatolii. *S. Iu. Vitte—diplomat.* Moscow: Mezhdunarodnye otnosheniia, 1989.

Iodfat, A. M'eamad hadat hyhudit bebryt-hamu'etsot vemilḥamah bah beshnot hashloshym. *Bḥynot* 2–3 (1972): 36–46.

Ioffe, Emanuil, and Beniamin Mel'tser. *Dzhoint v Belarusi.* Minsk: Magic Book, 1999.

Ioffe, Emanuel, and Viacheslav Selemenev. Jewish Refugees from Poland in Belorussia, 1939–1940. *Jews in Eastern Europe* 1, no. 32 (1997): 45–60.

Istoriia Belarusi v dokumentakh i materialakh. Edited by Igor' Kuznetsov and Valentin Mazets. Minsk: Amalfeia, 2000.

Istoriia Belorusskoi SSSR. Vol. 1. Edited by Vladimir Pertsev. Minsk: Akademiia nauk Belorusskoi SSR, 1954.

Istoriia Kazakhstana: Issledovaniia i dokumenty. Edited by L. Degitaeva. Almaty: Kazakhstan, 1998.

Isupov, Vladimir. *Demograficheskie katastrofy i krizisy v Rossii v pervoi polovine XX veka: Istoriko-demograficheskie ocherki.* Novosibirsk: Sibirskii khronograf, 2000.

Jelski, A. Rzeczyca. In *Slownik geograficzny Krolestwa Polskiego i innych krajow slowianskich,* vol. 10, edited by Bronisław Chlebowskiego and Władysław Walewskiego, 132–137. Warsaw: Druk Wieku, 1889.

Kabuzan, Vladimir. *Emigratsiia i reemigratsiia v Rossii v XVIII—nachale XX veka.* Moscow: Nauka, 1998.

Kaganovitch, Albert. The Attitude of the Czarist Administration to the Bukharan Jews and Their Legal Status in Turkestan in the Years 1867–1917. PhD diss., Hebrew University of Jerusalem, 2003.

———. Jewish Refugees and Soviet Authorities during World War II. *Yad Vashem Studies* 38, no. 2 (2010): 85–121.

———. *Rechitsa: Istoriia evreiskogo mestechka Iugo-Vostochnoi Belorussii.* Jerusalem: Mika, 2007.

———. Rechitsa v srednevekovyi period. In *Chatsvërtyia mizhnarodnyia doўnaraўskiia chytanni,* vol. 2, edited by Valentina Lebedzeva and others, 31–40. Gomel: Gomel University, 2004.

Kahan, Arcadius. Hyozmot hayhudit be-Rusyah hats'aryt. In *Yehudim be-kalkalah: Kovets ma'amarim,* Edited by Nachum Gross, 391–410. Jerusalem: Merkaz Zalman Shazar, 1985.

Kahanovich, Yahuda-Leib-Gershon. Homel. In *'Arim ve-'imahot be-Yisrael,* vol. 2, edited by Israel Leib Hacohen Fishman, 187–269. Jerusalem: Mosad Rav Kuk 1948.

————. *MiHomel 'ad Tel-Aviv: Zikhronot vedmuyot*. Tel Aviv: Hav'ad lehots'aat m'amarey Yahuda-Leib-Gershon Kahanovich, 1952.

Kalinin, Pëtr. *Partizanskaia respublika*. Moscow: Voen. izd-vo, 1964.

Kandybovich, Symon. *Razgrom natsyianal'naga rukhu ў Belarusi*. Minsk: Belaruski his-tarychny ahliad, 2000. http://kamunikat.org/halounaja.html?pubid=3658

Kappeler, Andreas. *The Russian Empire: A Multi-Ethnic History*. London: Longmans, 2001.

Karol', Tsvi, and Tsadok Linman. *Sefer Bet ha-kevarot ha-yashan be-Tel Aviv*. Tel Aviv: Ḥmu"l, 1940.

Kats, Ben-Tsiyon. *'Al' 'itonim ve'anashyim*. Tel Aviv: Tsrikover, 1983.

Katsenel'bogen, S. Evrei Minskoi gubernii. *Russkii evrei*, May 21, 1880, 806–810.

Katz, Dovid. *Words on Fire: The Unfinished Story of Yiddish*. New York: Basic Books, 2004.

Kaufman, A. Uchatsia li evrei. *Rassvet*, February 14, 1880, 269–271.

Khatskevich, Alexander. Vyniki raboty na praviadzen'i belarusizatsyi ў BSSR: Doklad na zasedanii prezidiuma Soveta natsional'nostei TSVK SSSR v 1927 g. In *Dva gady nat-syianal'noi raboty ў BSSR*, 58–75. Minsk: Natsyian. Kamisiia CVK, 1929.

————. Vyniki raboty siarod natsyianal'nykh menshas'tsiai ў BSSR: Doklad na zasedanii prezidiuma Soveta natsional'nostei TSVK SSSR v 1928 g. In *Dva gady natsyianal'noi raboty ў BSSR*, 76–92. Minsk: Natsyian. Kamisiia CVK, 1929.

Kholostiakov, Georgii. *Vechnyi ogon'*. Moscow: Voenizdat, 1976.

Khronologicheskii ukazatel' materialov dlia istorii inorodtsev Evropeiskoi Rossii. Edited by Pëtr Kennen. Saint Petersburg: Imperatorskaia Akademiia nauk, 1861.

Klier, John D. *Imperial Russia's Jewish Question, 1855–1881*. Cambridge and New York: Cam-bridge University Press, 2005.

————. *Rossia sobiraet svoikh evreev*. Moscow: Gesharim, 2000.

————. *Russia Gathers Her Jews: The Origins of the Jewish Question in Russia, 1772–1825*. DeKalb: Northern Illinois University Press, 1986.

————. Traditions of the Commonwealth: Lithuanian Jewry and the Exercise of Political Power in Tsarist Russia. In *The Vanished World of Lithuanian Jews*, edited by Alvydas Nikzentaitis, Stefan Schreiner, and Darius Staliunas, 5–20. Amsterdam: Rodopi, 2004.

Kniga pamiati voinov-evreev, pavshikh v boiakh s natsizmom. Vols. 1–7. Edited by Moisei Mar'ianovskii. Moscow: Narodnaia pamiat', 1994–2002.

Kniga pogromov: Pogromy na Ukraine, v Belorussii i evropeiskoi chasti Rossii v period Grazh-danskoi voiny, 1918–1922 gg.; sbornik dokumentov. Edited by Lidiia Miliakova. Moscow: ROSSPEN, 2007.

Kohut, Zenon E. The Khmelnytsky Uprising, the Image of Jews, and the Shaping of Ukrain-ian Historical Memory. *Jewish History* 17, no. 2 (2003): 141–163.

Kom, Chaim Shlioma. *Hyaye Shlioma*. Jerusalem: Moria, 1928.

Kom, Yehudah. Bereshet hanyitsul. *He'Avar* 22 (1977): 172–177.

————. *Derekh vedrakhim*. Tel Aviv: Shevivim, 1982.

————. *Shoresh ve-'Anaf*. Tel Aviv: Shevivim, 1971.

Kopysskii, Zalman. *Ekonomicheskoe razvitie gorodov Belorussii*. Minsk: Nauka i Tekhnika, 1966.

Korngol'd, C. E. Russkie evrei na voine 1877–1878. *Russkii evrei*, October 17, 1879, 227–230.

Korobkov, Kh. Statistika evreiskogo naseleniia Pol'shi i Litvy vo vtoroi polovine XVIII veka. *Evreiskaiia starina* 4 (1911): 540–562.

Kostyrchenko, Gennadii. *Tainaia politika Stalina.* Moscow: Mezhdunarodnye otnosheniia, 2001.

Kotik, Yehezkel. *Zikhronotav shel Yihzk'el Kotik.* Vols. 1–2. Edited by David Assaf. Tel Aviv: Ha-Makhon le-heker ha-tefutsot, Tel Aviv University, 1998.

Kotłubaj, Edward. *Życie Janusza Radziwiłła.* Vilna: Nakładem M. Mindelsohna, 1859.

Krivova, N. A. Vlast' i tserkov' v 1922–1925 gg. *Mezhdunarodnyi istoricheskii zhurnal* 17 (2001). http://history.machaon.ru/all/number_01/pervajmo/1_print/index.html.

Kukharenko, Iurii. Poles'e i ego mesto v processe etnogeneza slavian. In *Polese: Lingvistika, Arkheologiia, Toponimika,* edited by Viktor Marynov and Nikita Tolstoi, 30–46. Moscow: Nauka, 1968.

Kunin, Il'ia. Evrei v Moskovskom gosudarstve XV–XVII vv. In *Moskva evreiskaia,* edited by Konstantin Burmistrov, 304–310. Moscow: Dom evreiskoi knigi, 2003.

Lederhendler, Eli. Did Russian Jewry Exist prior to 1917? In *Jews and Jewish Life in Russia and the Soviet Union,* edited by Yaacov Ro'i, 15–27. Ilford, England: F. Cass, 1995.

Leizerov, Arkadii. Natsional'nyi sostav partiinogo, gosudarstvennogo, hoziaistvennogo apparata v Belarusi (20–50-e gg.). In *Aktual'nye voprosy gosudarstva i prava,* vol. 4, edited by Iurii Brovka, 100–105. Minsk: BGU, 1994.

Leksykon Hagvurah. Vols. 1–2. Edited by Yḅy'al Gernshtein and Moshe Kahanovich. Jerusalem: Yad Vashem, 1965.

Leshchinskii, Iakov. Dvizhenie evreiskogo naseleniia v Rossii. *Voprosy biologii i patalogii evreev* 2 (1928): 140–175.

Letopis' samovidtsa po novootkrytym spiskam: S prilozheniem trekh malorossiiskikh khronik. Kiev: Kievskaia vremennaia komissiia dlia razbora drevnikh aktov, 1878.

Levin, Vladimir. Yehudey Rusiah veshalosh hadumot har'ishonot: Habḅirot vesh'ela hayahudit bedumot 1906–1912. MA thesis, Hebrew University of Jerusalem, 1997.

Lipetski, E. Saiuz ruskaga naroda. In *Entsyklapedyia history Belarusi,* vol. 6, pt. 1, edited by Genadz' Pashkoў, 251–252. Minsk: Belarusskaia Entsyklapedyia, 2001.

List of Voters for Electors from Rechitsa uezd to the Second State Duma, 1906. http://www.jewishgen.org/databases/Belarus/DumaVoterLists.htm.

Litovskaia metrika. Vol. 1. Saint Petersburg: Arkheograficheskaia kommisiia, 1903.

Litvak, Yosef. *Plytym Yehudym miPolyin leBryt haMu'atsot 1939–1946.* Tel Aviv: Hakibbutz Hameuchad, 1988.

Liuban. In *Pinkas Slutsk ve-bnoteia.* Edited by Shimshon Nakhmani and Nakhum Khinits, 201–224. Tel Aviv and New York: Va'ad ha-Sefer, 1962.

Liubavskii, Matvei. *Ocherk istorii Litovsko-Russkago gosudarstva do Liublinskoi unii vkliuchitel'no.* Moscow: Khudozh. pechatnia, 1915.

Liutyi, Anatolii. *Sotsial'no-ekonomicheskoe razvitie gorodov Belorussii: V kontse XVIII–pervoi polovine XIX veka.* Minsk: Nauka i tekhnika, 1987.

Lopukhin, Aleksei. *Otryvki iz vospominanii.* Moscow: Gos. izd-vo, 1923.

Löwe, Heinz-Dietrich. *The Tsars and the Jews.* Chur, Switzerland: Harwood Academic, 1993.

Lozinskii, Samuil. *Sotsial'nye korni antisemitizma v srednie veka i v novoe vremia.* Moscow: Ateist, 1929.

Mahler, Raphael. Ha-Yehudim be-Polin erev ha-tkufat ha-khalukot. In *Kiyum ve-shever: Yuhudey Polin le-dorotyhem,* edited by Yisìra'el Bartal and Israel Gutman, 243–260. Jerusalem: Merkaz Zalman Shazar le-toldot Yisìra'el, 1997.

Marash, Iakov. *Ocherki istorii ekspansii katolicheskoi tserkvi v Belorussii 18 veka.* Minsk: Vysshaia shkola, 1974.

Marek, Pëtr. Administrativnoe delenie evreiskih poselenii v Litovski oblasti. In *Istoriia evreiskogo naroda,* vol. 11, pt. 1, edited by Alexander Braudo and others, 206–210. Moscow: Mir, 1914.

Materialy dlia geografii i statistiki Rossii. Vol. 3, *Vilenskaia guberniia.* Edited by Anton Korevo. Saint Petersburg: General'nyi shtab, 1861.

Materialy ob antievreiskikh pogromakh. Vol. 1, *Pogromy v Belorussii.* Edited by Zakharii Mindlin. Moscow: Evotdel Narodnogo Komissariata po delam natsional'nostei, 1922.

Materialy po evreiskoi demografii i ekonomike. Vols. 3–4. Moscow: Komzet, 1928–1929.

Meditsinskii otchiot po Minskoi gubernii za 1911 g. Minsk: Gubernskaia zemskaia uprava, 1913.

Mendelson, Ieguda. *Skvoz' dymku snov-vospominanii.* Jerusalem: Makhon Mendelson, 2001.

Minaev, Ivan. *Sviedieniia o stranakh po verkhov'iam Amu-Dar'i po 1878 god.* Saint Petersburg: Tipografiia V. S. Balasheva, 1879.

Minova, N. Problema antisemitizma v mezhnatsional'nykh otnosheniiakh na Gomel' shchine v 20–30-e gody XX veka. In *Evrei Belarusi,* vol. 6, edited by Inna Gerasimova, 152–159. Minsk: Chetyre chetverti, 2001.

Mironov, Boris. Traditsionnoe demograficheskoe povedenie krest'ian v XIX–nachale XX v. In *Brachnost', rozhdaemost', smertnost' v Rossii i v SSSR.* Edited by Anatolii Vishnevskii, 83–104. Moscow: Statistika, 1977.

Mitsel', Mikhail. *Evrei Ukrainy v 1943–1953 gg.: Ocherki dokumentirovannoi istorii.* Kiev: Dukhi Litera, 2004.

Motzkin, Leo. *Die Judenpogrome in Russland.* Vol. 2. Cologne: Jüdischer Verlag, 1910.

Mozeszon O. Material'noe polozhenie evreiskoi massy v Severo-Zapadnom krae. *Rassvet,* December 28, 1879, 610–611.

My nachinali eshchë v Rossii: Vospominaniia. Edited by Iehuda Erez. Jerusalem: Bibliotekaaliia, 1983.

Nadav, Mordechai. *The Jews of Pinsk, 1506 to 1880.* Edited by Mark Mirsky and Moshe Rosman. Stanford, Calif.: Stanford University Press, 2008.

Nakhmanovich, Vitalii. *Evreiskaia politika Tsarskogo pravitel'stva v 1870-kh gg.: Deiatel'nost' Komissii po ustroistvu byta evreev.* Moscow: Obshchestvo "Evreiskoe nasledie," 1998.

Nakrich, Yehuda-Leib. Yeshivat Beyt Yosef Denovrodok. In *Mosdot Torah be-'Eropah be-vinyanam uve-hurbanam,* edited by Samuel Kalman Mirsky, 247–290. New York: 'Ogen, 1956.

Nam pishut iz Rechitsy. *Russkii evrei,* October 24, 1879, 272.

Naselenie Rossii v XX veke: Istoricheskie ocherki. Vol. 1. Edited by Iurii Poliakov. Moscow: ROSSPEN, 2000.

Natanson, G. Neskol'ko slov o korobochnom sbore i ob otnoshenii ego k otbyvaniu voin-skoi povinnosti. *Russkii evrei*, October 17, 1879, 225–227.

Nathans, Benjamin. *Beyond the Pale: The Jewish Encounter with Late Imperial Russia*. Berkeley: University of California Press, 2002.

Noska, Mikhail. Pravoslavnoe hramostroitel'stvo v Rechice (vtoraia polovina XIX veka). In *Chatsvërtyia mizhnarodnyia doÿnaraÿskiia chytanni*, vol. 2, edited by Valentina Lebedzeva and others, 100–103. Gomel: Gomel University, 2004.

Oblastnoi pinkos Vaada glavnykh obshchin Litvy. Vol. 1. Edited by Semën Dubnov. Saint Petersburg: Tipografiia Lurie, 1909.

Obzor Minskoi gubernii za 1913 god. Minsk: Gubernskii statisticheskii komitet, 1914.

Ocherki po arkheologii Belorussii. Vol. 2. Edited by Vladimir Isaenko. Moscow: Nauka i tekhnika, 1972.

Olekhnovich, Galina. *Ekonomika Belorussii v usloviiakh Velikoi Otechestvennoi voiny, 1941–1945*. Minsk: BGU, 1982.

Osipova, Irina. *Khasidy "spasaia narod svoi . . ."* Moscow: Formica-C, 2002.

Osokina, Elena. *Zoloto dlia industrializatsii: "Torgsin."* Moscow: ROSSPEN, 2009.

Osvobozhdënnaia Belarus': Dokumenty iI materialy. Edited by Vladimir Adamushko. Minsk: NARB, 2004.

Otchet dlia okazaniia pomoshchi evreiam-pereselentsam za 1909 g. Minsk: Evreiskoe kolonizatsionnoe obshchestvo, 1910.

Otchet o deiatel'nosti po uporiadocheniiu evreiskoi emigratsii za 1910 g. Saint Petersburg: Tsentral'nyi komitet Evreiskogo kolonizatsionnogo obshchestva, 1911.

Otchiot o deiatel'nosti informatsionnogo biuro dlia emigrantov za 1907 g. Saint Petersburg: Evreiskoe kolonizatsionnoe obshchestvo, 1908.

Otchiot Rechitskogo evreiskogo obshchestva podaianiia pomoshchi i posobiia bednym za 1914–1915 gody. Rechitsa: Rechitskoe evreiskoe obshchestvo podaianiia pomoshchi i posobiia bednym, 1915.

Pamiat': Gomel'. Vol. 1. Edited by Piatro Rabianok. Minsk: "BELTA," 1998.

Pamiatniki diplomaticheskikh snoshenii drevnei Rossii s derzhavami inostrannymi. Vol. 35. Saint Petersburg: Sobstvennaia E.I.V. Kantseliariia, 1892.

Pamiats': Rechytski raion. Vols. 1–2. Edited by E. Hneuka and P. Rabianok. Minsk: "Belarus,'" 1998–1999.

Paperna, Abram. *Russko-evreiskii pis'movnik*. Warsaw: Tipografiia Aleksandra Ginsa, 1875.

Pashuto, Vladimir. *Obrazovanie Litovskogo gosudarstva*. Moscow: Akademiia nauk SSSR, 1959.

Patriarshaia ili Nikonovskaia letopis'. *Polnoe sobranie russkikh letopisei*. Vols. 9–10. Edited by Mikhail Tikhomirov and others. Moscow: Nauka, 1965.

Pazhitnov, Konstantin. *Gorodskoe i zemskoe samoupravlenie*. Saint Petersburg: P. P. Gershunin i Ko., 1913.

Perepis' evreev v Malorossii v 1736 g. *Evreiskaia starina* 6 (1913): 400–407, 526–536.

Pervaia vseobshchaia perepis' naseleniia Rossiiskoi Imperii 1897. Edited by N. Troinitskii. Vol. 22: Minskaia guberniia. Saint Petersburg: Tsentral'nyi statisticheskii komitet ministerstva vnutrennikh del, 1904.

Petrachenka, Iryna, and Aliaksander Kavalenka. Kameral'noe opisanie rechitskoi okrugi: 1796 iak istorichne dzherelo. In *Piatyia mizhnarodnyia doÿnaraÿskiia chytanni*, edited by Valentina Lebedzeva and others, 233–241. Gomel: Gomel'skii gosudarstvennyi universitet, 2005.

Petrov, Nikita, and Konstantin Skorkin. *Kto rukovodil NKVD, 1934–1941: Spravochnik.* Moscow: "Zven'ia," 1999.

Petrovskii-Shtern, Iohanan. *Evrei v Russkoi Armii.* Moscow: Novoe Literaturnoe Obozrenie, 2003.

Picheta, Vladimir. *Belorussiia i Litva XV–XVI.* Moscow: Akademiia nauk SSSR, 1961.

Pichukov, Viktor, and Mikhail Starovoitov. *Gomel'shchina mnogonatsional'naia: 20–30-e gody XX veka.* Gomel: Gomel'skii gos. Universitet, 1999.

Pinchuk, Ben-Zion. *Yehudey Bryit-Hamu'atsot mul' paney ha-Shu'a.* Tel Aviv: Goldstein-Goren Diaspora Research Center, 1979.

Pines, D. Stranichka istorii. *Gekhaluts* 15–17 (1926): 10–14.

Pinkas ha-kehilot: Romanyah. Vol. 1. Edited by Jean Ancel. Jerusalem: Yad Vashem, 1970.

Pinkas kehylot Lit'a. Edited by Dov Levin. Jerusalem: Yad Vashem, 1996.

Pipes, Richard. *Russia under the Old Regime.* New York: Collier Books, 1992.

Piriatin. In *Evreiskaia entsiklopediia*, vol. 13, edited by Semën Dubnov and others, 543. Saint Petersburg: Brokgauz-Efron, [1908–1913].

Pis'mo of Kostomarov, Kulish, and others. *Russkii Vestnik* 18 (1858): 245–247.

Polnyi khronologicheskii sbornik zakonov i polozhenii: Kasaiushchikhsia evreev, ot ulozheniia tsaria Aleksieia Mikhailovicha do nastoiashchago vremeni, ot 1649–1873 g. izvlechenie iz polnykh sobranii zakonov rossiiskoi imperii. Edited by Vitalii Levanda. Saint Petersburg: Tip. K. V. Trubnikova, 1874.

Polonsky, Antony. *The Jews in Poland and Russia.* 3 vols. Oxford: Littman Library of Jewish Civilization, 2010.

Pozner, Solomon. Armia v Rossii. In *Evreiskaia entsiklopediia*, vol. 3, edited by Semën Dubnov and others, 160–172. Saint Petersburg: Brokgauz-Efron, [1908–1913].

———. Evrei Litvy i Belorussii 125 let tomu nazad (k 125 letiiu nashestviia Napoleona). In *Evreiskii mir: Ezhegodnik na 1939 god.*, 72–88. Minsk: Gesharim, 2002.

Prakticheskoe razreshenie natsional'nogo voprosa v BSSR. Vols. 1–2. Minsk: Izdanie Natsional'noi Komissii TSIK BSSR, 1927–1928.

Predpisanie nachal'nika severo-zapadnogo kraia ob izuchenii evreiami russkogo iazyka. *Vestnik Zapadnoi Rossii: Istoriko-literaturnyi zhurnal* 11, no. 2 (1865): 106–107.

Promyshlennost' BSSR v diagramakh i tablitsakh. Edited by A. B. Shul'man. Minsk: Izd. VSNKh. BSSR, 1928.

Prot'ko, Tat'iana. Delo "Ob'edinënnogo antisovetskogo shpionsko-vreditel'skogo podpol'ia v BSSR" (1936–1937). In *Repressivnaia politika sovetskoi vlasti v Belarusi: Sbornik nauchnykh rabot*, vol. 1, edited by Iakov Basin and Igor' Kuznetsov, 122–152. Minsk: Memorial, 2007.

Protokol zasedaniia otdeleniia statistiki severo-zapadnogo otdela imperatorskogo Russkogo Geograficheskogo obshchestva ot 2 Dekabria 1872 g. In *Izvestiia Imperatorskogo russkogo geograficheskogo obshchestva*, 9:126–133. Saint Petersburg: Imperatorskoe russkoe geograficheskoe obshchestvo, 1883.

Protokol zasedaniia otdeleniia statistiki severo-zapadnogo otdela imperatorskogo Russkogo Geograficheskogo obshchestva ot 26 Marta 1873 g. In *Izvestiia Imperatorskogo russkogo geograficheskogo obshchestva*, 9:186–188. Saint Petersburg: Imperatorskoe russkoe geograficheskoe obshchestvo, 1883.

Pryzhov, Ivan. *Istoriia kabakov v Rossii v sviazi s istoriei russkago naroda*. Moscow: Book Chamber International, 1991.

Pushkin, Igar. Natsiianal'nyia menshastsi ў gramadska-palitychnym i kul'turnym zhytstsi Rechytskaga raëna 20-kh gg. In *Chatsvërtyia mizhnarodnyia doўnaraўskiia chytanni*, vol. 2, edited by Valentina Lebedzeva and others, 117–122. Gomel: Gomel University, 2004.

Raiskii, Vladimir. *Sud'by liudskie*. Gomel: Raiskii, 2003.

Raiskii, Vladimir, and Vladimir Gershanok. Evrei Gomelia v period NEPa. In *Belarus' ў XX stagoddzi*, vol. 3, edited by Yakov Basin, 73–85. Minsk: Union of Councils for Soviet Jews, 2004.

Ramanava, Iryna. Novaia historyia inkvizitsyi ў dakumentakh: NKUS BSSR ў 1938–1939 gg. In *Repressivnaia politika sovetskoi vlasti v Belarusi: sbornik nauchnykh rabot*, vol. 1, edited by Iakov Basin and Igor' Kuznetsov, 335–375. Minsk: Memorial, 2007.

Ransel, David L. Kul'tura detorozhdeniia u belorusskikh, evreiskikh i tatarskikh zhenshchin na territorii Belarusi kontsa XIX—nachala XX vekov. In *Zhenshchiny na kraiu Evropy*, edited by Elena Gapova, 74–88. Minsk: EHU, 2003.

———. *Village Mothers: Three Generations of Change in Russia and Tataria*. Bloomington: Indiana University Press, 2005.

Razvodovsky, Yury. All-Cause Mortality and Fatal Alcohol Poisoning in Belarus, 1970–2005. *Drug and Alcohol Review* 27 (2008): 562–565.

R.D. Oktiabr'skie pogromy v tsifrakh. *Evreiskoe obozrenie*, August 19, 1910, 11–17.

Rechitsa. In *Encyclopedia Judaica*, vol. 14, edited by Cecil Roth, 1432. Jerusalem: Keter, 1972.

Rechitsa. In *Evreiskaia entsiklopediia*, vol. 13, edited by Semën Dubnov and others, 755. Saint Petersburg: Brokgauz-Efron, [1908–1913].

Regesty i nadpisi: Svod materialov dlia istorii evreev v Rossii (80 g.–1800 g.). Vols. 1–3. Edited by Shimon Dubnov and others. Saint Petersburg: Obshchestvo dlia rasprostraneniia prosveshcheniia mezhdu evreiami Rossii, 1899, 1910, 1913.

Revoliutsionnoe dvizhenie v Belorussii 1905–1907 gg: Dokumenty i materialy. Edited by Anatolii Azarov and others. Minsk: Izd-vo Akademii nauk Belorusskoi SSR, 1955.

Revoliutsionnye komitety BSSR. Edited by V. Krutalevich and others. Minsk: Izdatel'stvo Akademii nauk BSSR, 1961.

Rogger, Hans. *Jewish Policies and Right-Wing Politics in Imperial Russia*. London: Macmillan, 1986.

Ro'i, Yaacov. The Jewish Religion in the Soviet Union after World War II. In *Jews and Jewish Life in Russia and the Soviet Union*, edited by Yaacov Ro'I, 263–289. London: Frank Cass, 1995.

Rokhlin, Lazar'. *Miestechko Krasnopol'e Mogilevskoi gubernii: Opyt statistiko-ekomomicheskago opisaniia tipichnago miestechka cherty evreiskoi osëdlosti*. Saint Petersburg: Evreiskoe kolonizatsionnoe obshchestvo, 1908.

Rokossovskii, Konstantin. *Soldatskii dolg.* Moscow: OLMA-PRESS, 2002.

Rosman, Moshe. *The Lord's Jews: Magnate–Jewish Relations in the Polish–Lithuanian Commonwealth during the Eighteenth Century.* Cambridge, Mass.: Harvard University Center for Jewish Studies, 1992.

Rospis' zhidom'. *Opisanìe dokumentov i bumag, khraniashchikhsia v Moskovskom arhive ministerstva iustitsii.* Vol. 4. Edited by Nikolai Kalachov. Moscow: Tipografiia L. Snegirëva, 1884.

Rothenberg, Joshua. *The Jewish Religion in the Soviet Union.* New York: Ktav, 1971.

Russko-evreiskii arkhiv: Dokumenty i materialy dlia istoriii evreev v Rossii. Vol. 2, 1550–1569. Edited by Sergei Bershadskiy. Saint Petersburg: Obshchestvo rasprostraneniia prosvieshcheniia. mezhdu evreiami v Rossii, 1882.

Russko-indiiskie otnosheniia v XVII veke. Edited by T. Lavrentsova and K. Antonova. Moscow: Izdatel'stvo vostochnoi literatury, 1958.

Rybtsevich, Iosif. *Gorod Rechitsa.* Minsk: Tipo-litografiia B. I. Solomonova, 1903.

Sahanovich, Henadz'. *Neviadomaia vaina, 1654–1667.* Minsk: Navuka i tekhnika, 1995.

Samoilov, R. Provintsial'noe evreistvo. *Rassvet,* January 4, 1913, 19–20.

Samusik, Andrei. Navuchal'nyia ÿstanovy Rechytsy ÿ XIX—pachatku XX stagoddziaÿ. In *Piatyia mizhnarodnyia doÿnaraÿskiia chytanni,* edited by Valentina Lebedzeva and others, 263–268. Gomel: Gomel University, 2005.

Sandler, Semën. Idish. In *Iazyki Rossiiskoi federatsii i sosednikh gosudarstv,* vol. 1, edited by Viktoriia Iartseva, 366–376. Moscow: Nauka, 2000.

Savinskaia, Maryna, and Mariia Aleinikova. Rechitsa v 20-e gg. XX veka: Nekotorye aspekty sotsial'no-ekonomicheskogo razvitiia. In *Chatsvërtyia mizhnarodnyia doÿnaraÿskiia chytanni,* vol. 2, edited by Valentina Lebedzeva and others, 140–150. Gomel: Gomel University, 2004.

Savitski, Eduard. Rechytskaia arganizatsyia RSDRP (b). In *Entsyklapedyia history Belarusi,* vol. 6, pt. 1, edited by Genadz' Pashkoÿ, 180. Minsk: Belarusskaia Entsyklapedyia, 2001.

Sbornik dokumentov, kasaushchikhsia administrativnogo ustroistva Severo-Zapadnogo kraia pri imperatritse Ekaterine II (1792–1796). Vilna: Vilenskaia komissiia dlia razbora i izdaniia drevnikh aktov, 1903.

Schneerson, Fishel. *Die katastrophale Zeit und die heranwachsende Generation.* Berlin: Schwetschke & Sohn, 1924.

Sefer gvura: Antalogia ha-Istorit-Sifrutit. Vol. 3. Edited by Israel Hylperyn. Tel Aviv: Am Oved, 1977.

Selemenev, Viacheslav, and Arkadii Zeltser. The Liquidation of Yiddish Schools in Belorussia and Jewish Reaction. *Jews in Eastern Europe* 1, no. 41 (2000): 74–111.

Sergii. Opisanie Markovogo monastyria. In *Pamiatnaia knizhka Vitebskoi gubernii na 1865 g.,* edited by Alexander Sementovskii, 3–74. Saint Petersburg: Vitebskii gubernskii statisticheskii komitet, 1865.

Shabad, Iakov. Gramotnost' evreev v Rossii. In *Evreiskaia entsiklopediia,* vol. 6, edited by Semën Dubnov and others, 756–759. Saint Petersburg: Brokgauz-Efron, [1908–1913].

———. Naselenie Rossii. In *Evreiskaia entsiklopediia,* vol. 11, edited by Semën Dubnov and others, 534–547. Saint Petersburg: Brokgauz-Efron, [1908–1913].

Shafir, M. Moi vospominaniia. *Evreiskaia letopis'* 4 (1926): 104–111.

Shafonskii, Afanasii. *Chernigovskago namestnichestva topograficheskoe opisanie s kratkim geograficheskim i istoricheskim opisaniem Maloi Rossii, sochinennoe v Chernigove 1786 goda.* Kiev: Universitetskaia tipografiia, 1851.

Shiper, Itskhak. Podatnoe oblozhenie evreev. In *Istoriia evreiskogo naroda*, vol. 11, pt. 1, edited by Alexander Braudo and others, 300–319. Moscow: Mir, 1914.

———. Rasselenie evreev v Pol'she i Litve ot drevneishikh vremën do kontsa XVIII veka. In *Istoriia evreiskogo naroda*, vol. 11, pt. 1, edited by Alexander Braudo and others, 105–131. Moscow: Mir, 1914.

Shipov, Alexander. *Khlopchato-bumazhnaia promyshlennost' i vazhnost' eia znacheniia v Rossii.* Vol. 2. Moscow: Tipografiia Volkova, 1858.

Shkandrij, Myroslav. *Jews in Ukranian Literature: Representation and Identity.* New Haven, Conn.: Yale University Press, 2009.

Shmeruk, Chone. Mashm'euta haḥevratit shel' hashḥitah haḥasidit. In *Mekarim be-toldot Yisira'el: Ba-'et ha-haḥdashah*, vol. 1, edited by Richard Cohen, 161–186. Jerusalem: Merkaz Zalman Shazar le-toldot Yisìra'el, 1995.

Shneer, Aron. *Plen.* Vols. 1–2. Jerusalem: Noi, 2003.

Shneerson, Fishel. *Sipurey hatglut hasyidyim.* Tel Aviv: Yazriel, 1976.

Shneerson, Isaac. *Lebn un kamf fun Yidn in tsarishn Rusland 1905–1917: Zikhroynes.* Paris: Edison Poliglot, 1968.

Shokhat, 'Azriel. Toldot kehilat Pinsk 1881–1941. In *Pinsk*, edited by Wolf Zeev Rabinowitsch, 5–297. Tel Aviv: 'Irgun Yotse'ei Pinsk-K'arlyin bemedinat Yisrael, 1977.

Shpilevskii, Pavel. *Puteshestvie po Polesiu i Belorusskomu kraiu.* Minsk: Polymia, 1992.

Shumatskii, Iakov. *Revoliutsinnaia provintsiia.* Moscow: Novaia Moskva, 1926.

Shybeka, Zakhar. *Garady Belarusi.* Minsk: EÿroForum, 1997.

Sifman, Roza. Dinamika chislennosti naseleniia Rossii za 1897–1914. In *Brachnost', rozhdaemost', smertnost' v Rossii i v SSSR*, edited by Anatolii Vishnevskii, 62–82. Moscow: Statistika, 1977.

Slonim, Manaḥem Samuel. *Toldot mishpahat ha-rav mi-Ladi: Megilat ha-yuhasin shel Ba'al ha-Tanya.* Tel Aviv: Ḥmu"l, 1946.

Smilovitsky, Leonid. Bor'ba evreev Belorussii za vozvrat imushchestva i zhilishch v pervoe poslevoennoe desiatiletie 1944–1954. In *Belarus' ÿ XX stagoddzi*, vol. 1, edited by Yakov Basin, 168–178. Minsk: Union of Councils for Soviet Jews, 2002.

———. *Evrei Belorusii: Iz nashei obshchei istorii, 1905–1953.* Minsk: Arti-Feks, 1999.

———. Evrei Belorussii v pervoe poslevoennoe desiatiletie. *Vestnik Evreiskogo universiteta v Moskve* 8, no. 26 (2003): 213–236.

———. *Evrei v Turove: Istoriia mestechka Mozyr'skogo Poles'i'a'.* Jerusalem: Tsur-Ot, 2008.

———. Jewish Religious Leadership in Belorussia, 1939–1953. *Shvut* 8, no. 24 (1999): 87–122.

———. *Katastrofa evreev v Belorussii, 1941–1944 gg.* Tel Aviv: Biblioteka Matveia Chenogo, 2000.

———. Pogrom in Rechitsa, October 1905. *Shvut* 5 (1997): 65–80.

———. Voskresnaia shkola v Rechitse. *Novaia evreiskaia shkola* 12 (2002): 164–172.

Snyder, Timothy. *The Reconstruction of Nations: Poland, Ukraine, Lithuania, Belarus, 1569–1999*. New Haven, Conn.: Yale University Press, 2003.

Sobolevskaia, Olga. Iudei v belorusskikh vladeniiakh Radzivilov v kontse 18–nachale 19 vekov. *Tsaitshryft* 6, no. 1 (1911): 23–40.

Sokolov, Dmitrii, and Vasilii Grebenshchikov. *Smertnost' v Rossii i bor'ba s neiu*. Saint Petersburg: Tip. M. M. Stasiulevicha, 1901. http://www.gvinfo.ru/node/31.

Sorkin, Ina. *Miastechki Belarusi u kantsy XVIII—pershai palove XIX st.* Vilnius: Eurapeiski humanitarny universitet, 2010.

Sorkin, Sidney. *Bridges to an American City: A Guide to Chicago's Landsmanshaften, 1870–1990*. New York: Peter Lang, 1993.

Soyer, Daniel. *Jewish Immigrant Associations and American Identity in New York, 1880–1939*. Detroit: Wayne State University Press, 2002.

Staliūnas, Darius. *Making Russians: Meaning and Practice of Russification in Lithuania and Belarus after 1863*. Amsterdam and New York: Rodopi, 2007.

Stampfer, Shaul. *Families, Rabbis and Education: Traditional Jewish Society in Nineteenth-Century Eastern Europe*. Oxford: Littman Library of Jewish Civilization, 2010.

———. *Ha-Yeshivah ha-Lita'it be-hithavutah*. Jerusalem: Merkaz Zalman Shazar le-toldot Yisìrael, 2005.

———. The 1764 Census of Polish Jewry. *Annual of Bar Ilan University* 24–25 (1989): 41–59.

———. What Actually Happened to the Jews of Ukraine in 1648? *Jewish History* 17, no. 2 (2003): 207–227.

Starovoitov, Mikhail. Osobennosti osushchestvleniia politiki belorusizatsii v Rechitskom regione (1927—nachalo 30-kh gg. XX v.). In *Chatsvërtyia mizhnarodnyia doŷnaraŷskiia chytanni*, vol. 2, edited by Valentina Lebedzeva and others, 156–166. Gomel: Gomel University, 2004.

Starozytna Polska. Vol. 4. Compiled by Franciszek Martynowskii and others. Warsaw: Orgelbrand, 1886.

Statut Vialikaha Kniastva Litouskaha 1588: Teksty, davednik, kamentaryi. Edited by Ivan Shamiakin. Minsk: Belaruskaia Savetskaia Entsyklapedyia, 1989.

Stepanov, Sergei. *Chernaia sotnia v Rossii: 1905–1914 gg.* Moscow: VZPI, 1992.

Stoletie Minskoi gubernii. Edited by Alexander Smorodskii. Minsk: Gubernskii statisticheskii komitet, 1893.

Stolpianskii, Nikolai. *Deviat' gubernii Zapadno-russkogo kraia*. Saint Petersburg: Vasilii Diriker, 1866.

Stupakevich, Marina. *Zhenskoe obrazovanie v Belarusi: Vtoraia polovina XIX veka–1917 god*. Grodno: Grodnenskii gos. universitet, 2006.

Subbotin, Andrei. *V cherte evreiskoi osedlosti*. Vol. 2, *Minsk, Vilna, Kovna i ikh raiony*. Saint Petersburg: Ekonomicheskii zhurnal, 1888.

Sudarskii, A. *Ekonomicheskoe polozhenie evreiskogo mestechka*. Moscow: Tsentral'noe pravlenie Ozet, 1929.

Surpina, Dina. Chto ia znaiu i pomniu (2007). http://evkol.nm.ru/d_surpina.htm.

Svatikov, Sergei. Evrei v russkom osvoboditel'nom dvizhenii. In *Evrei i russkaia revoliutsiia*, edited by Oleg Budnitskii, 31–160. Moscow: Gesharim, 1999.

386 Bibliography

Sverdlov, Fëdor. *Evrei—generally vooruzhënnykh sil SSSR.* Moscow: Sverdlov, 1993.

Tadger, David. *Entsyiklopedyiah le-halutsey ha-Yishuv ve-bonav.* 19 vols. Tel Aviv: Hotsa'at sfarim r'ishonim, 1947–1971.

Talmud-Tora. *Der Fraind* (December 10, 1903): 4.

Tauber, Kalman. *Svedeniia o sostoianii eshibota "Ramailes" v g. Vilne, zavedyvaemogo ravvinom K. Tauberom v 1889 g.* Vilna: Tip. I. Bliumovicha, 1890.

Teller, Adam. Hape'ilut hakalkalit shel hayehudim bePolin bemahatsit hasheniyah shel hame'ah ha17 uveme'ah ha18. In *Kiyum veshever: Yehude Polin ledorotehem,* edited by Israel Bartal and Israel Gutman, 209–224. Jerusalem: Merkaz Zalman Shazar letoldot Yisira'el, 1997.

———. *Kesef, koakh ve-hashp'ah: Ha-yhudim b'akhuzot beit Radzyvyl be-Lit'a be-m'ah ha-18.* Jerusalem: Merkaz Zalman Shazar le-Toldot Yisira'el, 2006.

Teter, Magdalena. Jewish Conversions to Catholicism in the Polish–Lithuanian Commonwealth of the Seventeenth and Eighteenth Centuries. *Jewish History* 17 (2003): 257–283.

Tikhomirov, Mikhail. Spiski russkikh gorodov, dal'nikh i blizhnikh. *Istoricheskie zapiski* 40 (1952): 214–259.

Tkachëÿ, Mikhail. Rechickiia umatsavanni. In *Encyklapedyia historyi Belarusi,* vol. 6, pt. 1, edited by Gennadzii Pashkou, 182–183. Minsk: BelEn, 2001.

Toldot anshei shem. Edited by Oscar Z. Rand. Vol. 1. New York: Hevrat toldot anshe shem, 1950.

Tolochko, Dmitrii. Faktor ob'edineniia Belarusi osen'iu 1939 g. v istorii Rechitskogo raiona. In *Chatsvërtyia mizhnarodnyia doÿnaraÿskiia chytanni,* vol. 2, edited by Valentina Lebedzeva and others, 166–173. Gomel: Gomel University, 2004.

Torgivlia na Ukraïni, XIV—seredina XVII stolittia: Volin' i Naddniprianshchina. Edited by V. M. Kravchenko and N. M. Iakovenko. Kiev: Naukova dumka, 1990.

Trudy gubernskih komissii po evreiskomu voprosu. Vol. 1, sec. 1, *Trudy Vilenskoi komissii,* and sec. 6, *Trudy Minskoi komissii.* Saint Petersburg: Vysochaishaia komissia dlia peresmotra deistvuiushchikh o evreiakh v imperii zakonov, 1884.

Trudy gubernskogo statisticheskogo komiteta: Istoriko-statisticheskoe opisanie deviati uezdov Minskoi gubernii. Vol. 1. Minsk: Gubernskii statisticheskii komitet, 1870.

Tseitlin, Hillel. Korotko o sebe. In *Baalei tshuva,* edited by Meir Khovav, 79–82. Jerusalem: Amana, 1991.

Tsekhanskaia, Kira. Rossia: Tendentsii religioznosti v XX veke. *Istoricheskii vestnik* 5 (1999): 59–69.

Udler, Evgenii, and Zinaida Dodina. Evrei Brianska vchera i segodnia. *Evrei Evrazii* (June–August 2002): 12–14.

Umetskii, Boris. *Rechitsa: Kratkii istoriko-ekonomicheskii ocherk.* Minsk: Gos. izd-vo BSSR, 1963.

Urusov, Sergei. *Zapiski gubernatora: Kishinëv 1903–1904 g.* Berlin: J. Ladyschnikow, 1907.

Usov, M. L. *Evrei v armii.* Saint Petersburg: Razum, 1911.

Ustav Rechickogo evreiskogo obshchestva podaianiia pomoshchi i posobiia bednym. Minsk: Rechitskoe evreiskoe dukhovnoe pravlenie, 1898.

Vakar, Nicholas P. *Belorussia: The Making of a Nation.* Cambridge, Mass.: Harvard University Press, 1956.

Velikii, Anatol'. Rechitskoe delo 1939 g. In *Tretsiia mizhnarodnyia doўnaraўskiia chytanni,* edited by Valentina Lebedzeva and others, 359–361. Minsk: Bel. knigazbor, 2002.

Vengerova, Polina. *Vospominaniia babushki.* Jerusalem: Gesharim, 2003.

Vilenskii, Ia., G. Izraelit, and I. Livshits. Iz Rechitsy. *Russkii evrei,* August 19, 1881, 1341.

Vishnitser, Mark. Evrei-remeslenniki i tsekhovaia organizatsiia ikh. In *Istoriia evreiskogo naroda,* vol. 11, pt. 1, edited by Alexander Braudo and others, 286–299. Moscow: Mir, 1914.

———. Obshchii ocherk politicheskoi i sotsial'noi istorii evreev v Pol'she i Litve. In *Istoriia evreiskogo naroda,* vol. 11, pt. 1, edited by Alexander Braudo and others, 21–104. Moscow: Mir, 1914.

Vishnitser, Mark, and Itskhak Shiper. Ekonomicheskii byt. In *Istoriia evreiskogo naroda,* vol. 11, pt. 1, edited by Alexander Braudo and others, 243–299. Moscow: Mir, 1914.

Vladimirov, Aleksei. O polozhenii pravoslaviia v Severo-Zapadnom krae. *Russkoe obozrenie* 20 (1893): 671–702.

Voenno-statisticheskoe obozrenie Rossiiskoi imperii. Vol. 9, pt. 4, *Minskaia gubeniia,* edited by Andrei Streng. Saint Petersburg: Departament General'nogo shtaba, 1848.

Voinilovich, Edvard. *Vospominaniia.* Vol. 1. Minsk: s.n., 2007.

Volfson, Semën. *Suchasnaia religiinas'ts'.* Minsk: Belorusskaia Akademiia nauk, 1930.

Vol'tke, Grigorii. Mestechki. *Evreiskaia entsiklopediia,* vol. 11. Edited by Semën Dubnov and others, 438–439. Saint Petersburg: Brokgauz-Efron, [1908–1913].

———. Vinnye promysly. *Evreiskaia entsiklopediia,* vol. 5. Edited by Semën Dubnov and others, 609–614. Saint Petersburg: Brokgauz-Efron, [1908–1913].

Vosemnadtsat'. Edited by Zeev Vagner. Jerusalem: Shamir, 1989.

V.R. Iz mira antropologicheskoi statistiki. *Voskhod,* 1881, no. 8, 49–78.

Vsenarodnoe partizanskoe dvizhenie v Belorussii v gody Velikoi Otechestvennoi voiny. Vol. 2. Edited by A. Kuz'min. Minsk: Belarus', 1973.

Vsia Rossiia na 1895: Russkaia kniga promyshlennosti, torgovli, sel'skogo khoziaistva i administratsii. Saint Petersburg: A. S. Suvorin, 1895.

Vsia Rossiia na 1902: Russkaia kniga promyshlennosti, torgovli, sel'skogo khoziaistva i administratsii. Saint Petersburg: A. S. Suvorin, 1902.

Vsia Rossiia na 1912: Spravochnaia kniga Rossiiskoi promyshlennosti, torgovli, sel'skago khoziaistva, administratsii, predstavitelei obshchestvennoi i chastnoi sluzhebnoi economicheskoi dieiatel'nosti i pr. Kiev: Izd. T-vo L. M. Fish, 1912.

Vstali my plechom k plechu . . . Edited by Inna Gerasimova. Minsk: Asobny Dakh, 2006.

Weeks, Theodore R. *Nation and State in Late Imperial Russia: Nationalism and Russification on the Western Frontier, 1863–1914.* DeKalb: Northern Illinois University Press.

Weinryb, Bernard Dov. *The Jews of Poland: A Social and Economic History of the Jewish Community in Poland from 1100 to 1800.* Philadelphia: Jewish Publication Society, 1973.

Wrangel, Nikolai. *Vospominaniia: Ot krepostnogo prava do bol'shevikov.* Berlin: Slovo, 1924.

Yahadut Lita. Vols. 1–3. Edited by Natan Goren. Tel Aviv: Hotsa'at 'Am ha-sefer, 1959–1967.

Yidn in V.S.S.R.: Statistishe materyaln. Minsk: Belaruskaia akademiia nauk, Iaÿreiskii sektar, 1929.

Zajka, Vital'. The Self-Perception of Lithuanian-Belarusian Jewry in the Eighteenth and Nineteenth Centuries. *Polin* 14 (2001):19–30.

Zakhar'in, Ivan. Vospominaniia o sluzhbe v Belorussii. *Istoricheskii viestnik: Istoriko-literaturnyi zhurnal* 15 (1884): 538–565.

Zakhoder, Boris. *Kaspiiskii svod svedenii o Vostochnoi Evrope.* Vol. 2. Moscow: Vostochnaia literatura, 1967.

Zaltsman, Shlyoma. *'Ayarati: Zikhronot u-reshumot.* Tel Aviv: Masada, 1947.

Zbor pomnikau historyi i kul'tury Belarusi: Homel'skaia voblasts'. Edited by Stanislau Martseleu. Minsk: Belaruskaia savetskaia entsyklapedyia, 1985.

Zelenskii, Illarion. *Materialy dlia geografii i statistiki Rossii: Minskaia guberniia.* Vols. 1–2. Saint Petersburg: Minskii gubernskii statisticheskii komitet, 1864.

Zeliankova, Ala. Dasiagnenni i prablemy shkol'nai spravy ÿ Rechytskim pavetse (1919–1926 gg.). In *Chatsvërtyia mizhnarodnyia doÿnaraÿskiia chytanni,* vol. 2, edited by Valentina Lebedzeva and others, 131–140. Gomel: Gomel University, 2004.

Zeltser, Arkadii. *Evrei sovetskoi provintsii: Vitebsk i mestechki, 1917–1941.* Moscow: Rosspen, 2006.

———. Jews in the Upper Ranks of the NKVD, 1934–1941. *Jews in Russia and Eastern Europe* 1, no. 52 (2004): 64–90.

Zemskov, Viktor. Zakliuchënnye, spetsposelentsy, ssyl'noposelentsy, ssyl'nye i vyslannye. *Istoriia SSSR* 5 (1991): 151–165.

Zhirnov, Evgenii. Proverka strakhom. *Kommersant-vlast'* (June 20, 2005): 70–76.

Zhivopisnaia Rossiia: Litovskoe i Belorusskoe poles'e. Edited by Pëtr Semenov-Tian'-Shanskii. Minsk: Belaruskaia Entsyklapedyia, 1993.

Zinger, Lev. Evreiskaia zhenshchina v narodnom khoziaistve Belorusskoi i Ukrainskoi SSR. *Tribuna evreiskoi sovetskoi obshchestvennosti* 10 (1936): 30–33.

———. *Evreiskoe naselenie v Sovetskom Soiuze: statistiko-ekonomicheskii obzor.* Moscow: Gos. sots. ekonomicheskoe izd-vo, 1932.

———. Gramotnost' evreiskogo naseleniia SSSR. *Tribuna evreiskoi sovetskoi obshchestvennosti* 20 (1928): 6–7.

———. Rodnoi iazyk evreiskogo naseleniia SSSR. *Tribuna evreiskoi sovetskoi obshchestvennosti* 16 (1928): 9–10.